W9-CNM-503

BUSINESS ENGLISH
AND
COMMUNICATION
SECOND CANADIAN EDITION
SI /METRIC

For a communication to do the job i
definite purpose. The communicator
about what he hopes to accomplish
to present facts to give directions
or to suggest ideas. Or he may wi
to entertain. Generally, he will
his major purpose, perhaps with
the newspaper reporter, for example
clear presentation of facts. But,
tain to the extent that buyers of
read his story with interest and
an idea; however,
ade, to criticize t
nd to persuade his
audience, his play
a major purpose, al
munication also has
common purpose that
kind of response i
business communication
in other words, all bu
designed to promote
communication i
the message
response
bine

Marie M. Stewart, Ph.D.

Formerly chairman of the Business Department at Stonington High School, Stonington, Connecticut, Doctor Stewart is now Executive Development Director for the Edmundite Fathers and Brothers of Mystic, Connecticut. Coauthor of six business English textbooks, she has taught in elementary, secondary, business, USAF, and university graduate schools. Doctor Stewart has served as communications consultant to businesses and has written many magazine articles on business education. She is in demand as a speaker by secretarial and office managerial groups, as well as by business teachers.

Frank W. Lanham, Ph.D.

Doctor Lanham is associate professor of business teacher education at the University of Michigan. His teaching experience also includes the secondary school, technical institute, and business college levels. Doctor Lanham is a writer and researcher in the areas of business communication, business teacher education, and school business administration. He served as editor of the National Business Education Association Yearbook No. 4 and is currently president of the Research Foundation of the Association.

Kenneth Zimmer, Ed.D.

Doctor Zimmer is chairman of the Department of Business Education and Office Administration at California State College at Los Angeles. Formerly director of the School of Business, Richmond Professional Institute of the College of William and Mary, he has also taught on secondary school and junior college levels. An editor for *Business Education Forum*, Doctor Zimmer has conducted training programs for business organizations and often speaks before business and professional groups.

BUSINESS ENGLISH
AND
COMMUNICATION

SECOND CANADIAN EDITION
SI METRIC

for a communication to do the job i
definite purpose. The communicator
about what he hopes to accomplish
to present facts to give directions
or to suggest ideas. Or he may wi
to entertain. Generally, he will
s his major purpose, perhaps with
he newspaper reporter, for example
clear presentation of facts. But,
tain to the extent that buyers of
read his story with interest and
f an idea; however,
ade, to criticize to
nd to persuade his
audience, his play
a major purpose, al
munication also has
common purpose that
ne kind of response in
business communication
In other words, all bus
designed to promote
communication i
the message
response
abl

FRANK W. LANHAM, PH.D.

MARIE M. STEWART, PH.D.

KENNETH ZIMMER, ED.D.

Revised by Kay Vanstone
Seneca College of Applied Arts & Technology

McGRAW-HILL RYERSON LIMITED
Toronto Montreal New York St. Louis San Francisco
Auckland Bogotá Düsseldorf Johannesburg London
Madrid Mexico New Delhi Panama Paris São Paulo
Singapore Sydney Tokyo

BUSINESS ENGLISH AND COMMUNICATION, Second Canadian Edition

Copyright © McGraw-Hill Ryerson Limited, 1977
Copyright © McGraw-Hill Company of Canada Limited, 1967
Copyright © 1967, 1961 by McGraw-Hill, Inc. All Rights Reserved
Copyright 1953 by McGraw-Hill, Inc. All Rights Reserved

ISBN 0-07-082543-2

890EP   65432

Printed and bound in Canada

This book is set in Fotosetter News Gothic. The Unit and Part titles are Standard Extrabold Extended with Standard Medium.
Design: Barbara Bert

The photographs on the display pages listed below are reproduced (from left to right) through the courtesy of the following organizations:

xiv-1	The Canada Life Assurance Company
2-3	American Telephone and Telegraph; Seneca College of Applied Arts and Technology; Michigan Consolidated Gas Company; Ford Foundation
4-5	Seneca College of Applied Arts and Technology; Northern Indiana Public Service Company
6-7	Northern Indiana Public Service Company; Seneca College of Applied Arts and Technology
30-31	Seneca College of Applied Arts and Technology
48-49	Seneca College of Applied Arts and Technology
63-64	Ewing Galloway; McGraw-Hill, Inc.
180-181	Ewing Galloway; McGraw-Hill, Inc.
240-241	McGraw-Hill, Inc.
270-271	McGraw-Hill, Inc.
294-295	The Canada Life Assurance Company
316-317	McGraw-Hill, Inc.
470-471	Randy Brown
498	Bell Telephone Magazine

PREFACE

In most of Canada the English language is the vehicle of effective communication. The educated person must have a functional command of this language that will enable him to express himself and to understand others.

Business English and Communication, Second Canadian Edition, is a textbook that trains students in *all* phases of communication—speaking, writing, listening, reading. Effective training in the four communication areas must be based on a solid educational foundation in English usage; vocabulary; punctuation; correct use of capitalization, abbreviations, figures; and in writing craftsmanship. This text provides both the broad, firm educational background and the specialized training needed for success in business careers.

Educating for Total Communication

Word Command Part 1 is concerned with **vocabulary;** and students are taught how to increase their command of words, how to use the principal word-building reference books, and how to choose the precise word for any given situation. Vocabulary is divided into two types: active and passive. The active vocabulary consists of words used when writing or speaking; the passive vocabulary, of additional words whose meanings are understood when listening or reading. Nothwithstanding, vocabulary cannot be built in a day or even a month. Therefore, the authors have made vocabulary expansion a continuing thread that runs through all succeeding units in the text. Every set of end-of-unit exercises has at least one vocabulary section.

Spelling is a corollary of vocabulary and is so treated in this textbook. In end-of-unit activities throughout the book, continuing spelling-improvement practices are presented. The spelling throughout this textbook is based on *Webster's Seventh New Collegiate Dictionary*. Note that in some parts of Canada there may be a preference to use the alternate form of spelling that is shown in the dictionary entry.

Listening and Reading Improvement Training for **listening** and **reading,** the sometimes neglected communication areas, in Parts 2 and 3, is another of the features of *Business English and Communication*. Students who use this text learn the listening habits, attitudes, and techniques that will make their education a more rewarding process—and will also prevent the embarrassing incidents caused by careless or faulty listening.

The reading-improvement units are of help to students who may have minor reading difficulties. Their main value, however, lies in the suggestions for increasing reading speed. To cope with the steadily growing mass of typewritten and printed material that streams daily into an office, every business employee must be able to read at a correspondingly faster rate.

Framework of Communication Part 4 of this text is a complete, but streamlined, course in **grammar;** it is a course in the grammar of communication. Students are required to learn only those functional principles that are used in speaking and in writing. The presentation is fresh and clear, and it is stripped of all confusing terminology. Wherever there is a hard-to-remember principle, an original and easy-to-understand learning device called a "Quick Trick" transforms a traditional rule into an always-remembered principle.

The Writer's Signals   Rules governing **punctuation, capitalization, abbreviations,** and **use of figures,** too often considered to be dull and meaningless, with the result that the rules are not assimilated, are logically presented as meaningful principles in Parts 5 and 6. The principles are taught as "the writer's signals," signals that he uses to guide a reader into correct interpretation of a written message. Students learn and remember these principles because they understand the "why" as well as the "how." Because of Canada's commitment to metrication, the "writer's signals" in *Business English and Communication,* Second Canadian Edition, are written in metric terms.

Writing   Parts 7 through 10, devoted to **writing craftsmanship,** present an original, unconventional, and interesting approach to the treatment of the art of writing. In these units, students are taught reader-oriented writing, the techniques of putting words together in such a way that the reader interprets a message in the exact manner intended by the writer. The teaching material is so simple, direct, and clear that students find learning easy—and enjoyable, too.

In business, most written communication is in the form of letters; therefore, in *Business English and Communication* the emphasis is on the writing of various types of letters. Students learn to write the letters that, as new employees, they would be expected to write. But the training does not stop there.

Students also receive basic training in the writing of more difficult letters; for instance, claim and adjustment letters; credit and collection letters; letters dealing with problem situations; sales and promotion letters. Aspiring writers learn the psychology of business writing. They learn that every letter they write is a personalized messenger by mail and is, therefore, a letter that sells the company and its goods or services. The authors believe—and teach—that no letter can be classified as "routine."

Techniques of writing communications other than letters—such as the "know-how" of writing memorandums, reports, news releases, minutes of a meeting, and telegrams—are also taught. Because of the modern, almost scientific, approach and thorough coverage, these units in written communication prepare students not only to enter upon their business careers but also to advance in those careers.

Speaking   The **oral communication** training provided in Part 11 prepares the student for effective speaking in the different on-the-job situations in which he will find himself as a business employee. An added value of this training is that it can be adapted to, and used successfully in, social, as well as business, activities.

Students learn how to "put their best foot forward" and also learn the voice mechanics of making themselves understood. The remaining four units teach the student effective speaking when meeting the public, either in person or by telephone; when participating in or leading conferences and meetings; when being interviewed for employment; and when giving a talk.

Metric Section

In this Second Canadian Edition a metric section covers the basic metric units, including a class practice exercise. This guides the student in the proper method of writing metric measurements. The table of metric terms familiarizes students with metric terms. Throughout the text, imperial terms have been converted to metric, reinforcing the learning of the metric system.

Canadian Postal Codes

Postal Codes have been added to all Canadian addresses, and instruction is given on the proper placement for inside and outside addresses.

Geographical Locations. Geographical locations include a wider Canadian representation. The section on grooming has been revised and updated.

Student Activities

Real learning takes place when students have an opportunity to put into practice the principles they have studied. In this text, the Application Exercises at the end of units supply students with the "do" experiences that make learning effective.

Present-day students read very little; consequently, their contextual sense is likely to be poor. To improve their ability to grasp the meaning of groups of words, many Application Exercises are set up in context form.

Student activities also include thought-provoking exercises called "Communication in Action," in which practical problem situations, both social and business, are presented for solution by students.

Supporting Materials

The **Workbook** that accompanies *Business English and Communication* is much more than the traditional workbook. It is a supplementary learning aid that combines enrichment with a continuous skill-building cycle. Each unit corresponds with the text in that it contains additional and advanced practice on textbook principles. Each unit also contains an exercise or exercises designed to enrich the learning of current and previous principles presented in the textbook. And, to reinforce skills and to keep them alive, this workbook features a carefully planned program of continuous review of principles taught in preceding units.

A **Test Booklet** is available for use with this text. In the booklet are nine objective tests covering the textbook presentation, plus a beginning inventory test and a comprehensive final examination.

The **Instructor's Guide and Key** contains full, complete answers to all exercises in the textbook, and a facsimile key to all workbook and test exercises. It also provides many helpful teaching suggestions for each of the units.

Marie M. Stewart
Frank W. Lanham
Kenneth Zimmer

CONTENTS

COMMUNICATION IN THE WORLD OF WORK   1

PART 1   WORDS WORK FOR YOU   6

UNIT 1   WORDS—CHIEF MEANS OF COMMUNICATION   9
What is a good vocabulary? Vocabulary in social life; How to improve your vocabulary; Our changing vocabulary; How to keep in step

UNIT 2   THE DICTIONARY—YOUR BASIC REFERENCE TOOL   17
Preview your dictionary; Word references, Reference section

UNIT 3   CHOOSING THE RIGHT WORD   23
How to study word confusions; Words commonly confused

PART 2   LISTENING AS A COMMUNICATION ART   30

UNIT 4   THE IMPORTANCE OF LISTENING   33
Listening in business and industry; Your need for effective listening; Listening versus hearing; Listening and the other communication arts

UNIT 5   HOW TO BE A GOOD LISTENER   40
Determine your purpose; Basic rules for listening; How to listen critically

PART 3   READING AS A COMMUNICATION ART   48

UNIT 6   READING AND YOUR GROWTH   51
Reading in your personal life—social life—professional life; Reading with a purpose

UNIT 7   YOU AND YOUR READING HABITS   57
Your eyes; Your reading environment; How to increase your speed; How to increase your comprehension

PART 4   THE FRAMEWORK OF EFFECTIVE COMMUNICATION   64

UNIT 8   WHY A FRAMEWORK IS NECESSARY   67
The importance of framework; Grammar, the framework of language; Framework promotes communication

UNIT 9   THE SENTENCE   73
What a sentence is; Subject and predicate; Simple and compound subjects; Normal and inverted sentence order

UNIT 10 VERBS, VERBS, VERBS   79
Words that assert;   Verb phrases, Principal parts of verbs;   Infinitives

UNIT 11 MORE VERBS   87
*"Being" verbs;   Transitive and intransitive verbs;   Troublesome verbs;   "If," "as if,"
"as though," "wish"*

UNIT 12 NOUNS—PLURALS   93
*Most common and less common plural endings;   Tricky plurals;   Nouns with two plurals;
Compound nouns;   Foreign plurals*

UNIT 13 NOUNS AND PRONOUNS—POSSESSIVE FORMS   103
*Principal use of the apostrophe with nouns;   Additional uses;   Possessives of personal
pronouns;   Possessive before a gerund*

UNIT 14 PRONOUNS—NOMINATIVE AND OBJECTIVE FORMS   111
*Forms of pronouns;   Nominative case;   Pronouns in compounds;   "We men" or "us
men"?   Objective case*

UNIT 15 PRONOUNS—MORE ABOUT FORMS   118
*Pronouns after "than" or "as";   "Self"-ending pronouns;   Pronouns as appositives;
"Who" and "whom," "whoever" and "whomever"*

UNIT 16 PREDICATE AGREEMENT WITH SIMPLE SUBJECT   128
General agreement principle;   Specific agreement principles

UNIT 17 MORE ABOUT PREDICATE AGREEMENT WITH SIMPLE SUBJECT 135
"A number," "The number" subject;   Foreign-noun subject;   Indefinite-pronoun subject

UNIT 18 PREDICATE AGREEMENT WITH COMPOUND SUBJECT   140
Subjects joined by "and";   Subjects joined by "or" or "nor";   Relative pronoun clause

UNIT 19 ADJECTIVES   147
*Comparison of adjectives;   Repeat the modifier;   Compound adjectives;   Adjective
pitfalls*

UNIT 20 ADVERBS   155
*Kinds of adverbs;   Adverb or adjective?   Adverb pitfalls;   Adverb and adjective
confusions*

UNIT 21 PREPOSITIONS   163
*Words requiring certain prepositions;   Troublesome prepositions;   Preposition
illiteracies*

UNIT 22 CONJUNCTIONS   171
*Coordinate conjunctions;   Correlative conjunctions;   Subordinate conjunctions;
Conjunction pitfalls*

PART 5   PUNCTUATION—THE WRITER'S SIGNALS   180

UNIT 23   THE PERIOD   183
Use a period;   Do not use a period;   Period pitfalls

UNIT 24   QUESTION MARK AND EXCLAMATION POINT   189
The question mark;   The exclamation point

UNIT 25   SEMICOLON, COLON, AND DASH   193
The semicolon;   The colon;   The dash

UNIT 26   THE COMMA: FUNDAMENTAL USAGES   202
In compound sentences;   In a series;   After introductory elements;   Before subordinate clause following main clause

UNIT 27   THE COMMA: USAGES TO INDICATE NONESSENTIALS   212
Interrupting elements;   Explanatory elements

UNIT 28   THE COMMA: ADDITIONAL USAGES   220
With adjectives;   For omissions;   Direct address;   Repeated expressions;   Unrelated numbers;   Names in filing order

UNIT 29   QUOTATION MARKS   226
Direct and interrupted quotations;   Quotation within a quotation;   Quoted expressions; Punctuation at end of quotations

UNIT 30   PARENTHESES AND THE APOSTROPHE   233
Parentheses;   The apostrophe

PART 6   CAPITALIZATION, ABBREVIATIONS, AND FIGURES   240

UNIT 31   CAPITALIZATION   243
First words;   Proper nouns and adjectives;   Names of places;   Titles of publications, Works of art;   Personal and official titles

UNIT 32   ABBREVIATIONS   252
Personal titles and firm names;   Punctuating abbreviations;   To abbreviate or not

UNIT 33   FIGURES   259
Numbers as words;   Numbers as figures;   Consecutive numbers;   Money;   Dates; Time;   House, street, Postal Codes;   Metric Measurements

PART 7   WRITING CRAFTSMANSHIP   270

UNIT 34   THE ART OF BEING EXPLICIT   273
Placement of words, phrases, clauses;   "Which" clauses;   The "who" and the "what"; Definite pronoun reference

UNIT 35 THE ART OF BEING POLISHED   281
Messages that flow; The "and" pitfalls; Balanced sentences

UNIT 36 ACHIEVING VARIETY IN WORD USAGE   288
Why aim for variety? Worst offenders; Key to the situation; Learn to use synonyms; Learn to use antonyms

PART 8 THE ART OF COMMUNICATING IN BUSINESS   294

UNIT 37 HALLMARKS OF EFFECTIVE COMMUNICATION   297
Empathy; Skill in human relations; Standards of business communication; Acceptance

UNIT 38 THE PSYCHOLOGY OF EFFECTIVE BUSINESS WRITING   302
Using psychology in routine letters; Using psychology in "problem" communications

UNIT 39 WRITING SKILL AND JOB SUCCESS   309
The need for writing skill; Types of business writing; The need for accuracy and authoritative reference sources

PART 9 EFFECTIVE LETTER WRITING   316

UNIT 40 MAKING BUSINESS LETTERS EFFECTIVE   319
Why write business letters? Kinds of business letters; Getting results from business letters

UNIT 41 QUALITIES OF EFFECTIVE LETTERS   326
What makes a letter effective? Ten requirements; Some expressions to avoid

UNIT 42 BUSINESS LETTER FORM—PARTS AND PLACEMENT   338
The heading; Opening; Body; Closing; Positioning of letter parts; Second page; Envelope; Postal Codes

UNIT 43 BUSINESS LETTER FORM—ARRANGEMENT AND PUNCTUATION STYLES   350
Arrangement styles; Punctuation styles; Style accessories

UNIT 44 LETTERS THAT ASK AND TRANSMIT   359
Everyday letters; Characteristics of asking letters; Typical asking letters; Courtesy carbons; Letters of transmittal

UNIT 45 LETTERS THAT ANSWER—ACKNOWLEDGMENTS   369
Why write acknowledgments? Acknowledging business papers and orders; Confirming appointments, orders, agreements

UNIT 46 LETTERS THAT ANSWER—RESPONSES   376
Opportunities to make friends; Types of letters of response; Rules for writing letters of response

UNIT 47 THE SECRETARY'S RESPONSIBILITY FOR CORRESPONDENCE 383

Routine for incoming mail; "To write or not to write"; Letters written for the employer; While-the-boss-is-away letters

UNIT 48 CLAIM AND ADJUSTMENT LETTERS 393

Claims; Writing claim letters; Adjustments; Writing adjustment letters; Classes of adjustments

UNIT 49 CREDIT AND COLLECTION LETTERS 403

Credit letters; Collection letters

UNIT 50 LETTERS FOR OTHER PROBLEM SITUATIONS 415

Incomplete inquiries; Unreasonable requests; Delays in filling orders; Refusals of orders; Invitation refusals; Information refusals; Refusing unearned discounts

UNIT 51 WRITING EFFECTIVE SALES LETTERS 424

Steps in planning; An effective letter plan; Follow-up letters

UNIT 52 USING WRITING SKILLS TO GET A JOB 439

The qualifications summary; Employment applications

UNIT 53 WRITING EMPLOYMENT LETTERS 446

The letter of application; Requesting references; Follow-up letters; The letter of resignation

UNIT 54 PUBLIC RELATIONS LETTERS 456

Characteristics of public relations letters

UNIT 55 SOCIAL-BUSINESS LETTERS 462

Why social-business correspondence? Kinds of social-business letters

PART 10 MEMORANDUMS, REPORTS, AND OTHER WRITTEN COMMUNICATIONS 470

UNIT 56 WRITING MEMORANDUMS 473

The tone of memorandums; Writing the memorandum; When are memorandums written? Displaying detailed matter

UNIT 57 WRITING REPORTS 478

What is a business report? Preparing a formal report; Tone of the formal report; Mechanics of report writing

UNIT 58 WRITING TELEGRAMS, MINUTES, AND NEWS RELEASES 486

Communicating by telegraph; Minutes of meetings; News releases

PART 11 THE ART OF EFFECTIVE SPEAKING 498

UNIT 59 SETTING THE STAGE 501
The setting is important; Dress and grooming; Posture and carriage; Facial expressions; Manners; Mannerisms

UNIT 60 DEVELOPING A FLEXIBLE VOICE 509
Your voice quality; The physical tools of speech

UNIT 61 ENUNCIATION AND PRONUNCIATION 515
What causes poor enunciation? Why we pronounce as we do; Frequent mispronunciations; Some tips to help you

UNIT 62 MEETING THE PUBLIC 523
Business people meet the public; Basic rules for meeting the public; Telephone techniques

UNIT 63 THE EMPLOYMENT INTERVIEW 531
Preparing for the interview; Conducting yourself during the interview

UNIT 64 PARTICIPATING IN CONFERENCES AND MEETINGS 538
The group member; The group leader

UNIT 65 GIVING A TALK 544
Preparing the talk; Delivering the talk

INDEX 551

"What you don't know won't hurt you."
"No news is good news."
"Silence is golden."

What would happen if your family, your friends, your teachers, your local businessmen, and others upon whom you depend for a variety of necessities and luxuries of living suddenly were to decide to guide their lives according to these familiar old saws? You and the rest of us soon would suffer the consequences of emotional, intellectual, and physical starvation. Why? Simply because we must communicate—exchange ideas and information with those around us—in order to satisfy ourselves as human beings. Languages were developed—and still exist—for the sole purpose of giving us a means to express ourselves and understand others.

Communication—the use of language to speak and write our thoughts and to read and listen to the thoughts of others—is not enough to satisfy us by itself. We also must occupy at least part of our time with activities that result in the production of goods and services that all of us require to satisfy a wide variety of needs. Therefore, with the exception of those persons of independent means, nearly all of us enter the world of work.

COMMUNICATION IN THE WORLD OF WORK

Today's world of work offers countless opportunities to choose from hundreds of interesting and rewarding careers in retailing, manufacturing, banking, insurance, advertising, real estate, automotive mechanics, and other types of business enterprises. The only "catch" to such opportunities is that you must be fully qualified to perform the duties of a secretary, a salesperson, an accountant, a cashier, a clerk-typist, a machine operator, a mechanic, or whatever other occupation you may choose.

Many of the qualifications you must have in order to enter and succeed in the world of work depend, of course, upon the kind of work you wish to do. Knowing how to operate a lathe, for example, isn't very likely to open many doors if you wish to be a secretary. On the other hand, being able to type or write shorthand won't be of much on-the-job help if you want to be a lathe operator. Obviously, all of us must decide sooner or later what we want to do and then take the steps necessary to prepare ourselves for the careers we choose before we enter the job market.

What does your ability to communicate have to do with your being qualified for the job you choose? No one in the world of work—regardless of his or her job title—works completely alone. Consequently, no

one is completely "communication exempt." Every employee receives instructions from supervisors, reports his progress to his immediate superiors, and exchanges ideas and information with his co-workers. And the duties of a great many employees bring them into contact with some segment of the public: customers, suppliers, dealers, visitors. In brief, everyone in the world of work has a basic need to speak and listen, to read and write.

To qualify as a secretary, for example, you will need to be able to type, take dictation, transcribe dictation, answer the telephone, receive visitors, write letters on behalf of your employer, requisition office supplies, keep records of appointments . . . . It takes a lot of listening, speaking, reading, and writing every day of the week to earn and keep a secretarial position, doesn't it?

One of the first things you would have to do as a salesperson is learn just about all there is to know about your company's products or services and also those of your competitors. Then you would have to put this knowledge to work by going out and meeting people and convincing them that they need and should buy your company's products or services. Whether you achieve your goal of writing up orders or not, you would have to prepare and submit reports of your discussions with

customers and prospective customers; plan and submit itineraries; keep and submit records of hotel, food, entertainment, and other necessary business expenses; and so on. Too, you would have to keep your eyes and your ears tuned to developments affecting the products or services you promote and the market to which you sell. To be a salesperson, you don't have to have the ability to "charm the birds out of the trees"; but you do have to have the ability to communicate effectively with people.

Communication is vitally essential to achieving the varied goals of total living, not just to fulfilling those connected with the world of work. To participate meaningfully in social, cultural, political, and other types of human activity, we must be able to speak, listen, write, and read effectively. To do this, we must learn a language and develop skills in using it. In a linguistic sense, none of us are born with the ability to communicate: expressions of the "born writer" type are as out of place in the world of work as are the axioms mentioned previously. An effective writer—like an effective speaker, listener, or reader—is simply a person who has mastered the art so well through thoughtful study and through continual practice that the rest of us think he has innate talent.

Our preparation for the world of work and for life in general is based to a large extent on the study of language and the development of language-arts skills. Beginning with the three R's of formal education—reading, 'riting, and 'rithmetic—all of us gain general communication competence through courses covering such subjects as spelling, penmanship, grammar, composition, and literature. However, those of us who aspire to entering and succeeding in the world of work need special competence in business English and communication. This course, therefore, deals with practical principles of communicating in person, by telephone, by letter, by report, by memo, and by other means commonly used in the world of work.

Setting Your Communication Goals

Is it true that one person's success may be another person's failure? Certainly, because the satisfaction and success each of us achieves depend mainly upon fulfilling goals that we set for ourselves, not upon meeting the standards of performance and achievement set by others. Thus, it is important to set realistic goals for your chosen career or profession and for your study of such courses as business English and communication. What are realistic goals for you? Only you can decide

by determining whether your answers to such questions as those below reflect goals that suit your personal interests, needs, and capabilities and that—with effort—you reasonably can expect to achieve.

1. What career or profession do you plan to enter when you attain the necessary qualifications? Briefly describe how your reading, writing, listening, and speaking skills will influence your on-the-job performance and success.

2. Do you agree with the statement, "The world in which we live and work is essentially a world of communication"? Cite specific examples that support your viewpoint.

3. Closely examine a copy of *Business Week, Maclean's, Time, Newsweek,* or some other news magazine. Of what value is such reading to you now? Of what value will it be to you when you enter the world of work?

4. The rapid development and refinement of communication systems and equipment has greatly affected our activities at home, in school, and at work. Does such progress make it more important or less important for you to master the principles and techniques of effective speaking, reading, writing, and listening? Why?

PART □ 1

Words Work for You □

In trying to describe a situation to others, have you ever found that you couldn't quite get anyone to see the situation as you saw it? Why weren't you able to make the description as vivid to your audience as it was to you? Probably you couldn't think of the particular words you needed. Word knowledge is also important when listening; you probably can think of some personally embarrassing experiences caused by your failure to know the meaning of words used by someone who was talking to you. There is no denying that words can work *for* you—or *against* you if your vocabulary is skimpy. The purpose of Part 1 is to help you to develop a good working vocabulary for school, business, and social situations.

Words—
Chief Means
of Communication

The chief means by which we communicate is through words. Only by having a large reservoir of words at our command can we communicate effectively. Words represent power—the power to convey facts and ideas, the power to influence others. The words we use can make another person happy or sad, angry or subdued, proud or humble. At the same time, our choice of words may label us as tactful or insulting, articulate or bumbling, up-to-date or old-fashioned.

What Is a Good Vocabulary?

The office employee, as an educated person, is expected to have a good vocabulary. What is a good vocabulary? Well, of course, it is a large store of words. But it is more than that. One's vocabulary may be described as good when it enables him to understand fully what he hears and reads, and to say and write precisely what he means. The key words here are *fully* and *precisely*. Weakness in either area results in mistakes and embarrassment.

A few examples will demonstrate how lack of a good vocabulary may be a handicap:

Michelle was asked to type a report in triplicate. Not knowing what "triplicate" meant, she prepared an original and one carbon copy and thought she had completed the work. Instead, she had to type another copy. This resulted in loss of time as well as in the impatience of her department head. *The possessor of a good vocabulary understands the meaning of the words most frequently used in business and in daily life.*

Two candidates for a certain job were asked to list in writing their previous experience. One applicant wrote simply, "Office work." Another wrote: "General clerical: typing letters and reports, using adding machine, opening and distributing mail, checking inventories." Which applicant probably made the more favorable impression? *The possessor of a good vocabulary uses precise words to express his meaning.*

Mr. Leroy told an employee to leave a memo on Mr. Kent's desk saying that he (Mr. Leroy) had gone out to Newton to inspect the two sites that had been suggested for their new factory building. Mr. Kent found this memo: "Mr. Leroy has gone out to inspect sights for the new factory." Would either Mr. Leroy or Mr. Kent be likely to feel that the writer of the memo would be an efficient secretary? *The possessor of a good vocabulary is familiar with those words that are pronounced exactly alike but are spelled differently and have different meanings.*

Gertrude wondered why people smiled when she said she thought the speaker's remarks were "inflammable." They knew, of course, that she meant "inflammatory"; but her embarrassing blunder was not soon forgotten. *The possessor of a good vocabulary distinguishes between words that look or sound somewhat alike.*

A thank-you note read: "Thank you for your generous donation to the Fresh Air Fund. This year, especially, such donations are greatly appreciated." The substitution of "gift" for the second "donation" would have varied the wording. *The possessor of a good vocabulary achieves variety in his communications by the use of synonyms (words that have the same or very nearly the same meaning).*

Jack told a friend he was going to stop at the photo shop to leave some "filums" to be developed. A mispronunciation like this instantly reveals slovenly speech habits. *The possessor of a good vocabulary pronounces words correctly.*

A stenographer's transcript contained the phrase, "seperate accomodations." When the misspellings were noticed, the stenographer had to retype the entire letter in order to insert the correct "separate accommodations." *The possessor of a good vocabulary spells words correctly.*

Vocabulary in Social Life

Most of the anecdotes just narrated pertain to office experiences. However, your ability to use words effectively is just as much an asset in school and social situations. If you can say or write exactly what you mean so that others will not misunderstand you, your ability to communicate, and thus to influence others, will be recognized. As a member of a club or an association, you probably will have many occasions to express opinions or to make suggestions during meetings. The person who can word a recommendation clearly or can summarize the feelings of a group precisely will probably be elevated to a position of leadership. As secretary, he or she would be responsible for keeping the minutes of meetings and for conducting club correspondence. Such activities are excellent preparation for the business world.

There are many other situations in which you will find a good vocabulary to be invaluable. Buying or selling goods, adjusting complaints, sending telegrams, using the telephone, expressing congratulations and sympathy—all these and many more offer opportunities to use your vocabulary effectively.

How to Improve Your Vocabulary

How do you acquire a good vocabulary? In at least four ways. You begin by becoming word-conscious. This means being alert for words that are new to you or for words that are used in unfamiliar ways. Next, you try to guess the meaning of the new word or expression from the words around it. Clues to its meaning may be found in the sentence in which the word appears, or in the surrounding sentences. Then, whether or not you were able to guess its meaning, you should consult a good dictionary for the appropriate definition and precise shade of meaning. And finally, you study each word and practice using it until it becomes part of your vocabulary.

Because a good vocabulary is so important to effective communication in all areas of life, we'll discuss each point separately.

Become Word-Conscious   Being word-conscious simply means being curious about, and interested in, words. The more you know about words—their origins, their development, their synonyms—the more swiftly your word reservoir will grow and the more words you'll promote from your passive (recognition) vocabulary into your active, working vocabulary.

The opportunities for cultivating word-consciousness are all about you. They are to be found on radio and television, in books, magazines, newspapers—even advertisements. They also come built-in with lectures and speeches, perhaps even in the conversations of friends and acquaintances.

Studies of successful persons show that they have in common this characteristic: a large vocabulary. It is logical, then, that you can increase your vocabulary by listening intently to the speech of such persons. Listen to your teachers or to the executives and department heads in your office—observe their choice of words. Take note of any word or expression that is not in your active vocabulary. Also, pay special attention to radio and television commentators. Broadcasts and telecasts are carefully prepared and offer excellent examples of well-chosen words. In addition, most commentators have had speech training; and their pronunciation is usually correct.

Find Meaning from Context   Discovering the meaning of a word or expression from the sentence in which it is used, or from the surrounding sentences, is called finding meaning from context. Many of you do this automatically. It is just common sense to guess at a word's meaning from the clues given, particularly when you do not have easy access to a dictionary. When you are sufficiently word-conscious, this type of detective work becomes fun.

For example: In reviewing a new novel, a literary critic referred to the author's "pedestrian style of writing that lacks the excitement deserved by the subject matter." To you, *pedestrian* probably meant "a walker." While this definition is a partial clue to the meaning of pedestrian in this sentence, it obviously is not sufficient. Probably the best clue here is the phrase, "lacks excitement." Put the clues together and you have "a walking style that lacks excitement." Now you're close. Reference to a dictionary tells you that *pedestrian* may mean "unimaginative" or "commonplace." These latter meanings are the proper ones in this context.

Consult Your Dictionary   Whether or not you are a skillful word detective, you'll want to check your dictionary to find if you guessed correctly and also to discover the precise shade of meaning for the word in question. Obviously, not all the definitions listed will be equally appropriate. You'll want to "try on for size" each definition in turn, until you find the most fitting one for the context. To do this, you may need to refer again to the sentence.

Knowing how to use the dictionary is so important to your vocabulary growth that the entire next unit is devoted to an examination of what your "word bank" contains. Another very important help to vocabulary building is a thesaurus, which is a collection of words and phrases arranged according to ideas. The thesaurus is discussed in Unit 36, "Achieving Variety in Word Usage."

Study, Practice   Absorbing a new word into your active vocabulary takes practice in using the word, as well as study. Keeping a notebook in which you write all unfamiliar words will make the process easier. When you write the word, be sure to note its spelling. Then say the word aloud. Write a sentence or two using the word, and then say the sentence aloud. Hearing the sound of the word will make it easier for you to use that word in conversation.

Our Changing Vocabulary

Just as the vocabulary of every person changes as he grows in knowledge and experience, the English language changes, too. It is a living language, and language must change and develop to keep pace with the people who use it. As people invent new things, make discoveries, enter into new relationships, and otherwise add to their store of experiences, they coin new words to express these experiences. They also borrow words from other languages, and they add new meanings to already existing words. As more and more persons use these new words and meanings, the latter gradually find their way into the dictionaries.

New Words Added Each Year   Every year, thousands of words are added to our dictionaries. In periods of great national or international activity and during times of great technical and scientific advances, as today, these additions are especially numerous. *Webster's Third New International Dictionary,* for example, contains 100 000 new words or new meanings. This remarkable unabridged dictionary was published in 1961, twenty-seven years after its predecessor; therefore, it represents an average of nearly 4000 recorded new words or new meanings a year!

Here are a few examples of new words or old words with added meanings that are found in the new *Webster's:* programming, tranquilizer, Medicare, countdown, sit-in, fringe benefit, beatnik, telecast, calypso, scuba, brainwashing, astronaut, spectacular (television show).

Usage Determines Acceptability   These new words and new meanings are absorbed into our language through usage. If enough people use them over a long enough period of time, they become an accepted part of the language. For example, some words that were once disdainfully called business jargon, like *mortician* and *beautician,* are now considered real words. Certain abbreviations—*auto, bus, taxi, gym*—also have come to be accepted as words. However, these clipped forms are more suitable in spoken or informal English than in formal writing. Note that, unlike real abbreviations, these shortened words are not followed by a period.

Ben Roth Agency

Why do we have to call it "fire"? Let's call it something realistic, like "ouch!"

It may surprise you to learn that some of our commonly used words were originally considered slang. For example, *mob, sham,* and *lynch,* once not considered "good" words, are now acceptable.

Words Change in Meaning   Changes in the meanings of words are nothing new in the development of our language. The English language always has been shifting. Who would think that *silly* once meant "good" or "happy," that *fond* meant "foolish," and that *curious* meant "careful"? The word *broadcast* originally meant "to sow seed."

In addition, the ways in which many words were used in sentences long ago differed from the ways in which they are used at present. In olden days, if *you* referred to one person, a singular verb was used. (Those today who are tempted to say "you was" would have felt right at home!)

Some Words Become Out of Date   Many words have been dropped from our working vocabularies because they no longer apply to our modern way of life. When gentlemen ceased to wear high boots, they no longer required *bootjacks* to help remove that type of footgear. Hence "bootjacks" is rarely used except in museum catalogues. Under our democratic way of life it is no longer fitting for the writer of a business letter to sign himself "Your obedient servant." It *was* fitting long ago when people were divided into masters and servants and a letter was written to an absent master by the servant in charge of the master's estate. Words like *erstwhile* and *quoth,* in common use a hundred years ago, just do not fit the direct speech and writing needed today.

How to Keep in Step

How are you to keep your vocabulary in step with changing times? How are you to judge which words, meanings, and pronunciations are up to date and which are acceptable? The answer is twofold: First, listen and observe; and second, suit your language to the occasion, the audience, and your purpose.

Listen and Observe   We stressed that you should listen to the speech of those persons who use language well—experts in various fields, speakers, executives, teachers, lawyers, and so on—in order to enlarge your vocabulary. The same process holds true for keeping up to date. Another way is to observe the vocabulary in well-edited newspapers and magazines. These persons and periodicals use what is commonly called *standard English*—the English generally used by educated people and that which you should use. Conversely, the language generally used by persons of little education is called *nonstandard English,* as are those words and usages that are very new, or are debatable.

Use Appropriate Language   Through such observation and listening you will learn to judge what is *appropriate* in language—what is suited to the times and to the people who live therein—and this is the key to using language well.

Formal and Informal English   Standard English can be either formal or informal, depending on how it is used. The proper degree of formality depends upon the occasion, the audience, and the purpose for which one speaks or writes. An executive writing a report for his company or a speaker addressing a large audience of educated persons would appropriately use formal English. On the other hand, friends having a chat or a person writing a letter to a close relative would use informal English.

The line between formal and informal English is not clear-cut. Informal English is used more often in speaking than in writing. However, it appears in newspaper stories and most magazine articles, in books of general interest, in many textbooks, and in most business letters. Informal English is characterized by an informal, conversational tone and by generally shorter sentences and a simpler vocabulary than is formal English. The word *you* pops up frequently in informal English.

Slang   Slang is considered nonstandard until it survives long enough to be accepted as standard informal English. However, "slanguage" is considered acceptable in informal speech when both speakers and listeners know each other well.

Be wary of slang, however, particularly in writing. Use it sparingly, if at all. Since many persons do not understand slang, you risk the danger of failing to make yourself understood. Also, the word that is on everyone's tongue today is hopelessly out of date tomorrow. (How many of you, for example, use the term *oomph* that was so popular a generation ago?) Perhaps the greatest danger of using slang is that the constant repetition of stock expressions to cover any and all situations impoverishes your vocabulary and weakens the exactness of your thinking.

Your conversation and writing can be fresh and modern without resorting to slang. Concentration on words is the antidote, and acquiring a stock of words can be fun. It also pays big dividends, for one of the surest ways of winning advancement in a job is by building a good vocabulary. A person who can use words effectively develops self-confidence and personality. Remember that the words you use interpret *you* to the world.

Communication Problems

Application Exercises

A ▪

Jane has formed the habit of characterizing anything of which she approves or about which she is enthusiastic as "terrific." Choose more meaningful words to describe each of the following specific nouns.

1	a friend's new hat	6	the new dramatic coach
2	an apple pie	7	the new English teacher
3	a motion picture	8	her department supervisor
4	a ball game	9	the majorettes' new uniforms
5	a new novel	10	dinner at a new restaurant

B ▪

The terms listed here are either new words or old words with new or added meanings. Refer to an up-to-date dictionary like *Webster's Seventh New Collegiate Dictionary* for the definitions. Then, for each word, write a sentence using the word appropriately.

1	fallout	5	featherbedding
2	finalize	6	structure (verb)
3	ghost (television)	7	exurbia
4	angle (in writing)	8	attaché case

C ▪

In each of the following sentences, choose the word in parentheses that correctly expresses the meaning.

1 My, but this (current, currant) jelly is good!
2 Yes, I (ought, aught) to open a savings account.
3 They searched the attic but found no one (their, there).
4 Two large ocean liners docked at adjoining (piers, peers) this morning.
5 As I don't pretend to be a (profit, prophet), I can't forecast the results.

6 At the end of the first (scene, seen) all the characters had been introduced.
7 We were (shone, shown) many courtesies in our tour through the plant.
8 No one is (aloud, allowed) through these gates!
9 Because of the high humidity, the pipes in our (seller, cellar) are dripping.
10 Stainless (steal, steel) is increasingly popular for tableware.

D ■

Here are ten frequently used words. Which are misspelled? Respell them correctly.

1	atheletic	6	controversy
2	parallel	7	nickle
3	priviledge	8	occurrence
4	recipient	9	Febuary
5	accidently	10	congradulations

E ■

For each of the following words, think of another word of similar meaning. The hints in parentheses may help you.

1 commence (a 5-letter word starting with *b*)
2 procure (a 6-letter word starting with *o*)
3 casual (a 7-letter word starting with *off*)
4 colossal (a 4-letter word starting with *h*)
5 approximately (a 5-letter word starting with *a*)
6 nevertheless (a 3-letter word starting with *y*)
7 courteous (a 6-letter word starting with *p*)
8 humorous (a 5-letter word starting with *f*)
9 scatter (a 6-letter word starting with *sp*)
10 frank (a 7-letter word starting with *s*)

F ■

The following words were used in this unit. Try to determine the meaning of each from its context. You will need to reread the sentence in which each word appears and, in some instances, the adjacent sentences. Check your guesses in a good dictionary.

1	reservoir	6	periodical
2	articulate	7	conversely
3	slovenly	8	stock
4	predecessor	9	impoverish
5	disdainfully	10	antidote

Communication in Action: *Giving Credit to Others*

Your supervisor, Mr. Nelson, says to you, "That was an excellent job you did in putting the vacation schedule together." But, in fact, you didn't prepare the schedule; the job was done by one of your co-workers, Floyd Moore. Reply to the supervisor.

The Dictionary— Your Basic Reference Tool

Should you say *'ad-ult* or *a-'dult?* Is the plural of *hero* formed by adding *s* or *es*? Do you divide *present*, when it comes at the end of a line, into *pre-sent* or *pres-ent?* What does *moratorium* mean? These are some of the kinds of questions that often confront even the most accomplished speakers and writers. The answers to these questions are to be found in a dictionary.

A Most Important Tool

All language is made up of words; and words are symbols for whatever ideas you wish to express through speaking and writing. Because a dictionary is the book that gives the most information about words, it is an important—perhaps *the* most important—tool of the communicator.

Quality Is Important   Just as the carpenter owns tools of high quality, so should you—as a beginning craftsman in the art of communicating—own a reliable, up-to-date dictionary. The best, most complete dictionaries are the unabridged ones, including *Webster's Third New International Dictionary* and Funk and Wagnalls *New Standard Dictionary.* These comprehensive works have approximately 450 000 word entries, but they are so large and expensive that they are found mostly in libraries and offices. Therefore, for personal use, a good standard desk dictionary would be an appropriate choice. Among these are *Webster's Seventh New Collegiate Dictionary, The Winston Dictionary, The Concise Oxford Dictionary,* and *The Heritage Illustrated Dictionary of the English Language.* Perhaps most useful for Canadian students is *The Gage Canadian Dictionary* as it emphasizes Canadian usage and includes many Canadian names, words, and idioms not found in other dictionaries.

But First, the Alphabet   Every once in a while, a teacher is shocked to find that a student in senior high school doesn't know his alphabet. You can readily see that the best dictionary money can buy would be of no use to such a student. Obviously, anyone who wishes to be a successful communicator, but who suffers from "alphabet blackout," must first learn the alphabet! Practice finding words in the dictionary until you can do this rapidly. You should be able to find in not more than twenty seconds any word you can spell. Be sure to make use of the guide words (the first and last word entries on each page) at the top of the page.

Preview Your Dictionary

Dictionaries differ in their number and arrangement of details; therefore, you should preview your dictionary before using it. First, study carefully the guides at the beginning of the book. (For illustrative purposes, all dictionary references in this text apply to *Webster's Seventh New Collegiate Dictionary.**)

Guide to Pronunciation   It is essential that you know how your dictionary denotes pronunciation. The pronunciation guide explains the vowel and consonant symbols—including the use of the schwa (ə) for the neutral "uh" sound, as in ba̱(ə)nan-a̱(ə)—which stand for all the sounds in our language; and the guide also explains the use of stress marks (') (,) for accented syllables.

Assume you want to know how to pronounce the verb *mediate*. Is it *mee-diate*, or *med-iate* (as in *medical*)? Upon looking it up, you find it to be *mee-diate*, because the dictionary indicates the *ee* sound by printing it *ē*, whereas the short sound of *e* (*bet*, *bed*) is indicated by the letter without any diacritical mark.

Explanatory Notes   Preliminary study of the explanatory notes will save you time and promote accuracy in using your dictionary. These notes explain the different typefaces and labels, the significant symbols and punctuation, and the other means by which a dictionary can achieve compactness. Take just one example, that of word division:

Suppose you want to know if the noun *blackout* is one word, two words, or a hyphenated word. When you look it up, you see *black·out*. The explanatory notes tell you that a centred period denotes a syllable break only; therefore, *blackout* is one word. If you looked up *self-conscious* you would find *self-con·scious*. This word, then, is hyphenated after *self* and syllabicated after *con*.

List of Abbreviations   So much information must be packed into a dictionary that abbreviations for proper nouns and explanatory words and phrases frequently are necessary; to get full use of your dictionary, you must know what these abbreviations mean. For instance, it is important for you to know that *obs* stands for *obsolete*, which means that this word is no longer in current usage. Knowing abbreviations for the parts of speech—*n*, *v*, *adj*, *adv*, and so on—may save you from making embarrassing mistakes in your speech and writing.

Although you need not attempt to memorize all the abbreviations, you should learn those most commonly used and also where to find the meanings of those used less often.

Word References

The main purpose of a dictionary, obviously, is to provide information about words. Every dictionary gives standard information, but not all dictionaries give the same

* Published by the G. and C. Merriam Co., Springfield, Massachusetts, 1963, and based on *Webster's Third New International Dictionary*, 1961.

variety of "extra" word information. For a sample of the information given in one dictionary, see the illustration on page 20.

Standard Information Every dictionary, no matter how small or how large, whether paper-covered or hardbound, shows the spelling, word division, pronunciation, and meaning or meanings of each word it lists. A good standard desk dictionary also gives what part of speech a word is; its origin; the ways in which it is used; synonyms; and certain irregular forms—for example, the principal parts of the verb *go* (*went, gone, going*), the plural of the noun *alumna* (*alumnae*); and the comparative and superlative forms of the adjective *gluey* (*gluier, gluiest*).

Bear in mind, however, that all dictionaries do not agree on preferred pronunciations. Since the standard of English pronunciation is based on the usage that prevails among educated people, this collective usage is hard to measure. Thus, in one dictionary you may find the pronunciation of *lever* given as 'lev-er (preferred), 'lē-ver; while in another you may find the opposite arrangement.

Supplementary Information It is extremely important that you know what extra help you can expect from your dictionary. For instance, you should know that you can find answers to problems in the following categories:

Capitalization Suppose you are writing advertising copy for a sale of women's bathing suits—one-piece, skirted, and bikini types. You happen to know that *Bikini* is an atoll of the Marshall Islands, and so you think you should capitalize the word. You check to make sure.

As you open the dictionary, you recall that the word entries are printed in small letters unless a word is capitalized almost always or more often than not. Therefore, when you see *bikini* and read the definition you know that the word as you are using it does not begin with a capital letter.

The main part of your dictionary, then, will help you with capitalization; but you may get further help from the rules for capitalization in the reference section.

Synonyms Although a dictionary is not a book of synonyms, it does give synonyms for some words; therefore, when you have a synonym problem, you ordinarily reach first for that "good old reliable" reference, your dictionary. In writing a letter, suppose you want to say that there has been no decline in sales, but you already have used the noun *decline* twice. In search of a substitute, you look up *decline* and find: "*n* . . . **syn** see DETERIORATION." Under *deterioration* you find synonyms for *decline* with their exact shades of meaning.

Noun Plurals The explanatory notes tell you that your dictionary gives any out-of-the-ordinary plural forms (plurals not formed by adding *s* or *es*, or by changing the final *y* to *i*). If you need to know the plural of *fungus*, for example, you will see given after that word in your dictionary this information: "*n, pl* **fun·gi** also **fun·gus·es**." And if it is the plural of *mother-in-law* that bothers you, you will find after that word: "*n, pl* **mothers-in-law**."

foretime

syllabicated word entry	**fore·time** \'fōr-,tīm, 'fȯr-\ *n* : former or past time
	¹**fore·to·ken** \'fōr-,tō-kən, 'fȯr-\ *n* : a premonitory sign
	²**fore·to·ken** \fōr-'tō-kən, fȯr-\ *vt* **fore·to·ken·ing** \-'tōk-(ə-)niŋ\ : to warn of in advance
numbered meanings	**fore·top** \'fōr-,täp, 'fȯr-, *in sense 2 often* 'fōrt-əp *or* 'fȯrt-\ *n* **1** : hair on the forepart of the head; *esp* : the forelock of a horse **2** : the platform at the head of a ship's foremast
	fore–top·gal·lant \'fōr-,täp-,gal-ənt, 'fōrt-ə-,gal-, 'fȯr(t)-\ *adj* : being the part next above the fore-topmast
	fore–top·man \'fōr-,täp-mən, 'fōrt-əp-, 'fȯr(t)-\ *n* : a sailor on duty on the foremast and above
	fore–top·mast \'fōr-,täp-məst, 'fōrt-əp-,mast, 'fȯr(t)-\ *n* : a mast next above the foremast
pronunciation	**fore–top·sail** \'fōr-,täp-səl, 'fōrt-əp-,säl, 'fȯr(t)-\ *n* : the sail above the foresail
	for·ev·er \fə-'rev-ər, fȯ-\ *adv* **1** : for a limitless time **2** : at all times
	for·ev·er·more \-,rev-ə(r)-'mō(ə)r, -'mȯ(ə)r\ *adv* : FOREVER
	for·ev·er·ness \-'rev-ər-nəs\ *n* : ETERNITY
parts of speech	**fore·warn** \fōr-'wȯ(ə)rn, fȯr-\ *vt* : to warn in advance **syn** see WARN
	fore wing *n* : either of the anterior wings of a 4-winged insect
	fore·wom·an \'fōr-,wùm-ən, 'fȯr-\ *n* : FORELADY
	fore·word \'fōr-(,)wərd, 'fȯr-\ *n* : PREFACE
	foreworn *var of* FORWORN
	fore·yard \'fōr-,yärd, 'fȯr-\ *n* : the lowest yard on a foremast
word origins	¹**for·feit** \'fȯr-fət\ *n* [ME *forfait*, fr. MF, fr. pp. of *forfaire* to commit a crime, forfeit, prob. fr. *jors* outside (fr. L *joris*) + *faire* to do, fr. L *facere* — more at FORUM, DO] **1 a** : something forfeited **b** : PENALTY **2** : FORFEITURE **3 a** : something deposited and then redeemed on payment of a fine **b** *pl* : a game in which forfeits are exacted
	²**forfeit** *vt* **1** : to lose or lose the right to by some error, offense, or crime **2** : to subject to confiscation as a forfeit — **for·feit·able** \-ə-bəl\ *adj* — **for·feit·er** *n*
run-on entries	³**forfeit** *adj* : forfeited or subject to forfeiture
	for·fei·ture \'fȯr-fə-,chù(ə)r, -chər, -,t(y)ù(ə)r\ *n* **1** : the act of forfeiting **2** : something that is forfeited : PENALTY
usage label	**for·fend** *also* **fore·fend** \fȯr-'fend, fōr-\ *vt* **1 a** *archaic* : FORBID **b** : to ward off : PREVENT **2** : PROTECT, PRESERVE
variant spelling	**for·gath·er** *or* **fore·gath·er** \fȯr-'gath-ər, fōr-\ *vi* **1** : to come together : ASSEMBLE **2** : to meet someone usu. by chance
	¹**forge** \'fō(ə)rj, 'fȯ(ə)rj\ *n* [ME, fr. OF, fr. L *fabrica*, fr. *fabr-*, *faber* smith — more at DAFT] **1** : a furnace or a shop with its furnace where metal is heated and wrought : SMITHY **2** : a workshop where wrought iron is produced or where iron is made : BLOOMERY
	²**forge** *vt* **1 a** : to form (as metal) by heating and hammering **b** : to form (metal) by a mechanical or hydraulic press **2** : to form or shape out in any way : FASHION **3** : to make or imitate falsely esp. with intent to defraud : COUNTERFEIT ∼ *vi* **1** : to work at a forge **2** : to commit forgery **syn** see MAKE
	³**forge** *vi* [origin unknown] **1** : to move forward slowly and steadily **2** : to move with a sudden increase of speed and power
	forg·er \'fōr-jər, 'fȯr-\ *n* **1 a** : FALSIFIER; *specif* : a creator of false tales **b** : a person guilty of forgery **2** : one that forges
	forg·ery \'fōrj-(ə-)rē, 'fȯrj-\ *n* **1** *archaic* : INVENTION **2** : an act of forging; *esp* : the crime of falsely and fraudulently making or altering a writing or other instrument **3** : something forged
principal parts of verb	**for·get** \fər-'get, fȯr-\ *vb* **for·got** \-'gät\ **for·got·ten** \-'gät-ᵊn\ *or* **forgot; for·get·ting** [ME *forgeten*, fr. OE *forgietan*, fr. *for-* + *-gietan* (akin to ON *geta* to get)] *vt* **1 a** : to lose the remembrance of. **b** *obs* : to cease from doing **2** : to treat with inattention or disregard : NEGLECT ⟨*forgot* his old friends⟩ **3** : to put out of mind
example contexts	⟨∼ it⟩ ∼ *vi* **1** : to cease remembering or noticing **2** : to fail to become mindful at the proper time ⟨∼ about paying the bill⟩ **syn** see NEGLECT — **for·get·ter** *n* — **forget oneself** : to lose one's dignity, temper, or self-control
	for·get·ful \-'get-fəl\ *adj* **1** : likely to forget **2** : CARELESS, NEGLECTFUL **3** : inducing oblivion ⟨∼ sleep⟩ — **for·get·ful·ly** \-fə-lē\ *adv* — **for·get·ful·ness** *n*
synonym study	**syn** OBLIVIOUS, UNMINDFUL: FORGETFUL usually implies a heedless or negligent habit of failing to keep in mind; OBLIVIOUS suggests a failure to notice or remember due to external causes or conditions or to a determination to ignore; UNMINDFUL may suggest inattention and heedlessness or a deliberate ignoring
	for·ge·tive \'fōr-jət-iv, 'fȯr-\ *adj* [prob. fr. ²*forge* + *-tive* (as in *inventive*)] : INVENTIVE, IMAGINATIVE
hyphenation	**for·get–me–not** \fər-'get-mē-,nät, fȯr-\ *n* : any of a genus (*Myosotis*) of small herbs of the borage family having bright-blue or white flowers usu. in a curving spike
	for·get·ta·ble \fər-'get-ə-bəl, fȯr-\ *adj* : likely to be forgotten
	forg·ing *n* **1** : the act of a forger **2** : a piece of forged work

Portion of a desk dictionary, indicating the variety of information it contains.

Reference Section

When considering the purchase of a dictionary, you would be wise to pay particular attention to the reference section, usually found in the back of the book. Dictionaries vary as to the amount and kinds of reference material they contain; therefore, because a dictionary is your basic reference source, you should invest in the one that will be of most help to you. Among the dictionary reference possibilities are the following:

Vocabulary of Abbreviations   Because newspapers, magazines, and other present-day publications are filled with abbreviations, anyone who reads and writes should have some source wherein he can find the whole words for which those abbreviations stand. Suppose you receive documents from your company's shipping agent showing "9 p.m. ETA." If you don't know what ETA stands for, you can discover from your dictionary that it is "Estimated Arrival Time." Now you know the shipment might arrive at 9 p.m., but that the arrival time is not definite. And what does *IRBM* mean? The answer is as near as your dictionary: "intermediate range ballistic missile."

Pronouncing Gazetteer   "Faraway places and strange-sounding names" will pose no pronunciation difficulties when your dictionary has a pronouncing gazetteer. Suppose your boss asks you to make travel arrangements for him to San Juan and Ponce (he's not sure how to pronounce it), Puerto Rico. You never heard of the latter place before, so you consult your dictionary. There you find that the correct pronunciation is "'pȯn(t)-(ˌ)sā." You also discover that it is a "city & port S Puerto Rico *pop* 114 286."

Biographical Names   Maybe you have need of a source where you can get information about persons of note. If so, be sure that the dictionary you buy has the biographical names section. Suppose, for instance, you hear a reference to Toulouse-Lautrec, and you want some information about him. Your dictionary will give, besides the correct pronunciation of his name, this information: "Henri 1864–1901 Fr. painter."

Rules for Spelling and Mechanics   If you lack technical English training or if your memory often fails you, you should own a dictionary that gives rules for spelling, punctuation, capitalization, italics, compounds, and formation of plurals.

Other Reference Material   Some of the other kinds of reference material furnished in dictionaries are arbitrary symbols and proofreaders' marks, forms of address, common English names, vocabulary of rhymes, and colleges and universities in the United States and Canada.

And now that you understand how valuable the various parts of a dictionary can be, you should be able to select the edition that will give you maximum use. After all, it's *your* dictionary.

Communication Problems

Application Exercises

A ■

Do you really know the exact order of the letters of the alphabet?

1 In your dictionary, locate the following fifteen words, taking each one in the sequence shown. Note the exact time when you start your search for the words and also when you finish. How many minutes did it take you?

intelligence	inference	conversation
contribution	phenomenal	persistence
alternate	interrogate	advantageous
residuary	subsidiary	environment
executor	equitable	realty

2 Now, write these words in alphabetic order.

B ■

The following words are to be found on one page of a dictionary. Without using a dictionary, write them in alphabetic order. Note your starting and finishing times. How long did it take?

parlous	parry	parody
parrot	parliament	Parmesan
parrakeet	parricide	parochial
park	parlay	parotid
parlor	parole	parlance
parity	parquet	paroxysm

C ■

Among the following words are several typical and common malformations (can you guess the meaning of that word?), which are caused, usually, by lack of attention to spelling. A few of the words are shown correctly. Respell those that are wrong.

ninty	existence	rhythm
ocassionaly	Philipines	prarie
occurence	vegitable	similiar
nineth		

D ■

Here are ten common words. You should know their breakdown into syllables so you will know where to divide them at the end of a line. Without consulting your dictionary, indicate syllable divisions in each. In words of more than one syllable, place a primary stress mark (') before the proper syllable. Check your choices in the dictionary.

fortunate	through	extraordinary
injurious	misrepresentation	Cincinnati
optimistic	aggressive	identity
incomparable		

E ■

The following words were used in this unit. If you are not already familiar with them, try to guess their meanings from the context of the sentences in which they were used. Then check your guesses in the dictionary.

express	diacritical	syllabicated
unabridged	preliminary	usage
denotes	promote	collective
illustrative	compactness	gazetteer

Communication in Action: *You Feel Responsible*

Your very good friend, Tom Egan, needed a job and asked you to speak to your boss about an accounting position with your firm. This you did, and Tom joined the staff. He has been at work for two weeks now, and you have noticed that his grooming is poor. You have also noticed that he makes rather frequent trips to the lounge and that he takes a few extra minutes for his coffee breaks. Because you helped him to get this job, you feel responsible for his performance. What, if anything, should you do?

In preparation for class discussion of the problem, jot down on paper some of the various courses open to you and indicate which action you would take.

UNIT □ 3

Choosing the Right Word

An amazing number of words in the English language are confused because they sound alike or look alike but have different spellings and different meanings. Some words are pronounced exactly alike, as *break* (to shatter) and *brake* (a device to stop motion). Some sound somewhat alike, as *respectively* (in the order given), *respectfully* (courteously), and *respectably* (in a conventionally correct manner). Others look somewhat alike. They may contain the same letters but in different order, as *diary* (a daily record) and *dairy* (a business that produces milk, butter, and cheese). One may have one letter where the other has two, as *ad* (the shortened form of *adver-*

tisement) and *add* (to increase). Or they may have other superficial resemblances, as *facetious* (witty) and *fictitious* (like fiction). This unit deals with a few of the groups of words often confused.

How to Study Word Confusions

In this unit are groups of words that are often confused because they either sound or look alike or sound or look similar. You will be helped in distinguishing between these and other words often confused if you will do the following:

1. Examine carefully how each word is spelled, noting whether the same letters occur but in different order, whether a letter is doubled in one word but not in another, and so on.

2. Learn how each word is pronounced. You will need to consult the dictionary to be sure. Note the phonetic spelling, which indicates the correct sounds, together with the stress marks that tell you which syllables are to be accented.

3. Knowing the part of speech of the word you seek will save you time in locating the precise meaning in the dictionary. This is important when two words are spelled alike, as *desert* (barren land) and *desert* (to abandon).

4. Study how the word is used in a sentence. This method of finding meaning from context often reveals the distinctions between words more easily than do dictionary definitions.

5. If you have any doubt about the meaning of a word, always look it up in a dictionary. Sift through the various meanings, becoming acquainted with the word's possibilities for use.

6. Form the habit of entering in your personal notebook any new group of words that are often confused. Head one section of your notebook "Word Confusions" and include brief definitions and illustrations for each entry. Enter any additional sentences you find that illustrate how these words are used. Some students find it helpful to underscore the letters that are the keys to the differences in meaning of the words in a group—for example, accept, except, expect.

Words Commonly Confused

The following combinations of words are commonly confused in spelling or meaning. Study them carefully. Be sure to look up the pronunciation of any word that is unfamiliar.

accede   To comply with. "We gladly *accede* to your request."
exceed   To surpass. "Our department budget may *exceed* $50 000."

accent   (*n*) Stress in speaking or writing. "The *accent* is on the first syllable."
        (*v*) To utter with accent. "*Accent* the first note sharply."
ascent   A rising or climbing. "The *ascent* to the summit was tiring."
assent   (*v*) To agree. "We *assent* to the changes in the contract." (*n*) Agreement. "Please get Mr. Ward's *assent* in writing."

accept   To approve; receive with favor. "We *accept* your bid."

except   *(prep)* Other than. "Everyone *except* Rudi passed." (*v*) To exclude. "In enforcing this rule, we can *except* no one."

expect   To look forward to. "I *expect* to graduate in June."

advice   (*n*; rhymes with *ice*) Information; recommendations. "I will seek the *advice* of a specialist."

advise   (*v*; sound of *ize*) To counsel. "I *advise* you to consult an attorney."

affect   (*v*) To influence. "The tornado did not *affect* us." To feign. "She *affects* the manners of a prima donna."

effect   (*v*) To bring about. "The new treatments often *effect* a cure." (*n*) Result. "The soothing *effect* of music."

assistance   Support. "He lent his *assistance* to the project."

assistants   Those who assist; helpers. "He volunteered the services of his *assistants*."

basis   A fundamental principle. "Character is the *basis* for credit."

bases   (*pl* both of *basis* and of *base*) The foundation on which something rests. "Respect and trust are the *bases* ('bā-ˌsēz) of a happy marriage." "The *bases* ('bā-səz) for the statues must be firm." (Note difference in pronunciation.)

capital   (*adj*) "*Capital* punishment." "*Capital* letters." "A *capital* idea." (*n*) "Ottawa is the *capital* (city serving as a seat of government) of Canada." "All his *capital* (money) is in long-term bonds."

capitol   The building in which a U.S. state legislature meets. When the word refers to the building in which the U.S. Congress meets, *Capitol* is capitalized.

chews   Masticates. "He *chews* on carrot sticks rather than on gum."

choose   To select; to prefer. "You may *choose* any one of these."

chose   (chōz) Did choose. "Last year the winner *chose* a camera."

cite   To quote; to refer to. "He *cited* many arguments."

site   Location. "The *site* for the new library."

sight   (*n*) Vision. "Following the accident, he had *sight* in only one eye." (*v*) To see. "At last we shall *sight* land."

close   ('kloz; *v*) To shut. "Please *close* the window." (*n*) The end. "At the *close* of the summer season."

close   (klōs; *adj*) Dense; tight. "The air in this room is *close*." "A *close*-fitting jacket." (*adv*) Near. "Their cottage is *close* by."

clothes   Wearing apparel.

cloths   Fabrics. "A sale of imported *cloths*."

commence   To begin.

comments   Remarks. "He plans to *commence* his talk with several favorable *comments* he heard recently."

complement Something that completes. "Our camp has its full *complement* of counselors."

compliment (*n*) A flattering remark or attention. "Please accept these roses with our *compliments*." (*v*) To express approval. "We *compliment* you on your record."

correspondence Letters. "Our *correspondence* has always been promptly handled."

correspondents Persons conducting correspondence. "The letters from our *correspondents* in the Far East are often amusing."

council (*n*) An assembly that deliberates on affairs. "The City *Council*." A member of a *council* is a *councilor*.

counsel (*n*) Advice. "We will seek the *counsel* of a specialist." A lawyer. "The *counsel* for the defendant." A lawyer who conducts cases in court is a *counselor*. (*v*) To give advice, especially on important matters. "My uncle *counseled* me not to act hastily in the matter."

consul A government official in a foreign country appointed to look after the interests of his country's citizens there. "I have a letter of introduction to the Canadian *consul* in Rome."

defer To put off. "I plan to *defer* my vacation for a month." To yield to authority. "We think it wise to *defer* to his judgment in this matter."

differ To disagree; to be unlike. "The twins *differ* both in temperament and in appearance."

dense Thick, compact. "A *dense* fog drifted in from the sea."

dents Small hollows resulting from a blow. "It will be costly to remove the *dents* from the body of the car."

dependence Reliance; trust. "Their *dependence* on their sister was touching."

dependents Persons who rely on others for support. "Since I have no *dependents*, I do not have your financial problems."

desert ('dez-ərt; *n*) Arid, barren land. "The Sahara *Desert* is in Africa."

desert (di-'zərt; *v*) To abandon. "To *desert* a friend in need." (*n*; usually in *pl*) Deserved reward or punishment. "He got his just *deserts* for betraying a friend."

dessert The last course of a meal. "I like ice cream for *dessert*."

dye (*n*) A stain or color. (*v*) To stain or color. (past, *dyed*; present participle, *dyeing*)

die (*n*) A tool for molding or shaping; one of a pair of dice. (*v*) To cease living; to wither. (past, *died*; present participle, *dying*)

formally In a formal manner. "He has not yet *formally* accepted the invitation."

formerly Previously. "He was *formerly* on the Stratford stage."

lead (led; *n*) A heavy metal. "A *lead* sinker is often used on fishing lines."

lead (lēd; *v*) (Past, *led*;) To guide. "The blind man asked me to *lead* him across the street."

loose   (adj) Unfastened; not compact. "A *loose*-leaf notebook." "*Loose* powder." "A *loose* bolt." (v) To set free. "He let *loose* the dog."

lose   (v) To mislay; fail to win; suffer the loss of. "I'd *lose* my head if it weren't fastened on." "I always *lose* at cards." "Don't *lose* sleep over it."

patients   Persons under medical care. "My doctor has many *patients*."

patience   The quality of enduring adversity or pain with fortitude; steadfastness. "Her *patience* seemed endless."

personal   Belonging to a particular person. "*Personal* property."

personnel   The staff. "We are proud of the attainments of our *personnel*."

precede   To go before. "The children *preceded* their elders in line."

proceed   To advance. "Let us *proceed* with the discussion." (*Pre* means "before," as in *prewar, preschool; pro* means "forward," as in *progress*.)

precedence   Priority in time or rank. "At formal functions, much attention is given to *precedence*."

precedents   Established rules; those things done that may serve as examples for subsequent actions. "There are no *precedents* to guide us in this case."

presence   Being present; bearing; mien. "Your *presence* is requested."

presents   Gifts. "Olga received many *presents* on her birthday."

principle   (n only) General truth; rule of conduct. "The *principles* of mathematics." "A man of high *principles*."

principal   (for all other meanings) (adj) Chief. "The *principal* reason for the failure." (n) A chief person or thing. "The *principal* of our high school." Money on which interest is paid or income received. "I wish to receive a larger return from my *principal*." One who hires another to act for him. "An agent has power to make contracts for his *principal*."

reality   That which is real. "In *reality*, this material is more expensive."

realty   Real estate.

residence   A house; dwelling place. "The Governor-General's *residence* is Rideau Hall."

residents   Those living in a place. "They are all *residents* of Hamilton."

right   (adj) Correct. "You know that's not the *right* answer!" (n) Privilege. "Next year I shall have the *right* to vote."

rite   Ceremony. "He received the last *rites* of the Church."

write   To inscribe. "Please *write* in my autograph album."

stationary   Fixed in position. "A *stationary* wall telephone is better suited to some locations than a desk phone."

stationery   Writing paper and envelopes.

superintendence   Management. ". . . under the *superintendence* of a district manager."

superintendents   Supervisors. "Mr. Little is attending the convention of school *superintendents* at Banff."

Communication Problems

Application Exercises

Now that you have studied the meanings of the words most commonly confused, see if you can apply them correctly. Study the list of words given for each exercise. From the list, select the words you would insert in the blank spaces within the sentences, and write those words on a separate sheet of paper. No word will be used more than once.

A ■

commence	loose	residence
comments	lose	residents
correspondence	patience	stationary
correspondents	patients	stationery

1 All our scientists are _____ of Chalk River.
2 Company policy is to process all _____ within 24 hours.
3 For note-taking you will need a _____-leaf notebook.
4 A _____ telephone is at times more convenient than one that can be moved about.
5 The Prime Minister's _____ is on Sussex Drive.
6 I do not have the _____ to check my work more than once.
7 We have heard several favorable _____ about the progress of the latest space project.
8 Anyone who meets the public cannot afford to _____ his temper.
9 Carbon paper can be purchased at any _____ store.
10 This textbook provides education and training for business _____ .

B ■

assistance	sight	personal
assistants	council	personnel
cite	counsel	precede
site	consul	proceed

1 In the academic procession, the faculty will _____ the seniors.
2 Can you _____ the sources for your statistics?
3 We recommend that you _____ the fugitive to give himself up.
4 The new library is to be built on this _____
5 We very much appreciate the _____ you gave our representative.
6 Let us _____ to the next topic on the agenda.
7 We received our information from the office of the Canadian _____ in Athens, Greece.
8 The Grand Canyon is indeed a _____ worth traveling to see.
9 Ms. Jordan is our _____ director.
10 How many _____ will Gilbert need to do the job well?

C ■

accede	bases	formally
exceed	basis	formerly
advice	desert	reality
advise	dessert	realty

1 Amy should come out of her dream world and face _____ .
2 The company will be pleased to _____ to any reasonable request.
3 Our president was _____ a college professor.
4 Your counselor will _____ you about scholarships.
5 Ali has never been known to _____ his post.
6 He was careful not to _____ his allowance.
7 Has Stephen Cobb _____ accepted the nomination?
8 Jealousy and envy are the _____ of many arguments.
9 Ice cream is a favorite Canadian _____ .
10 Before making a decision, you should seek the _____ of an older person.

D ■

affect	dents	right
effect	dependence	rite
capital	dependents	write
capitol	precedence	superintendence
dense	precedents	superintendents

1 All western accounts are under the _____ of the district manager.
2 Will the strike _____ your plans in any way?
3 The senior class set many _____ in scholarships.
4 Vancouver is not the _____ of British Columbia.
5 David's _____ on his brother is a handicap in making new friends.
6 The confirmation ceremony was an impressive _____ .
7 Will the strike have any _____ on your plans?
8 After the accident, there were several _____ in your fender.
9 How many _____ did you claim on your income tax return?
10 The visitor was much impressed with the architecture of the state _____ .

Communication in Action: Getting the Facts

A customer, behind in his installment payments, has been threatened via letter with repossession of his furniture. He comes to you, a clerk in the credit department, waving the letter and shouting, "You can't take my furniture back unless you return the $150 in payments I've made." His installment contract reads: "I, the lessee, hereby rent from the Ace Furniture Company the goods listed above.... The lessors agree that, if at the end of the term of the lease, the lessee has fulfilled all covenants, they will convey a free and clear title to the above articles to the lessee." What will you say to this customer? Be sure you understand the contract. *Hint:* Your company does not want to take back the furniture.

PART □ 2

Listening as a Communication Art □

Suppose you were asked to observe an audience being addressed by a well-known speaker and then to pinpoint the good listeners in the crowd. Would you select those persons who look steadily and intently at the speaker, those who furrow their brow, those who rest their chin on their palm, or those who whisper to their neighbor? Pinpointing good listeners on the basis of their physical reactions alone is somewhat like estimating the size of an iceberg: the surface evidence is only a rough indication of what lies beneath. In the next two units you will become even more aware that listening is a very complex physical-mental activity. You will also learn how you can become a more effective communicator by improving your skills in the important art of listening.

The Importance
of Listening

Communication is a two-way process: sending a message and receiving a message. In written communication, the writer is the sender; the reader is the receiver. In oral communication, the speaker is the sender; the listener, the receiver. There can be no communication unless a message sent is received. Thus, the book you do not read is not a communication; to you, the unread book might as well not have been written. The finest lecture to which you do not listen might just as well have been left unsaid, as far as benefiting *you* is concerned.

The effectiveness of every oral or written communication depends upon the proper functioning of the receiving process—both in business and social life. In this unit we shall stress the importance of receiving oral communication—and the responsibility of the receiver to develop his listening process.

Listening in Business and Industry

Habits of efficient listening contribute greatly to one's success in all areas of life, but particularly in business and industry. So important are habits of good listening that many large corporations—International Business Machines, General Electric, and General Motors among them—provide listening training for many of their executives and supervisory personnel.

A Supervisor Must Know How to Listen   These corporations know that management must know how to listen if it is to be effective. They know that the successful supervisor or manager doesn't just give orders; he also does a lot of listening. He listens to his employees to find out what they think—so he can help to settle grievances and establish good employee relations, and because he knows that employees often contribute time- and money-saving ideas when they have a sympathetic and appreciative audience.

Workers, Too, Must Listen   Listening is also extremely important below the management level. Many workers in business and industry rely on listening skills in order to carry out their daily assignments. Telephone operators must listen carefully so that they can handle the requests of the hundreds of callers daily. Sales people must listen just as carefully to determine the wishes of their customers.

One large retailing organization found that two out of every three former customers had taken their business elsewhere because its sales personnel were

Listening to supervisors and co-workers is an important part of every worker's job life. Here, a service-representative trainee receives on-the-job training from her supervisor.

Courtesy American Telephone and Telegraph

indifferent to customers' needs. Moreover, the organization found that much of the indifference was expressed through poor listening.

Have you ever had an experience like this one? In a shoe store, you ask the sales-clerk to show you a pair of brown loafers, size 8C. The clerk appears to have under-stood and proceeds to select from the shelves two or three boxes of shoes. To your annoyance, he brings you black dress oxfords, size 9C. Now you must again describe to him the shoes you want. The clerk's poor listening habits have caused you un-necessary delay and have made extra work for him. Such incidents of poor listen-ing are much too frequent in the business world.

Another who must depend upon effective listening for success in his work is the automobile service repair manager. When a customer brings his car in for repair, the service manager must listen and record what the customer thinks is wrong with the automobile. Sometimes he must even listen to the motor for clues to the diffi-culty. He must listen to find if, when, and where the repaired vehicle is to be delivered. After the work is completed, he must listen to the mechanics to find what repairs have been made and whether they have been made satisfactorily. The success of the service department manager depends greatly upon how well he listens in his role as liaison between customer and garage employees.

All employees who provide service of any kind—and that includes most—are partially, if not mainly, dependent upon their listening ability to carry out their duties. No one in business and industry is immune to the need for effective listening. Every worker—every secretary, accountant, shipping clerk, machine operator, maintenance person—receives much information and many instructions orally from co-workers, from supervisors, and from customers. Failure to listen results in errors and misunderstandings; and these are costly in terms of time, money, and goodwill.

Your Need for Effective Listening

Listening occupies more time than any other communication activity. One survey showed that approximately one-third of a person's waking hours are spent in listening—whether in school, in personal-social relations, or on the job.* The persons surveyed reported they listened three times as much as they read and that their listening time was one and one-half times that of their talking time.

The rewards of listening are great: they include increased knowledge, broadened experience, more and deeper friendships, increased job opportunities and promotions, development of facility in using language, and an increased appreciation of the spoken word.

Conversely, ineffective listening may have a disastrous effect in any of these same areas, with disappointments and failure the results. Frequently the potential school dropout fails in his studies, not because he can't learn but because he doesn't know how to listen. A snob or bore may not want to be unfriendly, but he just hasn't mastered the listening requirements inherent in successful social relations. An employee may be fired, not because he is unable to perform his job well but because he doesn't know how to listen to instructions.

Listening Efficiency Can Be Increased Tests have shown that immediately after the average person has listened to someone talk, he remembers only about half of what he heard. Two months later, he remembers only about a fourth of what was said. In other words, the average person is only 25 percent efficient in his listening skills. This means, therefore, that the average person has the potential for greatly increasing his listening efficiency.

What does all this mean to you? Well, suppose you are one of those "average" persons. But, through instruction and practice, you are able to double your listening efficiency. You become 50 percent efficient in listening, rather than just 25 percent. Consider what this improvement will mean in relation to your learning, your social life, your job.

Listening and Your Learning In high school today, as many as nine out of every ten hours in classes are devoted to listening or to discussions, which are largely listening. Doubling your listening effectiveness would greatly increase your learning productivity in those nine hours. It might eliminate much of the "burning of midnight oil" when you cram for exams. Efficient listening—resulting in improved learning and remembering—also would give you more time for other subjects and for extracurricular activities.

* Ralph G. Nichols and Leonard A. Stevens, *Are You Listening?* McGraw-Hill Book Company, New York, 1957, p. 6.

Listening and Your Social Life   Improved listening will also pay dividends in your social life. Everyone likes to be around a good conversationalist, and being a good listener is one of the latter's most valuable assets. Naturally, the good conversationalist listens to others because it is courteous to do so; but he listens also to keep abreast of conversational implications, trends, and the reasoning processes and emotionally colored statements of those talking. Such a listener gains friends and enriches and deepens his existing friendships.

Listening and Your Job   The rewards of improved listening are more tangible when you have a job—for often the rewards are in money. The beginning employee must listen to instructions and directions from his supervisor and fellow workers. He must listen to suggestions and criticisms in order to improve his job performance. To advance in a job, he must have an awareness of what's going on in his department and in the company; and this awareness results in part from intelligent listening. You can easily see that improved listening will enhance your chances of success in the world of work.

Listening Versus Hearing

Too often we equate listening with hearing, but there is a big difference. Whereas hearing is dependent upon the ears, listening utilizes the mind as well and often the eyes. The ears permit you to hear sounds; the mind enables you to decipher them, to recognize some of them as words, and to fashion the words into thoughts. With your mind you are able to perceive that an oral message is important, interpret the meaning of the message, and react to it.

Interpreting the message is a *thinking* act. It is dependent on both the listener's vocabulary and also on his attitude. The listener must *want* to grasp the meaning of the words.

You may not have considered the eyes to be an important tool in listening. Yet, what you see when a person is speaking is sometimes as important as what you hear. A smile, a quizzical glance, the appearance of boredom or exhilaration—all the facial expressions and mannerisms of a speaker may alter the meaning of his message.

The problem of improving listening is not one of improving the physical tools. Rather, it is a problem of improving the use of these tools so they become more effective in receiving messages.

Listening and the Other Communication Arts

The communication arts can reinforce one another to produce a higher degree of learning. Listening, for example, can be reinforced with reading, with speaking, and with writing to produce enhanced understanding and greater retention.

Listening and Reading   Listening, like reading, is a message-receiving skill. But listening is more difficult than reading because, generally, you cannot relisten to a spoken message as you can reread a written one. You must get the message right the first time or you lose it.

Reading about a topic in advance will enable you to listen more effectively to the speaker's message because you bring more knowledge to it and thus derive greater benefit from it. When planning to attend an important committee meeting, if you will examine the agenda and reread the minutes of previous meetings beforehand, you will be able to listen much more effectively during the meeting.

Listening and Speaking   Speaking reinforces listening in various ways. The good listener repeats to himself the speaker's important points, and he mentally rephrases them in his own words; this process adds to his understanding. Frequently, the good listener "speaks up"—he asks questions—in an effort to clarify what is meant.

Speaking is often an aid to memory, thus aiding listening retention. When you are introduced to a person, for example, you will be more likely to remember his name if you repeat his name orally and use his name in talking with him or in talking with others about him.

Listening and Writing—Note-taking   Writing, perhaps more than any other communication art, contributes to good listening. Frequently, the listener must take notes in order to retain for future reference the information he hears. The student attending a lecture, the secretary taking a telephone message, and the accountant receiving oral instructions from his supervisor are but a few of the persons who use writing—note-taking—to improve their listening.

However, notes should be made with discretion. If a listener spends too much

The ability to take notes, a part of every good student's stock-in-trade, is dependent upon his ability to listen. By listening carefully to his instructor's comments, this student will be able to understand his subject more easily.   *Courtesy Seneca C.A.A.T.*

time making notes, he may miss the heart of the message. And if he is too dependent upon his note-taking, he may be using his notes as a crutch to avoid real listening, rather than as a reinforcement to listening. In the next unit you will find specific suggestions for note-taking.

Communication Problems

Application Exercises

A ■

Choose a business position that you would some day like to hold. In a paragraph, describe some of the listening activities that would be required of you in order to carry out your job duties.

B ■

How much time do you spend in listening when you are in school? Keep an estimated record, hour by hour, of the listening activities in which you engage during one day of school. Then, figure the total listening time devoted to each activity, plus the total time you spend in listening during one day. When you come to class, compare your log of one day of school listening with those of the rest of the class. How do your results, individually and as a class, compare with the estimate of school listening on page 35?

C ■

Play a game of introductions. Divide the class into groups of five or six. Each person is to assume another name and to introduce himself to the others. After all introductions are made, how many of the group can you reintroduce by their assumed names? Missing one name is par for the game; if you miss more than one, you weren't listening.

D ■

Develop a one-minute skit to enact in class with another student. The scene: two friends are conversing; one is a poor listener (he wants to do all the talking); the other, although a considerate host, is obviously annoyed. First, enact the skit as you have written it. Then, reenact the same skit in which both persons are considerate and attentive conversationalists.

E ■

Be prepared to enact for two minutes another kind of listening skit in class: You, as the job applicant, are talking with the personnel supervisor. As the personnel supervisor describes the job requirements, you show that you are a poor listener. You're preoccupied with what you're going to say, you interrupt, you fiddle with your hands, etc. The curtain drops as the supervisor ushers you, the unsuccessful applicant, out of the office.

List specific listening techniques you *should* have used in the interview. Then, reenact the scene, practising these techniques of listening during the job interview.

F ■

Try a listening experiment. Go outdoors on a dark night. Consciously listen to all the night noises that surround you. See how many different ones you can distinguish. If you are in the city, you may hear such noises as the drone of traffic, the screeching of brakes, the faraway bark of a dog. If you are in the country, you may hear the trickling of water, the cry of a bird, the rustle of leaves in the wind, the hum of an airplane overhead. Be prepared to report to the class on your experiment. Tell which sounds you distinguished first, which next, and which last.

Word Study

A ■

The following words were used in this unit. Find each word, reread the sentence in which it appears, and try to guess its meaning from the context if you do not already know it. Then check your guesses in the dictionary, and use each word in a new sentence.

personnel	conversely	implications	decipher
grievances	disastrous	tangible	quizzical
liaison	potential	enhance	exhilaration
immune	inherent	equate	derive

B ■

In each of the following sentences, choose the word in parentheses that correctly expresses the meaning.

1 I have my mother's (receipt, recipe) for Christmas cookies.
2 The (trail, trial) through the woods was clearly marked.
3 He first (attend, attained) prominence during the campaign for alderman.
4 The first (addition, edition) of the novel has already been exhausted.
5 She is still (mourning, morning) the loss of her mink stole.
6 He was (prosecuted, persecuted) relentlessly by his political enemies.
7 I have just signed a (petition, partition) that we return to standard time.
8 He was unpleasantly (official, officious) in carrying out his duties.
9 There's no logic behind that (inane, insane) remark.
10 The rate of infant (morality, mortality) has been steadily declining.

Communication in Action: Accepting Criticism

John Barber, an accounting clerk, has been severely criticized by the chief accountant. "Look, John," the chief had said, "you're much too slow in making the sales recap. We need it by 10:30 every day. If you can't do it, we'll have to find someone else." John was furious—he couldn't take the criticism. Yet, John recognized that he was slow in making out the report because he didn't understand exactly where to find the information for it. Should John have been angry? What should he do or say to ensure that he learns how to collect the necessary information expeditiously?

UNIT □ 5

How to Be a Good Listener

Our ears are assaulted with sounds continually. We hear these sounds, but we don't listen to all of them. We can't; we would be inundated with sound if we did. In self-defense, we block off many sounds from our consciousness—we surround ourselves with a protective insulation of nonhearing.

This blocking off of sounds is a useful device, as it often aids concentration. But too often we also block off sounds to which we should be listening. Most of us have acquired bad habits of nonlistening, even when we are with our best friends; and these habits are very hard to dislodge.

Fortunately, they can be unlearned and good listening habits installed in their place. The first step in this process is to become *aware* of one's deficiencies in listening, and of one's need for good listening habits. When you have made this awareness a habit, you will be well on your way to becoming a good listener.

Determine Your Purpose

In the preceding unit, we said that the chief difference between hearing and listening is that the latter involves the mind as well as the ears. Another way of expressing this difference is that *listening has a purpose.* This purpose may be one of simple friendliness and sociability, as in party conversation; of obtaining information, as when listening to a lecture; or of critical analysis, as when observing a political debate.

Listening to a pep talk at a football rally is not the same as listening to a commencement address. Listening to an introduction prior to social conversation is not the same as overhearing someone's conversation on a bus. In an introduction you would want to listen carefully for the person's name, plus specific details that you can use as a basis for conversation. In listening to a commencement address, you would listen for main ideas and supporting facts. In a pep talk, you would listen for the general tone of the meeting, which you could easily anticipate; and the overheard conversation you might want to tune out after a few minutes.

One's listening in each situation calls for different skills and for different degrees of attentiveness. In each situation the demands are different because the purpose in listening is different.

As a rule, the more you "take" from a speaker, the more he wants to "give." In this way, you can be "selfish" in your listening attitude. On the other hand, you can always treat the listener as you would a guest. As a courteous host, you would recognize your obligation to be attentive to his pleasure and well-being; and this would include listening to him.

The main thing is that you decide on your purpose—any purpose, just so long as it makes sense to you. You will be a better listener as a result.

Basic Rules for Listening

While different purposes in listening imply different *kinds* of listening, most good listening skills are basic to all kinds. As we have just said, the first rule is to know *why* you are listening. Here are some others. They are closely related.

Get Ready to Listen   Good listening implies a *readiness* to listen. This requires that you prepare yourself for listening—physically, mentally, and emotionally. Literally turn your back on distracting sights and sounds, if necessary, and always give your-self maximum opportunity for listening by sitting near enough to the speaker to see and hear easily. If possible, read about a topic in advance, because the more you know about a topic, the more interested you will be in what the speaker has to say about it. Mental preparation, because it invariably supplies you with a purpose for listening, automatically leads to emotional involvement. And this, in turn, increases your readiness to listen.

Accept Your Share of Responsibility   Too often the listener approaches a speaker with a "show me" attitude; he dares the speaker to interest him in a speech. This kind of attitude is tough on the speaker, as well as being discourteous. The sooner you recognize that you as a listener share the responsibility for communication with the speaker, the sooner you will become a good listener. Not only will you be courteous to the speaker, but you will realize that the quality of your listening can affect his talking. It can even *control* his talking.

If you doubt this, pretend for a moment that you are in the midst of telling an interesting anecdote. One person in your group is flipping the pages of a magazine; two others are talking in low tones; another is openly yawning. How will you react? Will you go on with your story?

It is well known that a theater audience can greatly influence an actor's performance. It is perhaps less well known, but just as true, that an audience can influence the delivery, and even the length, of a speech. The reason is simple: we all crave good listeners, and we react accordingly.

Listen with Understanding   Be sure you understand the speaker's ideas fully and completely; don't jump to conclusions about a false, or half-true, idea. This means you must listen carefully. If necessary, ask questions to clarify anything that is vague or ambiguous.

Listen with an Open Mind   Keep your mind open when you listen; forget your biases and prejudices for the moment, and be ready to receive new ideas. Don't refuse to listen to new ideas just because they may conflict with those you already hold. Hear the speaker out; don't tune in only the parts you want to listen to. Of course, it is possible that your ideas may undergo change as a result, but you should be courageous enough to take the chance. After all, such changes may be for the better.

Listen Actively   Listening actively implies work on your part. Primarily, it means three things: concentration, relating what you hear to what you already know, and reading between the lines.

Concentration involves being selective about the sounds you hear. It enables you to focus your attention on what a speaker is saying and to disregard the noise of the pneumatic drill in the street outside. Being an active process, concentration takes both willpower and energy.

Relating ideas and facts just heard to your existing store of knowledge means that the latter will be changed in some way. It *must* be changed if learning is to take place. No change, no learning. And learning takes effort.

Reading between the lines—or sensing the implications of a speaker's message—is another rule of good listening. The good listener analyzes the speaker's word choice and observes closely the speaker's posture, facial expressions, tone of voice, manner, general appearance, etc.

Listen with Empathy   Empathic listening—listening with empathy—means putting yourself in the speaker's place so as to see his ideas through his eyes. Such listening requires imagination. Because it results in attentiveness that is very flattering to the speaker, this empathic listening serves to draw out the speaker and to help dissipate any shyness, suspicion, or hostility on his part. Thus, listening with empathy aids communication, and the rewards are great.

How to Listen Critically

Critical listening is a special kind of listening—listening with a view toward analyzing and evaluating what a speaker says and how he says it. It involves all the basic rules of listening, plus a few others: listening for main ideas and supporting details; reviewing points already made and anticipating what is coming next; and, finally, analyzing the evidence and accepting or rejecting the speaker's conclusions on the basis of this evidence.

Use Your Spare Listening Time   To listen critically may seem a large order, in view of the fact that you are expected to listen intently at the same time. However, it's entirely possible and reasonable, and good listeners do it all the time. They use their *spare listening time* to do just this.

All of us have this spare listening time because we think at a much faster rate than the average speaker talks. The rate of speech for most Canadians is around 125 words per minute; but we think at a rate that is four or five times that fast.

The half listener, or the nonlistener, generally uses this time to daydream or otherwise digress. Theoretically, this would be all right; but practically, it doesn't work out well. This type of listener usually finds his attention increasingly diverted from the speaker to these distractions. As a result, he misses some of the speaker's words. After missing certain portions of the speech, the listener becomes more and more disinterested, and he devotes more and more time to his increasingly interesting distractions. Again, he misses more and more of the speech, which becomes harder and harder to follow. Eventually, he may give up the listening effort altogether.

The good listener, on the other hand, uses his spare listening time to engage in thought processes that are closely related to what the speaker says; in other words, he listens actively. The result is that his understanding is enhanced and his retention increased. Following are some rules for utilizing your spare listening time.

Note Major Points   A well-prepared speech usually consists of a few major points. Often a good speaker may indicate these points near the beginning of his talk. Suppose he says the following:

"There has been a major technological revolution in the past fifteen years: a revolution in automated equipment and business practices that makes many traditional practices obsolete. Today, we shall deal with the effects of automation on the classroom in school. We shall discuss this technological upheaval as it relates to the preparation of young men and women to work in the automated world of work. As we discuss desirable changes in the preparation, let us consider three main topics. First, the power of automation in changing the way that work is performed. Second, the changing purposes for preparing people for work in automated business. And third, the changing classroom methods required to teach young people to learn."

Thus, the speaker reveals his outline, and you grasp it by noting his three main points:

1. The power of automation
2. The changing purposes of education and training
3. The changing methods of teaching

Recognize Details   As soon as you grasp the major ideas of a speech, you should recognize that everything else that is said is designed, or *should be,* to support these main ideas. The details will help you to fill in the structure of the speech and lead you to a better understanding of the speech as a result. Details will also tell you a lot about the way a speaker thinks.

In the following portion of a speech, note that while the sidelights add color and interest to the main idea, they are not separate ideas in themselves; only the italicized words comprise the main idea.

"Certainly one of the important cost factors in operating a plant is the cost of supplying the municipal government services. For instance, Newtown has a great many fine assets and would make an excellent location for certain types of operations; but perhaps one of its weaknesses is the debt position. At the present time its bonded indebtedness is $24 million, which amounts to more than $200 per capita. On the other hand, in Newtown this may not be serious since it is a fast-growing city and much of the debt will be absorbed by the expanding population. But then there is still another side to this financial picture of Newtown. Forty percent of the property within the city limits is either government-owned or tax free because it is owned by

public schools, churches, and other nontaxable institutions. This places an unusually heavy burden on individuals and companies who, in effect, help support the non-taxable property.''

In the above paragraph, note the words "For instance." Speakers often provide the listener with cues to indicate whether an idea is a new one or whether it merely adds support to an idea already presented.

Anticipate What Is Coming   Think ahead of the speaker, trying to anticipate what his next point will be. At the same time try to guess where the discourse is leading and what conclusions will be drawn.

Rephrase and Review   The effective listener works to retain the message of the speaker in two ways: he frequently rephrases silently the speaker's words in his own, and he reviews the major points of the speech from time to time. Both methods reinforce his comprehension of the speech and aid retention as a result.

The rephrasing process is similar to taking notes, except that you do it mentally: you concentrate on main ideas and summarize them as succinctly as possible. Note in the following illustration how you can mentally rephrase a speaker's words.

What the Speaker Is Saying	What You Are Saying to Yourself
I have read many books on selling. There are books that bring up every possible selling situation and give you ways and means to meet those situations—several hundred of them perhaps. But when you get in the presence of a prospect, you cannot recall any of them. But you can remember this formula: Ask yourself the simple question, "Just what does this prospect want?" If you cannot find out any other way, ask him. It is often that simple. Too many salespeople think they must do all the talking. Avoid it. Listen at least half the time and ask questions. It is only in this way that you can uncover unsatisfied wants.	You can't memorize ways of meeting every selling situation presented in books. You should find out what the prospect wants. Ask him what he wants, if necessary. You don't need to do all the talking—listen half the time and ask questions.

Detect Bias and Determine Motives   A biased viewpoint is a partial, or prejudiced, viewpoint. In business, bias and preconceived opinions are natural because a company wants to sell its product or service; this desire then becomes its primary motive. But the critical listener must learn to recognize this bias and this motive.

For example, an automobile salesperson may focus all his attention on the favorable attributes of a particular make of automobile; it is natural to do so. But you as a good listener must recognize his bias and, also, the fact that what you hear from the salesperson may not be the whole truth. The automobile salesperson would be foolish to disclose to you all the weaknesses of the car since his motive is to sell it; he would be just as foolish to extol the fine characteristics of some other car.

The warning *caveat emptor*, which means "let the buyer beware," applies equally to the listener: let the listener beware of biased or emotion-laden speaking.

Take Notes   Note-taking should be done as an aid to retention, not as a substitute for listening. If a listener spends too much time taking notes, he will miss the heart of the message. Therefore, notes should be made with discretion. Here are specific suggestions for note-taking.

1. Come equipped with plenty of note paper, a good pen, and an extra pencil or two.

2. Use a good, uncluttered writing surface.

3. Label your notes so that you can later identify them without difficulty.

4. Listen for such speaker's cues as "first," "second," and "third"; "another important consideration"; "finally"; "the most significant thing"; "on the other hand"; "in summary"; as well as questions posed by the speaker, pauses, intonations of voice, and gestures.

5. Flag important parts of your notes with brackets, underscores, arrows, or indentions.

6. Listen for special instructions.

7. Go over your notes promptly after the speech, to fix more firmly the major points in your mind.

Practise, Practise, Practise   Efficient listening, like the other communication arts, requires practise. To become a good listener, you must avail yourself of every opportunity to put these techniques into practice. In other words—practise, practise, practise!

Communication Problems

Application Exercises

A ■

On a separate sheet of paper, answer each of the following questions as "Yes," "Sometimes," or "No." The questions are designed to help you evaluate your own listening habits.

1   Do you have any hearing or eye weakness that has not been checked recently by a physician?

2   When you enter an auditorium to listen to a speech, do you consciously seat yourself where you can see and hear the speaker?

3   When listening, do you consciously observe the facial expressions of the speaker?

4   On the telephone, are you empathic toward the voice you hear, i.e., do you use your "mind's eye" to imagine the facial expressions of the speaker?

5 When in class, do you consciously listen and follow accurately all instructions and directions of the teacher?

6 When your teacher or others are speaking, do you pay alert and considerate attention to what they say?

7 When you do not understand what a teacher or another student has said in class, do you ask questions to clarify the meaning?

8 When another person is introduced to you, do you mentally practice saying and spelling the name to fix it in your memory?

9 In an introduction, do you use the new name in conversation with the person or with others to help fix it in your memory?

10 Do you consciously make a mental note of oral messages you need to remember?

11 In preparing for listening to a class lecture, do you read and think about the topic prior to the class meeting?

12 In listening to a speech or lecture, do you mentally repeat to yourself important points made?

13 In listening in class, do you rephrase what you have heard in your own words?

14 When you receive instructions or directions, do you write them down?

15 In your school classes, do you make effective notes of class discussions and lectures?

B ■

From the answers you have given to the questions in the previous exercise, prepare a 200-word written statement concerning your listening skills. Your statement should consider the following two points: (a) my listening weaknesses, and (b) what I can do to improve my listening.

C ■

Using the suggestions for taking notes (page 45) evaluate your note-taking skills. How can these skills be improved? Be specific.

D ■

If possible, in order to practise your listening skills, have someone read aloud to you the section headed "How to Listen Critically" beginning on page 42. Ask the reader to include all the paragraph headings. Describe to the class some of the *details* you remember about *one* of the major points in this section.

E ■

Be ready to report to the class from your "listening" in exercise D the *important ideas* you grasped and retained.

F ■

Write and be prepared to present orally a 30-second advertisement of some product or service as it would be presented on radio or television. From the oral presentations in class, discuss the advertisements in terms of bias and of motives of the speakers.

G ■

Make a list of rules for your class which, if followed, will promote good classroom listening.

Word Study

A ∎

The italicized words in list A, or forms of these words, were used in this unit. Match each verb in list A with the correct synonym in list B. If you cannot determine a word's meaning from the context given, then find it in the text and reread the sentence in which it appears. The verbs are listed in order of appearance in the unit.

A		*B*	
1	to *inundate* with sound	a	to take advantage of
2	different purposes *imply* different kinds	b	dissolve
3	to help *dissipate* any shyness	c	intensify
4	to daydream or otherwise *digress*	d	suggest, indicate
5	to *divert* his attention	e	include, contain
6	to *enhance* his understanding	f	to flood
7	to *utilize* your spare time	g	turn aside *from*
8	words *comprise* the main idea	h	make use of
9	to *extol* the fine characteristics	i	praise
10	to *avail* yourself of every opportunity	j	turn aside, deflect

B ∎

These nouns also appeared in this unit: *retention, empathy, bias, hostility, involvement, discretion.* If you do not know what they mean, reread the sentences in which they appeared and then fit them into the following sentences. Be very careful about your choices. Use each noun once. *Do not write in this book.*

1 His _____ with the story was so intense that he could not put down the book.
2 His _____ toward the group prevented him from joining in the singing.
3 The test is designed to measure reading_____ .
4 Jane showed _____ in her choice of a souvenir for her mother.
5 Having broken his arm a few months before, Joe could feel _____ for the accident victim.
6 The report was rejected because of the writer's strong_____ .

Communication in Action: Rush Job

Assume you are a receptionist in a large company. You are extremely busy at your desk when Mr. Abrams arrives to keep an appointment with the manager, Mr. Svoboda. You have been told that Mr. Svoboda is attending a meeting and will not be able to see Mr. Abrams for about ten minutes. Mr. Abrams is in a talkative mood—and you are frantically trying to finish typing a report. Suggest ways in which you can deal courteously with Mr. Abrams and still not lose too much time.

PART □ 3

As a student, you know that there is a close connection between school success and the ability to read well— but you may not realize that the same ability will be equally important in your life outside school. As long as you continue your studies and during your employment in business, reading will continue to play a significant part in your life. Business and professional people spend a large portion of their time reading all kinds of material—books, magazines, notices, reports, memorandums, letters, and many other forms of written communication. You therefore will be better equipped for your chosen career if you have improved your reading skill, suggestions for which are given here in Part 3.

Reading and Your Growth

Have you ever stopped to think how much reading has contributed to your accomplishments and pleasures in life? Without the ability to read, you would not have been able to reach your present educational level; and you would not be able to continue your education to the level required by your goal in life. You would not be able to drive a car; you would not be able to exercise that precious right of every citizen, the right to vote. You would not be able to follow the instructions on the cake-mix box or the instruction on a dress pattern. You could not read the sports section of the daily newspaper; you could not easily assemblea model airplane or automobile. Reading contributes much to your wealth of information as well as to many pleasurable hours.

Of course you already know how to read. Yes, but are you getting the maximum benefits from your reading? Can you improve your skills so that you can read more in less time and get more out of what you read?

Reading in Your Personal Life

To most of us, reading affords many pleasures. We may read the latest best seller, the daily newspaper, our favorite magazine. Many of us read to relax, to take our minds off the cares of the day. However, reading makes other contributions to our personal life. It furthers our effectiveness as citizens by enabling us to keep up to date on current happenings as reported in newspapers and magazines. The well-informed consumer reads advertisements carefully, as well as warranties and package labels. Many of us have learned to perform useful tasks because of our ability to read and to follow printed instructions.

Reading in Your School Life

As you well know, reading is an essential part of your school life. Since all knowledge cannot be obtained in the classroom alone, much of it must come from textbooks and reference and resource materials. Instructions concerning problems that have to be solved, tests that must be taken, and machines that must be operated have to be read and understood.

Students who have difficulty with some phase of reading find it hard to earn high grades. How often have you been severely penalized because you failed either to read an instruction at all or to comprehend it? Those of you who are college bound will soon learn that you need to do even more reading than you have been doing. It

Courtesy Seneca C.A.A.T.

Students read, read, read—in class and out. Handwritten notes, printed sheets, and textbooks all provide material for the above students to use in their studies.

is estimated that most successful college students spend about a thousand hours a year with books and that, during four years of college, an average student will read approximately thirty million words.

Reading in Your Professional Life

All successful persons in business spend a good portion of their working day reading. They read correspondence, instructions, reports, source documents for reports, reference books, memorandums asking for or giving information, and articles in professional or trade magazines. Whether you are planning to be a secretary, an accountant, a clerical worker, a salesperson—no matter what business position you hope some day to hold—reading will play an important part in your professional life.

A survey made by the American Management Association indicates that the higher a person's position in the business world, the more he reads. The so-called "self-made person," who has had very little formal schooling, usually has received much knowledge through extensive reading.

Executives Must Read Widely   Because of the increasing complexity of today's business world, the rapid progress and the new developments, today's business executive must read widely. The average top executive spends a little more than four hours a day in reading that is connected with his business. So important and so extensive is this need for reading that many firms are now giving their executives special courses to train them to read more rapidly. Why? A greater reading speed enables the executives to cut significantly the time they need to spend on essential reading. One firm found that this speedup in reading meant an annual saving of $40 000 in executive time that could be used profitably for other duties.

Business Workers, Too, Must Read   True, you will not start your professional career in an executive capacity. Nevertheless, you still will need to read a great deal. The following two examples will give you an idea of how two business workers use reading skills in their work:

Anne Beckley is a secretary for the firm of Mullins and Hepburn. Every morning Anne reads the mail that comes to her desk so that she will know how to sort it and arrange it in the proper order on her employer's desk. After she has taken dictation from her boss, Anne uses the dictionary and a stenographer's reference manual to help her transcribe the dictation. She looks up some information in a hotel directory. During her break and during the lunch hour, Anne reads *Today's Secretary,* a magazine she finds interesting and helpful in her work.

Paul Scott, assistant buyer in the men's furnishings department of a local department store, also uses his reading skills in many ways. During a typical day, he first checks the copy for the store's advertisement that is to appear in tomorrow's newspaper. Next, he reads the store's sales report for last month, comparing the sales in his department with those of similar departments and with his own department's record in previous months. Then, he reads a merchandising trade journal to get ideas for promotional plans to boost next month's sales. Afterward, Paul checks the labels on some sample sweaters left by a manufacturer's representative; and he reads carefully the literature describing those sweaters.

We have visited only two business employees during a small part of their working day, yet we can see many practical applications of their reading skill. Did you note the many different types of reading situations encountered by Anne and Paul? Each required a different *kind* of reading. Now let us examine more closely some of the *purposes* for which we read.

Reading with a Purpose

The way in which we read should be determined primarily by our purpose in reading. When we read for pleasure alone, our reading is different from those situations where we read to absorb information, as in studying. Therefore, we should always be aware of our reading purpose so that we can better determine *how* we should read. Among the many purposes in reading, the following are probably the primary ones.

Reading for Pleasure   When reading for pleasure, it is not necessary to absorb every detail, to remember all facts, or to read critically. Therefore, you may read at a rapid rate such material as most novels and biographies and many magazine articles. A desirable speed for pleasure reading is about 400 words a minute.

Reading for Specific Information   When hunting for information such as a name or date that is somewhere within a block of reading material, you should employ skipping and skimming in order to make the best use of your reading time. Skipping merely means jumping over large portions of material that are not pertinent to your reading purpose. Skimming means moving your eyes rapidly down a page of type, stopping to read only significant facts and phrases. When you wish to gain the main ideas and details of an article, but are not sure beforehand what the article will yield, you should both skim and skip. Most persons read newspapers largely by skipping and skimming.

Reading to Absorb Information   Reading to study—to absorb information—is always required of you as a student, whether the reading is from a textbook or from some resource material. It calls for your active participation, since you must read for meaning and remember what you read. So important to the student and the business worker is this type of reading that it will be discussed fully in the next unit.

Reading for Copying and Checking   Most secretaries, typists, and clerical workers do a great deal of this kind of reading. Every typing job, every set of inventory figures that must be checked, and every invoice that must be compared with receiving reports and purchase orders requires careful reading. Too often such reading is done without concentration and without attention to meaning. As a result, many errors are not detected. Of course, a typist or secretary would easily spot the error in the following sentence:

We did not receive hte letter until today.

Having skimmed the newspaper for the particular information they wanted, these people are now reading in detail and copying and checking their notes.

Courtesy Seneca C.A.A.T.

The *hte* is a typographical error and you do not have to be conscious of the meaning to detect it. However, the error in the following sentence is not quite so obvious. Unless you are reading for meaning, you might miss the error.

The two pencil are on the table.

Checking one copy against another or one column of figures against another calls for reading two sets of items almost simultaneously. This skill calls for a high degree of concentration.

How About You?

As indicated earlier, the average executive spends half his business day reading, and reading specialists say that he could cut two hours from this load by learning to read faster and with more comprehension. How about you? Does it take you longer to read your assigned work than it should? Do you approach reading with dread because you have a feeling of "plowing" your way through? Do you spend so much time trying to do the reading for some courses that you have no time for others?

If you said "yes" to any of these questions, then you can do something to improve your reading skills. The next unit will assist you in getting off to the right start.

Communication Problems

Application Exercises

A ■

Make a written list of the various uses you make of reading in your school and personal life. Indicate the approximate amount of time you spend daily in each of these reading activities.

B ■

On a separate sheet of paper indicate your professional goal. Write a short essay (about 350 words) on the topic of how you will use reading in your professional life and how this reading will contribute to your professional growth.

C ■

Secretaries, typists, clerical workers, copy editors, and advertising copywriters must learn how to proofread carefully. Proofreading calls for the reading of each word not only for spelling but also for its meaning within the sentence. Proofread the following paragraphs and on a separate sheet of paper make a list of all the errors. Then, rewrite the paragraphs so that they are free from error.

Thank you for you letter of May 25 and the cheque for $125 you enclosed. Every store appreciate the patronage of it's customers.

We have credit your account for the $152 and hope that their will be many opportunities for us to be of service to you.

D ■

The checking of amounts of money and other figures often results in problems because of reading carelessness. Compare the following two lists. On a separate sheet of paper, indicate which pairs of numbers do not agree. Follow the style of the example given.

	List A	List B		Do not agree
0	1234567	1235467	0	__x__
1	$768967	$768967	1	_____
2	987654	986754	2	_____
3	$3232.33	$3223.33	3	_____
4	654A765	654A765	4	_____
5	897898V	897889V	5	_____
6	R787899T	R787899T	6	_____

Word Study

A ■

One of the requirements of the skillful reader is the possession of a well-developed vocabulary. Indicate whether the correct word has been used in each of the following sentences. If not, what is the correct word?

1 *Personal* management deals with the handling of people.
2 The new amendment will *affect* shipping between provinces.
3 We could not *cite* a single case to uphold the law.
4 The Board of Directors *past* the motion without any discussion.
5 No one else will *except* the responsibility.

B ■

Should *ance* or *ence* be added to the following?

1	accord____	4	resembl____	7	correspond____
2	dilig____	5	appli____	8	abund____
3	experi____	6	remembr____	9	evid____

C ■

Should *er, or,* or *ar* be added to the following?

1	counsel____	4	collect____	7	supervis____
2	gramm____	5	propell____	8	profess____
3	betray____	6	advertis____	9	execut____

Communication in Action: *Following Instructions*

Laura Grant constantly got into difficulty because she failed to read correctly the memorandums that came from her supervisor regarding changes in procedures. When her supervisor finally had to speak to Laura regarding her failure to follow instructions, Laura glibly replied, "Oh, we get so many memorandums that I can't keep all of them straight in my mind." If you were Laura's supervisor, what advice would you give her to help keep the memorandums "straight"?

UNIT □ 7

You and Your Reading Habits

In Unit 6 you learned how important reading is and will continue to be in your personal, school, and professional life. Do you want to take some steps to improve your reading skills? Remember that such improvement will allow you more time for additional reading or other activities, as well as help you to get more out of your reading. In this unit you will learn how to improve your reading speed and comprehension—skills that will greatly aid your learning and retention.

First, however, you must make sure that your eyes have good care and that you have a good reading environment.

Your Eyes

There are many variations in each person's ability to see for reading. One person may have difficulty in seeing objects that are close to him, while another may find it hard to distinguish objects that are some distance away. If you find that you must hold ordinary written material either very close to your eyes or at arm's length in order to read it; if the material you are reading appears blurred; or if your eyes smart or become easily tired, then you should consult a qualified eye specialist. You may need to begin wearing glasses for reading, or you may need to have your present glasses adjusted.

Regardless of whether or not you wear glasses, you should practise good eye hygiene. Here are a few suggestions:

1. Rest your eyes every half hour or so by looking into the distance or by closing your eyes for a few minutes.

2. Exercise your eyes from time to time, particularly after doing close work. One good eye exercise is to rotate the eyes slowly, without moving your head. Move your eyes far to the right; then to the left; then up; and finally, down. These exercises will help to strengthen your eye muscles.

3. Avoid reading in bright sunlight or while riding in a car, train, or other vehicle.

4. Have eye injuries or sties attended to at once by a physician.

Your Reading Environment

Poor lighting conditions contribute to eye fatigue and the loss of visual acuity. Of course, good daylight is the best lighting for reading; and light-colored walls and furnishings allow for best utilization of daylight. The best artificial light for reading is an indirect light, which results in only a small loss of acuity compared with that of the semi-indirect and direct electric lights. Make certain there are no light bulbs visible to the eyes and that there are no glaring or shiny spots anywhere near you.

For best reading conditions, sit comfortably in a well-ventilated, not overheated, room. The room should be free of distracting sights and sounds. Above all, do not attempt to do serious reading with the radio, television, or record player on.

How to Increase Your Speed

As discussed earlier, how rapidly you should read depends upon the type of material you are reading and the purpose for which you read. Most "light" reading should be at the rate of at least 400 words a minute. Most studying and other serious reading should be at the rate of at least 200 to 250 words a minute.

There are technical helps for improving reading speed, and reading specialists may be consulted for assistance. However, there are a number of things you can do on your own to improve your reading speed. If you will follow these six suggestions, you should soon note an increase in your reading speed. (If you already are a fast reader, these suggestions will help you to read still faster.)

Read in "Thought Units"   When you read in phrases, rather than word by word, your eyes take in more words at each pause. Because you make fewer pauses on each line of type, you automatically read faster. As an experiment, read the following short lines:

> e   a   d   r   r   f   o
>
> meaning   for   read
>
> read for meaning

Undoubtedly, you read each line with ease, but reading the first line took longer than the second, and the second line took longer than the third. This was because in the first line you read individual letters; in the second, you read individual words; but in the third, you read a phrase.

You should be able to read a newspaper column line in one or two eye pauses and a book-width line in not more than four or five pauses. Now read the following sentence, noticing the difference in speed when you read it word by word and when you read it in phrases.

> You / are / more / likely / to / understand / and / remember / what / you / read / if / you / actively / participate / in / what / you / read.
>
> You are more likely / to understand and remember / what you read / if you actively participate / in what you read.

Reading in phrases means reading in *units of thought.* Reading in this way enables you to understand better what you read, because sentences—complete thoughts—are made up of these smaller thought units.

Increasing your reading speed in this way will also increase your understanding of what you read. Whereas the slow reader can think much faster than he can read —and thus allows his thoughts to wander and his concentration to flag—the phrase reader receives ideas from the printed page rapidly enough to keep his mind fully occupied with his reading. Therefore, the fast reader—the phrase reader—is the good reader.

Keep Eyes Moving from Left to Right   Once you have read a phrase, do not allow yourself to go back and read it a second time. Such backward movements of the eyes are called "regressions," and they slow the reader considerably. In the untrained reader, these regressions have become a habit. Force yourself to get the meaning of a phrase the first time; force yourself to concentrate. This calls for practice and discipline, as well as for eliminating all distractions that might interfere with your reading.

Keep Lips and Tongue Motionless   Don't spell or pronounce the words you are reading, not even inwardly. Such vocalization slows down your reading; it means you can read silently only as fast as you can read aloud.

Look at Word Beginnings   Can't you identify the following portions of words without seeing the entire word? *undoub— remem— partici—* (You can tell from the rest of the sentence whether the last word should be *participate, participating,* or *participation.*)

Keep Building Vocabulary   Follow the suggestions made in Unit 1 for increasing your vocabulary. The more words you have at your command, the fewer pauses you will have to make to check the meanings of words and the faster you will read. Also, when your mind instantly recognizes words, the better you will understand what you are reading.

Make a Continual Effort   Continual increase in reading speed means exercising your willpower and continually practising rapid reading. If you force yourself always to read a little faster than is comfortable, rapid reading soon will become a habit.

How to Increase Your Comprehension

Reading speed is very important to the student and business worker alike. However, of greater importance than speed is comprehension (understanding) and retention (remembering). Some of the suggestions for increasing your reading speed will also contribute to your greater comprehension. A well-developed vocabulary is one example. Reading in thought units is another. Both contribute immeasurably to comprehension as well as to speed. In addition, the following suggestions will help to improve your reading comprehension and also your ability to remember what you read.

Scan or Preview the Material   First, look over the material to be read, noting the main headings and subheadings, looking at the illustrations, and reading captions and numbered portions. This preliminary survey will help you to determine your purpose in reading, and it will also reinforce important points that you want to remember.

Read Actively   You will comprehend what you read more fully if you read actively—if you try to relate what you are reading to what you already know. You must also constantly keep in mind the problem you wanted to solve when you started to read. This takes a high degree of concentration. It demands that you be on the lookout for main ideas and also the way in which the author arranges these ideas to reach a conclusion.

Study all illustrative material, such as pictures, graphs, and charts, and also the footnotes; all these are designed to explain and amplify main ideas. Be sure, too, to read examples presented by the author. Often these examples will help to clarify an idea that at first may seem hazy to you. They will also help you to remember main ideas.

Make Notes   If you own the book or magazine you are reading, you may wish to underline or otherwise mark some key words or phrases. Or, you may wish to make marginal notes. If the publication is not yours, you may want to make notes in a notebook that you may use for future reference.

How do you select the essential material for note-making? Just record main ideas and related ideas. Never take verbatim notes, even if you know shorthand.

How do you find the main ideas? Usually, writers convey only one idea per paragraph. Often this main idea is in the first sentence, but sometimes it may be in the last sentence. Occasionally, there may be two central ideas expressed in a key phrase or sentence within the paragraph. If you have difficulty in finding a central idea, you may need to read the paragraph carefully two or three times.

In addition to the central idea, you should also note facts, examples, and other ideas that explain, support, and develop the central idea. The exercises at the end of this unit will give you practice in selecting the central idea from a paragraph.

Reread and Review   How often you reread or review the material you read will depend upon its difficulty and the use you plan to make of it. Often a quick skimming or rereading of your notes will be adequate for review if the first reading was done carefully.

If you will put into practice immediately the suggestions made in this unit, not only will you reap dividends in terms of improved school work but also will you see these dividends multiply in your professional life.

Communication Problems

Application Exercises

A ■

To get an idea of your reading speed, have someone time you with a stopwatch as you read the following paragraphs:

The aircraft to watch in the future is the helicopter, one of the most amazing machines we have. The fact that it can move straight up and down, as well as sideways and forward, qualifies it for so many jobs that we can expect this marvel to fill the skies in the years ahead. Right now the jet plane and the space missile take the headlines, but the day of the whirlybird is coming up fast; it is almost here.

The helicopter is not an impressive sight when you see it on the ground. A jet plane, now, with its long fuselage and needle nose, with its zooming tail and swept wings, has exquisite beauty built right into it. Not even the deepest fan of the whirlybird will say it is pretty. In the little models, the plexiglass cabin and long, sharp blades make it look, to be honest, like a mosquito; and the big rotors and oddly bent body of the bigger machine make it look too much like a huge grasshopper. No, the helicopter is not pretty.

But, whether the machine is pretty or not, it has made a performance record that is unquestionably impressive. It has lifted hurt climbers off the tops of mountains. It has transferred sick men at sea from one ship to another. During floods and storms, the helicopter has taken doctors and food and clothing where no other vehicle could go. The appearance of the machine has not mattered to the hundreds of wounded who have been snatched from the field of battle, to the crews whose planes have fallen at sea, to the men it has picked from drifting ice floes and forest blazes and endless jungles, or to the other legions whom it has saved.

For all the drama of these events, the real value that the helicopter offers the world is its use in routine work. The taxi service that the machine provides to many heads of state in their trips from capital to airport is well known, as are also the taxi flights that link the airfields around our cities, not only with each other but also with heliports in both downtown and suburban areas. Helicopters are being used in highway patrol and traffic control. They are serving to spray orchards, to drive cattle, to fight blazes, to hoist the top girders of skyscrapers. Watch in the future!* (400 words)

Note the time it took you to read the above selection. Then locate this time in the following chart. Your reading speed will be opposite the time. For example, if you read the above paragraphs in one minute, your reading speed is 400 words per minute; if it took you two minutes, your speed is 200 words per minute. Most material of a fair degree of difficulty, such as this, should be read at the rate of about 300 words per minute. How does your speed compare?

* Rowe, Lloyd, and Winger, *Gregg Typing, 191 Series,* Canadian Edition, Book 1, McGraw-Hill Company of Canada Limited, Toronto, 1965, p. 172.

30 seconds	800 wpm	2½ minutes	160 wpm
1 minute	400 wpm	3 minutes	133 wpm
1½ minutes	267 wpm	3½ minutes	114 wpm
2 minutes	200 wpm	4 minutes	100 wpm

B ■

Without rereading the paragraphs, write a brief synopsis. Use your own words. Then compare your summary with the selection. Were you accurate and complete?

C ■

Be prepared to read aloud in class the paragraphs on page 61, thus demonstrating your ability to read for meaning.

D ■

One good reading habit that will help you gain speed is to look only at the beginnings of familiar words rather than at the entire words. Test your ability to do this by reading as rapidly as possible the following paragraphs in which the endings of some familiar words have been omitted.

The abil— to read is taken so much for gran— that we hear with some surp— the state—: "Read— is and prob— always will be the most funda— skill taught and used in and out of sch—." Beca— elem—, high school, and col— study is great— affec— by the abil— to read, the stud— must be able to read quic— and thoro—.

Outside the realm of educa—, the ordin— individ— has an equal need for develop— read— skill. In the day's routine, he reads newspa—, street signs, recipes, movie captions, personal correspon—, writ— mater— pertain— to his busin—, and countless other pieces of prin— matter.*

E ■

Select the main idea in each of the following three paragraphs. On a separate sheet of paper, write each main idea in your own words.

1   Product improvement is a widespread form of competition in the Canadian economy. Creating new products and improving old products has frequently taken the place of price competition as the principal basis for economic rivalry. Accordingly, over the years the range of products and the opportunities for the exercise of consumer choice have steadily broadened. For example, wool suits now compete not only with other wool suits but also with rayon, Dacron, and cotton suits. Continued multiplication of grades and varieties of products has increased the range of substitution and inter-product rivalry.

2   In all provinces, Workmen's Compensation legislation provides for compensation for injury to a worker by accident arising out of and in the course of employment, or for disablement caused by a specified industrial disease, except where the worker is disabled for fewer than a stated number of days. The Acts of all provinces provide for a compulsory system of collective liability on the part of employers.

* Adapted from Sferra, Wright, and Rice's *Personality and Human Relations,* 2d ed., McGraw-Hill Book Company, New York, 1961, p. 28.

To ensure payment of compensation, each Act provides for an accident fund, administered by the province, to which employers are required to contribute at a rate determined by the Workmen's Compensation Board in accordance with the hazards of the industry.

3 If the Government decides to vary expenditures rather than taxes to correct cycles in income and employment, it must decide how to spend varying amounts of money. During the 1930s the Government spent large sums for relief payments and so-called "make-work" projects. But now these are not generally considered a basic part of a fiscal program for economic recovery. Relief spending is an emergency program designed to alleviate the acute suffering of the unemployed and to get the economy moving again. Although it reduced distress, the fabled "leaf-raking" of the 1930s was a slow way to restore public confidence in the ability of the nation to regain prosperity. The necessity for this "stop-gap" spending has been reduced by our present-day programs of unemployment compensation, farm subsidies, and aids to other groups.

Word Study

A ■

Without consulting your dictionary, indicate which of the two spellings you believe to be generally preferred for the words in the list that follows. Then check your selections with *Webster's Seventh New Collegiate Dictionary* and also with *The Gage Canadian Dictionary*. Which form of spelling is generally preferred in Canada?

1	acknowledgment, acknowledgement	6	traveller, traveler
2	instalment, installment	7	catalog, catalogue
3	quartet, quartette	8	canceling, cancelling
4	anaemic, anemic	9	advisor, adviser
5	flier, flyer	10	benefited, benefitted

B ■

Respell the following words by sound (phonetically) according to what you consider the correct pronunciations. Then check your forms with the dictionary.

1	apparatus	5	inquiry	9	avenue
2	apricot	6	juvenile	10	percolate
3	applicable	7	irate		
4	financier	8	height		

Communication in Action: *Reducing Reading Time*

Larry Shawn managed to make it through high school; but when he got to college, Larry began to have difficulty passing his courses. He had a great many reading assignments and often had to stay up until after midnight. Even then, he sometimes could not complete all the reading he was supposed to do. What advice would you give Larry so that he would not have to spend so much time on reading assignments and neglect both his much-needed sleep and some opportunity for recreation?

PART · 4

The Framework
of
Effective
Communication □

Let's face facts! All of us have a strong desire to win the respect and consideration of our associates, in business and in society at large. Therefore, we work very hard to correct any weakness that threatens our own personal prestige. Perhaps you already know that failure to use good English is a bar to attainment of status. Perhaps you have been in a group that tried to smother smiles when some speaker made a remark about "them things." Knowledge of principles of good English usage, then, is the framework for the kind of effective oral and written communication that will give you the standing you would like to have. This knowledge and this standing will be your reward for careful study of the English usage principles presented in the following 15 units.

Why a
Framework
Is Necessary

Suppose you were asked to build a house. Where would you start? This would be quite a challenge, wouldn't it? The reason is that there are too many things about house construction that you don't know. In the first place, what sizes of lumber would you buy? What thicknesses, lengths, widths? Would the lumber be pine, oak, hickory—or what? Would you need bricks and, if so, what kind? And even if you had the right building materials, would you know how to put them together in such a way that the framework would be solid?

Building a house requires special knowledge of many of the dozens of ingredients that go into its construction; it also requires blueprints. For, if the framework isn't constructed properly, the structure won't look right; and it certainly won't stand very long.

The Importance of Framework

Framework is extremely important in any kind of building. It is equally important in using language. If you are given a set of words and are asked to make an intelligent communication, you would have much the same decisions to make as would the man who builds a house. The difference is that the builder deals in boards, concrete, and nails; and the communicator deals in nouns, verbs, and other parts of speech.

No builder would attempt to erect a structure without knowing his materials and how to use them. On the other hand, however, many persons do just that when they speak or write. Often, a student protests, "I don't have to know the rules of grammar, punctuation, and capitalization in order to write well."

But he does need to know. Actually, the communicator needs to know how to fashion a solid framework just as surely as does the house builder. His communication will fall apart unless it has a solid foundation. In this case, a solid foundation means accuracy in using the ingredients of language according to accepted patterns.

Grammar, the Framework of Language

The communicator's framework of expression is language; and the structure, or pattern, of language is what is commonly called *grammar*. Specifically, grammar is the branch of the study of language that deals with the way words are put together into sentences and the forms these words take as a result.

"Why," you may ask, "do I need to know what a noun is?" The answer is simple. If you don't know the forms and functions of nouns, you may use language poorly. As a result, your reader may mistake your meaning. For instance:

In our store, the lady's lounge is on the fifth floor.

This is an incorrect message. As written, the lounge on the fifth floor belongs to or is for *one* lady. Mastery of noun plurals and possessives enables the writer to make the message clear:

In our store, the ladies' lounge is on the fifth floor.

If you don't know the forms and functions of verbs in language, you might make mistakes such as these:

The council are still in session. (*Council* is a collective noun and needs a singular verb. Written correctly, the sentence is this: *The council is still in session.*)

By the time we arrived at the airport, the plane had went. (*Gone,* not *went,* is the correct verb form.)

I wish I was in a position to grant your request. (The communicator who knows his verbs knows that *were* is always used with *wish.*)

We should like you to carefully and thoroughly study this report. (While use of a split infinitive is not a major error, the verb-wise communicator would write the sentence this way: *We should like you to study this report carefully and thoroughly.*)

Suppose you are not clear about pronoun usage. If so, you might be guilty of errors like the following:

Would you like Mr. Tracy and I to check the blueprint?

Sometimes *I,* the nominative case of the personal pronoun, is correct; sometimes *me,* the objective case form, should be used. In the above sentence, *me* would be correct. The trained communicator uses the correct form almost automatically. Note the pronoun in the following sentence:

"Yes, this is him speaking."

The person who answers the telephone in this manner is hazy about pronoun usage. He should say, "Yes, this is *he* speaking." Now, observe this message:

Of course your invited to the banquet!

Warm, isn't it? But it would be much more effective if the correct contraction of *you are, you're,* were used. *Your* means "belonging to you."

One of the most important reasons for understanding language framework is that *you know when you don't know.* What does this mean? Just this: Many persons, after uttering or writing a sentence, couldn't tell you whether it is correctly put together. Because they don't really understand language structure, they are always in doubt as to the correctness or appropriateness of their messages—a severe handicap to the writer of any communication. On the other hand, a person who knows enough to know that his sentence framework is shaky will doubtless know enough to discover how it can be improved.

Framework Promotes Communication

The function of language structure is to promote the clear, fluid communication of thoughts. Whenever you write or speak, you have a reason for doing so: you have something to communicate to someone. As a business worker, your success will depend upon how well you can express orally or on paper your facts and ideas.

To write messages that are clear and fluid, and to speak effectively, you will need to master certain techniques of putting words together. These techniques will help you guard against anything that would block or confuse your reader or listener or that would distract his attention from your central purpose.

Now, let's look at some additional illustrations.

> Our engineer span the wheel several times, but it still does not work free.

Did the verb *span* block you? The writer meant *spun*, the past tense of *spin*. And how about the adjective *free?* Did you visualize the wheel as being stuck in something that kept it from moving, something from which it could not work itself free? And if so, how could the engineer spin it? The meaning would have been perfectly clear if the adverb *freely* had been used. Just to show how to avoid confusing blocks, look at the sentence as it should be written.

> Our engineer spun the wheel several times, but it still does not work freely.

Now let's see how the choice of pronoun forms can aid or retard communication.

> Do you think you have given Bran Products just as much business as us?

> Do you think you have given Bran Products just as much business as we?

The first sentence is correct if the meaning is "just as much business as you have given *us*." The second sentence is correct if the meaning is "just as much business as *we* have given Bran Products." Can you see that the writer must know his "we's" and his "us's" if he is to avoid confusing his readers?

As just one more illustration of the way in which the framework of language affects communication, here is a sentence containing a misplaced adverb.

> I have permission only to sign Mr. Roche's name.

The meaning here is that the only permission I have is the signing of Mr. Roche's name. That seems somewhat ridiculous. But suppose I mean that I can't sign the name of anybody but Mr. Roche. I could communicate this meaning clearly by placing *only* in either of two other positions.

> I have permission to sign only Mr. Roche's name.

> I have permission to sign Mr. Roche's name only.

Now the meaning intended is the meaning expressed, because both these sentences are based on a solid framework.

If at this point you are saying to yourself, "Here we go again! More of the same old thing," you are wrong. In the next fourteen units you will study a streamlined version of the principles of language structure; and you will be asked to learn only those rules that will insure your effective use of good, standard English. You need not learn a single principle that you cannot put to use.

Communication Problems

Application Exercises

The framework of each of the following excerpts is shaky. Rewrite each excerpt, and supply any needed substitutions that will strengthen its structure.

A ■

From Minutes of a Meeting

The meeting was called to order by President Walsh at 8 p.m., and present was all members except two.

Under "Old Business," analyses of Mr. King's report on the summer swimming pool was presented by Mr. Juma and Mr. Ford. On a motion made by Mr. Gregg, seconded by Mr. Wong, it was unanimously voted to reserve one section for a children's wading pool; and the plans to be used are those that were drawn for the Jones' pool.

Decisions with regard to personnel were made. Rules to be observed by children and workers alike were lain out. A copy of the rules are attached to this secretary's report.

B ■

From a Letter

You will be sorry to hear that illness has caused David's prolonged absence. I had noticed that he wasn't looking good for some time; in fact, for weeks now he has acted as if he was drained of all energy.

David is a good student; but without he does his homework, I know that his problem may be identical to that of Ray Forbes. You may recall that, because of unavoidable absence from school, Ray was obliged to repeat his second year.

C ■

From a Report

I respectfully request that Pierre Bessette and Robert Stillman be assigned to help me with the research on computers. Although the project is a real big one, I am sure that between us the work will be done to your satisfaction.

We have all the supplys we need; our office is well ventilated and with plenty of light. Being that we have worked together on other projects, we perform like any well-organized team does.

D ■

From a Textbook

Many customers and vendors never see the letter writer or his place of business; consequently, they form their opinions entirely from the effect produced by letters. The tone of each letter, therefore, is very important; for it is tone that will determine whether or not the business relationships will be harmonious.

If the correspondent were talking to the readers of his letters, he would have the advantage of using facial expressions and voice inflections to stress his points and to make his meaning clear. In a written communication, the words on paper are the only means by which he can sell himself and his employer as honest, gracious persons—wonderful people with whom to do business!

Word Study

A ■

The following words are spelled phonetically as they are often mispronounced. Spell each correctly.

1	genuwine	5	anartik	8	genrilly
2	lenth	6	athaletic	9	Febuary
3	hoseree	7	akumpnement	10	histry
4	tremenjus				

B ■

The following brief definitions indicate frequently used words that contain silent letters. Spell the words. To help you, the number of letters in each word is given.

1 A body of land surrounded by water (6 letters)
2 To strike or rap (5 letters)
3 Unruffled; still (4 letters)
4 The opposite of day (5 letters)
5 The branch of medicine that deals with mental disorders (10 letters)
6 The opposite of right (5 letters)
7 A lien on property by which the property is made security for a loan (8 letters)
8 A song of praise (4 letters)
9 A twenty-fourth part of a day (4 letters)
10 A visitor (5 letters)

C ■

Here are ten pairs of definitions. The two words defined in each pair contain exactly the same letters, but in different order. What are the words?

1 A whitish metal. A sharp, thin fragment.
2 A pillar. To check; hold back.
3 Haphazard. Relating to a cause.
4 A heavy metal. To distribute; apportion.

THE FRAMEWORK OF EFFECTIVE COMMUNICATION

5 Stockings. Long-handled tools for weeding.
6 Disabled in leg or foot. Opposite of female.
7 A courageous deed. Destiny.
8 Pertaining to army life. Pertaining to marriage.
9 A thick slice of meat or of fish. A pointed stick driven into the ground.
10 A spiritual being. The area formed when two straight lines meet.

D ■

Should *ei* or *ie* appear in the following blank spaces to complete the correct spellings of these words?

1	gr__ve	5	bel__ve	8	c__ling
2	f__rce	6	rev__w	9	s__ge
3	rec__pt	7	w__ght	10	s__ze
4	n__ther				

E ■

Do the following words start with *des* or *dis?*

1	____cribe	5	____pondent	8	____cend
2	____astrous	6	____ease	9	____pise
3	____appoint	7	____solve	10	____prove
4	____troy				

F ■

Should *for, fore,* or *four* appear in the blank spaces in the following words?

1	____close	5	____gone	8	there____ (hence)
2	____ty	6	be____	9	____some
3	____man	7	____ward	10	____getful
4	____teen				

G ■

Should an *a*, an *e*, or an *o* appear in the blank space in each of the following words?

1	scen__ry	5	mem__ry	8	invent__ry
2	flatt__ry	6	machin__ry	9	satisfact__ry
3	liter__ry	7	volunt__ry	10	arbitr__ry
4	advis__ry				

Communication in Action: *Untangling Pompous Prose*

You are asked to revise and simplify a report that contains the following sentences. See if you can rewrite the paragraph in everyday language.

Subsequent to March 1 Miss Garvin terminated her employment with this organization after a considerable number of years of continuous and exemplary service. Apropos to her departure Miss Garvin stated that she had procured an infinitely superior connection in an executive capacity. We must employ perseverance in endeavoring to obtain a suitable replacement of comparable caliber.

The
Sentence

As a child, you learned first to say isolated words. As you grew older, you gained facility in the use of the language. You put words into sentences, and your efforts to communicate became more successful. At the age of five or six you went to school; and there, year after year, you studied some form of communication.

The English language is studied to improve communication between persons. Any courses involving reading and listening have as their objective an improvement in receiving messages. Courses in speaking or writing are offered to improve the sending of messages. Because communication is the primary purpose of language and because the sentence is the core of language—and thus, of communication—the logical starting place for your study of grammar is mastery of basic sentence essentials.

What a Sentence Is

In a dictionary a *sentence* is defined as a group of words expressing a complete thought. Such a group of words making sense when standing alone is also called an *independent* (or *main*) *clause*. You will learn more about clauses later.

To be a sentence, a group of words must mean something. If no meaning is received from what is supposed to be a sentence, communication will be disrupted and confusion will arise. It is therefore important that the words you write as sentences express complete thoughts.

※ QUICK TRICK No Sense, No Sentence

To see at a glance whether or not a group of words is a sentence, consider whether the words make sense. If they do make sense, there is a sentence; if not, there is no sentence. Just remember this: sense—sentence; no sense —no sentence. For example:

All bills must be paid within 30 days. (These words make sense; they express a complete thought. Therefore, they make a sentence.)

As we are not in a position to advertise now (Here is a "no sense" group of words. The words do not make sense because the thought they express is not complete. Therefore, this group of words is not a sentence.)

We are not in a position to advertise now. (In this instance, the thought is complete and the words do make a sentence.)

☐ CLASS PRACTICE 1

Throughout the entire grammar section, oral class practices and practices in proofreading are provided as a means of helping you to absorb the principles studied. Now tell which of the following groups of words are sentences and which are not. Just say, "Sense" or "No sense." For additional practice, make sense out of the "no sense" groups by adding words that will make them sentences.

1. The typists say that posture chairs are very comfortable
2. Promotion is the result of honest effort
3. Although the note is not yet due
4. Because of lack of warehouse space
5. Since we are not ready to advertise the new product
6. The stapler is a "must" in any office
7. Planned for quick reproduction of transcripts
8. That telephone operator has a pleasant voice
9. As we are in an embarrassing position

Subject and Predicate

Look again at the above groups of words you identified as sentences. Each of these sentences is composed of a subject and a predicate, and a review of subject and predicate is necessary at this point because it is the foundation for principles that will be presented in Units 16, 17, and 18.

The important point here is the subject; for if you are able to select the subject, you will then know that the rest of the sentence is the predicate. The complete subject is that part of the sentence that shows who is speaking or is spoken to or the person or thing spoken about. A subject may be a single word or a group of words.

The *predicate* is that part of the sentence that says something about the subject. The core of the predicate is the *verb*.

In each of the following sentences, the subject is enclosed in parentheses. Everything not in parentheses, including the italicized verb, is the predicate.

(I) *am going* to the bank this morning. (*I* is the subject of the sentence, the *person speaking.*)

(You) *are* to report to Mr. Bond. (*You* is the subject, the *person spoken to.*)

(The typist whom we hired last week) *is* very efficient. (*The typist whom we hired last week* is the subject, the *person spoken about.*)

(Our out-of-date typewriters) *have been sold.* (*Our out-of-date typewriters* is the subject, the *things spoken about.*)

☐ CLASS PRACTICE 2

Now, for a little practice, select the *complete subject* of each of the following sentences. Keep in mind that the rest of the sentence is the *predicate.*

1. Data processing equipment is in use in more and more offices.
2. Preliminary examinations are to be given tomorrow.
3. You will be pleased with the new carbon paper.
4. Ms. Paavola has decided to resign.
5. The purpose of the meeting is to determine the reason for increased cost of sales.
6. Many persons in their late teens are obtaining good office positions.
7. I am not sure about the wording of that order.
8. Improvements in electric typewriters are frequently being made.

Simple and Compound Subjects

You have now reviewed and practised selecting the complete subject of a sentence. The next step is to see whether you are able to isolate the simple or compound subject. Do not lightly assume that you know all about simple and compound subjects, for the principles presented in Units 16, 17, and 18 are based on your ability to select such subjects quickly and accurately.

A *simple subject* is the single most important word in the complete subject. For example:

> The *girl* in the blue dress is a new employee. (*The girl in the blue dress* is the complete subject. The most important single word is *girl;* therefore, *girl* is the simple subject.)

A *compound subject* consists of two or more words that are equally important and are joined usually by the conjunction *and, or,* or *nor.*

> The *debits and credits* in the trial balance must be equal. (*The debits and credits in the trial balance* is the complete subject. *Debits* and *credits* are the most important words, equally important, and are joined by the conjunction *and.* Therefore, *debits and credits* is the compound subject.)

☐ CLASS PRACTICE 3

In Class Practice 2, each sentence has a simple subject. Name those simple subjects.

☐ CLASS PRACTICE 4

See if you can select the simple or the compound subject of each of these sentences.

1. Jean Bennett is a graduate of our school.
2. Jean Bennett and her sisters are graduates of our school.
3. The stencil duplicator or the fluid duplicator may be used for this job.
4. The machine equipped with tape is a listing machine.
5. A few weeks spent in practice will increase your speed.

6. An outgoing personality and good manners are needed in business.
7. The tone of a person's voice could arouse resentment in a customer.
8. A desk in the outer office has been reserved for Mr. Ames.

Normal and Inverted Sentence Order

Many glaring errors in grammar are caused by the inability to identify the simple subjects of sentences, especially when sentences are in inverted order. The ability to recognize inverted sentence order and to change inverted order to normal order is a technique that you, when writing or speaking, can and should use to avoid making such errors.

A sentence is considered in *normal order* when the complete subject precedes the complete predicate. For example:

> The package in question disappeared somewhere in transit. (The complete subject is *the package in question*. It precedes the complete predicate, *disappeared somewhere in transit*.)

When the complete subject does not precede the complete predicate, however, the sentence is said to be in *inverted order*.

> Somewhere in transit, the package in question disappeared. (Here, part of the complete predicate, *somewhere in transit*, precedes the complete subject; therefore, the sentence order is inverted.)

To change inverted sentence order to normal order, simply rearrange the words so that the complete subject is written first, followed by the complete predicate.

> Down the avenue marched the parade. (Inverted order)

> The parade marched down the avenue. (Normal order)

Most questions are in inverted order.

> Where are we going? (Inverted order)

> We are going where? (Normal order)

> Can he get there on time? (Inverted order)

> He can get there on time? (Normal order)

When changing sentences to normal order, do not be disturbed that the changed construction may sound odd or may result in a different meaning. It is your ability to recognize sentences in inverted order and to change them to normal order that is important, for this technique will always enable you to find the subject.

☐ CLASS PRACTICE 5

Practice what you have learned by indicating which of the following sentences are in normal order and which are in inverted order. Then change to normal order all the sentences written in inverted order.

1. At the present time we are not quoting prices.
2. In the files you will find much valuable information.
3. Where are your letterheads?
4. A crowd of tired-looking girls surged out of the elevator.
5. To the beginning worker, the first day on the job is confusing.
6. Soon after his arrival, the telephones began to ring.
7. When should those letters be signed?
8. Luxurious furnishings are to be observed in some offices.
9. Did anyone here see Jim?
10. There is a run in your stocking.

Communication Problems

Application Exercises

A ■

Number from 1 to 20 on a separate sheet of paper. For each of the following sentences: (*a*) write the complete subject, and (*b*) draw a line under the simple or the compound subject.

The sentence: The sharpest pencils in the entire office are on Mr. Smith's desk.
Your answer: **The sharpest pencils in the entire office.**

1 Students who are graduated from our business course are well trained.
2 Time and tide wait for no man or woman.
3 In the morning June works very slowly.
4 The clerks in the brightly lighted office look very happy.
5 A scientist of renown and an engineer with a doctor's degree have been added to our staff.
6 Hundreds of packages of seeds were shipped today.
7 Paper and other supplies are stored in a special room.
8 Members of the office force have been invited to the picnic.
9 By using a flashlight, Mr. Aker was able to find his pen.
10 Willingness to work and ability to do the work are the basic job requirements.
11 In front of the receptionist stood two callers who did not have appointments.
12 Mr. Gunner and his daughter work in the same office.
13 At five o'clock the bell sounded for closing time.
14 Does the type on that typewriter stick in damp weather?
15 Pots of coffee and plates of sandwiches awaited the arrival of the guests.
16 A reference manual and a dictionary are tools of the stenographer's trade.
17 Bars of chocolate and boxes of candy will be on sale today.
18 An expert typist or a trained secretary is needed to help Miss Nichols.
19 A course for high-speed shorthand writers is being offered this year.
20 Are you going to the office party?

B ■

Some of the following groups of words are sentences; others are not. On a separate sheet of paper, number from 1 to 20 and then do the following: (*a*) Make a complete sentence out of any "no sense" group of words; (*b*) change to normal order any sentence that is in inverted order; (*c*) write the complete subject of each sentence, and (*d*) underline its simple or compound subject.

> *The sentence:* A new method of cost accounting is being considered.
> *Your answer:* A new **method** of cost accounting **(Complete subject with simple subject underlined.)**

> *The sentence:* Has the message about canceling the order been received yet?
> *Your answer:* **The message about canceling the order has been received yet.**
> **The message about canceling the order (Changed to normal order first.)**

> *The "sentence":* By sending us your cheque for $150.
> *Your answer:* **You can expedite delivery of your order by sending us your cheque for $150. You ("No sense" group first made into sentence.)**

1 Since he disliked bookkeeping.
2 Before cutting a stencil, you should clean your type.
3 Would you prefer a blue stencil?
4 Notwithstanding the severity of the weather.
5 Trembling and pale, Nancy went in to take her first dictation.
6 Each spring our office receives a thorough renovation.
7 By your carelessness in reading directions.
8 Did Mr. Evans buzz for his secretary?
9 In the warm sunlight, Mary's fingers seemed to move more slowly over the keys.
10 As we are making a very small profit.
11 Who was the first champion typist?
12 Strong and tanned and happy were the clerks returning from vacation.
13 After being praised by the office manager.
14 Has Mr. Hart been with our firm very long?
15 While I was typing the memorandum.
16 Here are the paper clips you lost.
17 Once a week, each file clerk gets an extra rest period.
18 Seating himself again.
19 Where is the wastebasket that belongs under my desk?
20 As if enjoying the work.

Word Study

A ■

Distinguish between the meaning and spelling of each of the following words that are often confused: mood, mode; command, commend.

B ■

What is the adjective form of each of the following words?

1	continue	**3**	invent	**5**	season
2	deride	**4**	work	**6**	imagine

C ■

Which of the following words are misspelled?

1	apologize	**3**	realise	**5**	exercise
2	merchandise	**4**	advertise	**6**	analyse

Communication in Action: *Name Game*

Has your ability to remember names after introductions improved lately? This is the time to find out. Have six of your classmates select assumed names and introduce themselves to you. You may ask one question of each as you try to fix the name in your memory. Then, introduce each one to another student. *Hint:* Try to associate face, appearance, dress, speech, etc., with names.

UNIT □ 10

Verbs, Verbs, Verbs

In the previous unit you learned that the predicate is that part of the sentence that says something about the subject and that the core of the predicate is the verb. The function of a verb in a sentence resembles the function of the motor in an automobile. Without a verb, the sentence will not go. With an incorrect verb, the sentence will not go where it is supposed to go. The verb principles that you will study in this unit and the next will be understood more easily if you think of verbs as the engines, or power-giving elements, of your sentences.

Words That Assert

A verb is a word that asserts or expresses action, a condition, or a state of being.

> He *ran* across the street. (Action)
>
> This milk *tastes* sour. (Condition)
>
> He *is* in the kitchen. (State of being)

In the following groups of words, keep in mind the idea of the verb as the motor of a sentence. Note that in each group the verb is missing.

The bird sweetly.

Mr. Adams his arm.

Brenda the best file clerk we ever had.

Did you get any message from these words? Did anything happen? Watch them *go* when verbs are supplied.

The bird *sings* sweetly.

Mr. Adams *broke* (*raised, scratched, hit*) his arm.

Brenda *was* (*is, discharged, snubbed*) the best file clerk we ever had.

☐ CLASS PRACTICE 1

Here is your opportunity to put into practice your understanding of verbs as motors for sentences. If the verb is missing in any of the following groups of words, supply a verb (and only a verb) for the group.

1. The store's basement needs redecorating.
2. Our information booth on the first floor.
3. This book important information about office etiquette.
4. The office boy the food for the coffee break.
5. Susan the pertinent file folders.
6. All tags show the prices clearly marked.
7. The executive the new dictating machine.
8. Reputable manufacturers the goods they have for sale.

Verb Phrases

In some cases, two or more verbs are needed to make the sentence "go." Whenever this is true, the sentence has a *verb phrase*.

Mr. Wood *was answering* the question.

You *should have asked* permission to use the telephone.

A verb phrase contains a *main* (principal) verb and one or more *helping* (auxiliary) verbs. Remember that, in a verb phrase, the *last* verb is the *main* verb. Study very carefully the following illustrations.

The caller *has been* here twice this week. (Main verb, *been;* helping verb, *has.*)

The bulletin *has been read* by the entire staff. (Main verb, *read;* helpers, *has* and *been.*)

Note that, in the first sentence, *been* is a main verb; but in the second sentence, *been* is a helper. This will present no problem if you have learned that the *last* verb in a verb phrase is the *main* verb and the preceding verb or verbs are *helpers*. Some of the more common helpers are shown in italics in the verb phrases:

am going	*do* go	*have* gone	*have been* going
are going	*did* go	*has* gone	*has been* going
is going	*can* go	*had* gone	*had been* going
was going	*must* go	*must have* gone	*must be* going
were going	*will* go	*shall have* gone	*should* be going
may be going	*may* go	*could have* gone	*could be* going

A knowledge of helpers and of verb phrases is necessary as background not only for the next topic you will study but also for some later topics.

☐ CLASS PRACTICE 2

To find out how well you understand the verb-phrase principle, select the verb phrase in each of the following sentences. Then tell which is the main verb and which is the helping verb or verbs.

1. Everybody should choose his career early in life.
2. The folders must be placed correctly in the file.
3. Have you written to Mr. James this week?
4. Your manner might be misunderstood by the customers.
5. Can you think of any necessary improvements?
6. You surely have been instructed in mailing routine.
7. Joan is failing in her efforts to keep up her production.
8. The calculator has been there for years.

Principal Parts of Verbs

The principal parts of verbs are the forms used for expressing the time of action, or *tense*, of a verb. Each verb has three principal parts: the *present*, the *past*, and the *past participle*. These three parts are used to form six tenses.

Tense   The *present* part is used to express *present time, future time,* and to make a statement that is *true at all times.*

We *answer* all orders promptly. (Present time)

I shall *answer* his letter tomorrow. (Future time)

They always *answer* in a courteous manner. (Statement true at all times)

The *past* part, or tense, of the verb is used to express *past time.*

We *answered* those letters last week.

The *past participle* is used to form the *present perfect tense,* indicating action that has been completed before the present time; the *past perfect tense,* indicating action completed before another past action; and the *future perfect tense,* indicating action that will be completed before a certain time in the future.

We have (She has) *answered* his request. (Present perfect)

She had *answered* the request before she received his second letter. (Past perfect)

I will have *answered* his request by that time. (Future perfect)

Regular and Irregular Verbs   Verbs are classified as *regular* or *irregular* according to the way their principal parts are formed. A regular verb forms the past tense and past participle by adding *d* or *ed* to the present form. For example:

Present	*Past*	*Past Participle*
walk	walked	walked
call	called	called

The principal parts of regular verbs do not require much study, as a mistake in the use of these verbs is rarely made.

Irregular verbs, however, form the past tense and the past participle in various ways—frequently by changing to a different word. Note the following examples:

Present	*Past*	*Past Participle*
sing	sang	sung
drive	drove	driven
go	went	gone
be	was	been
have	had	had

Errors in the use of irregular verbs occur often, particularly in speaking. A list of preferred forms for 60 important irregular verbs is on page 83. Memorize these forms if you don't already know them. If you are in doubt about any verb form, you can also consult the dictionary. The dictionary gives the past tense and past participle forms for all irregular verbs.

As you study irregular verbs, keep in mind that the past tense form is *never* used with a helping verb, whereas a past participle is *always* used with a helper—sometimes more than one. In the following examples, note how the verb *go* is used.

We *went* to the theatre Wednesday. (Past)

We have *gone* to the theatre many times since we moved here. (Past participle, plus helper *have*.)

We shall have *gone* three times in one week, counting tomorrow. (Past participle, plus helpers *shall* and *have*.)

In the sentence, "Julia has drew $10 on her pay," the verb phrase *has drew* is incorrect because the past form of *draw* is used with a helper, *has*. If the past form is retained, then no helper should be used. But, if the meaning to be expressed requires the helper *has*, then the past participle must be used.

Julia *drew* $10 on her pay.

Julia *has drawn* $10 on her pay.

Principal Parts of Verbs

Present	Past	*Past Participle	Present	Past	*Past Participle
be	was	been	hang (to put to death)	hanged	hanged
become	became	become			
begin	began	begun	hang	hung	hung
bid (to tell)	bade	bidden	hide	hid	hidden
bid (to offer)	bid	bid	know	knew	known
bite	bit	bitten	lay	laid	laid
blow	blew	blown	leave	left	left
break	broke	broken	lend	lent	lent
bring	brought	brought	lie	lay	lain
burst	burst	burst	pay	paid	paid
buy	bought	bought	ride	rode	ridden
catch	caught	caught	ring	rang	rung
choose	chose	chosen	rise	rose	risen
climb°	climbed	climbed	run	ran	run
come	came	come	see	saw	seen
do	did	done	set	set	set
drag°	dragged	dragged	shake	shook	shaken
draw	drew	drawn	shine°	shone	shone
drink	drank	drunk	shrink	shrank	shrunk
drive	drove	driven	sing	sang	sung
drown°	drowned	drowned	sit	sat	sat
eat	ate	eaten	speak	spoke	spoken
fall	fell	fallen	spring	sprang	sprung
fight	fought	fought	steal	stole	stolen
flee	fled	fled	strike	struck	struck
fly	flew	flown	swear	swore	sworn
forget	forgot	forgotten	swim	swam	swum
freeze	froze	frozen	take	took	taken
get	got	got	tear	tore	torn
give	gave	given	throw	threw	thrown
go	went	gone	wear	wore	worn
grow	grew	grown	write	wrote	written

*These parts of verbs must be used only with a helping verb.
* This is a regular verb, but wrong forms are often used in the past tense and the past participle.
° When *shine* means *to polish*, the parts are *shine, shined, shined.*

PROOFREADING PRACTICE 1

A competent proofreader must have an excellent background in the English language, for his job is to see and to correct errors in English, as well as typographical errors. For this error hunt, assume you are a proofreader who understands the correct use of principal parts of verbs. Find and correct all verb-form errors in the following sentences.

1. Joyce begun to wonder if she would ever finish transcribing.
2. Charles and Eugene done much for office morale.
3. That man was drove by his ambition to become vice-president.
4. The door opened and in come Martha.
5. Have you ever ate in the cafeteria on the first floor?
6. The train had went before he reached the station.
7. Beverly seen the first draft of the monthly bulletin.
8. Mr. Grimes has often spoke to Rosa about her untidy erasures.

Infinitives

A verb preceded by *to* is known as an *infinitive*.

to run	to do	to be
to say	to think	to have

Careful writers usually avoid placing any word or words between the *to* and the verb.

> *Poor:* to quickly run (split infinitive)   *Better:* to run quickly

Many English language authorities of today, however, do not consider a split infinitive the major error that it formerly was. Indeed, many well-known authors maintain that a split infinitive often adds force to a statement. Be that as it may, you as a beginning writer should avoid splitting infinitives whenever possible. However, if you are faced with a choice between a split infinitive and an awkward, unnatural construction, choose the split infinitive as the lesser evil.

☐ **CLASS PRACTICE 3**

See if you can identify the split infinitives in the following sentences. Then reword the sentences to avoid splitting those infinitives.

1. Robert was told to thoroughly clean the duplicator.
2. Helga was forced to quietly wait until Mr. Stein finished telephoning.
3. You would be wise to accurately proofread all typewritten work.
4. We thought the switchboard operator would try to at least be polite.
5. It is impossible to rapidly type in hot, sticky weather.
6. You should begin to, if you wish to succeed, develop good work habits.
7. The undesirable caller was persuaded to finally leave.

Communication Problems

Application Exercises

A ■

For each of the following sentences: (*a*) list the verb or verb phrase, (*b*) underline the main verb if you have listed a verb phrase, and (*c*) supply a verb for any group of words in which the verb is missing.

1 An impatient customer into the store.
2 Vendors of stockings announced the development of a new fabric.
3 The foundry has been purchased by Allen & Brown.
4 The word "parity" appears frequently in the newspapers.
5 The salesperson the coveted order.
6 We shall be glad to hear from you shortly.
7 Miss Morrow can take dictation at 140 words a minute.
8 Three telegrams from Mr. Downs have been received today.
9 Manufacturers usually allow a 30-day credit.
10 Delicious punch at the office party last Christmas.
11 For what company did the applicant last work?
12 Wheat is selling rapidly on the Exchange.
13 Do your customers like these linen napkins?
14 Has our request been given special consideration?
15 Our best customer an extension of credit.

Check: Did you change to normal order all the sentences that were in inverted order? If not, do so now.

B ■

If a sentence in the following exercise is correct, write "OK" on your paper. If it is incorrect, write the correction and give your reason for doing so.

1 Last week Bahn Brothers run an advertisement in the paper.
2 We are sorry that a misunderstanding about your account has arose.
3 Did you know that our president has broke his lease?
4 Angela has driven her own car for years.
5 Were you choosen to represent the office staff?
6 We were late getting home because the wind had blew hard all day.
7 Have you ever sang in a church choir?
8 Please try to never refuse a reasonable request.
9 After we had eaten our lunch, we hurried back to the office.
10 Prices have rose faster than wages.
11 The package you were looking for has came.
12 Steel companies have began to shorten working hours.
13 How much am I bid for this portable typewriter?
14 Have you payed your monthly dues?
15 The space bar on my machine is busted.

THE FRAMEWORK OF EFFECTIVE COMMUNICATION

C ■

The blanks within the following sentences should contain some form of these verbs: *begin, bid, drink, drive, hang, ride, ring, sink, speak,* or *tear.* Write the correct verb form for each sentence.

1   Has the cowboy ever _____ in the Calgary Stampede?
2   The hook on the fishing rod has _____ to the bottom of the pond.
3   When was the last time a convicted murderer was _____ in Canada?
4   The professor _____ us seniors to document all our term papers.
5   Don has _____ all the coffee in his vacuum bottle.
6   The November campaign has _____ to shape up very well.
7   Has the beginning-of-class bell _____ yet?
8   The manager has _____ to him several times about his untidy work.
9   While the decorator was here, our office was all _____ up.
10 The foreign student was _____ to the wrong railroad station.

Word Study

A ■

Distinguish between the meaning and spelling of the following words that are often confused: fineness, finesse; leased, least.

B ■

1   Which of the following words contains a silent letter (besides *e*): listen, February, telegraph, strength?
2   Which of the following words does *not* contain a silent letter (besides *e*): night, island, doubt, candidate?

C ■

Should *ancy* or *ency* be added to the following to complete the correct spellings?

1	effici____	3	emerg____	5	buoy____
2	hesit____	4	flu____	6	vac____

Communication in Action: Selecting the Right Word

Assume that the following sentences are taken from an office memorandum. Rewrite them, using correct words for those that have been used incorrectly or misspelled.

I respectively request that you permit us to put this procedure into affect at once. Our department likes sufficient staff to procure the datum we need to insure our customers of efficent service. Keeping seperate cost controls on each operation places a heavy bookeeping burden on our employees, but we will try to preform the task as good as possible.

More about Verbs

When the verbs you use not only "move" your sentences, but move them in the right direction, the next question is: Will your sentences move smoothly? Having a motor is one thing, but having a motor that is tuned up is another. The additional verb principles presented in this unit represent the tools you will need to keep your verb motor operating at peak efficiency.

To pave the way for some principles of grammar and usage that you will learn in Units 14 and 15, verbs are classified here in three ways: (1) "being" verbs, (2) transitive verbs, and (3) intransitive verbs.

"Being" Verbs

If you were to use the verb *be* in all its tenses and modifications, you would find the following different forms:

> am, is, are, was, were
>
> *be* with a helper: shall be, will be, may be, can be, would be, might be, etc.
>
> *been* with a helper or helpers: has been, have been, had been, shall have been, will have been, could have been, might have been, etc.

These forms of *be* are the "being" verbs. Probably the best way to learn them is to repeat them frequently until you have memorized them.

Remember, however, that these verbs are being verbs only when they are used as *main* verbs, not when they are used as helpers; and remember that the main verb is always the *last* verb in a verb phrase. For example:

> Mr. Goggin *was* not in the office today. (Since *was* is the only verb in the sentence, it has to be the main verb.)
>
> The winners of the bonus *should have been* Grace and he. (This verb phrase is a being verb because *been* is the last, and main, verb.)

The following sentences do not contain being verbs because the forms of *be* are used as helpers only.

> The reports *have been placed* correctly in the files. (Here, *have* and *been* are used as helpers. The last, and main, verb is *placed.*)
>
> Who *is going* to the demonstration? (The main verb is *going.*)

THE FRAMEWORK OF EFFECTIVE COMMUNICATION

☐ CLASS PRACTICE 1

Tell which of the following sentences contain being verbs. Name each being verb.

1. Your typewriter ribbon is worn out.
2. There must be some reason for his failing to check his work.
3. At the bottom of the wastebasket is a dollar bill.
4. When will the salesman be leaving for his trip?
5. The treasurer's reports were read and filed every week.
6. His cheque should have been in the mail this morning.
7. Next to our office is a large vacant lot.
8. Mr. Evans might be our next purchasing agent.

Transitive and Intransitive Verbs

A *transitive verb* is a verb that regularly has an *object*—a word that tells what or who receives the action expressed by the verb.

> The boy delivered the groceries according to schedule. (The object of *delivered* is *groceries,* so *delivered* is a transitive verb.)

An *intransitive verb* is a verb that does not have an object.

> The grocery boy winked as he passed. (The verb *winked* has no object; therefore it is intransitive.)

For ease in identifying transitive and intransitive verbs, study the following Quick Trick:

✳ QUICK TRICK   Ask "What?" or "Whom?"

If there can be an answer to the question "What?" or "Whom?" asked after a verb, that verb is transitive. If there can be no answer because an answer would not make sense, the verb is intransitive.

> The caller *placed* Ella in an embarrassing position. (Placed what? No answer. Placed whom? Answer: *Ella. Placed* is a transitive verb.)

> Birds *sing* sweet songs in the early morning. (Sing what? Answer: *songs. Sing* is a transitive verb.)

> Birds *sing* sweetly in the early morning. (Sing what? No answer. Sing whom? No answer. In this sentence, *sing* is an intransitive verb.)

Always Transitive   Whenever the past participle of a verb (for example, *done, broken, chosen*) has a being verb as a helper (*was done, has been broken, might be chosen*), that verb is always transitive because the subject is acted upon. This is automatic; therefore, in such a situation you need not ask "What?" or "Whom?" For example:

The statement *should have been sent* yesterday. (*Sent* is the past participle of the verb *send*. Although *should have been* is a being verb phrase, here it is used as a helper. Therefore, the verb phrase *should have been sent* is transitive.)

 CLASS PRACTICE 2

Name the verbs and verb phrases in the following sentences. Identify each as transitive or intransitive. (Remember to watch for any past participles of verbs that have being verbs as helpers.)

1. The rain has been falling gently all day.
2. That customer sent a cheque with his order.
3. All letters were typed before noon, despite interruptions.
4. Competition in modern times is becoming very keen.
5. Poor references eliminated the applicant before the interview.
6. The mail plane always circles the city before landing.
7. All the floors should have been polished after office hours.
8. The short circuit terrified the girls in the main office.

Troublesome Verbs

The verbs *lie* and *lay*, *sit* and *set*, and *rise* and *raise* are often called troublesome verbs because they are easily confused. In each pair, one verb is transitive and the other is intransitive.

You will have little trouble in choosing the right verb if you know the principal parts of each and if you can identify whether the verb is transitive or intransitive. The following Quick Trick will help you in deciding "which is which" almost immediately.

✳ QUICK TRICK   The "I" Verb Is Intransitive

First, review the principal parts of each pair. The following list includes the present participle, sometimes called the fourth principal part, of each verb.

Present	Past	Past Participle	Present Participle
lie	lay	lain	lying
lay	laid	laid	laying
sit	sat	sat	sitting
set	set	set	setting
rise	rose	risen	rising
raise	raised	raised	raising

In the first pair of verbs—*lie, lay*—which is the "I" verb; that is, the verb that has the "I" sound? The answer is *lie*. With what letter of the alphabet does the word *intransitive* start? I, isn't it? Then learn that the "I" verb in each pair is *intransitive*. Make this connection: *I* is the first letter of the word *intransitive; I*-sounding verbs are intransitive.

In the *sit, set* pair, which would you call the "*I*" verb? Your answer is *sit*. Then *sit* is the intransitive member of the pair. By now you can see that *rise* is the "*I*" verb in the *rise, raise* pair; and you know that *rise* is an intransitive verb.

Rather obviously, if you know which verb in the pair is intransitive, you know that the other verb must be transitive. Do not forget that a past-participle form with a being verb helper is always transitive.

Observe the reasoning by which the correct verb form is determined in the following illustrations.

Sue forgot that she (lay, laid) her notebook in the top drawer.

1. Which is needed here, a transitive or an intransitive verb? Answer—transitive.
2. Which verb is transitive? Answer—*laid*.
3. Which, then, is correct? Answer—*laid*.

Our dog (lies, lays) down at the first command. (Intransitive verb is needed; *lies* is intransitive; *lies* is the correct verb.)

Her margins were (sat, set) for a short letter. (There is no problem here. *Set* is correct because a past participle with a being verb helper is always transitive.)

☐ CLASS PRACTICE 3

Study the following sentences. For each sentence, determine whether you need a transitive or an intransitive verb. (Remember, a transitive verb has an object; an intransitive verb has no object.) Then name the correct verb.

1. During my lunch hour, I (lay, laid) on the couch in the clinic.
2. Please (sit, set) the vase on that table.
3. I have (lain, laid) the rough draft in its proper place.
4. The porter is (sitting, setting) the packages on the bench.
5. Our city (lies, lays) on the west bank of the river.
6. By sheer hard work, Mr. Rowe has (risen, raised) to his present position.
7. Those stencils have (lain, laid) in the box for a long time.
8. If you do not (rise, raise) an objection, Mr. Steers will think that you approve.

"If," "As If," "As Though," "Wish"

Sometimes it is correct to use *were* where ordinarily you would use *was*. This occurs after *if, as if, as though,* and *wish*. The rule is this: If the expressed condition is not true, is not possible, or is highly doubtful, use *were*.

The applicant acts *as if* she *were* a good worker. (But she is not a good worker.)

If I *were* you, I would look for another position. (But I am not you.)

If Kurt *were* here, he would find a way. (But Kurt is not here.)

Shirley talks *as though* Jane *were* subnormal. (But Jane is normal.)

On a day like this, Una *wishes* she *were* at the beach. (But Una is not at the beach.)

However, if the condition or situation expressed after *if* is true, or could be true, then use *was*.

If he *was* here, I did not see him. (He may have been here; the fact that I did not see him does not mean that he was not here.)

CLASS PRACTICE 4

By selecting the correct verb in each of the following sentences, you will discover how well you understand what verb is used after *if*, *as if*, *as though*, and *wish*.

1. I wish that Leo (was, were) going with us.
2. It seemed as though the type (was, were) out of line.
3. Betty acted as if she (was, were) disappointed.
4. If Kay (was, were) in my position, she would make the same decision.
5. If it (was, were) not for the accuracy of the accountants, our profits would not be so large.
6. I wish it (was, were) possible to type without errors.

Communication Problems

Application Exercises

A ■

On a separate sheet of paper, write the verb used in each of the following sentences and indicate whether it is transitive, intransitive, or being. Use "T" for transitive, "I" for intransitive, and "B" for being.

1   There were often a dozen or more callers in our small office.
2   Mr. Floss proudly nominated his secretary for the award.
3   Can't something be done about the stale air in this office?
4   Mr. Waters is confident of our support.
5   Our secretaries applied for the proofreading job.
6   Opposition makes Mr. Benton more persistent.
7   Eraser crumbs must be kept out of the type basket.
8   Miss Tripp has returned from her vacation.
9   We all like the new chief clerk very much.
10 You should have been here before 8:30.
11 Mr. Talcott was buying only from jobbers.
12 Did you return the original copy?

13 That applicant might be a competent person for the job.

14 We saw the vice-president at lunch.

15 Dirty type was the cause of her sloppy work.

B ■

Write "OK" on your paper for any correct sentences in the following. Rewrite the incorrect sentences, incorporating your corrections.

1 If Amy was at home, she did not answer the phone.

2 Very few housewives now set dough to raise.

3 It seemed as though the day was never ending.

4 Just let the stationery lay there.

5 Miss Brimmer always sits the pace for the other typists.

6 That machine looks as if it was ready to fall apart.

7 Has a time limit for this job been sat?

8 The duplicator has been lying idle all day.

9 I wish it was possible to show my deep gratitude.

10 Employers are rising their standards.

11 If I was in your place, I would check those figures.

12 The foundation for increased efficiency has been lain by the time-and-motion consultants.

13 I feel as though I was floating on air.

14 Our reception room is just like a private setting room.

15 My lunch lay in the locker all last week.

C ■

For each sentence, write the correct form of the verb enclosed in parentheses.

1 Reports make it appear as if Bob (be) going to resign.

2 Before noon the contractors had (lie, lay) the tile in the lounge.

3 Did you find the scissors (lie, lay) on the pile of clippings?

4 Undoubtedly Edward wishes he (be) getting a higher salary.

5 Bill said that he (lie, lay) in bed all day last Sunday.

6 The telescope should be (lie, lay) on the demonstration stand.

7 Can't something be (do) about expediting handling of the mail?

8 José looks as though he (be) infallible.

9 My new jacket does not (lie, lay) flat on my shoulders.

10 All fur coats have been (hang) in the storage vaults.

Word Study

A ■

These words are often confused, either as to spelling or as to meaning. Distinguish between them. Feet, feat; indite, indict.

B ■

The italicized words in the following sentences have been worn thin by overuse. Substitute a more precise word for each.

1   I'm *awfully* sorry I can't go to the dance.
2   I am *crazy* to study psychology.
3   The heat makes me feel *terrible.*
4   It was *nice* of you to invite me.
5   She was *real* pleased with the gift.

C ■

1   Which of the following words is *misspelled:* signify, testify, liquify, classify?
2   Which of the following words is spelled *correctly:* accomodate, privelege, embarrass, aquiese?

Communication in Action: *Following Company Rules*

Liz, an employee in the stenographic pool, believes that punctuation is a matter of personal taste. Her letters read as though she puts in commas and semicolons when the mood strikes her—not when they are needed. Her letters are frequently returned by the dictator for retyping. As her supervisor, you have spoken to her twice about punctuation; but apparently the results were negative. You will have to talk with her again. With another student, enact the drama as you think it should unfold. The door has opened and the employee has just entered.

UNIT □ 12

Nouns— Plurals

A *noun* is often defined in a dictionary as a word used to name a person, place or thing. A noun may be *common* or *proper,* depending on whether it names any one of a class of persons, places, or things (as *man, river, council*), or whether it names a specific person, place, or thing (as *Mary, Ed McAfee, Mackenzie River, UN Security Council*). Nouns also are *singular* or *plural,* depending on whether they name or represent one person, place, or thing, or more than one.

One of the obstacles presented by the English language is the spelling of the plurals of nouns, an understandable difficulty when you consider that there is no single way of forming plurals. Take this sentence: "Several cargoes of radios were shipped yesterday." The plural of *cargo* is *cargoes,* but the plural of *radio* is *radios*—although both singular forms end in *o.*

The purpose of this unit is to warn you that plural endings constitute a threat to a perfect spelling record. It is hoped that you will become aware of danger signals and that you will consult a dictionary when in doubt. Poor spellers are poor because they do not know enough to doubt. Therefore, you will be well rewarded by careful study of how the plurals of nouns are formed.

Most Common Plural Endings

The most common plural endings for nouns are *s* and *es*.

Most Nouns   Most nouns form the plural by adding *s* to the singular form.

table	tables	worker	workers
chair	chairs	pencil	pencils

However, singular nouns ending in *ch, sh, s, x,* and *z* form the plural by adding *es*. You should have little difficulty here, for the plural *es* form can be heard when the words are said aloud. As you read the following plurals, pronounce them silently. Do you "hear" the extra *es* sound?

church	churches	box	boxes
bush	bushes	chintz	chintzes
glass	glasses		

Proper Names   As with common nouns, the plurals of most proper names are formed by adding *s*.

(pod	pods)	Todd	the Todds
(paw	paws)	Shaw	the Shaws
(log	logs)	Fogg	the Foggs

However, the plurals of proper names ending in *ch, sh, s, x,* and *z* are formed by adding *es*. In the following examples, see how the *es* plural ending applies to proper names exactly as it does to common nouns.

(bench	benches)	Lynch	the Lynches
(brush	brushes)	Nash	the Nashes
(gas	gases)	Jones	the Joneses
(fox	foxes)	Tarbox	the Tarboxes
(topaz	topazes)	Schultz	the Schultzes

There is no reason for the confusion that so many persons experience when they are required to write the plural of a proper name. Just remember that the general rule that applies to plurals of common nouns also applies to plurals of names.

Titles with Names   When there is a title with a name, either the name or the title may be made plural. Never pluralize both the name and the title. With the title *Ms.* use the plural of the name. Here are some examples.

Mr. Ogden	*Messrs.* Ogden, the *Messrs.* Ogden, or the two Mr. *Ogdens* (*Messrs.* is the abbreviation for *messieurs*, the French word for *misters*.)
Mrs. Tate	The Mrs. *Tates* or *Mesdames* Tate (*Mesdames* is the French word that means more than one *Mrs.*)

Ms. Weinberg   Both the Ms. *Weinbergs*

Miss Park   *Misses* Park or the two Miss *Parks*

Doctor Nye   *Doctors* Nye or the Doctor *Nyes*

Nouns Ending in "y"   In English, the vowels are *a, e, i, o,* and *u.* The remaining letters of the alphabet are consonants. When a singular noun ends in *y* and the *y* is preceded by a vowel, the plural is formed by adding *s.* If, however, the final *y* is preceded by a consonant, the plural is formed by changing the *y* to *i* and adding *es.* This rule should be committed to memory, for the need for it arises often.

Final *y* preceded by a vowel:

attorney	attorneys	valley	valleys
monkey	monkeys	turkey	turkeys
toy	toys	key	keys

Final *y* preceded by a consonant:

facility	facilities	community	communities
supply	supplies	lily	lilies
remedy	remedies	laundry	laundries

NOTE: This rule does not apply to proper names. All names ending in *y* form the plural by adding *s,* as: *three Marys, the Averys.*

✔   PROOFREADING PRACTICE 1

If you understand how to use the most common plural endings, you will be able to find errors in the following sentences. Then substitute the correct plurals.

1. How many cup of coffee do you drink during the day?
2. Many industrys are moving to outlying communities.
3. What were the Messrs. Palmers doing in the office yesterday?
4. Many businesses failed during the depression years.
5. Did you see the puppys on sale at the kennel?
6. The Collinses have purchased a new car.
7. The potted bushs in the foyer are covered with dust.
8. There are no chimneys on any of the skyscrapers.
9. Are the Allenses going to open their new store soon?
10. Did you hear that the Smith's have resigned their positions?

Less Common Plural Endings

The following two rules concerning plurals may be less familiar to you. Study them carefully.

Vowel Changes   Some nouns form the plural by vowel changes.

woman	women	churchman	churchmen
mouse	mice	tooth	teeth
goose	geese	foot	feet

However, in a very few words ending in *man,* the plural is formed by adding *s.*

| German | Germans | | ottoman | ottomans |

A few plurals end in *en* or *ren.*

| ox | oxen | | child | children |

Figures, Letters, Words, Symbols   The plurals of letters, figures, symbols, signs, and words referred to as words are formed in the normal way by adding *s* or *es.*

Inga had only two *Bs* this term.

Everything seems to be at *sixes* and *sevens.* (OR: . . . at 6s and 7s.)

You have too many *ands* in that sentence.

Be sure to use & *s* when firms so print their names.

Sometimes, however, the addition of a simple *s* forms another word or may confuse the reader. Such cases are small letters, certain capital letters, and abbreviations with periods. *These are the only times an apostrophe is used in a plural.*

Remember to dot your *i's.* You may not get so many *A 's* next time.

Mr. Clay does not consider *f.o.b. 's* when figuring costs.

Remembering that an apostrophe *s* is used to form a plural only with certain letters and abbreviations will prevent your making errors that are frequently made by others. You would not, for instance, write a sentence like this: "The Smith's have invested heavily in company stock." You would know that the correct plural is *Smiths* because the apostrophe is used to indicate the plural only of letters and abbreviations when confusion would otherwise arise—and Smith is not one of these.

☐   CLASS PRACTICE 1

Before you are promoted to the Proofreading Practice level, you should practice the principles presented in the previous two topics. In each of the following sentences, select the correct word and explain why you chose that word.

1. How many (workmans, workmen) were employed to paint the house?
2. I cannot tell the difference between his (8s, 8's) and his (3s, 3's).
3. No (C.O.D.'s, C.O.D.s) will be accepted in the future.
4. What is the price of (gooses, geese) for Christmas?
5. Mr. Cort uses too many (*whiches, which's*) in his dictation.
6. My favorite period in history is the (1700s, 1700's).
7. When typing a dash, use two (-*s*, -*'s*).

✔   PROOFREADING PRACTICE 2

Now you should be ready to consolidate all that you have learned about noun plurals. In the following sentences, indicate which are correct and correct those that are wrong. Use this text or a dictionary if in doubt.

1. We think that the Harris are quite the nicest people in town.
2. The Professors Stewart must not be kept waiting.
3. Retired teachers often become active clubwoman.
4. Too many *ands* in a paragraph are boring to the reader.
5. All the Anns in the office have voted to form a club.
6. Our unsold turkies were stored in the freezer.
7. Attornies in large communities have many clients.
8. The Doctors Grants are in charge of the new clinic.
9. We received congratulations from the Benson's.

Tricky Plurals

Nouns ending in *o* and *f* or *fe* are tricky because they include so many exceptions to the rules for forming their plurals. Keep in mind that these nouns are not to be trusted. When in any doubt about their spelling, consult your dictionary.

Nouns Ending in "o"   When a singular noun ends in *o*, the plural is usually formed by adding *s*. (Interestingly enough, all nouns that relate to music add *s* for the plural: *pianos, solos, sopranos, trios.*) However, some singular nouns ending in an *o* that is preceded by a consonant form the plural by adding *es*. Others add *s*. Study the following examples, but keep in mind that the plural of a noun ending in *o* is not to be trusted.

Final *o* preceded by a vowel:

studio	studios	folio	folios
cameo	cameos	radio	radios

Final *o* preceded by a consonant:

echo	echoes	potato	potatoes
hero	heroes	embargo	embargoes

But note these exceptions:

piano	pianos	solo	solos
memento	mementos	zero	zeros
domino	dominos	lasso	lassos

Nouns Ending in "f" or "fe"   Some singular nouns ending in *f* or *fe* change the *f* or *fe* to *v* and add *es*. Others simply add *s*. Beware, then, of plurals of nouns ending in *f* or *fe*.

Final *f* or *fe* changing to *v* and adding *es:*

knife	knives	life	lives
half	halves	leaf	leaves

Final *f* or *fe*, adding *s:*

chief	chiefs	proof	proofs
safe	safes	sheriff	sheriffs

Nouns with Two Plurals

A few nouns have two plurals, but these plurals have different meanings.

brother	brothers (blood relatives), brethren (members of a society)
staff	staffs (personnel), staves (sticks, rungs)
index	indexes (to books), indices (symbols)

Plurals of Compound Nouns

A *compound noun*, as defined here, is a noun consisting of two or more words, whether hyphenated or unhyphenated. The plural of a compound noun is formed on the most important, or main, word. Study the following compound nouns and their plurals.

personnel manager	personnel *managers*
editor in chief	*editors* in chief
court-martial	*courts*-martial
man-of-war	*men*-of-war
son-in-law	*sons*-in-law
major general	major *generals*
notary public	*notaries* public

NOTE: The latest edition of a dictionary also lists *court-martials* and *notary publics* as acceptable, but the plurals listed above are preferred.

Exceptions to English rules are so frequent that you will not be surprised to learn that, in a very few compounds, the plural is added to both parts of the compound.

| gentleman usher | gentlemen ushers |
| Knight Templar | Knights Templars |

If a compound noun is written as one word, however, the plural is formed at the end, just like the plural of any other noun.

| stepchild | stepchildren | handful | handfuls |
| fisherman | fishermen | bookcase | bookcases |

☐ CLASS PRACTICE 2

Now is the time to find out how well you understand the last four rules for forming plurals. First, review the principles. Then select the correct word given in parentheses in each sentence.

1. How many (Governor Generals, Governors General) have held office since 1952?
2. Florida (tomatos, tomatoes) are now on the market.
3. During the storm all the (leafs, leaves) were blown from the   ees.
4. Petite Fashions is owned by my (sister-in-laws, sisters-in-law
5. Banana (cargos, cargoes) are profitable this winter.
6. Our (safes, saves) are burglarproof.
7. The report was given to the (brothers, brethren) of the chu   society.

✔ PROOFREADING PRACTICE 3

You have just studied and practiced several rules for forming plurals. Now tell which of the following sentences are correct and make corrections in the remaining sentences.

1. Use two tablespoonsful of butter in that recipe.
2. All the *zs* on those new machines are out of line.
3. The tornado was hard on the rooves of the houses.
4. His parents came to this country in the early 1900's.
5. Western heros always carry two guns.
6. The army record of your two courts-martial may affect your chances for civilian employment.
7. Have the Watrous's sent their cheque yet?
8. A conference of lieutenant-governors was held in Thunder Bay last month.
9. The customer was annoyed because the prooves of her pictures were not ready.
10. Why are there so many jokes about mothers-in-law?

Singular or Plural?

Knowing how to form the plurals of nouns will help you to spell correctly. To speak and write grammatically, however, you must also know the special rules that govern the singular and plural forms of certain nouns. You must know, for example:

1. That some nouns have exactly the same form in the singular and in the plural.

How many *reindeer* has Santa? (Not *reindeers*.)

Nouns of this type include the following:

Chinese	deer	odds	series
chassis	Japanese	politics	vermin
corps	moose	salmon	wheat

When used with numbers, the following nouns usually have the same form, whether they refer to one unit or more than one.

three *thousand*	four *score* (years)
two *yoke* (of oxen)	two *dozen* (apples)

2. That other nouns, even some that end in *s*, are always singular.

The *news* is good today. (Not *news are*.)

Here are some nouns that are always singular and with which you must use a singular verb:

statistics (course)	mumps (disease)	milk
economics (course)	measles (disease)	music
mathematics	molasses	news
whereabouts	aeronautics	civics

3. That still other nouns are always plural.

Where are my *scissors?* (Not *where is.*)

Nouns that are always plural and that therefore always take a plural verb include the following:

scales (for finding mass)	auspices	tidings
headquarters	trousers	grounds
credentials	proceeds	thanks
belongings	winnings	riches
hysterics	premises	goods
	scissors	tongs

Foreign Plurals

Some nouns of foreign origin have been given English plurals, some have only foreign plurals, and still others have two plurals—an English and a foreign. Where there is a choice of plurals, the foreign forms are used mainly in formal, scientific, and technical matter. If you are in doubt as to the plural of a foreign noun, consult your dictionary. The following words are used frequently in business.

Singular	Foreign Plural	English Plural
addendum	addenda	
alumna (fem.)	alumnae	
alumnus (masc.)	alumni	
analysis	analyses	
basis	bases	
crisis	crises	
criterion	criteria	criterions
datum	data	
formula	formulae	formulas
index	indices (see p. 98)	indexes
memorandum	memoranda	memorandums
parenthesis	parentheses	
terminus	termini	terminuses

NOTE: Some modern writers have a tendency to use *data* in most cases as a collective noun (one that names a group of persons or things—as *class, team, committee*) with a singular idea. These writers, therefore, use a singular verb with *data.*

☐ CLASS PRACTICE 3

Test your understanding of the principles just presented by selecting the correct word in parentheses in each of the following sentences.

1. Two (dozen, dozens) oranges were given to the first ten customers.
2. The data for the meeting (is, are) missing.

3. At school, economics (was, were) interesting to me.
4. In your opinion, (is, are) the bases of his argument weak?
5. The goods (was, were) completely sold by ten o'clock.
6. The Mesdames Craig (is, are) employed in our store.
7. (Credential, Credentials) presented by Julia (was, were) given to the personnel manager.
8. For some people, politics (makes, make) a fascinating career.

✓ **PROOFREADING PRACTICE 4**

In these sentences, correct any noun or verb forms that are incorrect. A dictionary may be used if needed.

1. Crises is forever arising in our office.
2. Riches has undoubtedly spoiled the contest winner.
3. Analysis of problems is beyond Mr. Perry.
4. We received notice that the premises is to be vacated May 1.
5. The western terminus of the Canadian Pacific Railway is Vancouver.
6. The whereabouts of the chief clerk are known.
7. Sanatoria for tubercular patients are plentiful in this province.
8. All the drum corpses in the province were asked to compete.

Communication Problems

Application Exercises

A ■

For each correct sentence in the following group, write "OK" on your paper. For each incorrect sentence, write your correction.

1 We simply must keep flys out of the lunchroom.
2 Who were the runner-ups in the office tennis league?
3 Please ask the Burchs to call at our credit department.
4 All the storeses on this street have been painted.
5 Chintzes are the drapery fashion this season.
6 Be sure to dot your "is."
7 The scissors is in my top left drawer.
8 The NATO force is made up of the armys of many nations.
9 Is the data ready for Mr. Dolan?
10 The president added the names of his three son-in-laws to the payroll.
11 Veal is the meat of calfs.
12 The briefing for bailiffs will be given Monday evening.
13 We must work evening's during the Christmas rush.
14 Is the mansion being converted into studioes?
15 The styli has been lost.

B ■

Beginning with this unit and continuing through Unit 22, each Application Exercise B will be a cumulative review. The following sentences are to help you review the grammar principles you have studied so far. If a sentence is correct, write "OK" on your paper. If it is incorrect, write the correction.

1 In an emergency, you can always depend on the Emerson's.
2 The new girl admitted that she had never did any filing before.
3 Erasers with brushs on them save much time.
4 Very few people know when to use *thats* and when to use *whiches*.
5 The company is reorganizing its sales territorys.
6 Be sure to carefully brush away all eraser crumbs.
7 Many old-fashioned remedys are still effective.
8 The Atom Smasher bowlers are quarters finalist in the tournament.
9 Candelabra is needed for the altar of the chapel.
10 Why do you capitalize your *a.m.*s?
11 It feels as though it was midwinter instead of July.
12 Has her belongings been taken out of her locker?
13 Winnipeg lies approximately 1500 km from Toronto.
14 The Mesdames Page is here to see you, Mr. North.
15 Files belonging to my two son-in-laws are out of date.

C ■

Read this paragraph and then rewrite it, correcting whatever errors there may be.

We recommend that you consult the Davis' about your management problems. They have specialized corps of assistants: attornies, notaries public, C.A.'s, statisticians—all the experts and facilitys needed to put your business on a paying basis. We ourselves have had occasion to use their services, and their analyses of all the points at issue has been most helpful.

Word Study

A ■

Words often confused: adverse, averse; preposition, proposition.

B ■

1 Does the suffix *ish* in *bookish, bluish, girlish,* and *devilish* impart to the words the meaning of: "resembling," "full of," "capable of," or "made of"?
2 Does the suffix *ee* in *employee, refugee, mortgagee,* and *nominee* impart to the words the meaning of: "a native of," "state or quality of," "the recipient of an action," or "having the characteristics of"?

C ■

How do you spell:

1 The verb meaning "to go before"?
2 The next number after one?

3 The adverb formed from *full?*

4 The capital city of New Brunswick?

Communication in Action: Word Problems

Answer the following questions from an employment test:

1. The auditor noted a *discrepancy* in the figures. Does this mean: (*a*) the figures are incorrect, (*b*) the company made too large a profit, (*c*) the figures are illegible, (*d*) the books are in balance?

2. Is *insolvent* nearest in meaning to: (*a*) rich, (*b*) indebted, (*c*) complacent, (*d*) secure, (*e*) impudent?

UNIT □ 13

Nouns and Pronouns— Possessive Forms

A noun or a pronoun (a word used to avoid repeating a noun) is in the possessive case when it shows ownership. Do you know that the apostrophe is the mark used to signal ownership? It is important to study the possessive case so that you know where to place the apostrophe—if one is needed.

Six apostrophe rules are presented in this unit. Knowing how to apply these rules will enable you to handle apostrophes with confidence.

Principal Use of the Apostrophe with Nouns

The apostrophe is used most often to show possession as applied to a noun; for example, *clerk's* salary, *bookkeeper's* office, *child's* toy, a *day's* notice. The rule that governs this most frequent use of the apostrophe consists of two parts:

1. If the word denoting ownership *does not* end in *s*, add apostrophe and *s*.

The *man's* hat was lost in the fire.

The *lady's* child is not well behaved.

2. If the word denoting ownership *does* end in *s*, add *only* the apostrophe.

Do you belong to any of the *girls'* clubs in the city?

Our *ladies'* lounge is on the fifth floor.

NOTE: Some authorities present the following exception: An apostrophe and *s* are added to a noun ending in *s* if an added syllable is heard when pronouncing the possessive; for example: *actress's behavior.*

The rule is very simple, but sometimes it is difficult to tell whether the word denoting ownership ends in *s*—or whether the word is singular or plural. It may be difficult to decide, for instance, whether the word in question is *lady* or *ladies.* The following Quick Trick will enable you to see immediately whether or not the ownership word ends in *s.*

✳ QUICK TRICK   Find the Ownership Word

The word following the word showing ownership represents something that belongs to that ownership word. For instance: "The man's hat was lost in the fire." The meaning here is *the hat belonging to the man. Man,* then, is the ownership word; and, since it does not end in *s,* an apostrophe and *s* are added.

The Quick Trick is to say the word following the word showing ownership and then say "belonging to" or "of the" ownership word. Thus you isolate the word about which you have doubts.

To fix this Quick Trick in your mind, give close attention to the following illustrations.

The (secretarys, secretaries) typewriter is seldom oiled. (Typewriter "of the" or "belonging to" the *secretary.* It is highly unlikely that a typewriter would belong to more than one secretary. *Secretary* does not end in *s;* therefore, the apostrophe and *s* are added—*secretary's typewriter.*)

The (secretarys, secretaries) typewriters have been exchanged for electric machines. (Typewriters "belonging to" or "of" *secretaries.* Here, the meaning evidently is more than one secretary, as it is doubtful that a secretary would have several typewriters. *Secretaries* does end in *s,* so only the apostrophe is added—*secretaries' typewriters.*)

NOTE: A trend is to omit the apostrophe in names of organizations and institutions except when the name ends in *men;* as: *Lions Club, Teachers Federation,* but *Businessmen's Club.*

☐ CLASS PRACTICE 1

In the following sentences, select the correct word given in parentheses in each sentence. If necessary, review the rules for the use of the apostrophe and study the Quick Trick.

1. (Children's, Childrens') toys are now displayed in the stores.
2. Mr. (North's, Norths') son is living in the (boy's, boys') dormitory.
3. I will give you my answer in three (week's, weeks') time.
4. The (boy's, boys') bicycles are in (everybody's, everybodys') way.

5. A (hero's, heroes') role is usually played by a famous star.
6. Our sale also includes (women's, womens') dresses and (girl's, girls') coats.
7. There are many (doctor's, doctors') offices in this building.
8. The (Olsen's, Olsens') new skyscraper is solidly built.
9. You must use the (customer's, customers') entrance.
10. Bill (Perry's, Perrys') resignation was accepted with regret.

✔ PROOFREADING PRACTICE 1

For practice on an advanced level, study the following sentences and see whether you can identify and correct any apostrophe errors.

1. The fishermens' boats were gaily decorated for the occasion.
2. Where is the patron's cafeteria?
3. Daniel Fuller's last pay cheque has not been cashed.
4. Mr. Greene can now loaf to his hearts' content.
5. Did the police recover the thief's tools?
6. The alto's voices were not strong enough to balance the chorus.
7. Have you seen the Burgess' swimming pool?
8. We are having difficulty finding stars to fill the heroine's roles for our next three pictures.

Additional Uses of the Apostrophe with Nouns

In addition to the basic rule for the use of the apostrophe with nouns, special rules cover noun possessives in certain situations. These rules follow.

Possessive of a Compound Noun   The possessive of a compound noun is formed on the last word of the compound. For placement of the apostrophe with this last word, follow the rule you have just learned.

His father-in-law's business is flourishing. (*Law,* the last word, does not end in *s.*)

Checking the timecards is someone else's job. (Job "of" *someone else.* The last word of the compound does not end in *s;* therefore, an apostrophe and *s* are added to *else.*)

Mr. Silva is president of the newly formed personnel managers' association. (Association "of" *personnel managers.* The last word of the compound, *managers,* does end in *s,* so only an apostrophe is added.)

Joint or Separate Ownership   *Joint ownership* is indicated by placing the apostrophe with the last word in the combination.

Gene and Sam's desk is usually cluttered with papers. (Gene and Sam share the same desk, as indicated by placing the apostrophe with the last word only.)

Have you received Ella and Rosa's supply list? (Ella and Rosa together are making out one supply list.)

Separate ownership is indicated by placing the apostrophe with each member of the combination. You might find it helpful to remember that separate apostrophes are used to show separate ownership. See how the preceding sentences have been changed to show separate ownership.

> Gene's and Sam's desks are usually cluttered with papers. (Gene's desk and Sam's desk. Each has a desk of his own. Note the plural *desks*.)

> Have you received Ella's and Rosa's supply lists? (Ella has a list and Rosa has a list. Note the plural *lists*.)

Appositive Showing Possession   Sometimes a noun that ordinarily would be in the possessive is followed by an explanatory word or words, called an *appositive*. In such cases, the apostrophe (or the apostrophe and *s*) is added only to the explanatory element.

> That is Miss Friden, the file clerk's, responsibility. (Note that the sign of the possessive is added only to the appositive.)

☐   CLASS PRACTICE 2

To fix in your mind the possessive-case principles that apply to compound nouns and joint and separate ownership, select the correct word in each of the following sentences.

1. You should not use (someone's else, someone else's) supplies.
2. There are no applications for the position of (editor's in chief, editor in chief's) secretary.
3. (Peter's and Raoul's, Peter and Raoul's) locker is jammed.
4. (Betty's and Eva's, Betty and Eva's) hair has been stylishly arranged.
5. Tom managed to reach the (runner's-up, runner-up's) position last week.

✔   PROOFREADING PRACTICE 2

If the preceding practice achieved its purpose, you should be ready to proof-read for errors in possessive-case forms of compound nouns and nouns showing joint or separate ownership. Prove your readiness by making needed corrections in the following sentences.

1. Lucy is joining her brother's-in-law counseling service.
2. Hill & Forbes products are sold in all leading stores.
3. The secretary-treasurer's position will be filled at the next meeting of the Board.
4. Not many voters recognize our Twin Cities need for a more adequate water supply.
5. Burnham & Case's hardware store now stocks paints.
6. In the competition, our drum corps performance was rated best.
7. There is no telephone in Bob's and Henry's office.

Possessives of Personal Pronouns

As already mentioned, a *pronoun* is a word that is used in place of a noun and that represents a person, place, or thing without naming it. (Examples: I, their, yours, that, anyone, nobody, who, those, some, himself.) There are, of course, many different kinds of pronouns.

What concerns us now are the *personal pronouns* (I, we, you, he, she, it, they) and, specifically, the possessive-case forms of personal pronouns (my, mine, our, ours, your, yours, his, hers, its, their, theirs) plus the pronoun *who* (*whose*).

Whereas the apostrophe is the signal of ownership when used with a noun, the possessive forms of personal pronouns *never take an apostrophe.* Look at the following illustrations:

> Every incoming letter has *its* own place. (*Its,* meaning "belonging to" *it.*)
>
> If it is misplaced, the fault is *yours.* (Note there is no apostrophe.)
>
> Alice, however, insists that the mistake is *hers.* (No apostrophe.)

Confusions to Avoid   The possessive-case forms of certain personal pronouns sound exactly like other words that have different meanings and different spellings. Such words are called *homonyms.* The possessive pronoun *its,* for example, sounds exactly like *it's,* meaning *it is.* Following is a list of pronoun possessives and their "sound alikes" with which they are too often confused. This confusion need not arise if you know when to use possessive pronouns and also how these pronoun forms are spelled. The first word of each pair is the possessive form.

Its, It's   The possessive-case form of the personal pronoun *it* is *its,* meaning "belonging to it." *It's* means simply "it is."

> *It's* a fact that every job has *its* discouragements. (*It is* a fact that every job has discouragements *belonging to it.*)

Their, They're, There   *Their* means "belonging to them." *They're* is the contraction of "they are." *There* may mean "in that place" or it may be used as an introductory word. It also has other meanings. If in doubt whether to use *there,* ask yourself if the meaning called for is *their* or *they're.* If neither fits, then use *there.*

> We suddenly found ourselves on *their* property. (Property belonging to *them*)
>
> *They're* the ones who posted the sign. (*They are* the ones)
>
> The book you want is over *there.* (Meaning *in that place*)
>
> *There* are several valuable coins in this collection. (Introductory word)
>
> You will find that *there* will be no difficulty about payment. (The meaning is neither *belonging to them* nor *they are,* so *there* must be correct.)

Your, You're   *Your* and *you're* sound alike, but the meanings are different. *Your* means "belonging to you"; *you're* means "you are." For instance:

When *you're* working in an office, *your* attitudes change. ("When *you are* working in an office, the attitudes *belonging to you* change.")

Our, Are   Clearly pronounced, *our* and *are* do not have the same sound; but because of careless pronunciation, they are often confused. *Our* means "belonging to us." *Are,*as stated before, is a being verb. To illustrate:

When *are* you going to present *our* petition? ("When *are* you going to present the petition *belonging to us?*")

Whose, Who's   *Whose* is a possessive pronoun meaning "belonging to whom." The possessive must not be confused with *who's,* meaning "who is." For example:

Who's the girl *whose* application was misfiled? ("*Who is* the girl . . . application *belonging to whom?*")

✔   PROOFREADING PRACTICE 3

See how many errors you can find in the following sentences. All errors will be in the use of the possessives of personal pronouns.

1. There incoming mail is delivered at nine o'clock.
2. Who's eraser is that?
3. Judith never admits that a mistake is her's.
4. You know that it's your duty to be punctual.
5. What are those folder tabs doing lying their on the floor?
6. We are looking forward to are holiday.
7. When your typing a stencil, be careful about your stroking.
8. Do you know who's making up the assignments?

Possessive Before a Gerund

A *gerund* is a verb form ending in *ing,* used as a noun; as: "*Swimming* is good exercise." "Ivo enjoys *walking* to work." If a noun or a pronoun precedes a gerund, the noun or pronoun must be in the possessive case. For instance:

Can you imagine *Ray's* being late? (*Ray's,* the possessive of *Ray,* is used before the gerund *being.*)

You can depend on *his* doing a thorough job. (*Doing* is a gerund; therefore, the pronoun *his* preceding it is a possessive.)

☐   CLASS PRACTICE 3

Select the correct word in each of the following sentences.

1. I was amazed at (Leon, Leon's) doing so well on the test.
2. Mr. Baker was much surprised at (Rose, Rose's) performing so poorly.
3. I disapprove of (you, your) being transferred to the sales department.

4. What do you think of (Dick, Dick's) winning the suggestion award?
5. (Him, His) coming was not expected.

Communication Problems

Application Exercises

A ■

These sentences were constructed to help you differentiate between plurals and possessives. If the Quick Trick of saying *belonging to* or *of the*, does not make sense, the word in question is a plural, not a possessive. On a separate sheet of paper, write the correct word for each choice given you.

1 Why have you never joined a (publisher's, publishers') association?
2 Mr. Wheeler's two (daughter-in-law's, daughters-in-law, daughter-in-laws) graduated from college.
3 (Children's, Childrens') (bicycles, bicycles') will be reduced next week.
4 Mr. Main's (letters, letters') are always well written.
5 The (secretary's, secretaries', secretarys, secretaries) desks are covered with all their paper and supplies.
6 The latest trade (journals, journal's) are in the bookcase by the (president's, presidents', presidents) filing cabinet.
7 You will find (lady's, ladies', ladies) coats on the third floor.
8 (Bookkeepers, Bookkeepers') like them are hard to find.
9 The (girl's, girls', girls) bowling teams defeated the men's teams.
10 When resigning your position, you should give two (week's, weeks', weeks) notice.
11 Right near the main entrance is a fashionable (lady's, ladies', ladies) hat bar.
12 Your carbon copies are full of (streaks, streak's, streaks').
13 The (Browns, Brown's, Browns') have bought a new car and have sold their old car to the Burnses.
14 Are all employees required to use a special (employees, employee's, employees') cafeteria?
15 (Womens, Women's, Womens') office duties usually require much detail work.

B ■

Proofread the following sentences carefully. If a sentence is correct, write "OK" on your paper. If it is incorrect, write the correction.

1 The boss's wives accompanied their husbands to the convention.
2 Why didn't you put yours' in Mr. Pike's personal file?
3 The Fritzes were pleased to hear of my promotion.
4 The Poe's attended the banquet given by the Rawlings Company.
5 Was the shift key broke before you arrived?
6 We do not stock misse's coats.

7 Mr. Foley is interested in my attending evening school.

8 John and Stanley's shorthand notes are illegible.

9 Did you see my shorthand pen laying on the table?

10 It's difficult for you to fully control your facial expressions.

11 The secretarys desks' should be tidied before the girls leave.

12 I wish I was able to type as fast as Monique.

13 Were the Regina chief's of police reports typed in this office?

14 Mr. Jordan surely was angry when he laid down the law to us.

15 If I was you, I would ask to be transferred.

C ■

Write the correct plural or possessive form of each word or phrase enclosed in parentheses.

1 Send the Chamber of Commerce a cheque for two (month) dues.

2 Please do not answer (anybody else) telephone.

3 (Lily of the valley) are my favorite flowers.

4 Information about fallout has found (it) way into many homes.

5 We now have a service contract for maintenance of (secretary) typewriters.

6 Is Doctor Rowe the scientist (who) research is being publicized so widely?

7 (Woman) office duties usually require much detail work.

8 My son said that the ("E") on his report card stand for "Excellent."

9 The Better Business Bureau reports that the (Jones) credit rating is poor.

10 Did the staff bulletin have any information about the annual (sheriff) conference?

Word Study

A ■

Words often confused: finely, finally, finale; expensive, expansive.

B ■

1 The following words are spelled as they are often pronounced. Which spelling indicates *correct* pronunciation?

vetran	tremenjus
incidently	purkolater

2 The following words are spelled as they are often pronounced. Which spelling indicates *incorrect* pronunciation?

temprament	rekogniz
lukshoori	partner

C ■

Some of the following words are preferably spelled with one *l*; some with two. Which should be changed?

1 cancellation		3 traveler		5 marvellous
2 cancelled		4 skilful		6 installment

Communication in Action: *The Error Is Yours*

You have proofread twice some material you typed on a stencil before it was dupli-cated. But there it is—a misspelled word on each of 1000 copies. You discover the error only after most of the copies are folded, inserted in envelopes to customers, and ready to mail. No one knows about the error except you. What do you need to know before deciding a plan of action? Should you tell your employer? If so, when?

UNIT □ 14

Pronouns— Nominative and Objective Forms

Would you say "Please return that book to *she* immediately"? "*Him* and *me* were planning to do it"? "That message is meant for *you* and *I*"? If you would, it would seem you are not sure of proper pronoun usage, for you are making a major error in grammar: that of using the incorrect case forms of pronouns.

Forms of Pronouns

Case refers to the form of a noun or a pronoun that indicates the relation of that word to other words in the sentence. In English grammar there are three cases: nomina-tive, objective, and possessive.

He threw the ball. (*He:* nominative case)

Ted threw the ball to *him.* (*Him:* objective case)

He said he wanted *his* ball. (*His:* possessive case)

In the preceding unit you saw that both a noun and a pronoun change form when they are in the possessive case. However, only a pronoun changes its form from the nominative to the objective case. The selection of the correct pronoun case form—nominative or objective—is the subject of this unit.

To simplify discussion and reduce learning time, only the principles governing pronoun usage for the nominative case will be emphasized here. Why only the nominative case? Because, if you know the rules for the use of the nominative case, you will also know when to use the objective case. In other words, if the nominative-case form of a pronoun cannot be used correctly in a certain situation, then the

Who shall I make it toom?

objective-case form of the pronoun must be correct. (Rules for the use of the objective case are given on page 116.) The rules that govern correct pronoun usage have been considerably simplified here; but remember that mastery of this usage depends on conscientious study and practice.

Now study the following list of pronouns. Be sure you know the case of each.

NOMINATIVE	I	you	he	she	it	we	you	they	who
OBJECTIVE	me	you	him	her	it	us	you	them	whom

You will note that the pronouns *you* and *it* do not change form from one case to the other. You, therefore, need to know only the nominative- and objective-case forms of the pronouns *I, he, she, we, they,* and *who*.

Nominative Case

Among the many rules for the use of the nominative case, only three are really needed for correct use of the nominative-case forms of pronouns.

Subject of a Verb   Any pronoun that is the subject of a verb is in the nominative case.

> *I* like apples. (Why do we say *I* and not *me?* Because the subject of the verb *like* must be in the nominative case. *I* is in the nominative case; therefore it is correct.)

> John and *he* are fine workers. (Here, *he* is part of the subject *John and he.* As a result, both *John* and *he* are in the nominative case.)

Predicate Nominative   A *predicate nominative* is a noun or pronoun that completes the meaning of a being verb (*am, is, are, was, were,* helper *be* and helper(s) *been*). Any pronoun that is the predicate nominative is in the nominative case.

Yes, this is *she*. (*She* completes the meaning of the being verb *is.* Therefore, *she* is a predicate nominative in the nominative case.)

It must have been *they* after all. (*They* is a predicate nominative because it completes the meaning of the being verb *must have been.* Therefore, the nominative-case form *they* is called for.)

Complement of Infinitive "To Be" When "To Be" Has No Subject   Any pronoun that follows and completes the meaning (is a complement) of the infinitive *to be* when *to be* has no subject of its own is in the nominative case. For correct application of this rule, there are two things you must remember:

1. This rule applies only to the infinitive *to be*. Do not try to use the rule in any other situation.

2. The infinitive *to be* will have a subject *only when a noun or a pronoun immediately precedes it.*

First, look at two sentences in which the infinitive *to be* does not have a subject.

Who would ever wish to be *I?* (Is there a subject—a noun or pronoun—immediately preceding *to be?* No. Then this *to be* has no subject; and the complement *I* is correct, because the pronoun must be in the nominative case.)

The visitors would seem to be *they*. (Since *to be* has no subject immediately preceding it, the complement of the infinitive *to be* must be *they*, not *them*, because *they* is in the nominative case.)

Now study the following sentences, in which the infinitive *to be* does have a subject.

Sam thought *me* to be pretty. (*Me* is the subject of *to be*.)

The receptionist mistakenly thought the *visitors* to be us.

 QUICK TRICK   NO Subject—NOminative Case

For a memory hook on which to hang the *to be* rule, make this connection:

NO subject—*NO*minative case

NO is the word you must remember, and *NO* starts the word *NOminative*. Think this over. You will be amazed to see that the Quick Trick promotes immediate application of the *to be* rule.

☐ CLASS PRACTICE 1

Select the correct pronoun in each of the following sentences. If you select the nominative-case form, give the reason for your choice. You need not give a reason for selecting the objective-case form; your only reason need be that the pronoun could not be in the nominative case. When making your choice, follow this reasoning process: Is the pronoun the subject of a verb? a predicate nominative? Is it the complement of a no-subject *to be?* If the pronoun is one of these three, the nominative case is correct. If the answer to the three questions is "No," the objective-case form must be correct.

1. Dorothy is often taken to be (I, me).
2. (She, Her) is going to the store.
3. If you were (I, me), would you look for another position?
4. Mr. Sims thought the blonde to be (she, her).
5. Why did you think it was (we, us)?
6. Who would ever wish to be (I, me)?
7. The large, awkward boys in the machine shop were (they, them).
8. Why did you say that it was (I, me) who was ill?
9. Who's there? It is (he, him).
10. The producer would not allow me to be (he, him) in the drama.

 PROOFREADING PRACTICE 1

As further evidence that you understand the three principles governing the use of the nominative case, find and correct any errors in the following sentences.

1. Whom is going to need the typewriter first?
2. It would be me who would make a mistake like that!
3. I should certainly not like to be her!
4. The most enthusiastic supporters of the plan were us.
5. The fastest checker seems to be her.
6. If it had not been him who told the story, I would have believed it.
7. It seems to be they over there in the corner.
8. Was it them who left the message?

Pronouns in Compounds

Many pronoun errors are made when the pronoun is part of a *compound*—two or more nouns or pronouns, or a noun and a pronoun joined by a conjunction. For example: *Mary and she, Mr. Jopson and me, Francis or him.* You will select the correct pronoun immediately if you learn the following Quick Trick.

✳ QUICK TRICK   Retain the Pronoun Only

Whenever a compound contains a pronoun, mentally omit everything in the compound except the pronoun. Then read the sentence again and see how the correct form pops right out.

Sam and (I, me) will carry out the invoice extensions. (Omit *Sam and,* and you must say: "*I* will carry out . . .")

Mr. Sears told Sam and (I, me) to carry out the extensions. (Once more, omit *Sam and;* and you must say: "Mr. Sears told *me* to carry out . . .")

"We Men" or "Us Men"?

The wrong pronoun is often used in such expressions (called "restrictive appositives") as *we men, us girls, we teachers.* Unfortunately, many writers and speakers seem to guess at the correct case form of a pronoun. You will have no difficulty with pronouns in restrictive appositives if you learn this Quick Trick:

✳ QUICK TRICK   Omit the Noun

When you are about to use a pronoun in a restrictive appositive, mentally omit the noun accompanying it. Read or say the sentence using *only the pronoun,* and the correct form will almost say itself. For example:

(We, Us) men must stick together. (Say the sentence, mentally omitting *men;* and you have: "We must stick together," as "Us must stick together" sounds ridiculous. The nominative form *we* is correct because *we men* is the subject of the verb *must stick.*)

Would you like (we, us) boys to shovel a path for you? (If you omit *boys,* you would say: "Would you like us to shovel a path for you?")

☐ CLASS PRACTICE 2

The first five sentences afford practice in using the Quick Trick for compounds; the remaining three, practice in using the Quick Trick for restrictive appositives. How rapidly can you select the correct pronoun?

1. Give the request to Mr. Avery or (she, her).
2. Thelma and (I, me) agree on most political issues.
3. Was that George or (he, him) in the private office?
4. The partners and (they, them) are discussing bankruptcy proceedings.
5. Mr. Todd asked his secretary to call Sarah and (I, me).
6. You students sometimes give (we, us) teachers a little trouble.
7. (We, Us) girls will be glad to work overtime tonight.
8. Every one of (we, us) clerks will do more work than the others.

✔ PROOFREADING PRACTICE 2

Now that you have practiced using the Quick Tricks, are you ready to proofread for pronoun errors in compounds and in restrictive appositives? If so, you will be able to correct whatever errors there are in the following sentences.

1. I told both Cora and she to be here on time.
2. The principal asked we teachers to read the daily bulletin.
3. I think that us girls have a chance to succeed.
4. Mr. Fortin appointed Owen and I to be tellers.
5. Could you persuade Eileen and she to check their work?
6. The manager and us two girls missed the last bus.
7. I encouraged Helen and her to take the lessons, too.
8. I wish you would let us bookkeepers find our own errors.

Objective Case

The objective-case forms of personal pronouns and of *who* (*whom*) are used when the pronoun is any of the following:

1. The object of a verb or of a preposition, or the subject or object of an infinitive

Susan introduced *him* at the meeting. (Object of a verb)

Whom did she introduce at the meeting? (Object of a verb)

Tony was introduced by *her*. (Object of a preposition)

They waited an hour for Mary and *me*. (Object of a preposition)

We wished *them* to get the prize. (Subject of *to get*)

Would you like to help *me?* (Object of *to help*)

Whom would you like to help? (Object of *to help*)

Ray taught *me* to like *them*. (*Me* is the subject of *to like; them* is the object of *to like*.)

2. The complement of the infinitive *to be* when *to be* does have a subject of its own

We wanted the winners to be *us*.

Communication Problems

Application Exercises

A ■

Indicate your reasons for selecting nominative-case forms, as: *subject of verb, predicate nominative*, or *to be, no subject* (meaning that the infinitive *to be* has no subject of its own).

1 The idea struck Agnes and (I, me) at the same time.
2 In her dress of gold, Alice was taken to be (she, her).
3 My brother and (I, me) were served with a summons.
4 I mistook the telephone operator to be (she, her).

5   It must have been (we, us) who have been neglecting this duty.
6   Mr. Banks selected both Freida and (she, her) as assistants.
7   Have you forgotten your childhood playmate? I am (he, him).
8   It surely ought to be (they, them) who qualify for the position.
9   I would not care to be (he, him), with all his money.
10 All secrets must be kept between you and (I, me).
11 It really was (they, them) who found the error.
12 When I was a child, I longed to be (he, him).
13 Are you absolutely sure that the visitor was (he, him)?
14 The men on the second shift would like to be (we, us), just for today.
15 Young bookkeepers like (he, him) need advice.

B ■

Correct any errors in the following sentences. Write "OK" for any sentences that
are correct.

1   Harriet feels that most mother-in-laws are difficult to know.
2   That letter was written to Mr. Baird and he.
3   Ross failed to fully understand my instructions.
4   Do you know who's record is up for review?
5   Where are Mr. Yang and him going to get the machinery we need?
6   The coffee had went long before noon.
7   I wish Ari had lain the report where I could find it.
8   I cannot imagine Mark's failing to check in this morning.
9   Us beginners in business have much to learn.
10 Did you say that you and him were not informed of the change?
11 Executive's courses in human relations will be offered soon.
12 What makes your secretary long to be her?
13 Roger rushed in as though he were afraid of being late.
14 Please ask Natalie and she to prepare the agenda for today's conference.
15 Barr and Brecks invention will speed the firing of ballistic missiles.

C ■

The pronoun that belongs in the place marked by the question mark is in either the
nominative or the objective case. If nominative, write "N" on your paper; if objective, write "O." Also, write the correct pronoun.

1   Gary mistook the telephone operator to be (?).
2   The agency sent (?) bachelors several invitations to community parties.
3   If I were (?), I should give the report to Mr. Voss.
4   Just between you and (?), what do you think of his "modus operandi"?
5   The coach and (?) boys will leave on the afternoon plane.
6   If anyone is disappointed, it will be (?)!
7   The most industrious workers in the office are (?) payroll clerks.
8   I like best to work with either Bob or (?).
9   It might have been (?) who lost the mailing list.
10 Did anyone inquire about the Edisons and (?) other special guests?

Word Study

A ■

Words often confused: sale, sail; intelligent, intelligible.

B ■

Each of the following sentences contains an expression that, though permissible in informal spoken English, should be replaced by a more acceptable expression in written or formal matter. What are the expressions? Suggest substitutions.

1 As soon as I am through with this filing, I will help you.
2 He got a kick out of the article.
3 His cheque was no good.
4 My brother is now located in Charlottetown.

C ■

What are the plurals of the following?

1	teaspoonful	3	company	5	memorandum
2	gas	4	mouse	6	radio

Communication in Action: *Short Sentences*

Simplify the following involved sentence taken from a rough draft of a report.

There are more misplaced papers in small offices, in proportion to the volume handled, than in large organizations and at first this is difficult to understand when you consider that the chances for error are greater in a large organization where more papers are handled and more people are involved, however, the realization of this error possibility causes large organizations to give adequate attention to the important aspects of filing routine, with a resulting increase in speed and accuracy of filing.

UNIT □ 15

Pronouns—More about Forms

In Unit 14 you learned to select the correct case form of a pronoun. You now have the background that will enable you, in almost all situations, to use the correct nominative- or objective-case forms of personal pronouns. To put the finishing touches on your training in choosing correct case forms for pronouns, however, you must be able to use *who* and *whom* correctly. In this unit you will learn three additional rules for case usage with personal pronouns and two specific principles for selecting *who, whoever, whom,* or *whomever.*

Pronouns after "Than" or "As"

When a noun or a pronoun appears in an incomplete clause and follows *than* or *as* in a statement of comparison, the correct form may be determined by supplying mentally the words that are not expressed. The following examples will show you how to supply the words that complete the meaning of the sentence.

> Charles says that he has more experience than (I, me). (If you complete the meaning of this sentence, you will have: "Charles says that he has more experience than *I have." I* is correct because it is the subject of an understood verb.)

> Unnecessary noise disturbs Mr. Reid as much as (I, me). (Supplying the missing words would give you: "Unnecessary noise disturbs Mr. Reid as much as *unnecessary noise* (or *it*) *disturbs me." Me* is the correct form. Why? Because not one of the rules for nominative case can be applied.)

Sometimes the selection of the correct pronoun form depends on voice emphasis. Italics are used for written emphasis, and italics are used in two of the following practice sentences where voice emphasis determines the selection of the correct pronoun.

☐   CLASS PRACTICE 1

Choose the correct pronoun in parentheses for each of the following sentences. Supply mentally any missing words in order to complete the meaning correctly.

1. You are much quicker at adding figures than (we, us).
2. I do hope they give *you* better treatment than (we, us).
3. I do hope *they* give you better treatment than (we, us).
4. Martha can do that job just as well as (she, her).
5. Do you think you have been as faithful as (he, him)?
6. Our office force works much harder than (they, them).

"Self"-Ending Pronouns

Myself, yourself, himself, herself, itself, ourselves, yourselves, and *themselves* are the *self*-ending pronouns. They have two uses: (1) to emphasize, and (2) to reflect a noun or pronoun already expressed.

To Emphasize   A *self*-ending pronoun is used to add force to a statement.

> Mary herself told me the news. (Do you see how *herself* adds power to an otherwise simple statement?)

> I did all the work *myself.*

When using a *self*-ending pronoun to emphasize, take care to place that pronoun where it will perform its emphasizing function. Careless placement of the pronoun may lead to distortion of a message. For instance:

Did you know that the home economics teacher cannot sew herself? (The message written correctly is not at all funny: "Did you know that the home economics teacher herself cannot sew?")

To Reflect   A *self* pronoun is also used to reflect some noun or pronoun that has already been named.

Jack mentally gave himself a pat on the back. (*Himself* refers back to the subject *Jack.*)

Public officials should not vote themselves increases in salary. (*Themselves* refers to *public officials.*)

Some persons use a *self* pronoun instead of a pronoun in the nominative or objective case because they are not sure which case form to use. Instead of saying "Be sure to write to Jan and *me*," the unsure person might say "Be sure to write to Jan and myself." However, this usage is not standard English.

☐   CLASS PRACTICE 2

Selecting the proper pronoun in the following sentences will help you to learn the correct uses of the *self* pronouns.

1. Both Sue and (myself, I, me) have been working steadily all day.
2. Would you like Ann and (myself, I, me) to mail those letters?
3. The man who can laugh at (himself, he, him) possesses the highest form of humor.
4. Mrs. Khan and (myself, I, me) are happy to accept your invitation.
5. Many executives literally work (themselves, they, them) to death.

✔   PROOFREADING PRACTICE 1

If the preceding practice fixed in your mind the correct uses of the *self* pronouns, you will be able to correct errors in the following sentences.

1. Lothar has decided to write himself.
2. Helen and I will treat ourselves to a good lunch.
3. Mr. Curtis asked Mark and myself to share the switchboard duty.
4. Both Paul and myself like to operate a calculator.
5. The president himself issued that order.

Pronouns as Appositives

An appositive, you will remember, is a word or group of words used to explain, or to give additional information about, a preceding word or phrase. For example:

Mr. Barnes, *the author and lecturer,* is one of my friends. (*The author and lecturer* gives additional information about *Mr. Barnes;* therefore, *the author and lecturer* is an appositive.)

Maria Carlos, *our secretary,* can tell you what you want to know. (The appositive is *our secretary,* which gives additional information about *Maria Carlos.*)

Note that there is a comma before and after the appositive. An important punctuation rule is this: An appositive is set off by commas.

When the appositive is a noun, no problem exists; but an error can be made in using pronouns as appositives. The rule is this: An appositive is in the same case as the word with which it is in apposition. Concentrate on the following illustrations and explanations.

These junior executives, Alfred and he, are pleasant co-workers. (The appositive, *Alfred and he,* is in apposition with the subject, *junior executives.* Therefore, the nominative case pronoun *he* is needed here.)

Mr. Bell frequently compliments our junior executives, Alfred and him. (Here the appositive is once more in apposition with *junior executives.* However, in this sentence *junior executives* is in the objective case, so *him* is correct.)

✔ QUICK TRICK   Pronoun in Appositive

Whenever the case form of a pronoun in an appositive must be determined, do this: Cross out the word or words with which it is in apposition. The correct pronoun will stand out immediately. For example:

These junior executives, Alfred and (he, him), are pleasant co-workers. (Cross out *these junior executives,* and the sentence reads: "Alfred and (he, him) are pleasant co-workers." *He* is quickly revealed as the proper pronoun.)

Mr. Bell frequently compliments our junior executives, Alfred and (he, him). (Once more, cross out *our junior executives.* You could also cross out the first part of the compound, *Alfred and.* You would have left: "Mr. Bell frequently compliments *him.*")

☐ CLASS PRACTICE 3

Before selecting the correct pronoun in each of the following sentences, review the case rule for appositives and the Quick Trick.

1. Our good neighbors, Pauline and (she, her), invited us to dinner.
2. The successful applicants were the first two, Barney and (he, him).
3. Mr. Niles put us, Brian and (I, me), in charge of the office.
4. The culprits, (he, him) and (I, me), were punished.
5. Mr. Park placed them, Duncan and (he, him), on probation.
6. The cleanup committee—Tony, Joe, and (I, me)—had to stay late.
7. Miss Yatom finally traced the story to its original authors, Mack and (I, me).

"Who" and "Whom," "Whoever" and "Whomever"

The pronouns *who* and *whoever* are nominative-case forms; *whom* and *whomever* are objective-case forms. If the pronoun in question is the subject of a verb, a predicate nominative, or the complement of a *to be* that has no subject of its own, use *who* or *whoever*. If the pronoun is none of these, use *whom* or *whomever*.

You may be helped in rapid selection of the proper pronoun form by using this Quick Trick.

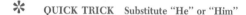

QUICK TRICK   Substitute "He" or "Him"

When faced with a choice between *who* and *whom* or *whoever* and *whomever*, do this: Mentally substitute *he* or *him*. If *he* could be used, the correct pronoun is *who* or *whoever*. If *him* could be used, the correct pronoun is *whom* or *whomever*. For example:

(Who, Whom) is going to sit here? ("*He* is going to sit here?" *Who* is correct because *he* can be substituted.)

For (who, whom) are you waiting? (Changing the order, the sentence would read: "You are waiting for (*him*) *whom*?" *Whom* is correct because *him* can be substituted.)

In Interrogative Sentences   In most instances a question containing *who* or *whom* will be in inverted sentence order. Your first job will be to change the order from inverted to normal, after which you will be able to see at a glance which form is correct. You already know how to make this change, for you studied inverted and normal sentence order in Unit 9.

Give close attention to the following illustrations.

(Who, Whom) is the man wearing the sport jacket? (Normal order: "The man wearing the sport jacket is *who*?" *Who* is correct because it is a predicate nominative.)

(Who, Whom) shall I ask to sit at this desk? (Normal order: "I shall ask *whom* (*him*) to sit at this desk." *Whom* is correct because no rule for nominative case can be applied.)

(Who, Whom) do you take me for? ("You do take me for *whom* (*him*)?" No nominative-case rule applies.)

(Who, Whom) are you supposed to be? ("You are supposed to be *who* (*he*)?" *Who* is the complement of a *to be* that does not have a subject of its own.)

However, some *who, whom* questions are not in inverted order. For instance:

(Whoever, Whomever) in the world would believe your story? (There is no way that the order can be changed. *Whoever* (*he*) is correct because it is the subject of a verb.)

(Who, Whom) is supposed to revise the filing system? (Once more, the order cannot be changed. *Who* (*he*) is correct because it is the subject of the verb.)

☐ CLASS PRACTICE 4

If you understand how to choose correctly *who* or *whom* when used in a question, you will have no difficulty with the following practice sentences. If the pronoun you choose is in the nominative case, give the reason for your choice.

1. (Who, Whom) did you bring with you?
2. (Who, Whom) will Mr. Ash have to help him?
3. (Who, Whom) is assigned to inspect the rockets?
4. (Who, Whom) did you meet at the conference?
5. (Who, Whom) will Mr. Abbott send to Edmonton?

✔ PROOFREADING PRACTICE 2

After practicing the previous *who, whom* questions, you surely will be able to detect any errors in the following questions.

1. Who is the better typist, Jane or she?
2. Who do you believe to be the better typist?
3. Who did they take Jerome to be?
4. Whom would you wish to be?
5. Who does he outrank in seniority?

In a Clause A *subordinate clause* is a group of words having a subject and verb, but forming only part of a sentence. The technique of determining the correct *who, whom* pronoun when that pronoun occurs in a subordinate clause depends on two preliminary steps: (1) Isolate the clause and (2) if the clause is in inverted order, arrange it in normal order.

Step 1 Isolate, or take out, the clause by selecting the group of words beginning with *who* or *whom*.

I do not know (who, whom) the applicant could have been. (Step 1—Isolate the clause: "(who, whom) the applicant could have been.")

The new typist is a girl (who, whom) everyone likes. (Isolate the clause: "(who, whom) everyone likes.")

Be courteous to (whoever, whomever) calls on the telephone. (The clause is "(whoever, whomever) calls on the telephone.")

Bess talks to (whoever, whomever) she meets on the bus. (The clause: "(whoever, whomever) she meets on the bus.")

Unfortunately, many students neglect to use this very basic technique, with the result that they never learn how to select the correct pronoun. Some students cannot isolate the clause, because they do not understand that the very first word in the isolation process is always *who, whoever, whom,* or *whomever* and that the pronoun is part of the clause to which it belongs and has nothing whatever to do with any other words in the sentence. If you are still a little hazy about Step 1, go over the illustrations again.

☐   CLASS PRACTICE 5

Isolate the *who, whom* clauses in the following sentences.

1. My question is addressed to (whoever, whomever) has the data.
2. Philip Jones, (who, whom) you met yesterday, has received the trophy.
3. (Whoever, Whomever) draws the short straw will win the prize.
4. Do you know (who, whom) will be selected to help Mr. Coe plan the advertising campaign?
5. Mr. Coe did not tell me (who, whom) he has selected to help him plan the advertising campaign.

Step 2   When you have isolated the clause, look to see if it is in normal order. If it is not, then arrange the clause in normal order. This will be easy if you remember that a verb can have only one simple subject. If a subject noun or pronoun—plus a *who, whoever, whom,* or *whomever*—appears before the verb, the clause is not in normal order. Consider the example clauses that were isolated in Step 1.

(who, whom) the applicant could have been. (Both *applicant* and *who, whom* come before the verb. This is your cue that the clause is out of order. The correct order is: "the applicant could have been (who, whom).")

(who, whom) everyone likes. (Do you have a subject plus a *who* pronoun? Yes, *everyone* and (*who, whom*). The normal order is this: "everyone likes (who, whom).")

(whoever, whomever) calls on the telephone. (Since the *whoever, whomever* is the only pronoun before the verb, this clause is in normal order; and no change in order can be made.)

(whoever, whomever) she meets on the bus. (There are two pronouns before the verb, *she* and (*whoever, whomever*). The correct order is: "she meets (whoever, whomever) on the bus.")

☐   CLASS PRACTICE 6

Using the clauses you isolated in Class Practice 5, indicate those that are already in normal order and change the others from inverted to normal order.

☐   CLASS PRACTICE 7

Now, using the same exercises, select the correct pronoun, giving your reason whenever you select a nominative-case form. Mentally substituting *he* for *who* and *him* for *whom* will be of great help to you here.

✔   PROOFREADING PRACTICE 3

If you are perfectly clear about the techniques described in this section, you should be able to select the correct *who, whom* pronoun immediately. Prove it by making any needed corrections in the following sentences.

1. Do you know who they will select?
2. Do you know who will be selected?
3. You are one of those who I saw at the dance.
4. Will you send whoever Mr. Peters says to send?
5. You may give the records to whoever you choose.
6. You may give the records to whoever asks for them.

Clause Within a "Who, Whom" Clause   Sometimes confusion arises because a parenthetical clause—*I think, he says, we believe*—occurs within a *who, whom* clause. Whenever you see a clause like this, mentally omit it. To illustrate:

Is that the man (who, whom) you said I should introduce to Dick?

First, isolate the *who, whom* clause: "(who, whom) you said I should introduce to Dick." Then omit the parenthetical clause *you said* and you have left: "(who, whom) I should introduce to Dick."

The next step is to arrange the resulting clause in normal order and substitute *he* or *him* for *who* or *whom*: "I should introduce (him) *whom* to Dick."

☐   CLASS PRACTICE 8

Identify and omit the "extra" clauses within the following *who, whom* clauses. Then select the correct pronoun. Give your reason if you choose a nominative-case form.

1. We invited Nigel, (who, whom) everyone knows is so popular.
2. Ralph is a man (who, whom) I believe will do satisfactory work.
3. Gilda is one stenographer (who, whom) I am sure can take Mr. Lyle's dictation.
4. I left the pen with the girl (who, whom) I thought had charge of lost and found articles.
5. You should select (whoever, whomever) you believe will best fit into our office atmosphere.

✔   PROOFREADING PRACTICE 4

Now see if you can find the *who, whom* errors in the following sentences. As you proofread, remember to omit any "extra" clause within a clause.

1. The advancement will be given to whoever we think deserves it.
2. Otto has a habit of flattering persons whom he thinks might be useful to him.
3. I listed the names of all whom she said had the necessary initiative.
4. The door opened and in came Ann, who we all thought was ill.
5. Has Horace, whom I believe finished school this month, obtained a position yet?
6. Sam, who was introduced to you yesterday, has won.

Communication Problems

Application Exercises

A ■

The following sentences furnish practice in applying the five additional pronoun principles presented in this unit. On a separate sheet of paper, write the correct pronoun for each sentence. If you select the nominative-case form, give the reason for your choice. Remember that italics indicate special emphasis.

1 Did you think that Sandra was older than (I, me)?
2 (Yourself, You) and your family are to be our special guests.
3 The messages might have been from them, Mr. Nye and (he, him).
4 On closer acquaintance, I find that I like *Harold* better than (he, him).
5 The guide explained to Flora and (myself, I, me) all about shipping room procedures.
6 The prom cochairmen, Ronald and (he, him), have called a meeting of the committee.
7 Julia wears more jewelry than (I, me).
8 Mr. Dixon always helps those less fortunate than (he, him).
9 My very best friends are they, Anita and (she, her).
10 Would you trust *Raquelle* rather than (she, her)?
11 The carnival manager asked Edna and (myself, I, me) to sell tickets.
12 We, Vincent and (myself, I, me), are civil engineers.
13 You know just as much about the atom as (he, him).
14 The only students who know anything about grammar seem to be Gladys and (myself, I, me).
15 The prize was given to Harry and (myself, I, me).
16 They are not so careful about detail work as (we, us).
17 Mr. Scott has been very kind to my sister and (myself, I, me).
18 That assignment was given to us, Dennis and (myself, I, me).
19 At the masquerade party, Mr. Howe is sure to recognize Bertha and (myself, I, me).
20 Nobody else in this office has so much concentration as (I, me).

B ■

Write "OK" on your paper for any correct sentence in the following. Rewrite the incorrect sentences, incorporating your corrections. Be sure to give your reason for each selection of a nominative-case pronoun.

1 Where are the experienced teachers, Ms. Reuben and her?
2 Who was the winner, Hiram or he?
3 Mr. Pine said that he knew it was her all the time.
4 Whom would René want to be in the drama?
5 Ken says that it is not who you are, but whom you know, that helps a person to succeed.

6 Etta brung flowers to Mr. Morey's desk.
7 Who do you suppose will get the order for jet planes?
8 Mr. Becker is better able to write the speech than me.
9 We found it difficult to determine whom was most worthy of promotion.
10 Mr. Percy's package has lain in the office for a week.
11 If Norman was you, he would spend that money for a new car.
12 We found it difficult to decide who to select for the promotion.
13 Did you know that mens' coats are on sale this month?
14 Whoever we select for the advancement will be criticized by other members of the staff.
15 Albin told his friends, Bruce and him, to ask for application forms.
16 Please ask her whom the chairman is to be.
17 Whom did you take me to be, Ellis or him?
18 Mr. Field always makes change's after letters have been transcribed.
19 To properly erase, you must know erasing techniques.
20 We shall be glad to receive whoever is sent by the committee.

C ■

Read the following paragraph; then rewrite it, correcting any errors.

We are having difficulty setting up preliminaries for the United Fund campaign. The planning assignment was given to us, Dennis and myself; but we feel that this is a problem that concerns you as well as us. Will you please tell us who you would like to have for an assistant. We shall be glad to work with whoever is selected. Any other suggestions as to personnel will be appreciated, for we realize that you know much more about fund raising than we.

Word Study

A ■

Words often confused: lean, lien; deference, difference.

B ■

Complete these proportions:

1 *True* is to *false* as *perfect* is to _____ .
2 *Familiar* is to *strange* as *major* is to _____ .
3 *Abundant* is to *scarce* as *natural* is to _____ .
4 *Conservative* is to *radical* as *valuable* is to _____ .

C ■

In the following words, what happens to the final silent *e* when the endings shown are added?

1 arrange + ing   4 advertise + er
2 change + less   5 concise + ness
3 expose + ure   6 hope + ful

Communication in Action: *Right Meeting, Wrong Report*

You are at a staff meeting. As the meeting progresses, it becomes apparent that you did not understand exactly the type of report you were to give at the meeting. What will you do when you are called upon? (*a*) Give the report you prepared? (*b*) Reveal your mistake to the group and ask for more time? (*c*) Blame your supervisor for giving you the wrong information? (*d*) Bluff your way, hoping no one will notice? (*e*) Or what?

UNIT □ 16

Predicate Agreement with Simple Subject

The sentence, "All our file clerks is experts," is awkward. Indeed, if you were to read this sentence in a letter, you would probably recognize it as having a major error in grammar. However, do you know why the sentence is incorrect? It is because the verb does not agree with the subject. When you have learned the principles of agreement presented in this and the following two units, you will be able to avoid making errors in subject-predicate agreement.

In Unit 9 you learned how to select the simple subject. You also learned that the predicate is the part of the sentence that remains after the complete subject has been determined. And, you know how to change a sentence from inverted to normal order as a technique for finding the subject. Thus, you already have some of the background knowledge that is needed for study of these three units on agreement. Be sure that you thoroughly understand each separate topic before you attack the next.

General Agreement Principle

The general principle regarding subject-predicate agreement is this: A predicate must agree in number and person with the simple subject. This means that the *verb* and any *pronouns* in the predicate that refer to the simple subject must agree with the subject. First, look at these examples illustrating subject-verb agreement.

> The executives who work in our building *are* assigned special parking spaces. (The simple subject is *executives*, which is plural; therefore, the plural verb *are*—not *is* —is used to agree with the subject.)

A man of many accomplishments *is* likely to succeed. (The simple subject is *man*, which is singular; therefore, the singular verb *is*—not *are*—is used to agree with the subject.)

Now look at an example of the agreement of a pronoun with its *antecedent* (the word to which a pronoun refers):

Our matron likes to have *her* opinions respected. (The simple subject is matron. Since *matron* is singular and is feminine, the correct pronoun is *her*.)

Choice of Pronoun   A pronoun must agree with its antecedent in *gender*, that is, a masculine antecedent requires a masculine pronoun, and a feminine antecedent requires a feminine pronoun.

Mr. Johnstone sent his mother a gift on her birthday.

Some words, however, such as *citizen, employee, president, typist*, could refer to men or women. It is correct to use *he or she, his or her*, or *him or her* in such cases, but sometimes, this creates very awkward sentences. For simplicity the masculine pronoun only is often used. At the time of writing, most company presidents have been men and most typists have been women, and it is often more practical in similar instances to use only *he* or *she*, whichever is more appropriate, if there is no definite indication of gender. However if you feel that the use of a single gender pronoun might be termed "sexist," you might prefer to rearrange your sentences to avoid the problem. Some alternatives are given below.

Every citizen is entitled to take *his or her* opinions to the polls.

Nobody knows what the future has in store for *him* or for *his* children.

Every president likes to feel that *he* is respected by *his* employees.

A good typist will check each letter carefully before *she* gives it to *her* boss.

Presidents like to feel that *they* are respected by *their* employees.

Check each letter carefully before *you* give it to *your* boss.

Letters should be checked carefully before *they* are submitted for signature.

Inverted Order   In Unit 9 you learned how to change the order of a sentence from inverted to normal order so you could find the subject more easily, and you reviewed this technique in Unit 15. This technique also is important to subject-predicate agreement.

Among the flowers (was, were) the missing girl. (Change the sentence to normal order: "The missing girl was . . . ." Do you see how much easier it is to find the subject and to determine the correct verb form when the sentence is changed from inverted to normal order?)

Where (is, are) all the bargains that you said would be offered? (Changed to normal order, the sentence reads: "All the bargains . . . are where?")

☐ CLASS PRACTICE 1

Select the correct words in the following sentences and state your answers this way:

The sentence: If a stranger (calls, call), treat (him, them) courteously.
Your answer: **Calls** and *him,* **to agree with** *stranger.*

1. One of them (is, are) surely not telling the truth about (his, their) absence.
2. The key to the desks (is, are) hidden in (its, their) usual nook.
3. Here (comes, come) two of my best friends, (his, their) eyes shining with excitement.
4. The file on Evans & Company (doesn't, don't) seem to be in (his, its, their) proper place.

✔ PROOFREADING PRACTICE 1

If you are sure that you understand the general agreement principle, you should have no difficulty finding and correcting whatever errors there may be in the following sentences.

1. Has every girl brought their walking shoes?
2. Behind the microphones are seated the principal speaker.
3. Not one of the candidates have agreed to state their platform.
4. The Ocean Beach parking lot don't accommodate many cars.
5. Each one of the players has signed his contract for next season.

Specific Agreement Principles

You have mastered the *general* rule governing predicate agreement. Now here are two *specific* rules. Be sure that you thoroughly understand the first before starting to learn the second.

Collective-Noun Subject   A *collective noun* is a word that refers to a group or collection of persons or things, such as *class, faculty, herd, committee, jury, company,* and *audience.* It is sometimes difficult to tell whether a collective-noun subject is singular or plural. If the group or collection is considered as *acting as a whole,* the subject is singular and takes a singular verb. On the other hand, if the group or collection is considered as *acting separately,* the subject is plural and takes a plural verb.

The jury *has been* out for nine hours. (A singular verb is used because the jury is considered as acting as a whole.)

The jury *are* arguing vehemently. (To argue, more than one person is needed. The plural verb *are* is correct because the jury members are acting separately.)

Also, when a collective-noun subject is the antecedent of a pronoun, the singular or plural number of the pronoun is determined by the same reasoning.

The jury gave *its* verdict almost immediately. (The singular pronoun *its*—not *their* —is correct because here the jury is acting as a whole.)

Do not try to apply this principle to any kind of simple subject other than a collective noun.

☐ CLASS PRACTICE 2

If the word or words you select are singular, name them and say, "to agree with the collective-noun subject (whatever it may be)." If you select a plural, state that plural form and indicate the word or words that caused you to decide that the collective noun must be considered as acting separately.

1. Every nation (looks, look) to (its, their) leaders for guidance.
2. Mr. Blake's audience (was, were) so small that the committee (was, were) embarrassed.
3. The public (has, have) widely divergent views on education.
4. The group (was, were) evidently at odds among themselves.
5. Our company (has, have) just completed (its, their) twentieth annual report.

✔ PROOFREADING PRACTICE 2

This is your opportunity to find out how well you understand predicate agreement when the simple subject is a collective noun. Make any needed corrections.

1. The Lions Club will hold their meeting on Monday.
2. Mr. Niles said that each group must make its own rules.
3. Did you know that the Nye Corporation have installed several electronic devices?
4. Surely the City Council has discussed this question among themselves!
5. The committee is handing in their various reports.

"Part," "Portion," or "Amount" Subject   When the simple subject is a word that indicates a part, a portion, or an amount of something, the number of the predicate —specifically the verb and any pronouns referring to the subject—cannot be selected until you know the answers to the questions: part or portion of what? amount of what? For instance, how can you select the correct verbs in the following sentences?

All (is, are) gone.

Half (has, have) been eaten.

Can you see that you must have more information before you can make the correct selection? This information is given you in the following sentences:

All the money *is* gone.   *But: All* the dimes *are* gone.

Half the cake *has been eaten.*   *But: Half* the cakes *were eaten.*

Here is the principle you are to learn: When the simple subject is a word that means part, portion, or amount, the number of the predicate is determined by the meaning of the complete subject, not of the simple subject alone. Again you are warned not to use this principle except with part, portion, or amount subjects.

☐ CLASS PRACTICE 3

After you have selected the correct word or words, be sure to indicate the word that influenced your choice.

The sentence: Nine-tenths of our office (is, are) adequately lighted.
Your answer: **Is, because of** *office.*

1. One-fifth of the clerks (has, have) returned to (its, their) respective offices.
2. Some of the reports (has, have) reached my ears.
3. Two-thirds of the beam (has, have) rotted away.
4. Part of the papers (was, were) in (its, their) folders and part (was, were) not.
5. Three-quarters of all stenographers tested (was, were) poor in spelling.
6. Half the machines (has, have) been moved from (its, their) original positions, and (it, they) must be returned.

✔ PROOFREADING PRACTICE 3

Find and correct errors in the predicates of the following sentences. If a sentence is correct, write "OK."

1. Four-fifths of the job were finished two hours before the deadline.
2. Most of the money has been invested in bonds.
3. Some of the avenues has been repaved.
4. All the cafeteria have been renovated.
5. Two-thirds of the nuclear physicists has his advanced degrees.
6. Half the rolls are attractively arranged in their boxes.

Communication Problems

Application Exercises

A ■

In the following sentences, indicate which verb and pronoun forms are correct. Follow your answers with a dash, plus the word or words with which your answer or answers agree. Your work, on a separate sheet of paper, will look like this:

The sentence: The man (is, are) taking the package with (him, them).
Your answer: **Is, him—man. (You have selected** *is* **and** *him* **as correct because they agree with** *man.)*

1 All travelers (stops, stop) at Winnipeg on (its, their) way east.
2 As long ago as last month, the council (was, were) ready with (its, their) findings.
3 All employees of the firm (takes, take) (its, their) vacations in July.
4 Do both companies (shows, show) increases in (its, their) inventories?
5 Every single officer of the Women's League (has, have) paid (his, her, its, their) dues.
6 In this modern age, nine-tenths of the offices (is, are) well furnished.
7 The outstanding bargain of the sale (is, are) the TV sets.
8 That family (does, do) (its, their) best to make a living.
9 One of our expert saleswomen (is, are) prepared to demonstrate (his, her, its) specialty.
10 Every city in the two provinces (is, are) conducting civil defence practices.
11 All the gasoline in the tanks (was, were) drawn off by vandals.
12 The committee (was, were) discharged because (it, they) disagreed on every point.
13 For how long (has, have) the two of them been married?
14 Half the offices (was, were) in (its, their) usual disorganized state.
15 Our best seller (is, are) broad-brimmed hats.

B ■

Correct the errors in the following sentences. If a sentence is correct, write "OK."

1 The football heroes, Carl and he, are very popular.
2 Every one of those tours were planned for a person of limited income.
3 Us industrialists must protest the added excise tax.
4 The committee have as their complement seven members.
5 Emily talks as though she were nervous.
6 The foundations of the problem goes back a few years.
7 No other girl in the office speaks so clearly as her.
8 The Board of Education recognize the need for increased school facilities.
9 All contracts will be given to whoever, in the opinion of the trustees, submits the best bid.
10 The day's routine had already began by the time we arrived.
11 In the corner by the window is the confidential files.
12 Has each of you women administrative assistants brought her notebook?
13 Plant worker's holidays are more frequent now than in past years.
14 The Board of Directors was all at the meeting yesterday.
15 The boy was instructed to leave the package with whomever answered the bell.

C ■

In these sentences the missing verb is indicated by a question mark. If the verb is singular, write "S" on your paper; if plural, write "P."

1 Revolutions that took place in that country (?) disastrous to farmers.
2 The jury (?) quarreling about the evidence.
3 After the introductory remarks (?) the real action.

4 Some of the machines on our order (?) not been delivered.
5 Ray, as well as Don and Jim, (?) working on the missile project.
6 The purpose of the meetings (?) to discuss cutting the cost of sales.
7 Every one of the ladies (?) willing to serve on the committee.
8 The clerk in charge of the files (?) very happy.
9 Every gem, as well as all the paste pieces, (?) polished for display.
10 A booklet with operating directions (?) distributed with every machine.

Word Study

A ■

Words often confused: staid, stayed; facilitate, felicitate.

B ■

Match the number of the following exercises with the letter corresponding to the correct answer.

1 Does the French word *résumé* mean: (a) something resumed, (b) a conversation, (c) a summary, (d) the main dish of a meal?
2 Does the Latin phrase *pro rata* mean: (a) for the rats, (b) according to the rates, (c) concerning, (d) proportionately?
3 Which of these means "for each person": (a) *per annum*, (b) *per capita*, (c) *per diem*, (d) *per se?*

C ■

In the following sentences, complete the incomplete words with either *ei* or *ie*.

1 The conc___ted manner of your n___ce was the ch___f reason for her dismissal, I bel___ve.
2 My fr___nd s___zed every l___sure moment to ach___ve his ambition.
3 The long-awaited for___gn fr___ght shipment has just been rec___ved at the p___r.

Communication in Action: *Modernizing Antique Writing*

In cleaning out some files you find the following letter, which is over fifty years old. Rewrite it in modern language.

Your letter of recent date received and contents duly noted. As per our agreement, enclosed please find my cheque in the amount of ten dollars ($10). I wish to advise that this is payment in full for membership dues for A.S.M.E. Please favor me with the date of the national meeting. I remain, Yours truly,

More about Predicate Agreement with Simple Subject

In Unit 16 you learned the general principle and two specific principles regarding subject and predicate agreement. Much emphasis was placed on the fact that the specific principles have no relation to one another but are separate and distinct rules. In this unit you will learn the four remaining specific principles governing agreement with a simple subject.

"A Number," "The Number" Subject   A *number* has a plural meaning; therefore, when *a number* is the subject of a sentence, the predicate must be plural. *The number* has a singular meaning, so the predicate must be singular. Modifiers that appear between *a* and *number* or *the* and *number* do not affect this principle.

> A number of people *have* been asking for you, Mr. Steele. (*Have* agrees with the plural *a number*.)

> The number of available stenographers *is* fewer than the Government needs. (The singular *is* agrees with *the number*.)

> A great number of young men *think* that earning *their* living is of no importance. (Both *think* and *their* are plural, to agree with *a number*. Note that the adjective *great* is disregarded.)

    QUICK TRICK   A Number, The Number

When confronted with the choice of singular or plural verbs and pronouns to agree with *a* or *the number*, you will have no time to sit and think about which is which. This Quick Trick will enable you to use them correctly—fast! Look at the following:

Plural	*Singular*
a	the

Which is the shorter word, *plural* or *singular?* Which is the shorter word, *a* or *the?* The shorter word *a* goes with the shorter word *plural*. The longer word *the* goes with the longer word *singular*. Therefore, *a number* is *plural;* and *the number* is *singular*.

THE FRAMEWORK OF EFFECTIVE COMMUNICATION

☐ CLASS PRACTICE 1

To see how well you can make the predicate agree with *a number* and *the number* subjects, select the correct words in the following sentences.

1. A number of mysterious accidents (has, have) occurred in our factory.
2. The large number of absences (has, have) held up production.
3. A great number of citizens (is, are) prone to criticize without knowing (his, their) facts.
4. A number of books (is, are) missing from the library.
5. The number of men who idle away their time (is, are) amazing.

Foreign-Noun Subject   In Unit 12 you studied plurals of nouns, among which were plurals of nouns of foreign origin. You will remember that, in some cases, a foreign noun ending in *um* is singular and the plural of that noun ends in *a*, such as: *memorandum, memoranda.* (The English plural of *memorandum,* however, is *memorandums.*) A foreign noun ending in *is* takes an *es* ending for the plural: *crisis, crises.* A singular noun ending in *us* becomes *i* in the plural: *alumnus, alumni.* Perhaps the most important thing you learned was that, if you are not sure whether the noun is singular or plural, you should consult your dictionary. When a foreign noun is the simple subject, you must know whether it is singular or plural. Otherwise, how can you make the predicate agree with the simple subject? Consider the following sentences.

An analysis of mailing-list returns *was* made. (*Was* is correct because *analysis* is singular.)

Analyses of mailing-list returns *were* made. (*Were* is correct because *analyses* is plural.)

☐ CLASS PRACTICE 2

For each of the following sentences, make the predicate agree with the foreign-noun subject by selecting the correct word in parentheses.

1. Put the parentheses in (its, their) proper (place, places).
2. The data (has, have) been carefully checked and can be found in (its, their) assigned drawer.
3. A very serious crisis (has, have) arisen in the Middle East.
4. (Is, Are) the sanatorium open for inspection?
5. Analyses of the production lag (is, are) ready for the meeting.
6. The highway oases (was, were) a welcome sight to hot, thirsty travelers.

✔ PROOFREADING PRACTICE 1

Errors in the following sentences concern agreement between *a number, the number,* and foreign-noun subjects with their predicates. Find the errors and correct them.

1. The addenda is ready for presentation on Monday.
2. The number of poor spellers in all walks of life are appalling.
3. The bases for your thinking is unsound.
4. The number of mediocre workers are greater than one would think.
5. The alumni of the University is having its reunion Friday.
6. A large number of credit sales are returned every day.

"There" at Beginning of Sentence or Clause   If a sentence or a clause begins with *there*, the subject usually follows the verb. Whenever you see a sentence or a clause beginning with the word *there*, look for the subject *after* the verb and see to it that the predicate agrees with the subject. A common error is the use of a singular verb when the following subject is plural.

> There *are* various ways of setting up a letter. (The subject *ways* comes after the verb *are*, which is plural to agree with *ways*.)

> Mr. Coe said that there *was* one letter still to be typed. (The singular verb *was* agrees with the subject *letter*. Note that *there* begins a clause.)

☐   CLASS PRACTICE 3

If you understand what to do when you see a sentence or a clause beginning with *there*, you will be able immediately to select the correct words in the following sentences.

1. There (is, are) always two sides to every question.
2. Have you been told that there (is, are) a right way to do every job?
3. Joe says that there (has, have) been ten men in the machine shop today.
4. (Is, Are) there eight or ten reams in that package?
5. The economist noted that there (is, are) plenty of jobs for everyone.

Indefinite-Pronoun Subject   The indefinite pronouns *each, either, neither, everyone, everybody, someone, somebody, anyone, anybody, nobody,* and *no one,* plus the words *a person* are singular in meaning. Therefore, whenever one of these indefinite words is the subject of a sentence, the verb and any pronouns referring to the subject will be singular. For example:

> Nobody *is* to take *his* confidential reports home with *him*. (*Is, his, him* to agree with the singular subject *nobody*.)

> Neither of the proposed solutions *is* good. (*Is,* to agree with the singular subject *neither*.)

> A person *is* not always able to have what *he desires*. (*Is, he, desires,* to agree with the singular subject *a person*.)

This is your last specific rule for agreement of the predicate with a simple subject. Remember that, although the predicate must agree with the simple subject, there are different kinds of subjects. For each separate type of simple subject there is a specific principle that applies only to that particular subject.

☐ CLASS PRACTICE 4

Take one more good look at the indefinite pronouns listed on page 137 and then select the correct words in the following sentences.

1. Neither of the girls (has, have) finished transcribing (his, her, its, their) notes.
2. Everyone who visits the exhibition (is, are) given a souvenir to take home with (him, her, it, them).
3. Nobody out of the entire group of listeners (seems, seem) interested in the speaker's ideas.
4. Each of the ten men already (has, have) (his, her, its, their) (mind, minds) made up.
5. Either of the synonyms (is, are) applicable here.

✔ PROOFREADING PRACTICE 2

Do you know what to do when you see the word *there* beginning a sentence or clause? Do you know the indefinite pronouns that are always singular? Then find the errors in the following sentences and rewrite the sentences correctly.

1. Neither of us are expected to work Saturday.
2. Did you realize that there are only a few silver dollars in circulation?
3. Nobody but Mary and me ever volunteer for the difficult jobs.
4. Somebody has to take their turn at the reception desk.
5. I looked in the warehouse, and there was only one bale of cotton left.

Communication Problems

Application Exercises

A ▪

Using a separate sheet of paper, select the correct word or words in each of the following sentences and indicate the simple subject with which the predicate agrees.

1   The focus of our thoughts (has, have) been on the strong points in the program.
2   Neither of the men (is, are) able to tie (his, their) bow tie.
3   Because of a lack of responsibility, a great number of working hours (is, are) lost every day.
4   Each of the three leaders (has, have) been trying to present (his, their) (stand, stands) to the public.
5   Where (is, are) the styli supposed to be?
6   There (has, have) been several service calls this morning.
7   Either of the typists (works, work) well under pressure.
8   A number of reasons (has, have) been given for the decision.

9   Neither of those executives (is, are) in (his, their) (office, offices) when you need (him, them).
10 That opening parenthesis mark (is, are) not correctly placed.
11 You will find that there (is, are) two mistakes in the letter.
12 Everybody in this office (knows, know) that (he, she, they) (is, are) to help reduce overhead.
13 The large number of graduates this year (is, are) impressive.
14 Mr. Hyde's order is that everyone (is, are) to use (his, her, their) own supplies.
15 Arthur cannot do the work because the needed data (is, are) not available.

B ■

If a sentence is correct, write "OK" on your paper. If it is incorrect, write the correction.

1   Many heroes have fell on the field of battle.
2   The number of office workers who patronize our cafeteria are truly gratifying.
3   Mr. Latif sent for the three of us—Ivan, Clyde, and I.
4   You must have laid the special delivery letter on top of the chute.
5   If a person does not enjoy working here, they should resign.
6   I will provide help for whomever is in need of assistance.
7   Both Fred and myself are eligible for the promotion.
8   Are the memoranda in their usual neat form?
9   The jury was arguing among themselves as to whether it should postpone the verdict.
10 Today, there is more jobs than people to fill them.
11 There are only two private secretaries in our firm, Ms. Carey and I.
12 Someone has left their notebooks on my desk.
13 Meet me at Peck's and Harding's office.
14 Behind our flag stand many patriotic citizens.
15 I reminded you that there was two appointments that have been canceled.

C ■

In some of these sentences, the question mark indicates a missing *verb;* in others, a missing *pronoun.* Write "S" if the omitted word is singular in number; write "P," if plural.

1   There (?) ten orders that came in the morning mail.
2   Everybody must bring to the meeting (?) notes on the article about atomic power.
3   Usually, the number of applicants (?) not very large.
4   Analyses of claims made during the past month (?) of much help to the purchasing department.
5   Neither of the women would admit that (?) lost the receipts.

Word Study

A ■

Words often confused: billed, build; deduce, deduct.

B ■

Which of the numbered items in the following sentences correctly matches the italicized business term?

1 *Agenda* means: (a) a list of the officers of a corporation, (b) a summary of the company's financial condition at the end of the year, (c) a list of topics to be discussed at a meeting, (d) the history of the company.

2 A *charter* is: (a) a person who draws charts, (b) a document granting a corporation rights or privileges, (c) a seal attached to legal documer' ., (d) bylaws.

3 "The decline of the market wiped out thousands of dollars of *paper profits.*" Does this mean: (a) profits listed in newspapers, (b) profits of paper manufacturers, (c) unrealized profits, (d) profits on the sale of paper and stationery?

C ■

How do you spell?

1 The *ing*-ending form of *sue?*
2 More than one *basis?*
3 The state of being unable to pay one's debts?
4 The past tense of *see*, as in "I _____ him yesterday"?

Communication in Action: *Urgent Message*

You receive this telephone message: "Tell Mr. Mason I've been called out of town and can't see him until Thursday." Mr. Mason, your boss, is on the way to the airport to board a plane to the city of the caller. The plane is to leave in 45 minutes. How would you relay this urgent message to your boss? List alternate methods in case your first attempt fails.

UNIT □ 18

Predicate Agreement with Compound Subject

In Units 16 and 17 you learned the principles of predicate agreement with different kinds of simple subjects. However, a subject may also be compound. What will you do about predicate agreement if your sentence contains a compound subject?

This unit completes the "agreement" story. Here you will learn to use the correct predicate verbs and any pronouns that refer to the subject when you have singular or plural subjects joined by *and, or,* or *nor.* Mastery of these principles is the task ahead.

Subjects Joined by "And"

A compound subject joined by *and* takes a plural predicate.

> The letter *and* the envelope *have* been separated.

> Jack *and* Owen *have* their plans made.

Perhaps you would almost automatically use a plural predicate when you have a subject joined by *and.* However, there are two instances where a subject joined by *and* takes a *singular* predicate. Watch for these exceptions.

Exception 1   When the parts of a compound subject joined by *and* denote the same person or thing, a singular predicate is used.

> Pie *and* ice cream *is* my favorite dessert. (This is commonly one dessert—a piece of pie with ice cream on top.)

Exception 2   When a compound subject joined by *and* is modified by *each, every,* or *many a,* a singular predicate is used. For instance:

> *Every* file clerk, typist, *and* stenographer *is* expected to have certain basic training as part of *his* educational background. (The singular verb *is* and the singular pronoun *his* are correct because the subject joined by *and* is modified by *every.*)

> *Many* a young man *and* woman *has* risen in the profession.

☐   CLASS PRACTICE 1

Now that you know the rule and the two exceptions governing the number of the verb and of the pronouns to be used with a subject joined by *and,* you will be able to select the correct words in the following sentences.

1. Each accountant, stenographer, and clerk (is, are) happy to be of service to you.
2. Accuracy and speed (is, are) both important to the typist.
3. Many a girl and boy (has, have) been eager to advance (himself, herself, themselves).
4. Joe and Tom (avails, avail) (himself, themselves) of all (his, their) opportunities.
5. Ham and eggs (makes, make) a substantial breakfast dish.
6. Both the workers and the work (is, are) wholly unorganized.
7. Every man, woman, and child (was, were) frightened when the plane broke the sound barrier.

Subjects Joined by "Or" or "Nor"

When a compound subject is joined by *or* or *nor*, match the verb and any pronouns referring to the subject with that part of the subject nearer (or nearest) the verb.

Neither the *parents nor* the *child was watching* the traffic signals. (The subject is *parents nor child.* Do you see that the singular *child* is nearer the verb than the plural *parents?* Therefore, the singular *was* is correct, to agree with *child.*)

Neither the *child nor* the *parents were watching* the traffic signals. (Here we have the same sentence—with one important difference. This time, *parents* is nearer the verb, so the plural *were watching* is used to match the plural *parents.*)

✳ QUICK TRICK   Start with the Last Part

When the compound subject is joined by *or* or *nor*, start with the second or last part of the subject and read the rest of the sentence; like this:

Either *Max or* the other *men* (is, are) to be asked to show (his, their) workshop products. (*Men* is the part of the subject nearer the verb. Starting with *men,* the sentence reads: "*Men are* to be asked to show *their* workshop products." The plurals *are* and *their* are needed to agree with *men.*)

Correct predicate use with compound subjects is a matter of seeing *and, or,* or *nor.* When *and* is seen, the "*and*" rule or exceptions are applied. When *or* or *nor* is seen, the "*or, nor*" rule must be applied. Take time now to fix in your mind each compound-subject rule. Then do the following class practice.

⬜ CLASS PRACTICE 2

How well you understand the agreement of a predicate with a subject joined by *or* or *nor* will be revealed to you as you select the correct words in the following sentences.

1. Neither Wanda nor the two boys (was, were) responsible for the ink spot.
2. Either you or he (is, are) to be transferred to the main office.
3. Neither Gus nor I (am, is, are) ready to start filing.
4. Neither Thomas nor David (avails, avail) (himself, themselves) of all (his, their) opportunities.
5. Either the saleswomen or Frank (has, have) to have (his, her, their) time-cards checked.
6. Neither Leo nor the twins (does, do) good work after (his, their) lunch hour.

✔ PROOFREADING PRACTICE 1

Make the necessary corrections in the following sentences. You can do this only if you are clear as to the correct number of the predicate to be used with (a) compound subjects joined by *and* and (b) compound subjects joined by *or* or *nor.*

1. Each pencil, paper, and pen are to be returned to the box.
2. Jane and I are ready to type the lists now.
3. Mercury or alcohol are used in most thermometers.
4. The hours and salary mentioned in the advertisement is not satisfactory to me.
5. The comma or the semicolon are usually required between the parts of a compound sentence.
6. Neither she nor you is in danger of overworking.

Relative-Pronoun Clause

The principle that governs agreement in a clause introduced by a relative pronoun might be called an "orphan" rule, for it cannot be classified under predicate agreement with a simple or a compound subject. Remember, a *clause* is a group of words having a subject and a verb, but forming only part of a sentence. Before learning the rule that applies to a clause introduced by a relative pronoun, consider these preliminaries:

1. The relative pronouns are *who, which,* and *that.*
2. A relative pronoun is called "relative" because it refers to a word called an "antecedent."
3. The antecedent is the noun or pronoun usually occurring immediately before the relative pronoun.

The following illustrations will help you to recognize a relative pronoun and to identify its antecedent. This you must be able to do before you can apply the principle.

The man *who* lives there is my roommate's uncle. (In the clause *who lives there, who* is a relative pronoun because it relates, or refers back, to its antecedent *man.*)

I'm going to the opera Saturday, *which* is my birthday. (In the clause *which is my birthday,* the relative pronoun *which* refers to *Saturday,* its antecedent.)

In the following sentences, the antecedents of the relative pronouns are a little less obvious. Note that the antecedents come immediately before the relative pronouns.

Ellen is one of those stenographers *who* think their methods are the most efficient.

Where can I buy one of those erasers *that* have brushes attached to them?

In the following sentences, can you see that *who, which,* and *that* are *not* relative pronouns? They cannot be, because they do not relate to anything. They have no antecedents.

Who is that man carrying the brown brief case? (*Who* is not a relative pronoun because it has no antecedent.)

Do you know which word is correct? (*Which* here is not a relative pronoun.)

Mr. Reid said that the man has much in his favor. (*That* is not a relative pronoun because it has no antecedent.)

Now that you have this basic information, you are ready for the rule that governs predicate agreement in clauses introduced by relative pronouns. Here is the rule: The predicate of a clause that is introduced by a relative pronoun agrees *with the antecedent of that pronoun*, not with the relative pronoun itself.

He is the man (*who*) *carries a brown briefcase.* (The relative clause is *who carries a brown briefcase.* The verb *carries* agrees not with the relative pronoun *who* but with its antecedent, *man.*)

✳ QUICK TRICK Omit the Pronoun

You will apply the principle more quickly if you omit the relative pronoun and use the antecedent as the subject of the clause, like this:

Ralph is one of those *students* who (thinks, think) (he, they) can get along without doing (his, their) homework. (Omit *who*. Start with the antecedent *students* and make your selections: "*Students think they* can get along without doing *their* homework.")

Note that the clause that follows *one of those* always has a plural predicate.

Now use the Quick Trick with these sentences:

Ellen is one of those *stenographers* (who) *think their* methods are the most efficient. (*Stenographers think their* methods . . . .)

Where can I buy one of those *erasers* (that) *have brushes* (not *a brush*) attached to *them?* (*Erasers have brushes* attached to *them.*)

☐ CLASS PRACTICE 3

Before you select the correct words in this class practice, answer these questions: Can you identify a relative pronoun? Can you select the antecedent? Do you know that the predicate of a relative-pronoun clause agrees with the antecedent? Now, in each of the following sentences, omit the relative pronoun, start with the antecedent, and choose the word or words that agree with the antecedent.

1. My sister is one of those reckless drivers who (is, are) always taking chances.
2. Your duty is to paint the fence posts, which (is, are) being delivered today.
3. The lion is one animal that (is, are) known for the restless padding of (his, its, their) (cages, cage).
4. Mr. Barker bought one of those lawn mowers that (does, do) not break up the turf with (its, their) sharp knives.
5. Sam is one of those men who (makes, make) friends wherever (he, they) (goes, go).

✔ **PROOFREADING PRACTICE 2**

If you can make the necessary corrections in the following sentences, you will know that you *really* understand the relative-pronoun agreement principle.

1. It was his favorite pipes that was destroyed in the fire.
2. Juliette is the kind of file clerk who think they own the files.
3. Responsibility is given to those people who has this very desirable trait.
4. The boss called my attention to some raised capitals, which is found in many typed communications.
5. Mr. Floyd is one of those golf enthusiasts who are always talking about their last game.

Communication Problems

Application Exercises

A ■

On a separate sheet of paper, write the correct word or words in each of the following sentences. Then make a dash; and write the noun, nouns, or pronoun with which your choice agrees.

The sentence: Neither they nor Tom (knows, know) what (he, they) (is, are) supposed to do.

Your answer: **knows, he, is—Tom**

1 Either you or Ilsa (is, are) to deliver the message.
2 On upper Pine Avenue (is, are) the best drugstore and the best department store in the city.
3 Hans is one of those beginners who (thinks, think) (he, they) (knows, know) everything.
4 Neither Edward nor the other bookkeepers (gives, give) (his, their) services willingly.
5 Bacon and eggs (is, are) my most satisfactory breakfast dish.
6 Eric is a man who (takes, take) excellent care of (his, their) property.
7 Either the President or the Vice-President (is, are) usually in Washington.
8 Each chair, desk, and cabinet (is, are) in need of repair.
9 Let's read one of those books that (was, were) recommended by the librarian.
10 Ravi said that there (was, were) present only Ricardo, Denise, and she.
11 Is it John and George who (has, have) the latest filing equipment?
12 Ruby and Thelma (is, are) taking (her, their) work home with (her, them).
13 You know very well that it is not I who (brings, bring) in the mail.
14 Either the manager or the members of the board (has, have) been approached about that directive.
15 A block and tackle (is, are) of great help to construction workers.

B ■

Find and correct any errors in the following sentences. If a sentence is correct, write "OK" on your paper.

1 Their will be a long holiday weekend for us in July.
2 Everyone is judged by the quality of their work.
3 Mr. Ayres has great respect for whomever he thinks is dependable.
4 Each man and woman is obligated to do a good job.
5 We women take just as much pride in our work as them.
6 Is that book one of the five that was recommended by Julia?
7 Production of plastic materials has risen steadily.
8 How would you like to have to pay the Quinns' heavy overhead?
9 Bread and butter are my favorite afterschool snack.
10 Mr. Craig is one of the salesmen who calls regularly on Ray.
11 Here are the folders you asked me to get for you.
12 Many an executive and a secretary have refused to read mimeographed letters.
13 You can trust Jack and myself to do our best for you.
14 High grades are given to whoever earns them.
15 Either Betty or the male accountants has to take his examination.

C ■

Edit and rewrite the following paragraph.

Neither the administrative assistants nor the president himself approve the procedures outlined in your report of May 6. Each point you made and each recommendation you submitted were considered carefully. Defining the responsibilities of staff members is one of those areas that need more-than-average thought, time, and study. We should appreciate your revising this report with a view to keeping any overlapping to a minimum.

Word Study

A ■

Words often confused: fair, fare; undo, undue.

B ■

1 If your dictator told you to *delete* the second paragraph of a letter, would you: (a) indent it, (b) enclose it in quotation marks, (c) omit it?
2 A *centimetre* is: (a) an insect having many legs, (b) a unit of measure, (c) a meter that counts cents.
3 A *presentiment* is: (a) the sending of something in advance, (b) a representation, (c) a premonition.

C ■

Which spelling in each of the following groups is right?

1 succeed, sucsede, succede
2 mimiced, mimicked, mimmiced

3 conscientous, conseinshus, conscientious
4 auxillary, auxiliary, auxillaree
5 maintainance, mantenance, maintenance
6 rythm, rhythm, rhythym
7 perserverance, perseverence, perseverance

Communication in Action: *The Chronic Complainer*

You work in the purchasing department. Seated at the desk immediately behind you
is an older man who is a chronic complainer. He mumbles constantly about his aches
and pains, the poor lighting, the unfairness of the manager, overwork, the shortcomings of other employees, and so on. For a while you overlook the problem, but
it is beginning to affect your work. What would you do? Would you talk to him? to
the supervisor? What would you say?

UNIT □ 19

Adjectives

An *adjective* is a word that modifies a noun or pronoun. Adjectives are of two general types:
  1. Descriptive adjectives, which are picture-making words (*leather* couch, *green*
dress, *small* apartment, *weary old* man) that answer the question "What kind of?"
  2. Limiting adjectives, which point out an object or indicate its number or quantity
(*this* hat, *that* newspaper, *the* answer, *a* dog, *six* books, *first* day). They answer the
questions "Which?" or "How many?"
  Study of the picture-making function of adjectives, while important, is not the
total of what must be learned about adjectives. If you would speak and write standard English, then you must master the rules that will enable you to use adjectives
correctly. These rules have to do with the fact that most descriptive adjectives are
capable of being compared.

Comparison of Adjectives

Most adjectives change their forms to express different degrees of quality. This
modification is called "comparison." There are three forms or degrees of adjective
comparison: (1) *positive*, used when the adjective is not compared with anything
else; (2) *comparative*, used to express a higher or lower degree than expressed by
the positive degree; and (3) *superlative*, used to denote the highest or lowest degree.

Forms of Adjective Comparison   Adjectives may be compared in one of three ways:

1. By adding *er* and *est* to the positive form.

Positive	*Comparative*	*Superlative*
fine	finer	finest
friendly	friendlier	friendliest
strong	stronger	strongest

2. By adding *more* and *most* (or *less* and *least*) to the positive form.

Positive	*Comparative*	*Superlative*
patient	more (*or* less) patient	most (*or* least) patient
personable	more (*or* less) personable	most (*or* least) personable
amusing	more (*or* less) amusing	most (*or* least) amusing

3. By changing the form of the word completely.

Positive	*Comparative*	*Superlative*
much, many	more	most
little	less	least
good	better	best
bad	worse	worst

Selection of Correct Forms of Comparison   Adjectives of one syllable are compared by adding *er* and *est;* adjectives of three or more syllables, by adding *more* and *most.* However, adjectives of *two* syllables are sometimes compared by adding *er* and *est* and sometimes by adding *more* and *most.* Usually you can tell which form is right by the sound. If in doubt, however, consult an unabridged dictionary for the correct forms.

The new typewriter is the *prettiest* machine in the office. (Not *most pretty.*)

The electric typewriter is *more useful* than the manual machine. (Not *usefuler.*)

Choice of Comparative or Superlative Degree   When referring to two persons, places, or things, use the comparative degree.

Both courses are good, but I think this is the *better.*

When referring to more than two persons, places, or things, use the superlative degree.

All courses are good, but I think this is the *best.*

Double Comparison   Note that adjectives may be compared in any one of three ways. Avoid the error of double comparison, which occurs when two comparisons are used at the same time.

Mr. Grayson is a kinder (not *more kinder*) man than Mr. Hall.

I think that this is the worst (not *worstest,* not *most worst,* not *most worstest*) of all the ideas.

☐   CLASS PRACTICE 1

Select the correct words in the following sentences. Give your reasons.

1. Which picture is the (larger, more larger), hers or mine?
2. Both girls have lovely voices, but Barbara's is the (lower, lowest).
3. Who is the (most efficient, most efficientest, efficientest) secretary in the organization?
4. Heather cannot make up her mind which is the (better, best) position for her, bookkeeper or secretary.
5. Nancy cannot make up her mind which is the (better, best) position for her—nurse, laboratory technician, or dental assistant.

"Other" and "All" in Comparisons   When comparing a particular person or thing with a group of which it is a part, use the comparative degree and the word *other* or *else*.

There are *more* office workers in New York City than in any *other* city in the world. (Since New York is a city in the world, failure to use the word *other* would mean that New York has more office workers than any city including New York.)

Bob worked harder than anyone *else* in the group. (The word *else* is needed to distinguish Bob from the others in the group.)

When using the superlative degree, however, *other* is not used. Neither is *any*. Use *all* after the superlative form.

Sandra is the *most* industrious of *all* our clerks. (Not of *any* of our clerks. *Any* means *any one*, and Sandra could not be the *most industrious* of *any one* of the clerks.)

Adjectives That Cannot Be Compared   Some adjectives, called "absolute" adjectives, cannot be compared because in the positive degree they are already the ultimate. For instance, if you had a *full* glass of water, your friend could not have a glass that was *fuller;* nor could someone have the *fullest* glass of all. Some examples of absolute adjectives are these:

complete	immaculate	round
conclusive	level	spotless
correct	perfect	square
dead	perpendicular	supreme
eternal	perpetual	unanimous
final	right	unique

Sometimes there is need to indicate the degree to which a person or thing approaches the top represented by the positive degree. In such case, use *more nearly* or *most nearly*.

John's circle is *more nearly* round than Tony's.

Leon's answer is the *most nearly* correct.

☐ CLASS PRACTICE 2

Now is the time to see if you understand *other* in comparison and if you know what to do about adjectives that cannot be compared. Select the correct word in each of the following sentences and give the reason for your choice.

1. (No, No other) manufacturing company has a better reputation than ours.
2. Mr. Hill's office is the (emptiest, most nearly empty) of furniture.
3. Jan works longer hours than (any, any other) girl in the bank.
4. This is the (most, most nearly) unique letter setup that I have ever seen.
5. Dora does the best mimeograph work of (all the, any of the) girls in the duplicating room.

✔ PROOFREADING PRACTICE 1

Test your understanding of the four principles presented so far in this unit by finding the errors in the following sentences.

1. Your story about the returned goods is funnier than any story you have ever told.
2. Which master carbon is the best, the black or the purple?
3. Your letters are neat, but I think mine are more neater.
4. Brenda has the calmest disposition of all the girls who have worked for Mr. Larke.
5. Both girls are efficient, but Diane is the most poised.
6. With the windows closed, the office became a little more warm.

Repeat the Modifier

When you wish to make clear that two or more persons or things are meant, then repeat a modifier such as *a*, *the*, or *my* before each successive noun.

> A stenographer and *a* typist have arrived. (There are two persons, one a stenographer; the other, a typist.)

On the other hand, if it is your intention to indicate that only one person or thing is meant, place a modifier before the first noun only.

> A stenographer and typist has arrived. (Here we have one person who is both a stenographer and a typist.)

Compound Adjectives

A *compound adjective* consists of two or more words that act together as a single thought unit that modifies a noun. Many compound adjectives are hyphenated. Others are written as one word or as two words.

When a compound adjective occurs *before* the noun it modifies, the adjective is usually hyphenated. For example:

air-conditioned room	*middle-aged* man	*twenty-second* floor
first-class typist	*sixty-day* tour	*up-to-date* methods
high-grade goods	*ten-storey* building	*well-known* person

On the other hand, certain well-known compounds are not hyphenated when used as adjectives. For example:

business reply envelope	*high school* teacher
charge account customer	*social security* benefits

Whether or not to hyphenate is a puzzler for most students, even though they memorize the exceptions to the rule. To help you decide when to use the hyphen, follow the reasoning shown in this Quick Trick:

 QUICK TRICK   To Hyphenate or Not

Take an example like the following:

The senior play was a *first* (?) *rate* production.

Your problem is whether to hyphenate *first* (?) *rate*. First, find the noun modified by *first* (?) *rate*. The answer is *production*. Then ask yourself, What kind of production? Your answer cannot be *rate* only. This answer would not make sense. Both words, *first* and *rate*, are needed to convey the one thought; they cannot be separated. Therefore, you should hyphenate *first-rate*.

 CLASS PRACTICE 3

Fix in your mind the rules governing the omission of a modifier and the hyphenation of compound adjectives by selecting the correct words in the following sentences.

1. A black and a gold fountain pen (has, have) been found in the ladies' lounge.
2. It is too bad that your building is so far (out of the way, out-of-the-way).
3. There, too, they faced the (ever present, ever-present) problem.
4. The army and the navy (was, were) somewhat lax at Bell Harbor.
5. The secretary-treasurer of the company (has, have) (his, their) office on the tenth floor.
6. The red tape that had confronted us intermittently was now ever present.

 PROOFREADING PRACTICE 2

Find the errors in the following sentences.

1. A blue and a red blouse is to be put away for that customer.
2. China is sold on the twenty first floor.
3. The cab and the driver is waiting for Mr. Evans.
4. Hit or miss methods caused the failure of that firm.
5. She was frequently complimented on her peaches-and-cream complexion.

6. There are good workers and not so good workers in our office.
7. The red and black ribbon was removed from your typewriter.
8. A blue and red blouse are to be put away for Mrs. Graves.

Adjective Pitfalls

There are two common errors in the use of adjectives that are made primarily in speech. So that you may not be guilty of these illiteracies, either in speaking or in writing, study carefully the following presentation.

Those and Them. *Those* is an adjective; *them* is a pronoun. Use *those* if there is a following noun; use *them* if there is no following noun.

> Please take those papers (*not* them papers) to Mr. Hall. (The noun *papers* follows the word in question, so the adjective *those* is correct.)

> Please take them to Mr. Hall. (*Them* is correct because there is no following noun.)

You understand, of course, that the adjectives *these* and *those* are equally correct, the choice being a matter of position. *These carbons* would be used when the carbons are near the speaker. *Those carbons* are at a distance from the speaker.

Kind(s) and Sort(s). *Kind* and *sort* are singular nouns; *kinds* and *sorts*, plural nouns. A singular adjective must be used with the singular noun; a plural adjective, with the plural noun. For example:

> The careful employee does not make (this, these) kind of error. (*This kind* is correct. *Kind* is singular and must be modified by the singular adjective *this.*)

> Why does Julia make (that, those) sorts of errors? (The plural noun *sorts* must be modified by the plural adjective *those*. *Those sorts* is correct.)

☐ CLASS PRACTICE 4

How well do you understand the difference between *those* and *them* and the correct adjective to use with *kind(s)* and *sort(s)*? To find out, select the appropriate words in these sentences.

1. Did you deposit (those, them) cheques for Mr. Martin?
2. Cynthia likes this (kind, kinds) of letterhead best of all.
3. Why do you always use those (kind, kinds) of paper clips?
4. I should like you to get (those, them) for me immediately.
5. Those (sort, sorts) of machines were discarded by Mr. Hamil.
6. You ought not to associate with these (kind, kinds) of people.
7. Please pick up (these, them) business reference books.
8. What is the name of that (kind, kinds) of type cleaner?
9. Have you filed (those, them) sales letters yet?
10. Have you tried (that, those) kinds of cookies?

Communication Problems

Application Exercises

A ■

Before you select the correct words in the following sentences, be sure that you have taken time to study all the principles in this unit.

1   This is the (valuablest, most valuable, most nearly valuable) proposal that I have ever received.
2   The clothing sold in that store is (low priced, low-priced).
3   Why did you buy the (costliest, most costliest) ring in the showcase?
4   The shipment contained only (those, them) sizes specified in your order.
5   The famous author and lecturer (gives, give) (his, their) (talk, talks) this evening.
6   Of the two cities we visited, we thought London was the (cleaner, cleanest).
7   Adjectives are (picture making, picture-making) words.
8   Please hold the tape in a (more, more nearly) perpendicular position.
9   Will (that, those) kind of blanket be warm enough for camp use?
10 Marge has (lovelier, more lovely, more lovelier) manners than she.
11 You should use stainless steel, for it will resist rust and pitting better than (any, any other) metal.
12 Mr. Fyfe is really a much (happier, more happy, more happier) person than he looks.
13 You returned two books, but you surely do not expect full credit for (those, them).
14 In our main office, the receptionist sits at the desk (nearer, nearest) the entrance.
15 A red and a black typewriter ribbon (was, were) missing from the shipment.

B ■

Correct all incorrect sentences. Write "OK" for all correct sentences.

1   A new baby's outpatient clinic has been opened at the hospital.
2   Do these kinds of oranges come from Florida?
3   The sales group are meeting in Parlor A.
4   Please do not order any more of them carbons.
5   Whom would you like to see take part in the discussion?
6   Just telephone my secretary or I for an appointment.
7   Owena is the most friendliest girl in our sorority.
8   Where shall I set these boxes?
9   Of the three buildings, ours is nearer the corner.
10 Celia's spelling grade was the most perfect.
11 Are the runners-up Bill and myself?
12 Our company pays higher wages than any other firm in the province.
13 None of the accused men was actually guilty.
14 Our office sent two delegates, Dick and he, to the convention.
15 That file clerk and typist has little time for conversation.

C ■

Rewrite the following paragraph, correcting the errors you find.

Thank you very much for your courteous reception of me last Monday. My instructions were to consult a scientist and engineer; and for the engineer, you were the "pick of the crop." You answered my questions about many details that puzzled me, those kind of technical particulars that were outside my experience. At least, I now have a sort of self-starter grasp of the engineering phase of our problem.

Word Study

A ■

Words often confused: shoot, chute; desolate, dissolute.

B ■

1   In which of the following words is the *u not* pronounced as in *human?*

gratitude   student
utterance   revenue

2   In which of the following words is the *ou not* pronounced like the *oo* in *noon?*

souvenir   acoustics
cantaloupe   coupon

C ■

Here are definitions of five words that rhyme with *hole.* How are these "ole" words spelled?

1   A black, solid mineral used as a fuel
2   One and only
3   A round, deep, hollow dish
4   To have one's name recorded on a list
5   The spiritual part of a person

Communication in Action: Social Etiquette

Discuss the following statements. Are they correct or incorrect? Consult a modern etiquette book in the library if you need help.

1. When walking on the sidewalk, the boy should walk on the "outside" of the girl—that is, next to the street.

2. A woman should never extend her hand when being introduced to a man.

3. At the formal dinner table, do not begin to eat until your hostess does.

Adverbs

Perhaps you know that an *adverb* is a word that describes, explains, or limits a verb, an adjective, or another adverb. But there are other facts about adverbs that you should know also. For example, an adverb follows the same rules for comparison as an adjective (*clearly, more clearly, most clearly*); while most words ending in *ly* are adverbs, not all adverbs end in *ly* (*here, there, never, not, down, quite*, etc.). An adverb usually answers such questions as When? Where? How? Why? How much or how little? To what extent?

You must also know the principles covered in this unit if you are to use adverbs with confidence.

Kinds of Adverbs

According to the way they are used, adverbs are classified as *simple* or *conjunctive*.

Simple Adverbs   A simple adverb is used as a modifier only, and this unit is concerned primarily with simple adverbs. Here are some common simple adverbs:

soon	quite	immediately	never
too	very	clearly	now
here	nearly	always	then

We can *easily* drive that distance in an hour. (*Easily* is a simple (or modifying) adverb and answers the question "How?" or "To what extent?")

Conjunctive Adverbs   A conjunctive adverb connects a subordinate clause to the main clause, and it also acts as a regular adverb in that subordinate clause. Knowledge of this twofold use will be helpful to you when you study punctuation. Some of the most commonly used conjunctive adverbs are these:

after	however	therefore	when
as	moreover	since	while
before	then	thus	yet

Study the following illustrations of simple and conjunctive adverbs.

Since you did not send us your cheque, we will cancel the order. (*Since* is a conjunctive adverb that introduces the clause *since you did not send us your cheque*.)

Time passes *quickly when* one is busy. (*Quickly* is a simple, modifying adverb answering the question "How?" *When* is a conjunctive adverb introducing the clause *when one is busy*.)

☐ CLASS PRACTICE 1

Stop here to get some practice in identifying adverbs. Use the "adverb questions" and see how quickly you can select the correct words in these sentences.

1. You will remember that we asked you to fill our order (immediate, immediately).
2. The wind blew (furious, furiously), and all ships made for the harbor.
3. I knew it was Jon, for he always tramps so (noisy, noisily).
4. The snow fell (quiet, quietly), and by morning the streets were covered.
5. When the farmer entered the barn, the cattle lowed (soft, softly).
6. Jet planes fly (swifter, more swiftly) than the older models.

Adverb or Adjective?

Some writers do not know whether to use an adverb or an adjective after *linking* (no-action) *verbs*, such as *seem, appear, sound, taste,* and *smell.* You will be sure which is correct if you understand that in some sentences the verbs are action verbs and in other sentences the same verbs are no-action verbs. Since you will be greatly hampered unless you understand this double function—action and no-action—of some verbs, you will do well to study very carefully the following illustrations.

The milk *tastes sour.* (*Tastes* is a no-action verb here. If it were an action verb, the milk would have a tongue and would be tasting with it.)

Kate *tastes* all hot liquids *cautiously* before drinking. (Now this same verb *tastes* is an action verb. Kate has a tongue and is using it.)

Mary feels so *bad* when June is ill. (Is Mary actually feeling or touching? No. Since the subject is not performing any action, *feels* is a no-action verb here.)

Until the lights are turned on, Mary *feels* her way *carefully* through the rooms. (Can you see the difference? Here you get the picture of Mary performing an action—feeling, groping her way through the dark rooms. In this sentence, *feels* is an action verb.)

The following Quick Trick may be helpful in determining whether the verbs in question are action verbs that are modified by adverbs, or whether they are no-action verbs that are followed by adjectives.

❋ QUICK TRICK Lucky Coincidence

Look at the following pairs:

Action	*No-Action*
Adverb	Adjective

Isn't it a coincidence that *action* has the same number of letters as *adverb* and that *no-action* and *adjective* have the same number of letter spaces? This hookup will help you to remember which calls for which.

☐ CLASS PRACTICE 2

Keeping in mind *action—adverb* and *no-action—adjective,* select the correct word in each of the following sentences.

1. A receptionist must have a voice that sounds (clear, clearly) over the telephone.
2. Because of the heat, even our best stenographers looked (dejected, dejectedly).
3. The stenographers looked (dejected, dejectedly) about the office at all the letters that had to be rewritten.
4. Jerry thought that the coffee tasted (strong, strongly).
5. The trucks appeared very (sudden, suddenly) at the entrance to the store.

✔ PROOFREADING PRACTICE 1

If the preceding class practice did what it was supposed to do, you should be able with confidence to make any necessary corrections in these sentences.

1. Your work seems satisfactorily in all respects.
2. The disappointed customer looked angry.
3. Ella said that she felt confidently about winning the contest.
4. I thought she seemed happily to make the appointment.
5. The disappointed customer looked angrily at the bare counters.

Adverb Pitfalls

Three types of adverb errors crop up frequently in speaking and writing. These are (1) placing the adverb in the wrong position in the sentence; (2) misusing *never* for *not;* and (3) using double negatives.

Position of Adverbs   An adverb should be placed as near as possible to the word it modifies. Failure to do this may cause the meaning of a sentence to be obscured or changed entirely. For instance:

Only my boss sold his car last week. (Nobody else sold a car, only my boss. The car dealers must have had a poor week.)

My *only* boss sold his car last week. (Lucky me! Some people have several bosses, but I have only one.)

My boss *only* sold his car last week. (He didn't trade it in, polish it, repair it, or anything except *sell* it.)

My boss sold *only* his car last week. (He didn't sell his house, his ring, his clothes— only his car.)

My boss sold his *only* car last week. (Some people have two or three cars, but my boss owned only one.)

My boss sold his car *only* last week. (It was just last week that he sold his car.)

THE FRAMEWORK OF EFFECTIVE COMMUNICATION

 PROOFREADING PRACTICE 2

Yes, correct placement of the adverb is a help in making a message clear. To express precise meanings, what changes would you make in the following sentences?

1. After payday, Pierre has a cent hardly to his name.
2. This is the first time I have met him only.
3. I knew the dessert was a success when Tami took three helpings alone.
4. The building lot was not even sold for $8000.
5. We just expect to leave in five minutes.

"Never" and "Not"   Both *never* and *not* are adverbs, but their meanings are quite different. *Never* means "not ever; at no time; not in any degree, way, or condition." It is a strong word.

We have *never* offered a special discount to any of our customers.

Not is simply a word that expresses negation. *Never* is used all too frequently and incorrectly instead of *not*. For instance:

We have *not* received your cheque. (Not "We *never* received your cheque.")

Mr. Hanley did *not* order us to arrange the names geographically. (Not "Mr. Hanley *never* ordered us . . . .")

Double Negatives   *Scarcely, only, hardly, but,* and *never* are negative in meaning; and *no other negative* should be used with them. For example:

It is so foggy that you *can scarcely* see the white lines on the road. (Not *you cannot scarcely* . . .)

I *have only* one comment to make. (Not *haven't only* . . .)

Why *doesn't* the manager *ever* use the front entrance? (Or "Why *does* the manager *never* . . ." but not "Why *doesn't* the manager *never* . . .")

☐ CLASS PRACTICE 3

Select the correct words in these sentences. Remember that your aim is to avoid double negatives and to use *never* and *not* appropriately.

1. I couldn't (help but think, help thinking) of all the hours Mr. Baird spends on his work.
2. Alice said that she (wasn't, was) scarcely sixteen when she graduated from high school.
3. You (did not tell, never told) us to ship C.O.D.
4. Roy (didn't earn but, earned but) $400 last summer.
5. Diane (hasn't, has), according to Joe, hardly a relative left.
6. I (never said, did not say) that it was true.
7. Mr. Harper (didn't give, gave) only $5 to the Community Chest.

And I tell you we don't NEED no set of grammar books.

Ben Roth Agency

Adverb and Adjective Confusions

The word pairs that you will study in this section are sources of frequent errors. You may be helped in using them by remembering that, in each pair, the first word is an adjective; the second, an adverb.

Sure, Surely; Real, Really. The choice of *sure* or *surely*, or of *real* or *really*, depends on whether you need an adjective or an adverb. *Sure* and *real* are adjectives; *surely* and *really* are adverbs. For rapid selection of the correct word, note the following Quick Trick:

  QUICK TRICK Substitute "certainly" or "very"

Remember this: If you can substitute the word *certainly* or *very*, the correct word is *surely* or *really*. *Certainly* and *very* end in *y*, and so do *surely* and *really*. If you cannot make the substitution, use *sure* or *real*. For example:

You *surely* have been a success here. (*Surely* is correct because you can say *you certainly have been . . . .*)

Mr. Sanders has a *real* affection for his friends. (*Real*, not *really*, is correct because you would not say he has a *very* affection.)

Good, Well. *Good* is the adjective and *well* is the adverb, except when referring to health. If the question "How?" can be answered, use *well;* if not, use *good.* However, when speaking of health, always use *well.* Say, "I don't feel *well* (not *good*)." To illustrate:

Is this a *good* time to ask about a salary increase? (*Good* is an adjective modifying the noun *time.* It does not answer the question "How?")

The Addressograph is now working *well.* (Working how? *Well.*)

You do not look *well* today. (Referring to health, use *well.*)

Some, Somewhat. *Some* is an adjective and *somewhat* is an adverb. A Quick Trick will help you decide which to use.

✳ QUICK TRICK   Substitute "A Little Bit"

Use *somewhat* if you can substitute the words *"a little bit";* otherwise, use *some.*

Lillian was *somewhat* hesitant about asking for an appointment. (She was *a little bit* hesitant.)

I should like to order *some* stationery for my own use. (*Some,* because *a little bit* cannot be substituted.)

Most, Almost. *Most* is an adjective, the superlative form of *much* or *many.* *Almost* is an adverb meaning "not quite" or "very nearly."

Before I knew it, we were *almost* there. (We were *not quite* or *very nearly* there.)

Most employees have spent *almost* all their pay shortly after they receive it. (Many, more, *most* employees have spent *very nearly* all their pay . . . .)

Do not fall into the error of using *most* as a contraction for *almost.*

☐ CLASS PRACTICE 4

To fix in your mind the differences between the pairs discussed in this section, select the correct words in the following sentences.

1. The (real, really) story is (real, really) shocking.
2. Bill has (most, almost) finished (most, almost) of his work.
3. (Some, Somewhat) typists are (some, somewhat) careless about proofreading.
4. The (good, well) secretary performs (good, well) even under trying circumstances.
5. You are (sure, surely) justified in making a complaint when you are (sure, surely) of your facts.
6. (Good, Well) work cannot be done (good, well) when the worker is not feeling (good, well).

✔ PROOFREADING PRACTICE 3

Here you have an opportunity to find out whether you really know what you need to know about using adjectives and adverbs and about avoiding double negatives. Make the necessary corrections. If you make a mistake, be sure that you study carefully the point that you evidently do not understand.

1. Catherine is wearing a real pretty dress today.
2. Did you notice that Joan couldn't help but smile at Cam's foolish antics?
3. If you do not feel good, ask for permission to go home.
4. Ron complains that he has learned scarcely anything in that course.
5. Mr. St. Cyr's letters are some longer than Mr. Cabot's.
6. It's sure a good thing for you that you checked those figures.

Communication Problems

Application Exercises

A ■

Before you select the correct words in the following sentences, review all the topics presented in this unit. Write your answers on a separate sheet of paper.

1 The experienced mason spreads cement (even, evenly).
2 We were (sure, surely) glad to see Mr. Acton's secretary return to the office.
3 The sale was so successful that the grocer (has, hasn't) scarcely a pound of sugar left.
4 Bess (only needs, needs only) ten more points to win the contest.
5 Yvette felt the cloth (careful, carefully) before making her purchase.
6 Mr. Harkin's reply was that he (had, hadn't) only one comment to make.
7 Mr. Nash is (real, really) delighted that you are able to come to work.
8 At the camp, fresh milk was delivered (regular, regularly).
9 Rufus always tastes hot food (cautious, cautiously) before taking a mouthful.
10 Such an arrangement (could, couldn't) hardly satisfy even the best of employers.
11 Our supervisor can do all the office jobs very (good, well).
12 Edith said that the coffee tasted (bitter, bitterly).
13 There (are, aren't) but five more days before Christmas.
14 Bad news seems to travel (quicker, more quickly) than good news.
15 Frances looked (beautiful, beautifully) in her new spring outfit.

B ■

Follow the usual directions.

1 Danny, along with two other boys, was selected to represent the purchasing department.
2 Are the messenger's bicycles their own property?
3 That house needs a coat of paint very much.

4 Who did you ask for the key to my supply room?

5 Mr. Exeter is one of those men who are conscientious about completing their assignments on time.

6 The boss had no criticism of the efficiency of we personal shoppers.

7 In the files were the data for the specifications.

8 We checkers felt badly about the error.

9 My salary has been risen twice in the six months I have worked here.

10 Because the announcer does not talk clear, I miss much of the news.

11 Three-quarters of the mechanics were in no condition to work in that intense heat.

12 Both Sam and myself need to use a calculator.

13 My plan is really much more simpler than it sounds.

14 Almost all clerks will give you the best of service.

15 About four o'clock, the important records are lain in the safe.

C ■

If a word represented by a blank within the sentence should be an adjective, write "adj." on your paper; if an adverb, write "adv."

1 In some situations, Henry does not act very _____.

2 We were glad we sent for the new doctor. He looked _____.

3 We can _____ complete the job by noon today.

4 It is no wonder that Pat looks tired; he has been working _____ all day.

5 Ray felt _____ when he received his report card.

6 The children on our street play quite _____.

7 Angela was _____ sorry to leave your employ, Mr. Rowe.

8 For shipment overseas, be sure to pack large boxes _____.

9 The half-starved dog looks _____ at the side of beef.

10 Don't feel too _____ about making that error.

Word Study

A ■

Words often confused: disburse, disperse; equable, equitable.

B ■

Match each word in column A with the term in column B that is nearest it in meaning.

A		*B*	
1	repetitious	a	with rainbowlike colors
2	iridescent	b	enduring
3	obscure	c	unreal
4	permanent	d	transitory
5	axiomatic	e	monotonous doing or saying
		f	critical
		g	indistinct
		h	self-evident

C ■

How are each of these words spelled when *ed* is added?

1	admit	**3**	develop	**5**	refer
2	acquaint	**4**	appall	**6**	embarrass

Communication in Action: *Grooming*

There was an unfortunate occurrence in your office yesterday. One of the newer office workers was sent home because she had arrived with her hair in curlers and a scarf over her head. It has always been an unwritten rule that both men and women in your office dress in an acceptable manner for business. Prepare a one-minute talk on one phase of good grooming: makeup, appropriate clothing, matching colors in dress, grooming accessories, cleanliness, men's wear, and so on.

UNIT □ 21

Prepositions

By way of definition, a *preposition* is a connecting word that shows the relationship between a noun or a pronoun (called the *object of the preposition*) and some other word in the sentence.

> We received the news *from* him *by* telephone. (The preposition *from* shows the relationship between the pronoun *him* and the noun *news; by* relates *telephone* to *received.*)

Remember, too, that a preposition is always followed by a noun or a pronoun and that the preposition and this object of the preposition, together with any modifiers, are called a *prepositional phrase.*

> We met a shaggy dog *on the way.* (The preposition *on,* the noun *way,* and the adjective *the* compose the prepositional phrase.)

There are, however, additional facts that you should know in order to avoid errors in using prepositions. To help you recognize prepositions, study the following list of those in common use.

about	before	by	like	to
above	below	except	of	under
after	beside	for	off	up
against	between	from	on	upon
among	but (meaning	in	out of	until
at	"except")	into	over	with

Words Requiring Certain Prepositions

Certain words require specific prepositions following them. Other words require one preposition for one meaning and an entirely different preposition in another situation. For example:

abide *by* a decision	*But:*	abide *with* a person
conform *to*	*But:*	in conformity *with* or *to*
convenient *to* (near at hand)	*But:*	convenient *for* (suitable)
enter *upon* duties	*But:*	enter *into* agreements
wait *for* someone	*But:*	wait *on* a sick person
in compliance *with*		inferior or superior *to*

Now study these word combinations that are used frequently in business communications:

Agree with (a person), *to* (a plan). Use *agree with* when the object of the preposition is a person; use *agree to* when the object is not a person; as:

Mr. Taylor *agreed with* the other members of the committee.

Mr. Taylor *agreed to* the proposal made by the committee.

Angry with (persons), *at* (things or conditions). Use *angry with* when the object of the preposition is a person; use *angry at* when the object is not a person. For instance:

Are you *angry with* me or *with* the other girls?

I get so *angry at* my machine when I make an error.

Part from (a person), *with* (a thing). Use *part from* when the object of the preposition is a person; use *part with* when the object is not a person.

Naida *parted from* Ben at the bus stop.

Sue hates to *part with* her stationery.

Discrepancy in (one thing), *between* (two things), *among* (more than two things). Use *discrepancy in* when the object of the preposition is singular; use *discrepancy between* when the object denotes exactly two in number. To illustrate:

Did you note any *discrepancy in* the Polaris report?

There is a *discrepancy between* your total and mine.

In Regard to; With Regard to; As Regards. The three phrases are equally correct. It makes no difference whether you write *in regard to the plan, with regard to the plan,* or *as regards the plan.* The common error is the use of *regards* with *in* or *with.*

We should like to talk with you *with regard* (or *in regard*) to your proposal. (Not *with regards* or *in regards.*)

As regards personnel policies, Mr. Ames has no authority. (This is correct because both words—*as* and *regards*—end in *s*.)

Different from; Identical with; Plan to; Retroactive to. No tips can be given to help you master the correct prepositions in the first three phrases. You will have to go over them again and again and plant them firmly in your mind. Perhaps you will be helped by knowing that *retroactive* means "extending to a prior time." Before you start to memorize, study the following illustrations.

Your ideas about proper dress are very *different from* mine. (Not *different than*.)

Bob's problem is *identical with* mine. (Not *identical to*.)

You should *plan to* join some of the office activities. (Not *plan on* joining.)

Is the directive *retroactive to* January 1? (Not *retroactive from*.)

CLASS PRACTICE 1

The following sentences should help you in using the particular prepositions selected for special study. Select the appropriate words or phrases.

1. Did you see how angry Mr. Gomez was (with, at) the way Sally treated that customer?
2. The blouse Ella bought is identical (with, to) Jean's.
3. Our city editor plans (to put, on putting) out a special edition.
4. Why isn't the salary increase retroactive (to, from) May 15?
5. Mr. Burke wishes to see you (in regard, in regards) to taking inventory.
6. Has your mother ever parted (from, with) any of the letters your father wrote to her?
7. The discrepancy (in, between) what Mr. Hayes says and what he does is very apparent.
8. In what way is Lee's personality different (from, than) Jane's?

 PROOFREADING PRACTICE 1

Now look for errors in preposition usage in these sentences.

1. Our old product is much inferior to the new one.
2. Mr. Emmet becomes so angry at people who do not listen to him!
3. Do you agree with accepting her as a member in good standing?
4. Lucy's boss is not planning on making any promotions just yet.
5. All employees should be glad to conform with established policies.
6. The second statement is different than the first.
7. In a democracy, citizens are supposed to abide with any fair decision that is made.
8. At the end of the year, most teachers are loath to part with their pupils.
9. Gracious compliance to office rules will be appreciated by your employer.
10. In his younger days, Mr. Ellis was employed for $15 a week.

Troublesome Prepositions

In order to use prepositions appropriately, you must sometimes make a choice between two prepositions. Then, too, there are times when a preposition should be expressed and other times when that same preposition should be omitted. This introduction may make preposition usage sound more difficult than it really is, as you will soon discover.

Between, Among. *Between* is commonly used when referring to *two* persons, places, or objects; *among,* when referring to *more than two.*

> *Between* you and me, I think he should apologize.
>
> The work was divided *between* the two clerks.
>
> The work was divided *among* the three clerks.

Between also may express the relation of one thing to each and all of several related things; as:

> An agreement has just been reached *between* our company and the retailers, jobbers, and wholesalers handling our product.

Beside, Besides. *Beside* means *by the side of,* and *besides* means *in addition to.*

> Stack the finished letters *beside* the tray for outgoing mail. (Meaning *by the side of* the tray.)
>
> Who, *besides* Bill, is being promoted? (Meaning who, *in addition to Bill.*)

Inside, Outside. Do not use *of* after *inside* or *outside.* When referring to time, use *within,* not *inside of.* For example:

> You will find the receptionist's desk just *inside* the door. (Not *inside of.*)
>
> Do you do much work *outside* office hours? (Not *outside of.*)
>
> May we have your cheque *within* a week. (Not *inside of.*)

All, Both. After *all* or *both* use *of* only when *all* or *both* is followed by a *pronoun.* Omit *of* if either word is followed by a *noun;* thus:

> *All of* us are eager to make *all* the money we can. (*All of* is followed by the pronoun *us,* but only *all* precedes the noun *money.*)
>
> *Both of* them reported that *both* the machines were in need of repair. (*Both of them,* but *both the machines.*)

At, To; In, Into. *At* and *in* denote position. *To* and *into* signify motion.

> Mr. King was *at* his desk early this morning. (No action is involved here.)
>
> Mr. King went *to* his office early this morning. (Can you see Mr. King moving toward his office?)

The lost letter was *in* the wrong tray, as I discovered when I went *into* the office. (The letter was right there *in* position. I was moving; therefore, I went *into* the office.)

NOTE: When either *at* or *in* refers to a place, use *in* for larger places; *at* for smaller; as:

Rita lives *in* Vancouver and works *at* the Bayshore Inn.

Behind, In Back Of. Use *behind*, not *in back of*. Oddly enough, *in front of* is correct. For instance:

Mr. Higgins likes best to work *behind* closed doors, so his secretary stands guard *in front of* his office. (Odd language, English, isn't it? *In back of* is incorrect, but *in front of* is correct.)

From, Off. *From* is used when referring to persons; *off*, when referring to things; as:

Borrow a pen *from* Jim, if you can get him to take his feet *off* the desk long enough to lend you one. (*From Jim*—person; *off the desk*—thing.)

☐ CLASS PRACTICE 2

By selecting the correct words in the following sentences, you can discover just how well you understand the appropriate use of prepositions.

1. Was Mr. Hake (at, to) the bank when you went (in, into) town yesterday?
2. Nobody (beside, besides) Patrick would stand (beside, besides) Mr. Ryan in the controversy.
3. (Both of, Both) us realize that (all of, all) the other offices close during the very hot weather.
4. Take some money (from, off) the table and buy some coffee (from, off) Jake.
5. Pete's desk is just (behind, in back of) David's.
6. Personality is said to be (outside, outside of) a person, while character is (inside, inside of) a person.
7. Just (between, among) the two of us, do you think Lora is popular (between, among) her many acquaintances?

Preposition Illiteracies

Certain preposition errors are indicative of lack of education or of gross carelessness. If you want to speak standard English, you should recognize these errors and avoid making them.

Of, Have. *Of* is a preposition; *have* is a verb. Writing or saying *of* when *have* is correct is a common error. As with many other errors, this one may be charged to mispronunciation. For instance, people say, "You shuduv paid your bill." Is it any wonder that the written sentence frequently is, "You should of (for *have*) paid your bill"? Think this over and remember to use *have*, not *of*, when that verb should be used.

Where. Remember that neither *at* nor *to* should be used with *where*. For example:

Do you know where Alex is? (Not *where Alex is at*.)

Where in the world did that girl go? (Not *Where . . . did that girl go to?*)

Help. Do not use *from* after *help*.

Edith cannot help asking all these questions. (Not *cannot help from asking . . . .*)

It is evident that Henry just cannot help throwing his money away. (Not *cannot help from throwing . . . .*)

Opposite, Opposite To. Do not use *to* after *opposite* unless you mean *contrary*.

Arthur's desk is opposite mine. (Meaning *on the other side of*)

His beliefs are opposite to mine. (Meaning *contrary*)

Off. Never use *of* or *from* after the word *off*.

Did you push the atlas off the shelf? (Never *off of*.)

You may take the stapler off my desk. (Never *off of*.)

Borrow a dollar from Judith. (Never *off from Judith* or *off of Judith*.)

☐ CLASS PRACTICE 3

The following practice sentences will help you to learn to avoid preposition illiteracies.

1. If you know where Mr. Collins' folder (is, is at), please get it for me.
2. Why did you shove the packages (off, off of) the receiving table?
3. Eva could hardly (help, help from) laughing at the man's silly question.
4. The apartment house (opposite, opposite to) the Schultzes has some vacant suites.
5. Donald's entry should not (have, of) won the prize.
6. You can get the data (off, from, off of) Mr. Flynn's secretary.

✔ PROOFREADING PRACTICE 2

To consolidate your learning with regard to (1) choosing the appropriate preposition and (2) avoiding serious preposition errors, correct the errors in these sentences.

1. Your choice lies between Sue, Ann, and her.
2. Everybody borrows paper clips off of Grover.
3. The customer was so rude that I could scarcely help from losing my temper.
4. There are many men besides us who are loyal to the company for which they work.
5. You should of consulted the post office guide.
6. Do you think I can find Mr. Keane to home today?
7. Surely, more than one person in this office knows where the petty cash box is at!
8. Both the plans are satisfactory to all of us.
9. Go into the private office, and just inside of the door you will see the new table.
10. We will let you know our decision inside of a week.

Communication Problems

Application Exercises

A ■

On the basis of your study of the topics presented in this unit, make your selection of the correct words in the following sentences. Use a separate sheet of paper.

1 Your debit total should be identical (to, with) the credit total.
2 We shall divide the doughnuts (between, among) the two of us.
3 Why were you so angry (at, with) Mr. Lynd this morning?
4 (Beside, Besides) Gavin, two other salesmen exceeded their quotas.
5 One of the covenants of the League of Nations was that nations would not enter (upon, into) private agreements.
6 Had I known how hot the weather was going to be, I wouldn't (of, have) gone.
7 If Sonja could have a new machine, she would gladly part (from, with) her old one.
8 He answered from his special hiding place (inside, inside of) the barn.
9 Discrepancies (in, between) Bill's and Jack's statements were obvious to all of us.
10 Would it be convenient (for, to) you to see me this morning?
11 Did you mean that (all, all of) the envelopes must be retyped?
12 When Mr. Loft rushes through the office, I often wonder where (he is going, he is going to).
13 We are writing you (in regards, in regard) to your request for an extension of credit.
14 Isabel can be found anywhere except (to, at) her desk.
15 Kay is so punctual that no one ever has to wait (on, for) her.

B ■

If a sentence is correct, write "OK." If incorrect, write the correction.

1 Nylon does not feel very softly to the touch.
2 On days like this, I wish I were lying on the beach.
3 In our office, one clerk does nothing beside filing.
4 Edwin receives a higher salary than him.
5 There is the man who we thought was too ill to work.
6 Had we not been delayed, we surely would of been here sooner.
7 Are the Baileys' moving their machinery to the new location?
8 Our best customers, Mr. Bell and he, have gone out of business.
9 All of the telegrams received this morning contained cancellations.
10 This vase is expensive because it is made of hand-blown glass.
11 The Boy Scout troop are preparing for the court of awards.
12 When the parade passed our building, Mr. Adams was talking to Henry and myself.
13 Some of the applicants for the position of head scientist is married.
14 John is quite different from his brother, isn't he?
15 To which of our artists, Eric or he, did I give the layout?

C ■

On a separate piece of paper, supply the specific prepositions and word combinations that are used appropriately with the words in italics.

1 Your December pay cheque will be substantially larger because, as you know, your salary increase is *retroactive* _____ July 1.
2 Occasions that call for casual dress are quite *different* _____ those where formal dress is appropriate.
3 Mr. Dunn's temper contributes nothing to a pleasant office atmosphere. Very often he becomes *angry* _____ the members of his staff and _____ the many small, but necessary, interruptions.
4 The Secretary of State refused to make any comment _____ *regard* _____ the royal commission.

Word Study

A ■

Words often confused: pact, packed; facetious, fictitious.

B ■

Mary described the singer whom she had heard last evening with, "I enjoyed listening to him. His voice is so *redundant*." What did she mean to say?

C ■

The following sentence contains five misspelled words. Find them. How should they be spelled? "It was a privilige to recomend him for the goverment begining bookeeping position."

Communication in Action: *Understanding Big Words*

You may have to use a dictionary to understand the following passage. Can you summarize in two sentences the major idea of the paragraph?

A few years ago, the market for children's toys was inundated with cheap, inferior items. Because it was virtually impossible to exercise any control over the content of the original source materials in these toys, the plethora of malfunctioning and dangerous goods that infiltrated the market caused great concern to those involved in protecting the consumer. A standard had to be set, and testing procedures had to be established that would prevent any recurrence of this most upsetting situation. Finally, procedures were implemented whereby all manufacturers wishing to sell children's toys in this market had to submit samples for rigid testing before licences to produce those particular toys would be issued.

UNIT □ 22

Conjunctions

A conjunction is a word used to connect words (Maria *and* Sandra), phrases (on the blotter *or* in the tray), or clauses (Joe was very tired *because* he had been running.). There are three types of conjunctions: *coordinate, correlative,* and *subordinate.*

In this unit you will study how coordinate and correlative conjunctions are used, and you also will become familiar with the more common subordinate conjunctions as a prelude to your study of punctuation principles in Part 5.

Coordinate Conjunctions

Coordinate conjunctions connect *like* grammar elements, such as: two or more *words,* two or more *phrases,* or two or more *clauses.* Study the following list of some of the most common coordinate conjunctions.

accordingly	hence	now
also	however	or
and	likewise	so
as well as	moreover	so then
besides	neither	therefore
but	nevertheless	thus
consequently	nor	wherefore
either	notwithstanding	yet

A study of conjunctions used in business correspondence would probably show that the most frequently used coordinate conjunctions are *and, but, or,* and *nor.*

Correlative Conjunctions

Correlative conjunctions are conjunctions used in pairs:

both . . . . and	not only . . . . . . but
either . . . . or	not only . . . . . but also
neither . . . . . . nor	whether . . . . . . or

As with coordinate conjunctions, correlatives connect words, phrases, or clauses of equal value. Note that *or* is used with *either* and *nor* is used with *neither*.

Either an eraser *or* an ink eradicator may be used to correct the error.

Neither Tom *nor* his sister knew we were coming.

Subordinate Conjunctions

Subordinate conjunctions connect clauses of *unequal* rank or value, as illustrated in the following sentences.

Please type this letter *whenever* you have time. (*Whenever you have time* is a subordinate clause. It does not make sense without the rest of the sentence.)

While we are about it, we may as well cover all the machines. (This sentence starts with the subordinate clause *while we are about it.*)

Since we are junior clerks, we must expect to do routine work. (The subordinate clause is *since we are junior clerks.*)

Some of the common subordinate conjunctions are listed here. Study them carefully, because you will need to recognize them in order to punctuate accurately.

after	inasmuch as	though
although	in case that	till
as	in order that	unless
as if	on condition that	until
as soon as	otherwise	when
as though	provided (*not* providing)	whenever
because	since	where
before	so that	whereas
even if	supposing	wherever
for	than	whether
how	that	while
if	then	why

CLASS PRACTICE 1

Can you recognize the different kinds of conjunctions? Find out by selecting the conjunction in each of the following sentences and classifying it as *coordinate*, *correlative*, or *subordinate*.

1. Is this your own work, or did someone else do it for you?
2. When Mr. Hyde enters the office, everybody becomes very busy.
3. Bring me both the originals and the carbons of the letters to salesmen.
4. If Henry is late just once more, he will find himself out of a job.
5. Branch offices are located in Victoria, Calgary, and Halifax.
6. Be sure that all corrections appear not only on the original but also on all carbons.

Parallel Structure

Ideas of equal importance should be expressed in parallel structure; for example, a noun should be paralleled with a noun, an adjective with an adjective, a phrase with a phrase, and so on.

> Michael works quickly and quietly. (Coordinate conjunction *and* connects adverbs *quickly* and *quietly*.)

> He can be found at his desk or in Mr. Fry's office. (Coordinate conjunction *or* connects phrases.)

Because parallel structure (sometimes called "parallelism") must be used with coordinate and correlative conjunctions, now is the time to learn the principle of parallel structure. It is part of the background you will need when you study business correspondence.

With Coordinate Conjunctions   First, review the coordinate conjunctions listed at the beginning of this unit. Then learn that coordinate conjunctions must connect *like* elements. For instance, if *and* has a noun before it, then a noun or pronoun must come after it. Just remember that the elements that are written before and after a coordinate conjunction must match. Study the following illustrations and explanations.

> *Poor:*   Martin is honest, capable, and ought to be promoted. (Before the *and* there are two adjectives—*honest* and *capable;* but after the *and,* there is a verb—*ought to be promoted.* The elements connected by the coordinate conjunction do not match.)

> *Better:*   Martin is honest, capable, and worthy of promotion. (This is a parallel structure, because *and* connects three adjectives.)

> *Better:*   Martin is honest and capable, and he ought to be promoted. (Here is another matching possibility—independent clause, *and,* independent clause.)

> *Poor:*   Our firm is noted for its excellent reputation and because it treats the employees fairly. (Do you see that the elements connected by the coordinate conjunction do not match? The construction is prepositional phrase, *and,* subordinate clause.)

> *Better:*   Our firm is noted for its excellent reputation and for its fair treatment of employees. (Now a prepositional phrase is matched with another prepositional phrase.)

☐ CLASS PRACTICE 2

In the following pairs of sentences, one represents a violation of parallel structure; the other is correct. Select the correct sentence and tell why it is correct.

1. Our office is well ventilated and well lighted.
   Our office is well ventilated and with plenty of light.
2. The executive told us that we should learn the vocabulary of the business and to keep a shorthand notebook of these words.
   The executive told us to learn the vocabulary of the business and to keep a shorthand notebook of these words.
3. Finding a vacancy is one thing, but preparing for an interview is quite another.
   Finding a vacancy is one thing, but to prepare for an interview is quite another.
4. A girl may think she is unattractive if she has big ears, flat feet, or with a pug nose.
   A girl may think she is unattractive if she has big ears, flat feet, or a pug nose.

With Correlative Conjunctions Remember that correlative conjunctions are conjunctions used in *pairs*. Parallel structure demands that whatever kind of element is written *after* the *first* member of the pair must match the element that is written *after* the *second* member of the pair. Note the following illustrations:

Poor: I *both* need the originals *and* the carbons. (*Both . . . and* is a correlative conjunction. In this sentence there is a verb after *both* and a noun after *and.* Thus there is no match.)

Better: I need *both* the originals *and* the carbons. (Now there is a match—*both,* noun; *and,* noun.)

Poor: You must *either* go to the post office *or* to the bank. (The structure here is not parallel because *either* is followed by a verb and *or* is followed by a prepositional phrase. There is no match.)

Better: You must go *either* to the post office *or* to the bank. (Here is parallel structure—*either,* prepositional phrase; *or,* prepositional phrase.)

☐ CLASS PRACTICE 3

As in Class Practice 2, one of the following pairs of sentences is correct; the other, incorrect. Select the correct sentence and tell why it is correct.

1. That department store has neither a good stock of dresses nor hats.
   That department store has a good stock of neither dresses nor hats.
2. Miss Cone is one of those women who talk either too much or too little.
   Miss Cone is one of those women who either talk too much or too little.

3. Ronald has neither the personality nor has he the background for that job.
   Ronald has neither the personality nor the background for that job.
4. Jack was undecided whether he should take the test now or to wait until next week.
   Jack was undecided whether to take the test now or to wait until next week.

 PROOFREADING PRACTICE 1

If you thoroughly understand parallel structure with coordinate and correlative conjunctions, you should be able to find the errors in the following sentences. When you make a correction, tell why you make it.

1. I agreed to accept the increase and that I would try to be worthy of Mr. Dunn's confidence.
2. The wastebaskets have been emptied by neither the office boy nor the porter.
3. Mr. Dean is the man who managed the business and later rising to the position of president.
4. I find writing advertising copy is more interesting than to work with figures.
5. Every business person not only must be courteous but also tactful.
6. Our typing teacher told us to double-space and that we should leave wide margins.
7. The new salesman proved himself to be not only likable but also a man who was very capable.

Conjunction Pitfalls

Many errors in grammar occur when a speaker or writer, faced with a choice of conjunctions, is unable to select the one that properly conveys his meaning. Another pitfall is occasioned by being uncertain whether to use a conjunction or a preposition. If you would avoid these pitfalls, *do not use the following:*

"And" for "But." Whenever there is a contrasting or opposing idea, no matter how faint, use the conjunction *but*—not *and.*

> You are young, *but* I am old.

> I should like to go with you, *but* I must finish this work.

"And Which" or "And Who (Whom)." When using *which* or *who,* the conjunction *and* is superfluous; do not use it. Remember to use *who* to refer to persons; *which* to refer to objects, and *that* to refer to persons, animals, or objects.

> In the morning mail was the announcement, *which* made Andrea's engagement official. (Not *and which.*)

> Yesterday I met the head salesperson, *whom* you have often mentioned. (Not *and whom.*)

"Because," "Where," or "Like"—for "That." Say "the reason is *that*," not "the reason is *because*." Say you "read in the paper *that*," not you "read in the paper *where*." Say you "pretend *that*," not you "pretend *like*."

The reason the girl failed is *that* she was poorly prepared.

Did you read in the paper *that* our company is going to expand?

Pretend *that* you do not see her.

"Being that"—for "Since," "Because," or "As." Using *being that* for *since, because,* or *as* is not acceptable. There is no such conjunction.

Because the ability to speak well is so important, you should devote more time to English grammar. (Not *being that the ability* . . . .)

A caller entered; and, *as* I was nearest the door, I greeted him. (Not *being that I was* . . . .)

"Like"—for "As," "As If," or "As Though." When like is used as a preposition, it takes an object—a noun or a pronoun. It should not be used as a conjunction to introduce a clause. Therefore, do not use *like* when *as, as if,* or *as though* would be correct.

Wardens taste good, *as* a cigarette should. (Not *like*.)

You type *as if* you were angry. (Not *like you were* angry.)

It looks *as though* it would be a good day tomorrow. (Not *like it would be* . . . .)

The children look *like* their mother and me. (This is correct. Here *like* is used properly—as a preposition.)

"Without" or "Except"—for "Unless." This error is the same type as that discussed in the preceding paragraph. Do not use the prepositions *without* and *except* when the conjunction *unless* is called for.

Do not make any changes *unless* you tell me first. (Not *without you tell* me . . . . However, *without* would be used correctly as a preposition if the sentence read: "Do not make any changes *without telling me first.*")

You may not leave *unless* Mr. Pike gives you permission. (Not *except Mr. Pike gives* . . . . Or, the sentence could be written: "You may not leave *without Mr. Pike's permission.*")

"As . . . As"—for "So . . . As." The correlative *as . . . as* should be used when the statement made is *positive;* such as, "Helen transcribes just *as* fast *as* I do." The correlative *so . . . as* should be used when the statement made is *negative;* such as, "Helen does *not* transcribe *so* fast *as* I do."

This duplicated report is *as* clear *as* it possibly could be.

Duplicated reports have *never* been *so* clear *as* they should be.

☐ CLASS PRACTICE 4

So many points of usage have been discussed that you should take time to review them before you work this class practice. After reviewing the seven conjunction pitfalls, select the correct words in these sentences.

1. Mr. Ames looked (like he was, as if he were) keeping his temper with difficulty.
2. The reason for the change in position is (because, that) business now demands desirable personality traits.
3. Do not leave (without, unless) you first turn out the lights.
4. Pretend (that, like) you do not notice the new clerk's nervousness.
5. I intended to close the books this morning, (and, but) Mr. Bohn needed me for some special work.
6. Edna's car was not equipped with snow tires, (and which, which) most drivers use.
7. I read in the daily bulletin (that, where) no shift will work on Saturday.
8. (Being that, Since) the bus would be a little late, we decided to have some lunch.

✔ PROOFREADING PRACTICE 2

This is the "proof of the pudding." If you can easily make the necessary corrections in these sentences, you will have little difficulty with your home study of principles of conjunction usage.

1. You look like your mother did when she was young.
2. Are you pretending like you're too busy to talk to me?
3. Outside our office there is a new sign, and which is the gift of the employees.
4. You are not so familiar with conjunctions as you are with verbs.
5. Being that your quotation was too high, the contract has been awarded to Harvey.
6. The reason Vera went home was because she was ill.

Communication Problems

Application Exercises

A ▪

After you have studied every point that was made in this unit, select the correct words in the following sentences. Write your answers on a separate sheet of paper.

1 Next Saturday (either we shall go, we shall go either) fishing or swimming.
2 The package was delivered to the Hotel Royal, (and which, which) was not the correct address.

3 Miss Alison (neither wants, wants neither) your help nor your pity.

4 We are going to take inventory tomorrow, (and, but) a more important job is scheduled for today.

5 The reason I refused to buy the house was (because, that) it was too expensive.

6 Writing a speech is sometimes easier than (to deliver, delivering) it before an audience.

7 I saw in the notice near the clock (that, where) the plant will close during the first week in August.

8 Miss Dane always (pretends like, pretends that) she is very efficient.

9 (It is our policy not, It is not our policy) to frighten witnesses, but to win their confidence.

10 (Being that, As) his jaw was broken in the accident, a wiring job had to be done.

11 Use that machine (like, as) you were instructed.

12 Our boss enjoys winter sports like sleighing, skiing, and (to skate, skating).

13 Blanton's store will not be able to continue in business (except, unless) there is an upturn in the recession.

14 The cost of building the school was not (as, so) great as was estimated.

15 The studio couch (was neither the, neither was the) regular size nor the right color.

B ■

Write "OK" for any correct sentence. Correct any incorrect sentence.

1 Who is Mr. Phelps interviewing now?

2 I both like to teach and to work in an office.

3 Whom the next president would be was a closely guarded secret.

4 Mr. Blake prefers to deal with Hake & Company rather than they.

5 All the Harrises' children have college degrees.

6 Simon works like he was a machine.

7 The rest of the money have been locked in the safe.

8 Our vice-president's speech was well received.

9 Either of the salutations are correct for this letter.

10 No other duplicator works as well as our old model.

11 The letter I had been looking for was lying under the tray.

12 The reason you make that mistake is because you are not familiar with business reference books.

13 The applause was for the baseball players, Hugh and him.

14 Everyone seems to think that Tom and myself have plenty of time to chat.

15 Roger told me that he read in the confidential report where our company is rated among the top ten.

16 Whomever you suggest will be hired by me.

17 Jan is quiet, ladylike, and should be pleasant to have around.

18 I like my typewriter better than her's.

19 The mob was gathered around the speaker.

20 Is Mr. Beebe a graduate of a four-year college?

C ■

Here is another editing job for you. Revise and rewrite this paragraph.

We strongly urge you to reconsider your decision to decline nomination for the presidency of the Chamber of Commerce. The reason you were selected for the position is because you are the man best qualified for this high office, and which is the most important post in the organization. Knowing you as we do, we feel confident that you would find the work interesting and a challenge. The members of the nominating committee also feel that the Chamber both needs your personal drive and your public-relations experience. May we call on you Monday morning for further discussion?

Word Study

A ■

Words often confused: fate, fete; census, senses.

B ■

Each of the following phrases may be replaced by a single word that conveys the same thought. What are the words?

1	Without meaning to	**4**	Without thinking
2	Of his own free will	**5**	From time to time
3	With great emphasis	**6**	Lost consciousness

C ■

Substitute for the following italicized phonetic spellings the correct spelling of the words.

1 Greek is no longer *taut* in most high schools.
2 As I *fot* my way through the snowbanks, I *thaut* I should miss my bus.
3 North York is one of the five *buros* of Metropolitan Toronto.
4 The police *kot* the fugitive after they had searched the house *thoroly*.
5 As the delivery entrance was closed, my furniture was *brot thru* the *wrot*-iron gates of the front entrance.

Communication in Action: A Club Project

The Women's Club in your company plans to take orders for Christmas trees from employees in the plant. The proceeds are to be used for food baskets to be given to needy families. Write an announcement to go into your monthly employee magazine, describing the why, what, where, when, how, and who (make up your own set of circumstances) for purchasing a tree. Appeal to the employees to purchase their trees from the Club.

PART · 5

Punctuation--
the Writer's
Signals□

In theory, a speaker has many more things "going for him" than does a writer. The speaker can pause to let the audience catch up with a particular thought. He can use a lower tone of voice to indicate that certain words are on a lower level of importance. He can shift his position to show that he is about to introduce a new thought. Actually, though, the experienced writer also has techniques for indicating many of the oral and visual signs that are the property of the speaker. The writer uses punctuation marks—written signs and signals that are as effective as the speaker's pauses, voice inflection, and shifting of position. You will learn how to master these signs and signals as you study the next eight units.

The
Period

In the writing process, the *period* is a full stop, much like a red traffic signal. Knowing when to use this red light, and when not to use it, is very important if you wish to make your written messages clear. To simplify your study of the use of the period, this unit is divided into three main topics: (1) when to use a period, (2) when *not* to use a period, and (3) pitfalls in the use of the period.

Use a Period

A period is used after declarative and imperative sentences, after indirect questions, and after requests phrased as questions.

After Declarative and Imperative Sentences   In order to help you classify sentences, remember a *declarative sentence* is a statement and an *imperative sentence* is a command or a request. A period is used at the end of each.

> The mail has not yet come. (Declarative sentence—it makes a statement.)
> Please bring in the mail. (Imperative sentence—it makes a request.)

After an Indirect Question   An *indirect question* is really a statement, because it rewords a direct question in the speaker's or writer's own words. Therefore, an indirect question requires a period at the end.

> Mr. Ryan asked, "Have the letters been mailed?" (The quoted portion is a direct question, for Mr. Ryan's actual words are used.)
>
> Mr. Ryan asked whether the letters had been mailed. (Indirect question)

After Requests Phrased as Questions   Sometimes a request or a suggestion is written in question form for the sake of courtesy. Such a request or suggestion should end with a period.

> May we have your reply immediately.
>
> Will you please verify this information.

No direct questions are intended here, but to say "Reply to this letter" or simply "Verify this information" would be extremely impolite, as well as abrupt and dictatorial.

☐ CLASS PRACTICE 1

Decide whether or not to use periods to end these sentences:

1. Mr. Doe asked how much I could afford to pay
2. Will you please send us a cheque for your Order No. 434 before the end of the month
3. Can you see the clock from where you sit
4. Will you have your cheque certified before mailing it to us
5. The file you want is in the lowest drawer
6. She asked if you would appear in her place

Do Not Use a Period

Six instances in which periods should *not* be used are the following:

After Headings or Titles A period should not follow any centred heading.

Unit 23: The Period (Chapter heading)

Swiss Family Robinson (Centred title)

After Roman Numerals Written with Names No period should follow a roman numeral used with a name or with a title.

Elizabeth II is surely loved by the British.

I think that Chapter IV is the most exciting chapter in the book.

In tabulations or outlines, however, roman numerals *are* followed by periods, as shown in the skeleton outline below.

After Numbers or Letters Enclosed in Parentheses "Enclosed in parentheses" are the important words in this heading, as illustrated in the following skeleton outline.

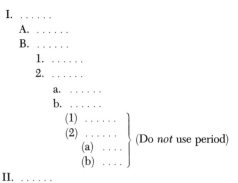

```
I. ......
   A. ......
   B. ......
      1. ......
      2. ......
         a. ......
         b. ......
            (1) ......  ⎫
            (2) ......  ⎬ (Do not use period)
                (a) ....  ⎪
                (b) ....  ⎭
II. ......
```

After Items in Tabulated Lists or in Outlines If the items are incomplete sentences, no periods are used after them.

Unit 23 is divided into the following main parts:
1. When to use a period
2. When not to use a period
3. Period pitfalls

However, if each item is a complete sentence, a period should be used.

The important points for you to remember are these:
1. A period brings the reader to a full stop.
2. Correct uses of the period are part of a writer's stock-in-trade.

After Even Amounts of Dollars   In general writing, do not use a period or a period and two zeros after even amounts of dollars.

The consultant expects to arrive before 10 a.m.

After Even Amounts of Dollars   Except in tabulations, do not use a period or a period and two zeros after even amounts of dollars.

The price of the table is $98.60. The cost to you will be $95 if you send a cheque with your order. (Note $95, *not* $95.00.)

   PROOFREADING PRACTICE 1

The usual class practice is omitted because the points just presented are not very difficult. Now, find whatever errors there may be in the following sentences.

1. The following are headings or titles. Indicate the punctuation you would use.

> The Edge of Night
> *Business English and Communication*
> Use of the Period

2. The prices of the various chairs are $58.40, $78.00, and $98.89.
3. "The Wives of Henry VIII." was an excellent play.
4. We are sending you our cheque for $10, which represents the difference between the $80 due on your account and the $90 cheque you sent us.
5. By now, you know that you learn best when you: (*a.*) study and learn one principle at a time, (*b.*) study all principles before attempting to work a homework assignment, and (*c.*) review frequently.

Period Pitfalls

Using a period when no period is necessary and using a comma when a period is called for are two common errors in punctuation.

The Period Fault   Placing a period at the end of a group of words that rightly belong in a preceding or in a following sentence is called a *period fault*.

Mr. Lloyd stayed at the office until eight o'clock. Hoping thus to get his work done.

Does *hoping thus to get his work done* make sense? No? Then it is not a sentence. (If you need to refresh your memory in selecting "sense" and "no sense" groups of words, turn back to Unit 9.) Here is the sentence written correctly.

Mr. Lloyd stayed at the office until eight o'clock, hoping thus to get his work done.

Condensed Expressions   The use of a period after *condensed expressions*—such as answers to questions or phrases that lead into another thought—is *not* a period fault. These expressions do not rightly belong in another sentence. If a condensed expression is declarative or imperative, it is followed by a period.

Are we planning to reduce our sales staff? Not for a few weeks. (*Not for a few weeks* is the answer to a question. Since it does not belong in another sentence, it can stand alone and is correctly followed by a period.)

One part of our problem has been solved. Now, for the next part. (*Now, for the next part* is a transitional phrase leading into the next topic. It correctly stands alone, although it is not a complete thought.)

The Comma-for-Period Fault   The *comma-for-period fault* is the use of a comma where a period should be used. When this error is made, there is no full stop at the end of a complete, finished thought. Instead, two different thoughts are hitched together. The result is one cloudy message.

Miss Niles is an excellent teacher, she received her education and training at our local university.

If you read this again, you will see that you have two complete "sense" groups; therefore, a period should be placed after *teacher*. (Not a comma.)

✔   PROOFREADING PRACTICE 2

As a test of your understanding of the correct use of a period at the end of a sentence, find any errors in the following sentences. Be sure to explain why you think they are errors.

1. I get so annoyed by that old question of whether the hen or the egg came first?
2. For years we have ordered parts from you, they have always given satisfaction.
3. Please send Mr. Spears the references he requested.
4. Many members of the staff are attending the play tonight, they like comedies.
5. We are returning your affidavit dated June 1. This paper being unsuited to our needs.
6. Will you please fill in and return the enclosed form soon.
7. A last-minute demand for gloves was noted. With suedes and double-woven cottons wanted.

Communication Problems

Application Exercises

A ■

Using a separate sheet of paper, write your selection of the correct alternate in each of the following sentences, together with the reason for your choice. For example, suppose the sentence to be: *Please find the letter from the (S.P.C.A.., S.P.C.A.)* Your answer would look like this:

> *S.P.C.A.* Only one period should be used at the end of a sentence.

1 Mr. Evans asked how I knew the story was true (. ?)
2 According to instructions from the merchandise manager, all coats marked ($150.00, $150) or higher are to be moved to the ($120.00, $120) rack.
3 The package fell into the wastebasket (. ,) (where, Where) it remained until the janitor cleaned the office.
4 You must hurry, for the safe-deposit vaults close at 3:30 (p.m., p.m..)
5 Will you please write us about your procedure for sending statements to customers (. ?)
6 Before Chapter (III., III,) the story was rather dull.
7 The letter had been filed (. ,) Jean could not find it.
8 My supervisor questioned me about the revised price list (. ?)
9 We are extending our store hours (. ,) (although, Although) the increase in business may not justify the increase in overhead.
10 Will you please have your cheque in the mail by noon on Monday (. ?)
11 The customer asked whether the cafeteria was open on Tuesdays (. ?)
12 Will you please return the report to me as soon as you have read it (. ?)
13 We are sending you a cheque for the ($49.00, $49, $49.) due on our order of June 15.
14 Our typist is well satisfied with your carbon paper (. ,) (she, She) has asked us to order twelve more boxes.
15 Before you take that long trip, you should become a member of the (C.A.A.., C.A.A.)

B ■

Some of the following sentences are correct; others are incorrect. On a separate sheet of paper, indicate your corrections and explain why you are making them.

1 Everybody should read instructions. Before proceeding to complete the project.
2 We have decided to engage the services of a C.P.A..
3 You must increase your typing speed, you must work harder than you have been working.
4 Please ship collect. As we do not wish to wait until you investigate our credit references.
5 Will you please return the enclosed papers to me within twenty-four hours after their receipt?

6 Just send a cheque for $46., and the mattress will be shipped immediately.

7 May we have Mr. James' references by Monday of next week?

8 Making decisions takes time, we must wait another week before answering your question.

9 Remember that the price quoted is f.o.b. Montreal.

10 You must master the principles of punctuation. If you wish to paint a clear picture.

11 To carry through the theme of your story, Chapter IX. must be rewritten.

12 May we have your specifications before the bids are advertised.

13 Was George V. the father of Elizabeth II?

14 Our salesman called on Mr. Lane, this customer is very difficult.

15 George III hired Hessian mercenaries to fight the early settlers.

C ■

Clarify the following message by copying and punctuating the paragraph.

In your May 6 letter you made reference to your latest promotional material specifically you asked if we like the new poster design there must have been a slipup somewhere we have not received your new presentation but we are interested in seeing it and are right now very much in need of new ideas may we have the promotion kit by May 15

Word Study

A ■

Words often confused: recent, resent; reference, reverence.

B ■

Choose the correct definition for the italicized word in each of the following sentences.

1 An *idiom* is an expression: (a) that is used by illiterate persons, (b) that cannot be explained by the usual rules of grammar, (c) that is now considered obsolete.

2 An *antecedent* is a word: (a) that immediately precedes another word, (b) that has an opposite meaning, (c) to which another word refers.

3 A *suffix* is: (a) one or more syllables joined at the beginning of a word to change its meaning, (b) one or more syllables joined at the end of a word to change its meaning, (c) the second element of a compound word.

4 A *direct question* is: (a) a question in its original form, (b) an impertinent question, (c) a request in question form.

C ■

Which of the following place names are misspelled?

1	Fredricton, N.B.	**4**	Winnipeg, Man.
2	Charlotetown, P.E.I.	**5**	Ottowa, Ont.
3	St. Catharines, Ont.	**6**	St. John, N.B.

Communication in Action: *Storyteller*

A good conversationalist has a knack for selecting incidents of human interest to tell: the strange or extraordinary happening, the embarrassing moment, the ordinary happening with a humorous twist, and so on. From your own personal experience, select one such event to describe to your class. Limit yourself to one minute. Relate your story as though you were giving an after-dinner talk.

UNIT □ 24

Question Mark
and
Exclamation Point

The question mark and the exclamation point are the two remaining full stops in your study of punctuation traffic signals. Like the period, they are red lights. The principles relating to these "Stop" signs are relatively few, but you will need to know how to use the question mark and the exclamation point correctly in order to convey a clear message.

The Question Mark

In this section you will study the use of the *question mark* after a direct question; after a short, direct question following a statement; and in a series of queries. In addition, you will review two related principles that you studied in the preceding unit.

After a Direct Question   A question mark is used after every *direct question.*

> When shall we release the advertising?
>
> What kind of type is used in this book?

After a Short, Direct Question Following a Statement   Sometimes a sentence will begin as a statement but will end in a question, usually a short question. The correct end punctuation is a question mark.

> You will bring the book tomorrow, will you not?
>
> Mr. Baxter expects to go to the meeting, doesn't he?

In a Series of Questions   If a sentence contains a series of questions, use a question mark after the last member of the series only.

Who is to make the decision—the office manager, the advertising manager, or the sales manager?

Review of Related Rules   In the preceding unit you learned that a period, not a question mark, is correct after an indirect question and after a sentence written in the form of a question just for the sake of courtesy. To refresh your memory, study the following illustrations.

Mr. Peabody asked her where she was going. (Indirect question.)

May I have my bill just as soon as you can get it to me. (A request. In fact, it is practically an order.)

☐   CLASS PRACTICE 1

Indicate the correct punctuation for the following sentences. Explain your reason for each selection.

1. You expect to take the cash to the bank before closing time, do you not (. ?)
2. Will you please let me have the first draft by noon tomorrow (. ?)
3. Would you like to live in Ottawa, in Banff, or in Saskatoon (. ?)
4. Mr. Towne asked her how much difference there was between the debit and credit totals (. ?)
5. What address did you type on that envelope (. ?)

The Exclamation Point

An *exclamation point* is used after a word, phrase, or sentence that expresses strong feeling. Only the writer can use it accurately because only he knows how much emotion and what meaning he wishes to convey.

After a Sentence   The same sentence may be either an exclamation or a question, depending upon the writer's intent. A declarative or an imperative sentence may also be an exclamatory remark, depending upon the inflection of the speaker.

Where in the world has that girl gone? (No strong feeling here—just a question.)

Where in the world has that girl gone! (The writer is thoroughly exasperated, as he shows you by using the exclamation point.)

This water is cold.   *or*   This water is cold!

Go to your room.   *or*   Go to your room!

Caution: The exclamation point should be used sparingly, particularly in business correspondence. Never use two or more marks together.

After a Word or Short Phrase   The exclamation point may be used after a single word or a short phrase. The sentence that follows the exclamation, however, is punctuated in the usual way.

Congratulations! You surely deserve the promotion.

Well, now! Where do we go from here?

After "Oh"   The exclamation point is used directly after the exclamation *oh* when it stands alone. However, if the group of words containing *oh* is the exclamation, *oh* is followed by a comma. Note that *oh* is capitalized only at the beginning of a sentence.

Oh! What a relief! (Both *oh* and *what a relief* are exclamations.)

But, oh, so sad! (The entire group of words is the exclamation.)

☐ CLASS PRACTICE 2

What is the correct punctuation for each of the following sentences? Why do you think so?

1. Help (. !) Man overboard (. !)
2. Great Scott (. !) Are you sure that letter was mailed on Tuesday (? !)
3. Stop (. !) You are using the wrong copy (. !)
4. Not on your life (. !) Saturday has always been my day of rest (. !)
5. Oh (. !) How could you find time to do that (? !)
6. What delightful news (. !) You must come and tell me all about it (. !)

Communication Problems

Application Exercises

A ■

Both this group of exercises and the next contain several sentences that review the use of the period. On a separate sheet of paper, indicate your selections and give the reasons for your choices.

1 Is there any difference between a bookkeeper and an accountant (. ?)
2 What a tremendous saving we made by changing to electric typewriters (. ? !)
3 If the fault does not lie with the shipping department, where does it lie (. ? !)
4 Will you please send this remittance before April 15 (. ?)
5 Of what value to a salesman is a knowledge of psychology (. ?)
6 If businessmen did not have integrity (. ,) (there, There) would be no business.
7 Does your company carry hospitalization insurance for its employees (. ?)
8 Oh (. ? !) Where did you learn the wonderful news (. ? !)
9 Can you guarantee that shipment will be made before the first of the month (. ?)
10 Our cheque was mailed on Monday (. ,) (You, you) should have received it by Wednesday.
11 Do you think you will be able to send your remittance by April 15 (. ?)

12 Harry will be sure to lock up when he leaves, will he not (.?)

13 When are you planning to hold your anniversary sale (. ?)

14 Do you spend your leisure time in playing golf, in relaxing, or in puttering around the yard (. ? !)

15 Mr. Perez asked me to find out what the largest city in Quebec is (. ?)

B ■

Using a separate sheet of paper, make the necessary corrections in these sentences. Explain why each correction is made. If you do not make a correction, explain this, too.

1 Mr. Abbey wants to know where the new warehouse is located.

2 What a pleasure it is to see a letter properly punctuated?

3 If we follow these instructions, how can we reduce our inventory.

4 Atlases are now in our library, we needed them very much.

5 In your opinion, were his data accurate.

6 You are sure that no letters remain to be filed, aren't you.

7 What interesting news did you see in the trade journal!

8 Well! Are you satisfied now?

9 The manufacturer asked whether it is a fact that previous generations were more industrious than the present generation.

10 Will you please let us have your answer by January 1?

11 Sara will be able to finish those letters this afternoon, won't she.

12 Here, now! How often have I told you to clean your keys daily.

13 How do you like typing, filing, and answering the telephone.

14 Art came to work for us only a year ago, his advancement has been remarkably rapid.

15 Will you please use the enclosed envelope when replying to this letter?

C ■

Is the punctuation in the following paragraph correct? If not, copy the paragraph and punctuate it correctly.

What are we going to do about Bill Emerson. His work has been unsatisfactory for about a year now, hasn't it. He cannot be depended on to follow through on any job, and he seems to think that he is entitled to frequent rest periods. What an attitude? I really think that we cannot afford to carry him any longer, and I ask that you give me authority to dismiss him. If you agree that Bill is costing us money, will you please send me soon a memo to the effect that he is to be discharged.

Word Study

A ■

Words often confused: expand, expend; assistance, assistants.

B ■

By adding a short prefix to each of these words, change the word to one having a negative meaning.

1	normal	**3**	proper	**5**	literate
2	engage	**4**	noble	**6**	enchanted

C ■

How are the following pairs of words spelled when *ing* is added?

1	hop, hope	**3**	mop, mope	**5**	bar, bare
2	plane, plan	**4**	dote, dot	**6**	pine, pin

Communication in Action: *Taking Notes*

Your instructor will read a short article. Pay close attention, taking appropriate notes as you listen. From your notes, write a brief summary of the article.

UNIT □ 25

Semicolon, Colon, and Dash

The semicolon, the colon, and the dash are *partial* stops. You might think of these marks as traffic signs that say, "Yield." Partial stops show that, while the thought of a sentence is continuous, there is a pause in that thought.

The Semicolon

When the eye sees a *semicolon*, the mind receives a signal to take a breath, a little rest; for the semicolon is a sign that tells the reader to come to a partial stop. The semicolon is used mainly in compound sentences.

In Compound Sentences A *compound sentence* is a sentence that has two or more independent clauses. In other words, if a sentence has two or more parts, each of which could stand alone and make sense, the sentence is compound.

> Telephones rang incessantly, and the switchboard operators could not get a moment's rest. (Here are two parts, each of which would make sense if it stood alone: *telephones rang incessantly* and *the switchboard operators could not get a moment's rest.*)

> Mr. Kerr does not wish to be a candidate, but he will serve if elected.

Because the clauses in a compound sentence are of equal value or rank, the connective used is a coordinate or a correlative conjunction. (Turn to Unit 22 to review coordinate and correlative conjunctions.) Although a coordinate conjunction—as *and* and *but* in the preceding sentences—is usually the connective used in a compound sentence, a correlative conjunction may be used. Consider this sentence:

> Either this machine is not properly adjusted, or we do not know how to operate it. (There are two parts to the sentence, and each one makes sense by itself. The connective is the correlative *either . . . or.*)

Now that you can recognize a compound sentence, you are ready to study four uses of semicolons in compound sentences.

To Show Omission of Conjunction If the connecting conjunction is omitted in a compound sentence, a semicolon is used to show that omission. For example:

> The bell rang; the light flashed; the whistles blew. (No conjunctions connect these three complete thoughts. Semicolons are signals that conjunctions are omitted.)

Before Second Clause Starting with Introductory Word In some compound sentences, the second clause starts with an introductory word. Here are some common introductory words:

accordingly	consequently	moreover
again	furthermore	nevertheless
also	however	otherwise
besides	indeed	therefore

A semicolon signals the partial stop before a word that introduces the second clause.

> Miss Hughes understands bookkeeping; *therefore,* she has a foundation for learning to operate a calculator.

> The samples of material you sent are of excellent quality; *however,* the designs are too flamboyant.

When a Clause Contains One or More Commas If a compound sentence contains one or more commas in either clause, a semicolon is used to separate the clauses.

> If you need replacements, write us immediately; and we will send them in the very next shipment. (A semicolon separates the clauses because there is a comma in the first clause.)

> I think we can get the five o'clock train; but, if we miss that, there is one at six o'clock. (Here there are two commas in the second clause.)

When One or Both Clauses Are Very Long Remembering that the semicolon is a partial-stop sign, you can understand its use in a long sentence. There must be some stopping place that will clearly separate the parts of the sentence. In the following illustration, can you see that you would be lost in a maze of words if the semicolon were not used?

We feel somewhat embarrassed in making the following request of a customer who has been so prompt about paying his bills for so many years; but this record is the very thing that leads us to feel that our last statement has either gone astray or been overlooked.

Before Explanatory or Enumerating Words A semicolon is also used to signal the approach of words that explain or enumerate. Some of these words are *as, for example, for instance, namely, that is,* and *that is to say.* Again, the semicolon fulfills its function as a partial stop by furnishing the rest period needed by the reader before he gives his attention to the words that follow the comma.

The most common typing error is the striking of a nearby key for the letter desired; for example, *k* for *l*, *v* for *b*, and so on. (The semicolon says, "Take a little rest and then look at the illustrations.")

CLASS PRACTICE 1

In each of the following sentences, choose the correct punctuation mark within parentheses and give a reason for your choice.

1. Concord was the home of four famous authors (; , .) namely, Thoreau, Alcott, Emerson, and Hawthorne.
2. One brother sold stationery (, ;) another operated an employment agency.
3. Miss Thorne is the senior member of the staff (; ,) therefore, she should be given first consideration.
4. Since your order arrived only this morning, we shall be unable to ship to-day (, ;) but we can promise to put the merchandise on the truck within three days.

The Colon

Whenever you hear a fanfare of trumpets you automatically prepare yourself for something that is coming, don't you? A *colon* is the written blare of trumpets that says: "Now, hear this! Here comes something for your special consideration." The various uses of the colon are the following:

Before Listed Items A colon serves to introduce a list of items, either within a sentence or in tabulated form. Often it is preceded by one of these expressions: *as, as follows, the following, thus,* or *these.*

To make neat corrections, the typist needs the following tools: a thin card, a typewriter eraser, a pencil eraser, and an erasing shield.

The most important factors to be considered in selecting filing equipment are the following:
1. Durability
2. Safety from fire
3. Adaptability
4. Convenience

The most important rule connected with the colon is this: Use a colon before a listing whenever you wish to make that listing stand out.

> Duties of the general clerical worker are these: filing, typing, recordkeeping, and opening mail.

Before Sentence to Be Emphasized   Also, a colon may be used before a complete sentence if you wish to place strong emphasis on that sentence; as:

> The most important rule for the colon is this: Use a colon before any listing of items that you wish to emphasize.

Right here is probably the best place to learn the rule for capitalization after a colon. The rule is this: Capitalize the first word of a complete sentence following a colon if you wish to emphasize the statement or if the sentence states a formal rule. In the following illustration, see how the colon performs its role.

> Remember this: The person who practices the Golden Rule finds himself comfortable to live with. (Do you feel the strength here? Do you know why *The* is capitalized?)

Period Instead of Colon   If the last words in a sentence *do not lead directly into* a listing or a statement, use a period after those words, not a colon.

> A cheque book balance may not agree with the actual cash balance for one of the following reasons, which are here enumerated in a convenient order for checking. (The *last words* do not lead directly into the listing; therefore, a period, not a colon, is correct.)

Also, use a period, not a colon, if another sentence follows the sentence containing the lead-in.

> If you do the family buying, keep the following rules in mind. By heeding them, you can help to "stretch" your income. (1) Take a shopping list with you. (2) Examine each article carefully before buying it. (3) Consider the cost of upkeep and of repairs of substantial items. (The sentence immediately before the listing *does not lead into* the listing.)

☐ **CLASS PRACTICE 2**

Correctly punctuate the following sentences and explain your choices.

1. In your order you failed to specify the following (no punctuation, colon) the length and width of the floor, the height of the ceiling, and the number of doors and windows.
2. The following suggestions are recommended for your study. You will be well repaid for your time (. :)

3. Please send the following items (. , :) one set of dishes, one tablecloth, and a dozen matching napkins.
4. You are invited to consider the following facts, which are the result of an extensive study by our staff (. :)
5. I simply must have these (no punctuation, colon) a room for the night, some warm clothing, and a good dinner.
6. The office-training areas, as enumerated in the following outline, should be included in all clerical practice courses (. :)

✔ PROOFREADING PRACTICE 1

To find out how well you understand the use of the semicolon and the colon as partial stops, make the necessary corrections in the following sentences.

1. The successful candidates were the following. Mayor Thomas, General Holmes, and Councilman Kirby.
2. The house was dilapidated; the yard was neglected; the front gate hung by one hinge.
3. I have finished all my business, accordingly, I shall be able to sail tomorrow.
4. Both jobs can be filled by a man already in our employ, namely, Fred Jackson.
5. The question that Mr. Alton very much needs to ask himself is this, Am I improving or destroying the morale of the personnel?
6. Your merchandise has been deteriorating steadily in quality, moreover, your service is very slow.
7. The following words are often misspelled. *Receive, separate, accommodate,* and *chief.*
8. We were obliged to refuse delivery of our Order No. 825, however, we are sending a reorder that contains more explicit specifications.

The Dash

Forcefulness is the trademark of the *dash.* The writer uses it to snip off the message abruptly, so that the following words burst upon the reader with special impact. The difference between the colon and the dash is that the colon gives warning, leads into something; but the dash cuts off the message *without warning* in order to make the following words conspicuous.

Purpose Determines Use If you are in doubt as to whether to use a semicolon or a dash or whether to use a colon or a dash, you must first decide what effect you wish your words to have. Do you wish to hold your reader's attention long enough for him to absorb the first part of your message before going on to the second part? Then use a semicolon. Do you wish to build up the second part by warning your reader that something important is coming? Then use a colon. If, however, you want to snip off the message so that the following words will have special impact, then use a dash. Look at the following sentence:

The box for petty cash contains coins of these denominations: pennies, nickels, dimes, quarters, and half dollars. (The colon warns the reader that a listing is coming.)

The above sentence is a good one, but the following sentence is stronger.

The box for petty cash contains coins of nearly all denominations—pennies, nickels, dimes, quarters, and half dollars. (Do you see that the use of the dash, with no introductory word, makes the listing more forceful?)

Forceful Expression, Summarizing, Repetition   Remember that the dash is the partial stop that you, the writer, use to make your words stand out in the mind of the reader. Is there a certain fact or message that you feel *must* be made to register? If so, use the dash before stating that fact or message.

Bill just walked in and asked for an increase in salary—and got it. (The point you wish to make forcefully is the amazing result of Bill's casual request.)

Will a summing up of what you have just said cause the reader to pay particular attention to your words? Then use the dash to separate a summarizing word from the listing that precedes it.

The monotonous checking operations, the tiresome copying and recopying, the constant addition of new material—all were forgotten when the finished report was so enthusiastically received. (The word *all* summarizes the drudgeries listed.)

If you strike the same note a second time, will the reader retain a deeper impression of the message? Use of a dash will strengthen the repetition.

Congratulations! You have made a fine record—a very fine record, indeed. (The outstanding thing about the person definitely is his *fine record*—as you show by the repetition after the dash.)

With Afterthoughts   You may use a dash before a *planned* afterthought to add variety to your writing, to soften a statement that could give offense, or to prepare the reader for some topic that will be discussed in a later letter. For example:

We are unable to adopt your suggestion—that is, without further study. (To soften refusal.)

On the other hand, the budget of the purchasing department needs revision—but we won't go into that now. (But we will later, so be prepared for it.)

Punctuating Material Set Off by Dashes   Except for quotation marks, no other mark of punctuation is used *before* words that are set off by dashes.

You need to know, however, the principles governing punctuation at the close of a sentence that ends with "dashed" material and punctuation of words enclosed in dashes.

At End of Sentence   Whenever "dashed" material ends a sentence, the regular end-of-sentence punctuation should be used—not the ending dash.

Who is the tall girl in the outer office—the one in the blue dress? (This is an interrogative sentence.)

What a gift for a bride—or for yourself! (Exclamation point ends this exclamatory expression.)

Words Enclosed in Dashes   Use commas where needed within the material that is set off by dashes.

Most employees—and John, of course, is no exception—do not like to work overtime.

The question mark, the exclamation point, and quotation marks are the only punctuation marks that are used *before the ending dash*. No other marks are correct. Note these illustrations:

Their cashier—what did you say his name is?—entered an incorrect total on the deposit slip. (The words within the dashes ask a question. Note that the interrupting sentence begins with a small letter.)

Here are pure-silk ties—yes, think of it!—for as little as $4.98. (An exclamatory expression is enclosed in dashes.)

His talk was called "Errors and How to Avoid Them"—not a very original title.

☐   CLASS PRACTICE 3

Tell where and why you would use a dash in each of the following sentences.

1. Louis is reasonably sure of a promotion though promotions are unusual at this season because of his work on the project.
2. When Mr. Lewis arrived, George, no, it was Ray, met him.
3. This is a "super" opportunity, one that we cannot afford to neglect, according to our broker.
4. Two of the attendants were on duty, you know, the ones who were there last Friday.
5. Tickets for the play can be obtained at the box office, yes, also at the agencies.
6. Tennis, rowing, hockey, these are Mr. Fort's favorite sports.

✔   PROOFREADING PRACTICE 2

You can test your knowledge of the correct punctuation to use with "dashed" words by finding whatever errors there are in these sentences. Justify every correction.

1. I cannot reconcile these two claims—or any of the others, for that matter, —can you?
2. Did you receive our designer's sample color schemes—two for your living room and three for your bedroom.

3. So far as I am concerned, her word is good—and always will be!
4. With your health, intelligence, and youth, you should never think of failure —never.
5. Your letter—was it dated June 3—was very welcome.
6. Yesterday—and what a day it was—went so fast that I just could not find time to answer your letter.

Communication Problems

Application Exercises

A ■

Each of the following sentences contains one or more question marks to indicate missing punctuation. On a separate sheet of paper, indicate whether you would use a colon, a semicolon, a dash, or another mark of punctuation at those points.

1 You have a choice of these three models (?) the small table model, the large table model, and the two-door console.
2 When you have complicated tabulation jobs (?) for example, payrolls, personnel analyses, market surveys (?) call on us.
3 Mr. James was handicapped by entering college a month late (?) furthermore, he lacked sufficient funds.
4 The qualities that I admire in Ethel are these (?) her industry, her graciousness, and her integrity.
5 I prefer transcribing letters to typing tabulations (?) but, since my job involves both duties, I give them equal attention.
6 Mr. Knapp operates his office on the barber shop principle (?) first come, first served.
7 A good sales letter will do the following (?) attract attention, create desire, and motivate action.
8 Little Tommy has decided to become a musher (?) one who drives dog teams.
9 Miss Bates is a victim of wanderlust (?) that is, she yearns to see more of the world.
10 You, too, can have color television—and for only 10 cents a day (?)
11 Department stores are so called because they are divided into various departments (?) men's clothing, household furnishings, yard goods, jewelry, and many others.
12 My complaints are as follows (?) no instructions for assembling the unit, wrong nails, and insufficient amount of tar paper.
13 Shorthand and typing skills, punctuation, spelling, grammar (?) these are "musts" for the good secretary.
14 Ms. Arnez has been with us only a month (?) therefore, she is not acquainted with all the personnel.
15 Please send me another atlas (?) an atlas without missing pages.

B ■

On a separate sheet of paper, indicate corrections for any of the following sentences that may be incorrect.

1 Your machine is very satisfactory, in fact, we think it is the best on the market.
2 Lucy asked how ice skating differs from roller skating?
3 Your letter went to Mr. Martin, then he referred your request to Mr. Carlin.
4 Mr. Jenkins has worked long and faithfully on the missile project—and for what?
5 If Edna had taken the overseas job, she would have had a very different kind of life; because she enjoys meeting people of various backgrounds.
6 Will you please send me very soon a copy of your latest price list.
7 Miss Ash started as a pool stenographer, then she became secretary to Mr. Perry.
8 We shall be glad to change your billing date to the second week of the month. If that would be more convenient for you.
9 Harry seems to have only one pleasure—eating.
10 The housewares exhibit will be held in our store, very likely there will be a large audience.
11 Oil paints, linseed oil, small brushes. These are the supplies I need most.
12 The concrete blocks having hardened. The plasterers began their work.
13 Our city is considering several ways of raising money; increasing property taxes, levying an income tax, and increasing the sales tax.
14 Will you please send us names and addresses of three references?
15 Our most respected executives—Mr. Lee, Mr. Archer, and Mr. Blinn,—will represent us at the annual meeting.

C ■

Insert the correct punctuation in the places marked (?).

Right now we are unable to take advantage of your special discounts (?) however (?) we would appreciate your keeping us on the list for any future offers. We would be particularly interested in your prices on these items (?) letterheads, outside envelopes, and return envelopes. As for some of the other stationery items—carbon paper, carbon packs, masters—(?) our inventory is large enough to carry us for one full year. Thank you for thinking of us (?) and please continue to do so.

Word Study

A ■

Words often confused: peace, piece; specie, species.

B ■

What are the singular forms of the following plural nouns?

1	parentheses	3	passersby	5	p.m.'s
2	teeth	4	notaries public	6	flies

C ■

Column A lists six words containing prefixes. Column B lists the meanings of many of the most commonly used prefixes. Match the words with the meanings that refer to their prefixes.

A		B	
1	*sub*way	a	before
2	*contra*dict	b	against
3	*post*script	c	around
4	*in*convenient	d	between, among
5	*ante*date	e	one
6	*inter*state	f	beyond
		g	under
		h	above
		i	after
		j	not

Communication in Action: *Writing a Radio Announcement*

As a public service, your local radio station devotes 30 minutes daily to announcing community events of public interest. Up to one minute is allowed for each event. Write a one-minute announcement of the play, "Charley's Aunt," a comedy that is to be presented by the drama club of your school. Supply details as to time, place, etc.

UNIT □ 26

The Comma: Fundamental Usages

Commas are the "Slow" signs that guide your reader into absorbing one part of a thought before going on to another part. Unless you use commas correctly, your message will not be clear to the reader. Confusion leads to waste of time and money—additional letters must be written, goods may be delayed, and friendly relations with customers are threatened.

To show you how garbled a message can be if a comma is misplaced, look at this copy of a newspaper announcement:

> Because of the holiday, tomorrow the stores of Anton will remain open tonight until 8:30. (Use of the comma after *tomorrow* would have slowed down the reader at the appropriate point. As the sentence is written, the reader must back up and reread in order to get the meaning.)

Failure to use a comma when the reader should be slowed down also causes confusion, as illustrated in the following sentence:

> In order to balance the statement would have to be rewritten. (A second reading is necessary here. If the reader is slowed down after *in order to balance*, the message is clear.)

Training in the use of the comma is provided here and in the next two units.

In Compound Sentence

A compound sentence, as was stated in the previous unit, is a sentence that contains two or more independent (main) clauses.

Between Independent Clauses   Use a comma between the clauses of a compound sentence joined by the coordinate conjunctions *and, but, or,* or *nor.* Note that the comma comes *before* the conjunction, not after.

> Your cheque must reach us before the first, *or* we shall take legal steps to collect the balance of your account.

> A machine may cost $100, *but* in a month it may be difficult to realize $75 on this same machine.

✳   QUICK TRICK   No Subject, No Comma

The rule for this use of the comma can be simplified if you will do this: Concentrate on four words—*and, but, or, nor.* Whenever you see one of these words, look to see if there is an *expressed* (as opposed to *understood*) subject after it. If there *is* an expressed subject, use a comma before the *and, but, or, nor.* In other words: no subject, no comma.

> We have ordered radios from you before, and they have always given satisfaction. (There is a comma before *and* because the following main clause contains the expressed subject *they.*)

The following sentence is not a compound sentence: it is merely a simple sentence with a compound predicate. Therefore, a comma should not be used before *and.*

> We wired him at his hotel and asked him to call you. (The words *asked him to call you* do not make sense because they do not contain an expressed subject.)

Exceptions   Note, however, that there are two exceptions to this use of a comma in compound sentences. They pertain to very short clauses and to semicolons.

Very Short Clauses   If the clauses of a compound sentence are very short, the comma may be omitted.

We wired him but we received no answer.

Clara likes the office and she is happy there.

Semicolons   In Unit 25 you studied the uses of the semicolon, and you learned three uses that concerned compound sentences. Turn now to Unit 25 and review those semicolon principles.

☐   CLASS PRACTICE 1

Tell where and why you would insert commas or semicolons in the following sentences.

1. If you ask John, he will open the door for you but he refuses to leave it unguarded.
2. All of us were interested in the blueprints for the new car but it was the motor that particularly interested Peter.
3. Bess typed all the letters left by Alice and still had time to transcribe her own letters.
4. In the morning the janitor cleans the entrance to the office building but in the afternoon, of course, his wife has to repeat the process.
5. The seniors toured Ottawa and visited the Houses of Parliament and the Mint.
6. Marvin went to school but he was late.
7. Checking is my job operating the duplicator is yours.

In a Series

A series consists of a minimum of three succeeding items, which may be three words, three phrases, or three clauses. A comma is used to separate the parts of a series; and, to ensure message clarity, a comma is used before the conjunction that precedes the last item in a series. For example:

The dress makes up well in cotton, nylon, or rayon acetate. (Series of words. Note the comma before *or*.)

Our offices are located in Vancouver, in Edmonton, in Regina, and in Winnipeg. (Series of phrases.)

Type the letter, sign it in my absence, but do not mail it until tomorrow. (Series of clauses.)

The art school will offer the following subjects: figure sketching, fashion design, interior decorating, and advertising layout and typography. (Use of the comma after *decorating* tells the reader that *advertising layout and typography* is one subject and the last item in the series.)

However, when the conjunction is repeated before each item of a series, no commas are used to separate the items.

At our camp you will have an entire week of swimming *or* boating *or* fishing *or* just sitting.

No comma is used at the end of a series unless the sentence structure demands a comma at that point. Such occurrences are rare. For instance:

A jurist, an economist, and an explorer were the speakers.

A jurist, an economist, and an explorer, each known for his contribution to society, were the speakers. (Here the sentence structure demands a comma after *explorer*.)

When "Etc." Ends a Series If a series ending in *etc.* occurs in the body of a sentence, a comma is placed *after*, as well as before, the *etc.* Of course, if *etc.* ends the sentence, the period denoting the abbreviation is the ending punctuation mark.

There is a temporary embargo on butter, milk, eggs, ice cream, etc., as well as on certain vegetables.

A meeting has been called to discuss increase in wages, decrease in working hours, expansion of fringe benefits, etc.

Ben Roth Agency

Speaking for myself, I'm trustworthy, loyal, helpful, friendly, courteous, kind, obedient, cheerful, thrifty, brave, clean, and lost.

Watch that you do not fall into the common error of writing *and etc.* Because *et cetera* is the Latin for *and so forth,* writing *and etc.* would be saying *and and so forth.*

Semicolons in a Series   In Unit 25 you learned that a semicolon is used to separate the main clauses of a compound sentence when the clauses are long, when the conjunction is omitted, or when the clauses contain one or more commas. A semicolon rather than a comma is used because a comma does not provide a long enough break to prevent confusion in the message. It is logical, then, that the semicolon should be used in a *series* when the items are very long or when the items contain commas. For example:

> Goods must be transported to the place where they are to be consumed; sometimes they have to be stored for a time; often they must be rearranged into shipping units; and the sound wares must be culled from the damaged and spoiled. (With so many words, a partial stop is needed between items.)

> During our vacation trip last year, we stopped at the following places: Indiana, Pennsylvania; Holland, Michigan; Paris, Illinois; Mexico, Missouri; and Midwest City, Oklahoma. (Visualize commas here instead of semicolons, and you can imagine the perplexed state of the reader.)

CLASS PRACTICE 2

Practice what you have learned about the use of the comma and the semicolon in series by telling where you would insert what punctuation in the following sentences and why.

1. You can get the data from Lija or Kurt or Harry.
2. Books papers pencils magazines etc. were strewn on the floor.
3. Ann swept the floor with an old, worn-out broom Marie dusted the furniture when Ann finished sweeping and Henry chopped stove-length sticks for the fireplace.
4. Please check all invoices statements bills of lading etc.
5. The hail beat against the windows rattled on the roof and flattened the flowers in the garden.
6. This is what you must do: Prepare a data sheet, with a list of references attached write a covering letter of application and send them to Miss Atwood.

After an Introductory Word, Phrase, or Clause

A comma is used after an introductory word, phrase, or clause as a signal to the reader to slow down.

Introductory Word   Use a comma to set off *introductory words,* the most common of which are the following:

accordingly	fortunately	naturally	otherwise
actually	further	next	perhaps
also	however	nevertheless	personally
besides	indeed	no	say
consequently	meanwhile	now	theoretically
finally	moreover	obviously	therefore
first	namely	originally	yes

The one-syllable adverbial connectives *hence, still, then, yet, thus,* and *so* usually do not require a comma after them unless the connective demands special emphasis.

> Several of the items you ordered are out of stock; *so* we are holding the entire order.

> You shouldn't be without this soap powder another day; *so,* the first thing tomorrow morning ask your grocer to send you a package. (In this sentence *so* is used to emphasize the message that follows and is, therefore, set off by a comma.)

An introductory word may occur at the beginning of a sentence, or it may introduce a clause within the sentence.

> However, we do feel that the slight price increase is justified.

> Our production costs are mounting steadily; consequently, our prices must be increased comparably.

Do not take it for granted that these words are always introductory and, therefore, are always followed by commas. Sometimes the word modifies a word that follows, as in the following sentence:

> However worthy the cause, we feel that we can contribute only to the Community Chest. (*However* here is part of the message *however worthy the cause.*)

Introductory Phrase   When a phrase—prepositional, infinitive, or participial—is used to introduce the thought that follows, place a comma after that phrase.

> For various good reasons, we have decided to change our style of letterhead. (Introductory prepositional phrase.)

> To mention just one objection, our office is too small to accommodate such a large machine. (Introductory infinitive phrase.)

> Speaking before a special committee, the treasurer gave reasons for decreasing the dividend. (Introductory participial phrase.)

Whether to use a comma after an initial prepositional phrase is something of a problem. If the phrase is very short or if it flows swiftly into the main thought, do not use a comma. If it is a long phrase, use a comma.

> In the spring we plan to open a new store. (Short phrase that flows into the main thought—no comma.)

> With the addition of the new wing, the building will cost more than we had planned. (Not only is this phrase long, but it is also obviously introductory to the main thought.)

Introductory Clause   An *introductory clause* is a subordinate clause that precedes the main thought. Use a comma to slow the reader after an introductory clause.

> Although Mr. Ash has lived in the city for many years, his greatest ambition is to own a farm.

> When the messenger returns, please ask him to deliver the package.

Study the following list of conjunctions that introduce subordinate clauses. You will then be able to recognize an introductory clause on sight, because the conjunction will signal that such a clause is coming.

after	even if	provided	until
although	for	since	when
as	how	so that	whenever
as if	if	supposing	where
as soon as	inasmuch as	then	whereas
as though	in case that	till	wherever
because	in order that	though	whether
before	otherwise	unless	while

CLASS PRACTICE 3

In the following sentences, tell where you would place commas.

1. Your suggestion was very valuable; therefore we are writing to thank you for it.
2. Having forgotten the previous unfortunate experience Mr. Dove ordered a year's supply of stationery.
3. When I give the signal start to type.
4. Personally I would not risk hiring a man without references.
5. To tell you the truth I had completely forgotten the time.
6. Perhaps you would like us to send you some swatches of the new dress materials.
7. We concede that your proposal would do much for us; nevertheless we do not feel that we are in a position to adopt it.

Before Subordinate Clause Following Main Clause

There is no question about using a comma after an introductory clause, but there may be a question about using the comma before a subordinate clause that *follows* a main clause. If this clause is an essential part of the message, no comma is used.

> She plans to go home if he comes before six. (No comma needed because her going home is contingent upon his arriving before six.)

However, if the subordinate clause is not necessary to the meaning—just "tacked on"—a comma is used.

We should appreciate your sending us the home address of your sales manager, if you will be so kind. (*If you will be so kind* is not essential; therefore, the comma is used.)

✔ **PROOFREADING PRACTICE 1**

Study these sentences and tell whether they are correctly punctuated. Then make any necessary corrections.

1. This item should be charged to selling expense if you wish to be technical about it.
2. Since I do not write shorthand I shall be unable to take notes as quickly as may be necessary.
3. You must not leave unless you have permission to do so.
4. The slight improvement is only temporary as we all realize.
5. There are three things about the meeting to remember; namely the time, the place and the purpose.

Keep Moving

A written message is snarled if commas slow the reader at the wrong places. A writer must know when *not* to use the "Slow" sign; he must know when to keep a thought moving. He must observe the following rules:

1. *Do not separate the parts of a compound by a* single *comma.* A compound subject, a compound object, or a compound verb must contain at least two commas—or none at all. For example:

The president and the treasurer will discuss the decrease in sales. (Compound subject.)

The president and, of course, the treasurer will discuss the decrease in sales. (Here the compound subject is separated by the interrupting expression *of course,* which is set off by *two commas.*)

2. *Do not separate a subject from its predicate by a* single *comma.*

The complaint of the new employee was submitted to the grievance committee. (No comma needed.)

The complaint of the new employee, in addition to those of some of the older staff members, was submitted to the grievance committee. (This sentence is correct because *two* commas set off the interrupting prepositional phrase between subject and predicate.)

3. *Do not use a comma before an ampersand (&) in a firm name.*

Wool, Sharpe & Wool (*Not* Wool, Sharpe, & Wool.)

Communication Problems

Application Exercises

A ■

On a separate sheet of paper, write the correct punctuation for any sentences that are incorrectly punctuated and give your reasons for the corrections. If a sentence is correct, write "OK."

1   We went early and left early.
2   The string, paper clips, rulers etc. on our Order No. 432 have not been delivered.
3   We could not possibly get the report out yesterday; moreover we were not the only ones who did not meet the deadline.
4   The Scouts swam ate sang and danced away their week at camp.
5   To think well is admirable to act well is more so.
6   However poor the service is we feel that it is better than none.
7   We could not find our tickets or we would have been at the theatre earlier.
8   To hold our trade we must give better service.
9   Digest the letters we received from Harding Adams & Polk.
10 Certain foods are high in protein; for instance meat and cheese.
11 On Friday we shall celebrate our tenth anniversary.
12 Ms. Beck contributed $100 the staff gave an equal amount.
13 From our office window there is a fine view of the river and on a clear, sunny day even the smaller boats can be seen.
14 If you accept this position, typing letters and envelopes typing from corrected rough drafts setting up and typing tabulations etc. will be your duties.
15 Some of the natives of India will not eat anything that is fish flesh or fowl.

B ■

On a separate sheet of paper, make whatever corrections are necessary and explain in your own words why you made them.

1   Fred is cheerful and carefree, his brother is very reserved.
2   A shopper should never be without a charge plate, or a cheque book, or a reasonable amount of cash.
3   Ilya, Sol, Edgar, and I, are always the first to arrive.
4   Please give us a choice of three dates, and if we can possibly arrange to see you, we shall make a definite appointment.
5   You may obtain your passport by making application to the local office, or by writing directly to Ottawa.
6   On our tenth floor you will find a complete stock of chairs, tables, lamps and etc.
7   Unless granted permission, you must not take any materials off my desk.
8   Roman always did his work better than the rest of us, that is the reason for his rapid promotions.
9   Leila knows very well that she must go, that she would like to go and that she will go.

10 To win the bonus you must exceed your quota by 10 percent.

11 Will you please send the requested information immediately.

12 We have canceled Mr. Salem's account with us, moreover, we have reported him to the Better Business Bureau.

13 I should like to know whether the new type cleaner is satisfactory?

14 However, fast a train may go, a plane can go much faster.

15 Mr. Ferry handed me the paper, thrust a pen at me and told me to sign on the dotted line.

C ■

You have been promoted! Beginning with this lesson, the Application C exercises will require that you edit for all kinds of writing errors—framework, spelling, vocabulary, punctuation. The quality of your written revisions will show whether you deserve the promotion.

Ambition, enthusiasm, training and hard work, are the ingredients for success in any career. However there is one other factor that effects a worker's pay cheque, he must be able to get along well with all his associates. Obviously the associates of a writer include the readers of all his communications, therefore, a business writer has particular need for good personal relationships.

Word Study

A ■

Words often confused: lightening, lightning, lighting; respectively, respectfully.

B ■

What nouns ending in *ty* are related to the following adjectives?

1	rare	**3**	entire	**5**	facile
2	real	**4**	anxious	**6**	notorious

C ■

To each of the following, add the termination that is pronounced "shun."

1	expan_____	**3**	comple_____	**5**	discus_____
2	connec_____	**4**	func_____	**6**	suspi_____

Communication in Action: *Gobbledygook*

High-sounding words and phrases cloud the meaning of your writing and speaking. They are called "gobbledygook." For example, "Extinguish the nocturnal illumination" means, in everyday language, "Turn off the light." Rewrite the following example of gobbledygook so that it is easy to understand.

It is anticipated that the writer will be reimbursed upon lapse of a reasonable interval of time. The amount of $685 is considerably in arrears, and it is contemplated that compensation will be forthcoming in due course. If complete reimbursement is not feasible immediately, perhaps an arrangement could be consummated whereby intermittent installments would be acceptable.

The Comma:
Usages to Indicate
Nonessentials

One very important use of commas is to indicate which parts of a message are separable from the main thought. In this unit you will learn to set off by commas expressions that are not essential to the intended meaning.

To "set off" means to place a comma after the nonessential expression when it comes at the beginning of a sentence; before the expression when it comes at the end of a sentence; and both before and after the expression when it comes in the body of a sentence.

> *Having heard the weather report,* they decided not to go.
>
> They decided not to go, *having heard the weather report.*
>
> They decided, *having heard the weather report,* not to go.

Whether to set off words, phrases, and clauses depends on whether they are *restrictive* or *nonrestrictive*. In this context, *restrictive* means "essential"; so, since the prefix *non* means "not," *nonrestrictive* means "nonessential."

The rule is this: Set off nonrestrictive elements in a sentence by commas.

When in doubt, ask yourself two questions: Are these words essential to the intended meaning? Could I omit them and still say what I mean to say? If the words are not essential—if you could omit them without affecting the completeness of the main message—these words are nonrestrictive and are set off by commas.

The use of the comma with nonessential elements is divided here into two parts: *interrupting and parenthetic elements* and *explanatory elements*. In each case, keep in mind that all words, phrases, and clauses not absolutely essential to the meaning of a sentence are set off by commas.

Interrupting Elements

An interrupting element does exactly what the name indicates—it interrupts the message. An interruption makes no contribution to the *basic* message; it might be called "excess baggage." All such "excess baggage" words are set off by commas.

> You knew, *of course,* that we were without funds at the time.
>
> Our best sources of sulphur, *for example,* are in Alberta.

Such expressions as *for instance, of course, as we said, for example, to tell the truth,* and *on the other hand,* as well as those interrupting words and clauses used to explain or qualify a statement, are set off by commas. Although they often make the sentence smoother or add additional information, these elements are not necessary to the basic meaning of the sentence; therefore, they interrupt it. (Some of these expressions are parenthetic and others are interrupters used in a parenthetic sense.)

Parenthetic Expressions An expression inserted in a sentence by way of comment is a parenthetic expression *if the meaning of the sentence is complete without it.* The words may be used to qualify or to amend the message. The aim of the writer may be to take away some of the sting of his words. The words may also be used to point out a contrast. Whatever the reason for their use, parenthetic expressions are set off by commas.

> The incident, as far as I am concerned, is closed. (*As far as I am concerned* qualifies the message. Apply your test questions: (1) Are these words essential to the basic meaning? (2) Can you omit them and still have a complete message?)

> The mailing list must be checked very carefully, not just inspected casually, if the revision is to be of any use. (The words expressing a contrasting thought are correctly set off by commas.)

Actually, you do not have to analyze these expressions to see whether they are qualifying, amending, or emphasizing a contrast in order to know you should set them off by commas. All you have to do is to recognize that they are "excess baggage."

Other Interrupters Certain phrases, such as *so to speak, to say the least,* and *after all,* are nearly always treated as parenthetic and set off by commas. So, too, are the conjunctive (transitional) adverbs *nevertheless, therefore, however, consequently, moreover, furthermore,* and so on, when they come in the middle of a sentence or clause. (When they introduce a sentence or clause, of course, they are called introductory words.)

> The sales tax, *moreover,* went into effect in April.

> A cheque for the full amount of your bill would, *therefore,* be very welcome.

Occasionally, however, these same words and phrases are used as basic parts of the sentence. Then, of course, they are not set off by commas.

> He could not budge the log however hard he tried.

NOTE: Words ordinarily considered interrupting may occasionally be written without commas for special effect. However, you will be wise to follow the more acceptable pattern in your writing.

CLASS PRACTICE 1

Now, see if you recognize words and expressions that are not essential to the meaning of a sentence. Indicate the punctuation you would use and why.

1. On this decision then rests our authority to proceed.
2. We are of course prepared to stand behind our guarantee.
3. The rumor we are convinced is without foundation.
4. The due date on your note however was July 8.
5. The ceramics factory is according to my information operating three shifts daily.
6. The samples were definitely shoddy, and we are therefore requesting you to cancel our order.
7. We are asking you therefore to cancel our order.

✔ PROOFREADING PRACTICE 1

You have just had practice in setting off by commas all "excess baggage" words. You should be ready, therefore, to find errors in the following sentences. Tell why you make the corrections.

1. The new model it is generally conceded contains the best features of preceding cars in addition to some new features.
2. George Edsen it is reported will be a candidate in the coming mayoralty election.
3. We will, though it is against our rule, allow the discount.
4. The new posture chairs are very desirable for but not absolutely necessary to the comfort of the typists.
5. The rest of the typewriters too are to be serviced when your repairman calls.
6. You can obtain the information fortunately from our office in Victoria.
7. Errors like these cost money. You will therefore check all figures three times.
8. All stenographers not clerks are to work seven hours a day.
9. The restrictions regarding credit as you can well imagine have seriously affected installment buying.
10. Shipments however are to be made according to the current schedule.

Explanatory Elements

Some sentences contain words that give additional information but are not necessary to the meaning. Your comma problem regarding explanatory elements is to recognize them as such and to know when to set them off by commas.

Mr. Anderson, who has had twenty years' experience in the shoe business, will join our staff on March 1. (Omission of the clause set off by commas leaves this: *Mr. Anderson will join the staff on March 1.* This makes sense; so you know that the words set off by commas were used to give additional information.)

Now attack the problem from another angle. You have written the following sentence, and you wonder whether you should have used commas.

> The salesperson who joined our staff on March 1 has had twenty years' experience in the shoe business.

Should you have used commas to set off *who joined our staff on March 1?* If you did, you would have this left: *The salesperson has had twenty years' experience in the shoe business.* You would leave yourself open to the natural question, "Which salesperson?" The clause in question is needed to identify the salesperson about whom you are talking; it is a restrictive clause so no commas are used.

☐ CLASS PRACTICE 2

Decide which of these sentences contain words that are not essential to the meaning. In the sentences where additional, nonessential information is given, indicate the places where you would use commas.

1. In the South where temperatures are milder there is no demand for the heavier line of coats.
2. In sections where temperatures are milder there is no demand for the heavier line of coats.
3. We received their bid after the time for filing bids had expired.
4. We received their bid this afternoon which was after the time for filing bids had expired.
5. The results of the test mailing are as disappointing as you prophesied they would be.
6. The results of the test mailing are disappointing as you prophesied they would be.

"That" vs. "Which" Careful writers make a distinction between the use of *that* and *which*. Clauses that are *not* essential to the meaning of a sentence are introduced by *which* and are set off by commas. Clauses that *are* essential are introduced by *that* and are not set off by commas. For example:

> We are sending you our new catalogue, *which* contains all the new items we manufacture. (*Which* introduces a clause that gives additional information.)

> The catalogue will give you an idea of the many new items *that* we are featuring. *(That* introduces an essential clause needed for identification.)

Appositives In Unit 15 you studied the correct case form for appositives, and the signposts you used to recognize appositives were the commas that set them off. You already know, too, that appositives give additional information.

There are, however, some instances where the identifying term is very, very closely connected with the principal term; and in such cases commas are not used. For these closely connected terms, use your test: *If the term is needed for identification, no commas are used.* If the element can be omitted without affecting the meaning of the sentence, set it off by commas. The following examples show you when to use commas and when not to use them.

> Our representative, Mr. Charles Daniels, will call on Monday. (Omit the words set off by commas and you have this: *Our representative will call on Monday.* In this instance the man's name is not needed for identification.)

> In 1945, the year World War II ended, the Toronto Argonauts won the Grey Cup. (*The year World War II ended* is not needed to identify the year. It is, therefore, set off by commas.)

> My sister Eileen works for the new plastics company. (If you omit *Eileen,* your reader will not know which sister you mean. *Eileen* is necessary for identification and is not set off by commas.)

> William the Conqueror found the English people very uncooperative. (Omission of *the Conqueror* would leave the reader wondering which William you meant. This closely connected term is needed for identification and, therefore, is not set off by commas.)

Degrees, Titles, Other Explanatory Terms   *Ph.D.* after a person's name gives additional information about that person—it indicates that he holds a Doctor of Philosophy degree. *Ltd.* after a firm name tells you that the company has been incorporated. *Jr.* after a man's name gives the information that he has the same name as his father. Because degrees, titles, *Inc., Ltd.,* etc., give additional information, they are set off by commas.

> The newest book on the subject is by John Doe, M.D., who is a former member of the faculty at the University.

> Amos Garfield, Jr., was elected chairman of the board.

> Make out the cheque to William Seton & Company, Ltd., and send it by registered mail.

Calendar Dates   Whenever the year is included in a date, set off that year by commas—that is, use a comma before *and after* the year. Really, the year is explanatory, telling which May 1 or April 10 is meant or which May or April is meant.

> July 14, 1976, is a date I shall never forget.

> Are you thinking of May, 1965, or May, 1975?

Provinces, Cities   If the name of a city is followed by the name of the province, the name of the province is set off by commas.

> Lethbridge, Alberta, is my hometown.

> Would you rather live in Cornwall, Ontario, than in Cornwall, P.E.I?

☐ CLASS PRACTICE 3

Some of these practice sentences contain "additional information" words, words that should be set off by commas. Other sentences contain words essential to the meaning, words that are not set off by commas. Take a few minutes to study them and then tell why and where you would insert commas.

1. Judith herself told me the good news.
2. My pocket dictionary which never failed to help me out of a difficulty has been mislaid.
3. Please call at our office in Truro Nova Scotia for your registration card.
4. A student who works his way through college appreciates his education.
5. Send the tax notice to Edward Bessette, Jr. rather than to Edward Bessette, Sr.
6. The manuscript which was beautifully typed was accepted for publication.
7. The agreement signed July 18, 1967 is still in effect.
8. Harold was in spite of this failure a studious and an intelligent young man.
9. Philip Black, D.D.S. is the way he prefers his name to be written.

✔ PROOFREADING PRACTICE 2

Now that you have had practice in using commas with elements that give additional information, find errors in the following sentences.

1. I am returning your article, which I read last evening and thoroughly enjoyed.
2. The books, that contain the records, are in Mr. Boyd's file.
3. Our manager sensing the situation sent out of the office the stranger who was causing the trouble.
4. Mr. Gibson my next-door neighbor has formed a car pool.
5. This is the book that I told you about yesterday.
6. Sherbrooke, Nova Scotia is a smaller town than Sherbrooke, Quebec.
7. The words appearing in red ink fairly shout their message.
8. Joe's friend who was also his cousin made the arrangements.

Keep Moving

In Unit 26 you learned that a subject must not be separated from its predicate by a *single* comma. Now learn the companion rule: A verb should not be separated from its object or complement by a *single* comma. There should be either two commas or no comma.

He is, I believe, a talented actor. (*Two* commas set off the parenthetic expression *I believe.*)

I am returning to you for your files the record for the plaintiff in the case of Martin *vs.* Larsen. (A comma after *files* would be incorrect.)

Communication Problems

Application Exercises

A ■

Keeping in mind the general rule that you set off by commas any words or expressions not essential to the meaning and that you do not use commas with words or expressions that are necessary to the meaning, punctuate these sentences. Indicate on your paper your reasons for making the corrections.

1 We cannot however approve such action until we know more about the circumstances.
2 Fred Wills who has been largely responsible for the success of the sale has asked me to type his report.
3 Yours is a legitimate though somewhat unusual excuse.
4 Some adults like many children fear to meet new situations.
5 John P. Quirk, LL.D. is a professor at Simon Fraser University.
6 Excise taxes by the way are to remain at their present level.
7 Under the circumstances therefore we do not feel that we can make an exception in your case.
8 July 1, 1867 is a date that is known to every Canadian.
9 Charles the only son Mr. Coe had at home has joined the army.
10 The biography of the poet Shelley is now published in a paperback edition.
11 Our offices are in Brandon, Manitoba and Thunder Bay, Ontario.
12 Ceramics, Ltd. is the name of the firm that has bought the Barrows Building.
13 Then too he feels that Bill will advise us about the contract.
14 The cellar or basement of his new house is very dry.
15 The machine although old and ugly does a very satisfactory job.

B ■

Beginning with this unit and ending with Unit 33, the second learning exercise is a cumulative review of the principles presented in Part 5. For each Application Exercise B, you are to write "OK" on your paper if a sentence is correctly written. If a sentence is incorrect, write your corrections and give reasons for making them.

1 Perhaps Mr. Singh was too ill to attend the meeting.
2 Place all bills face up, that is, with the portraits on top.
3 Our guest entertained us with many exciting stories of World War II, he had been a newspaper correspondent.
4 Books, and papers, and pencils were strewn on the floor.
5 A man should be judged by what he does, not by who his ancestors were.
6 James will go to the bank, and make the deposit for you.
7 The really happy person knows, that work is a blessing.
8 Elsa works as a typist during the day, and attends school at night.
9 In the summer, when June cannot skate or ski she plays tennis and golf.

10 However, gratifying the attendance may be at the next meeting, it will probably fall short of the goal we have set.

11 Your service has always been excellent; and we are, therefore, recommending your transportation facilities to Evans & Bates.

12 You can expect to be happy in almost any job. If you are interested and conscientious.

C ■

Remember that you are now editing for errors of all types.

Mr. Bell plans on moving to Dauphin, Manitoba, next March and would like to buy a small house in the suburbs. His son, John R. Bell Jr., lives in Ashville which is only 15 km from the centre of Dauphin. Mr. Bell, as well as his parents, are interested in looking at houses that are on or near a bus line. Will you please follow up on this lead immediately? We can discuss commission details at our next meeting.

Word Study

A ■

Words often confused: quiet, quite; explicit, implicit.

B ■

For each word in group A there is a word in group B that means very nearly the same thing. Match the words.

A		B	
1	discordant	**a**	unstable
2	incessant	**b**	ridiculous
3	absurd	**c**	inharmonious
4	careless	**d**	negligent
5	artificial	**e**	abusive
		f	diffident
		g	unnatural
		h	unceasing

C ■

How are the following words spelled when the "uhble"-sounding suffix is added?

1	detest_____	**3**	inexhaust_____	**5**	siz_____
2	indestruct_____	**4**	unspeak_____	**6**	reduc_____

Communication in Action: Testing Your Tact

Marge has just returned from vacation. She begins to give you the full details of her two weeks of relaxation and fun. You're mildly interested; but you have a long letter to type, and your boss is waiting impatiently for it. How would you handle the situation? Exactly what would you say?

UNIT □ 28

The Comma: Additional Usages

This final unit on the use of the comma presents some important principles that are not related to any of the others you have studied. For best results, concentrate on each separate use and understand that use thoroughly before proceeding to the next principle. The unit is planned and arranged to help you with this study method. When you have learned these five additional uses, you will have achieved mastery of the comma. Your message then cannot be misinterpreted, for you will know how to use the "Slow" signs that will guide your reader into understanding the meaning you intend your words to express.

With Modifying Adjectives

If you use two or more adjectives to modify a noun, separate the adjectives by commas—if each one separately modifies the noun.

> The blue, red, and yellow sweaters belong to the three girls taking the entrance test. (*Blue* modifies *sweaters; red* modifies *sweaters; yellow* modifies *sweaters.*)

> The 1916 automobile was a high, cumbersome vehicle. (The automobile was a *high vehicle* and was also a *cumbersome vehicle.*)

When in doubt as to whether to use a comma in a situation like this, try a Quick Trick:

✳ QUICK TRICK   Can You Substitute "And"?

> If you can mentally use correctly the word *and* between the adjectives, a comma should be used. If you cannot insert *and*, no comma should be used. Using this Quick Trick with the preceding illustrations, you would say this:

> The blue *and* red *and* yellow sweaters

> A high *and* cumbersome vehicle

Knowing this Quick Trick will help you avoid the common error of placing a comma after the last modifying adjective. You know it would be incorrect to write: "the blue, red, and yellow, sweaters" because you would be saying: "the blue *and* red *and* yellow *and* sweaters."

There is another instance in which it would be wrong to use a comma with modifiers.

The rule is this: Do not use a comma before the last adjective in a series when this adjective is thought of as part of the noun.

> Our spring is noted for its cold running water. (Why is there no comma after *cold?* Because the meaning is not cold *and* running water. *Cold* modifies the idea of *running water;* and no comma is placed between *cold* and *running.*)

☐ CLASS PRACTICE 1

These sentences help you understand when to use, and when not to use, a comma with modifiers. Punctuate the sentences correctly.

1. Eva got the information from a polite helpful man at the reservations desk.
2. You have been recommended as a progressive wide-awake dealer.
3. We never offer shopworn defective goods for sale.
4. Miss Harding is wearing a bright pretty scarf.
5. Our department store is a modern well-stocked and well-run business.
6. At last the wearisome monotonous checking job was finished.
7. Mr. Ahern is a short stout good-natured man.
8. A detailed comprehensive report is required.

✔ PROOFREADING PRACTICE 1

Here is an opportunity to prove how well you understand the use of commas with modifying adjectives. Find any errors in the following sentences.

1. Mr. Ladd is a true, loyal, honorable, man.
2. The article was written by a renowned mining engineer.
3. Our visitor had a long pointed head.
4. The new cabinets are beautiful practical roomy models.
5. A feeble, old, man was begging on the corner.
6. Miss Harding is wearing a bright nylon scarf.
7. The people who can least afford to do so eat desserts topped with sweet thick snowy whipped cream.
8. Two heavy square wooden boxes were delivered at the office this morning.

To Indicate Omissions

Writers sometimes omit words without confusing the message, for the omitted words are clearly understood from the sense of the sentence. However, whenever such words are left out, a comma is used to slow down the reader, so that he knows there is an omission.

> Men's overcoats are marked down to $49.50; boys', to $39.50. (The meaning, very clearly, is *boys' overcoats are marked down to $39.50.*)
>
> To err is human; to forgive, divine. (To forgive *is* divine.)

In Direct Address

Names or terms used in speaking directly to a particular person or group of persons are said to be used in *direct address*. Any names, words, or phrases used in direct address are set off by commas.

It is my privilege, members of the Rotary Club, to introduce Dr. Armando Sabatini.

There is no more important question in the whole field of politics, my friend, than that of levying taxation.

Very probably you would automatically set off by commas any words used in direct address, even without being familiar with the term "direct address." You have already learned to set off by commas any words that are not essential to the meaning, and words used in direct address are not necessary words. The preceding illustrative sentences make perfect sense when written like this:

It is my privilege to introduce Dr. Armando Sabatini.

There is no more important question in the whole field of politics than that of levying taxation.

☐ CLASS PRACTICE 2

To clarify your understanding of the use of the comma to indicate omissions and to set off words used in direct address, punctuate the following sentences.

1. We are gratified to tell you that in May this year our sales jumped 15 percent over last year's; in June 20 percent; and in July another 20 percent.
2. Will you teach me to operate the machine Jacques?
3. Something has been added. What we are not sure.
4. Yes sir, I will have the data for you by Monday.
5. The reports show that in 1969 the company had fifteen salesmen; in 1973 forty; and in 1976 seventy-five.
6. We wish Mr. Downes that we were able to grant your request.

✔ PROOFREADING PRACTICE 2

If you can find whatever errors there are in these sentences, you will prove to yourself that you have a fine understanding of the two comma rules you practiced in the preceding sentences.

1. You can readily understand gentlemen that our expenses, too, are increasing.
2. The price of the first table is $100; of the second $90; and of the third $75.
3. Do you agree with me Ms. Rosen that we must automate our accounting procedures?
4. The average person when young is venturesome; when old, less daring.
5. We are glad to offer you courteous reader an opportunity to buy these books at a 10 percent discount.

In Repeated Expressions

Sometimes, effective writing can be achieved by repeating a thought or an idea. If you should repeat for emphasis, use a comma to set off the repetition; like this:

Yours is a splendid idea, a splendid idea.

Such a discount policy is foolishness, utter foolishness.

Between Unrelated Numbers

When two unrelated numbers written in figures follow each other, they should be separated by a comma. Without the separating comma, the two numbers would run together and be confusing to the reader. Sometimes the confusion can be avoided by rearranging the sentence.

In 1976, 1736 persons requested free samples of our soap.

In 1976, free samples of our soap were requested by 1736 persons.

With Names in Filing Order

Where names appear in *filing* or *indexing* order (that is, with the surname first), a comma separates the surname from the rest of the name.

Natural Order   Filing Order

Louise E. Larkman   Larkman, Louise E.

Matthew Williamson   Williamson, Matthew

☐ CLASS PRACTICE 3

In the light of your study of commas with repeated expressions, names in filing order, and between unrelated numbers, punctuate these sentences.

1. Never never write a cheque before filling in the stub.
2. In the year 1929 387 companies in this kind of business failed.
3. We are pleased with your report really pleased.
4. The label on Robert J. Burnsley's file should read "Burnsley Robert J."
5. You must always always observe the rules of the office where you work.

✔ PROOFREADING PRACTICE 3

Now, find any punctuation errors in the following sentences.

1. On April 15 456 cases were received in our warehouse.
2. You will find Miss Byrne an intelligent girl, unusually intelligent.
3. The following names are in filing order: Roberts Jan; Suzuki George; and Van Dyk Dick.
4. Above all, this project needs to be better organized much better organized.

Large Numbers

Do **not** use a comma to separate thousands, millions, billions, and so on. Instead, in figures of five or more digits leave a *space* between groups of three digits. No space is necessary if there are only four digits unless the number appears in a column with larger numbers where spaces are necessary.

2200 (four digits)   13 874 $ 1 350 000   56 113

9 825 (four digits in column)

135 567

Keep Moving

Do **not** use a comma or leave a space in years, page numbers, house and street numbers, American ZIP codes, policy numbers, and other serial numbers unless they appear with spaces on the original document. The Canadian postal code must, of course, have a space, and telephone numbers are usually written with a hyphen.

in 1976   11212 Elm Street   page 1004   Policy No. 387546   Model 57954

But: Soc. Ins. No. 434 595 618   Postal code N8H 1A6   Telephone 221-5185

Do **not** use any punctuation when writing units of measurement that refer to *one* measurement.

We made the flight in 4 h 50 min 10 s.

Communication Problems

Application Exercises

A ■

The following sentences afford practice in using all the comma principles presented in this unit. On a separate sheet of paper, indicate where you would place commas and tell why.

1   The typist has long hours of sitting; the file clerk long hours of standing.
2   We can allow only our customary regular discount.
3   Hans won $98 000 $29 400 of which had to be set aside for income tax.
4   Friday is the deadline for the report Mr. Anderson.
5   The Gila monster is a sluggish poisonous lizard.
6   Don't you agree that we have been lenient in this case too lenient?
7   In England the statesman was revered; in France despised.
8   Alice arranged six golden daffodils in a gray bowl.
9   Mr. Mohr can you spare some time for me this morning?
10   A large number of customers attended the sale an unusually large number.
11   We cannot use the small model that adds only to 99999.
12   We do hope Mrs. Grant that you will be pleased with your new stereo.

B ■

Write "OK" on your paper for each correct sentence. Correct each incorrect sentence.

B ■

Write "OK" on your paper for each correct sentence. Correct each incorrect sentence.

1 The last shipment, however, is not up to our standards.
2 Mr. Lee complains that his secretary is slow, and inefficient.
3 The teapots nevertheless did arrive in good condition.
4 Visits to art museums have cultural value, they help pupils to enrich their classroom study.
5 The treatment was in line with the latest, scientific discoveries.
6 We manufacture locks, bolts, and screws, and we can supply hardware dealers in all parts of the country.
7 The television hero offered his enemy three choices: draw, fight with fists or run.
8 Our interviewer objected to her voice, not to her manner.
9 Will you please pay your future bills by cheque by cheque only.
10 A week before business showed a slight improvement.
11 Hosiery, gloves, neckwear, etc., will go on sale next week.
12 Mr. Wilton has been appointed manager of the new company; Mr. Higgins purchasing agent; and Mr. Barr chief accountant.

C ■

Here's another opportunity to develop your editing skill.

You are one of the very special customers who we are inviting to our advance showing of new, fall styles. The colors this year are jewel-like—ruby, sapphire, emerald; the styles conservative. We think that you Mrs. Roberts will be particularly interested in our fine selection of clothing for shorter women. We look forward to seeing you on the afternoon of August 17. Tea will be served from four to five.

Word Study

A ■

Words often confused: manner, manor; emanate, eminent, imminent.

B ■

Which of the words that follow each of these sentences is nearest in meaning to the italicized word in that sentence?

1 Her reply to his question was most *perfunctory*. (secretive, exhaustive, mechanical, insolent)
2 The suggestion that he is well fitted for the job is *ludicrous*. (imposing, ridiculous, irresponsible, indefinite)
3 Do not *procrastinate* longer if you expect to win. (delay, criticize, daydream, rebel)

C ■

Rewrite the following announcement, correcting the spelling and any errors in grammar. Improve the wording, making the message as concise as possible.

Pleas announse to all of the students in your classes that a meeting for a organisation of a proffessional nature will be held on January 10th, 19-- in room 2436 accrost from the lounge at 7:30 p.m. in the evening. All of the students in your classes are wellcome. Any other students are also invited.

Communication in Action: *To Bluff or Not to Bluff*

You are asked to give your opinion about the value of increasing the number of merit ratings, a topic brought up at a staff meeting. The trouble is that you don't know current company practice about merit ratings. Should you bluff your way through, saying something you hope makes sense; or should you admit that you don't have an informed opinion? What would you say?

UNIT □ 29

Quotation Marks

A writer uses various signals to cue a reader into the proper interpretation of a written message. The writer's signals mark the reader's thinking route and prevent the reader from straying.

This unit is concerned with the use of quotation marks. These signals are used principally to tell the reader: "These are the actual words spoken or written by a specific person." This and other uses of quotation marks, together with related pointers, are explained under the following topics.

Direct Quotations

When you record word for word what someone has said or written, enclose the words in *quotation marks*. If the quotation is brief, use a comma to separate it from the rest of the sentence.

> Mr. Scott's comment was, "That will be satisfactory."

> "That will be satisfactory," said Mr. Scott.

If you wish a quoted sentence to strike the reader forcibly, or if the quotation is a long one, use a colon before the portion quoted.

The letter contained just one sentence: "We are now ready to discuss a new lease with you." (The colon emphasizes the direct quotation.)

Secretary Pine, on his return from Europe yesterday, said: "If the free peoples of the world are to remain free, they must rally to a cause that will unite them." (The colon precedes a long direct quotation.)

Interrupted Quotations

If a direct quotation is interrupted, quotation marks are placed around the quoted words only.

"Neither the manufacturer nor the jobber," continued the letter, "can supply the goods in time to fill the order." (Commas set off the interruption.)

If the quotation ends with a question mark or an exclamation point, these marks of punctuation are used instead of the comma.

That sign, "Dangerous Curve Ahead!" could not be overlooked. (The exclamation point is part of the quotation and is used here instead of the comma.)

If a semicolon or a period occurs at the interrupting point, place the semicolon or the period *after the interruption.*

"Our sales staff should be enlarged," he recommended; "our showrooms should be modernized."

"Our sales staff should be enlarged," he recommended. "Also, our showrooms should be modernized."

When you enclose material in quotation marks, that material must be quoted exactly as it was written or spoken. Even if you know that the grammar or the punctuation is wrong, you should make no corrections. Otherwise, you would not be quoting.

Quotation Within a Quotation

A quotation within a quotation is enclosed in single quotation marks. (These are made on the typewriter by striking the apostrophe key.)

The student reported, "We now know the difference between 'adapt' and 'adopt.' "

Quoted Terms and Expressions

Quotation marks are used with some expressions and terms to signal that the quoted words have some special significance. You, the writer, can direct the reader's interpretation of your message by plainly marking his route with quotation marks. Follow closely the topics and discussion given here, so that you will be able to quote correctly and effectively.

Words Explained or Defined   Words and phrases accompanied by their definitions or introduced by such expressions as *so-called, known as, termed, marked, entitled, signed, the word*, and similar words and phrases are enclosed in quotation marks.

A contest in a court of law is termed "litigation" by attorneys.

You should have used the word "but," not "and."

This is an example of their so-called "hands-off policy."

Strictly speaking, "manuscript" refers to handwritten documents.

"Yours for profits" is an unusual complimentary closing. (You draw special attention to this unusual complimentary closing by enclosing it in quotation marks.)

NOTE: This rule applies to material that is to appear in typewritten form, as in letters or reports. If the material is to be set in type, however, expressions of this kind should be underscored and the quotation marks omitted. Underscoring indicates to a printer that the expressions are to be set in *italic* type.

Terms Unfamiliar to the Reader   Whenever you use terms that you assume are unfamiliar to the reader, those terms should be enclosed in quotation marks. There may be a question as to whether you should use such terms. As your primary aim is to make your message clear to the reader, the use of technical or trade terms unfamiliar to the reader may not promote clarity. If you do use them, however, enclose them in quotation marks.

All our newspaper "cuts" become the property of the newspaper using them. (*Cut* is a technical term meaning "an engraved block or plate for printing.")

This new locomotive will make it possible to eliminate "pushers" up the westbound grade. (*Pusher* is a technical term used in railroading.)

NOTE: Be careful not to overuse quotation marks. Do not use them to enclose well-known words, phrases, and expressions familiar to the reader. (In the examples above, quotation marks would not be used with *cuts* or *pusher* if the intended readers were journalists or railroad workers.)

Keeping up with the Joneses may not be worth the cost.

Slang, Humor, Poor Grammar   Sometimes writers use slang or poor grammar just to make their writing more interesting. Too, sometimes writers like to use words that they intend to be interpreted as humorous. In such cases, these expressions are enclosed in quotation marks.

The price quoted in our letter of May 3 was surely a "boner."

All this is an indication of the fact that the "world do move." (This quoted expression illustrates both poor grammar and a questionable attempt at humor.)

When writing to a person who is a total stranger, it is safer not to use slang or poor grammar. Also, perhaps you should not try to be funny. He may not appreciate your humor.

Translations of Foreign Words   Whenever you give a translation of a foreign word, enclose that translation in quotation marks; like this:

> *A la mode* means "after the fashion."

> "As it should be" is the translation of *comme il faut*.

☐   PROOFREADING PRACTICE 1

The following sentences illustrate the use of quotation marks with various expressions and terms. See if you can find the errors, make the corrections, and explain why you made the corrections.

1. In material descriptive of automobiles, the term automotive is frequently used.
2. Remember that the only safe way is to check and double-check.
3. The words principal and principle are frequently confused.
4. Sandhogs is the name given to men who work under compressed air, as in digging tunnels.
5. This is confidential—to at least a thousand people.
6. Noninterference is the free translation of *laissez faire*.

Titles

Enclose in quotation marks the following titles: parts or chapters of books (but not *titles* of books), short plays, lectures, articles, essays, sermons, short poems, toasts, mottoes, paintings, sculptures, and names of ships, planes, and trains.

> Chapter V, "Inquiry Letters," appears in Part I, which deals with "Business Letter Writing." (Title of a chapter and title of a section of a book.)

> Professor Gray will address our club on the topic, "This Competitive Era." (Title of a lecture.)

> My personal motto is, "I'd rather be ready and not go than go and not be ready." (Exact words of a motto.)

> Did you get reservations on the "Queen Elizabeth"? (Name of ship.)

Underscore titles of complete printed works: books, booklets, magazines, newspapers, long poems, and full-length plays. In material that is to be set in type, underscoring indicates to the compositor that such titles are to be set in *italics*.

> Dr. Henry Van Dyke's <u>Work</u> (*Work*) contains much inspiration for those who must work to live. (Title of a book is underscored, not quoted.)

> <u>The Financial Times</u> (*The Financial Times*) carried the announcement today.

NOTE: If the titles of complete printed works occur frequently in business correspondence, an acceptable alternative to underscoring such titles would be to type them in all capitals. This would be a timesaving device. Putting titles in all capitals is also used as an eye-catching device in advertising and sales promotion copy.

Do *not* enclose in quotation marks (nor underscore) the following: titles of documents, annuals, reports, proceedings, and such words as *Preface, Introduction, Contents, Appendix,* or *Index* of a book. For instance:

Have you seen the Report of the Committee on Law Enforcement?

Don't forget to read the Preface in *Westward, the River.*

☐   PROOFREADING PRACTICE 2

To be sure that you are clear about which titles should be underscored (italicized) and which should be enclosed in quotation marks, test yourself by finding errors in the following sentences.

1. Adam Smith's great work was his Wealth of Nations.
2. Please save me your copy of "Life."
3. Romeo and Juliet is both a play and an opera.
4. Business before pleasure is our motto.
5. "I have read your article, 'The Continuing Business Pattern,'" reported Mr. Pierre.
6. The subscription price of "Today's Post" has not been increased.

Punctuation at End of Quotations

Are punctuation marks at the end of quoted words, phrases, and sentences placed inside or outside the quotation mark? Here are the three principles that cover all ending-punctuation situations.

1. *Periods and commas* are placed *inside* the closing quotation mark to avoid the appearance of a dangling mark.

Our new model reproduces sound from records without "chatter." (Not "chatter".)

To eliminate "chatter," purchase one of our new models. (Not "chatter",)

2. *Colons and semicolons* are placed *outside* the closing quotation mark.

The following are "Current Assets": cash, accounts receivable, furniture, and equipment.

The person who is being sued is known as the "defendant"; the one who is bringing the suit, as the "plaintiff." (Note that the period is placed inside the ending quotation mark.)

3. *Question marks and exclamation points* are sometimes placed inside and sometimes outside closing quotation marks, depending on the following conditions:

a. If the quoted matter is a question or an exclamation, the question mark or the exclamation point is placed *inside* the closing quotation mark.

I am sending you a copy of the next chapter, "What Are the Flowers Saying?" (Placing the question mark inside the quotation mark is only sensible. The question mark is part of the chapter title, and it is the title that is enclosed in quotation marks.)

My message to you is "Stand fast!" (Since the exclamation point is part of the quoted material, it must be placed *inside* the ending quotation mark.)

b. If the entire sentence is a question or an exclamation, the question mark or the exclamation point is placed *outside* the ending quotation mark.

What have you done with your "excess baggage"? (The question mark here is *not* part of the quotation. It is used to end a sentence that asks a question.)

Jim is an out-and-out "parasite"! (The exclamation point is placed *outside* the quotation mark—at the end of the exclamatory sentence, where it belongs.)

✔ PROOFREADING PRACTICE 3

The following sentences were written to help you with the punctuation used with quotations. If punctuation is omitted or incorrectly placed, say so and tell why you think so. Capitalize letters where needed.

1. It looks like rain said the farmer. we certainly can use some.
2. Please "rush:" 1 dozen packages mixed flower seeds, 4 lawn mowers, and 6 garden rakes.
3. The purchasing agent said I very much regret the decision.
4. The friendly feeling of the public for a firm is known as "goodwill;" without it, no business can long endure.
5. "May we look forward to receiving your order soon" is an excellent way to close a sales letter.
6. Is this stock one of the "Blue Chips?"
7. Mr. Jelton said that he very much regretted the decision.

Communication Problems

Application Exercises

A ■

On a separate sheet of paper, indicate where quotation and other punctuation marks should be inserted in the following sentences. Be prepared to give a reason for every mark you insert.

1 A solid or screened plate used in printing tints is called a tint block.
2 The general's words were, I shall return.
3 His next article will be titled Save It—It May Be Valuable.
4 In the May issue of Business Advertising outline the material on the following pages 120, 121, 225, and 226.
5 Our lawyer said that he did not wish to bring suit unless it was absolutely necessary.

6 Which paper is delivered to your house, the Morning Record or the Evening Sun?

7 The most important part of the order read like this "Buy 100 shares of General Oil at market."

8 The mere fact that a package is marked Fragile is not enough to guarantee safe transportation.

9 The next chapter of Are You Listening is entitled Listening To High Pressure.

10 The words stationery and stationary are called homonyms.

11 I have read your book, What Is Ahead for Small Business

12 In the column headed "Total" place the amount owed at the end of the month.

13 His secretary asked Shall I mark this cablegram Deferred Rate

14 Look up some synonyms for nice; it is an overworked word.

15 Please do not feel that we are trying to rook you.

B ■

Find and correct the errors in the following sentences. If a sentence is correct, write "OK" on your paper.

1 If Henry can still type that typewriter should suit him.

2 "We, the People of the United States," etc., begins the Preamble to the Constitution of the United States.

3 A group of cold, hungry, Boy Scouts reached camp long after dark.

4 Your credit standing is excellent, and if you wish to purchase goods on open account, we shall be happy to have you do so.

5 I cannot understand the luck that some people have, last year my neighbor won an automobile that cost him only ten cents.

6 We are proud of the reputation we enjoy and will do everything in our power to maintain and increase our prestige.

7 Many writers cannot spell the word recommend.

8 No discount is to be taken when a bill is paid in 30 days. As is clearly printed on all our invoices.

9 Trees, shrubs, flowers, etc. are all parched for rain.

10 However successful the results, the methods used are questionable.

11 May we have your answer within a week?

12 He replied that "their company is no longer manufacturing this machine."

13 Mr. Maine urged the applicant to begin drawing his chair nearer to the prospective employee.

14 Mr. Brant prefers to read his speeches; Mr. Atwater to talk from notes.

15 The report made public by the committee on June 2, shows gross inefficiency at all levels of the bureau.

C ■

Follow the usual "edit and revise" instructions for Application C exercises.

In today's mail you should receive a copy of our brochure, "Home Gardener". I was happy to meet yourself and Mrs. Ames at the banquet last Tuesday and to learn of your interest in horticulture. Surely if camera enthusiasts are called Shutterbugs, us gardeners might be known as Flowerbugs—or is the pun too much for you? At any rate, please accept the brochure with our compliments and please feel free to consult us whenever you have a gardening problem.

Word Study

A ■

Words often confused: human, humane; forgo, forego.

B ■

In Exercise 1, match the correct definition with the term in italics. In 2 and 3, match the correct term with the definition in italics.

1 *To garnishee* is: (a) to attach wages to pay a debt, (b) to appropriate an employer's money, (c) to try to enforce by legal process, (d) to try to effect an agreement.

2 *One to whom a debt is owed* is: (a) a creditor, (b) a cashier, (c) an auditor, (d) a referee.

3 *One who has authority to represent another in a business transaction with a third person* is: (a) a notary public, (b) a jobber, (c) an agent, (d) a financier.

Communication in Action: *Helping a New Employee*

A new employee, Frank Hart, is assigned to the desk next to yours. Your supervisor was called to a meeting before he could introduce Frank to you or any of the others. Courtesy demands that you take action. What are your responsibilities? Enact a typical introduction. Make a list of other things you could do to introduce this person to his new situation.

UNIT □ 30

Parentheses and the Apostrophe

In this unit you will study two more signals, *parentheses* and the *apostrophe*. When you have learned the uses for these signals, you will have two added tools for ensuring clear and accurate interpretation of your written messages.

Parentheses

Parentheses are used mainly to enclose words that give additional information. You will recall that commas and dashes are also used for this purpose; however, each of the three marks serves its own special function. The peculiar function of parentheses is to tell the reader, "This is something I am repeating or adding, but it has very little connection with the main thought." In other words, parentheses are used to *de-emphasize* the importance of the additional information.

> You will receive 25 percent off the list price (our usual trade discount) on these articles. (Although the parenthetical element gives additional information, the parentheses imply that *the usual* discount is nothing extraordinary.)

Commas and dashes, on the other hand, are used to set off material that is related more closely to the main thought of the sentence. In contrast to parentheses, dashes are used to *emphasize* the importance of this additional material.

> We have turned your problem over to our advertising department, located in Toronto, for expert solution. (While *located in Toronto* is not essential to the meaning, it provides knowledge helpful to the reader.)

> If we were offering you just a course in merchandising—even an unusually good one at an unusually good price—it would not be surprising if you did not buy it. (While the words set off by dashes may be omitted, without them the sentence would lose color and emphasis.)

Besides setting off additional information not pertinent to the main thought of a sentence, parentheses also are used: (1) to acknowledge authority for a statement made; (2) to enclose references or directions; (3) to indicate enumerated items and items beyond the fourth level in an outline; and (4) to enclose a question mark to express doubt and an exclamation point to show disbelief, sarcasm, or surprise.

To Indicate Authority, References, Directions   Enclose in parentheses the name of an authority for a statement and all references or directions.

> Goodwill: the favor or advantage in the way of custom that a business has acquired beyond the mere value of what it sells. (Webster)

> Because of unusually heavy losses this quarter (see the attached financial report), we are not able to proceed as planned.

> The steps in the sales presentation have already been discussed (see page 57).

With Enumerated Items   In Unit 23 you learned that the period is not used after numbers and letters that are enclosed in parentheses. At the same time, you had a preview of this principle: Enumerated items and some items in outlines are enclosed in parentheses (as shown below and in the skeleton outline on page 184).

> The following instructions are intended for: (1) senior bookkeepers, (2) junior bookkeepers, (3) ledger clerks, and (4) statistical clerks. (Equally correct for enumerating items would be the use of the letters (*a*), (*b*), (*c*), and (*d*).)

To Express Doubt and Surprise   Some writers enclose in parentheses a question mark to express doubt and an exclamation point to show disbelief, sarcasm, or surprise.

> The applicant is a Romanian (?) refugee. (*Meaning:* I am not sure that he is Romanian. He may be of some other nationality.)
>
> You will find that this is a harmless (!) treatment. (*Meaning:* I say "harmless," but you will probably find it quite different.)

Caution: While question marks and exclamation points enclosed in parentheses have a place in the punctuation repertoire of the skillful writer, he knows that too frequent use of marks enclosed in parentheses can make his messages boring, even annoying, to his readers. He uses this device only when it is exactly the right punctuation for some precise situation.

☐ CLASS PRACTICE 1

In the following sentences, insert parentheses where needed.

1. That novel was written toward the close of the nineteenth century 1893.
2. The office of comptroller chief accountant is sometimes filled by a person who is a qualified C.A.
3. Insert the carbon pack into your machine be sure that paper edges are even and start typing on line 10.
4. It was in 1899 ? that we started to manufacture marine engines.
5. Your attention has previously been called see Unit 23 to enumerated items and to items in outlines.
6. The population of Canada grew from a total of 5 371 315 in 1901 to a total of 14 009 429 in 1951. Canada Year Book, 1961.

With Other Marks of Punctuation   Principles governing punctuation of words enclosed in parentheses are here divided into: (1) punctuation of parentheses-enclosed words when they are part of a sentence, and (2) punctuation of such words when they stand alone.

Parenthetical Element Within a Sentence   When the words enclosed in parentheses are part of a sentence, follow these rules:

1. Do not use any mark of punctuation *before* the opening parenthesis mark.

> If there is good reason for writing (and I think there is), we will do so tomorrow.

2. Place *after* (outside) the end parenthesis mark any regular sentence punctuation—comma, period, question mark, exclamation point, colon, or semicolon.

> If you will call us tomorrow (625-2319), we will have the information for you.
>
> Does your firm specialize in office equipment: desks, chairs, tables, files (all makes)? (The sentence is a question; therefore, the question mark is placed *after* the end parenthesis mark.)

3. Place *inside* the end parenthesis mark any question mark, exclamation point, or abbreviation period that belongs with the words enclosed in parentheses.

The Kelly Mills have moved to Charlottetown (or was it Halifax?). (Here the parenthetical words are a question. Note that the regular sentence punctuation, the period, is placed *after* the end parenthesis mark.)

The taxi driver (the wretch!) claimed to have no small change. (Since the words enclosed in parentheses are exclamatory, the exclamation point is placed inside the end parenthesis mark.)

4. Do not capitalize the first word of a parenthetical element unless that first word is a proper noun. This is true even when the words are a complete sentence.

The account may be withdrawn by giving advance notice (this is usually two weeks).

Congratulations on the new job (I should say "position")! (*I* is always capitalized.)

Parenthetical Element Standing Alone When words enclosed in parentheses are not part of a sentence, but are entirely independent, the first word is capitalized and the end punctuation is placed *inside* the end parenthesis mark.

No further action was taken on the Cass case. (See the enclosed annual report for details.) (The parenthetical words are entirely separate and complete.)

Please accept my best wishes for your new work. (How does it feel to be boss?) (Since the parenthetical words are a question, the question mark is placed *before* the end parenthesis.)

☐ CLASS PRACTICE 2

Now it is time to practice the punctuation principles just presented. Insert punctuation marks and capital letters as needed in each of the following sentences.

1. When you reach Windsor (it will probably be near noon) be sure to telephone the office.
2. Please select one of the following colors (they are all that are offered) gray, blue, or red.
3. Please send me the proper quality of ribbon (is it No. 1 or No. 2) for my typewriter.
4. I was delighted to receive a salary increase (and retroactive to January 1)
5. Would you be interested in our introductory offer of twelve treatments for $25 (regularly $3.50 a treatment)
6. President Barr did not mention moving (a great many things required his attention yesterday) but, so far as we are concerned, we can be ready at short notice.
7. A thrifty person estimates his income and expenditures for a given period. (this is known as "budgeting" and is explained in Chapter V)

The Apostrophe

In Unit 13 you studied the use of the apostrophe to indicate possession. In Unit 12 you learned that the apostrophe is used to form plurals of certain letters, symbols, signs, and words used as words. As a brief refresher, these uses are illustrated below.

> Men's and boys' swimming trunks are sold in our sportswear department. (Swimming trunks belonging to men and to boys—the apostrophe indicates possession.)
>
> Your *a's* are not written plainly. *(a's,* plural of *a.)*

Other uses of the apostrophe are as follows:

In Contractions   Use an apostrophe to indicate contractions—shortened forms of one or more words; as: *nat'l* for *national; don't* for *do not;* and *o'clock* for *of the clock.* Some words formerly considered contractions are now recognized as complete words; for example, *phone* and *cello.*

For Omission of Figures   Use the apostrophe to signal the omission of the first figures of a year: '77 for 1977.

For Invented Words   A word that is devised from a letter or an abbreviation must be signaled as being an invention. To do this, add an apostrophe and *d* or *ing* to the coined verb.

> The order was OK'd before we sent it to you.

☐ CLASS PRACTICE 3

Practice the several uses of the apostrophe by correctly inserting apostrophes in these sentences where necessary.

1. The "Three Rs" are the subject of many magazine articles.
2. We just cant get the shipment out today.
3. Charles mother had previously met the manager of the office.
4. I know for a fact that Mr. Alger was born in 99.
5. Some unions advocate that workers birthdays be paid holidays.
6. One of Miss Doe's duties is the OKing of requisitions.

Communication Problems

Application Exercises

A ■

On a separate sheet of paper, indicate for these sentences the correct marks of punctuation.

1   We cannot consider your recommendation until after July 1 (the beginning of our fiscal year) therefore, please write us after that date.
2   The hurricane of 38 was more disastrous than the blizzard of 88.
3   If you call before eleven on Monday, we shall be able to make a definite appointment for you. (our number is 737-6558)
4   I cannot read the name, for it has been Xd out.
5   What amount was entered in the bankbook (passbook)
6   Mr. Acton uses too many "so's" in his speeches.
7   The man repaired my radio free of charge (can you beat it)
8   Whos to be notified to attend the meeting?
9   Mr. Bell is not of legal age (if we can believe the records) but he has been made a member of the city council.
10 Please arrive at the pier in ample time (the ship sails at 10 a.m.)
11 There are two "ts" in *committed*.
12 At this point I recommend do you follow me? that we revert to our old policy.
13 The bank may refuse to honor pay or cash the cheque when it is presented.
14 Since the Everglades are low (swampy) high winds and rains bring floods.
15 Final reports will be ready Monday (or is it Friday?) and as soon as they are assembled, we will call you so that you may analyze them.

B ■

Find and correct the errors in the following sentences. If a sentence is correct, write "OK" on your paper.

1   Within the offices had that look of bustling prosperity.
2   We cannot send you the catalogue immediately. As it is not yet off the press.
3   Note these special features (operated from the keyboard): (1) margin set, (2) tab clear, (3) tab set, and (4) electric carriage return.
4   Bill failed the final examination, and had to take another one the following year.
5   Did you characterize your warehouse as "bursting with activity?"
6   Judith has developed into an excellent proofreader, Miss Akers was her special office teacher.
7   The Rapido one of the finest trains in the country runs daily between Toronto and Montreal.
8   I shall be glad to lend you my copy of "Where Do We Go Now?"
9   Show me a typist who X's out errors, and I will show you a person who is not long for the job.
10 It seems to me that these are the character traits, that will make you a valued employee.
11 You are to be commended for an excellent job a really excellent job.
12 The appliance then called "radio," would be a museum piece today.
13 The Japanese beetle is not very troublesome in its native country (Japan); however, in America it is a most destructive insect.
14 Our manager made this strong statement: "Our product is suitable for domestic trade only".

15 "The stock market," reports the financial sheet, "suffered another 'sinking spell' yesterday."

C ■

Edit and revise this paragraph.

Where else but at Blanton's can you find such beautiful gifts (and at such reasonable prices?) As a frequent caller at the Blanton Gift Shoppe you know that bargins galore will be available at the pre-Christmas sale on November 28. Do come in and browse around, you won't be wasting your time.

Word Study

A ■

Words often confused: access, excess; forbear, forebear.

B ■

What is the difference in the meaning of these pairs of words?

1 consummate ('kän-sə-mat) and consummate (kən-'səm-ət)
2 invalid ('in-və-ləd) and invalid (in-'val-əd)
3 refuse ('ref-yüs) and refuse (ri-'fyüz)
4 entrance ('en-trən(t)s) and entrance (in-'tran(t)s)

C ■

Should *y*, *i*, or *ie* appear in the blank spaces in order to complete the following words?

1 bus ___ ness   3 occup ___ ing   5 trolle ___ s
2 dr ___ ness   4 rel ___ ance   6 tr ___ s

Communication in Action: *Supervising People*

As department head, you receive the following written report from a supervisor: "I cannot recommend Miss Allison for a salary increase. During her first six months as my assistant, she tried. Then she lost interest. Now my work is taking second place to her long coffee breaks and her personal visits and telephone calls. It took three hours yesterday to get a simple, six-page report typed. I request that you talk with her."

You have asked Miss Allison to come to your office. What will you say to her? Enact the scene with another student.

PART 6

Capitalization, Abbreviations, Figures ▫

Now that you know how to use punctuation signals, you are almost ready to go to work. Remaining, however, are three more signaling tools whose use you must master. You must know how to convey a message by capitalizing or not capitalizing; for instance, that "West" means a particular section of the country, but "west" denotes direction. You must know when, and when not, to abbreviate. You must know how to write numbers correctly, because lack of such knowledge could result in serious loss of time and money. Your mastery of principles presented in Part 6 will give you full command of all the essential technical signs and signals used by a writer.

Capitalization

In this unit you will learn how to use the last of the signals that you need in order to make your written messages perfectly clear—the capitalization signal. The principles you are asked to study are basic principles followed by most people. When starting a new job, however, keep in mind that some businesses may modify these rules slightly. Check any capitalization about which you are in doubt.

First Words

Capitalize the first word of (1) a sentence or a group of words used as a sentence; (2) a direct quotation; (3) each item in an outline; and (4) each line of poetry.

> Her new car was dark red.
>
> No, not now. (Group of words used as a sentence.)
>
> He exclaimed, "Turn out the lights!" (Direct quotation)
>
> Business Letter Form
>> I. The Heading
>>> A. The Letterhead
>>> B. The Dateline
>>> C. Typed Headings
>> II. The Opening
>
> Do you fear the force of the wind,
> The slash of the rain?   —*Hamlin Garland*

Proper Nouns and Adjectives

Capital letters are used mainly to signal *proper nouns*, which name particular persons, places, or things, and *proper adjectives*, which are the adjectives derived from those names. Remember that all-important word *particular*. It may be of help to think of capitalized words as denoting private property. For instance: Your name is capitalized because it is your private property; *Spain* is capitalized because that name is the private property of that country; *Bureau of the Census* is capitalized because that name is the private property of that bureau.

Names of Persons   A person's own name is very important. Therefore, if you do not write a person's name as he wishes it to be written, you run the risk of causing ill will. If you have any way of checking—via the files or current incoming letters—

be careful to write a name exactly as written by the person who owns it. Lacking such information, use these rules:

1. *O', Mc, Mac.* The prefixes *O'* and *Mc* are always followed by a capital letter without extra spacing: *O'Neil, McCaffery.* The prefix *Mac* may or may not be followed by a capital, depending on the style used by the owner of the name: *MacNamara, Macmillan.*

2. *D, da, de, della, di, du, la, le, lo, van, von.* Whether or not to capitalize these prefixes depends on these two factors:

a. If only the last name is used, the prefix is capitalized: *Du Pree, De Frias, Von Ribbentrop.*

b. If a first name *or a title* is used with the last name, the prefixes are not capitalized. *François de la Croix, Madame la Salle, Elsa von Veer.*

☐ CLASS PRACTICE 1

In the following sentences, indicate which words should be capitalized and explain why.

1. many of our most successful businessmen started out as office boys.
2. will van hoch be in the office on Monday?
3. the manager said, "your sales approach was commented on favorably."
4. mary obrien is my best friend.
5. indeed, yes.
6. mr. de lancy does not approve of chewing gum.

Names of Places Capitalize names of places as follows:

1. Capitalize the names of countries, geographical localities, streets, parks, rivers, and buildings: *Switzerland, North Africa, Northwest Street, Stanley Park, the St. Lawrence River, the Confederation Building.*

2. Capitalize points of the compass—*North, West, Southeast*—when those names denote a particular section of the country. When compass points refer simply to direction, they are not capitalized.

The West is the heart of the oil industry. (*West* is a name of a particular section of the country.)

We are thinking of going south this winter. (*South* is not capitalized because it indicates direction.)

3. Capitalize the word *city* only when it is part of the corporate name of a city: *Dawson City,* but *the city of Edmonton.*

4. Capitalize the word *province* only when it is used in imaginative or special names: *La Belle Province,* referring to the province of Quebec.

5. Capitalize the word *the* in names of places only when *the* is part of the official name: *The Pas* (a town in Manitoba), but *the Maritime Provinces.*

☐ CLASS PRACTICE 2

In these sentences, capitalize the names of places that you think should be capitalized.

1. The "Nautilus" traveled under the north pole.
2. Crystal city is in the province of Manitoba.
3. When you go to the Netherlands, be sure to visit the Hague.
4. The west offers a visitor scenery unlike that in any other part of the country.
5. Our offices are in the Globe building.

Names of Organizations   Capitalize the names of particular companies, associations, societies, commissions, committees, bureaus, boards, departments, schools, political parties, conventions, fraternities, clubs, religious bodies, and so on.

International Typographical Union	East High School
McGraw-Hill Book Company	Liberal Party
Canada Council	Buddhists
Vancouver City College	Canadian Red Cross
Meridian City Council	Better Business Bureau

If in doubt as to whether to capitalize the name of a certain group or organization, ask yourself this question: Is this a name that is the private property of a particular organization? Look at the following illustrations.

Mr. Fyfe's family attends the First Methodist Church. (The name *First Methodist Church* is the private property of this particular institution.)

Mr. Fyfe's family attends the first church that was built in this city. (Is there any name here that is the private property of any particular institution? No. Then there is no particular name to capitalize.)

Note that some names of organizations are preceded by *the*. Capitalize *the* when it precedes a name only when it is part of the recognized official name. If you do not know whether *the* is part of an organization's official title, check to find out.

I have applied for membership in The National Secretaries Association (International). (The official name is *The National Secretaries Association (International)*.)

Do you know the mailing address for the Canadian Institute on Public Affairs? (The official name is *Canadian Institute on Public Affairs*.)

Names of Government Bodies   Capitalize names of international organizations; of national, provincial, and city government bodies and their branches; and of positions of high-ranking government people.

Minister of Finance	Unemployment Insurance Commission
United Nations	Department of Education

Names of Commercial Products Names of commercial products are capitalized—*Griffin Shoe Shine, Master's Coffee, Moon Radio*. Some writers have difficulty recognizing the difference between the proper nouns that are part of the official title of a commercial product and common nouns that name the general class to which the nouns refer. The following illustrations should help to make this difference clear to you.

> Have you considered looking at the Gelidaire washing machine? (*Washing machine* it not part of the official title; so it is not capitalized.)

> I have heard that the Weston Launderquik does a most satisfactory job. (The name that is the private property of this particular product is *Weston Launderquik*.)

Names of Historical Events and Documents Capitalize names of important historical events; of movements; of periods; and of specific treaties, bills, acts, and laws: *World War II, the British North America Act, the Dark Ages, Medicare*.

Names of Items in Sequence Capitalize nouns identifying items used in numerical or alphabetical sequence: *Model No. 757, Invoice 3478, Exhibit A*. (NOTE: the abbreviation *No.* for *number* is always capitalized.)

Names of Holidays, Months, Days of Week Names of holidays, both legal and religious, are capitalized—*New Year's Day, National Education Week, Easter, Yom Kippur*—as are names of the months and the days of the week. Note, however, that the seasons are *not* capitalized, nor are the earth, sun, and moon.

Thursday	*but:*	the *spring* sales
February		the new *fall* styles
Labor Day		a soft landing on the *moon*

□ CLASS PRACTICE 3

Find out how well you can apply the rules for capitalizing names of things by capitalizing the correct words in the following sentences.

1. The north atlantic council is the governing body of NATO.
2. The Canada labour relations board reports to the minister of labour.
3. When may we expect delivery of the blue rose coffee requested on our purchase order no. 423?
4. How many times has the supreme court reversed its decisions?
5. The unemployment insurance act has been amended a number of times.

Proper Adjectives Since proper nouns are capitalized, adjectives derived from proper nouns are also capitalized. These are called *proper adjectives*.

> In Mexico, the language used is Spanish. There seems to be no Mexican language as such. (*Spanish* and *Mexican* are proper adjectives derived from the proper nouns *Spain* and *Mexico*.)

French restaurant	Georgian architecture
British humor	South American countries

NOTE: Through long use, certain adjectives are no longer capitalized because they have lost their association with the proper nouns from which they were derived; for example, *french* dressing, *india* ink, *turkish* towel, *panama* hat. Always check a dictionary to make sure whether or not to capitalize such adjectives.

Substitutions   We in Canada often devise nicknames for persons and places if somebody or some place attains prolonged prominence. Such a descriptive term is capitalized if (1) it is generally known and recognized, and (2) you can lift out the term and substitute the name of the actual person or the actual place.

Mr. Martin has gone to the Lakehead for a few days. (Lakehead, describing Thunder Bay and the area around that city on the northwest shore of Lake Superior.)

In 1873, the Father of Confederation was re-elected as Prime Minister. (Sir John A. Macdonald is known by the descriptive term *Father of Confederation*. You can substitute *Sir John A. Macdonald* for the *Father of Confederation* in this sentence.)

CLASS PRACTICE 4

In the following sentences, capitalize the words that should be capitalized and tell why.

1. How many times have you crossed the american border?
2. The happy warrior was known to be a wise politician.
3. The weather over the labor day weekend was fall-like.
4. It is interesting to read of korean customs and culture.
5. The African Campaign was noted for the brilliance of the desert fox.

Shortened Forms   Occasionally, instead of writing out a complete name for some particular person, place, or thing, a writer will use only part of that name. In such a case, the shortened form is capitalized to indicate that a *particular, specific* person, place, or thing is meant.

You are to report to the Admiral immediately upon termination of your leave. (The capitalization of *admiral* signals that one *particular* admiral is meant. The sentence could have been written: "You are to report to Admiral James A. West immediately upon . . . .")

Does the trip you mention include four days on the Lakes? (*Lakes* is the shortened form for *Great Lakes*, or other specific lakes understood by the reader.)

Mr. Shaw is the youngest member of the Commons. (*Commons* indicates the *House of Commons*.)

Theatre audiences stand during the singing of The Queen. (Capitalizing *The Queen* denotes the anthem, *God Save The Queen*.)

☐   CLASS PRACTICE 5

Before you indicate capitalization of the words in the following sentences, think about this principle: Capitalize a shortened form when you can replace that form by the full name of a particular person, place, or thing.

1. The association voted to contribute to all charity drives.
2. Has the prime minister announced the new cabinet members?
3. In Canada, functions of the crown are discharged by the governor general.
4. Mr. Dodds is a member of the legislative assembly.
5. The ambassador has claimed diplomatic immunity.
6. We have invited a judge, a senator, and a colonel to join our organization.
7. Please prepare a list of members of the house of commons.
8. When you are in Vancouver, be sure to take time to see the bridge.
9. We like to boast that we have the best high school in the province.

Titles of Publications, Works of Art

Many writers (and typists) do not know how to capitalize a manuscript heading or the title of a publication. To them, when to capitalize and when not to capitalize are complete mysteries. The rule is this: Capitalize the first word and all main words in the titles of books, articles, poems, works of art, and musical compositions; but *do not capitalize* articles *(a, an, the)*, conjunctions, and short prepositions. A "short preposition" is one having five or fewer letters. Obviously, if the preposition has six or more letters, it should be capitalized.

Teaching Principles and Procedures for Gregg Shorthand (And is a conjunction; *for* is a three-letter preposition.)

The Case Against War (Against is a preposition of more than five letters and is, therefore, capitalized.)

A problem may arise when a heading or a title contains a hyphenated compound word. Capitalize a hyphenated compound just as you would if it were not a compound.

"How to Use High-Speed Tools"

"Readings from Sixty-Three Books"

Personal and Official Titles

The following principles will tell you whether or not to capitalize titles used with names of persons.

Titles Preceding Names of Persons   Capitalize professional, business, executive, civic, military, religious, and family titles that *precede* names of persons. More simply, whenever a person has a title that you write *before* his name, capitalize that title.

The invitation list includes Professor Edward Seton, Chief Justice Fred A. Vine, and Captain Robert McCaffery.

Titles Following Names of Persons   Titles written *after* names of persons are always capitalized on envelopes and in inside addresses; for example:

Mr. John W. Dolan, City Editor
The Westerly Sun
Edmonton, Alberta T6E 3L2

In all other cases where titles *follow* names, capitalize the titles only when they belong to high Government officials.

The Right Honorable Lester Pearson, when Minister of External Affairs, won the Nobel Peace Prize. (Note the capitalization of title preceding the name of a person, as well as capitalization following the name of a person who is a high government official.)

The Honorable Mr. Jean-Jacques Blais, Postmaster General, forewarned of a further increase in postal rates. (Postmaster General is capitalized because an office in the Cabinet is a high government position.)

John J. White, mayor of Chatham, is much interested in fire-fighting procedures. *(Mayor* is not capitalized because it is not a *high* government position.)

Hyphenated Titles   When *ex-* and *-elect* are joined to titles, they are not capitalized. Although not hyphenated, *former* and *late* also are not capitalized when used with titles. To illustrate:

The welcoming address will be given by Mayor-elect Rogers.

Did former Mayor Williams receive a pension from the Government?

Mr. Harper, the late Minister of Health, retired to his ranch in Alberta.

☐   CLASS PRACTICE 6

As a check to see how well you understand capitalization of titles used with names of persons and titles of books and articles, indicate which words in the following sentences should be capitalized.

1. Recommendations will be solicited from treasurer-elect Sherman.
2. The annual cleanup campaign was announced by Harold Thorpe, health commissioner.
3. David B. Sloan, chairman of the Appropriations Committee, has a new secretary.
4. Anton's book, *the English-speaking nations,* will be published in two volumes.
5. You will have to ask chairman Grant for a ruling on the question.
6. Mr. Henry W. Powers, treasurer of the Milford Storage Company, is best qualified for the position.
7. You really should study the article, ''how to read the financial page.''

Miscellaneous Rules

Letter Parts In the salutation of a letter, capitalize the first word and any title. In the complimentary closing, capitalize only the first word.

Dear Mr. Bradley: Very truly yours,
My dear Mr. Bradley:

Family Titles Capitalize words denoting family relationships only when they are used as a part of a person's name or as a substitute for a person's name.

Mother   *but:*   my mother
Uncle Harry   his uncle

School Subjects Capitalize the names of languages and of specific numbered courses. Do not capitalize the names of subjects, except for any proper nouns or adjectives in the subject name.

French   *but:*   journalism
Algebra II   Canadian history

"I" and "O" Always capitalize the pronoun *I* and the interjection *O*. But do not capitalize the interjection *Oh* unless it begins a sentence.

Communication Problems

Application Exercises

A ■

On a separate sheet of paper, indicate the correct capitalization of words in the following sentences.

1   Our new fashion consultant is Paul De beaumont.
2   The easter and passover holidays occur about the same time.
3   The treasurer-elect quickly assembled his office staff.
4   Mr. Burgess is a veteran of the battle of the Marne.
5   All my graduate work was done at the university.
6   The liberal national convention will be held in Toronto.
7   If you write a personal letter to the mayor, he will probably accept your invitation to speak.
8   Can you recite the poem "the owl and the pussycat"?
9   For best results do this: check the capitalization of any words that do not conform to the capitalization rules you have learned.
10 Many people have never visited the caribou country.

11 The security council of the united nations has great influence on the peace of the world.

12 The lakehead is noted for its beautiful scenery.

13 "Results of the twenty-first investigation" was the title of Anderson's report.

14 The people of the far east have a lower economic level of living than those of Canada.

15 Without exception, the staff members are loyal to the company.

B ■

Correct all the errors in the following sentences. If a sentence is correct, write "OK" on your paper.

1 Did Mr. Blaine say, "Turn west" or "Turn left?"

2 The strait of Magellan was named for the man who discovered it.

3 The heading of Chapter X is "The War between the States."

4 We know that you will be interested in this type of job (secretarial); your training has prepared you for it.

5 There is no opening in our office just now, nevertheless, we shall be glad to place your name at the top of our list.

6 The new member of the Cabinet has no comment to make.

7 Mr. Houston handles all our adjustments, he will be glad to discuss your problem with you.

8 Mr. Andrews has invested in some Montana Copper Mines.

9 Winnipeg, Manitoba, is a well-known railroad terminal.

10 Mr. Bergen the new controller has his office on the tenth floor.

11 The author worried about having the manuscript ready for the printer hired additional typists.

12 We certainly did enjoy la Follette's speech.

13 Here is an easy way to multiply by 75: first multiply by 100 and divide by 4; then multiply the result obtained by 3.

14 Is the new doctor a member of the Association?

15 The best seller was written by James B. Douglas, former chief justice of the Supreme Court of the United States.

C ■

"To capitalize or not to capitalize" is your main problem here, but not your only problem. Find and correct errors in punctuation, and in mechanics as well.

You will be interested to learn that the main speaker for the writers' club banquet will be Ex-Mayor John P. Crowley, his topic will be Humor Is From Within. As toastmaster you might like to gather data on the mayor's accomplishments as a humorist. If there is anything I can do to help you may call on me at any time.

Word Study

A ■

Words often confused: credible, creditable; metal, mettle, medal, meddle.

B ■

Two of the words in each of the following groups are synonymous. Pair the words.

1 genuine, commodious, spacious, fabulous
2 prestige, knowledge, attainments, renown
3 superficial, ridiculous, shallow, serious
4 disparage, value, discredit, distrust

C ■

Indicate whether the following words are masculine or feminine; also give the correct spelling for the word of opposite gender.

1	executrix	3	comedienne	5	heroine
2	actor	4	alumna	6	host

Communication in Action: *Correcting an Error*

The salesclerk had written $7 on a sales check instead of $9. As cashier, you find the error when the customer comes to pay you. Exactly what will you say to this customer to correct the error and yet retain goodwill?

UNIT □ 32

Abbreviations

An abbreviation is a signal used in place of a word or several words. In business communications, some terms are always abbreviated, as *f.o.b.* for "free on board" and *C.O.D.* for "collect on delivery." Such terms are few, however. For most business writing, abbreviating is frowned upon, as the primary aim of business writing is to make a message absolutely clear; and abbreviating is a threat to the clarity of the message. The reader may not understand the abbreviation or may misread it.

Personal Titles and Firm Names

If you are thinking of abbreviating a person's name or the name of a company, check the files or current incoming letters to see how the person or the firm wishes the name to be written. Lacking a means of checking, spell out a name rather than abbreviate it. Your motto could well be: "When in doubt, spell it out."

Titles After Names Always abbreviate the following titles when they are written *after* a name: *Jr.* (for "Junior"), *Sr.* (for "Senior"), *B.S.* (for "Bachelor of Science"), *Ph.D.* (for "Doctor of Philosophy"), and other degrees.

Melvin E. Stone, M.D.   George S. Miller, A.M., Ph.D.

Titles Before Names Always abbreviate the following titles when they are written *before* a person's name: *Mr., Messrs., Mrs., Ms.,* and *St.* for "Saint." *Miss* is not included in this list because it is not an abbreviation.

Messrs. Newton, O'Malley, and Buonono   Ms. van Dyk   St. Christopher

Titles Before Full Names When a title precedes a *full name,* practice differs. In formal usage, such titles should always be spelled out; and many writers prefer to spell them out under all circumstances. In business correspondence, technical writing, tabulations, or wherever brevity is desirable, abbreviated forms are commonly used.

Dr. Amos F. Cutler   Prof. William T. Green
Lt. S. Henry Archer   Supt. T. Alan Crowe

Titles Before Last Names Only Write in full any titles that you use with just the last names of persons. Remember this when you are writing the salutation of a letter.

Doctor Strong   Governor Farnsworth
Professor Green   Captain Winter

Titles of Respect and Dignity *Reverend* and *Honorable* are titles of respect and dignity used in addressing clergymen and government officials of any rank. Spell out these titles, except in addresses, lists, and notices. *The* will precede the titles in formal usage but may be omitted in addresses, lists, and notices. In the following illustrations, note that a first name or another title follows *The Reverend* or *The Honorable.*

The Reverend Carl Worcester   The Honorable Jay F. Arnold
The Reverend Doctor Worcester   The Honorable Mr. Arnold

But: Rev. Carl Worcester
         2200 McBride Crescent
         Prince George, British Columbia
         V2M 1Z7

Firm Names As mentioned earlier in this unit, a part of a firm name is abbreviated only when you are sure that the abbreviation is used by the company in question. Only when you have so seen it in print would you abbreviate the words *Company, Corporation, Association, Brothers, Railroad, Railway, Manufacturing,* or any other part of a firm name.

☐   CLASS PRACTICE 1

In the following sentences, indicate words that should be abbreviated and abbreviations that should be spelled out.

1. The data were obtained from Prof. Ives.
2. We have received a report from Mr. Geo. D. Macafee describing recent economic developments.
3. The name of the marshall of the parade is General Arnold G. Braintree.
4. When you arrived at the scene of the accident, had a dr. been called?
5. Be sure that you reserve a place on the platform for the Rev. Doctor Cragan.
6. You should have used the salutation "Dear Dr. Cutler."

Punctuating Abbreviations

Most abbreviations are written with periods, but some are not. Following is a discussion of current trends plus specific rules.

Names of Associations, Government Agencies   Probably because of the need to save time, abbreviations for names of associations are used increasingly and are considered correct. If you use such abbreviations, be sure that they are in general use and will not be misunderstood.

C. N. I. B.	Canadian National Institute for the Blind
S. P. C. A.	Society for the Prevention of Cruelty to Animals

The trend in writing abbreviations for government agencies and for certain organizations that are best known by their initials or abbreviated forms is to write them "solid"—with no periods and no spacing. The letter designations or abbreviations of radio and television stations are always written solid.

CBC	Canadian Broadcasting Corporation
NATO	North Atlantic Treaty Organization
CLC	Canadian Labour Congress
CAA	Canadian Automobile Association
CFAM	(Radio station)

Letters Used Instead of Names   Sometimes letters are used to designate a person or a thing, and in such cases no period follows the letters; as: *Mr. B, Exhibit D,* and so on.

You really save money by buying Grade A vegetables.

Shortened Forms   Because of long and frequent use, certain shortened forms have become accepted as complete words. Some of these forms are *ad* for *advertisement, gym* for *gymnasium, phone* for *telephone,* and *lab* for *laboratory.*

The medical secretary should be familiar with terms used in lab work.

To Abbreviate or Not

Whether to abbreviate or not to abbreviate is a question you'll have to answer again and again in business correspondence. To guide you, here are several clear-cut rules.

Always Abbreviate   Always abbreviate the following:

A. D. and B. C. in Year Dates   Important historical dates are often accompanied by the abbreviation *A. D.* (for *anno Domini*, "in the year of our Lord") or *B. C.* ("before Christ"). Note that *A. D.* is written before the year, but *B. C.* is written after the year.

> 400 B. C.   A. D. 1967

a.m. and p.m. in Statements of Time   Although you will see *a.m.* and *p.m.* written in capital letters, the preference is for small letters with no spacing. Be sure that (1) you do not use the word *o'clock* with these abbreviations, and that (2) you do not use the abbreviations without figures.

> You will please report at 9 a.m.
>
> He is to arrive at eight o'clock. (But not *8 o'clock,* or *8 o'clock p.m.*)
>
> Sue will come tomorrow afternoon. (Not *tomorrow p. m.*)

NOTE: The abbreviation for noon is either *n.* or *m.* (for *meridies*, the Latin word meaning *noon*); however, noon is usually spelled out, as *12 noon*.

Number as No. Before Numerals   Before numerals, the word *number* is always abbreviated as *No.*, except when it comes at the beginning of a sentence. Then it is spelled out.

> We are enclosing your Policy No. 345987.
>
> Number 34567 has been assigned to your latest policy.

☐   CLASS PRACTICE 2

Now is the time to see how well you have assimilated the previous topics. In the following sentences, make the necessary abbreviation corrections and explain your reasons for doing so.
1. Have you ever visited any sessions of the U. N. when you were in New York?
2. Is 10 o'clock p.m. the official closing time for the sessions?
3. There are too many "f.o.b.'s" in your advertising copy.
4. An appointment has been made for you at 1 o'clock on Tuesday.
5. Julius Caesar was assassinated in B. C. 44.
6. No. 3 now moves into first place.
7. Box number 483 weighs 10 pounds.

Never Abbreviate   Never abbreviate the following:

Names of Cities, Provinces, States   First on the list of terms that you will never abbreviate are (1) names of cities, no matter how long the names may be; (2) names of the provinces and states unless space is very limited. If you must abbreviate, be sure you know the correct abbreviation!

Names of Cities, Certain States First on the list of terms that you will never abbreviate are (1) names of cities, no matter how long the names may be; and (2) names of these states: *Alaska, Hawaii, Idaho, Iowa, Maine, Ohio,* and *Utah.*

NOTE: The U.S. Post Office Department has adopted two-letter abbreviations that may be used for all states with ZIP Codes. However, these abbreviations should be used only in addresses on envelopes; as: *Alaska, Ak.; Hawaii, Hi.; Idaho, Id.; Iowa, Ia.; Maine, Me.; Ohio, Oh.; and Utah, Ut.*

"Fort," "Mount," "Point," and "Port" in Names of Places Never abbreviate *Fort, Mount, Point,* and *Port* in place names. Instead, write *Fort Erie, Mount Forest, Point Edward,* and *Port Colborne.* Always check "Saint" before abbreviating: *Saint John,* but *St. John's.*

Terms of Measure Except in technical work and on invoices, spell out the names of the common units of weight, length, capacity, area, volume, temperature, and time. In ordinary business writing you would write *50 pounds, 7 yards, 4 square miles, 8 dozen,* and the like.

Compass Points In business communications, a compass point used in a sentence should be spelled out. You would write, "The new building is at the *northeast* corner of Elm and Cutler Streets." However, compass directions used in a specialized business, such as surveying would be written as *N., NE., SSE.,* and so on.

Avoid Abbreviating Avoid abbreviating the following:

Names of Streets In the message part of business writing, do not abbreviate names of streets, roads, avenues, and so on. For reasons of space, however, these names may be abbreviated in lists, in inside addresses, and on envelopes.

Geographical Names Preferably, spell out all geographical place names.

Days and Months Names of days of the week and months of the year are preferably spelled out. Because of lack of space—as in a table or a list—you may be forced to abbreviate. *May, June,* and *July,* however, are never abbreviated.

☐ CLASS PRACTICE 3

Using your knowledge of the topics just presented, correct the following sentences. Explain each correction you make.

1. Mr. Drake plans to go to Tor. on Monday of next week.
2. We have found that Oct. is our worst month for sales.
3. The prov. of Nfld. was our tenth province.
4. Is the store you mention on the W. side of Front St.?
5. Ft. St. James was the original capital of B.C.

Plurals of Abbreviations

In Unit 12 you learned to use an apostrophe and *s* to indicate the plural of an abbreviation consisting of letters. You would write: two *C.O.D.'s*, *f.o.b.'s*, *C. P. A.'s*, and the like. To form the plurals of most other abbreviations, *s* is added to the singular form; as: *yds.*, *lbs.*, *depts.* Some abbreviations, however, are the to the singular form; as: *depts.*, *Nos.*

Communication Problems

Application Exercises

A ■

Each of the following sentences contains an error in the use of abbreviations. On a separate sheet of paper, correct each error and justify the correction.

1   Mr. Ash calls his assistants Miss A. and Miss B., for he can never remember names.
2   Our guest of honor will be the Hon. Charles E. Hyde.
3   The customer asked that the fob point be shown on our quotation to him.
4   The school gym. is the best place for the football rally.
5   Have you asked the Off. Mgr. for a copy of the new form?
6   Their new executive officer is Lieutenant Peter Clinton.
7   The Middle Ages are generally considered to have begun in 400 A. D.
8   F. B. Axton, Junior, is the man who ordered the hampers.
9   Is Pt. Alberni on Vancouver Is.?
10 Martha Simmons, Master of Arts, is writing a textbook.

B ■

Find and correct the errors in all incorrect sentences. Write "OK" on your paper for every sentence that is correct.

1   Our firm specializes in the georgian style of architecture.
2   This food has an alkaline (nonacid) reaction in the body.
3   "What are your reasons"? challenged the chairman.
4   I should like very much to accept, however, circumstances force me to decline.
5   The Alderman will meet with his constituents on Monday at the City Hall.
6   Your erasures, on the other hand, are always very neat.
7   The C.P.P. became effective January 1, 1966.
8   Many of our executives do not use our teletype, they seem to prefer to use the commercial wire service.
9   The mts. have a grandeur all their own.
10 I am happy to contribute to the fund. Since so many of our group will benefit from it.

C ■

The realtor who wrote the following paragraph asks you to revise it for him.

The house at 116 Tipping Rock Rd. is not NHA-approved. Although one of the oldest houses in the community (1779 A.D.), it has never been restored. No. 120, on the other hand, has been modernized, therefore, it meets the standards set up by NHA. The latter house is for sale and is presently owned by Mr. Ray A. Cole Superintendent of the local schools. Would you like me to make arrangements for you to look at the Cole house with a view to buying it.

UNIT □ 33

Figures

If you have mastered all the various punctuation "Stop" signs and signals, you can write with confidence, knowing that your words will not be misunderstood. But what about the numbers you use? Will you write them in words or *figures?*

In business correspondence, numbers are more often written in figures than in words, but the writer must know when to use words and when to use figures.

Numbers Written as Words

In general, write in words all isolated numbers that can be expressed in not more than two words.

Numbers One Through Ten   Always write numbers from one through ten in words when such numbers are used in isolated instances.

Miss St. John has had four years' experience as a secretary.

Numbers one through ten *must* be written in words when used in isolated instances, but numbers eleven through one hundred *may* be written in words. If your eye is offended by "So far this month, there have been 18 instances of absenteeism," you may write "eighteen instances."

Even and Approximate Numbers   Even and approximate numbers are written in words.

We have received exactly one thousand applications.

Approximately two million refugees will be affected.

When spelling out even numbers over one thousand, express the numbers in the fewest possible words:

fifteen hundred (*Not:* one thousand five hundred)

Numbers That Begin Sentences Write in words numbers that begin sentences.

Twenty-six executives attended the planning session.

Of course, if writing out the number is awkward, the sentence may be rephrased so as to change the position of the number.

Fractions That Stand Alone; Mixed Numbers When a fraction stands alone (is not used with a whole number), write that fraction in words.

Approximately two-thirds of the building is in need of water-proofing.

When spelling out a mixed number (a whole number and a fraction), be sure to use the word *and* to separate the whole number from the fraction.

Our turnover is two and one-half times that of the other firms in the city.

Centuries and Decades In formal writing, numbers referring to centuries or decades are written in words.

The United States did not feel the effects of the Industrial Revolution until the nineteenth century.

Life must have been exciting in the Gay Nineties.

Metric Measurements

By "going metric" Canada has introduced a new vocabulary to most Canadians. Some metric terms are familiar by now, and some you will only need to know if you are involved in scientific work. As you prepare for work in an office, however, you will need to know how to use the common metric symbols and what they mean.

Metric Units The most common metric units are the *metre, gram,* and *litre.* These measure length, mass, and liquid volume. To these words are added prefixes to make larger or smaller units. Highway speeds are measured in kilometres per hour, and temperature is measured in degrees Celsius. The table on page 261 sets out the units you are most likely to meet and their application.

Writing Metric Measurements Metric symbols are *not* abbreviations and are therefore not followed by a period unless they come at the end of a sentence. Neither is it correct to pluralize metric symbols. Leave *one* blank space between the quantity figure and the metric symbol.

Flight baggage limits are 20 kg for economy and 30 kg for first class.

The unit names are written out in full only when they do not appear with any number. Whenever numbers are used, they are written in figures followed by the appropriate symbol.

How many kilometres is it from here to your cottage? It's only 50 km.

Speeds In speeds, the word *per* is used when quoting general terms; when using exact figures, write the symbols separated by the solidus stroke (/).

Speeds may be stated in metres per second or in kilometres per hour.

A speed of 10m/s is equal to 36 km/h.

☐ CLASS PRACTICE 1

How clear is your understanding of these occasions where numbers are written in words? Correct the following sentences and explain why you made your corrections.

1. About 200 typists are employed by that insurance company.
2. We found that 2 of the dozen shirts you sent us were marked "seconds."
3. The job breakdown shows that ⅖ of her time is spent in checking.
4. 110 applications were received for this high-level position.
5. Within an hour after opening for business, we had 10 calls about our advertisement.
6. Approximately 1,800 registration forms were mailed to members.
7. I can remember only that World War II ended sometime in the 40's.

Numbers Written in Figures

Numbers over Ten Previously, you learned that isolated numbers one through ten *must* be written in words, and that numbers from eleven through one hundred are preferably written in figures but *may* be written in words. You would be wise to find out which form your employer prefers.

By the end of the year we expect to have 11 new designs. (This is correct according to the rule.)

By the end of the year we expect to have eleven new designs. (Your employer prefers the number spelled out; he feels the word looks better than the figure.)

Numbers over one hundred, with the exception of round numbers, are written in figures.

The book you mention has 212 pages.

Numbers in a Series When you write a sentence containing a series of numbers, some of which must be written in figures and others that should be written in words, write *all* numbers in figures so that their form will be consistent.

TABLE OF METRIC TERMS

Quantity	Unit	Symbol	Relationship
length	kilometre	km	1 km = 1000 m Length of a brisk 10 min walk Vancouver to Victoria is 100 km.
	metre	m	1 m = 100 cm Half the height of the average door
	centimetre	cm	1 cm = 10 mm About the width of a little fingernail 3 cm = a light snowfall
	millimetre	mm	1000 mm = 1 m A dime is 1 mm thick.
mass(*)	tonne	t	1 t = 1000 kg A Volkswagen has a mass of about 1 t.
	kilogram	kg	1 kg = 1000 g Sugar is packaged in 2 kg bags.
	gram	g	1 g = 1000 mg A small tube of toothpaste has a mass of 40 g.
	milligram	mg	1000 mg = 1 g About 300 mg is the mass of an Asperin.

(*)**Mass** is the amount of matter in an object and replaces "weight" in metric terminology.

liquid volume	kilolitre	kL	1 kL = 1000 L Used to measure liquid content, as in a swimming pool or gasoline truck
	litre	L	1 L = 1000 mL Milk comes in 1 L, 2 L, or 3 L cartons.
	millilitre	mL	1000 mL = 1 L A small tube of toothpaste contains 25 mL of toothpaste.
speed	kilometres per hour	km/h	City speed limits will be 50 km/h and highway speed limits will be 80 km/h — 100 km/h.
temperature	degrees Celsius	°C	Water freezes at 0°C and boils at 100°C. Normal body temperature is 37°C.

Of the more than 200 members of the graduating class, 59 plan to become nurses; 65, secretaries; 8, dietitians. The remainder have not made known their plans. (Note *8* dietitians, not *eight.*)

Time Connected with Discount or Interest Rates   For clarity and emphasis, periods of time mentioned with terms of discount or interest rates are written in figures.

If you will pay for the goods within 10 days, they will cost you just $126. (Figures make *10* stand out as the time during which the discount may be taken.)

Percentages   Percentages that appear in isolated instances in sentences should be written in figures followed by *percent.*

The 6 percent method of calculating interest is simple to learn.

When percentages occur in pairs, they are written in figures, with *percent* following the second figure.

NOTE: *Percent* written as one word is preferred practice today over *per cent* (representing the two Latin words, *per centum*).

Our discounts range from 2 to 10 percent.

When percentages occur frequently, use the % sign and repeat that sign with each figure; like this: *discounts of 2%, 5%, and 10%.*

In general business correspondence, fractional percentages are written as common fractions rather than as decimals; as: *33⅓ percent* or *5½%.* In technical work, however, these percentages are usually expressed decimally; as: *5.5%.*

Decimals   Decimals are always expressed in figures. *7.5; 45.5.* A cipher is placed before a decimal marker if the number is less than one, e.g., 0.2568. A space is left between groups of three digits in large decimal figures, e.g., 3.141 597.

☐   CLASS PRACTICE 2

By correcting the following sentences, you will test your understanding of the additional principles relating to the use of figures.

1. Living costs have increased 30 percent to 50 percent.
2. Please send us these items: 15 reams typing paper, ten gros shorthand notebooks,six boxes erasers, and 24 dozen nylon typewriter ribbons.
3. The members of some religious denominations contribute ten percent of their income to the support of their churches.
4. Mr. McKenna's new contract calls for a twenty-five % increase.
5. In decimal, three-fourths is written as 0.75.

Temperatures   When writing temperatures in degrees Celsius, *no* space should be left after the number.

His temperature rose to 38.6°C and we called the doctor.

☐   CLASS PRACTICE 3

Can you correct any errors in writing measurements in these sentences?

1. Box No. 483 has a mass of 10 kilograms.
2. The material is ninety centimetres wide.
3. Today's temperature rose to 28° C.
4. How many litres of milk does that jug hold?
5. The painter needed 8 l of paint to cover the walls.

Consecutive Numbers

If one number immediately follows another, a comma should separate the numbers. Better still, the sentence should be worded so that the numbers do not immediately follow each other.

> In 1960, 3 206 164 t of salt were produced in Canada. (Even with the comma, the sentence looks confusing.)
>
> Canada produced 3 206 164 t of salt in 1960. (The rewording prevents confusion.)

If two numbers form one item, however, rewording is not feasible. In this case, one number is written in words; the other, in figures. Usually, the number that would make the shorter word is spelled out.

> 75 four-cent stamps   two 3 cm nails

Sums of Money

In business communications generally, sums of money are written in figures. Only in specialized writing, such as legal documents, is money written both in words and in figures.

Dollars   You learned in Unit 23 not to use the period and two zeros with even sums of money. However, if you are tabulating, the period and two zeros are used to even the columns.

ITEM	AMOUNT
1 dress	$19.95
1 skirt	14.00
1 scarf	2.89

Whenever you write a *series* of sums of money, use the dollar sign with each member of the series.

> Our new fall blouses are priced at *$15, $17.50,* and *$20.*

Cents   Isolated amounts of cents that appear in a sentence are written in figures followed by the word *cents.*

Take *50 cents* from the petty cash for carfare.

However, to be consistent, use the dollar sign and the decimal point with amounts under $1 if those amounts occur in a series with other sums made up of dollars and cents.

I spent $4 for stamps, $2.50 for stencils, and *$0.60* for file cards.

The symbols ¢ and @ on your typewriter are used only in price quotations and in technical communications.

The Conway Construction Company's bid was for 250 cement blocks @ 75¢ and 4 bags of cement @ 98¢.

Million, Billion   As an aid to clarity, present practice in writing extremely large sums of money is to spell out *million, billion,* and so on. The number of millions or billions, however, is written in figures.

"Foreign sales by our company so far this year exceed $2 billion." (This number could also be written 2 *billion dollars.*)

☐   CLASS PRACTICE 4

Here is an opportunity to practice the preceding principles. Correct the errors in the following sentences.

1. Is the correct price of the coat $79.00 or $89.00?
2. Many items that formerly cost five cents are now priced at 7 cents.
3. Be sure to order 10 2 kg bags for Mrs. Thomas.
4. We shall be happy to sell you gift certificates in the amounts of 5, 10, and $25.
5. The postage due on your last order amounts to 38¢.
6. Soon, Canada's population will exceed twenty-five million persons.
7. In 1975 125 463 subscribers were added to the mailing list.

Dates

The term *ordinal ending* is frequently used in this section pertaining to dates. Ordinal endings are *st, d,* and *th* following figures: *1st, 2d, 3d, 15th,* and so on. Note particularly *2d* and *3d.* The styles *nd* and *rd* are considered old-fashioned.

Day Following Month   When the day follows the month, that day is written in figures, without ordinal endings.

April 15   January 2   July 27

Day Preceding Month   When the day precedes the month, the day is written in figures, *with ordinal endings, or written out as a word.*

the 15th of April   the 2d of January

☐   CLASS PRACTICE 5

Some of the following sentences contain errors in the writing of a date. Find the errors and correct them, stating your reasons for making the corrections.

1. The Adams salesman visits us each year on April 3d.
2. The reorganization will take place on the eleventh of July.
3. We very much appreciate your order of November 20th.
4. Our sale will end on the 22 of January.
5. This year the annual house furnishings sale will be held on the second of May.
6. Did you read carefully the bulletin issued on January 1st?

Ages

Use words when writing numbers that represent ages of people if expressed in years only.

> In our company, any employee who becomes sixty-five years of age is eligible for a pension.

> The Dodds Engine Company is celebrating its fortieth year.

Figures should be used, however, when a person's age is given in years, months, and days.

> At the time of the accident, the insured's age was 45 years 7 months and 5 days. (Because the age is considered as a single unit, no commas are used in the series.)

Time

Units of Time   When referring to time units, spell out single, isolated numbers.

> four years of work   seven months to pay

Time of Day   With the word *o'clock*, spell out the number representing the time. With *a.m.* and *p.m.*, use the figure.

> All employees must be back from lunch by one o'clock. (But never *one o'clock p.m.*)

> Our closing time is 5:15 p.m.

24-hour Clock   The use of the 24-hour clock is becoming more and more prevalent, particularly in travel schedules and notices of formal meetings. Times are expressed by four digits separated by a colon. The first two digits represent the hours since midnight, and the last two represent the minutes in that hour.

> Ms. Bernier's flight is at 08:45; she should arrive in Winnipeg at 10:00.

> The meeting began at 14:15 and was adjourned at 16:30.

NOTE: The word *o'clock* and the abbreviations *a.m.* and *p.m.* are *not* used when stating times on the 24-hour clock.

☐ CLASS PRACTICE 6

Test the degree to which you have learned the last four principles by correcting the following sentences. Tell why you made the corrections.

1. Do you ordinarily begin work at 8 o'clock?
2. Mr. O'Brian has served 30 years as engineer for our company.
3. A person of 40 may have difficulty in obtaining a position.
4. This will be the 30th year that Mr. Eaton has been on the Boy Scout Court of Honor.
5. Flight 461 from Jamaica arrives at 15:15 p.m.
6. This firm has been in operation for 18 years.
7. The executive session is called for 2000 this evening.

House, Street, Postal Code and ZIP Code Numbers

With few exceptions, in business correspondence house and street numbers are written in figures. Postal codes and the United States Zip Code numbers are always written in figures.

House Numbers House numbers are written in figures, with the exception of the number *one*. Neither the abbreviation *No.*nor the sign # should be used with house numbers or with R. R. numbers.

> The Gray Publishing Company has moved from 3846 Portage Avenue to One Park Place, not 14 Park Place.

Numbered Streets When streets have numbers one through ten as their names, write those numbers in words.

> We often shop in the Fifth Avenue stores. (Not *5th Avenue.*)

> There is a transfer point at the Tenth Street bus station.

Numbered street names over ten are written in figures. To separate the building number from the numbered street, leave an extra space between the street number and the street name; or use a hyphen to mark the separation.

> *1718-86th Street*

Also in the interest of readability, *East, North,* or any other word that precedes the numbered name of a street should be spelled out.

> Marcia's new address is 1462 East 125th Street.

Consider just one more item about names of numbered streets. There is a growing trend toward writing these numbers without the *st*, *th*, and so on. Marcia's address could thus have been written *1462 East 125 Street*. Dispensing with the ordinal endings makes the name of the street stand out and thus promotes clarity.

Postal Code and ZIP Code Numbers   The postal code numbers and American ZIP code numbers are always written in figures and follow the name of the province or state, with no punctuation preceding the code or in the code.

☐   CLASS PRACTICE 7

To practise the principles just presented, find and correct the errors in the following sentences.

1. A branch of our store is to be opened at West 1st Place.
2. The most desirable business address in the city is 1 Broad Street.
3. Address the package to R.R. #2, Trail, British Columbia V1R 2Y8.
4. Be sure that you note the change in address to Hartford, Ohio, 45234.
5. Blankton's number is 1826 Front Street, not No. 1836.
6. Do you think 1333 N. 168th Street is too far out for a business to locate?

Communication Problems

Application Exercises

A ■

Each of the following sentences contains an error in the use of figures. On a separate sheet of paper, indicate the errors and make the corrections.

1   We allow trade discounts of 5, 10, and 15%.
2   Your subscription expires in 2 months.
3   5,000 questionnaires were sent out on Saturday.
4   An employee *may* retire at 65, but he *must* retire at 70 years of age.
5   About 1 000 extra shipfitters are needed to build the new submarine.
6   Depending on quality and workmanship, we can offer you bedspreads at $18, 25, 35, and 50.
7   The cost of the manila envelopes is only seven cents each.
8   Your note will fall due in sixty days.
9   Do not expect a definite answer from us before the twenty-first of October.
10   Is a speed of 70 km. per hour too fast on city streets?
11   We are making your appointment for 10:00 a.m. on Monday.
12   We have no 11 o'clock appointments open until after Labor Day.
13   The temperature did not fall below 5° C last night.
14   We have received proxies from ⅓ of the stockholders.
15   We have 3 questions to ask you, 2 of which relate to business and 1 to personal affairs.

B ■

Write "OK" for any correct sentence. Find and correct the errors for any incorrect sentences.

1   Your letter was dated April 12th, not April 10th.
2   My next job is to type the speech to be given at the Kiwanis Club meeting.
3   The Hon. John Faulkner will present the trophies.
4   Miss Archer has designed 6 new shirt patterns.
5   Essential secretarial traits may be mentioned here without comment (analysis): tact, initiative, discretion, and poise.
6   The office force presented the bride with a large, old-fashioned, inlaid, desk.
7   There are 400 of our employees who rate the salary increase.
8   The Vikings carried a flag, that bore a black raven on a field of white.
9   The information, not the money, was requested by Mr. Drake.
10 Is the price of the material $2.75 per metre?
11 The good executive listens attentively to all complaints, he realizes that knowing about and preventing dissatisfaction will promote good employee morale.
12 Instead of ten 40 folders were taken from the stock room.
13 Canada now has a population of over 23143000 people.
14 Bill wanted to know, whether it would be possible to ship the goods on Monday.
15 The Nelson River, which flows into Hudson Bay, is twenty-five hundred km long.

C ■

This is the final editing exercise—your last chance to show your ability to revise material written by other persons.

I am writing to confirm our telephone conversation of this morning. We at 1 Park Avenue will be happy to be your hosts at the conference with Dr. James P. Kenney on June 2d at ten a.m. We consider ourselves priveleged to be able to obtain the services of 2 outstanding authorities on nuclear power. If there are any materials that must be prepared before the meeting please send us a list of whatever you will need.

Word Study

A ■

Words often confused: deceased, diseased; risky, risqué.

B ■

These signs appeared in various places—in stores, in ads, along highways. What's wrong?

1   Tourists accomodated.
2   If Its a Camera You Want, We Have It.
3   Carmel Sunday, 25 cents.
4   Our Vanishing Cream is more effective than any cream.
5   Clearance Sale of Mens' and Boys' Suits.

C ■

How are the following figures written in words?

1	19	**3**	⅑	**5**	3,900
2	90	**4**	²³⁄₂₄	**6**	2⁹⁄₁₄

Communication in Action: Making Facts Meaningful

Paul believed in giving the facts about his company to anyone who would listen. Often he was assigned the job of taking visitors through the company plant. Here is part of his talk: "Five years ago, we had only 127 production workers. Today, we have 1 270. Those workers produced 1 635 fans a month. Today, the workers produce 247 000 a year. Five years ago, we were losing $1 000 a week. This year, our profits will be about $250 000." Assuming these facts are important, could Paul give them in such a way that his visitors would grasp them more quickly?

PART · 7

Writing Craftsmanship

Would you say that anyone who can plug a leaking pipe is entitled to call himself a plumber? No, there is a difference between someone who does a makeshift job and someone who is adept at his trade, whose completed work represents perfection. So, too, can almost anyone put words on paper; but jotting down words does not make him a writer. A writer, like a plumber, must be a craftsman. And to be a craftsman, a writer must be expert in using words and in putting those words together; he must be able to give a finished, polished performance. When you have learned to apply the principles presented in the next three units, you will find that your own writing efforts are on the way to true craftsmanship.

UNIT □ 34

The Art of Being Explicit

If art can be said to have a main purpose, that purpose is communication. The artist, be he painter, architect, musician, sculptor, or writer, wishes to show others what he himself sees—whether with his eyes or in his mind. To communicate successfully, however, the artist needs more than talent; he needs special education and training. And you, the future writer of business communications, need special training, the elements of which are presented in this part of your textbook.

One of the marks of the trained correspondent is his ability to put down on paper a message that the reader can interpret in only one way, the way intended by the writer. Lack of such ability can cause confusion and misunderstanding. For instance, the person who received this message, "The manager told Mr. Edwards that he will soon visit your territory," would have to write a letter asking whether the manager or Mr. Edwards will visit the reader's territory. Letters that must be written to straighten out mix-ups increase the cost of doing business.

Because of garbled messages, goodwill may be lost and prestige dimmed. For example, what do you think would happen to the prestige of a newspaper reporter who wrote this item: "Yesterday Fred King was struck by an automobile wearing a cub scout uniform"? The utter absurdity of an *automobile wearing a cub scout uniform* would cause the newspaper's readers to lose some respect for the reporter and the paper.

The purpose of this unit is to help you to be explicit. Mastery of the following principles will enable you to say exactly what you mean and to construct messages that mean the same thing to your reader as they do to you.

Placement of Words, Phrases, Clauses

One cause of confusing and ridiculous messages is that the writer fails to place a word, a phrase, or a clause with the unit of thought to which it belongs. As you study the following presentation, keep in mind the all-important "thought unit."

Words A word carelessly placed can change the meaning of a sentence; but when that word is written with its correct thought unit, the intended message is clear. For instance, consider this message:

This is the first time I have met him only.

Although the meaning might possibly be that this is the first time that I have met nobody else but him, the odds are that the correct thought unit is *only the first time:* "This is only the first time I have met him."

Now suppose that the following advertisement appeared in your local paper.

CORDUROY BOYS' TROUSERS ON SALE TOMORROW

Wouldn't you be amused by the thought unit "corduroy boys"? And how simple it would have been to write the correct thought, "boys' *corduroy trousers*"!

Phrases Incorrectly placed phrases, too, can completely change the meaning of a message. For example:

I sat watching the helicopter fly by in my office.

"Helicopter fly by in my office" presents a fantastic picture. But place the phrase *in my office* with its proper thought unit, and we have:

I sat in my office watching the helicopter fly by.

Equally ridiculous is the following question:

Did you see a man in the bus with a black sombrero hat?

Here you have the thought unit "bus with a black sombrero hat." Of course, the inquirer meant "man with a black sombrero hat."

Did you see in the bus a man with a black sombrero hat?

Clauses Errors of all kinds are more likely to be made in long sentences, and misplaced clauses are no exception. The reason may be that there is such a string of words that the writer loses sight of the thought unit. Evidently that is what happened in this sentence:

The maintenance man installed a fluorescent light over Mr. Shay's head that was recessed.

What do you think of the thought unit "head that was recessed"? And how do you think Mr. Shay would feel about it? The writer could have omitted the clause *that was recessed* and could have written the message clearly, like this:

The maintenance man installed a recessed fluorescent light over Mr. Shay's head.

Not quite so funny, but just as inexact, is the following message:

He gave the book to his brother that was bound in leather.

What was bound in leather? The book, wasn't it? Then the thought unit "brother that was bound in leather" is incorrect. The sentence could have been written correctly in any of the following four ways. The last two are preferable because they are less wordy.

He gave the book that was bound in leather to his brother.

He gave his brother the book that was bound in leather.

He gave the leather-bound book to his brother.

He gave his brother the leather-bound book.

"Which" Clauses

There is nothing wrong in using "which" clauses, provided those clauses are explicit in meaning. When used to refer to an entire thought or when incorrectly placed, however, "which" clauses can confuse the message. As is the case with any other kind of thought-unit violation, misplaced clauses can play havoc with communication.

I refused to exchange the goods, which greatly disappointed the customer.

The meaning of this sentence is not entirely clear because the "which" clause refers to the entire idea of "I refused to exchange the goods," the reason that the customer was disappointed. Viewed as a thought unit, "goods, which greatly disappointed the customer," is also confusing. Either of the following revisions would make the meaning of the sentence explicit.

I refused to exchange the goods, much to the disappointment of the customer.

The customer was greatly disappointed by my refusal to exchange the goods.

Always be very careful with the placement of a "which" clause. Good writers are aware that a grotesque meaning may be conveyed when a "which" clause is not written with its proper thought unit. See what happens in the following sentence:

The sandwiches were wrapped in aluminum foil, which we ate hungrily.

Aluminum foil, which we ate hungrily sounds pretty silly, doesn't it? Now see the revision, which makes clear that *sandwiches* were eaten and that they came wrapped in aluminum foil.

We hungrily ate the sandwiches, which were wrapped in aluminum foil.

Note the correct use of the "which" clause—to give additional information—as contrasted with a "that" clause. Use of *that* would mean that we ate *only the sandwiches wrapped in aluminum foil*—no other sandwiches. Remember that *that* introduces a clause needed for identification and that, therefore, it is not set off by a comma.

We hungrily ate the sandwiches that were wrapped in aluminum foil. (But we didn't eat those wrapped in waxed paper.)

☐ CLASS PRACTICE 1

Stop now and see how well you understand the presentation thus far. Discuss and revise the following sentences.

1. Tom sat around talking with persons who had no business with us until four o'clock.
2. Do you carry a stock of pink ladies' gloves?
3. We can sell you this table at a very attractive price, which has a leather top.
4. Bob found a note in the dictionary that was written by his boss.
5. We will ride to the airport when the time comes in a limousine.

The "Who" and the "What"

Another way to prevent needless expense caused by writing obscure messages is to be explicit as to *who* did, will do, or is expected to do *what*. The main cause of this type of confusion, as in many others, is lack of understanding of the thought-unit principle that applies to this particular problem. The following illustrations and explanations will help you to indicate clearly the *who* and the *what*.

> Having paid his fine and retrieved his driver's licence, the judge gave the defendant a severe lecture.

Exactly *who* was it that paid his fine and retrieved his driver's licence? The thought unit as written is this: "Having paid his fine and retrieved his driver's licence, the judge."

Did the judge pay his own fine and retrieve his own driver's licence? Or did he pay the defendant's fine and retrieve the defendant's licence? Obviously, the judge did neither. Command of the *who did what* principle would enable a writer to make his meaning clear:

> After the defendant paid his fine and retrieved his driver's licence, the judge gave him a severe lecture.

Confusion as to the *who* and the *what* also arises when a sentence is constructed in such a way that the thought unit shows an object to be the doer of an action instead of a person. Here is an illustration of this type of fuzzy writing:

> Being a bit nervous, the speech given by the author was not very convincing.

By now you can readily distinguish the thought unit as written: "Being a bit nervous, the speech." The absurd meaning here is that the speech was nervous. Written correctly, the thought unit would make plain the fact that the *author* was nervous; as:

> Being a bit nervous, the author gave an unconvincing speech.

There are instances where the *who did what* confusion can be highly amusing, as you will agree after reading this example:

> Our operator recognized the caller looking up from the switchboard.

Of course, the caller *could* be a contortionist, but a more probable idea is the following:

> Looking up from the switchboard, our operator recognized the caller.

Definite Pronoun Reference

The last part of this unit on the art of being explicit concerns pronoun reference. When you use *it, he, she, they, this* or another pronoun to refer to somebody or something, you must pinpoint the person or the thing meant by that pronoun. Do not make the reader guess at your meaning.

To be definite, you must avoid the indefinite. Some specific pronoun-reference pitfalls that you must learn to avoid are the following:

Indefinite "It"   Inept writers use the pronoun *it* as a sort of vague, catchall word. They frequently use *it* as a substitute for something that should be clearly stated. Consider the use of *it* in this sentence:

> We are offering credit to reputable persons, because it means more sales for us.

Do you see that the *it* in this sentence forces the reader to stop and think of what *it* stands for? The reader will understand the message immediately when the writer uses a definite reference.

> We are offering credit to reputable persons because *such practice* means more sales for us.

Even more indefinite and crude is the use of the *it* in the following illustration:

> If you can sail a boat, please teach it to the Boy Scouts.

As you read the following revision, note that the writer is much more explicit.

> If you can sail a boat, please teach the Boy Scouts how to handle that kind of craft.

Indefinite "He," "She," "They"   Vagueness in the use of these pronouns, in all their different forms, is also a common writing fault. Sometimes their references are so uncertain that the reader is faced with a serious interpretation problem; as in this example:

> Mr. Ash told Peter that his cousin has been asked to join the staff.

Whose cousin has been asked to join the staff? Is it Mr. Ash's cousin or Peter's cousin? Now look at two possible revisions, either of which would be explicit.

> Peter learned from Mr. Ash that the latter's cousin has been asked to join the staff.

> Mr. Ash told Peter that his, Peter's, cousin has been asked to join the staff.

Then, too, there is the favorite, but slipshod, "they say" expression.

> They say that the economy will take an upswing during the last quarter of the year.

Who is meant by the "they" in this sentence? A person who knew what he was talking about would have been specific about who said what.

Dr. Roy Bryce (an economist) says that the economy will take an upswing during the last quarter of the year.

Indefinite "This" Even experienced writers are sometimes careless about using *this* to refer to an entire preceding thought. In such an event, the reference is so hazy that the reader may have to reread in order to be sure of grasping the meaning. For example:

When our sale opened yesterday morning, crowds of customers jammed all the entrances and exits. This created a safety problem.

The above message exemplifies sloppy, as well as inexact, writing. A moment's reflection on the part of a skilled writer would produce something like the following:

When our sale opened yesterday morning, the crowds of customers who jammed all the entrances and exits created a safety problem.

CLASS PRACTICE 2

Test your ability to handle *who did what* and *indefinite pronoun reference* situations by discussing and revising the following sentences.

1. Mr. Lee's father entered the contracting business when he was a baby.
2. Sue found a tiny mouse uncovering her typewriter.
3. If your dog will not eat raw meat, cook it.
4. A personnel manager selects all the application letters that impress him and calls them for interviews.
5. While setting the time lock, the door swung open.
6. One way to clarify messages is to be explicit as to *who* did *what*. This is known by all trained writers.

Communication Problems

Application Exercises

A ■

All these sentences contain incorrect thought units. For each sentence, copy the thought unit that you think is confusing.

1 I sat issuing orders to the shipping clerk at my desk.
2 While waiting for my change, the fire alarm started.
3 The angry player approached the referee with fire in his eyes.
4 After returning from his vacation, the entire office force welcomed Mr. Haynes.
5 Pete scarcely has a word to say during working hours.
6 You need not show how angry you are in the claim letter you write.
7 Occasionally, some customers will be granted credit who abuse the privilege.

8 Mr. Coe took an order from his wallet, which he gave to the salesman.
9 Mr. Fields rented the house in which he died a year ago.
10 The police chief saw a fat little pig going to the station.
11 A pencil sharpener is on my wall made of aluminum.
12 The campers sat watching the tide go out on their veranda.

B ■

Now revise the sentences, writing words, phrases, and clauses in their proper thought units.

C ■

The following sentences need revision, too. Rewrite each one, making the meaning explicit.

1 You will be glad to hear that Mr. Post sold the building to Mr. Forbes just before he left.
2 Our uncle once tried sheep raising, but he made no money out of them.
3 The cashier informed the accountant that his balance was incorrect.
4 Our guest gave an account of his life, which was very interesting.
5 I offered to help the new clerk, but he refused it.
6 All taxes levied by our town for the current tax year were paid on time. This is most unusual.
7 Do they have many rules and regulations in your office?
8 Further delay in payment will impair your credit, which neither of us wants.
9 Mr. Walsh dictated all morning, but his secretary transcribed only two of them.
10 In our office manual it says that secretaries are to use open punctuation.

Word Study

A ■

Do you really know the exact order of the letters of the alphabet?

1 In your dictionary, locate the following words, taking each one in the sequence in which it is shown. Note the exact time when you start your search and the exact time when you finish. How many minutes did you need?

inconvenience	interfere	collateral
confident	pamphlet	prominent
accrue	incidentally	appropriate
repetition	supersede	extension
eligible	erroneous	recommend

2 Now write these words in alphabetic order.

B ■

Among the following words are several typical and common malformations (*Hint:* Look up the meaning of that word!) caused, usually, by lack of attention to the letter-by-letter spelling of the word. A few of the words, however, are shown correctly. Respell those that are wrong.

1	govenor	6	embarass
2	acummulate	7	conceed
3	posession	8	endevor
4	comeing	9	alleged
5	difference	10	familar

C ■

Here are ten words that you are likely to encounter almost every day. If you are a typist, you must know their breakdown into syllables in order to be able to select the points at which to divide at line ends. Accents also have a bearing on choosing the best division points. Therefore, without consulting your dictionary, indicate the syllable divisions and the accent marks. Place each accent mark before the syllable to be accented. Then using the dictionary, check the accuracy of your choices.

1	committee	6	maintenance
2	intelligence	7	accommodate
3	occurrence	8	existence
4	miscellaneous	9	necessary
5	thought	10	eliminate

⌐D ■

Ten frequently used foreign expressions are listed in column A. Match these with the correct meanings in column B.

A		B	
1	carte blanche	a	for each person
2	bon voyage	b	a social blunder
3	faux pas	c	common spirit of a group
4	esprit de corps	d	social knowledge
5	à la mode	e	solid ground
6	per capita	f	unlimited authority
7	ex cathedra	g	luxurious
8	terra firma	h	a good journey
9	de luxe	i	after the fashion
10	savoir-faire	j	with authority
		k	one by one
		l	unexcelled
		m	to the manner born

Check your selections against the choices in the dictionary.
Copy in your notebook the phonetic spelling of each expression.

Communication in Action: *Making Introductions*

How would you introduce each of the following: (1) a young man to an older man? (2) a boy and girl the same age? (3) a fellow accountant to a very important business or government executive? (4) a stenographer to a new employee? A quick look at page 506 will help you. Enact the various situations described.

The Art
of Being
Polished

Although music has its own place as one of the arts, there is a kind of music in all the other arts. A ballet performance, for instance, can be considered music in motion. The flowing lines of a beautiful building give the viewer a sense of rhythm, which is the music of architecture. Writing is raised to the level of an art when stimulating ideas are borne along by means of a smooth, almost musical flow of words. Writing that meets the highest standards, then, must have the fluidity and polish that characterize good music.

In business communications, polish is a secret ingredient that may make a very important contribution to increased profits. For example, every business message carries with it the company "image": an impression of the firm whose name is on the letterhead. A polished communication conveys the image of a top-quality firm.

Mastery of the principles that govern this phase of the art of writing—the principles that you will study in this unit—will help you to become a polished writer.

Messages That Flow

Each type of communication—letter, report, news release—usually has one main thought that is developed throughout; consequently, the entire communication should flow smoothly from beginning to end in order to show the logical development of that thought. Sentences within each paragraph must be written so the paragraph hangs together, and all paragraphs must glide along the main-thought track.

To be a polished writer, then, you must be skilled in taking the reader by the hand and leading him gently along the thought track of your message. One way to accomplish your purpose is to learn how to use transitional, or "bridging," words and phrases. These are simply the conjunctive adverbs and the parenthetical expressions that you have studied previously. Note the following examples:

accordingly	for this purpose	notwithstanding
after all	furthermore	on the contrary
also	hence	on the other hand
at the same time	however	otherwise
besides	in addition	similarly
consequently	meanwhile	still
for example	moreover	therefore
for instance	nevertheless	yet

Flowing Sentences   To understand the importance of "bridging" expressions within sentences, study carefully the following illustration and explanation.

We have a staff of five correspondents; bottlenecks are frequent.

Can you see any connection between having five writers and having frequent bottlenecks? Something is needed to tie this sentence into a smooth, meaningful message; and that "something" is a suitable transitional word. Let's try *nevertheless*.

We have a staff of five correspondents; nevertheless, bottlenecks are frequent.

Now you can see that the bridging word *nevertheless* ties the meaning of the second clause to the meaning of the first clause.

Remember that a comma always follows an introductory transitional, or bridging, expression. *Nevertheless* is considered introductory because it introduces the second clause.

Transitions Between Paragraphs   Failure to use transitional expressions to introduce new paragraphs can affect the flow of the entire message exactly as such failure affected the smoothness of the single sentence you have just studied. With "thought bridging" in mind, consider the following paragraphs taken from a letter replying to a question about the writer's inactive account.

Yes, we have done business with your firm for more than 20 years; and we, too, have enjoyed the friendly relations that have always existed between us.

We feel that we must take advantage of prices quoted by your competitors. Three times within the last month, we have been able to purchase quality merchandise at a price that was significantly lower than yours.

We think it only fair to tell you that, in the future, ours will probably be an inactive account. If you can meet the quotations of the competition, be assured that you will be our preferred vendor.

Let's polish this letter by using transitional expressions to introduce the second and third paragraphs and to link the first and second sentences of the third paragraph.

Yes, we have done business with your firm for more than 20 years; and we, too, have enjoyed the friendly relations that have always existed between us.

Nevertheless, we feel that we must take advantage of prices quoted by your competitors. Three times within the last month, we have been able to purchase quality merchandise at a price that was significantly lower than yours.

Consequently, we think it only fair to tell you that, in the future, ours will probably be an inactive account. If, *however,* you can meet the quotations of the competition, be assured that you will be our preferred vendor.

The "And" Pitfalls

Boring, repetitious, and incorrect use of the word *and* is a common writing fault that you must learn to avoid. The "and" pitfalls are the following:

And, And, And   "And" is one of the most important conjunctions. There is no reason for a writer to avoid using it, but there is a very good reason for him to watch lest he overuse it. A message consisting of sentence after sentence containing two or more clauses joined by *and* is monotonous and boring. A skilled writer avoids this pitfall by varying his sentence structure. For instance, he would not write a paragraph like this:

> We received your letter of May 1 this morning, *and* it was most welcome. All the tellers in the bank read it, *and* they like the suggestions you made. We think that your idea for expediting the cashing of cheques is excellent, *and* we are putting that idea into operation immediately. Your suggestions are always helpful, *and* we give priority to letters from Management Consultants, Ltd.

Now let's vary the sentence structure. Study the following revision and note the use of subordinate clauses.

> Your very welcome letter of May 1 arrived this morning. We passed it on to all the bank tellers, who liked the suggestions you made. You will be interested to learn that your idea for expediting the cashing of cheques is so good that we are putting the idea into operation immediately. Your suggestions are always helpful; therefore, we give priority to letters from Management Consultants, Ltd.

And So   Using *and so* to introduce a clause is using the expression as a conjunction; yet *and so* does not appear in any list of conjunctions. This incorrect expression is another common writing fault. Some writers constantly use *and so* to introduce a reason-giving clause; they do not know that there are other expressions that would be just right for reason-giving. Some transitional words that may properly be used for this purpose are: *hence, therefore, consequently, accordingly.* Now study the following illustrations and revisions.

> *Poor:*   When the goods left our factory, they were in perfect condition; *and so* the carrier must be at fault.

> *Poor:*   The Walshes arrived on time; *and so* they heard the entire lecture.

> *Poor:*   Your letters have been returned marked "Undeliverable"; *and so* we removed your name from our mailing list.

In the first sentence, either *hence* or *therefore* would have been a good addition; in the second, *consequently* or *therefore;* and in the third, *accordingly* or *therefore.*

> When the goods left our factory, they were in perfect condition; *therefore,* the carrier must be at fault.

> The Walshes arrived on time; *consequently,* they heard the entire lecture.

Written without the *and*, however, *so* is an acceptable conjunction. Like any other conjunction, it must not be overused. The following sentence illustrates the *so* usage; but *therefore, consequently,* or *accordingly* would be just as effective.

> Knowing yourself is the starting point in looking for a job; *so*, start taking inventory of your knowledge and skills.

And Which, And Who, And Hence   Do not use *and* with *which, who,* or *hence*. Such use of *and* is a glaring grammatical error. For example:

> *Poor:*   Your letters have been returned marked "Undeliverable"; and hence, we removed your name from our mailing list.

> *Better:*   Your letters have been returned marked "Undeliverable"; therefore, we removed your name from our mailing list.

Balanced Sentences

When you want to emphasize a comparison or contrast or when you want to emphasize a particular idea in a forceful way, you may want to use a "balanced" sentence. This type of sentence is one in which ideas of equal value are expressed in parallel, or similar, constructions.

Balancing Comparisons   To be balanced, comparisons must contain all necessary words; therefore, omission of necessary words causes lopsided comparisons. Look at the following sentence:

> Mr. Allen appreciates your work just as much, and maybe more, than I do.

Remember that words set off by commas are considered excess baggage and can be omitted without affecting the basic meaning of the sentence. In the above illustration, however, omission of the words enclosed in commas would produce this meaning: "Mr. Allen appreciates your work just as much *than* I do." The use of *than* in this sentence is completely inappropriate; hence, the meaning of the sentence is obscured.

If, however, you correctly insert the second *as*, and if you place the commas correctly, you will have the following balanced comparison:

> Mr. Allen appreciates your work just *as* much *as*, and maybe more than, I do.

To fix this principle in your mind, study one more illustration and explanation.

> Do you think that men spend more time reading newspapers than women?

As written, this question is a request for your opinion as to whether men spend more time reading newspapers than they spend reading women. For balance and clarity the comparison should be phrased this way:

> Do you think that men spend more time reading newspapers than women do (spend)?

Balancing Modifiers   Although you would say *a boat,* you would not say *a apple.* When writing words in a series, do not omit modifying adjectives if the first adjective will not serve for the entire series. For instance:

The sportsman has stashed away a camera, radio, fishing rod, and umbrella.

Because *a* is used only before the first item in the series, the meaning is that he has stashed away a camera, a radio, a fishing rod, and *a* umbrella. However, the first modifier is not correct for all members of the series, so the sentence should read: "a camera, a radio, a fishing rod, and *an* umbrella."

Balancing Verbs   Some sentences contain verb phrases such as *will make, have sent, was shipped,* and so on. Some sentences may contain two verb phrases, as does this sentence:

You *will go* to the bank and (*will*) *get* a cashier's cheque.

Note that the *will* is omitted before *get,* because the *will* in the first verb phrase serves correctly for the second part of the compound verb phrase.

Verbs will not balance, however, if a sentence has two verb phrases and any necessary part of one of them is omitted or if the tense or number of both is not the same. For example:

Poor: Your order *was* received yesterday and the goods (was) shipped today.

These verb phrases do not balance because the *was* that is correct for *received* is not correct for *shipped. Order* requires a singular verb; *goods* requires a plural verb. Correctly written, the sentence is this:

Your *order was received* yesterday, and the *goods were shipped* today.

Now consider balance in relation to a compound verb:

Poor: I never *have,* and never *will, understand* the T-1 income tax form.

While only one form of the main verb phrase, *will understand,* is expressed, the two forms are not the same. Adding the unexpressed *understand* to the first part of the compound would give this awkward construction: "I never *have understand.*" Thus, omission of part of a verb phrase destroys verb balance. The sentence should have been written this way:

I never *have understood,* and never *will understand,* the T-1 income tax form.

Balancing Prepositions   Different words call for different prepositions to go with them. For instance, you would say *conform to,* but *in compliance with.* Balancing prepositions means that if different prepositions are required to accompany words used in a compound, each preposition must be stated. For instance:

Some men drivers have little respect or faith in women drivers.

Consider the preposition *in* as used in this sentence. *Respect or faith in* means *respect in* and *faith in.* But *respect in* does not make sense. Omission of a preposition, therefore, caused a mismatch; and the sentence should have been written like this:

> Most people have little respect *for* or faith *in* drug users.

Now study this second illustration:

> I cannot understand why Mr. Kent has no understanding or interest in golf.

Can you see that *understanding (in) or interest in* is not balanced? The sentence must be written as "understanding *of*, or interest *in*."

Incomplete Clauses   Although omitting part of a clause may be good writing, in many cases such an omission can really confuse a reader. In this sentence, for example, "Sally is much more adept than I," the meaning "than I (am)" is clear.

But read the following sentence and see what an omission in a clause can do to the clarity of a message.

> Did Mr. Payne shoot the burglar or his wife?

What do you suppose this writer means? He may want to know whether Mr. Payne shot the burglar or shot his, Mr. Payne's, wife. On the other hand, he may want to know whether Mr. Payne shot the burglar or the burglar's wife. The polished writer would have asked clearly and simply:

> Which one shot the burglar, Mr. Payne or his wife?

Now see how absurd is the following illustration, as a result of the incomplete clause.

> Did Bill send in the request or his brother?

The interpretation could be this: "Did Bill send in the request or did he send in his brother?" To make the meaning clear, the complete clause should be written like this:

> Did Bill send in the request, or did his brother send it in?

Communication Problems

Application Exercises

A ■

Revise each sentence and supply a "bridging" word or expression that will make the thought flow smoothly and correctly.

1   I thought the report much too long; I read until I finished it.
2   All written communications should be free from errors in grammar; lack of predicate agreement.

3 We do not like convertibles; and so we have never purchased one.
4 There is an error in this invoice total; please recheck it.
5 Your order arrived after the sale had ended; we are filling it at the sale price.
6 Many industries are consumers of textiles; the automobile industry.
7 George refused to obey the order; and so he lost his position.
8 Pete is afraid to travel by plane; he flew to Toronto last week.
9 The commuter train was late last night; I arrived home on time.
10 There was a long line in front of the window; Bill couldn't get our tickets.

B ■

Rewrite the following paragraph, avoiding the *and, and, and* pitfall.

I am happy to recommend Mr. Ray Burns for a position with your firm; and I do so as a friend, as well as an employer. Ray has been our chief accountant for the past five years, and his work has always been "tops." In addition, he has a fine personality; and he gets along well with his associates. His character is above reproach, and he is respected in his business and in his social life.

C ■

Rewrite and polish the following sentences:

1 Mr. Foley's cheque has not arrived, and which I forget to tell you.
2 Ray always has and always will like daylight saving time.
3 Mark is as well educated, if not better educated, than the other executives in our company.
4 Being accurate is more important than to be speedy.
5 Angus has great appreciation, but little education, in art.
6 We are converting to automated accounting, and hence the delay in sending your statement.
7 A new constitution has been drawn up and new bylaws prepared.
8 Did the manager write the letter or Mr. Coffey?
9 Please requisition for my personal use a pen, bottle of ink, and envelope large enough to hold two file folders.
10 Give the caller either the choice of waiting or being called later.
11 Our product is better, not equivalent, to the best on the market.
12 The men should have confidence and respect for their supervisors.

Word Study
A ■

Words often confused: confidently, confidentially; lesser, lessor, lessee.

B ■

Some of these sentences contain errors in expression. Spot them and indicate correct substitutions.

1 I'm bringing this mail down to Mr. West.
2 He inherited considerable from his aunt.

3 I can't hardly wait for tomorrow.
4 There lay the purse just where I had dropped it.
5 She hadn't ought to have done it.

C ■

Should *ei* or *ie* appear in the blank spaces in these sentences?

1 The w___rd case was very dec___ving because it w___ghed nearly 50 pounds, yet was only a little over a foot in h___ght.

2 Th___r large f___ld y___lds a var___ty of crops.

3 In old front___r towns on the prair___ , n___ghbors often banded together for protection against f___rce animals.

Communication in Action: I, Me, and My

Personal conceit is often revealed by the overuse of personal pronouns such as *I*, *me*, and *my*. Eliminate as many references to self as you can in the following sentence: "I think my department would improve if I could have three of my people rearrange my furniture I have in my office."

UNIT □ 36

Achieving Variety in Word Usage

Why Aim for Variety?

Do you realize that you may be using the same words over and over to express a variety of situations, events, or emotions? You could, for example, describe your boss, last evening's TV program, the weather, a new coat—almost anything you approve of or are enthusiastic about—as *nice* (or anything you don't like as *not nice*). You probably intend one of these meanings for *nice*:

Your boss: *considerate, even-tempered, pleasant, agreeable, patient, appreciative*

Last evening's TV program: *amusing, well acted, exciting, dramatic, thrilling, true to life, informative*

The weather: *pleasant, fair, exhilarating, stimulating*

A new coat: *becoming, practical, comfortable, stylish, smart, chic*

How much more interesting, informative, and vivid your descriptions would have been had you chosen the really descriptive term rather than the vague, outworn *nice*.

Some of the Worst Offenders

Other overused words include the following:

good	awful	big	say	know	come
lovely	fine	little	think	fix	go

Now don't think that these words are entirely taboo. They are essential for many occasions, but they are abused by overuse. To prove this, in each of the following sentences substitute for the italicized word the words in parentheses.

The stenographer made a *bad* mistake in her transcript. (inexcusable, serious)

The Armed Forces are always seeking *fine* young men. (promising, alert, spirited)

We both had a *lovely* time at the party. (delightful, enjoyable)

Dad has an *awful* cold. (heavy, persistent)

"Mary has lost her purse!" *said* Jane. (exclaimed, shouted)

The old man *went* slowly down the road. (limped, shuffled, hobbled, crept)

You surely will agree that the substitution of the parenthetical words would give more accurate, interesting, and vivid pictures in these sentences.

Consider, also, the difference that the improved sentences would make to a listener. He would understand precisely what the speaker had in mind instead of having to infer or guess the meaning.

Then there are those hackneyed phrases that were originally apt and mildly amusing but that have long since lost all element of surprise or sincerity. Some of these expressions are worn-out figures of speech like *cold as ice, the staff of life, green with envy*. Saying *chilled, bread,* and *envious* is more direct and meaningful. Other timeworn expressions are proverbs or threadbare quotations like "Truth is stranger than fiction," "He who hesitates is lost," "Variety is the spice of life," and so on. You can express yourself so that the meaning is entirely apparent without using such trite sentences.

The Key to the Situation

Why do people keep on using these weak, outworn words and expressions? One word gives the answer—laziness. The users just do not have sufficient interest to take the time and trouble to select more accurate words and expressions. They follow the line of least resistance and utter the same old words over and over and over.

There is no doubt that, by the time you have reached this course, you have encountered many of the words that you need to add variety to your speech and writing. Unquestionably, also, you have heard a great many of these words from your teachers, your employer, and speakers on radio and TV. All you need to do is to start using these more effective substitutions.

Learn to Use Synonyms

What, exactly, is a synonym? A *synonym* is a word that has the same or nearly the same meaning as another word—*glad* is a synonym for *happy*, for example. Most synonyms, however, are not *completely* synonymous; that is, though they have the same *basic* meaning, each synonym has a slightly different shade of meaning. Look up the word *get* in your dictionary. You will find the following listed as synonyms: *obtain, procure, secure, acquire, gain, win, earn.* Notice that each of these words, although it has the fundamental idea of *get*, has its own shade of meaning. For example, you would *obtain*, not *win*, a position; you would *win*, not *acquire*, a prize. Because the English language was derived from so many other languages—Latin, Greek, French, German, Anglo-Saxon, and others—it is exceedingly rich in synonyms; therefore, it is possible to express fine shades of meaning by choosing the appropriate synonym.

Your prime source of help in learning to differentiate the meanings of synonyms is your dictionary. Form the habit of noticing whether synonyms are listed at the end of the entry under any word that you may look up. If they are, try to understand the differentiations in meaning of the various synonyms and try to frame sentences or phrases using the synonyms. For example, suppose you have looked up *occurrence* (perhaps in order to check on the number of *c*'s and *r*'s in the word). Notice the list of synonyms: *event, incident, episode, circumstance.* From the differentiations given, you can "concoct" these phrases and sentences: "The final *event* that led up to World War II was . . . ," "We have completely forgotten the unpleasant *incident*," "The *episode* of launching the first world satellite," "Missing my bus was the first *circumstance* in a long series of delays."

If you will follow this plan of conscientiously learning the differences between synonyms, you will be surprised by your growing awareness of distinctions in meanings that you had never thought of before.

The Thesaurus Many students, as well as writers and editors, overlook the help to be obtained from that most useful reference book, the thesaurus. Roget's is the classic work.

A thesaurus is a collection of words and phrases arranged according to *ideas*. The function that it serves is different from that of a dictionary. A dictionary gives the meaning of the *word* that one has in mind. A thesaurus enables one to find the word with which to express an *idea* one has in mind. In other words, a thesaurus goes one step farther than a dictionary. In using the dictionary or a book of synonyms, one must have at least one word in mind; in using a thesaurus, one can start with a general idea from which comes one word that will start you on the hunt for the exact word you need.

Suppose, for example, that you are the school chairman for the Junior Red Cross drive, which will start on a Tuesday and continue for the rest of the week. During the preceding week you will make daily announcements over the school amplifying system; but you want to do something different on Monday, something that will start the drive off with a bang.

You decide to pass out to all students slips of paper containing a mimeographed message. As you wrestle with the message, you seem unable to get away from the verb *give;* so you turn to a thesaurus for help. In the Index you find several verb synonyms under *give,* but the synonym *present 816.12** is the one you think you want. Turning to "12" under "816," you find:

> Verbs 12. give, present, donate (chiefly U.S.), tip (slang, except as a gratuity), slip (slang), let have; bestow, confer, award, allot, render, bestow on, impart, communicate; grant, accord, allow, vouchsafe, yield, afford; tender, extend, issue, dispense, administer; serve, help to; deal, dole, mete; give out, deal out, dole out, mete out, hand out (coll.), dish out (coll.), fork out (slang), shell out (slang); make a present of, gift, give as a gift.

As you read the listing, you realize that you hadn't thought of using slang, but that slang would appeal to your audience of teenagers. From then on, the message almost writes itself: TOMORROW'S THE DAY TO SHELL OUT FOR THE JUNIOR RED CROSS. LET'S MAKE IT THE BIGGEST COLLECTION IN BLAIR HIGH SCHOOL HISTORY!

Learn to Use Antonyms

An antonym is a word that has an opposite meaning. There are two types of antonyms. In one type, a prefix meaning *not* has been added to the word for which the antonym is desired. For example:

By adding	to	the result is
in	active	inactive
im	mature	immature
ig	noble	ignoble
il	literate	illiterate
ir	responsible	irresponsible
ab	normal	abnormal
dis	satisfied	dissatisfied
non	sense	nonsense
un	natural	unnatural

The three prefixes *in, non,* and *un* are widely used to "manufacture" almost any word of opposite meaning that may be desired. However, the person who has a wide enough vocabulary to choose an entirely different word as the antonym is a master of words. Such a person, wishing to characterize a certain statement as not correct, might describe it as *erroneous* instead of as *incorrect.*

* *Roget's International Thesaurus,* 3d ed., Thomas Y. Crowell Company, New York, 1962, p. 536.

Communication Problems

Word Study

A ■

Substitute specific or emphatic words for the italicized words in these sentences.

1 He *walked* slowly down Main Street.
2 I *said* that I would meet George at ten o'clock.
3 I consider that a *good* plan.
4 That store has a *poor* policy in dealing with its customers.
5 The results *show* what can be done if one tries.
6 He is building a *small home* near the lake.
7 The *route* home led through the woods.
8 I *saw* my first robin this morning.
9 He *ate* his supper in five minutes.
10 She bought some *beautiful* vases in France.

B ■

Match each word in column A with its synonym in column B.

A		*B*	
1	remuneration	a	infer
2	undue	b	congratulations
3	accelerate	c	pay
4	cryptic	d	wealthy
5	felicitations	e	speed up
6	deplete	f	excessive
7	apathy	g	fascinating
8	category	h	classification
9	opulent	i	indifference
10	surmise	j	exhaust
		k	mysterious

C ■

Substitute words of opposite meaning for the italicized words below.

1 Jane *answers* entirely too many questions.
2 Her physician told the patient to *descend* the stairs slowly.
3 The forged cheque proved the prisoner's *innocence*.
4 Between the hills nestled an *artificial* lake.
5 His *definite* recommendations left us confused.
6 The high wind *collected* leaves all over the lawn.
7 Her suggestion was much too *conservative*.
8 We have an *inadequate* supply of everything we need.
9 Miss Drew is very *strict;* otherwise I should not have passed the exam.
10 Because of the *scarcity* of talent, the play was a hit.

D ■

Substitute a more precise adjective for the overworked *awful* in these expressions.

1	an awful cold	**6**	awful manners
2	an awful hurry	**7**	an awful meal
3	an awful storm	**8**	an awful-looking room
4	an awful hat	**9**	an awful pain
5	an awful mistake	**10**	an awful boss

E ■

Convert the following negative statements into positive statements.

1   That is no small task.
2   This is not a bad idea.
3   The building will be started at no distant date.
4   She is no ordinary typist.
5   He is nobody's fool.
6   The crate must contain no fewer than 5 dozen eggs.
7   I wish a shade no darker than this sample.
8   She is no novice.
9   Her popularity is due in no small measure to her sunny disposition.
10   I was not a little surprised at the results.

F ■

In these six groups of four words each, three of the four words in each group have similar meanings. Which word is the intruder?

1   showy, gaudy, delicate, pretentious
2   discouraged, depressed, dejected, elated
3   enlarge, contract, expand, amplify
4   evening, dusk, dawn, twilight
5   hesitant, brave, dauntless, intrepid
6   erudition, scholarship, learning, sensibility

G ■

Consult the thesaurus for additional substitutions that might be selected in place of any four of the italicized words in Exercise A.

Communication in Action: *Vocabulary Game*

It is better to know big words than to use them. Consider this gem: "Simians indigenous to Zamboanga are destitute of caudal appendages." This means that monkeys in Zamboanga have no tails! The game of changing popular sayings into difficult words, such as in the example, is fun and will add to your recognition of words. Use a dictionary to find difficult and clever synonyms for words in three popular sayings. Try them out on your class. Discuss the desirability of having a larger vocabulary than you use in everyday speaking or writing.

PART □ 8

The Art of Communicating in Business □

While writing serves many purposes, in business one goal predominates—to get results. In many business communications, we can quickly see whether our goal has been achieved. If our communication attempts to sell a product, do we make the sale? If our goal is that we be given the opportunity to be interviewed for a job, do we get the opportunity or does our request go un-heeded? The purpose of Part 8 is to help you learn how to get the desired results from your communication in business, regardless of the form of communication used.

Hallmarks
of Effective
Communication

An effective communication is one that does the job intended by the communicator. For example, if an advertisement persuades people to buy the product advertised, that advertisement is effective. If a speech prompts listeners to feel that they have profited from the message, that speech is effective. Anyone can transmit a message, but to do so in such a way as to bring about the desired result is an art.

In this unit we shall discuss the characteristics, or hallmarks, of effective communication—particularly business communication—together with the standards of such communication.

Effective Communication Has a Purpose

In order for a communication to do the job intended, it must have a definite purpose. The communicator must be perfectly clear about what he hopes to accomplish with his communication. He may wish primarily to present facts, to give directions, or to suggest ideas. Or he may wish to persuade, to criticize, or to entertain. Generally, he will have one of these six aims as his major purpose, perhaps with one or more others as minor purposes.

The newspaper reporter, for example, may have as his primary aim the clear presentation of facts. But, he also wishes to entertain to the extent that buyers of his newspaper will read his story with interest and perhaps will even approve his knack of putting words together. A playwright may have as his major purpose the presentation of an idea; however, unless he writes also to entertain and to persuade his audience, his play is not likely to be very successful.

It Promotes Acceptance

Besides having a major purpose, all communication also has a common purpose— that of promoting some kind of response in the receiver. The common aim of all business communication is to promote not only a response, but also a favorable response. In other words, all business communication is designed to promote *acceptance* of the message.

For example, if you write a letter to sell insurance, your primary aim is to convince the recipient that he will be better off by choosing your company's insurance. You want him to *accept* what you have written and then to purchase insurance from you. If you are being interviewed for a position, your major aim (assuming you want the job) is to persuade the interviewer that you are the person best qualified to fill that job—you want him to *accept* you. In these two instances, the major purpose—persuasion—and the common purpose—to gain acceptance—are identical.

A person may seek acceptance openly by means of selling—as in the situations just mentioned—or he may employ more subtle means of influencing others.

Direct Persuasion Saying that much business communication is selling doesn't imply that a "fast pitch" is incorporated into everything spoken or written. It does mean that much communication is *direct persuasion*. What we say or write is intended to sway the thinking or the feelings of another so that he will act as we want him to act, think as we want him to think, feel as we want him to feel. To accomplish this purpose, we as communicators must weigh our words carefully, choose phrases that are positive and pleasant, and inject into our speech and writing a tone favorable to our purpose.

If you want to convince your family that you should have the car for an out-of-town trip with your friends, your approach must be a sales approach. Think of all the reasons why you should be given this privilege, and then try to express these reasons in a way that will make refusal difficult.

Indirect Persuasion Every person who speaks or writes effectively employs numerous subtle as well as direct means to modify the thinking of others. If a person states his point of view forcefully but tactfully, this force and tact may dispose others to believe what he says. Moreover, others are likely to be influenced favorably by his ability to express himself and by knowledge gained from his reading and listening. In person-to-person contact, a speaker's appearance, his manners, his tone of voice—all *indirectly* help to persuade. In writing, *how* the writer says something may be nearly as important as *what* he says. His word choice can convey tact, friendliness, warmth, respect—nearly any impression the writer wishes.

Indirect persuasion involves sensitivity to the needs of others and to the probable effect of a person's words on his listeners or readers. Indirect persuasion, as well as direct persuasion, involves *empathy*.

It Shows Empathy

There is an old rhyme often quoted by sales managers to teach new salespersons the basic art of selling:

> "To sell John Smith what John Smith buys
>
> You must see John Smith through John Smith's eyes."

What does this rhyme mean? It means that if you hope to sell a product to a customer you must first put yourself in the customer's place. You must look at the situation—and the product—the way he might look at them. You must have empathy for the customer.

The same goes for "selling" a point of view to your boss or to a fellow worker. You will get nowhere by demanding that he do something, or by insulting him, except to make him angry. Neither will you sell an idea to him just because *you* think it is a good idea. What you must do is to try to look at the idea as you imagine your boss might look at it. If you can put yourself in his place—have empathy for him—you can go a long way toward accomplishing your aim.

It Furthers Human Relations

Harmonious relations are vital to good office production. Employees must work together to get the job done; and no one likes to work with a disagreeable, discourteous, and tactless person. Such a person hinders the smooth flow of work. To be successful in business, a person must show courtesy, tact, consideration, and a genuine respect and liking for his co-workers. These qualities are good human-relations ingredients that are expected of all who work in business or serve the public.

Good human relations, both inside and outside the company, spring from an appreciation for the feelings of others. This appreciation will result in selecting the most tactful words and phrases to put across a point of view and in saying and writing things in ways that are understandable, reasonable, accurate, and pleasant.

Effective communication contributes enormously to good human relations—with customers and the public and among people working together in a company. Whether the communication is a letter or a personal greeting, a newspaper advertisement or a telephone conversation, the communication can be effective only if it recognizes that human beings are involved. If you are insensitive to others' feelings and show this lack in your communication, you'll drive away customers. You also will have a hard time getting people to cooperate with you in your daily work.

Skill in human relations as revealed in written communication will be discussed in the next unit.

Standards of Business Communication

We have given you some major characteristics of effective business communication, both oral and written. No one knows the exact words and phrases that will achieve the desired effect on everyone. Human beings vary too widely. If there were a magic formula, then the business of communicating effectively would be simple indeed. However, there are certain yardsticks that, if applied consistently, will surely put the odds in your favor.

Simplicity and Clarity   All communication should be clear. For practical, everyday use, communication should also be simple. Usually the simplest way of expressing an idea is the clearest.

Consider the following complex sentence taken from a letter of application:

"I beg to inform you that I saw your most attractive position of accountant described interestingly in a current issue of the local newspaper and in reference to which I wish you to consider herewith my application for a job in your firm."

Obviously, this long, involved sentence is neither simple nor clear. This applicant has a poor chance of being considered for the job. On the other hand, a simple statement like "I hereby apply for the position of accountant that you advertised in last night's *Smithville Hour*" is clear.

Consider this statement:

> "Mr. Wilson is planning a trip to Regina to see Mr. Jackson because he needs assistance in selecting a factory site."

Who needs the assistance, Mr. Wilson or Mr. Jackson? How much clearer the meaning becomes in this statement:

> "Mr. Jackson, of our Regina office, needs help in selecting a factory site; and Mr. Wilson is going there to assist him."

Accuracy and Completeness Effective communication is accurate and complete. In business, time is money; and time spent in communicating adds up to a tidy sum. Whenever an error is made because of an inaccurate communication, time is wasted.

Suppose Mr. Wilson's secretary were asked to send a telegram for Mr. Wilson (see the previous examples) telling Mr. Jackson in Regina that Mr. Wilson is arriving by plane tomorrow morning and wants to be met at the airport. The secretary sends the following message: WILSON ARRIVING REGINA TUESDAY MORNING. PLEASE MEET HIM. What would Mr. Jackson need to know in order to be sure of meeting Mr. Wilson at the airport? He will need to know the name of the airline, the flight number, the exact time of arrival, and the date. Such a communication as this one will require a follow-up by Mr. Jackson and will result in unnecessary expense and delay at both ends.

The effective communicator makes sure his facts are complete before he speaks or writes. Incomplete or inaccurate communication is expensive and time-consuming, and it often makes enemies.

Standard English Few persons are influenced favorably by communications that depart from standard English. Inaccuracies in the use of language mark the communicator as unskilled, or at best, careless. Accurate use of language is essential for effective communication. Your language habits can build confidence in you on the part of your readers and listeners, or your use of language can destroy that confidence completely.

Communication Problems

Application Exercises

A ■

What is meant by the statement, "Effective business communication promotes acceptance"? Be specific.

B ■

"Every business communication we write is actually a sales message." What does this statement mean? Is it true? Why or why not?

C ■

How can the effectiveness of a communication be measured? Give examples.

D ■

Rewrite the following excerpt from a business letter so that it is simple and clear.

We are in receipt of your communication under date of August 2, and in reply we wish to state that our delay in shipping your appliances was regrettably unavoidable and we will endeavor to overcome similar occurrences in the future. Same being sent forward presently, and we trust will be satisfactory.

E ■

Suppose you received the following memorandum. What additional information will you need if you are to comply with the instructions?

There will be a meeting next Thursday at eight o'clock. All employees in the department are expected to be there.

F ■

Criticize the use of language in the following sentences. Find the error in each, tell why it is an error, and remedy it.

1   Please reserve a place at the head table for Miss Fields and I.
2   Are you as efficient as him?
3   I disapprove of you using a worn-out typewriter ribbon.
4   Both jobs are so difficult that I cannot decide which is the hardest.
5   Our company pays higher wages than any company in the city.
6   Writing advertising copy is more interesting than to work with figures.
7   Not one of the men were aware of the error.
8   We shouldn't compare one report to the other.
9   There seems to be a difference of opinion between the three branch managers.
10 I saw in the office news bulletin where we are not going to work next Friday.

Word Study

The following words were used in this unit. Tell what each word means, either orally or in writing; then use the word in a sentence.

A ■

transmit	achieve	employ
primary	involved	modify
tactfully	inaccurate	subtle
privilege	insensitive	dispose
influence	harmonious	standard

Communication in Action: *What Should He Have Said?*

Some examples of poor human relations are shown in the following incidents. Decide (1) what the probable reaction was in each situation, and (2) suggest what he or she should have said in order to maintain or further good human relations.

1 Young man who has just been bumped into by a messenger carrying a large, heavy box: "Why don't you look where you're going?"
2 From a letter to a customer: "You are wrong. The mistake was yours, not ours."
3 Secretary, on the telephone: "Mr. Melrose is tired of having people show up late for meetings. Could you manage to be on time for once?"
4 Salesclerk to customer: "Well, what do you expect of a $40 phonograph? Why don't you spend more and get a really good one?"
5 Clerk in a hardware store: "If you hadn't misused that saw and had followed the directions I gave you, you wouldn't have had this trouble."

UNIT □ 38

The Psychology of Effective Business Writing

Business writing has an enormous effect on human relations. After all, what one says in writing is every bit as important as what he says aloud. *How* he says it can be even more important in writing since a letter cannot be accompanied by a friendly expression—a memorandum cannot smile. Yet, some persons who carefully guard what they say orally give only slight attention to what they write.

Each written communication requires all the skill in human relations and all the persuasive reasoning the writer can muster. Being able to express a point of view in such a way that your reader accepts it and is still your friend is an art. These are the three magic words: *still your friend.* As you write each letter, memorandum, or report—especially those that require you to break unpleasant news—ask yourself this: Will the recipient still be my friend after he reads this? Of course, it is sometimes impossible to keep a friend when you have to tell him "No," no matter how hard you try. But you should assume that you can.

Skill in human relations—we might call this skill "using psychology"—is what makes for effective business writing. Following are some hints for acquiring this skill.

Using Psychology in Routine Letters

Even so-called routine letters and memorandums are potential dynamite in terms of human relations. Suppose you must inform members of the Recreation Committee that you want everyone to be on time at the meeting next Wednesday morning. Simple? Yes. But see how you might lose friends and influence people negatively.

> There will be an important meeting of the Recreation Committee in the second floor Conference Room on Wednesday, May 18, at 10:30 a.m. You are expected to be on time.

What is wrong with this memorandum? The first sentence is fine, but the second sentence is demanding and tactless. It implies that the members have been arriving late at previous meetings. (They may have been, but demanding promptness isn't likely to foster goodwill.) If the writer wants to make sure that each person arrives promptly, he should first decide how *he* would like to be reminded to arrive on time. Then he might word the memorandum this way:

> There will be an important meeting of the Recreation Committee in the second floor Conference Room on Wednesday, May 18, at 10:30 a.m. I know we all want to get started on time, so I hope everyone will arrive promptly.

Do you see the difference in tone? There is no demand—only a tactful request. The second example will not wrinkle the brow as the first one surely would. What is even more important, the second example is likely to get better results!

Ask, Don't Demand   If you want to get people to do things (and getting other people to do things will be an important part of any job you have), you must not demand—you must ask. "Get me that report from the files" is a demand that will arouse resentment, but "Would you please bring me the Miller report from the files?" would probably elicit a cheerful response.

Beware of Accusations   Accusations are especially dangerous in communications. "You are wrong," or "You have made a serious mistake," or "I don't like the way you handled that customer," are accusations; and accusations destroy good human relations. On the other hand, statements like the following help to maintain good human relations: "Would you mind checking those figures again?" "Let's find out where our figures don't agree; I believe there is an error." "May I make a suggestion concerning the way in which you responded to that customer?"

Using Psychology in "Problem" Communications

There are many "problem" communications in business—that is, letters or memorandums that refuse requests or state a point of view not entirely pleasing to the reader. Naturally, these require empathy and tact. Experience has shown that, when composing them, the writer has a better chance of accomplishing his mission if he will follow these suggestions:

Give Reasons Tell a person why his request has been refused. He may be disappointed, but he is not so likely to be resentful if you give reasons for the refusal. In business as elsewhere, resentment destroys goodwill. Every refusal should therefore be accompanied by logical—and truthful—reasons.

Suppose you asked your father to let you use the car on Monday night, and he said simply, but explosively, "No!" How would you feel? Now suppose he answered like this: "I'm sorry, but your mother and I need the car to visit your Aunt Sally, who is in the hospital at Ardway." Wouldn't this reply make a difference in your reaction?

The following reasons for not granting requests were given in letters. Are they logical?

1. ". . . neither would it be fair to you if we made an exception in allowing another customer a discount to which he was not entitled."

2. ". . . so it would not be ethical to reveal information that we have pledged our distributors to keep confidential."

3. ". . . and, therefore, because so many of our employees were out ill during the epidemic, we are about ten days behind in filling our orders."

4. ". . . so it is only because we have many articles on the same subject that we must return your manuscript to you."

The letter on page 305 illustrates good human relations. Mr. Farr, the writer, is eager to get some material from a manufacturer of drugs; and the manufacturer is late in sending it. Note that Mr. Farr does not accuse, demand, or insult. Instead, he gives the manufacturer a reason for his urgency, and a very tactful one at that.

Have the Right Attitude It has been said that anyone who has the right attitude can write effectively, but that it is impossible for a good writer to do so if he has a sour attitude. What is the right attitude? It is looking at situations fairly. It is displaying genuine interest in what you are doing. And most important, it is caring about the results of your actions.

If you have a "Let-George-do-it" or a "Why-should-I-worry?" attitude, you can hardly expect to handle effectively the correspondence for problem situations. If you are indifferent, you show that you do not care what others think of you or of your supervisors or company. Only those who care about people and about their work can become skilled communicators.

Having the right attitude also means avoiding a negative attitude. Never write when you have a chip on your shoulder. To do so might cost your company money—and cost you your job!

Suppose you work for a mail-order house and a customer writes, requesting that she be allowed to return for credit a pile coat she ordered recently. The coat is an inexpensive one costing $68.95 and the customer complains about its "matty fur" and "cheap look." You think to yourself that the customer should know she can't expect real fur at so low a price. A good fur costs hundreds, even thousands, of dollars. Besides, the catalogue describes the coat as "economical," and "made of a fur-like fabric that will wear well if not steamed." Your company's policy is not to accept wearing apparel for refund unless the garment proves defective in workman-

Southwestern **DRUG** Corporation

Full-Line Full-Service Wholesale Druggists

GENERAL OFFICE
P.O. BOX 6099
DALLAS, TEXAS   75222

My five-year-old daughter

asked me this morning, "Daddy, who are we mad at today?"

First I told her it was "whom," and then I gave her a
long list of names .... yours was included. But I explained to her that at this point we were only "play
mad." You see, Kathy wants to go to California this
year and visit Disneyland. I've been hearing about it
since January. Well, her old man is unable to take his
vacation now. He can't until Southwestern Drug's Christmas Trade Catalogue is "put to bed." And some of our
good friends have not yet sent their catalogue page inserts to us.

Our deadline was July 8. Then we had a final deadline
of July 15. For our "kissing cousin type" friends we
shall have an absolutely final deadline of July 22. But
that's it!

> By July 22 we must receive your 3 500 inserts--
> measuring 8 1/2 x 11, trimmed--if we are to in-
> clude them in the catalogue.

We both lose sales if your sheets don't arrive on time.
Let's both of us try to prevent that.

Now, Kathy doesn't appreciate your problems or my problems. She just wants to go to Disneyland--and in a
hurry.

Drop me a note--today--and let me know when your sheets
will arrive, please.

Best regards,

Fred E. Farr

Fred E. Farr, Director
Advertising and Sales Promotion

Courtesy Southwestern Drug Corporation

Chatty and ingenious, this letter uses a positive approach to bring results.

ship. What will be your attitude as you begin to write your reply? Will you be annoyed—and show it? If you experience anger or impatience, you are likely to write something like this:

> Dear Mrs. Antoine:
>
> You claim that the pile coat you purchased from us is of poor quality and does not measure up to your expectations. What do you expect from a $68.95 coat? I refuse to believe that anyone could be so unreasonable as to think he can buy a mink coat at such a ridiculously low price.
>
> Besides, if you don't take care of your coat, no wonder the fur has begun to mat! Surely you don't expect . . . etc.

The customer who receives this letter doubtless would become extremely annoyed after reading the first sentence. Upon reading the second sentence, she would be insulted. From then on, no matter what you say, you are not going to "get through" to her because you have lost her goodwill, and thus, her attention. Even though a customer is wrong and has no basis for expecting an adjustment, the writer has not even made allowance for the possibility that the customer simply doesn't know any better. Arguing with a customer or insulting him hinders rather than helps human relations; it merely magnifies in the customer's mind his original complaint. In fact, a letter like this supports the customer's belief that the company is not a good one to deal with! He is lost forever as its customer.

Now look at a reply that reflects a positive attitude. The situation is the same— the customer is wrong and company policy will not change, but the letter says so in an entirely different manner.

> Dear Mrs. Antoine:
>
> Thank you for writing us about the coat you purchased recently. We like our customers to be satisfied with their purchases.
>
> The "Storm Queen" is one of the finest deep-pile coats that can be found anywhere at the low price of $68.95. Of course, it is not fur; a fur coat would cost at least several hundred dollars. The "Storm Queen" was specially designed to combine the luxury of a mink-like fabric with chic styling and finished workmanship. While the "Storm Queen" is cut from surprisingly good-quality fabric for an inexpensive garment, it was not intended to compare with real furs. You will find a full description of the coat on page 1184 of our Fall and Winter Catalogue. You will also note in this description that our policy does not permit us to accept the garment for credit.
>
> Perhaps you have found that you would prefer a fur coat after all, Mrs. Antoine. If this is the case, I should like to call your attention to the fine fur creations described on pages 1186 to 1192. These coats are highly recommended, and I know you would be very much pleased with one of them.
>
> Sincerely yours,

Negative words indicate negative attitudes, which can be distressing to a reader. Therefore, avoid such phrases as the following:

your error	you are dissatisfied	your unfavorable reaction
your failure	your poor credit record	I regret our delay
your displeasure	our product gave you trouble	our unsatisfactory merchandise

Know Company Policy   Company policy reflects the company's attitude toward its customers, its employees, and the public at large. In short, its policies are its rules for doing business. Major policies are sometimes put into writing in employee manuals—policies regarding credit, refunds, contributions to charitable organizations, discounts, purchasing procedures, personnel relations, and so on. Other policies are merely understood. When there is an established company policy, of course, you must follow it. If your firm does not allow sales discounts after ten days, there is not much you can do except refuse to allow such discounts when customers ask for them. Remember these five rules concerning interpreting company policy:

1. Be sure you have all the facts before you write.
2. Regardless of your answer, always be courteous and tactful.
3. Never lose your temper.
4. Give reasons for your actions.
5. In the absence of established rules, do the thing you believe is best for your company.

Communication Problems

Application Exercises

A ■

In each of the following situations, indicate in a written statement how you would say "No." Remember that you want to retain the friendship of the person making the request.

1   Jim wants to borrow Lex's history textbook overnight, but Lex plans to use it.
2   Jack already owes Tom $2.50, and he asks to borrow another dollar from Tom.
3   Roxanna is invited to a dance by Art; but she would rather go with Ed, who has also invited her.
4   Ken works in Solomon's Record Shop. A customer wants to return a record because it is scratched. There is a conspicuous sign on the store wall saying: "Records may not be exchanged or returned. Examine them carefully before making your purchase."

B ■

In the following letter, indicate the negative words and attitudes that should be avoided. Rewrite the letter, showing positive attitudes and expressions.

Dear Mrs. Thompson:

We were sorry to get your letter of complaint about the error in sending you the wrong set of dishes. Our order clerk failed to read the order ticket properly and made the mistake of thinking "Maxton" was "Marston."

We will rectify this mistake if you let us know when it will be convenient for us to pick up the wrong set of dishes.

Please accept our regrets. We hope we have not incurred your displeasure.

Very truly yours,

C ■

Restate tactfully the following statements and questions. The first four apply to office situations.

1 "Shut that window; it's cold in here."
2 "Why are you so slow about getting that report done?"
3 "That's not the right way to address envelopes."
4 "Let me have those figures; I'll give them to Anne, because I know I can trust *her* to add them correctly."
5 While the family is watching a television comedy, Mike jumps up and suddenly switches the channel, saying, "There's a good movie on Channel 7 that I want to see."

D ■

Rewrite the following, using what you believe to be good psychology.

1 "I have instructions from Mr. Brady to make sure that you close this display room promptly at three o'clock."
2 "It has come to my attention that many of you are using expensive bond paper for mimeograph work. This will not be tolerated."
3 "How can you expect faster delivery in view of the fact that we had a serious fire in our factory last week?"
4 "You neglected to give us the catalogue number, and we would like to know just which lamp shade you want."
5 "Don't blame us because your furniture order has not arrived; there's a rail strike, you know."

Word Study

A ■

Words often confused: threw, through, thorough; device, devise.

B ■

Three of the four words in each line are synonymous. The fourth is an antonym. Spot the intruder in each group.

1 Flexible, pliable, inelastic, malleable
2 Exhaustive, superficial, complete, thorough

3 Counterfeit, genuine, real, true
4 Reputable, honorable, estimable, base
5 Alleviate, augment, allay, lighten

C ■

Complete the following by adding *ar*, *er*, or *or*—whichever is correct.

1	cig___	**3**	simil___	**5**	partn___
2	ledg___	**4**	aviat___	**6**	col___

Communication in Action: *Conflicting Instructions*

An older employee in your department has been watching you as you make out a sales summary report. "The way you are doing that report is wrong," she says. "The cost price, rather than the selling price, should be used." Your supervisor has asked you to use the selling price, and you made note of it at the time you were instructed how to do the job. What should you say or do?

UNIT ■ 39

Writing Skill and Job Success

The Need for Writing Skill

Writing is often the only practical means of communication possible in the business world. When you must "talk" to a person who is not personally present, for instance, you can reach him via a letter or memorandum. Through letters and memorandums, you can "talk" to people all over the world; and each person written to can "hear" the message at his convenience. In business situations where it is necessary to remember what has been said, writing provides "visible" memory. Most contracts for sales and purchases and many other important agreements are put into writing to provide proof and a permanent record of terms or conditions agreed upon. Writing helps people think more clearly; for it permits a person to organize and summarize his thoughts and, thus, to solve problems. Indeed, the business world needs so many different kinds of writing that employers consider writing skills of first importance in hiring a business worker.

Types of Business Writing

In a visit to a business office, you would observe a multitude of written communications. Thousands upon thousands of letters, interoffice memorandums, and reports are stored in long rows of files. On each desk, file baskets are stacked with current papers. Catalogues, reference books, magazines, and similar written materials line bookshelves accessible to most workers. Near each desk, wastepaper baskets, often overflowing before the end of the day, collect discarded writing. Business people write, write, write!

As a business worker, you'll soon realize how much your success depends upon writing. The following are just a few of the typical situations arising during an ordinary business day—situations that require writing.

"Take a letter, please, to . . ."

"Please confirm my telephone conversation with . . ."

"Write a memo to everyone about the meeting."

"I like the idea, but PIW (put it in writing)."

"Please send for a new catalogue and price list."

"Give me a report comparing our absence rate with that of other companies."

"Wire Jones that I'll see him on Tuesday."

"Please write up the minutes of the Research Committee meeting."

Each of the example situations requires a different type of written communication. Some types of written communication are used so frequently and are so important in every business job that they deserve a brief introduction. They are the following:

1. Business letters
2. Interoffice memorandums
3. Reports
4. Telegrams, minutes, and news releases

Business Letters   In business the letter is used more extensively than any other type of written communication. Letters are written to buy and sell goods, to welcome new customers, to ask for information, to answer inquiries, to request or to make adjustments, to collect overdue accounts, and to build a friendly attitude toward a company and its products. Letters are also written to get jobs. Just about everyone in business writes these kinds of letters. In fact, just about everyone writes some of these letters in his everyday living, too. The knowledge and practice you need to develop your letter-writing skills, then, are extremely valuable to you. Being able to write a good letter has boosted the chances for advancement in business affairs of thousands like you. You'll receive specific information about and practice in writing all types of business letters in Units 40 to 55.

Interoffice Memorandums   The interoffice memorandum, as illustrated on page 476, is an important type of business letter, with one big difference: a memorandum is written by a person in the company to communicate with someone else in the same company. Because a memorandum is circulated within the company, it is likely to be less formal than most letters that are mailed to people outside the company.

A vacation schedule may be released; notice of a meeting may be sent to certain executives; plans for expansion of the company may be revealed to employees—all these messages for people within the company would be written in the form of memorandums. Before entering business, you should know how to prepare inter-office memorandums. They are discussed in Unit 56.

Reports A company relies heavily on the many reports written about the activities carried on in its various departments. A report is usually more detailed and follows a more rigidly prescribed form than other kinds of written communication. Reports are often prepared to summarize business activities. For example, each department head may be asked to write a report—monthly, quarterly, or annually—that describes the important accomplishments of his department. These reports, like the balance sheet and other financial statements prepared by the accounting department, tell management what has happened.

Many other "study reports" are used to help solve company problems. The advertising department, for example, may be requested to study and report on proposed changes in the advertising budget. The sales department may study and, by means of a report, may recommend redistributing sales territories and sales quotas. The research and development department may report on research in the proposed use of plastics instead of metals in a particular product. Accountants doubtless will present reports on the differences between expected production costs and actual costs. And the credit department will report on delinquent accounts and the proposed action to be taken in each instance. As you can see, the business report is an important document. You will learn about writing business reports in Unit 57.

Telegrams, Minutes, and News Releases Telegrams, minutes of meetings, and news releases represent a wide variety of miscellaneous business communications that you will need to know how to prepare. Although not used so frequently as other forms of writing, they are important in the conduct of a successful business. And every business employee must know how to compose them.

A *telegram* or *cablegram* is a type of letter used when time is highly important. The delivery of a telegram is faster than it is for any other written communication. Because the cost of sending telegrams is high, you need to learn how to write them to convey your message in as few words as possible.

Minutes of meetings are a special form of report used to record important proceedings. In large firms, much of the internal business is conducted through small groups and committees. The discussions of these groups are recorded in minutes that serve as a memory, or record, of the meeting. Knowing how to write concise and clear minutes of meetings is important to all who enter business.

News releases concerning some phase of its business operation are an important form of public relations for a company. Whenever a newsworthy event occurs, the company announces this event through the columns of local newspapers and trade magazines and, sometimes, through radio and TV. Such an event may be the opening of a new branch office, the promotion of an executive, the development and marketing of a new product, or an expanded or a different type of service offered by the company. Whatever the event, news media editors prefer—and are more likely to publish—news items prepared in news release form.

Each of these miscellaneous forms of business writing—telegrams, minutes, and news releases—is considered in detail in Unit 58.

The Need for Accuracy

To obtain your first full-time job and to be ready for an early promotion, you must use every opportunity now to develop your writing skill. And you can't expect to write clearly and accurately if you don't understand language structure, which you have recently reviewed in Units 8-22. You must be sure when you know and when you *don't know* what is standard English; and to have such confidence, you must master the fundamentals of grammar and usage. As you proceed in this course, you will be given additional opportunities to review language fundamentals.

You also must be sure of yourself when it comes to the other essential tools of written communication—punctuation, capitalization, and the use of abbreviations and figures—discussed in Units 23-33. A large vocabulary, a knowledge of grammar, and the ability to read and listen effectively—all may be for nothing if you do not understand the rules of punctuation. Often the effective writer—especially the secretary—is distinguished from the ineffective one by his ability to punctuate and capitalize correctly.

The Need for Authoritative Reference Sources

No one can be absolutely sure of the accuracy of all aspects of language usage in every situation. That is why outstanding secretaries keep authoritative reference sources close at hand. It is the mediocre secretary or writer who is over-confident and who won't bother to look things up even when he isn't sure.

The following reference works are recommended:

1. *A good secretarial handbook.* A secretary's handbook not only gives the rules of correct language usage, but also contains valuable suggestions as to office procedure, accepted styles of various types of written communication, postal information, legal forms, and the like.

2. *A reference manual for stenographers and typists.* Hundreds of thousands of office workers use a concise reference manual for matters of grammar, style, and punctuation. There are several excellent manuals, a popular one being the *Reference Manual for Stenographers and Typists,* Canadian Edition, by Ruth E. Gavin and William A. Sabin, McGraw-Hill Company of Canada Limited, Toronto, 1970.

3. *A handbook of grammar.* If you write a great many letters, memorandums, and reports, you would be wise to have handy a complete handbook of grammar. Several good ones are available.

4. *A good dictionary.* You can't get along in an office without a good dictionary. Not only is the dictionary helpful for looking up spellings and definitions, but it also contains information on word division, pronunciation, synonyms, geographical locations, abbreviations, and miscellaneous information.

Communication Problems

Application Exercises

A ■

In a concise statement, describe the function of each of the following types of written communication. Do some serve more than one function? If so, mention all functions.

1 A marriage licence
2 Minutes of a club meeting
3 A catalogue from a mail-order house
4 A catalog from a mail-order house
5 A newspaper advertisement
6 A textbook on writing
7 An outline for a speech
8 Class notes and reading notes
9 Business letters (a file drawer full)
10 A report on letter-writing practices in your office

B ■

Analyze the following sentences. Tell what is wrong with each, and state briefly the areas of language usage or mechanics in which the writer in each case needs additional study and practice.

1 As you requested in your letter of May 16 we are sending you duplicate statements as for Feb March and April.
2 I have before me your letter of July 9, and I thank you for writing me this letter.
3 The correspondents from Milford Company don't seem to be in it's usual place.
4 In 1976 3 people left our company for Overseas work.
5 I am eager to have your opinion on the Carter proposal; I am also eager to have your opinion about the length of the contract, because your opinion is important to forming an opinion of my own.

C ■

Decide what type of written communication (letter, memorandum, etc.) would be required to fulfill each of the following oral requests. For each request, tell what information will be needed to prepare the communication.

1 "Please get a hotel reservation for me."
2 "Will you inform the members of the committee about the next meeting."

3 "We want people in the community to know about the new factory we are going to build."

4 "Let Mr. Baker know immediately that I am taking the two o'clock plane to Montreal."

5 "A complete record should be made of what went on in that meeting."

6 "Please send a copy of that bulletin to every branch office."

7 "Please order me the book advertised on page 17 of the *Production Managers Journal*."

8 "If Mrs. Langan calls while I'm out, take a message."

9 "Explain to Mr. Furney in Revelstoke why I can't meet him in Duncan next month."

10 "Please confirm my appointment for next week with Mrs. Goldberg when I'm in Peterborough."

D ■

What type of written communication would you use:

1 To tell Mrs. Whitcomb that she has been accepted as a charge customer at your store?

2 To inform the payroll department in your company of the number of hours worked during the week by each employee in your department?

3 To cancel an appointment in another city today because of bad flying conditions?

4 To explain to a customer in another city why you cannot make a cash refund on a purchase he would like to return?

E ■

Obtain from your library, from a secretary, or from your business teacher a copy of a secretary's handbook or reference manual and a handbook of grammar. In a brief report, tell specifically what kinds of information each book contains.

Word Study

A ■

How are the following words spelled when the syllables indicated are added?

1	stop + ing	**6**	perform + ance
2	occur + ence	**7**	drug + ist
3	cancel + ed	**8**	brief + est
4	credit + or	**9**	control + able
5	bag + age	**10**	install + ment

B ■

Which words in the following ten lines are misspelled? Respell them correctly.

1 requirement, truely, changeless, feild

2 managment, enterprize, suitable, recording

3 meaning, acheive, regretable, curious

4 becomeing, amplifier, payed, resistence
5 approximately, excelence, analize, patience
6 arguement, beged, terrible, complexion
7 receipt, solicitted, embarrassment, ancester
8 merryly, agreeing, ladilike, superceed
9 envyous, location, forgivness, daily
10 changeable, label, fully, interruptting

C ■

Add the termination pronounced "shun" to each of the following words.

1 deprecia_____   4 colli_____   7 comple_____
2 dimen_____   5 expul_____   8 deduc_____
3 resigna_____   6 techni_____   9 occas_____

D ■

Choose *ize*, *ise*, or *yze* for the ending of each of these words.

1 item_____   4 monopol_____   7 util_____
2 ar_____   5 franch_____   8 emphas_____
3 civil_____   6 disgu_____   9 anal_____

E ■

How are the following words spelled when the "uhble"-sounding suffix is added?

1 receive_____   4 accept_____   7 advise_____
2 convert_____   5 reverse_____   8 sense_____
3 sale_____   6 value_____   9 move_____

F ■

Which of the following words ending with the sound of "seed" are misspelled? Spell them correctly.

1 precede   6 receed
2 superceed   7 exceed
3 intercede   8 cede (to assign)
4 seed (the grain of plants) 9 sesede
5 succeed   10 procede

Communication in Action: *Being Blamed for Mistakes of Others*

You and another stenographer take dictation and write letters for the same executive. When you take in some letters that you have just typed, your boss is checking others—not typed by you—and calls your attention to several mistakes. What will you say or do?

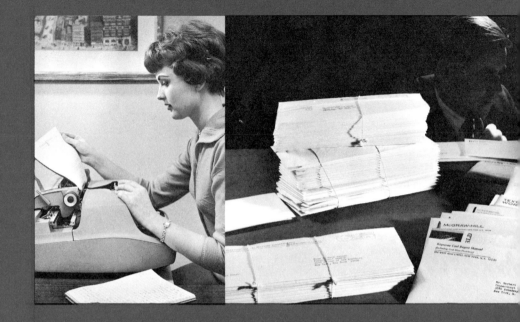

PART · 9

Effective Letter Writing ·

Letters are probably the most common type of written communication used by business people. Because there are so many reasons for the writing of letters, you should be familiar with the varied purposes served by business letters and with the "know-how" of writing letters that most effectively meet these purposes. While you may never need to write some of the types of letters discussed in Part 9, you should be prepared for any assignment that is given to you. In any case, learning how to handle *all* types of letters will definitely contribute to your writing education.

Making
Business Letters
Effective

Why do you write letters to friends and relatives who live out of town? You write because you want to keep in touch, and it isn't possible to make a trip every time you want to exchange news and information; that would be time-consuming and expensive. Telephoning, too, becomes expensive if you talk very long. Your letters, then, are substitutes for personal visits. They convey messages, and at the same time they build new friendships or maintain old ones.

Why Write Business Letters?

Business letters are written for much the same reasons as personal letters. A businessman can't afford the time for, nor the expense of, a personal visit each time he wants to transact business in various parts of the country; so he makes phone calls or writes letters instead. He depends on the written word to keep him in touch with his customers and business associates and to preserve on paper his "conversations" with them. Thus, his letters become his "paper representatives."

To Conduct Business It is estimated that 85 percent of business is conducted wholly or partially by mail. That is why the business letter is so important: it is the primary means by which goods and services are exchanged freely.

To Build Goodwill When a business is sold, the purchaser may pay much more for it than the worth of the physical assets; he also pays for the good reputation of the business—often called "goodwill." This reputation doesn't just happen; it has been consciously built over the years.

Goodwill is a friendly feeling—a feeling of confidence in an organization that makes a customer trade with it rather than with another. Goodwill is not a tangible thing; but it is extremely important to a business.

You may have a favorite store in which you like to shop. Perhaps you prefer this store because it gives superior service, or because it is more conveniently located than other stores, or because the people who run it are exceptionally pleasant. These factors all add up to a good feeling on your part toward the store. And this is what the store wants and works hard to maintain. Its management wants you to think of this store when you need merchandise.

Building goodwill—and maintaining it—is an important job of the business letter. Because many of the people to whom you write never enter your place of business, never see you or talk to you, their impressions of your business are formed entirely through the letters they receive from you. Your business letter, therefore, is not only your business representative; it is also your ambassador.

Kinds of Business Letters

The employee in business writes many types of letters. He may write letters to ask for information, advice, or favors; he may write letters to send information, to collect money, to apologize for a mistake; and he may write letters to say "No" to an unreasonable request, to apply for a job, or to sell his company's products or services. One could hardly name all the types of letters written—the list is practically endless. While some letters are easier to write than others (you can more easily maintain goodwill when granting a request than when refusing one), you cannot say that one letter is more important than another. Every letter is important.

The following kinds of business letters are among those most frequently written.

"Asking" Letters   *Asking* letters may also be called "please send me" letters. They are the simple requests for information, literature, favors, appointments, reservations, and so on. Secretaries and stenographers often write such letters for their employers.

Another type of asking letter is written to order merchandise or services. It is commonly called an *order letter.* Many large companies use a form called a purchase order for this purpose, but thousands of small companies place orders for goods and services by means of letters. These letters often comprise the only authorization needed by the supplier to ship the merchandise. Secretaries often write order letters for special office supplies—accounting forms, typewriter ribbons, and reference books, for example.

Letters Answering Requests   Just as a business firm often writes letters asking for something from another organization, it also receives a great many such letters. Usually the replies to these letters are not difficult to write. For example:

> Here are the color swatches you asked for when our salesman, John Brodie, called on you last week. I hope you will find among them the exact shade you want to match your new office furniture. If you would like to see other samples, please let us know.
>
> You will see that the swatches are numbered. If you decide to order one of these fabrics, just send the number and specify the yardage you will need. We can make delivery on any of these fabrics within two weeks.

Form letters and postal cards are often used to acknowledge routine requests if the reply does not require a personal message.

Some letters answering requests are not so easy to write. You may sometimes have to tell a customer that his order will be delayed because the merchandise is out of stock, or you may have to refuse a customer's request for a special favor simply because you cannot possibly grant it. These letters require the utmost tact and courtesy.

Letters answering requests give the letter writer one of his best opportunities for making friends and building goodwill. They are, therefore, among the most important communications in business.

Claim and Adjustment Letters   However hard people try to avoid them, mistakes will occur in business. A furniture store receives a shipment of lamps and several are broken. A disappointed mother feels that the tricycle she ordered for her young son does not look new—the paint has been scratched in several places. A shoe store manager receives too many shoes in size 6A and too few in size 5B. These are typical situations in which the person who has been inconvenienced or offended writes a letter in protest. Although these letters are called *claim letters*, they really are *complaint letters*. All businesses receive—and send—them.

Letters written in response to claims are called *adjustment letters*. When the adjustment asked for is not granted (it isn't always; the claim may be unreasonable or unjustified), you must write the claimant a letter refusing to make the adjustment. In order to retain goodwill, you must always give a logical reason for the refusal. Because adjustment letters are among the most difficult to write, they require special understanding of people, plus extensive knowledge of the company the writer represents.

Credit and Collection Letters   A large percentage of business transactions in this country are handled on a credit basis. Letters must be written in response to requests for credit. Usually, the responses are favorable: "We are pleased to welcome you as a new charge customer at Elliot's." Sometimes, however, requests for credit must be declined because the applicants are not good credit risks. These are perhaps the most difficult of all letters to write. No one wants to be told that he is a poor credit risk!

Collection letters are written because a very small percentage of those who are given the privilege of credit violate that privilege. Therefore, they must be reminded, reasoned with, and sometimes threatened, before they will pay what they owe. Collection letters are among the most challenging to the letter writer—their effectiveness is measured by the amount of money they bring in from forgetful or careless customers.

Sales Letters   In a sense, every letter a businessman writes is a *sales letter* because it automatically becomes a showcase for himself and his company. However, there are letters written for the specific purpose of selling a product or a service. You probably have received a great many of these yourself. A publisher wants to sell you a subscription to a magazine; a record company tries to persuade you to join its record club; an insurance company asks you to buy a policy. Millions of such letters are written every year.

Other sales letters come under the heading of "promotion letters." These don't attempt to make *direct* sales; their primary purpose is to make friends and to create a good feeling between the company and its customers. In the long run, of course, the desired outcome is an increase in customers—and in sales.

Employment Letters   *Employment letters* deal with getting a position. They are written by everyone, not only by those who expect to work in business. Employment letters include letters inquiring about a position, letters of application, letters thanking an employer for an interview, and letters of resignation.

Social-Business Letters   Many letters of a social-business nature are written to maintain friendly relationships with customers and business acquaintances. Typical social-business correspondence includes letters of congratulation, letters of sympathy, invitations, letters of friendship, and thank-you letters. Since they show thoughtfulness on the part of the writer, social-business letters do a great deal to build goodwill.

Getting Results from Business Letters

Business spends millions of dollars each year corresponding with customers, prospects, dealers, suppliers, and the public at large.

Measuring the Cost   Special studies have shown that, for many businesses, the cost of writing a single letter is more than $3.50. When this amount is multiplied by the great volume of letters written, the cost is considerable. Such factors as the executive's time, the stenographer's time, the paper consumed, the postage, and miscellaneous expenses contribute to the total cost. Yet letters must be written. The question the businessman asks himself about the correspondence that goes out from his office every day is, "Will this letter get results?" If it doesn't, a great deal of time and money is being wasted. If his communications get the results he is after, however, the businessman is not so concerned about the cost.

Measuring Results   An effective letter is one that stimulates in the recipient the most favorable reaction possible. Of course you can't expect every reader to be overcome with joy at the contents of every letter he receives. That is why the word *possible* is included in the definition of an effective letter. An effective business letter, however, makes a friend—or keeps one.

Measuring the effectiveness of a business letter usually is not easy. Every reader is different, and a letter that appeals to one reader will not always appeal to *all* readers. The good letter writer knows this and tries to adapt his message to each individual reader. He is a student of human nature. A good letter writer is essentially a person who understands people—what motivates them, what "ruffles" them. He is usually a tactful person who respects the feelings of those around him. Good letter writing cannot be separated from good human relations. Someone has said that "effective letter writing is good human relations—*on paper.*" This statement may be oversimplified, but there is a great deal of truth in it.

Planning Leads to Better Results

Why Plan? If you were going to take a long trip, would you just hop into your car and take off? Not very likely. Your car might break down shortly after you started; you might run out of money before you reached your destination; and you might waste much valuable time by traveling on the wrong routes. Many things could go wrong because you had not planned ahead.

A blueprint helps the carpenter to build a house; a pattern helps the dressmaker to make a dress. Without the blueprint and the pattern, the builder and the dress-maker would be lost. When you write a letter, your "blueprint" can be of great help to you, for an effective letter does not just happen—it is a combination of knowledge, experience, and careful planning.

How to Plan The first step in any planning process is to gather together all the materials you will need to do the job. In writing a letter, these materials may include the letter to which you are replying, a good dictionary, and pertinent information such as prices and delivery dates. Only when you have all the necessary tools and information at hand can you plan an effective letter.

Using this information, you may wish to make brief notes—either on a scratch pad or on the letter to which you are replying. From these notes you can prepare a rough draft of your letter.

First, however, you should prepare an outline of what you wish to say; for an outline will help you to organize your thoughts. This practice will save you time and money, for it should prevent the necessity for writing follow-up letters to add information or explain something that was not clear in the original.

Using your outline, you should next prepare the rough draft of the letter. Then, check this draft for correct spelling and grammar and for completeness and accuracy of details. You may wish to improve the wording or change the order of some sentences so that your meaning is clear, your words vivid, and your ideas fluid. This is the process of revision.

Probably you will want to prepare still another draft, and perhaps even another before you arrive at a final draft. In each, you will incorporate the changes made in the preceding draft. This procedure is time-consuming, but it makes for a better letter.

As you gain experience in letter writing, you will find that you need to spend less and less time in detailed planning; in time, many facets of the letter-writing process will become almost automatic.

A Successful Example An outline for a letter quoting wholesale prices on transistor radios to a retail store might look like this:

1. Acknowledge letter of May 1 from Midtown Radio and TV regarding Clarion Transistor Radios.
2. Send catalogue of complete line of Clarion Radios.
3. Whipporwill, with eight transistors, is model we recommend for Midtown's special sale.

4. Quote price of $15.95 in lots of less than 50, and $14.60 in lots of 50 or more.
5. Explain extra charge of 20 cents each for batteries.
6. Promise delivery within one week after receipt of order.

Eventually, when you have had more experience in planning and writing business letters, you will need only brief notations to direct you. Your condensed outline then might look like this:

1. Acknowledge inquiry, send catalogue
2. Whipporwill $15.95 each in lots of less than 50, and $14.60 in lots of 50 or more
3. Batteries 20 cents each
4. Delivery in a week

Here is the letter written from the outline:

Dear Mr. Leonard:

Thank you for your letter of May 1 asking about Clarion Transistor Radios. We are pleased to send you today our catalogue describing the many models available.

For your special anniversary sale we recommend the Whipporwill, an eight-transistor beauty. It is described on page 9 of the catalogue. The Whipporwill wholesales for $15.95 in quantities of less than 50, for $14.60 when purchased in lots of 50 or more. Batteries are extra at 20 cents each.

We predict that the Whipporwill will be a big seller for you, Mr. Leonard. Retailers have reported great success with this fine transistor. You can expect delivery of your Whipporwills within one week after your order is received.

Cordially yours,

Communication Problems

Application Exercises

A ■

1 List all the types of letters you have received during the past year.
2 List and describe the types of letters that the following persons might write in a typical month:

Housewife	Clothing store owner
Dentist	Manager of a garage
College dean or school principal	Librarian

B ■

Bring to class examples of as many types of letters (try to bring at least four) as you are able to collect at home or from business friends. Be prepared to discuss:

a The kind of letter it is
b Why the letter was written
c The overall appearance of the letter

C ■

Divide a sheet of paper into two columns. Label each column as follows:

Message Conveyed	*Goodwill Feature*
Your answer: **The price of the radio is $25.95.**	*Your answer:* **We sincerely hope you will give us an opportunity to serve you.**

From each letter used in Exercise B, select one sentence that conveys a message to the reader, as in the above example. Write this sentence in the column headed "Message Conveyed." Then select a sentence or phrase that attempts to develop goodwill and write this feature in the opposite column.

D ■

Discuss each of the preceding letters as to clarity, completeness, and correctness.

E ■

For each of the following situations, tell the kind of business letter you would write.

Your answer: **To welcome a charge customer, you would write a** *credit letter.*

1 To obtain a college catalogue
2 To sell a power lawn mower
3 To report that a radio you ordered was received in damaged condition
4 To apply for a position with the Raymore Company
5 To congratulate a business acquaintance who has been elected president of the Lions Club
6 To answer a customer who wrote to you for the price of slipcovers
7 To open an account to buy on credit
8 To order 500 boxes of stationery
9 To remind a customer that his account is overdue
10 To send a customer a catalogue he requested

Word Study

A ■

Words often confused: intense, intents; insoluble, insolvable, insolvent.

B ■

Should *raise* or *rise* be used in these sentences? (Some sentences require the past-tense or past-participle forms.)

1 John, will you please _____ the shades.
2 At what time will the sun _____ tomorrow?
3 Last year we _____ both cucumbers and tomatoes in our garden.
4 The price of coffee has _____ several times this year because the growers _____ their prices.
5 The last speaker _____ a doubt as to the wisdom of the decision.

C ■

Which of the following frequently used words are here misspelled? Spell each one correctly.

1	sandwitch	**5**	questionaire	**8**	amature
2	untill	**6**	parallel	**9**	alright
3	anonymous	**7**	inoculate	**10**	alledge
4	grammer				

Communication in Action: *Avoid a Mistake*

You overhear the new salesclerk promise a customer that the latter's new dress will be delivered to her home the following evening. As an experienced clerk, you know that the alterations will not be completed for three days and that it will take another day for delivery. How can you convey the correct information to the customer without causing the new clerk to "lose face"?

UNIT □ 41

Qualities of Effective Letters

On what basis do you select your friends? How do you decide what food to pick from an appetizing display in a cafeteria? How do you decide what suit or dress to buy?

In each case, the person or the article you choose possesses certain qualities or characteristics that appeal to you. The friend may be thoughtful of other people—and thoughtfulness is a trait you like. The salad may simply look appetizing—and appearance helps you make the choice. The suit or dress may be of an interesting texture—and texture influences your decision. These are only a few of the factors that help us choose one person or thing rather than another. There are many others. We react favorably to some characteristics and unfavorably to others.

What Makes a Letter Effective?

The same is true when you read a letter. The qualities it possesses will cause you to react either favorably or unfavorably. One of the main objectives of all business letters is to prompt favorable reaction in the recipient.

But, you may ask, every person does not like the same things; so how can a letter please everyone? All of us do not like spinach; we do not all like the color yellow; not everyone likes Beethoven's music. How, then, can one write a letter that will appeal to *every* reader?

You cannot predict exactly how your words will affect another person. From your own experience in dealing with friends and classmates, however, you know what kind of behavior and personal characteristics affect *most* people favorably. You know that friendliness usually wins friends, but sarcasm and indifference do not. You know that a "sharp" appearance, a ready smile, and good listening habits usually attract people; but shoddiness, glumness, and nervous jabber drive them away. There are certain qualities in business letters, too, that will call forth successful results.

Ten Requirements

If each of your letters meets the following ten requirements, the chances are that you will be a successful letter writer. A good letter does the following:

1. Creates a favorable first impression
2. Appeals to the reader's point of view
3. Is correct in every detail
4. Is courteous, friendly, and sincere
5. Promotes goodwill
6. Is clear and complete
7. Is concise
8. Holds together
9. Is well paragraphed
10. Avoids jargon

Creates a Favorable First Impression   When you meet a person for the first time, you probably form some quick judgment about him on the basis of his appearance. So it is with a letter. Your first impression is often influenced by the letter's appearance, and that impression stays with you as you read the message. If the physical characteristics of the letter create a favorable first impression, you will probably react more favorably to the contents. Therefore, every letter you write should look inviting. An attractive platter of food stimulates your appetite to eat; an attractive letter stimulates your desire to read. The factors that help to create a favorable impression include the quality of the stationery, the attractiveness of the letterhead, the neatness of the typing, and the form of the letter.

Appeals to the Reader's Point of View   Many letters are written to get the reader to do something the writer wants him to do. If your letter is of this type, then you should put your words together in such a way as to prompt the reader to act in the way you want him to act. Some people react quickly if their pride is at stake; health or happiness motivates others; financial gain is still another incentive to get people to act.

Producing an action-getting letter will be easier for the writer who puts himself in the reader's place. As he composes the letter, the writer can pretend that he is the *reader*, asking, "What do *I* get out of this? What will it do for *me*?" The writer will then find that he uses the pronoun *you* more often than *I* or *we*. He puts the reader's interest first. He shows how taking the desired action will be to the advantage of the reader.

Suppose you wrote as follows to a customer who was tardy with a payment:

Please send *us* your cheque for $16.89 so that *we* may balance *our* books.

Is there anything in this sentence that would move the reader to sit down, write the cheque, and mail it? Probably not. The typical customer doesn't care whether the company's books are balanced or not. Certainly, he can't see any advantage in it for him. Nearly always there is a better chance of collecting the bill if the customer himself is brought into the picture. For example, here is an appeal to the customer's pride:

Your cheque for $16.89 will balance *your* account and help *you* to maintain *your* good credit standing.

Is Correct in Every Detail   Errors in a letter can prevent the letter from doing the job it sets out to do. Of course, errors are never intentional; even so, there is little excuse for them. Reasons for errors fall into two main categories:

1. *Carelessness, such as the following:*

    Typographic errors—wrong letters, strikeovers, errors in spacing
    Uneven typing—some letters light, others dark
    Poor margin balance—top and bottom and right and left sides out of balance
    Poor erasing

2. *Failure to consult reference sources, with these results:*

    Misspelled words and names (All misspellings are serious; misspelled names are unforgivable.)
    Errors in selection of words
    Errors in dates and figures
    Errors in capitalization and punctuation

Some errors, such as those involving dates and amounts of money, can cause a great deal of harm. Such errors not only irritate the reader (especially if they cause him loss of time or money), but they also cause him to lose faith in the company sending the letter. You can see the harmful effect on goodwill if your letters contain errors. Therefore, you should proofread every letter carefully and correct all errors before you send it.

Is Courteous, Friendly, and Sincere   Would you continue shopping in a store where your patronage was not appreciated? A famous chain of cigar stores displays this sign at all cash registers: "Your purchases are free if we fail to say 'thank you.'"

The owners claim they have never lost any money but have won thousands of friends. They do not take their customers for granted. No doubt you can remember some person for whom you were always delighted to do favors. Why? Probably this person always showed his appreciation, and his *expression* of gratitude made you want to help him. Yes, everyone wishes to be treated courteously—to be told that he is appreciated.

Of course, good manners are not reflected merely in a "please" or "thank you." The *way* in which you say or write "please" or "thank you"—the tone—makes the difference. The tone of your letter tells many things about you—your attitude, your sense of fair play, your desire to be of service. Such expressions as the following help to give your letter a desirable tone:

"You were most thoughtful to . . . ."
"We are indeed happy to . . . ."
"Thank you for . . . ."
"We appreciate your . . . ."
"You are entirely right in saying . . . ."
"We were gratified to learn that . . . ."

Of course, these phrases do not in themselves make a courteous letter. Your letter must "talk" to the reader as if he were a guest in your home.

Friendliness is an important quality of the good letter. Friendliness and courtesy are related, but they are not synonymous terms. You may use courteous words and yet not be very friendly. For example, the person who wrote the following was not actually discourteous. But he does not sound very friendly, does he?

We cannot honor your request for a discount. We can grant discounts only on the regular items listed in our catalogue. Please send us your cheque for $5.76.

You can inject warmth into your letters by writing as you would talk, by keeping the reader's point of view, and by using friendly sounding words and expressions. Now let's try to inject a friendly tone into the preceding letter:

No doubt, Mrs. Holcomb, you assumed that our usual discount applied on these rose bushes. Perhaps this was not entirely clear in our advertisement. I know you will understand, however, that, because we are selling these Beverly Beauties below cost, our usual discount does not apply. May we, therefore, expect your cheque for $5.76?

Sincerity is another quality your letter should possess. Sincerity means that you really do wish to be of service to your reader—you have a genuine interest in him. Assumed sincerity, however, will show through. Sincerity must be genuine. If you are sincere, the customer will not take the attitude that your courtesy and friendliness are prompted by a selfish desire to get what you want. Rather, your sincerity should make him feel that *he* will benefit by acting as you request. When you are sincere, you mean what you say; and your letter reflects this feeling. To write a sincere letter, you must believe in people, in your company, and in yourself. You must talk *with*, not *at*, people. Following are examples of expressions that help to reflect sincerity:

> "Please accept my apology for the delay in sending . . . ."
> "Your problem is quite understandable, and . . . ."
> "We would like to make an exception in this case; however, . . ."
> "I am pleased to explain the situation more fully . . . ."
> "Certainly, you have every right to expect better service; and I . . . ."
> "I agree with you that two weeks does seem a long time to . . . ."

Promotes Goodwill   Every letter you write should help to promote goodwill for your firm. Goodwill results from:

1. Good products or services
2. Ethical conduct
3. Superior service to customers
4. Prompt attention to details, such as correspondence

Remember that every letter you write *is* the company insofar as the reader is concerned. Your letter sells—or unsells—the reader on your firm.

When you write letters for your company you should have a thorough knowledge of that company and of the goods or services it offers. You also should have loyalty toward your company: you should believe in it and its goods and services. If you are sincere in this belief (and also a good letter writer), then your faith will doubtless show in your letters. Goodwill must necessarily follow.

Loyalty toward your company is dependent upon the company's ethical conduct—its honest and upright dealings in all situations. A company's reputation for high ethical standards must also include keeping its word, never taking advantage of any other firm or person, and paying its bills promptly. In carrying out your duties for the company, you should reflect your company's ethics in what and how you write.

It is ironic that customers expect good service, but when they receive it they are flattered. When they get poor service, on the other hand, they react negatively; and their outrage soon makes itself felt. In no time at all their goodwill is lost and, eventually, their business. Most progressive firms make top service a company policy, for they know that consistently excellent service keeps old customers and makes new customers out of prospects. Your business letters should stress this "service-mindedness" of your company.

One secret of building a reputation for "super" service is prompt action. When an order comes in, it should be filled immediately. When a request comes in, it should be answered within forty-eight hours. If a customer has a complaint, it should be attended to without delay. Failure to reply quickly to a letter is a sure way to destroy goodwill. Such negligence implies to the customer that he is not important enough to merit your attention. Therefore, even if you are unable to answer all the writer's questions within forty-eight hours, you should write him anyway, giving what help you can and indicating when his remaining questions will be answered.

Is Clear and Complete   Have you ever received a message that you did not understand? How did you feel—confused, and maybe a little angry? What kept the message from being clear? Was something left unsaid? "Meet me tomorrow at 4 p.m.," Jim writes. But Jim does't tell you *where* to meet him. So his message is not clear because it is not complete. You can see, then, that completeness contributes to clarity in letter writing—that a clearly written message is vital if your letter is to achieve its purpose. You can't meet Jim if you don't know where to meet him. And Miller Brothers can't fill your order for shirts if you don't tell them the size you want. Incomplete letters can be costly, for they lead to errors and often cause delays in filling orders.

Clarity is also influenced by the words you use and the way you use them. First, you must have a clear idea in your own mind of what you want to say. Then, you must decide how you are going to say it. In general, the writer should use the simplest everyday expressions—those he is sure the reader will understand. Contrast the following:

Poor: "It is obligatory that you confirm this outstanding indebtedness and, if no discrepancies exist, that you expedite remittance."

Better: "Please let us know if your records and ours do not agree. If you find that they do, won't you send us your cheque right away?"

Is Concise   A concise letter—a letter that covers the subject in the fewest possible words—is more certain to convey the message than a rambling, verbose letter. But do not think that *concise* and *brief* mean the same thing; brevity is only a part of conciseness. To be concise, a message must be both brief and complete. Look at the following letter:

Please send me a pair of the desert boots advertised in last Sunday's Record-Gazette. My cheque is enclosed.

This letter certainly meets the test for brevity; but could the order be filled? No, because the size (and perhaps color) desired has not been specified. Brevity is desirable; but it must not be used at the expense of clarity or completeness.

Conciseness means saying all that needs to be said and no more. In business, time is money—and few business people have time to read irrelevant details.

Holds Together   A letter should hold together; that is, each part should be related to the other parts. This cohesiveness helps the reader to follow your thinking because each sentence flows smoothly into the next, and each paragraph connects with the one preceding and the one following. On the other hand, a rambling letter that has no guide lines—like a rambling speech—is hard to follow.

Logical sequence of thought is the most important factor in achieving cohesiveness. You will be helped in thinking logically if you first number the points you wish to make and then expand each point into a paragraph. In other words, make an outline of your thoughts before you begin.

In making the transition from one sentence to another or from one paragraph to another, you will be helped by using connecting or linking words or expressions, such as the following:

however	in the first place	furthermore	next
therefore	nevertheless	at any rate	thus
of course	on the other hand	for example	finally

Don't expect these words to work miracles for you, however. Using them to link sentences that embrace disconnected thoughts will fool no one.

Is Well Paragraphed   Good paragraphing is an essential part of effective business letters. However, there is no formula for determining how many paragraphs a letter should have. Many believe that every letter, no matter how short, should contain at least two paragraphs. This is a pretty good rule to follow in most cases. However, the rule does not always work. Consider the following:

Enclosed is my cheque for $8.60 for a two-year subscription to <u>Sportsman</u> magazine.

This letter is complete (assuming that the writer's name and address are included elsewhere), and there is no need to say more. If you have to contrive a message just to make two paragraphs, then you should forget about the two-paragraph rule.

There are three main guiding principles in paragraphing letters:

1. Convey only one principal idea in a paragraph.
2. Hold paragraphs to not more than six or eight typewritten lines. Long paragraphs make your message *look* hard to read, whether it is or not.
3. Don't overparagraph. Too many paragraphs make a letter look choppy, and detract from the smoothness of the message. The typical full-page letter contains three or four paragraphs.

Avoids Jargon   Within any trade, profession, art, or science there develops a vocabulary of technical terms commonly called *jargon*. Because jargon is often obscure and meaningless to the layman—and because it serves to cloud the mind of the writer as well as the reader—jargon should be avoided in business letters.

Some Expressions to Avoid

Contrast the following italicized expressions. Those on the left are pretentious and old-fashioned and are to be avoided. On the right are more appropriate expressions for the same ideas.

To Be Avoided	*Preferable*
1. *Acknowledge receipt of*	1. *I received* or *Thank you for*
"This is to acknowledge receipt of your letter."	"Thank you for writing me about . . ."
2. *Advise*	2. *Say, tell, let us know*
(a) "Please advise us of the action you intend to take."	(a) "Please let us know what action . . ."

To Be Avoided	*Preferable*
(b) "I cannot advise you as to when the contract will be ready."	(b) "I cannot tell you when the contract will be ready."
3. *Am (are) in receipt of*	3. *Thank you* or *I have received*
"We are in receipt of your cheque for $81.20."	(a) "Thank you for your cheque for $81.20."
	(b) "I have received your cheque for $81.20, and appreciate . . ."
4. *As per*	4. *As, according to*
"We are crediting your account as per instructions."	(a) "As you instructed, we are crediting your account."
	(b) "We are crediting your account, according to your wishes."
5. *At an early date*	5. *Soon,* or give a specific date
"You will hear from us at an early date."	(a) "I expect to write you soon about your delivery date."
	(b) "You will hear from me by August 15 about the new delivery date."
6. *At this time, at present, at the present writing*	6. *Now,* or omit entirely
"My opinion at this time (or at present) is that the meeting will take place."	(a) "I now am of the opinion that the meeting will take place."
	(b) "I believe that the meeting will take place."
7. *Attached hereto*	7. *Attached, here,* or *enclosed*
"Attached hereto is the agreement for your signature."	(a) "Attached is the agreement for your signature."
	(b) "Here is the agreement, which I hope you will sign."
8. *Beg*	8. *Ask, request, hope,* etc.
"I beg your indulgence in this matter."	(a) "I should like to ask for an extension of time."
	(b) "I hope you will allow me another month in which to pay this bill."
9. *Due to the fact that*	9. *As, because, since*
(a) "Due to the fact that our factory is on strike, we cannot . . ."	(a) "Because our factory is on strike, we cannot . . ."
(b) "You have been placed on our preferred list of customers due to the fact that you always pay promptly."	(b) "Since you always pay your bills promptly, we are pleased to place you on our list of preferred customers."
10. *Duly*	10. Do not use. Superfluous.
"I received your order of February 8, which I duly acknowledge."	"I appreciate your order of February 8."

To Be Avoided	*Preferable*
11. *Enclosed please find*	11. *Enclosed,* or *here*
"Enclosed please find your copy of the minutes of our last meeting."	(a) "Enclosed are the minutes . . ."
	(b) "Here are the minutes . . ."
12. *I have before me*	12. Do not use. Superfluous.
"I have before me your reminder of the deadline for my article."	"I am grateful for your reminder of the deadline for my article."
13. *Herewith*	13. Do not use.
"I am sending you a duplicate bid herewith."	"Enclosed (or attached) is a duplicate bid."
14. *In re*	14. *Regarding, concerning, as to*
"In re the freight charges, I believe they are high."	"As to the freight charges, I believe they are high."
15. *In the event that*	15. *In case,* or *if*
"In the event that you cannot arrive on Tuesday evening, I shall schedule the conference for Wednesday."	"If you cannot arrive on Tuesday evening, I shall schedule the conference for Wednesday."
16. *In this matter*	16. Do not use. Superfluous.
"I shall await your action in this matter."	"I shall await your action."
17. *Kindly*	17. *Please*
"If our substitution is not satisfactory, kindly let us know."	"If the substitution we are sending is not satisfactory, please let us know."
18. *In the amount of*	18. *For*
"Our money order in the amount of $6 is enclosed."	"Our money order for $6 is enclosed."
19. *Party* (referring to a person)	19. *Person,* or use a name or title
"According to another party in your firm, our record is satisfactory."	"According to your credit supervisor (or another person, or Mrs. Black), our record is satisfactory."
20. *Same*	20. *It, they, them,* or omit
"I have received your letter and thank you for same."	(a) "Thank you for your letter."
	(b) "I have received your letter and I thank you for it."
21. *State*	21. *Say, tell,* or omit
(a) "In response to your inquiry, I wish to state that we can furnish you with the items you specified."	(a) "We can furnish you with the steel plates you need."
(b) "In your letter you state that you want a ripple finish on the letterheads."	(b) "In your letter you say (or you tell us) that you want a ripple finish on the letterheads."

To Be Avoided	*Preferable*
22. *Take the liberty of*	22. Omit
(a) "I am taking the liberty of sending you the beige, rather than the desert tan, drapery material."	(a) "Therefore, I am sending you the beige, rather than the desert tan, drapery material."
(b) "May I take the liberty to tell you how much we value your business."	(b) "May I tell you how much we appreciate your business."
23. *Thank you in advance*	23. Do not use. It is presumptuous to thank a person in advance.
"Thank you in advance for any courtesies you can extend Mr. Philips."	"I would appreciate any courtesies you can extend Mr. Philips."
24. *The writer*	24. *I, me, my*
(a) "The writer wishes to acknowledge receipt of the book."	(a) "Thank you for sending me the book."
(b) "Please send the samples to the attention of the writer."	(b) "Please send the samples to me."
25. *Trust*	25. *Hope, know, believe*
"I trust my suggestion will be satisfactory."	(a) "I hope my suggestion will be satisfactory."
	(b) "I believe you will agree with the action I have taken."
26. *Under date of*	26. Omit.
"I have your letter under date of October 9."	"I have your letter of October 9."
27. *Under separate cover*	27. *Shall send, am sending, in another mail,* etc.
"I am mailing the back issues under separate cover."	(a) "I shall send the back issues to you today."
	(b) "In another mail, I am sending the sample you requested."
28. *Up to this writing*	28. *So far,* or omit
"Up to this writing, I have had no word from the Wilson Company."	(a) "So far, I have had no word from the Wilson Company."
	(b) "I have not heard from the Wilson Company."
29. *Would ask, would remind, would say*	29. Do not use *would* in this way.
"As to a better delivery schedule, I would ask that you bear with us."	"As to a better delivery schedule, I hope you will understand why it will be delayed."

Communication Problems

Application Exercises

A

Rewrite the following letter. Paragraph it correctly and use connecting words that will aid clarity and make the ideas flow better.

> Your order No. 7432 for pencil sharpeners was received today. We do not manufacture pencil sharpeners. We cannot fill your order. We looked up the nearest manufacturer. We found it to be the McMillan Sharpener Company. Their address is 701 Wharf Street, Halifax, Nova Scotia. We are sending you a catalogue of our products. Perhaps we can be of further service to you in the future. Thank you for writing to us.

B ■

Each of the sentences below is "writer slanted"; that is, each takes the writer's point of view. Rewrite each sentence so that it is "reader slanted."

1 We are eager to receive your order.
2 Help us meet our sales quota by sending us your order now.
3 Send your remittance now so that we may balance our books.
4 Your overdue account prevents us from paying our bills promptly.

C

Criticize this letter on the basis of the 10 requirements for a successful letter listed on Page 327.

> Dear Mrs. Barker:
>
> We do not believe you have any cause for complaint concerning the shipment of your order for Princess Priscilla blouses. Our seamstresses have been working night and day trying to catch up on a multitude of orders. It is not our fault that the blouses you ordered have been so popular that everyone wants them. Besides, you should have ordered them earlier. We are just not prepared for the big run on our stock. One of the problems was that at first the textile mills were not sending us enough of the yard goods from which the blouses are made. So, they were behind; but they have caught up now. If you will just be patient, we will do our best to get your order shipped. You ask whether you can have these blouses in time for Easter. That is a good question. It looks like we could and I am sure you will, but still one never knows, do they? As a matter of fact, our production manager said this morning that we will ship all orders by the end of next week. This means you would be receiving them two weeks before Easter.
>
> Yours truly,

D

Each of the following messages lacks some important information. Rewrite the message, providing the information that will make it clear and complete.

1 Meet me at 9 tomorrow.
2 Please send 3 doz. lamp bulbs.

3 Reserve a room for me in your hotel.
4 I would like your travel agency to plan a trip to California for me for next summer.
5 Please let me know how much your blue book costs.

E ■

Revise the following sentences, using more effective wording.

1 Due to a recent change in accounting procedures, you will receive your bill on the tenth of the month instead of on the first.
2 We trust that you will agree with us.
3 Please advise as to what disposition you wish to make of order No. 684.
4 We are replacing the broken gasket and will rush same to you.
5 The goods were shipped as per your order of June 5.
6 Thanks for your esteemed favor of April 2.
7 I want to acknowledge receipt of your order which arrived today and thank you for same.
8 I expect to hear from you at an early date.
9 I beg to advise you that we cannot ship your order at this time due to the fact that our plant is on strike.
10 Enclosed hereto is my cheque in the amount of $62.20 for which the writer thanks you.

Word Study

A ■

Words often confused: deprecate, depreciate; bow, beau, bough.

B ■

Many of our most frequently used words are derived from Latin or Greek roots. Using the root in the first column, add two or more words to each word in the third column.

Root	Meaning	Words Build on Root
1 graph-	write	graphic
2 duc-	lead	ductile
3 spec-	look at	spectator
4 phon-	sound	phonograph
5 fin-	end	finish

C ■

Change the present-tense forms of the verbs within parentheses to the past-tense forms.

1 It (begin) to snow about seven o'clock.
2 I (hear) the faint sound of bells in the distance.
3 She (choose) a slightly darker shade of blue for her new suit.
4 Tim (swim) to the raft and back several times.
5 I (forget) my report card.
6 My sweater (shrink) when I washed it.

Communication in Action: *Contract for an Orchestra*

You have been asked to arrange for an orchestra to play at the annual Accounting Department dinner dance. Make a list of the information you will need to give and get as you telephone an orchestra leader to engage his group for this event.

UNIT □ 42

Business Letter Form— Parts and Placement

When a musician writes a song, he is concerned with a number of things—the title, the notes, the key, the beat, and the verse, to mention a few. These parts all must fit into their proper places on his sheet of music if the song is to make sense.

The letter writer is concerned with many letter parts, too: the address, the salutation, the closing, and the message, to mention some of them. These parts, also, must be arranged in a sequence that will make the letter meaningful. Usually, a letter is divided into four parts. These sections, each of which contains several essential and a few optional parts, are the following:

1. The Heading
2. The Opening
3. The Body
4. The Closing

The Heading

Except in unusual situations—when proof of the mailing date is important, for example—envelopes are not retained and filed in business offices. Therefore, information that the reader needs to answer a letter must be included in a *letterhead* and *dateline*. These are the essential heading parts referred to when the reply is written and, frequently, after the letter has been filed.

The Letterhead   Practically every company uses high quality stationery with its name, address, and telephone number printed on it. These identifying items, and often such additional data as the names of the company's top executives, its slogan, and so on, are referred to collectively as the *letterhead.*

Letterheads, showing a variety of styles. Note the difference in feeling of each.

In addition to providing identification of the writer's company, the content and design of the letterhead help to project the company's image. While the reader is primarily interested in getting to the writer's message as quickly as he can, he is almost sure to glance at the letterhead first. In doing so, he forms an opinion (perhaps subconsciously) about the company: It's old-fashioned or it's modern; it's futuristic or it's ultraconservative; it's middle-of-the-road or it's ultraprogressive; and so on.

It is for these reasons that practically every company hires a professional artist to design its letterhead. Various styles and sizes of type and different layouts serve to project different images. Naturally, every company wants to make the most favorable impression that it can—even if only for a fleeting second in a reader's mind.

The Dateline   It is often *very* important to know when a letter was written—important to both reader and writer. With the flood of mail that every business office receives and sends, it is unwise to assume that you or your reader will remember the exact order of events related to a particular matter. And, there are many instances in which the writer gives no precise indication of time in the message he conveys. Every letter should therefore carry a dateline consisting of the month, day, and year.

There are two widely used dateline styles—one for ordinary business correspondence and one for military correspondence. In neither style is it acceptable to use an abbreviation or number to indicate the month—even if the letter is written to a military organization or individual. Do not use *st*, *nd*, *rd*, *th*, or *d* after the day of the month. (In letters originating within the military services, however, the month is sometimes abbreviated.)

	Correct Styles	*Incorrect Styles*
BUSINESS	January 10, 1977	Jan. 10, 1977
		1/10/77
MILITARY	10 January 1977	
	10 Jan. 1977	10/1/77

Typed Headings   Office people become so accustomed to using printed letterheads, which are "return addresses," that they sometimes forget to type this information when they write personal business letters on plain paper. A personnel manager for a well-known industry once remarked, "I received a splendid letter of application today. I'd certainly hire that girl if only I knew her address."

For a typed heading, use one of the following forms:

> 1224 Lawrence Avenue West
> Toronto, Ontario M6A 1E4
> June 15, 19—

or

> JOHN J. FRANKLIN
> 1224 Lawrence Avenue West
> Toronto, Ontario
> M6A 1E4

> June 15, 19—

The Opening

The functions of the *opening* are to direct the letter to a specific individual, company, department, or whatever, and to greet the reader. The *inside address* directs the letter, as does an *attention line*, if used; and the *salutation* greets the reader. Both parts are essential in every letter style except the simplified letter style (illustrated on page 352).

From the reader's point of view, the opening is assurance that the letter is intended for him and that the writer is thoughtful enough to say "hello" before be-

ginning to talk business. In addition to serving a practical need, the opening therefore serves the purpose of courtesy and helps establish the overall letter tone.

The Inside Address   The name of the addressee, which should always be preceded
by a courtesy title (except in the case of M.D.'s and a few others), is usually the
first line of the inside address. It is also common courtesy to include the person's
job title when it is known—either on the same line as his name or on a separate line
in the inside address. The name of the addressee's company; the street address;
the city, province, and postal code are also included. If the letter is addressed to the
United States, the ZIP Code number is required, and is placed three typewriting spaces
after the state name.

The following are examples of accepted inside-address styles:

Mr. Edward W. Hampton, President
Hampton Home Appliances, Ltd.
1740 Fullerton Avenue
Lethbridge, Alberta
T1K 3L5

Miss Ellen M. Hertzfeld
Home Economics Department
Riverside High School

151 Riverside Drive
Thompson, Manitoba R8N 0X3

Richard P. Rodriguez, M.D.
2850 West End Avenue
Chicago, Illinois   60624

Mrs. Mildred K. Pierce
1294 Allerton Boulevard

Victoria, B.C. V8R 3C2

The Salutation   There are several accepted forms of salutations, and each form
reflects a different "tone." The following are examples of salutations and the tones
they reflect:

Singular Form	Plural Form	Tone
Sir:	Sirs:	Extremely formal—"cold"
Madam:	Mesdames:	
Dear Sir:	Dear Sirs:	Still very formal—"cool"
Dear Madam:	Dear Mesdames:	
Dear Mr. Allen:	Dear Messrs. Allen	Formal but cordial
Dear Mr. Cooper:	and Cooper:	
Dear Mrs. Allen:	Dear Mmes. Allen	
Dear Mrs. Cooper:	and Cooper:	
	Gentlemen:	Very commonly used when the
	Ladies:	letter is addressed to a
		company or to a group
		consisting entirely of
		men or of women
Dear Bill:		Very informal—implies a
		personal friendship

The Attention Line   When a letter is addressed to a company or to a department
within a company, rather than to a specific person, an *attention line* may be used

to speed up handling of the letter. This line is typed *below the inside address* and above the salutation. The following are various styles of attention lines. Remember that an attention line, even if it includes the name and/or title of a specific person, has no bearing on the salutation. (Because the salutation agrees with the first line of the inside address, "Gentlemen:" (or "Ladies:") is the correct salutation.)

ATTENTION: Mr. Jonathan J. Morgan   Attention Mr. J. J. Morgan

Attention of the Personnel Manager   ATTENTION—Sales Department

The Body

The body of the letter is, of course, the most important section of the letter—from both the writer's and the reader's point of view. It is here that the writer makes every effort to get his thoughts across to the reader effectively.

In the discussion here, the important thing to remember is that the body of the letter consists essentially of the *message* and may optionally include a *subject line.*

The Subject Line   If the writer wishes to give the reader advance notice of what the letter is about, he can do so in a displayed subject or *in re* line that precedes the message. The following are examples of two subject-line styles.

SUBJECT: Salesmen's Incentive Compensation Plan

IN RE: Policy No. 714CL070

The Message   The message is the "body and soul" of the whole letter—all the other parts are appendages, arms and legs, that support and help make the message work. By using the techniques discussed in Units 44–55, the writer gives the message a purpose that is meaningful to him and to the reader.

The message of every business letter usually consists of at least two paragraphs—even if the second paragraph is nothing more than "Thanks and best wishes to you," or something along that line.

The Closing

Just as a person usually says "Good-bye" or "So long" when he has finished a conversation, so a writer usually uses a *complimentary closing* in a business letter. The only thing that is different is the way in which he says "So long" or "Good-bye."

The Complimentary Closing   Complimentary closings, like salutations, vary in form and tone. The important thing to remember is to match the tone of the complimentary closing with that of the salutation as closely as possible. "Dear Lil" and "Very truly yours," for example, obviously would make a rather absurd combination in a business letter—or any other letter. The most used forms, ranging from formal to informal, are these:

Very truly yours,	Yours very sincerely,	Very cordially yours,
Yours very truly,	Yours sincerely,	Yours very cordially,
Very sincerely yours,	Sincerely yours,	Yours cordially,
		Cordially yours,

Simmons & Waters

200 Clinton Avenue
Regina, Saskatchewan
S4R 3R7
Phone: 555-0135

September 10, 19-- (2)

Treeman-Hughes Chemicals, Ltd.
(3) 1535 King Avenue
Bathurst, New Brunswick
E2A 1S7

ATTENTION: PLANNING ENGINEERS (4)

Gentlemen: (5)

Subject: Opportunities in Saskatchewan (6)

Do you know that over a quarter of the vast industrial expansion
in the West during the past ten years went into new chemical
facilities? The abundant raw materials for chemical production,
fair labor rates, and economy of transportation are just three
reasons why chemical manufacturers are moving to the West.

Two other reasons are the many low-priced tracts of available
property suitable for industrial development, and favorable
privileges regarding taxation of new industrial enterprises.
Aren't they worth investigating? (7)

We are pleased to offer you our services in conducting your
investigation of opportunities in Saskatchewan, which is fast
becoming the nation's centre for chemical facilities. Because we
have been established here for three decades, because we are fully
informed of existing properties, and because we have already
serviced three other chemical companies, we believe we can offer
you the most authoritative service available.

We look forward to having the opportunity to be of service to you.
Meantime, do read the enclosed pamphlet!

(8) Very truly yours,

SIMMONS & WATERS (9)

F. H. Waters

F. H. Waters, President (10)

(11) FHW/pm
(12) Enclosure
cc J. C. Maloney (13)

1	**Letterhead**	5	**Salutation**
2	**Date line**	6	**Subject line**
3	**Inside address**	7	**Message**
4	**Attention line**	8	**Complimentary closing**

9–10	**Signature block**
11	**Reference initials**
12	**Enclosure notation**
13	**cc notation**

The parts of a business letter. Parts 1, 2, 3, 5, 7, 9, 10, and 11 must be included
in every letter. Parts 4, 6, 12, and 13 are optional—to be used only when needed.

Notice that the closing *Yours truly* is not included in the list. This closing, although still used by many, is considered abrupt by experienced letter writers. Notice, too, that *yours* is usually included in the complimentary closing of business letters.

If you are writing to someone to whom you wish to show great respect, you may use "respectfully" closings—*Yours respectfully* or *Respectfully yours*. (You must not, however, make the error of using *respectively* for *respectfully*.)

The Company Signature   The typed name of the company—the *company signature*—is usually considered an optional part of the closing. Some companies require that the typewritten name of the firm appear, on the theory that the company, not the writer, is the legal entity. Other companies feel that it is pointless to repeat information that already appears in the letterhead.

If the company's name is shown, it would appear in a form such as one of the following:

MARTINSON'S COMPANY LIMITED   THE PAULSON SUPPLY COMPANY

McPHERSON & DINSMORE, LTD.   MORRIS RESEARCH ASSOCIATES

Writer's Signature   This is simply the handwritten signature of the writer.

The Writer's Identification   In most instances, the name of the writer and his title (and/or department) are typed below his signature. Sometimes only the writer's title and/or his department are used. Here are several examples of styles:

Morris J. Sternberg, Manager

A. Phillip Carmichael
Senior Vice-President

Manager, Credit Department

President

Mrs. Frances Allison
Administrative Assistant to
Robert F. Paulson

Accounting Department

L. K. Lambert, Manager
Payroll Section

Reference Initials   If the writer's name is included in the writer's identification, his initials *may* be omitted in the reference initials. However, the initials of the typist or secretary should be included unless the writer specifically requests that they be omitted. If the writer's name is not included in the writer's identification, his initials or his full name may be indicated in the reference initials. The reference initials serve an administrative purpose only, and they are seldom of interest to anyone but the writer. Various styles follow. Remember that, when used, the writer's name or initials are written first:

P. F. Thorns/cmg   PFT:CMG   PFT/cmg

cmg   PFT/law/cmg   (These initials indicate that
                            PFT signed the letter, *law*
                            wrote it for him, and that
                            cmg typed it.)

Enclosure Notation   When something is included with the letter in the same envelope or container, this fact should be indicated by an *enclosure notation*. Such a notation is helpful to the writer and to his secretary, as well as to the recipient and his secretary in confirming that all the enclosures are there when the letter is received.

These are widely used enclosure-notation styles:

Enclosure	Enclosures (2)	Enclosures: 1. Contract
Enclosure: Contract	Enclosures:	2. Cheque
	Contract	3. Return Envelope
	Cheque	4. Memo

cc (Carbon Copy) Notation   When the writer wishes to send a copy of the letter to one or more persons and wishes the addressee to know that he is doing so, a *cc notation* is indicated on the original and all duplicate copies of the letter. This may be accomplished in these ways:

cc: Mr. Jeffrey H. Paley   cc Legal Department
    Mr. Robert Johnson

bcc (Blind Carbon Copy) Notation   This notation never appears on the original copy of a letter. It appears only on carbon copies and is used only when the writer wishes to send a copy to a person other than the addressee, but does not want the addressee to know that he is doing so. All *cc* and *bcc notations* should appear on the copy that the writer retains for his files.

Mailing and Other Notations   When some special postal service, such as *registered mail* or *special delivery* is to be used in mailing a letter, a note indicating the special service should appear on all copies of the letter. Too, if the letter is of a *confidential* or similar nature, this fact should be indicated on all copies of the letter. Such notations may be typed either below the date or below the reference initials. An example notation is shown in the blocked letter on page 353.

P.S. (Postscript)   If the writer has unintentionally forgotten to mention something in the message, he probably will add a *P.S.* rather than have the letter completely retyped. Some writers feel that using a postscript is an effective way of drawing the reader's attention to a particularly important point. A postscript therefore functions as part of the *body*, but it is always positioned in the closing section of the letter. It is treated like other paragraphs, except that it is preceded by the letters *P.S.*

Positioning of Letter Parts

The sequence in which the letter parts occur in a business letter is indicated by the order in which they have just been discussed. Their horizontal positioning—whether typed to begin at the left margin or the centre, for example—is determined by the letter's arrangement style, which will be discussed in the next unit. The vertical spacing of the letter parts, however, is relatively fixed.

Spacing   The spacing between the various parts of a letter has become more or less standard for all letter styles. One blank line is left before the salutation, each paragraph, the complimentary closing, and the company signature, if used. If an attention line or a subject line is included, one blank line precedes and follows these parts.

The writer's identification should be preceded by at least three blank lines, to allow room for the signature; and at least one blank line usually separates the writer's identification from the reference initials. Generally, no blank lines separate the reference initials from the enclosure and carbon copy notations.

A *postscript*, if used, would be preceded by one blank line; and a *bcc* notation would be typed about 2.5 cm from the top of the (carbon copy) page.

All of these parts except the postcript are shown in the sample letters on pages 352-354.

Horizontal and Vertical Placement   The placement of the whole letter on the page can do much to enhance or to destroy the impact of the message on the reader. If the left and right margins are approximately even, the letter looks balanced horizontally; if not, it looks as though it were ready to fall sideways off the page. The same is true of vertical placement. If it ends too high on the page, it looks as though it were hanging at the top of a cliff. If it ends too low, it looks as though it were sliding right off the page. The letter should be balanced visually—with approximately equal margins on all four sides.

To help you balance your letters visually on a page of standard-size stationery, here are a few suggestions. If you are using one of the many special sizes of paper that are available, you will have to make adjustments to give your letter a well-balanced appearance.

Date   The date is typed on line 15 from the top edge of the paper. If the letterhead is very deep, leave two blank lines below the lowest line of printing and type the date on the next line.

Inside Address   The inside address starts at the left margin five lines below the date.

Message   The length of line used for typing the body of the letter will determine the width of the margins and will depend on the number of words in the letter. The table at the top of page 347 will help you in deciding the length of line to use, depending on whether your typewriter has *pica* or *elite* type. With a little experience you will soon be able to judge where your margins should be set to give your letter that balanced look.

	Length of Writing Line	
Words in Body of Letter	**Pica**	**Elite**
Under 100 words (short)	40 strokes	50 strokes
100-200 words (average)	50 strokes	60 strokes
Over 200 words (long)	60 strokes	70 strokes

Letters are usually typed single space with one blank line between paragraphs. If, however, a letter is very short consisting of perhaps only one or two short sentences, double spacing could be used to give the letter a better appearance. Always indent the first line of every paragraph in double-spaced material and leave *one* blank line between paragraphs.

To balance your letters visually on a page, follow the suggestions given in the chart on the opposite page. The chart suggests desirable line lengths, according to the total number of words in the letter and the size of stationery used. The chart also tells how far from the top the date and inside address should be typed when using various sizes of stationery.

The Second Page

Sometimes letters cannot be completed on one page and the message must be continued on a second and, sometimes, even a third page. When this happens, *plain* (not printed letterhead) paper of the same size and quality as the letterhead sheet should be used for continuation pages.

Side Margins   All continuation pages should have the same side margins as the first page. Since there would be over 200 words in the body of a two-or three-page letter, the right and left margins would be about 10 to 12 typewriter spaces each.

Top and Bottom Margins   Six blank lines should be left for the top margin of a continuation page (start typing on line 7). At least six—preferably nine—lines should be left blank at the bottom of each continuation page. The last page of a letter may, of course, have a much deeper bottom margin.

Continuation-Page Heading   A heading consisting of the name of the addressee, the date, and the page number should appear at the top of each continuation page. Two of the commonly used arrangements for such headings are illustrated below. Remember that two or three blank lines should be left between the last line of the heading and the first line of the continued message.

Mr. S. R. Emerson   2   December 1, 1977

Mr. S. R. Emerson
Page 2
December 1, 1977

When dividing a paragraph at the bottom of the first page, leave at least the first two lines on the page and carry at least three lines to the continuation page. If this isn't possible, carry the whole paragraph over to the continuation page. Avoid dividing the last word on any page.

The Envelope

The information contained in the envelope address should be identical with that in the inside address. As a general guide, begin the mailing address halfway down and halfway across the envelope. Special mailing services and any attention line are typed at least two lines below the return address.

If the envelope does not have a printed return address, be sure to type a return address in the upper left corner—not on the back of the envelope.

Postal Codes All addresses in Canada must include the postal code. If a postal code is not known, it can be found in postal code directories available from the Post Office. Some points to remember about the postal codes are the following:

1. The postal code is always the last item of the address.
2. The postal code may appear on the last line by itself or two spaces after the province.
3. It must not be lower than 2 cm from the bottom edge of the envelope.
4. The letters are typed in block capitals with one blank space between the two parts of the code, and no punctuation marks.
5. No writing of any kind should appear below the postal code on the envelope.

ZIP Codes   Envelopes being mailed to the United States must show the ZIP code number. This is typed three blank spaces after the name of the state (on the same line) with no punctuation preceding or following the number.

Province, State   Wherever possible, the province or state should be written in full; however, these may be abbreviated to give a more balanced look.

Dr. Ralph Magee	Mr. Robert Doe	Ms. A. Wong
17 Queen Street	34 Willow Lane	4 Ayres Road
Charlottetown, P.E.I.	Minneapolis, Minn. 55421	Winooski, VT 05404
C1A 4A2		
REGISTERED MAIL		
ATTENTION: W. J. Hendricks		

A correctly addressed envelope, with attention line and mailing notation.

Courtesy Business Week

B\W\ BUSINESS
WEEK A McGraw-Hill Publication

Suite 1507
Carlton Towers
2 Carlton Street
Toronto, Ontario, Canada
M5B 1L2

REGISTERED MAIL

ATTENTION: W. J. Hendricks

                    Fine Papers Division
                    Inland Lake Paper Co. Ltd.
                    P.O. Box 389
                    Sault-Ste-Marie, Ontario
                    P6A 5M1

Communication Problems

Application Exercises

A ■

The following were selected from actual business letters in the files of a large company. Many of these letter parts contain errors. Rewrite each, making corrections wherever necessary.

1 Dr. Robert Allen, M.D.

2 Dear Prof. Nestor

3 September 5th, 19—

4 My Dear Agnes,

5 Yours very cordially,

6 Yours truly,

7 Mr. John Bennett
   Field, B.C. V0a 1g0

8 William Smithers
   1563 5 Ave. E.
   Vancouver, B.C. V5N 1L6

9 Velvet-Smooth Ribbon Company
   83 Lynn Avenue
   New York, New York   10007
   Attention: Mr. R. E. Ellwood
   Dear Sir:

B ■

Write the salutation and complimentary closing for each of the following.

1 A letter to a good customer, Edwin Murray, congratulating him on his recent marriage

2 A letter to a firm composed exclusively of women, inquiring about a new product it has just distributed

3 A letter to a senator asking him to support an important bill in which you are particularly interested

4 A letter to a friend, inviting him to a party

5 A letter to your doctor, thanking him for his recent attention when you were ill

C ■

Obtain five No. 10 envelopes, or cut paper to size (24 cm by 11 cm). Make whatever corrections are necessary in each of the following and prepare the envelope as it should appear.

1 Ferris Window Co.
   1283 Yonge St.
   Toronto M4T 1W6

2 John J. Cotter
   249 King St.
   Charlottetown, P.E.I.

3 Mr. Thomas Fallon
   President
   Ames Desk Company
   411 Bouvin Blvd.
   Granby, P.Q. J2G2L2

4 Cochran Furniture Company
   Fredericton, N.B. E3B 4Y2
   Attention/J. M. Smith

5 Doctor L. E. Douglas, M.D.
   Professional Building
   1313 Cary Street
   Norman, Oklahoma—73069

Word Study

A ■

Words often confused: pursue, peruse; populous, populace.

B ■

Give the nouns that may be formed from the following verbs:

1	compel	**3**	govern	**5**	unite
2	refuse	**4**	annoy	**6**	denounce

C ■

Spell the words that are pronounced

1	trāl	**3**	sēs	**5**	mōd
2	vāg	**4**	kwit	**6**	sēz

Communication in Action: *New Chairman*

Jamie Lawrence has been elected chairman of an important committee in the club to which he belongs. Jamie has not served as a chairman before and does not know how to conduct the meeting of his committee properly. What advice would you give Jamie to help him become more familiar with the procedures for conducting a meeting properly?

UNIT □ 43

Business Letter Form— Arrangement and Punctuation Styles

Just about all the everyday things that we use are available in a wide variety of styles or models. Clothing for men is made to achieve the "Continental Look," the "Italian Look," and so on. The range of clothing styles or "looks" for women is much wider than it is for men. Therefore, when buying a suit, a dress, or some other article of clothing, you try to select the style that meets your preference and that best reflects *you*.

The same is true of styles for business letters. You may select from among six commonly used styles of arrangement and from among three punctuation patterns. There is no standard by which the appropriateness or inappropriateness of a specific style can be firmly established. However, some companies adopt one particular arrangement and punctuation style; and in such instances, as an employee you would be expected to conform. In all other situations—as in selecting clothing, for example—the choices are for you to make from these arrangement and punctuation styles.

Arrangement Styles:

1. Full-Blocked (also called "Block" or "Extreme Block")
2. Simplified
3. Blocked (also called "Modified Block")
4. Semiblocked (also called "Modified Block with Indented Paragraphs")
5. Indented
6. Hanging-Indented (also called "Inverted Paragraph")

Punctuation Styles:

1. Open
2. Standard (also called "Mixed")
3. Closed

Arrangement Styles

The arrangement style of a letter depends upon the *horizontal* placement of the various letter parts. The order or sequence in which the parts are positioned is, as indicated in Unit 42, fixed in a logical pattern that is normally not altered to suit individual tastes.

Full-Blocked Letters   Letters in which *all* the parts begin at the left margin are written in the full-blocked arrangement style. This style, which is illustrated on page 352, saves typing time since the typist doesn't have to use the tabulator in setting up the letter.

Simplified Letters   The Administrative Management Society, formerly the National Office Management Association, developed and advocates the use of the simplified letter style—shown on page 352. In arrangement, it is the same as the full-blocked style. The differences are these:

1. The salutation and the complimentary closing are omitted.
2. Subject and writer's identification lines are always typed in all-capital letters.
3. Listings in the message are indented five spaces, except when the items in the listing are numbered or lettered. When the items are identified by letters or numbers, they are blocked, and no periods are used after the numbers.

The chief purpose of the simplified letter style is to save time. The claim is made that the use of this style saves 10.7 percent of the time required to type a 96-word letter in some other style. Efficiency is not, however, the sole criterion for selecting a letter style. Many writers consider the simplified style cold and impersonal; and, as a result, they use one of the traditional styles.

Full-Blocked
VIGOROUS, AGGRESSIVE
Letter Style

With a subject line and open punctuation

March 6, 19--

Mr. Roger S. Patterson
Western Life Company
433 Wellington Street
London, Ontario N6A 3P7

Dear Mr. Patterson

Subject: Form of a Full-Blocked Letter

This letter is set up in the full-blocked style, in which every line begins at the left margin. A few companies modify it by moving the date to the right, but most firms use it as shown here. Because this style is the fastest to type, it is considered very modern. It is natural, although not necessary, to use "open" punctuation with this style of letter.

This letter also illustrates one arrangement of the subject line, which may be used with any style of letter. Like an attention line, a subject line may be typed with underscores or capitals. In a full-blocked letter, it must be blocked; in other letter styles, it may be blocked or centered. It always appears after the salutation and before the body, for it is considered a part of the body.

Legal firms and the legal departments of companies sometimes prefer to use the Latin terms Re or In Re instead of the English word Subject.

Yours very sincerely

Mary Ellen Smith

Mary Ellen Smith
Reference Department

urs

Simplified
THE EFFICIENCY EXPERT'S
Letter Style

With open punctuation and full-blocked design

March 6, 19--

Mr. Richard W. Parker, Jr.
Humphrey Lumber Company
1520 Southview Terrace
Kamloops, B.C. V2B 7R4

THE SIMPLIFIED LETTER

Several years ago, Mr. Parker, The Administrative Management Society (formerly NOMA) designed a new letter form that they called the "Simplified Letter." This is a sample.

1 It uses the full-blocked form and "open" punctuation.

2 It contains no salutation or closing. (AMS believes such expressions to be meaningless.)

3 It displays a subject line in all capitals, both preceded and followed by two blank lines. Note that the word "Subject" is omitted.

4 It identifies the signer by an all-capitals line that is preceded by at least four blank lines and followed by one--if further notations are used.

5 It seeks to maintain a brisk but friendly tone, partly by using the addressee's name at least in the first sentence.

Perhaps, Mr. Parker, as some say, this form does not really look like a business letter; but its efficiency suggests that this style is worth a trial, especially where output must be increased.

Ralph C. Jones

RALPH E. JONES, TRAINING CONSULTANT

urs

Semiblocked
CONSERVATIVE, EXECUTIVE
Letter Style
With attention line and cc notation

March 7, 19--

Savard, Foster & Company
17 Westminster Avenue
Amherst, Nova Scotia
B4H 3V1

ATTENTION TRAINING DIRECTOR

Gentlemen:

For a letter design that is both standard and
distinctive, try this style: semiblocked (one of the two
most popular styles) with the paragraphs indented ten
spaces (instead of the usual five).

This letter also shows you an alternative
arrangement for the attention line: centered, in all
capitals (instead of being blocked at the left margin and
underscored). In two regards, however, the use of the
attention line here is standard: it is accompanied, as it
should be, by the salutation "Gentlemen"; and it is typed
above the salutation.

Worth noting also in this letter are the following:
(1) positioning the date at the margin, as an alternative
to starting it at the center; (2) the use of "standard"
punctuation, which calls for a colon after the salutation
and a comma after the complimentary closing; and (3) the use
of the "cc" notations at the bottom to indicate to whom carbon
copies of the letter are being sent.

Yours very truly,

(Mrs.) Elsie Frost

Elsie D. Frost, Director

URS
cc Miss Filene
cc Dr. Young

Semiblocked style is exactly the same as the blocked style except that the first line of each paragraph is indented.

Blocked
THE MOST FLEXIBLE
Letter Style
Some persons call this the "Modified Block Style"

10 March 19--

Mrs. Elizabeth Carr, Chairman
Committee on Standardization
The Palliser Hotel
Calgary, Alberta T2V 3S8

Dear Mrs. Carr:

There is no doubt that the blocked letter style is the one
most commonly used in business today. But there is no reason
why any company could not modify the basic blocked design to
incorporate some special point of letter distinction. For
example:

1. You might adopt the "military date" shown above, with
   the day preceding the name of the month.

2. You might devise a special arrangement for the closing
   lines, perhaps like the display below.

3. You might establish a policy that enclosures should
   always, or usually, be enumerated.

With a little ingenuity, you should easily be able to develop
a letter arrangement that would give you the look of a standard
business letter, along with the efficiency of the blocked
arrangement and some special touch of unique individuality.

Cordially yours,

CORRESPONDENCE COUNSELORS

Harry B. Silverman

Regional Director

HBS/urs
Enclosures:
1. Booklet
2. Reply Card
REGISTERED MAIL

Blocked style is most nearly "standard" letter form. Note enclosure and mailing notations and standard punctuation.

Hanging-Indented
FOR SUPER-DISPLAY SALESMANSHIP
Letter Style   With paragraphs and signer's name displayed

March 9, 19--

To All the Typists Who
Need a Way to Display
A Special Sales Letter
So It Looks Special

Dear Ready-for-Rescue:

Yes, this is a hanging-indented letter, with a key word "hanging"
in the margin at the start of each paragraph and with other
lines indented.

Yes, this letter style takes attentive production. You set a
tab stop some appropriate number of spaces in from the
margin and indent all lines except the first one in each
paragraph.

Yes, the hanging-indented style is designed solely for sales
promotion--this form is too cumbersome for ordinary correspondence. Since the whole point of the display is
to feature those paragraph starters, the letter has to
be prepared especially to fit this arrangement.

Yes, indicating the signer's name in the reference position,
as below, instead of below the space where he signs the
letter, is a procedure that may be used with any form
of letter. It is a good device to use when a signer has
a signature he likes but which is illegible!

Yours very truly,

LETTER DISPLAY, INC.

Louis Leslie

Vice-President, Sales

LTLeslie/urs

Indented
THE ULTRACONSERVATIVE
Letter Style   With 5-space indentations and closed punctuation

March 8, 19--

Mr. Harold V. Faunce,
2810 Forest Avenue,
Brandon Man itoba.
R7B 2N5

Dear Mr. Faunce:

This letter illustrates the indented form, as you see
by a glance at the inside address and the closing lines. In
each of these groups, the lines are tab-indented in steps of
five spaces; and the paragraphs are each tab-indented five
spaces, too.

One care to be exercised when you use indented letter
form is to make sure that none of the final lines projects
into the right margin; you must start the complimentary
closing far enough to the left to assure that there is room
for all the closing lines.

This letter also illustrates the "closed" form of
punctuation. Each of the displayed opening and closing
lines is "closed" by a punctuation mark.

Neither the indented arrangement nor "closed"
punctuation pattern is commonly used, but they are both
very popular (especially when used together) in Mexico
and Europe.

Yours very sincerely,

INTERNATIONAL SUPPLY COMPANY,

George H. Chalmers

George Heard Chalmers,
Training Director.

urs:
Enclosures (3).

Hanging-indented style is similar to blocked style except that the second and succeeding paragraph lines are indented.

Indented style is distinguished by indented inside address and closing lines. It is shown here with closed punctuation.

Blocked Letters   In arranging a letter in blocked style, the typist usually changes the position only of the dateline, complimentary closing, company signature, and writer's identification. All these parts usually start at the horizontal centre of the page. However, the date may be aligned to end at the right margin, and the subject and attention lines may be centered, or indented five or ten spaces. A letter in blocked style is illustrated on page 353.

Semiblocked Letters   Semiblocked letters are exactly the same as blocked letters except that the first line of each paragraph is indented, usually five or ten spaces. This style is also illustrated on page 353.

Indented Letters   The indented letter style is perhaps the oldest letter arrangement, for it was the style principally used when all letters were handwritten. The first line of each paragraph and the second and succeeding lines of *each part* of the letter are indented, usually in a series of 5-space steps. As in most other letter styles, the date may be started at the centre, centred, or positioned to end at the right-hand margin. This, of course, is the most time-consuming style to type because of the many paragraph and other indentions required. A letter in indented style is shown on page 354.

Hanging-Indented Letters   The hanging-indented style is not widely used except in advertising or sales letters, to attract the reader's attention. This style, which is illustrated on page 354, is similar to the blocked style with this exception: the second and all other paragraph lines are indented five or ten spaces. The first line of each paragraph is *not* indented.

NOTE: There is still another arrangement style—the "formal" or "personal" style—in which the inside address is placed at the bottom of the letter. (See illustration below.) The inside address is typed from two to five spaces below the signature, at the left margin. No reference initials are used.

```
                        Respectfully yours,



                        Joseph P. Warner



       Dr. Leo. K. Purdy
       Institute of Commerce
       475 Granville Street
       Summerside, Prince Edward Island
       C1N 4P7
```

Formal, or personal, letter style with inside address at the bottom of letter.

Punctuation Styles

There are three commonly used punctuation styles for business letters.

1. Open
2. Standard (also called "Mixed")
3. Closed

It is important to remember that the punctuation of the *message* is the same, regardless of which style is used for the other letter parts.

Open Punctuation Letters This style, shown on page 352, requires that *no* punctuation be used after any part of the letter except the message. Open punctuation is frequently used with full-blocked arrangements, as both styles are considered timesavers for the typist.

Standard Punctuation Letters In the standard punctuation style, only the salutation and the complimentary closing are followed by a mark of punctuation. The salutation is followed by a colon, and the complimentary closing is followed by a comma. This style, which is the most commonly used one, is shown on page 353.

Closed Punctuation Letters The closed punctuation style requires that a punctuation mark appear at the end of every line of every part—except the message—of the letter. This style, shown on page 354, is perhaps the least used of the three styles.

Style Accessories

As important as the letter style are two accessories:

1. The stationery
2. The quality of the typewriting

These accessories, together with the letterhead and the arrangement and punctuation styles, contribute to the first impression made by a letter upon its reader. Therefore, considerable care should be taken to see that these accessories create the desired effect.

Stationery Good-quality stationery is a wise investment. It gives the impression that the firm attaches importance to its correspondence, while poor-quality paper may give the reader the opposite impression. Thus, cheap stationery may endanger prestige.

The size, color, and quality of stationery selected is a matter of individual preference. Frequently, the type of business the firm is engaged in will determine what size, color, and weight of paper should be selected. For most uses, white bond paper is preferred, although a conservative tinted paper would be acceptable in some instances. For example, a florist or gardening supply house may wish to use light-green stationery instead of white. A bond paper with some rag content is of better quality than very lightweight paper with no rag content. Again, however, there are circumstances when lightweight paper may be very appropriate. Certainly, if a firm sends multipage letters or many airmail letters, a thinner paper may be more appropriate and economical than a heavier paper. The second sheet should be of plain paper that matches the letterhead stationery in quality and color.

Envelopes also should be of the same quality and color as the letterhead paper.

Carbon copies for the files are typed on inexpensive paper that is firm enough to give a good carbon impression. Either onionskin or a lightweight yellow second-sheet paper is generally used.

Typewriting Quality   The quality of the typescript is governed by three factors: the evenness of touch, the typewriter ribbon, and the neatness of erasures. An even touch will produce typescript of even density—not a sprinkling of light and dark letters across the page. A well-adjusted electric typewriter guarantees consistent density of typescript, since each key strikes the paper with the same force, regardless of how much or how little pressure is used by the typist. Cleaning the type keys regularly prevents dust-and-ink-clogged letters from marring the appearance of the typescript.

A good-quality ribbon should be used, one that is suited to the type of typewriter —standard or portable, manual or electric. When the ribbon has been used so frequently that there is insufficient ink to produce clear typescript, the ribbon should be replaced. Ribbons come in a variety of colors, but black is the color most frequently used. With tinted stationery, however, a colored ribbon of the same hue might be used. For example, the florist who uses light-green stationery may prefer to use a dark-green ribbon.

Of course, erasures should be kept to a minimum. And, if there are noticeable erasures, the letter should be retyped. Some erasures are usually necessary, but these should be made so neatly that they are not noticeable. Good erasing tools are as essential to the typist as a good set of carpentry or plumbing tools is to the carpenter or the plumber. A good typing eraser and a typing shield that will prevent the smudging of adjacent letters help to make the erasing process easier.

Communication Problems

Application Exercises

A ■

If your employer permitted you to use whatever letter style you prefer, which would you use? Why?

B ■

Design a letterhead that you think would be suitable for a local business of your choice. Use pencil, pen, typewriter—whatever tools you need.

C ■

Bring to class as many samples of letterheads as you are able to obtain (try to get at least five). Be prepared to discuss the appropriateness of each.

D ■

Using a separate sheet of paper for each, set up a letter in each of the following letter styles:

1	Indented style	4	Semiblocked
2	Full-Blocked	5	Blocked
3	Simplified		

Use the inside address and company name and signature given below. Select an appropriate salutation and complimentary closing. In place of the body of the letter, use lines to represent the copy as:

_____

_____

_____

_____

Inside Address:

514 Keats Avenue
Ottawa, Ontario
K1G 0T2

Company Name and Writer's Identification

Marvelon Rug Company
James A. Burkett
Vice-President

E ■

Visit two different firms in your community. Find out what letter style each uses and why. If possible, obtain a sample of the letterhead, envelopes, and second-sheet paper used by each. Use these samples to prepare a bulletin board display.

Word Study

A ■

Words often confused: attendance, attendants; intolerable, intolerant.

B ■

Which of the words that follow each of these sentences is nearest in meaning to the italicized word in the sentence?

1. Louise's remark *insinuated* that the guest had invited herself to the luncheon. (1) denied, (2) hinted, (3) claimed, (4) questioned.
2. My aunt *deprecates* the loss of the little niceties of life. (1) undervalues, (2) appreciates, (3) regretfully disapproves, (4) misses.
3. My grandfather *ceded* some of his land for the new college campus. (1) assigned, (2) sold, (3) purchased, (4) mortgaged.

4 Because of Mr. Clark's many *commitments* for December, he regrets that he will be unable to address your group on the 15th. (1) trips, (2) financial burdens, (3) commissions, (4) promises to do various things.

5 We are weary of those *perennial* jokes about mothers-in-law. (1) stupid, (2) far-fetched, (3) unceasing, (4) tasteless.

C ■

Which spelling in the following groups is correct?

1 vegitable, vegatabel, vegetable
2 relavant, relevant, revelent
3 occasionally, ocassionaly, ocasionally
4 chaufeur, shoffeur, chauffeur
5 Philipino, Filipino, Fillippino

Communication in Action: *Learn to Like It*

Give a one-minute talk on the following statement by King George V of England. State reasons why you agree or disagree. Use dramatic examples if you can.

"The secret of finding happiness is not to do what you like to do, but to learn to like what you have to do."

UNIT □ 44

Letters
That Ask
and Transmit

Have you ever run across a magazine or newspaper advertisement that invited you to send for something free? Maybe you have listened to a radio or television commercial that tempted you to write for a free sample or giveaway. If you yielded to any of those temptations, you probably wrote an *asking* letter unless you merely filled out a coupon. Asking letters are letters that request something.

Many asking letters are written in every business. Of course, they are not always in response to advertisements, but many are of this same type. A businessman writes to a supplier, asking for a catalogue or a price list; to a publisher, asking for reprints of an article, or to be listed as a subscriber; to a hotel, asking that a conference room be reserved for a meeting; to another executive, asking for an appointment, and so on.

Business people also write many letters that *transmit* (send) something. For example, when a cheque is sent to a supplier in payment of a bill, it is accompanied by a short letter of *transmittal*. The same is true of a contract or other important business paper.

Everyday Letters

Asking letters and letters of transmittal are classified as *everyday* letters, because such letters are very common and do not present special problems. Writing every-day letters does not require a great deal of literary talent—they are usually quite simple to write—but this does not mean that they are not important.

If you work in a business office, you are likely to write many everyday letters. In fact, most of the letters that beginners in business write fall into the *everyday* category. You will write some on your own initiative, and others will be suggested by your employer. Some people call these letters "routine." You should not look upon everyday letters as routine, however. No letter is routine if the word *routine* suggests that the letter does not warrant your best writing effort. Regardless of its purpose or length, every letter requires careful planning and thoughtful writing in order to do the job intended.

Characteristics of Asking Letters

In writing a letter requesting something, you must ask yourself this all-important question: What kind of letter would I like to receive if I were being asked for some-thing? You would probably decide that you would want the writer to be as *brief* as possible—to avoid wasting your time trying to determine what he wants. On the other hand, you would want the writer to give you *complete* information so that you wouldn't need to write him for more details. And you would probably expect the writer to be courteous and tactful—no "do-it-or-else" demands.

While these characteristics are applicable to any kind of business letter, they are especially important in asking letters—particularly when you want a favorable response to a request that will benefit you.

Brevity   Some people are inclined to ramble in a simple letter. Consider the following example of aimless verbiage:

Gentlemen:
Last Monday when I was shopping with my best friend, Myrtle Frobosch—she is really not my best friend, although I like her very much—we saw some of the cutest blue kitchen curtains in your store. You know, the ones that have a panoramic picture effect across the top border—Monterrey, Mexico, I think, and the most

cunning tie-backs. Myrtle preferred the peach ones and I liked the red ones. But then our kitchens are not the same color. Besides, I never did like peach. It has no distinction — no splash, you know.

What I really want to know is, may I exchange the red curtains I bought for the blue ones? The price is $8.75, and they are called Fiber Mist.

Sincerely yours,

Ridiculous? Of course. This letter is an adaptation of one that appeared on the joke page of a national magazine some years ago. The letter serves to illustrate the pitfall into which many writers fall: going into unnecessary detail. You have already seen that the entire first paragraph of this letter could have been omitted—with much better results!

Look at the following letter. Note that it says what needs to be said—no more, no less—then stops.

Gentlemen:

I should like to subscribe to <u>Sport Car Magazine</u>. A money order for $13.50, the special two-year subscription rate, is enclosed.

Please send the magazine to Kenneth J. Hammert, 81 Kensington Drive, Moncton, New Brunswick E1E 3J7.

Very truly yours,

Completeness   In striving for brevity, the writer should not overlook the fact that he must give complete information. Business firms often receive letters that contain no return address (and frequently the writers of such letters are the most vocal about the poor correspondence habits of the firm to which they have written!). Other important information may be lacking, too. Suppose you were the reservation clerk of the hotel that received the following letter. It was written by a beginning stenographer, asking for a hotel reservation for her boss.

Gentlemen:

Please reserve a room in your hotel for May 15.

Sincerely yours,

While this letter certainly passes the brevity test, it is lacking in necessary details. What questions need to be answered before an intelligent reply can be given? Of course, the hotel needs to know the name of the person who is to occupy the room. If there are other persons in the party, their names should be given. Does the guest want a single room or a double room? What time will he arrive? (Rooms are usually not held after 6 p.m. unless the person making the reservation asks that it be held "for late arrival.") The hotel will also want to know how long the guest plans to stay.

Other information that might be given—although it is not always essential—is the guest's preference for a room location, the price he expects to pay, and any special services he may require.

Here is the letter a competent secretary would have written:

Gentlemen:

Please reserve a single room for Mr. Harold Mansett, treasurer of our company, for the evening of May 15.

Mr. Mansett will be arriving about 7:30 p.m., so please hold the reservation for late arrival. Mr. Mansett prefers a room facing the St. Lawrence River.

Please confirm this reservation.

Very truly yours,

If Mr. Mansett has other preferences that his secretary knows about, she will, of course, make them known to the hotel.

Tact and Courtesy   Pleasant words like "thank you," "please," "grateful," and "appreciate" will do more to make the reader want to go out of his way to help you than will a brusque demand. Here are some typical beginnings for effective asking letters:

"May I please . . . ."
"I shall be grateful if you will . . . ."
"Will you please . . . ."
"I should appreciate having . . . ."
"Please send me . . . ."

Following are typical endings for effective asking letters:

"I am certain we can count on your cooperation."
"Your suggestions would be genuinely appreciated."
"I would appreciate this help."
"We shall be grateful for this special service."

When Should Reasons Be Given?   When the stated reason for a request will prompt the reader to give you better service, then you should state such a reason in your letter. For instance:

Dear Mr. Parker:

Last week you gave a set of records, "Typing to Music," to the people who attended your press conference on new discoveries in self-instruction typewriting. Unfortunately, I was not able to be at that conference; but I would very much like to have a set of the records. Several of our employees are brushing up on their typewriting, and I have an idea that records such as these would be very beneficial to them. At least, I should like to listen to the records and prepare a descriptive write-up about them for our personnel bulletin.

I shall be grateful, Mr. Parker, if you can arrange to send me these records. Incidentally, I understand the press conference was most successful; and I regret that I had to miss it.

Cordially yours,

If the reason for a request is obvious, and the reader is expected to grant it without question, there is no need to state the reason. For example:

Gentlemen:

Please send me the free reprint, "New Dimensions in Stereo Sound," which you offered on last night's Frank Morrison TV program.

Thank you.

Very truly yours,

Typical Asking Letters

Examples of various kinds of asking letters are given on the following pages. Here are specific suggestions for writing letters of this type:

1. Write to a particular individual, if possible, rather than to a company. If you do not know the name of the person, you can help to speed the handling of your request by indicating the department you think will handle the matter. For example, if your letter concerns employment, you would address the Personnel Department; if it concerns an order, you would address the Sales Department; if it concerns advertising or customer relations, you would probably address the Advertising Department or the Public Relations Department.

Above all, be sure you have spelled all names correctly and have written them exactly as the addressee prefers to have them written.

2. Be sure that *you* are clear in your own mind as to what you want to know. You are then much more likely to make your request clear to the reader.

3. "Thank you" is always in good taste, but do not write "Thank you in advance" or, worse still, "Thanking you in advance."

4. Do not make unnecessary work for the reader by asking for information that you could have obtained from reference books or other sources available to you.

5. If the reply is to be a special favor, a stamped, self-addressed envelope should be enclosed.

Here are some examples of typical asking letters. Notice how these letters carry out the suggestions just made.

For Information

Gentlemen:

Would you please give me the name of your dealer in the Brockville area? We are interested in getting estimates on water-softening equipment and supplies for our hosiery plant.

We shall appreciate having this information as soon as possible.

Very truly yours,

For Literature or a Free Service

Gentlemen:

Please send me a copy of "Beauty Magic for Modern Homemakers" advertised in yesterday's <u>Herald Examiner</u>. I am also interested in a booklet you published several months ago, which I recently saw at a friend's home. It was <u>Make Your Own Rug</u>. Do you have a copy to send me?

I have learned a great deal about home decoration from your various publications; and I, as well as my friends, appreciate this wonderful service.

Sincerely yours,

Often a postal card will serve as well as a letter in making routine inquiries; in fact, many companies prefer them. For instance:

Gentlemen:

Please send me <u>Filing Secrets</u>, the booklet advertised in this month's <u>Modern Methods</u> magazine.

Thank you.

Sincerely yours,

Ordering a Product or Service   Most business firms of medium and large size use a purchase order form when ordering goods. Such a form centralizes in the hands of one department the responsibility for ordering merchandise and helps to eliminate the possibility of any Tom, Dick, or Harry's ordering goods on his own initiative. Too, a purchase order form is quicker to prepare than a letter.

Orders may also be placed on an order blank supplied by the company from which goods are being bought. A number of small companies use these order forms.

A third way of ordering merchandise, used widely in small companies, is by means of letters and postal cards.

In preparing order letters, accuracy is extremely important. Figures and items must be checked and rechecked. To make an order letter easier to read and to check, the smart typist places each order item on a separate line. For instance:

Gentlemen:

Please send us hand stamps as follows:

Quantity	Item
2	No. 613 B (PAID)
4	No. 721 X (Company name to be: ARNESON NOVELTIES, LTD.)
1	No. 41 (Name: HORACE T. ARMENTIER)
1	No. 41 (Name: J. FRIEDA CUFFNEY)

Our cheque for $28.80 is enclosed. May we have these stamps by September 18.

Very truly yours,

Requesting Appointments   In business, usual practice is to make appointments by telephone or letter when you wish to call on an executive at his office. Of course, if the appointment is local, the use of the telephone is quicker and less expensive. Out-of-town appointments are often made by letter.

> Dear Mr. Jackson:
>
> I am planning to spend the day in Fort Garry on April 14 and should like very much to talk with you or one of your associates while I am there. We are setting up a wage-incentive program in our organization, and I have been told that you have a very effective plan at Hoffman.
>
> Would you find 10 a.m. on the 14th a convenient time to see me? An hour of your time should be sufficient and would mean a great deal to me.
>
> Cordially yours,

Asking Special Favors   Still another type of asking letter that often must be written is one requesting a special favor. Such a letter is usually a little more difficult to write than those already discussed, for here you are asking a person to do something he may not have expected to do. In business, customers are expected to write for catalogues or to make appointments. Sometimes, however, a businessman receives a request that is a little out of the ordinary.

Of course, these letters must contain the same characteristics as any other asking letters. However, they must have an added "something"—an appeal that will make the reader want to grant this special favor. In the letter below, can you find this special "something"?

> Dear Mr. Gardner:
>
> The Neosho Chapter of the NSA is having its annual Boss-Secretary Night on Thursday, November 18. We should like very much to have you as our guest speaker.
>
> Our members and their bosses (we expect about 80 people in all) have expressed a particular interest in hearing a lively talk on "Better Letters." We are especially interested in having our bosses hear something about what the secretary can do to help her employer with his communications problems. Our program calls for a forty-minute presentation from the speaker; but you may take a little more or a little less time, as you wish. Probably you know that this night is the highlight of our year's meetings and, while it has a serious purpose, is usually on the "lighter" side.
>
> Several of us enjoyed your very interesting article in the August issue of <u>Your Girl Friday</u> magazine. In fact, you can build your speech along the very same lines, if you wish.
>
> I hope you can accept this invitation, Mr. Gardner. If you can, I will write you again giving you all the details—time, place, and complete program plans.
>
> Cordially yours,

Using Courtesy Carbons

To make it easy for those from whom favors are being asked by letter, carbons are frequently used. For example, in a letter requesting an appointment, a carbon copy accompanies the original; the recipient may simply check and return the carbon. (Often a stamped, addressed envelope is included, too.) Following is an example of a courtesy carbon.

Dear Mr. Wilson:

Would you or one of your associates be free for an hour beginning at 9:30 a.m. on February 6?

I should like to talk with you about your employee publications, which we consider to be outstanding examples of good personnel services. Your experiences will be very helpful to us in inaugurating our own plan.

For your convenience, I am sending you an extra carbon. Please indicate your answers in the spaces provided and return the carbon to me in the enclosed envelope.

Sincerely yours,

Please check ($\sqrt{}$)
or insert time

1. Yes, 9:30 a.m. on February 6 is a good time to meet me at my office. _____

2. Sorry, 9:30 a.m. on February 6 is not convenient, but I can see you on that date at _____

3. I shall be unable to see you on February 6. _____

Letters of Transmittal

A cheque, a money order, or an important business paper sent by mail should always be accompanied by a letter. A letter helps to identify what is being sent so that the recipient knows exactly what you *intended* to send. The letter also provides a valuable record for future reference. When remittances or business papers are accompanied with a letter, the carbon copy answers the question: "I wonder whether I sent that salary survey to Johnson as I promised?" or "How many copies of the Mayberry agreement did I send to Lawford and Hines?"

Transmitting letters should do the following:

1. Identify *what* is being sent and *how many* (if money, the *amount*)
2. Specify any action necessary on the part of the recipient
3. If transmitting money, identify the purpose for which the money is to be used —to apply on account, in payment of a certain invoice number, for services rendered, or for purchases made

Note the following example.

Dear Mr. Rencroft:

Enclosed are the original and one copy of the contract for your manuscript, A Boy's Story of the War Between the States. Please sign both copies, return the original to me, and retain the carbon.

The review of your manuscript by Bosley Carruthers was extremely complimentary. As you know, our target date for publication is October 15. I'll be in touch with you when editing begins.

Sincerely yours,

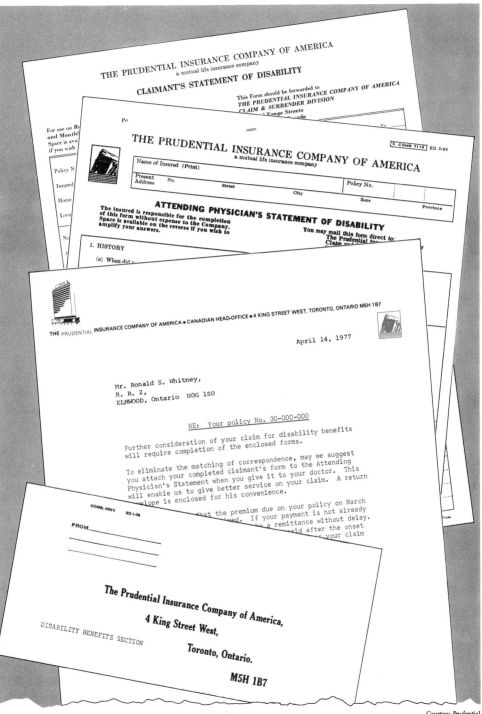

THE PRUDENTIAL INSURANCE COMPANY OF AMERICA
a mutual life insurance company

CLAIMANT'S STATEMENT OF DISABILITY

This Form should be forwarded to
THE PRUDENTIAL INSURANCE COMPANY OF AMERICA
CLAIM & SURRENDER DIVISION
Yonge Streets

THE PRUDENTIAL INSURANCE COMPANY OF AMERICA
a mutual life insurance company

C COMB 7110   ED 3-64

Name of Insured (Print)

Present Address   No.   Street   City   Policy No.   Zone   Province

ATTENDING PHYSICIAN'S STATEMENT OF DISABILITY

The insured is responsible for the completion of this form without expense to the Company. Space is available on the reverse if you wish to amplify your answers.

You may mail this form direct to:
The Prudential In
Claim

1. HISTORY

(a) When did

THE PRUDENTIAL INSURANCE COMPANY OF AMERICA ● CANADIAN HEAD-OFFICE ● 4 KING STREET WEST, TORONTO, ONTARIO M5H 1B7

April 14, 1977

Mr. Ronald S. Whitney,
R. R. 2,
ELMWOOD, Ontario   N0G 1S0

RE: Your policy No. 30-000-000

Further consideration of your claim for disability benefits
will require completion of the enclosed forms.

To eliminate the matching of correspondence, may we suggest
you attach your completed claimant's form to the Attending
Physician's Statement when you give it to your doctor. This
will enable us to give better service on your claim. A return
velope is enclosed for his convenience.

that the premium due on your policy on March
ived. If your payment is not already
a remittance without delay.
aid after the onset
your claim

COMB. 4001G   ED 1-38

FROM

The Prudential Insurance Company of America,

4 King Street West,

DISABILITY BENEFITS SECTION

Toronto, Ontario.

M5H 1B7

This transmitting letter identifies enclosures and specifies required action.   *Courtesy Prudential*

Communication Problems

Application Exercises

A ■

In a magazine or a newspaper, find an advertisement offering a free pamphlet or booklet that you might like to have. Clip the advertisement. Then write a letter requesting the booklet or pamphlet and attach the advertisement to your letter. After your letter has been returned to you by your teacher, you may want to send for the booklet or pamphlet.

B ■

Write a letter to Mr. Anderson Reid, personnel manager of the Tyler Manufacturing Company, 1238 Robin Street, Montreal, Quebec H2L 1W5. Request a career booklet, *Your Future at Tyler,* which you saw mentioned in an article in *Reader's Digest,* current issue.

C ■

Write a letter to the Town House Hotel, 148 McKenzie Avenue, Prince George, British Columbia V2L 4N4, in which you make a reservation. You will be attending a convention at the Town House, and you will be staying three days. Supply dates and other details.

D ■

Assume that you work for Mr. Kenneth Fremont, a lawyer who has a small office in a rural community, and that you need to order some supplies from your nearest stationer, the Wadley Stationery Company, 14 Montcalm Street, Drummondville, Quebec J2B 2X6. One of the salesmen, William Andrews, usually handles your order. You need the following items: 12 boxes of paper clips, 2 bottles of permanent blue ink, 6 reams of white bond paper, 6 black typewriter ribbons, and 1 ream of onionskin paper. Write the order letter.

E ■

You have been asked by your supervisor to send a duplicate invoice requested by a customer in his letter of July 9. The customer is the Potter Envelope Company, 179 Nipissing Street, North Bay, Ontario P1B 4L3. The customer was sent an original invoice, but apparently misplaced it. The number of the invoice is KX362.

Word Study

A ■

Words often confused: elicit, illicit; key, quay.

B ■

Are these statements truthful?

    1 A possessive is never written without an apostrophe.
    2 Two singular nouns connected by *and* used as the subject of a sentence require a plural verb.

3 Synonyms are words that have exactly the same meaning.

4 The prefixes *counter* and *contra* impart the meaning of "against" to a word.

5 The same expression may be written sometimes as two words and sometimes as a hyphenated word.

C ■

In which of the following words should an *e* appear in the blank space?

1	sens___ble	**3**	judg___ment	**5**	griev___ance
2	notic___able	**4**	courag___ous	**6**	liv___liness

Communication in Action: *Still a Stranger*

Mary Landreaux had been working in the office of Andruss and Company for more than two months, yet she felt like a stranger. None of the other girls with whom she worked seemed very friendly. They all ignored Mary during the rest periods and in the cafeteria at lunch time. Yet the girls seemed friendly enough with one another. Mary was both perplexed and unhappy. What advice would you give Mary?

UNIT □ 45

Letters That Answer— Acknowledgments

Suppose at Christmas an aunt sends you a cheque for $20, for which you are very grateful. You can use the money! You would be ungracious, wouldn't you, if you did not write her a letter of thanks? In fact, you probably would not let many days go by before getting the letter in the mail—while the thought was fresh in your mind.

Why Write Acknowledgments?

A usual business practice—and always very good business—is to acknowledge by letter any money or business papers received, favors granted, appointments made, and agreements reached orally.

To Show Courtesy The first reason for writing letters of acknowledgment is that writing such letters is the courteous thing to do. A letter from you acknowledging something or confirming something tells the recipient that he need not worry—you have received safely what he sent.

To Avoid Misunderstanding   A second, and equally important, reason for writing acknowledgment letters is to avoid misunderstandings or mistakes. If you have received an order and will make shipment as soon as possible, the customer will want to know. If he does not hear from you, he may assume that you did not receive his order, or he may wonder what you are doing about it if you did. A written acknowledgment assures him that you have the merchandise in the quantity he requests and that you are going to fill his order quickly.

To Provide a Record   A third reason for writing acknowledgment letters is to provide a record. Records are the memory of business. You would not want to trust your own memory as to the date on which you promised delivery of an order; the carbon copy of your acknowledgment, therefore, provides the information.

Acknowledging Receipt of Money

When money is received, it usually should be acknowledged. Remember these special rules when writing letters acknowledging the receipt of money:

1. Express thanks for the money, even though payment may be long overdue.

2. Be sure to mention the amount that is received. This letter provides a valuable record for the future. Rather than just saying, "Thank you for your cheque," say, "Thank you for your cheque for $88.95."

3. When appropriate, mention how the money is to be used—to apply on account, to be used as full payment for merchandise or services, or whatever the purpose of payment.

4. If you can think of something pleasant to say to the sender, doing so is always in good taste. "We appreciate your prompt payment," or "Doing business with you is always a pleasure," or "I hope you will enjoy your new Visi-View floor lamp."

Following are typical examples of letters acknowledging the receipt of money.

Dear Mr. Roundtree:

Thank you for your cheque for $16.75. This amount has been applied to your account, leaving a balance of $33.50.

We appreciate your promptness in making your payments, Mr. Roundtree; and we are always pleased to serve you.

Sincerely yours,

Dear Miss Krasna:

Thank you for being so prompt in sending the $10 money order for 20 copies of Adventures in Sound.

I hope that you and other members of the Listeners Club are deriving much enjoyment from these materials. Over 15.000 copies of the booklet have been sent to listeners all over the world.

Cordially yours,

Acknowledging Business Papers

Important business papers—such as contracts, securities (stocks and bonds), notes, insurance policies, bids, and the like—should always be acknowledged promptly, since they are often just as important as money. In writing such letters, be specific as to just what was received and the identifying number. If any action is required on the part of the recipient, this should be made clear in your letter. Here is an example:

> Dear Mr. Horn:
>
> I received today two copies of the signed contracts for servicing our office machines for the coming year. Thank you.
>
> As indicated by our agreement, we shall expect service to begin on September 1. I hope this will be the beginning of a mutually profitable association.
>
> Cordially yours,

Acknowledging Orders

Some business firms acknowledge all orders for goods or services they receive. Form letters or postal cards may be used for this purpose in larger companies, and many hotels and motels use form letters or printed cards like this one to acknowledge reservations.

Typed inserts complete this printed form acknowledging hotel reservation.

Courtesy The Royal York Hotel

THE
ROYAL YORK
TORONTO CANADA
A CANADIAN PACIFIC HOTEL

Please Note — Should a room not be available at the rate requested the next available rate will be assigned.

CONFIRMS WITH PLEASURE YOUR RESERVATION FOR:

DAY.	ARRIVAL	DEPARTURE DATE	TYPE OF ACCOMMODATION
Monday	May 25/77	May 26/77	Single, Standard

. (late arrival)
Mr. Samuel P. Johnson
675 Hastings Street West
. Vancouver, B.C. V6B 1M2

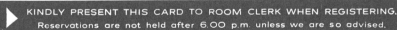

KINDLY PRESENT THIS CARD TO ROOM CLERK WHEN REGISTERING.
Reservations are not held after 6.00 p.m. unless we are so advised.

However, individually written letters are much more effective. Customers, especially, appreciate the "extra touch" of a personal letter.

When a customer places an order, he is interested primarily in one thing: when will he get the merchandise? This information should be supplied early in the letter. A formula for writing acknowledgments of orders usually includes the following:

1. A "thank you" for the business received
2. A statement concerning the time and method of delivery
3. Any special instructions
4. An offer to be of further service

Notice how this formula is put to work in the following letter:

Dear Mr. Cartright:

Thank you	Thank you for your order for a Power House Outboard Motor. The
When shipped	motor is being shipped today by prepaid freight.
and how	Would you do us—and yourself—a favor? Just as soon as your Power House "37 Plus" arrives, please fill out the card attached to the
Special	motor and mail it back to us. Receipt of this card will tell us that the
instructions	motor arrived in good condition and will also serve as a record of our special two-year guarantee.
Offer to be of	I hope you have many happy hours of motor boating. Let us know
further help	how we can help you further. Incidentally, Neptune Marina, in Norfolk, carries a complete line of parts and accessories for your Power House "37 Plus."

Sincerely,

Confirming Appointments, Orders, Agreements

Orders and agreements made orally (in person or by telephone) or by telegraph should be confirmed by letter. Appointments made by telephone, at meetings, or over the luncheon table are usually confirmed in writing. If the persons making an appointment by telephone are at their desks, a note on the desk calendar is usually a sufficient reminder. Otherwise, the safest policy is to follow up with a letter. By providing a written record of appointments, agreements, and orders, letters perform a most valuable function in business.

Confirming an Appointment

Dear Bob:

I was glad to meet you at Rotary in Toronto last Tuesday, and I enjoyed chatting with you about some of the problems of handling volume correspondence.

You promised to tell me more about how you have improved correspondence procedures in your offices and suggested that we get together for lunch on the 16th. Unless I hear from you, may I assume that our appointment is still "on"? I'll plan to arrive at your office about 12:15.

Sincerely,

CARL FORSLUND, (Father and Three Sons) Furniture
122 EAST FULTON STREET – – GRAND RAPIDS MICHIGAN 49502

PHONE GL 9-8101 AREA CODE 616

Thursday morning
June 30, 19--

Scattered sunshine ----

Good morning, Mr. Zimmer:

How pleased we are to have your nice
order, and thank you very much. This
has been entered on our number C24710
as shown on the enclosed acknowledgment.

Should there be any need to write us
about this particular order, will you
please refer to the above number; this
helps to locate your order quickly.

Again our thanks for shopping with us,
Mr. Zimmer; it's a pleasure to serve
you.

                    Sincerely,

                    Carl Forslund

CARL FORSLUND
CF/kf
Enclosure

Courtesy Carl Forslund, Furniture

Informal letter acknowledging an order. Note original letterhead and date line.

Confirming a Telephoned Order

Dear Mr. Hughes:

Thank you for telephoning us your order this morning. We are shipping by book post to-day the following:

250 copies of Better English, by Corwin
100 copies of Reading Faster, by Walsh and Kirkley
175 copies of Your Speech Shows, by Morey

We appreciate your placing this order with us and hope these books will be fast sellers for you. Our invoice will follow in a few days.

Yours very truly,

Confirming a Telegram

Dear Mr. Hackett:

This morning I wired you as follows:

CAN SUPPLY 100 VISI-GIDE LOOSE-LEAF BINDERS IN WESTERN SADDLE LEATHER BY OCTOBER 16 AT $3.70 EACH.

We shall be happy to have your order, Mr. Hackett. Would you please let us know by October 1 whether you wish us to ship these binders. Our stock is low, and the demand is heavy right now.

We have this same binder in imitation morocco in either blue or black. The price of the morocco binders is $3 each.

Cordially yours,

Communication Problems

A ■

Now that you have had practice using postal codes, these will not always be given in the exercises. Remember, however, that every return address and inside address must include the postal code. Where can you find a postal code if you do not know it?

The Walters Manufacturing Company follows the policy of acknowledging every order and every payment it receives from customers. On the other hand, the Reliable Desk Company does not believe in acknowledging the receipt of orders or payments because this procedure adds to the cost of doing business. Which company has the better policy? Why?

B ■

Rewrite this inept letter from a wholesale hardware firm to acknowledge an order from a retail hardware dealer for 100 waste cans, 25 hammers, and 75 boxes of 15 mm screws. The order was shipped today.

Dear Sirs: Thanks for your recent order. We're glad to have your business.

We will send your order just as soon as we can. Begging to remain, Yours Truly,

C ■

Suppose you work for the Sound of Music Company, Ltd. The A-1 Record Store, Corner Brook, Newfoundland, ordered ten diamond phonograph needles last month and must now send payment (invoice No. 11-433) for $50.

1 How should the money be sent? Should they use cash? Why or why not?
2 Should a letter be sent to accompany the payment? Why or why not?
3 Now, assume the cheque was received by Sound of Music. Write an appropriate letter of acknowledgment to the A-1 Record Store.

D ■

Acknowledge the following order:

> Gentlemen: Please ship us 20 Rite Time Clocks, No. 3Y42, at your special price of $9.40 each. We would like ten white and ten brown. WELLS SUPPLY COMPANY, Windsor, Ontario.

Information you will need: You will ship immediately by truck freight. You appreciate the order, and you will offer a discount of 2 percent if the invoice is paid within 10 days. There is a one-year guarantee on each clock. You are also sending them, in a separate mailing, one of your new catalogues describing other clocks you manufacture.

E ■

Assume that you work at the reservation desk of the Vacationer Hotel in Summerside, Prince Edward Island. You receive a request for a double room for Mr. and Mrs. Edward Sabin for the week of July 6. The Vacationer Hotel makes it a practice of acknowledging reservation requests by personal letter. Write the letter. Supply any details you wish, such as rate, special events in the area during the week of July 6, new hotel facilities just completed, and so on.

Word Study

A ■

Words often confused: fiscal, physical; holy, holey, wholly, holly.

B ■

In the following words, which syllable should receive the primary accent?

1 dis-charge
2 ap-pli-ca-ble
3 ex-qui-site
4 pos-i-tive-ly
5 su-per-flu-ous
6 ac-cli-mate

C ■

If you wished to contract the following words and phrases, what forms would you use?

1 national
2 we are
3 I shall
4 I will
5 they have
6 continued
7 does not
8 it is
9 department

Communication in Action: *Responding to Gossip*

Today in the lunchroom an office gossip made several uncomplimentary remarks about your supervisor—her poor taste in clothes, her general appearance, and her bad disposition. Six other employees at your table heard the remarks, and everyone looked at you as if he expected a retort. What would you say, if anything?

UNIT □ 46

Letters That Answer— Responses

Pick up a copy of any popular magazine or newspaper, and you will see pages and pages of advertising. Some advertisements gently nudge you; some are persuasively convincing; some try to shock or startle you. All hope to do one thing: build interest in the advertiser's product or service. Your favorite radio or TV program is probably paid for by advertisers who hope to convince you that you will benefit from choosing their products. Advertising is all around us. Every company aims to develop friendly attitudes on the part of the buying public, because businessmen know that these attitudes are the means by which customers are made.

Letters of Response: Opportunities to Make Friends

Everyone employed in business—the salesperson, the deliveryman, the switchboard operator, the receptionist, and the letter writer—is expected to do his part in making friends. One of the main purposes of advertising is to get readers and listeners so interested in a product that, if it isn't readily available, they will make a trip to their dealer for a closer look; or they will write a letter asking for more information. The businessman, therefore, welcomes customer inquiries about products or services as opportunities to make friends—and to sell. What a waste of the advertiser's money if, on this "last mile" between the customer's casual interest and his decisive action, someone failed to do his share in getting the desired results!

Types of Letters of Response

Letters of response are among the most important—and are probably the most numerous—of business letters. They are written in response to coupons that have been clipped from advertisements or containers; in response to business reply cards that accompany sales letters; in response to orders; in response to requests for information or favors.

Suppose you work for a company that recently began to distribute a new sports car—the Porpoise. Advertisements have appeared in national magazines, in newspapers, and on nationwide radio and TV. The company is delighted, of course, when letters start coming in, because these letters are proof that the company's ads are attracting interest that can eventually turn into sales. Such questions as the following arrive:

> What is the name of a dealer near Midville? What models are available? What is the cost of a convertible? How many litres per hundred kilometres will this car consume? How long will it take to get delivery? What colors are available? Are parts easy to get? Where can I get more information?

Form Letters   If such inquiries are many, the company will probably develop a form letter (either printed or typed on an automatic typewriter) that may be sent to all those who request information. In addition, to save money as well as to present the product in the most favorable light, the company will probably prepare special booklets comprising photographs, descriptive information, and sales arguments. Often, a printed letter is the first page of such a booklet. In any event, some type of letter or response is needed to accompany the booklet. And the more personal the letter can be made to look, the more successful it will be.

Here, for example, is a form letter sent in response to coupons, cards, and general inquiries about the Porpoise sports car:

> Dear
>
> Naturally, we are delighted that you are interested in the Porpoise. Thank you for giving us a chance to tell you more about this fine new sports car that has just received Sports Car National's "Best Newcomer of the Year" Award.
>
> The enclosed booklet, <u>Continental</u> <u>Contemporary</u>, was prepared especially for you and others like you whose taste runs to the bold, the daring, the unusual—the discriminating. Only in the Porpoise does the true sports car lover find all his dreams come true!
>
> May I suggest that you visit your dealer,   to test drive the Porpoise "Flamenco" or the Porpoise "Matador." Only when you get behind the wheel of the Porpoise can you fully appreciate the sensational advantages of this little masterpiece. You will be thrilled with its daring lines, its sauciness, its verve.
>
> Of course, you are always welcome to write us for any additional information you may need.
>
> Cordially yours,

Note that space was provided in the salutation and on the first line of the third paragraph for inserting the name of the addressee and the dealer, respectively. In addition to form letters, fill-in cards are often used to answer inquiries.

Individual Letters   Many inquiries, of course, cannot be answered by a form letter or a postal card. And even if they could, some companies consider inquiries important enough to deserve individually written replies. Note the following inquiry and response:

Gentlemen:

Please send me a copy of Connecticut Kitchens advertised in Restful Living magazine. I am interested in remodeling my kitchen in Western Pine.

While I am at it, I am also thinking of having my kitchen floor recovered. Do you have any suggestions for colors that would blend with pine?

Sincerely yours,

Dear Mrs. Larkin:

We are delighted to send you a copy of Connecticut Kitchens as advertised in Restful Living magazine.

Western Pine is a versatile and highly practical paneling for your kitchen, Mrs. Larkin. It will blend beautifully with just about any color or decorating scheme you choose. A striking example of color harmony is illustrated on page 9 of the enclosed booklet. The floor is in Brownstone Red, a new color that is very popular with decorators. The paneling is finished in Puritan Pine "Wax-Nu." Several other possibilities are shown on pages 3, 4, 7, and 12.

May I suggest that you visit Goldman's Lumber Company, our dealer in Yellowknife, to ask him to help you plan your kitchen. Many Connecticut Kitchen dealers offer a free decorating service to customers.

Thank you for writing.

Sincerely yours,

Rules for Writing Letters of Response

You have already seen that letters of response are essentially sales letters, and the rules for writing them are the same as those for other letters whose aim is to persuade. There are, however, four rules that are worth special mention.

Be Prompt There is nothing that says so well, "We are interested in you" as a prompt reply to an inquiry. Some companies insist that all mail be acknowledged within forty-eight hours after it is received; others set twenty-four hours as the maximum length of time before a reply is sent. Even if a reply cannot be given to a customer's inquiry, the inquiry at least should be acknowledged and the writer told when he will have his answer. For example:

Dear Mrs. Quigley:

I appreciate very much your letter asking about the proper way to care for leather-topped furniture.

Because we have had so many similar requests from lovers of Paxon's leather-topped originals, we have prepared a special booklet giving complete instructions. It is called Leather Magic, and we expect delivery of this booklet from the printer within ten days.

You may be sure, Mrs. Quigley, that a copy of Leather Magic will be sent to you just as soon as possible. In the meantime, let me call your attention to Roger Wilton's newest creation—"Wide Open Spaces," the outdoor furniture of the year. It is being featured this month at Bampton's, in Penticton.

Sincerely yours,

Some letters must be referred to another person or to a branch office in another city. If the reply is likely to be delayed several days, the person who originally received the letter should acknowledge it, telling the customer how the request is being handled. For example:

Dear Mr. Phillips:

Your request for information about delivery of the new Electric Eye Hair Dryer has been referred to our Maritime district office. You see, Mr. Phillips, each district office is supplied with a quota of this fast-moving dryer. In some areas, dealers are well supplied; in others, sales have run much higher than expected and stocks are temporarily low.

Mr. Mark Griffith, manager of our Halifax office, will write you within a few days telling you exactly what the situation is in that area. In any event, I am sure that you will not have to wait long for delivery once your order is placed. Our factory is now operating at full capacity. We are certain that you will find the Electric Eye Hair Dryer worth waiting for!

Cordially yours,

After sending this letter to Mr. Phillips, the writer will attach a carbon copy of it to Mr. Phillips' original letter (or a photocopy) and send both to Mr. Griffith, the manager of the office in Halifax. This will help Mr. Griffith attend to Mr. Phillips' request more quickly.

Be Helpful   Montgomery Ward and Company, in a special bulletin to its employees, once wrote, "When you are writing a letter to a Ward customer, remember—you are talking to your boss." For this reason, you should provide the customer with as much help as you think he will need. As you have seen, providing special printed information is one way to be helpful. Other special helps might include price lists, catalogues, samples, and the like. Most important of all, however, is a willingness on the part of the writer to "reach out" and find ways to be helpful. The little extras on the correspondent's part often mean the turning of a simple inquiry into a sale. These extras are lacking in the following:

Dear Mr. Mackenzie:

I am sorry that we cannot help you. We do not manufacture aluminum doors and storm windows. We make only aluminum paneling for building construction.

Yours truly,

This letter wasn't very helpful, was it? The thoughtful letter writer might have handled the situation in this manner:

Dear Mr. Mackenzie:

Thank you for writing to National Aluminum about aluminum doors and combination windows.

No doubt, Mr. MacKenzie, you have confused us with another firm of a similar name. We manufacture only aluminum paneling for building construction. The organization to which your letter should be addressed is National Home Aluminum Specialties, Ltd., 1303 Jackson Avenue, Saskatoon, Saskatchewan S7H 2M9.

Sincerely yours,

P. S. You might be interested in the enclosed folder that describes our products.

Be Complete When writing a letter of response, you should be certain that you have answered the inquirer's questions as fully as possible. If your company provides printed information that is sent to those who write, make sure it answers all the questions asked. Often, the customer will have a special problem not covered in the printed information. In this case, the letter might be written as follows:

Dear Miss Holbrook:

We are delighted to know that you are interested in the new Lektrawax Polisher. Most of the questions you raise are answered completely in the illustrated booklet enclosed. I hope you will read it carefully, noting the various models and the special features of each.

As to your question about a trade-in allowance for your old polisher, may I suggest that you discuss this matter with your dealer in Lethbridge—Younker's department store. Policies on trade-ins vary from store to store.

Thank you for writing.

Cordially yours,

In some cases where a form letter is used, a P. S. may be individually typed at the bottom of the letter. For example:

P. S. Because of the already low price of the Watkins office clock, we are unable to offer any special discounts for quantity purchases.

Be Courteous and Friendly It costs nothing in money or time to be courteous and friendly when writing letters of response. Observe how the following letter is friendly, courteous, and sales-slanted:

Dear Ms. Greene:

We are so pleased that you thought of Lowry's Town House for the annual "Secretary-Boss Night" of the Westbrook Chapter of The National Secretaries Association.

We have two excellent private dining rooms—the Plantation Room and the Garden Court. Each is decorated in a distinctive motif, and each is perfectly suited to a group such as yours. Many organizations hold their monthly and annual banquets in these delightful rooms. Each banquet room seats 100 to 125 persons and is equipped with a loudspeaker system, a piano, and a movie projector and screen. The Plantation Room also has a raised dais where the speaker's table may be placed. Both rooms are still available for May 10.

The decor of both the Plantation Room and the Garden Court assures you of delightful dining in an absolutely private atmosphere. Each is air-conditioned and sound-conditioned. As you know, Lowry's Town House has an excellent reputation for the finest meals and service. I am enclosing our banquet menu, featuring full-course dinners ranging from $5 to $8.50

I should be happy to show you these two lovely dining rooms, Miss Greene, when it is convenient for you to visit Lowry's Town House. Would it be possible for you to have lunch here with me one day next week? Just telephone me at 737-2491.

May I urge you to make your reservations early. We do not know just how long these facilities will be available for the May 10 date, and we would like to have you with us.

Cordially yours,

The writing of answering letters may be a daily routine in many offices; but such letters should not be handled in a routine, mechanical fashion. They are very important because each person who writes to the firm is already interested in the product or service sold by the company. Firms spend thousands of advertising dollars each year just to create customer interest. So when interest is evidenced by an inquirer, be sure to capitalize on it by answering with a polished, sales-promoting letter.

Communication Problems

Application Exercises

A ■

Rewrite this poorly written letter in answer to an inquiry.

Dear Dr. Brown,

Your letter of the 10th received and contents noted. Thanks for your interest in our pianos.

We do not know what size you want, the type (upright, baby grand, spinnet) or the kind of wood. Please let us know.

When we receive this info. we will send you full particulars. Trusting to hear from you real soon, we are

Very truly yours,

B ■

You are secretary of a motorcycle club. You receive an inquiry from a person interested in becoming a member, requesting information about how to join, how often the group meets, where it meets, what activities it has, and what the dues are. Write a letter to this person, giving all the information requested.

C ■

You are employed by the Spicewood Novelty Company, in Rocky Point, North Augusta, Ontario, which makes wood carvings for sale to gift shops in all parts of the country. You have received a letter from the Old Lyme Gift Corner in St. John's, Newfoundland. Respond to the letter, referring to a catalogue and price list that you are sending. Your company would like very much to do business with the Old Lyme Gift Corner, so make your letter friendly and persuasive.

D ■

You work in the order department of the Markham Publishing Company. An order arrives from a bookstore requesting 50 copies of a book, *Making Costume Jewelry for Pleasure and Profit*. This is not one of your publications, and you cannot fill the order. You can easily find out, however, who the publisher is. What would you do? Write the letter, enclosing one of your own catalogues.

E ■

Assume that you are employed as a correspondent for the Millington Leather Company, in Trail, British Columbia. You have received a letter from Mr. Fabio Garcia, of San José, Costa Rica, in which he asks about ordering a large stock of your luggage for his store. All trade with Latin American countries is handled by your Halifax office. Write a letter to Mr. Garcia, telling him that you are referring his inquiry to Miss Martha Lanin, manager of the Halifax branch of your company. What steps should you take to let Miss Lanin know that you are sending the inquiry to her?

Word Study

A ■

Words often confused: raise, raze, rays; costume, custom.

B ■

Indicate the prepositions that should be used in the blank spaces in these sentences.

1 My sister has a prejudice _____ mystery stories.
2 *Dread* is synonymous _____ *fear*.
3 The game was so exciting that I became completely oblivious _____ time.
4 I am not at all satisfied _____ the results of the investigation.
5 The supervisor does not approve _____ the behavior of the new typist.
6 His property is adjacent _____ my father's.

C ■

Add an "e" at the end of—

A word meaning:	To result in a word meaning:
1 Pertaining to or characteristic of mankind	Kind, merciful, tender
2 Relating to a choir or chorus	A simple tune sung in unison
3 Ethical	A confident state of mind
4 Melodious, harmonious	A social entertainment featuring music
5 Characteristic of cities	Smoothly polite

Communication in Action: *Positive and Friendly*

Positive statements are more likely to win friends than negative ones. Rewrite the statements below to make them more friendly.

1. Really, Mrs. Jones, you can't blame us if you didn't follow the printed instructions included with each mower.

2. I'm sorry, but we can't make an adjustment unless you return the merchandise in a reasonable length of time.

UNIT □ 47

The Secretary's Responsibility for Correspondence

One of the most important responsibilities of the secretary, and of other assistants to executives, is handling correspondence. The busy executive depends on his secretary to receive, open, and sort incoming mail and to handle all the details necessary to get letters written and sent. Many secretaries spend over half of their time working with correspondence. The ability to handle effectively the routines of correspondence is one of the qualities that distinguish the private secretary from the stenographer.

This unit, however, is not intended just for those who expect to be secretaries. Other office workers—bookkeepers, clerks, stenographers, and typists—also have

MACHINE FOUNDRY COMPANY

50 Madison Avenue
Hamilton, Ontario
L8L 5Y4

January 11, 19--

Mr. George Ames
Atlas Manufacturers
Sarnia, Ontario N7T 7K7

Dear Mr. Ames:

Thank you for your prompt attention to our order
No.16438 for ten lathes.

After uncrating the lathes, we found that the setup
instructions were not included. Would you be good enough
to send us ten copies of setup instructions for X13-14-86
lathes. In addition, we should very much like to have your
service supervisor check our setups when he is next in our
vicinity. When is he scheduled to be in this area?

We know that we can count on your usual good service
to handle these matters for us.

Very truly yours,

Howard Lawrence

HOWARD LAWRENCE

HL:TM

*Send 10
copies
pamphlet
#X13-5014 ?
Johnson in
Hamilton
2/8 - 2/11*

A letter that has been date-stamped, underlined, and annotated by a secretary.

the responsibility for handling mail and, in some cases, for writing letters on behalf of their employers. Therefore, this material is valuable for all students aspiring to office jobs.

Routines for Incoming Correspondence

Most employers expect their secretaries to open and sort incoming mail. In smaller offices, the secretary may receive and distribute the mail for the entire organization. In a large company that has a central mailing room, letters are sorted according to departments; and the receptionist or another employee within the department re-sorts and distributes mail—unopened—to the appropriate persons. The secretary's step-by-step procedure for handling incoming mail for her employer is as follows:

1. Letters marked "Personal" or "Confidential" are separated from the rest of the mail. These letters should be delivered unopened.

2. Other letters are opened, preferably with a letter opener to avoid damage to the contents.

3. The envelope is examined carefully to make sure that any enclosures mentioned in the letter are included. If an enclosure is missing, this fact should be noted in the margin of the letter and initialed.

4. The letter should be checked to see that it contains the return address of the sender; if not, the envelope should be attached to the letter.

5. To be sure the envelope is empty before it is thrown away, it should be held to the light and carefully examined. Some companies require that envelopes be opened on three sides before they are thrown away.

6. All incoming mail should be date-stamped. Note the date stamp on the letter on page 384. In many offices, the time element is so important that the hour, as well as the date, is stamped on incoming mail. An electric clock-dating machine is used in many large firms.

Reading the Mail The secretary can often save time for her boss by reading the mail carefully before delivering it to him. Some employers prefer that the secretary underline the important points in each letter so that he may read it more quickly; also, these underlined passages serve as signals to him when he is dictating a reply. The secretary may also make marginal notations concerning action that has been taken. You will find examples of underlining and marginal notations on page 384. The secretary should also verify figures, dates, and computations in incoming mail. If previous letters or other documents will help the employer to understand what the letter is about, the secretary should attach them to the incoming letter.

An employer who has a large volume of correspondence may instruct his secretary to digest the important letters for his quick reading. Such a digest (shown on the next page) is especially helpful when the boss is away and a large volume of correspondence awaits him upon his return.

DIGEST OF IMPORTANT MAIL

May 6-10, 19—

The following items need your attention. All mail has been acknowledged. The item checked is urgent.

May		
6	Mr. Gordon Fuller	Wants an appointment with you when you return.
7	Memo from Credit Dept.	Wants your recommendation on several customers whose accounts are delinquent.
$\sqrt{10}$	Mr. Leon Graves, Essex Mfg.	Very upset about not having received his order.

Delivering Mail to the Employer　The mail should be placed on the employer's desk in order of importance. For example:

1. Telegrams (on top)
2. "Special Delivery," "Registered," and "Certified" mail
3. Mail marked "Personal" or "Confidential" or of a personal nature
4. Regular first-class mail
5. Circulars and advertisements
6. Magazines and newspapers

If there is much traffic in the boss's office, place the letters in a manila folder so that they will not be seen by others. If there is a great volume of mail, the secretary may also separate the different types in different manila folders.

"To Write or Not to Write—"

Some executives appreciate having the routine mail answered by the secretary; others prefer to dictate every letter. The new office worker will soon learn his employer's preferences. If your employer has entrusted letter-writing responsibilities to you, he may indicate his wishes right on the incoming mail; or he may prefer that you tell him which letters you can answer. An executive secretary may write a rough-draft reply to routine correspondence, attaching it to the incoming letter before the employer has an opportunity to read it. Or she may simply make the notation "I will answer" on the incoming letter or tell her boss how she proposes to answer, thus: "I'll tell him you will be away on the 18th" or "Will send."

Even if the boss dictates all his correspondence, he may expect the secretary to edit his letters—that is, smooth out his writing style and correct any errors in grammar, punctuation, and computations. "This is about what I want to say—you 'fix it up'" is a direction often given to the secretary.

But not all executives feel this way about correspondence. Some want every word, every comma, every paragraph to appear just as they dictated it—wrong though they

Maybe I did invent some of the words I dictated, but I still think you
should have tried to spell them better.

may be. The best advice for the new secretary is to transcribe the boss's dictation
just the way he gave it. If she discovers errors, she might tactfully say, "Mr.
Jamison, don't you think it would be better if we itemized those directions in 1-2-3
order? They might be easier to follow." Gradually, the executive will trust his secretary to use her best judgment in polishing his dictation—if she can back up her suggestions with effective performance.

If the employer is in the office, he will probably prefer that letters composed by
the secretary be written for his signature. This poses the question: "Should I write
the letter the way I think it should be written, or do I write it the way I think
he wants it?" As long as the secretary is writing *for her employer,* she must write
the letter as she thinks *he* would write it. She should study the carbon copies of
previous letters so that she can match his style as closely as possible.

Sometimes the employer will ask the secretary to sign his letters for him, in
which case it is customary for her to place her initials immediately below the signature. Some employers, however, would rather the secretary fake his signature—
especially when writing to people whom he does not know personally. Whichever
procedure is followed is a matter of individual preference and often depends on
how much the employer trusts his secretary and also on how well she can match
his signature.

Here is an example of a letter written by a secretary for her employer.

Dear Mr. Atkins:

Mr. Watson has asked me to acknowledge, with gratitude, the copy of <u>Fifty</u> <u>Years</u> <u>of</u> <u>Ship-building</u>—the <u>Story</u> <u>of</u> Perkin-Bullmer. He was very pleased to have it.

I am sure you know that Mr. Watson has been very busy with the reorganization of the Danbury Ridge plant. During this month, he has been out of the office more than he has been in. I know he will want to write you just as soon as he has a "breather."

The book is beautifully illustrated and looks very interesting. I know Mr. Watson will enjoy reading it.

Very truly yours,

Linda Raglan

Linda Raglan
Secretary to Mr. Watson

Types of Letters Written for the Employer

The types of letters written most often by the secretary include letters making reservations, asking letters, letters referring matters to others, thank-you and acknowledgment letters, letters about appointments, transmittal letters, and follow-up letters. You have been introduced to several of these already. Some are so important to the secretary that they will receive additional emphasis in this unit.

Making Reservations   In making hotel and travel reservations, either the employer's signature or the secretary's may be used. Refer to Unit 44 for additional information on writing letters making reservations.

For the Employer's Signature

Gentlemen:

Please reserve a single room for me for July 8, 9, and 10. I shall be arriving about 16:00 on July 8 and will leave the morning of July 11.

I should like an outside room, with shower, at a rate not exceeding $24.

Very truly yours,

Asking Letters   Asking letters may be written for the secretary's signature or for the employer's, depending on his preference. The message is only slightly different. For example:

For the Employer's Signature

Gentlemen:

Last week I was on Air Canada 614 from Toronto to Montreal. During a conversation with me, the stewardess mentioned a kit of materials containing luggage stickers, maps, and a set of "Junior Pilot" wings that Air Canada gives to passengers with youngsters.

When I deplaned, I forgot to pick up the kit. I think my nephew would enjoy having these souvenirs, since he is very much interested in planes.

If you can possibly send me a kit, I would be very grateful—and you would make a five-year-old boy very happy!

Sincerely yours,

For the Secretary's Signature

Gentlemen:

Last week, Mr. Millard E. Watson was on Air Canada Flight 614 from Toronto to Montreal. He meant to take with him one of the kits containing luggage stickers, maps, and a set of "Junior Pilot" wings when he deplaned but did not remember to do so.

Can you possibly send Mr. Watson one of these kits? He very much wants to present it to his five-year-old nephew, who is extremely interested in planes. Both Mr. Watson and his nephew would be very grateful, I am sure.

Very truly yours,

Letters Referring Matters to Others   The executive may not be able to give personal attention to letters that are really meant for someone else. In that case, the secretary nearly always writes an acknowledgment letter for her own signature and attends to any necessary follow-through with the other person. Here is an example:

Dear Mrs. Blanford:

Thank you for writing about your article describing your recent sailing trip to Tortola. It sounds very interesting.

Our publication, Fleet Owner, is a magazine circulated to owners of fleets of trucks and buses for commercial hauling and transportation. We do not feature articles of consumer interest and, of course, our magazine is limited to land transportation.

There are several consumer magazines that feature articles such as the one you describe. Two of the most popular are The Yachtsman, 44 East 20th Street, and Ahoy!, 688 Lexington Avenue, both in New York City.

Very truly yours,

Follow-Up Letters   The secretary is expected to follow up on correspondence for her employer. Enclosures mentioned in an incoming letter may not have been included; the secretary's request for an appointment for her boss may have gone unanswered; promised materials may not have arrived; expected action may not have taken place; and so on. Such letters are usually written by the secretary for her own signature. Here are some examples:

Gentlemen:

In your letter of May 14, you mentioned that you were sending us the deed to the Harper estate. However, the deed was not included in the envelope.

Just as soon as we receive this deed, we shall be able to complete the final arrangements for the transfer of title.

Very truly yours,

Dear Mr. Judson:

Will you be able to see Mr. Pickens when he is in Windsor on Friday of next week? He had hoped to hear from you before he left on a ten-day trip this morning. Since he did not, he has asked me to inquire and to let him have the information before he leaves Chatham on Tuesday.

I expect to be in touch with Mr. Pickens by telephone later this week. Please wire collect, telling me whether you can see him when he is in Windsor.

Cordially yours,

While-the-Boss-Is-Away Letters

Whether the secretary writes letters for her employer or not, when he is out of the office she is expected to acknowledge important letters and explain any delays caused by his absence. While-the-boss-is-away letters are usually brief, courteous, and noncommittal. By *noncommittal* is meant that the secretary should be careful not to reveal private company matters in her acknowledgments. Often, this means not saying where the boss is or what business he is on. She must also be careful not to express opinions that may be in disagreement with those of her employer.

For example, if she works for a publisher and receives a magazine article in her boss's absence, she would *not* say:

Thank you for sending us the article, "Ceramic Magic." It is extremely good, and I know Miss Talbert will want to publish it in the next issue of Busy Hands magazine.

If her boss feels differently about the article, this letter will put her (or him) in an embarrassing position. The noncommittal, but courteous, letter the secretary might write is as follows:

Dear Mrs. Wolpert:

Thank you for sending us the article, "Ceramic Magic." It is extremely good, and I know Ms. Talbert will want to publish it in the next issue of Busy Hands magazine.

The editor, Ms. Ida Talbert, is out of the office on a short business trip. When she returns, you may be sure that she will write you.

Sincerely yours,

Note that the secretary has said that Ms. Talbert "is out of the office on a short business trip." It is usually best not to reveal more than this. Such information as "Ms. Talbert is in Banff on vacation" or "Ms. Talbert is in Haney this week visiting a new printing plant" would not be appropriate. The safest phrase, when in doubt, is: "Ms. Talbert is out of the office this week."

Here is another example of tact and discretion used in writing a noncommittal letter for the employer:

Dear Mr. Erskine:

While Mr. Stimson is out of the office, I want to acknowledge receipt of your bid on the Fullerton shopping area project and the report that accompanied it.

Shortly after Mr. Stimson returns (he is due back on August 12), I know he will get in touch with you.

Yours very truly,

When the employer is away and the correspondence cannot wait for his return, letters are often referred to another individual in the company. Before referring letters to another executive, however, the secretary must be sure that she has his permission to do so—as well as that of her boss. Only urgent or highly important letters will usually deserve this action.

Dear Mr. McGinnis:

Thank you for your letter of April 17 to Mr. Kent.

Mr. Kent will be out of the office for about two weeks, so I am referring your letter to our Sales Manager, Mr. T. J. Loring. You will be hearing from Mr. Loring just as soon as he has had an opportunity to study your proposal.

Cordially yours,

Communication Problems

Application Exercises

A ■

The boss leaves the following handwritten letter for you to type. Make the necessary corrections and prepare a perfect copy, preferably typed.

> Bill Jones, Mgr.
> Essex Fire Co. Ltd
>
> Dear Bill
>
> Rec'd your letter and was glad to hear from you, however, I'm sorry I can't see you next week. I'll be out of town on business the first part of the week the latter part I start my vacation. Would like to talk over the matter of the increased tire orders so perhaps you and I can get together over the luncheon table when I return. I'll phone you when I get back and arrange an apointment.

B ■

Assume that your boss, Richard King, sales manager of King Furniture Co., is on a three-week vacation in Hawaii. On July 8 you receive the following letter from a very good customer. Your boss is not due back from his vacation until July 25. How would you handle the situation?

> Dear Mr. King:
>
> The fifteen bookcases we ordered arrived today. However, only one of these bookcases has glass doors. Our order No. 1653, dated June 2, definitely specified glass doors for all fifteen of the bookcases.
>
> Since we need these bookcases for our sale beginning July 23, we are wondering what you can do about this situation. We are already overstocked with bookcases without doors, so we cannot use the additional ones that were sent to us by mistake.
>
> We hope we will hear from you immediately regarding the action you are taking.
>
> Very truly yours,

You investigate the matter and you find that an error was made. You will send 14 bookcases with glass doors by truck immediately, and you will pick up the 14 sent in error. (Your authority for this action is the assistant manager.) Write the appropriate letter to the customer for your own signature.

C ■

Your employer, A. N. Steinberg, has been invited to be a guest at a luncheon meeting at the Civitan Club on July 14. Write the president, Mr. Wilson Livingston, explaining that Mr. Steinberg cannot attend; he will be in Toronto on business at that time.

D ■

In each of the following situations, indicate whether you think a secretary should compose the letter or whether the boss should write it.

1 Your boss would like a sample copy of *The Executive's Monthly Magazine.*
2 A customer would like to have an extension of time to settle his account.
3 A customer is having trouble with a machine purchased from your firm.
4 Your boss would like a reservation for a single room at the Sheridan Hotel in Niagara Falls, Ontario, for May 5, 6, and 7.
5 Your boss is sending a cheque for $10 to cover a year's subscription to *The Executive's Monthly Magazine.*

E ■

Write a letter for each of the above situations that you indicated the secretary should be able to handle.

Word Study

A ■

Words often confused: extent, extant, extinct; collision, collusion.

B ■

Are these statements true?

1 A period always follows an abbreviation.
2 Indirectly quoted remarks are not enclosed in quotation marks.

3 *Come and* is considered nonstandard for *come to.*

4 In dividing words, you should never separate beginning two-letter syllables from the rest of the word.

5 Nouns ending in *s* are always plural and require a plural form of verb.

C ■

To each of the following, add the termination pronounced "shun."

1 illustra_____   **3** electri_____   **5** coer_____

2 provi_____   **4** repeti_____   **6** aver_____

Communication in Action: *Greeting a Customer*

A salesperson in a bookstore that sells only paperback books approaches each customer with a greeting such as "What are you looking for?" or "What do you want?" or simply "Yes?" Suggest more effective greetings for customers who seem to be puzzled about where to find what they want.

UNIT □ 48

Claim and Adjustment Letters

No matter how efficient a business firm tries to be, mistakes will happen. The customer may receive the wrong merchandise, slow service, invoices or statements that contain errors, even discourteous treatment at the hands of employees. A letter in which a complaint is expressed—that is, one in which the customer indicates that he feels he has a claim against the company—is called a *claim letter.*

The company for which you work undoubtedly will receive some claim letters; in turn, the company will have occasion to write claim letters to those from whom it buys. To promote the company's and your own best interests, you need to be familiar with claim situations and with the principles of writing effective claim letters.

The Nature of Claims

Customer claims generally deal with one of the following:

Merchandise—Orders incorrectly filled; unsatisfactory quality of merchandise; goods damaged or delayed in shipment

Amounts of Money—Errors in statements and invoices; misunderstandings regarding price or terms of payment

Service—Delays in filling orders or requests for service; improper treatment by employees; failure to follow up

Goal: Satisfaction   The person writing a claim letter is interested in one thing: satisfaction. If the merchandise is faulty, he wants it replaced at no cost or inconvenience to him. If the service is poor, he wants an apology and assurance that service will improve; he may even want some compensation for the inconvenience caused him. If an error has been made, he wants it corrected.

In order to get satisfaction, the claimant must present his case carefully and thoughtfully to the person he feels is at fault. Suppose you ordered a lamp from a mail-order house, specifying a light-green shade. When the lamp is delivered, you are disappointed to find that a pink shade was sent—and a pink shade simply will not do. You become quite upset and a little angry, asking yourself, "How could they make such a stupid mistake?"

Anger Works Against You   How would you begin your letter? In the first place, you should not write the letter while you are angry. Cool off first. You can do a much more convincing job when you are calm and can see the situation in a reasonable light. The mistake was not intentional; mistakes never are. If your letter were written in anger, it might begin like this:

> It was certainly careless on somebody's part to send me a pink lamp shade when I asked for a green one. Don't your order clerks know how to read? I simply do not understand . . . .

Such a letter would do more harm than good. After you had had time to think, you would be sorry you had written it. And you would surely get much more willing cooperation from the seller if you had been courteous. You can imagine how much sympathy you would get from the order clerks with your insulting remarks! A letter like the following would accomplish your purpose and do it much more successfully:

> The new milk-glass lamp I received today (your invoice No. 753291) had a pink lamp shade instead of the green one specified in my order.
>
> Would you please send me the green shade ordered (your catalogue No. 21G1044) and tell me how to dispose of the pink one.
>
> With guests arriving in our home on April 10, we shall appreciate your promptness.

Rules for Writing Claim Letters

Five basic rules should be followed in writing all claim letters:

1. Explain carefully and tactfully what is wrong.
2. Include any details necessary to identify your claim—dates, catalogue numbers, styles, order numbers, and the like.
3. Indicate the loss or inconvenience you have suffered (if any), but don't exaggerate.

4. Explain, in general, what you believe the company should do about your claim; but don't be unreasonable in your request.

5. Avoid negative accusations or threats, such as "I demand," "I must insist," "you will have to," "unless you," "why can't you," etc.

Here is an example of a claim letter to a nurseryman that follows these rules:

Dear Mr. Valder:

This morning I received your statement covering my purchases from March 16 to April 12. The statement does not show credit for the 12 "Lycoming Beauty" rose bushes that I returned on March 1.

I assume that there was no question about these rose bushes—they appeared to be dead, a fact that did not come to light at the time I accepted them from the driver. I gave them to your truck driver when he was here on March 1, and he left me a receipt for them. There has never been any difficulty in the past when I returned unsatisfactory merchandise in this manner.

My cheque for $317.20 is enclosed. You will note that the cost of the 12 rose bushes that were returned—$24.60—has been deducted. If you need additional information, please write me.

Your azaleas are real beauties this year! I shall have to get a new supply when your driver makes his next trip to Lawrence; they are selling very fast.

Very truly yours,

Remember that in writing claim letters you are likely to get better service, more consideration, and more satisfaction if you explain the situation calmly and in a reasonable manner. Do not jump to conclusions. Assume that the company to whom you are writing will accept your side of the story—and not that it will be on the defensive. Usually, the company will be on the defensive only if you are unreasonable.

The Nature of Adjustment Letters

In writing *adjustment* letters, you are on the other side of the fence. Your customer has the claim and he writes *you*. He may be dissatisfied with your merchandise, your service, or your general efficiency.

Opportunity to Remedy Faults   A good company welcomes customer comments because they afford an opportunity to remedy faults that may exist. It is your job to see that the customer receives fair treatment—fair to him, of course, but also fair to your company. Since adjustment letters sell satisfaction, too, they are really sales letters.

Policies Differ   Most firms have established broad policies for making adjustments. Some are very generous and practice the motto, "The customer is always right." Others are not so eager to please the customer, especially if he is in the wrong. Even in the most generous organizations, there will be numerous occasions when claims cannot be granted. And regardless of the fact that established policies exist for most adjustment situations, there will always be exceptions. For example, an old customer who has dealt with a firm faithfully over the years is likely to receive a little more consideration than a new customer who is merely shopping around for the best buy. Many factors enter into the decision as to whether or not an adjustment will be granted. Often there is simply no policy to cover an adjustment situation, so the letter writer must weigh all the evidence and then do what he thinks is fairest to his customer and to his employer.

Rules for Writing Adjustment Letters

The writer of adjustment letters must, under all circumstances, use patience, tact, and diplomacy in his replies. These four principles should always be observed in writing adjustment letters:

1. Reply promptly.
2. Show the customer that you understand his problem.
3. Tell the customer exactly what you are going to do about the problem.
4. Avoid negative words and accusations.

Reply Promptly   The longer a customer waits for a reply to his claim, the angrier he gets and the harder it is to soothe his ruffled feelings. Show the customer that he is important enough to warrant your immediate attention to his problems. For instance:

"Right after I finished reading your letter of June 10, I looked into the matter of . . . ."

"We lost no time tracing the discrepancy in the invoice you wrote about . . . ."

"Good news! The lawn mowers arrived this morning, and they are already on their way to you."

"To make sure that there would be no slip-up this time, I personally saw to it that your order . . . ."

"Your letter arrived this morning, and we have already started a tracer on your shipment."

Show Understanding   Those who have claims to make want, first of all, to have someone understand why they feel as they do. Your letter will be more effective if it expresses empathy. For example:

"We know how you feel about . . . ."
"You are entirely right about . . . ."
"Indeed, we can understand that . . . ."
"Your point is well taken, and . . . ."
"We ourselves have been in the same situation, and . . . ."
"Surely you have a right to feel that . . . ."

Be Exact   Tell the customer exactly what you are going to do about his claim. If you are in a position to grant it, say so immediately and describe how you are going about it. For instance:

"Our cheque for $16.04, which is a refund on Invoice No. A 1428, will be sent to you this week . . . ."

"Within a day or two you will have your new green lamp shade to replace the pink one you received . . . ."

"You have been given full credit for the eight dead batteries, amounting to $73.15. While these batteries were carefully inspected when they left our warehouse, they . . . ."

"We are pleased to replace the plastic hose on your Royal Vacuum Cleaner with a new 'Tite-Nit' hose made of nylon. Several of our customers reported the same difficulty with the plastic hose and . . . ."

"You are entirely right. The discount to which you were entitled was not shown on your February statement. You may be sure, however, that . . . ."

Even if you are not able to grant the claim, you should be exact in telling the customer why, as:

1. We wish we could offer you an adjustment on this clothing, but our inspection shows that the suit has been worn several times and is soiled. You can understand, of course, that . . . .

2. Time slips by so fast that we can understand how it happened that your May 8 cheque contained a discount deduction of $12.70—although the 10-day discount period had expired. Would you like to send us a cheque for $12.70, or shall we add this amount to your next statement?

3. Nothing would please us more than to accept your "Jolly Jack" guitar for refund, but we are bound by the terms of the guarantee that you received with your instrument. If you check, you will find that the guarantee mentions . . . .

Avoid Negatives   Negative words tend to put an unhappy claimant in an even more irritable frame of mind. On the other hand, positive, pleasant words help to take the edge off his irritation. In fact, you should try to conclude your letter with a positive statement that will build goodwill. In the following examples, notice the difference in tone in the positive statements as compared with the negative ones.

Positive:	Thank you for your helpful letter of June 3.
Negative:	We have received your complaint of June 3.
Positive:	We are so glad that you called our attention to the late arrival of your order No. 4286.
Negative:	We are sorry to hear of the unfortunate delay in the delivery of your order No. 4286.
Positive:	Thank you for the friendly suggestion made in your letter of July 8.
Negative:	Your July 8 criticism has been received.
Positive:	We will check even more carefully than usual all your future orders.
Negative:	Please accept our apologies for sending you unsatisfactory goods.
Positive:	Our driver brought your parcel back to the store because the house number was omitted from the address.
Negative:	Because of your failure to give us your house number, our driver had to bring back the parcel, thus delaying delivery for three days.

Classes of Adjustments

The writer of adjustment letters is faced with four different types of problems:

1. When the company for whom he works (the seller) is at fault
2. When the person making the claim is at fault
3. When the responsibility is divided between the seller and the customer
4. When a third party, such as the transportation company, is at fault

When the Seller Is at Fault   If you are the seller of goods or services and you are entirely at fault in an adjustment situation, you will usually, of course, grant the claim. And you should do so willingly. Just as you have greater respect for the person who readily admits his mistakes, the customer respects the company that cheerfully fulfills its responsibilities without quibbling about it. When you must grant a claim because it is your fault, follow an outline such as this:

1. Tell the customer the good news immediately—preferably in the first paragraph.

2. Explain how the mistake happened (if you have an explanation). Don't be afraid of embarrassment—it is folly to try to save face when you are unquestionably wrong.

3. Express appreciation to the customer for his understanding and assure him that you will do your best to see that he receives better treatment in the future.

> Dear Mr. Lathan:
>
> On Friday of this week we will send you by parcel post, special handling, 200 "Cougar" pennants to replace those that were printed in white instead of yellow. There will be, of course, no charge for these.
>
> I have tried to find out what caused the confusion, but I have no explanation—or excuse. The only possible reason I can offer is that two members of our production department were ill last week, and we had to use inexperienced help for two or three days.
>
> Please excuse us this time, Mr. Lathan. We can take a little solace from this situation: we have started a new training program for all those who are likely to be called into emergency service in the production department. We expect that this precaution will help us to give you better service.
>
> You may dispose of the 200 pennants that you received. It is not necessary to return them to us. Thank you for giving us an opportunity to be of service to you.
>
> Very truly yours,

When the Customer Is at Fault   In many instances, the customer's request for an adjustment is not justifiable and his claim must be refused. Of course, this fact must be established conclusively before a letter is attempted. You cannot automatically *assume* that the customer is wrong; therefore, all the facts should be obtained and weighed carefully. "Make sure you are right, and then go ahead" is good advice in writing letters of this type. Even though you know you are right and the customer is wrong, however, this type of letter is still one of the most difficult to write. Somehow you must convey to the customer the idea that you are following the only course open to you and that, as a reasonable person, he will agree with you.

Suppose a customer writes that he wishes to return for credit several items of merchandise he purchased several months ago. The reason he gives for his return is that the merchandise he received was not that which he specified in his order. Of course, you are skeptical immediately. Why did he wait so long before reporting the error to you? After looking up the order, you find that he did receive the merchandise he asked for; he even paid the bill. You conclude that he is merely trying to unload some stock that he can't sell. In this particular case, you cannot accept the merchandise for credit.

In writing the reply to this claim, follow an outline something like this:

1. Thank the customer for writing you, restating the adjustment he believes should be made.

2. Explain why it is not possible to grant the adjustment.

3. Offer helpful advice, if possible.

4. Assume that the customer accepts your position as fair, and close the letter on a friendly note.

The letter might read:

Dear Mr. Krause:

Thank you for writing us about the "King Comfort" hassocks that you wish to return for credit. Immediately after receiving your letter, I rechecked your order of May 11. Your order specified 12 "King Comfort" hassocks in beige. The bill of lading matches your order in every respect. In fact, you have already paid the invoice for this shipment.

Under the circumstances, we are unable to accept these hassocks for credit. This particular line was discontinued by the manufacturer in July, and we are now featuring "Royal Rest" hassocks. Several of our dealers, however, reported considerable success in moving the "King Comfort" line. Premier Furniture, in Oceola, found that one of the biggest sales features is that the hassocks can be used with both indoor and outdoor furniture. The plastic cover included with each hassock makes this a really all-purpose item. Have you tried running an ad on these hassocks in connection with your summer furniture clearance sales? I think you will find doing so profitable.

Several new items of furniture for fall have arrived. Particularly exciting is the new line of Radwick Maple originals for every room in the house. Look over the enclosed folder describing some of these authentic period pieces. People everywhere are talking about Radwick. This line promises to be among the best sellers we have had in years.

Sincerely yours,

As explained previously, you will sometimes grant adjustments even though the customer is clearly at fault. The risk of turning down a good customer may be too great, or the amount in question may be so small that refusing to make the adjustment would be poor business. In such a case, you should take full advantage of the opportunity to "give in" gracefully and to build goodwill. For example:

Dear Mr. Braun:

We'll be glad to make an adjustment on the invoice you wrote us about in your letter of March 6. Would you please return the invoice to us.

When we advertised the reprints of the article "You Can't Automate People!" we mentioned that in quantities of 1000 the reprints could be purchased for 40 cents each; in less than 1000 lots, the price is 50 cents each. In each case, these are actual costs to us. However, I can see now that this was not entirely clear in our advertisement; and I am happy to give you the 40-cent price on the 100 you ordered. As soon as we receive your invoice, we shall issue a new one for $40.

Thank you for writing us. I hope you will be able to make effective use of these reprints. The demand for them has been exceedingly heavy.

Cordially yours,

When the Fault Is Divided   Occasionally, the seller and the customer share the responsibility for error. For example, the customer may have misunderstood your policy because it was not stated clearly or because the salesman calling on him gave him the wrong impression. Of course, you should cheerfully acknowledge your error; at the same time, you may try to convince the customer that he shares some of the responsibility, too.

Dear Mrs. Baker:

I am pleased to write you about the high-fidelity Angel recording (Mendelssohn's "Elijah" by the Huddersfield Choral Society) that you returned recently.

Upon examination of the records, our inspectors found that Sides 1 and 2 were apparently played with a blunt needle. May I suggest that you examine the needle of your phonograph before playing any records. A record is only as good as the needle playing it.

I am sending you a replacement for the first record; the other two have been checked by our inspectors and are in excellent condition.

I am also enclosing a booklet describing the various needles recommended by Angel— available at any authorized Angel record dealer.

Very sincerely yours,

In the foregoing example, the customer may have been entirely to blame; but just where the responsibility lies is not clear. At any rate, note that the seller gives the customer the benefit of the doubt—in a gracious manner—but suggests that similar occurrences in the future will be the fault of the customer.

When a Third Party Is at Fault   Quite often the roots of a claim lie neither in the customer's nor in the seller's actions but in the carrier's. Since the carrier assumes responsibility for safe delivery of any shipment accepted, the customer's claim is usually against him rather than against the seller, who has a receipt showing that the merchandise was in good condition at the time it was released to the carrier. When a shipment arrives in a damaged condition or is "short," the company to whom the claim is made may do one of two things:

1. Take the responsibility for the adjustment, and make a claim against the carrier.
2. Suggest that the customer enter a claim with the carrier, since the matter is really between the buyer and the carrier.

Following is an example of a letter from a supplier to a dealer who received a badly damaged television set:

Dear Mr. Lamar:

We are sending you today by Maywood Shippers a LaForge Crestwood television set to replace the one damaged in shipment. I know you have a customer waiting for this set, and I want you to have it as soon as possible.

We are entering our claim against the Rapid Truck Lines Ltd. for the set you received. Will you please leave this set in a convenient place until the inspectors from Rapid Truck call on you.

Cordially yours,

Communication Problems

Application Exercises

A ■

The following letter of complaint was received by the Ace Radio-Television Company.

Gentlemen:

I recently purchased a Claridge High-Fidelity Phonograph from you. When it arrived, it was badly scratched. The tone is horrible and the playing arm squeaks. In addition, your repairman is not able to do anything with it. I just think it is cheap merchandise, which is probably all you carry. I should have known better than to buy anything from your "junk" shop.

Very truly yours,

1 Criticize this letter, pointing out all its faults.
2 Write the letter you think should be written in reply if the customer had a legitimate claim.

B ■

Suppose you had purchased a washing machine from the Albemarle Appliance Store and, after you used it four or five times, the washing machine broke down and required adjustment. You were billed $17.50 for the adjustment and felt that the charge was not justifiable since this was a new washer. You wrote to the store, and this is the letter you received in reply.

Dear Mr. Sinclair:

We are sorry that we cannot cancel the $17.50 charge for adjusting your Rex Washing Machine.

We have to pay our repairmen high salaries, and we must account for every call they make. Since the adjustment necessary was probably due to your overloading your washer, we feel that it was your fault, not ours. Therefore, why should we suffer the loss?

Yours very truly,

1   How would you feel if you received this letter?
2   What is wrong with the tone of the letter?
3   Indicate several possible ways this claim might have been adjusted.
4   Assume that you are granting the claim. Write the letter.

C ■

A mirror you purchased from a factory in another city arrives with a large crack through the centre of it. The mirror was well crated and marked "Glass—Handle with Care."

1   Write the letter making your claim.
2   Compose the adjustment letter you would write if you were employed by the shipper, who found that the Springville Trucking Company was at fault in carelessly transporting the mirror.

Word Study

A ■

Words often confused: disposition, deposition; disprove, disapprove.

B ■

Substitute the correct forms for any incorrect styles of numbers in these sentences.

1   The price range for this type of ranch house is $20,000–35,000.
2   Please deliver my order to my home, 1,350 Broad Street, this city.
3   In just five years this neighborhood has deteriorated tremendously.
4   450 catalogues were mailed yesterday.
5   At three-fifteen the thermometer registered ninety-five degrees.

C ■

Should one or two *l*'s be used in the blank spaces in these words?

1	acce___erate	4	inte___igent	7	Phi___ippines
2	appa___	5	misce___aneous	8	vani___a
3	bu___etin	6	mo___asses		

Communication in Action: Write as You Talk

Saying something aloud before writing it helps to give naturalness to your expression. Rewrite the following paragraph as you would *say* it. See how much your writing can be improved.

"In accordance with your request of July 6, a cheque was made in your favor and mailed on that date. Failure to respond earlier was an oversight on the part of the accounting department. Measures have subsequently been taken to avoid such an occurrence in the future."

Credit and Collection Letters

Canadians from every walk of life enjoy many things today that they probably would not have if it were not for credit privileges. Perhaps the house you live in, the family automobile, your television set, and much of your clothing were purchased on credit. A conservative estimate reveals that more than 75 percent of all business in Canada is transacted on credit. The housewife buys merchandise on credit from the retail store; the retail store purchases its stock on credit from a wholesaler; the wholesaler, from the factory; and the factory purchases its raw materials from various suppliers—also on credit. The chain is almost endless, and the use of credit continues to grow. Many Canadians travel, dine, and obtain hotel accommodations on a credit basis merely by producing a convenient credit card.

Even though millions of dollars' worth of business is done on credit each year, the losses from bad debts are surprisingly small. Most businessmen estimate that, of their total charge accounts, fewer than 1 percent will be uncollectible. One reason for this small percentage of "bad debts" is that credit privileges are not granted in a hit-or-miss fashion. Before businessmen grant credit, they make reasonably sure that they will be paid for the goods they sell; each prospective charge-account customer is investigated carefully before credit is extended to him. Another reason for the small number of uncollectible accounts is, of course, that most people are fundamentally honest.

Credit Letters

A person wishing to establish credit will usually go to a store's credit department for an interview, or he will write or telephone for a credit application form. Such an application is illustrated on page 404.

When the store receives the applicant's credit application, the credit manager immediately begins to investigate the references that have been supplied. In some cases, he will merely ask for a credit investigation by the local Retail Credit Bureau of which he is a member. Or, he may write or call the stores that have been listed by the applicant as places where he has previously bought on credit. Usually, these reference letters are form letters, such as:

Gentlemen:

Mr. Gordon Rodgers, of 1010 Franklin Street, Hampton, _____ has requested credit privileges from us and has given your firm as a reference.

We should very much appreciate your answering the following questions about _____ Mr. Rodgers _____ :

1. How long has he had an account with you? _____

2. Was there a maximum amount allowed? _____ If so, how much? _____

3. Did he make payments according to your terms? _____

4. Does the applicant still owe you? _____ If so, how much? _____

5. Do you consider him:

_____ An excellent credit risk

_____ An average credit risk

_____ A poor credit risk

A return, stamped envelope is enclosed.

Very truly yours,

MOISTEN HERE AND SEAL

application for a Holt Renfrew charge account

Mr. ☐   Mrs. ☑   Mr. & Mrs. ☐   Dr. ☐   Dr. & Mrs. ☐   Ms. ☐   Miss ☐   *Please make sure marital status is indicated*

Applicants. Family Name: _DOE_   First Name _JANE_

Telephones: Home _536-7240_ Business _226-1971_   Spouse First N. _JOHN J._

Home Address: _120 ELMHURST BLVD. TORONTO_ _M 9 W 2 K 3_ Postal Code _17_ YRS. How Long

Previous Address: _1440 AVENUE ROAD, TORONTO_

Your Employer: _TORONTO BOARD OF EDUCATION_ Position: _TEACHER_ _10_ YRS. How Long

Spouse's Employer: _HILTON FABRICATING LIMITED_ Position: _DIE MAKER_ _12_ YRS. How Long

Name of Bank and Address: _MONTREAL, 1127 BATHURST ST._ Account number: _592 6251_

Personal Reference: _MRS. SARAH KING_

Address: _91 HUMBERSIDE AVENUE_

Credit Reference Firm & Account No. _EATON'S #372-201_   _SIMPSON'S #956712_

Credit Limit Requested $ _500—_   Sales Person or Credit Interviewer's Name & Number _____

HOLT RENFREW & CO., LTD.

If this application is accepted and a credit card issued I agree to abide by the terms of the account agreement of which I have received a copy, I have read and understood.

See examples of monthly payments and credit charges schedules on reverse side.

Date: _MARCH 10, 19—_

I request Holt Renfrew credit card(s) and renewals or replacements thereof from time to time. THE UNDERSIGNED CONSENTS TO THE OBTAINING OF CREDIT INFORMATION BY HOLT RENFREW OR BY A CREDIT REPORTING AGENCY REQUIRED AT ANY TIME IN CONNECTION WITH THE CREDIT HEREBY APPLIED FOR OR ANY RENEWAL OR EXTENSION THEREOF.

(Mrs.) Jane Doe
Signature

John J. Doe.
Spouse Signature

Courtesy Holt Renfrew

Credit application form, showing employment and listing bank references.

Letters Granting Credit   If the decision regarding an applicant's request for credit is favorable, the letter writer faces one of his most pleasant writing tasks—that of telling the customer the welcome news. The following outline may be used as a guide in writing letters granting credit:

1. Welcome the customer, expressing your wish for a pleasant association.
2. Describe the special privileges to which he is entitled.
3. Explain the terms of payment.
4. Encourage him to use his new charge account and offer any special assistance.

Dear Mrs. Larkin:

We take great pleasure in opening a charge account at Capwell's in your name. I feel sure that this will be the beginning of a long and mutually pleasant association.

As a charge customer, you will enjoy many privileges at Capwell's. For instance, our charge customers receive advance notices of special sales, so that they may take advantage of wonderful bargains before they are offered to the public at large. Charge customers, too, are entitled to free gift wrapping on any purchase of $15.00 or more. Your account plate is good at our Terrace Restaurant, at our Calorie-Watcher's Bar, and in our Book Rental Department. Use your plate for anything and everything!

On the first of each month, you will receive an itemized statement of your purchases made through the 25th day of the preceding month; purchases made after the 25th appear on the following month's bill. Remittances are expected by the 10th.

I hope you will make regular use of your charge account. Remember, everyone at Capwell's is dedicated to the slogan that is taken from the first three letters of our name—CAP: "Capwell's Always Pleases." Let us know if we ever fail to measure up to it.

Sincerely yours,

Many stores notify acceptance of applications for credit by a printed announcement card.

Letter Refusing Credit   If the credit manager determines from the information he has gathered that a credit applicant is a poor risk, he will have to write a letter turning down the request. No letter is more difficult to write. Regardless of what is said, the writer is, in effect, telling the customer that he does not warrant the store's faith. Of course, a letter refusing credit must be very tactful. Remember, you want the customer to continue buying from you on a cash basis.

Some credit men believe that you should not come right out and tell the applicant that he is being refused credit. They feel that such an uncomplimentary statement violates the trust and confidence of those who supplied information about the applicant. Therefore, they hide behind generalities, hoping the applicant will come to the store in person to discuss the matter. Such a noncommittal letter follows:

Dear Mr. Peterson:

Your desire to open a charge account at Young's is a real compliment.

On the basis of the information we have received regarding your credit standing, we feel that we cannot give you a definite decision at this time. There are several matters that should be discussed in person with you before we can make a commitment.

I shall be glad to talk with you about credit privileges when you can visit us.

Very truly yours,

Other credit men believe that it is not ethical to use this subterfuge—that the writer should, in the applicant's own interests, set forth the exact reason for the refusal. For example:

Dear Mr. Peterson:

You have paid us a compliment by requesting credit privileges at Young's.

As in the case of all those who apply for credit, Mr. Peterson, we made a careful investigation of your capital resources and your ability to handle additional credit. I believe you will agree that purchasing on installment a new car, two large appliances, and a piano—while making payments on a new home—is stretching your present income a little too much. I know you will understand why you should not endanger your credit reputation by additional credit obligations.

Please continue to allow Young's to serve you on a cash basis until such time as you are able to reduce your present obligations. When the circumstances are more favorable, you may be sure that we shall welcome the opportunity of considering your application again.

Cordially yours,

Letters Stimulating Credit Business   Business firms welcome the opportunity to grant credit—to the right people, those who will use it wisely. In fact, because they know that credit customers are bigger buyers and generally more loyal customers, stores often put on special campaigns to encourage credit customers to make more frequent or larger purchases. These letters are combined goodwill-sales letters, in that they stimulate both interest and sales for the firm.

Retail stores often will invite steady cash customers to open charge accounts on the theory that they will like the convenience of shopping in this manner and will, of course, be encouraged to make more frequent purchases. Here is a letter encouraging a cash customer to avail herself of a charge account:

Dear Mrs. Perkins:

You are cordially invited to open a charge account at Benson and Black.

Hundreds of our customers enjoy the convenience of a charge account. They are able to shop without having to carry large sums of money; and often, too, they enjoy the convenience of shopping more easily by mail or by telephone. Merchandise that you really need now can be purchased now, and you will not have to defer the pleasure of using it.

Benson and Black "pampers" its charge customers in many ways, and you will be delighted with the personal attention you will receive. Why not come in and let us show you how easy it is to open an account—and use it immediately.

Sincerely yours,

Collection Letters

Most of the people who have been granted credit pay their bills faithfully and on time. Some people, however, need to be reminded when their accounts are past due. The person who writes collection letters must assume that every customer is fundamentally honest and fair and that he intends to pay his bills. This attitude is necessary to maintain the basic principle of credit—mutual faith. Therefore, the experienced credit man practises the philosophy that "the customer *is* trustworthy until he is proved otherwise."

Gentle Reminders   Most stores send out statements each month to those who have charge accounts. These statements serve as reminders to pay. At the same time, they furnish the customer with a record of his purchases.

At one time, charge customers looked upon the statement as a "dun"—and that is what it was called. Today, however, we expect to receive a statement of our account each month; and we welcome it.

A statement of account is all that most people need to prod them into paying. No additional reminders are necessary. But sometimes statements are mislaid or forgotten. If the store does not receive payment within a specified number of days after the statement is sent, they may simply send a second statement, marked *Second Statement,* and hope this will be sufficient. The second reminder may be a form letter or a card reminder, such as that illustrated here.

Form reminder slip from department store, with impersonal but friendly message.

Courtesy Rich's

A Reminder . . .

Just a word of appreciation for your business and a friendly reminder that the balance shown on the enclosed statement includes purchases for which you were billed three months ago.

If your account has been paid within the last few days, please accept our thanks and disregard this notice.

RICH'S

RA

You will notice that these reminders are very impersonal and very gentle. There is a good reason for this. At this stage of collection, the credit manager doesn't want the customer to feel that he is being singled out. Otherwise, the customer's attitude may be "Why is he picking on me? I'm only a few days late." Because of this attitude, a personalized message is not so effective as a printed notice or a form letter in this situation.

More Persuasive Letters   If the various notices just discussed do not bring results, additional reminders will be necessary. The procedure to be followed from this point depends greatly on the customer. If his credit record is good, the store may continue to remind him with gentle hints. If there is some past history of tardiness in paying, the next reminder may be more forceful. If the store, because of past dealings with the customer, suspects that he will be difficult to collect from, stiffer reminders may be written earlier. Also, the number of days allowed between reminders will depend on the store's experience with the customer; quick-paying customers are usually given more time between reminders. There is no standard pattern for all customers or for all businesses; many factors determine the frequency and the type of letters sent to collect past-due accounts.

Following is a typical pattern in a collection system:

	Number of Days After Regular Billing
1. Second statement	30
2. Stronger request	45
3. Urgent request	60
4. Threat of legal action	75
5. Letter from attorney or agency	90–100

To illustrate a collection situation, let us assume that Mrs. Marvin Jones has a charge account with Dell's Department Store. Dell's records show that Mrs. Jones, whose husband is a building contractor, has had an account for about a year. She has made frequent purchases since that time and has always paid her bills; but each month, two or three reminders were necessary before the account was paid.

During June, Mrs. Jones purchased a rattan chaise longue and a redwood dining set for outdoor use. The amount of her purchase was $287.88. A statement was sent on July 1, followed by a routine form letter on July 31 with no results. What type of letter should now be sent to Mrs. Jones? This will depend on the kind of person the store thinks Mrs. Jones is. Obviously, a more personal message than has been sent heretofore is now required, so that Mrs. Jones will know that the appeal is being made directly to her. But, if the store considers her merely careless or forgetful rather than deliberately slow, they will be careful not to offend her—she is still a profitable customer.

Dear Mrs. Jones:

Haven't you overlooked something? According to our records, you received a statement of your account in early July. On July 31 we sent you a reminder that your balance of $287.88 had not been paid.

I know that this matter is merely an oversight and that you will mail us your cheque right away. Better still, why not come to the store in person to take care of the account? While you are here, stop in to see the new shipment of barbecue grills we have just received. In gleaming aluminum, these grills are as handsome as they are practical.

Cordially yours,

Notice that this letter gently chides the customer for her oversight. Note, too, that she is indirectly complimented by the implication that there is no cause for worry on your part—you know she will pay. The letter ends with a sales message, because at this stage you wish merely to plant an idea, not to offend the customer by overdoing your plea.

If this letter does not get results (and in most cases it will), you will have to use a different approach. Again, the time elapsed between the letter just illustrated and the next one will depend upon the customer and the store. In most cases, the time between letters grows progressively shorter. If there is a problem in receiving payment, the store does not wish to drag the matter out; the customer may get the impression that prompt payment really isn't important.

Appeals There are several appeals the store may use in writing the next letter if the "it-was-merely-an-oversight" letter does not get results. The one most often used for the next step is the appeal to *fair play:* "We have kept our part of the bargain— won't you keep yours?" The following letter illustrates this appeal:

Dear Mrs. Jones:

Suppose a good friend of yours wanted to borrow your new outdoor redwood dining set for a lawn party she was giving. Because you like her and wish her party to be a success, you gladly consent—even offer to help her move the furniture to her house for the occasion. Of course, it is understood that the furniture will be returned promptly after the party.

How would you feel if your friend kept the furniture and said nothing about returning it? if she even ignored a couple of reminders from you that it should be returned? My guess is, Mrs. Jones, that you would be somewhat bewildered—and a little annoyed.

We find ourselves in a similar position regarding your account. We granted you credit because we felt you would not abuse the privilege. Yet, you have not paid for your June purchases; and you have not responded to the three notices we have sent you. We are naturally curious to know why. We sold you a chaise longue and a redwood dining set in good faith, and we have tried to see that you were pleased in every way. But we believe you also have a responsibility to show us that our faith in you was justified.

Won't you send us your cheque (the amount is $287.88) right now—this minute, while it is fresh in your mind? If you can't pay the entire amount, why not come in and discuss payment with us? Perhaps we can arrange a plan whereby part of the amount due may be paid now and the balance later.

Sincerely yours,

Notice the strong appeal to the sense of fair play. Also notice the store's willingness to make suitable arrangements for partial payment.

DINERS CLUB

10 COLUMBUS CIRCLE / NEW YORK, N.Y. 10019 / TELEPHONE: (212) CI 5-1500 / CABLE: "DINCLUB" N.Y.

<u>Re:</u> Credit Card #
Balance Due $

Dear

Since you cannot be here in person . . . . .

won't you consider this as a personal interview -- one in which we frankly present our side of the case.

In all our pleasant dealings with you, we did our best by offering a wide variety of establishments throughout the world where our credit card was accepted. When your account became delinquent, we did our best in friendly reminders and letters to collect or discover some reason for not paying.

Frankly, the only thing we know to do, unless we hear from you within the next few days, is to turn the account over to a collection agency. If this becomes necessary, the account will be entirely out of our hands.

Sincerely yours,

Collection Department

CS-7

Courtesy Diners Club

Impersonal reminder letter with appeal to recipient's sense of fair play. Left to be inserted are the date, inside address, credit card number, and balance due.

If this appeal does not bring the desired results, the credit manager has some cause to be worried about the intentions of the customer. His next letter will be much stronger. Some stores would make the next letter an ultimatum: "Either pay us now or we will turn your account over to our collection agency." (A collection agency is an organization whose business is to collect delinquent accounts for other businesses. The agency makes its income by retaining a percentage of the money it collects on each account.) Indeed, some stores would not have waited this long before sending a threatening letter. If the customer is to be given one more chance before he is sent a "pay-or-else" letter, this letter should be an appeal to his pride.

Dear Mrs. Jones:

If we received an inquiry concerning your credit, we would like to say: "Of course, Mrs. Jones is an excellent charge customer—she always pays her account and, what's more, she pays it on time." If we received such an inquiry today, however, we unfortunately would not be able to be so positive.

You have been a good Dell customer, Mrs. Jones, and we value your friendship. For some unexplainable reason, though, you have given us reason to doubt your intentions concerning settlement of your account. Frankly, we cannot imagine what is wrong.

Please help us to help you. Your credit reputation is a valuable asset, and we do not want to see it damaged. Your credit reputation is in danger, however, unless you send us your cheque immediately. The amount is $287.88.

Very truly yours,

If the foregoing letter does not elicit immediate payment, the credit man has no alternative but to assume that the customer does not intend to pay. Usually, however, he will give the customer one last chance before placing the matter in the hands of a collection agency or in the hands of the store's attorney, who will bring suit against the customer. The letter of ultimatum may read as follows:

Dear Mrs. Jones:

Will you please mark the date of September 15 on your calendar. This is an important date to you, because, unless your account is paid by that time (the amount is $287.88), we shall be forced to place your account in the hands of a collection agency. I am sure you realize that this is a drastic step, and it is taken only when we have reason to believe that a customer does not intend to pay his account.

Of course, such a step will damage your credit reputation; and we wish it were not necessary for us to take it. There is only one way you can stop us: send us your cheque immediately, or at least let us know your intentions. This is the last notice you will receive from us.

Very truly yours,

Collection-Letter Series   As you have seen, collection letters are often written in a series. There may be as many as six letters in a series, beginning with the first reminder and ending with the final ultimatum. Many large department stores and mail-order houses have developed several series of collection letters—as many as five or six different series. Each series may be independent of the others, or letters in one series may be interchangeable with one or more in the others. For example,

Letter 3 in Series A may be substituted for Letter 4 in Series B and so on. Collection-letter series are usually duplicated form letters; the typist merely fills in the name and address. Some firms, however, prefer to give their collection letters a more personal touch (these command more attention) by having them typed on an automatic typewriter. Each letter in a series is given a code number, and a careful record is kept of those that have been sent to the customer.

Acknowledging Payment When a customer responds to a collection letter by making full payment of his account, some stores write him a special thank-you letter. For example:

Dear Mr. Lubeck:

I was pleased to have your cheque for $116.20. It has been credited to your account, which is now completely clear.

All of us at Roth's appreciate your cooperation, Mr. Lubeck. We hope you will continue to let us serve you in every way we can.

Sincerely yours,

Sometimes a customer sends only a portion of the amount due. This payment should be acknowledged by letter. At the same time, the customer should be asked very tactfully when the balance may be expected. Since the partial payment indicates a willingness to pay, drastic steps should not be necessary to recover the remainder due.

Dear Mr. Carter:

Thank you for your cheque for $100 to apply on your invoice of July 11 for $156.25.

Your account has been credited for $100, leaving a balance of $56.25. We know you will send us your cheque for this balance very soon. Would you let us know when we may expect it?

Cordially yours,

Sometimes a recipient of a collection letter admits frankly that he cannot pay. Of course, the credit manager is not greatly concerned about retaining such a customer; but he is very much interested in getting the money due. Writing an angry response to such an admission will have no results. Bringing suit will be costly and unpleasant. The only alternative is either to grant a delay and request small weekly or monthly payments or to have the customer sign a note for the amount due. Sometimes both are demanded. The following is an example of such a letter:

Dear Mr. Carter:

Thank you for writing us about your inability to pay your account of $150. I appreciate your being so frank with us.

I know you are sincere in wanting to meet your obligations, and I want to be just as sincere in helping you to do so. We can arrange for you to make monthly payments of $50 until your account is settled in full. If you will sign the enclosed 90-day promissory note, we will set up your account in three monthly payments.

Sincerely yours,

The Esterbrook Pen Company

BOX 230, CHERRY HILL, NEW JERSEY, U. S. A. 08034
TELEPHONE: 609-424-1710

Gentlemen:

    If you keep "fiddling around" with payment of your past-due balance . . .

    . . . it will take more than a fire extinguisher to put out the conflagration blistering your credit background.

    Playboy Nero didn't "care" - but I'm sure your business reputation is important to you.

    So, who wants to call out the "legal smoke eaters"?

Re:

                B. E. Van Dyke
                Credit Manager

AMERICA'S OLDEST PEN MAKER

Courtesy The Esterbrook Pen Company and The Dartnell Corporation

This letter in a collection series has urgent tone and is close to being an ultimatum. Inside address and amount due are to be individually inserted.

Communication Problems

Application Exercises

A ■

As a wholesaler of electric appliances, you receive a request from a retailer to open an account. Investigation of the retailer's business activities, particularly his credit experience, reveals that he would make a poor credit risk. He has many outstanding debts and is a slow payer. Write a letter to him turning down his request but attempting to retain him as a cash customer.

B ■

The Carolina Manufacturing Company has sent you two orders accompanied by cheques. You have made some discreet inquiries and have learned that the firm is a good credit risk. You would like to add the firm to your list of charge customers. Write a letter inviting the firm to open an account with you.

C ■

You write letters for a department store. Mrs. Thomas F. Lawson has been a very good customer, but for the last three months she has purchased very little. Write a letter designed to encourage her to use her account.

D ■

Assume that you are the credit manager for the Wilding Clothing Store. Prepare a series of four collection letters that may be used for delinquent accounts. Leave blank the amounts and dates in the body of the letter.

E ■

George T. Dumont has given your name as a credit reference. He has always paid you, but he never pays on time. Although you have kept him on your books, you consider him "slow pay." Write a reply to a reference request from Dundee Jewelry Store.

F ■

Mr. Walter Campbell, one of your customers, sends you a cheque for $200 on a long overdue account for $350. Write Mr. Campbell, thanking him for the cheque and inquiring tactfully when you may expect the balance.

G ■

One of your new customers, Mr. Clark Bronson, writes that he cannot pay the $150 he owes you. Prepare a letter to Mr. Bronson.

Word Study

A ■

Words often confused: conscious, conscience; cereal, serial.

B ■

For what words or phrases do the following frequently used abbreviations stand? Consult the abbreviations section of your dictionary, if you need to.

1	approx.	4	contd.	7	r.p.m.
2	ctge.	5	atty.	8	vs.
3	km/h	6	Messrs.		

C ■

The following "words" appear as they are pronounced. How are they spelled?

1	lăm	4	ku	7	kē
2	trŏf	5	thō	8	ī
3	gōst	6	nōn		

Communication in Action: *Punctuation Discussion*

"When I have the slightest doubt about the need for a comma or a semicolon, I always put one in," says Freda Moore, a secretary. "But my boss says that overpunctuating is worse than no punctuation at all. In fact, he thinks that just the opposite rule should apply: 'Don't punctuate unless failure to do so will cause the reader to misinterpret what you say.' " Discuss these points of view. Is either of them entirely correct? If not, formulate a rule of your own.

UNIT □ 50

Letters
for Other
Problem Situations

You already have learned that some letters are easier to write than others. Letters that comply with requests, for example, are not too difficult to write because they tell the reader what he wants to hear. They say, "Yes, we are pleased to do as you request." Sometimes, however, you cannot comply with a request, because:

1. Information you need is missing.
2. The request made is unreasonable.
3. Circumstances prevent your granting the request.

Incomplete Inquiries

Suppose you receive an inquiry that is not clear or complete. Any attempt on your part to answer such a letter fully will probably fail to satisfy the customer. What you must do is write to the customer, asking him for the information you need. Such a situation must be handled tactfully, without giving the correspondent the impression that he was negligent or careless. Suppose, for example, that you work for a photographer who receives this letter from a customer:

Dear Sir:

I would like to have some photographs made of myself. I am unable to get to Vernon until late this month, and I would like to know in advance of my trip how much the photographs would cost.

Very truly Yours —

In order to supply the correct information, you must know more about the customer's needs. Here is a tactful, helpful, and courteous response.

Dear Mrs. Allan:

Thank you for writing us about your photographic needs. I know that we can please you with our superior work—and at modest prices.

In order to give you the price information you need, please answer the following questions and return this letter to us in the envelope enclosed. No postage is required.

1. What size photograph would you like?

    Passport or identification
        (5 x 6 cm) _____
    Miniature (8 x 10 cm) _____
    Standard size:
        8 x 15 cm _____
        10 x 12.5 cm _____
        12.5 x 18 cm _____
        20 x 25 cm _____

2. How many copies do you plan to order? _____

3. Please check one of the following:

    Black and white _____ Brownette _____ Color _____

4. Metal frame_____ Silver plate frame_____
    Cardboard matting_____

Just as soon as we receive this information from you, we shall be happy to send you complete prices.

We hope you will give us an opportunity to serve you very soon.

Sincerely yours,

Note that the writer makes it easy for Mrs. Allan to send the necessary information. And in no way is an implication made that Mrs. Allan was at fault by not supplying all the details in her letter of inquiry.

Unreasonable Requests

Businesses sometimes receive unreasonable requests for information or service. Note the following:

> Gentlemen:
>
> I am interested in buying one of your Electro Percolators. A friend told me he could get me one wholesale.
>
> In order to know whether I'm getting a good price or not, I would appreciate having the wholesale price of the Electro Percolator.
>
> Very truly yours,

This request is not a reasonable one, since wholesale prices are confidential between manufacturer and dealer. Nevertheless, you should not tell the correspondent that his request is unreasonable, even though it is. You must attempt to retain his interest in your product. Look at this tactful reply that tries to sell the customer on buying through regular channels.

Dear Mr. Herbert:

Your interest in buying an Electro Percolator pleases us very much. You have selected the finest coffee maker available anywhere at any price.

The suggested retail price of the Electro is $29.95; and once you have seen the Percolator, you will agree that it is well worth every cent. This low price allows only a modest profit for the manufacturer and the dealer.

I wish I could tell you the wholesale price of the Electro Percolator; but standard business ethics, Mr. Herbert, require us to keep this information confidential between the manufacturer and the dealer. I know you will understand the reasons behind this policy.

Four stores in St. Catharines carry Electro appliances—Goodson's, Star Appliances, Reid Hardware, and Friedman-Jones Department Store. All these dealers are featuring Electro products this month. I hope you will let one of them show you his complete line. When you buy from an authorized dealer, you are sure of getting service on the product.

You will be delighted with the Electro Percolator. Once you have tried it, you will know why discriminating coffee lovers say, "I didn't know coffee could taste so good!"

Sincerely yours,

Delays in Filling Orders

When a customer has been "sold" on your firm to the extent that he places an order, he has a right to expect fast, courteous service. Unfortunately, delays do happen; and the letter writer has little control over them. He does what he can to satisfy the customer and hopes that the customer will understand. For example, here is a letter acknowledging an order from a new customer. The writer wants very much to give the customer good news—but he is unable to do so.

Dear Mr. Hathaway:

We were naturally very pleased to have your first order for Tempo Sports Shirts. You are most thoughtful to comment on our advertisement in Men's Wear magazine. Apparently, a good many others saw the ad, too, because we have been swamped with orders for the Tempo line.

I am sending you today two dozen each of small, medium, and large sizes in assorted colors. The remaining four dozen of each will be shipped on Monday of next week.

I am embarrassed, Mr. Hathaway, that you should be inconvenienced on your very first order; but I know you will understand that we were not prepared for the large quantity of orders received. You may be sure that our factory is now geared for round-the-clock production in order that we may keep all our dealers supplied.

I hope you find it just as hard to keep Tempo Sports Shirts in stock—they are so very popular! Why not place your order now for a new supply? We promise our usual prompt service on your next order.

Sincerely yours,

In writing letters of this type, observe these rules:

1. Always tell the customer first what you *can* do, then what you *can't* do. (We are sending some shirts now; the rest will have to be sent later.)

2. Keep the tone positive. Even though you must apologize for the delay, don't overdo it. Assume that the customer understands. (This rush of business naturally caught us unprepared.)

3. Reestablish the customer's confidence in your firm by encouraging him to place additional orders. (Place your next order now. We will give it our *usual prompt* service.)

Refusals of Orders

The primary purpose of any business, of course, is to sell goods or services for a profit. Usually, nothing makes a business happier than to receive an order. Under some circumstances, however, orders must be refused. The most common instance is that of a consumer who tries to purchase directly from a wholesaler. The wholesaler must refer him to a retail store. This type of letter is not so much a refusal as an explanation and a referral. In writing it, the correspondent should follow three steps:

1. Thank the customer for his order.
2. Tell the customer why his order cannot be accepted.
3. Tell the customer where he can obtain the merchandise and encourage him to buy while his interest is high.

Following is a typical letter refusing an order. The letter was sent by a national manufacturer to a customer who ordered directly from him.

Dear Mrs. Warren:

Thank you for your order for a Worksaver Steam Iron. We are delighted that you chose this fine product. Worksaver does, indeed, live up to its motto, "Takes the dread out of ironing."

Since we distribute our products through local dealers only, we are unable to serve you directly, Mrs. Warren. I am pleased, however, to refer you to the Lincoln Appliance Centre at 115 West Main Street in River Grove. The Lincoln people will be delighted to show you their complete line of steam irons and many other fine Worksaver appliances.

I am returning your cheque for $25.95 and hope that you will make a trip to Lincoln Appliance Centre right away for your new Worksaver. You will find that our steam iron is one of the wisest investments you have ever made.

Sincerely yours,

Invitation Refusals

A business organization and its employees receive numerous invitations to participate in exhibits, to speak before groups, or to take part in various kinds of community activities. Most businessmen feel that it is wise to participate in these affairs—they help to build goodwill for the business. However, not all such invitations can be accepted because of time or financial limitations. In writing a letter refusing an invitation, you should include these three important points:

1. Express appreciation for the invitation.
2. Give a logical reason for having to refuse.
3. Keep open the possibility of accepting a similar invitation in the future (if desirable).

Note the following example of a letter refusing an invitation to speak:

Dear Mr. Miller:

I was pleased and flattered to have your invitation to speak at the October meeting of the Retired Men's Club of the Paxton YMCA.

Unfortunately, Mr. Miller, I shall not be able to accept your invitation because I shall be out of town during the last two weeks in October. This is an important company business trip that cannot be postponed. I am genuinely sorry that I cannot be with you.

It would be a pleasure to appear before your group at some later date. If you wish me to do so, I hope you will let me know at least a month in advance. Incidentally, the subject of "How to Make Your Retirement Income Go Further" suits me just fine.

Cordially yours,

Information Refusals

Businesses sometimes receive requests for information that must be refused. The request may be unreasonable, or the information sought may be confidential. For example, a physician or a hospital cannot divulge medical information about a patient; a bank will not give information regarding its depositors except to those authorized by the depositor to receive such information. Letters refusing to give information are usually brief and to the point. Study the following examples:

Dear Mr. Wargo:

I am sorry that I am unable to send you information about Miss Sally Moreno. Personal data concerning our employees is considered highly confidential, and only our personnel department is permitted access to it.

Very truly yours,

Dear Mr. Frosch:

I appreciate your letter in which you ask for information concerning markup rates on drug products sold in our store. Markup rates vary considerably, Mr. Frosch, and it is impossible for me to give you a figure that would apply to all drug products. Putting together detailed information would require more time than we can afford just now.

I should like to refer you to Service Bulletin No. 16, Markups in the Drug Industry, issued by the Business and Consumer Information Publishers in Gatt. This 25-cent booklet contains markup rates for the drug industry as a whole, and I am sure it will be helpful to you.

Cordially yours,

Refusing Unearned Discounts

Occasionally, a customer may figure the discount on his bill incorrectly; or he may attempt to take advantage of a discount when he is not entitled to it. The company may do one of three things:

1. Return his remittance and request a cheque for the correct amount.
2. Accept the remittance and ask for an additional remittance to make up the difference.
3. Accept the remittance and add the difference to the customer's next bill.

In any event, a letter must be written to the customer. Under no circumstances should the situation be ignored. In fairness to other customers who abide by the rules, the business cannot afford to make exceptions. In writing the customer, point

Fairfield's **THE MAGAZINE OF TODAY**

2920 rue de Bordeaux   Montreal, P.Q. H2K 3Y9

August 3, 19--

Mr. Kenneth Barton
38 Albion Street
Winnipeg, Manitoba
R3B 1E7

Dear Mr. Barton:

    Thank you for giving me an opportunity to read your manu-
script, "Safari to Shangri-La." I have shared the manuscript
with several assistants on the editorial staff, and they all
found it immensely enjoyable.

    Unfortunately, Mr. Barton, we find that our readers can
"take" only two or three adventure stories each year; and our
files are bulging with at least a dozen good adventure articles
awaiting publication. While yours is good enough to add to the
others, I do not think it fair to you to keep your manuscript
when we have no idea if and when we can use it. Therefore, I
am returning the manuscript with the hope that you can sell it
elsewhere.

    Your writing style is delightful. Have you ever done
anything in the area of whimsical family humor--articles on
commuting, gardening, entertaining, and so on? We can't seem
to get enough manuscripts on these topics, and I think you have
the talent for doing some good writing. Why not try your hand
at one of these topics and let me see it.

                Cordially yours,

                Roger Hawer

                Roger Hawer
                Editor

RH:msj
Encl.

**When rejecting a manuscript that has been submitted for publication, the letter writer
must be very tactful and diplomatic. Note positive tone of this letter.**

out the error tactfully and appeal to his sense of fair play—doing both without offending him. Study this example:

Dear Mr. Wheaton:

Thank you for your cheque for $2450 in payment for your March invoice. We appreciate the many opportunities you have given us to serve you.

We notice that, in the past, you have always paid your invoices within the discount period in order to take advantage of the saving. As you know, we can afford to give this discount because prompt payment enables us to make a similar saving on our purchases.

When a customer does not make payment within the discount period, we do not make any saving either. In this instance, you have waited seventeen days before making payment. Of course, this is seven days beyond the maximum allowed.

Because you are a good customer and because this is the first time you have gone beyond the discount period, we should like to allow the discount. However, if we did so, we should be unfair to our customers who pay within the 10-day period. They would lose confidence in us, and so would you.

Therefore, Mr. Wheaton, will you please send us with your next remittance the $50 remaining on your account?

Very sincerely yours,

Communication Problems

Application Exercises

A ■

Assume that you are employed by the World-Wide Travel Agency and receive this inquiry from William Tucker, 114 Forrest Avenue, Winnipeg, Manitoba.

Gentlemen:

Please send me information about vacations in New Brunswick, including prices, etc. Thank you.

Very truly yours,

1 Criticize Mr. Tucker's letter, telling why you think it is a good or a poor letter.
2 What information should you have from Mr. Tucker in order to be of the greatest help to him? Make a list of everything you should know.
3 Write to Mr. Tucker requesting the information you need.
4 What aids would you use in answering Mr. Tucker after he supplied the necessary details?

B ■

The following letter was sent in reply to a request for information about the wholesale price of Koolray summer rugs. It is against company policy to reveal wholesale prices other than to authorized dealers. What is wrong with this letter? Rewrite it as you think it should have been written.

Dear Sir:

We are sorry that we cannot tell the wholesale price of Koolray summer rugs. Wholesale prices are the personal business of our firm and our authorized dealers only. Frankly, we are surprised at your request.

Yours truly,

C ■

Your firm receives an order for 50 Delta porch gliders from a furniture store that has not previously done business with you. You welcome the business, but unfortunately you are out of stock on the gliders. It will take about ten days to fill this order. How would you handle the situation? Write the kind of letter you would like to receive if you were the company placing the order.

D ■

The Mi-Ty Explosives Company receives a request for a school group to tour its plant to see how explosives are made. Because of the danger involved, however, the company prohibits visitors from entering the plant. Write a letter turning down the request but retaining the goodwill of the correspondent.

E ■

Criticize the following letter. Then rewrite it as you think the letter should be written.

Sir:

We can't accept your order for one of our Gaxton mixers. Only The Wilson Dept. Store in your city is authorized to handle the sale of Gaxton products. We are, therefore, returning your cheque for $39.95.

Yours truly,

F ■

The Brentwood Ladies Society requests a donation from your firm for their Building Fund Drive. This is one of hundreds of similar requests received by your firm. You are asked to compose a letter that your employer might send refusing the donation in such a way that none of the members, many of whom are good customers, will be offended.

Word Study

A ■

Words often confused: appraise, apprise; pretend, portend.

B ■

Correct the capitalization in these sentences:

1   We fear that mayor horton will not be able to attend.
2   I have just bought mother a gift for mother's day.
3   They waited several hours before the Prime Minister's house.
4   I am looking forward to studying Chemistry.
5   Hudson bay, in Canada, is 1360 km long.

C ■

What are the plurals of these words?

1	witness	**3**	1950	**5**	kg
2	century	**4**	foot	**6**	assets

Communication in Action: *Telephone Conversation*

Criticize the following telephone conversation. Then rewrite it as it should have been handled.

Person Answering: Hello.
Caller: Who is this?
Person Answering: Whom do you want?
Caller: I was trying to get the advertising department.
Person Answering: This is the advertising department.
Caller: Is Ralph Pearson there?
Person Answering: Yes.
Caller: May I speak to him, please?

UNIT □ 51

Writing Effective Sales Letters

Every business letter you write is a sales letter. That is, every letter has something to sell—whether it is merchandise, service, an idea, a point of view, or simply good-will. When you write a letter announcing a new location of your firm and inviting customers to come to see you, you are selling goodwill. When you write a collection letter, you are hoping to sell the customer the idea of paying his account. A letter explaining why your delivery schedules were late this month sells a point of view. Even a letter applying for a job is a sales letter—the writer is selling his abilities.

Usually, however, the term *sales letter* is used in connection with selling merchandise or service. "Experience the thrill of stepping from your bath and wrapping yourself in a luxuriously fluffy, absorbent Marcan towel" or "Your car is in safe, reliable hands when you bring it to Ronnie's Garage for service" are typical of the sales statements you are accustomed to hearing or reading. As you study this unit, which emphasizes the writing of letters selling merchandise or service, you should keep in mind that the very same principles apply to writing letters that sell ideas, goodwill, or points of view.

Steps in Planning

A sales letter is effective if it achieves its purpose. The purpose may be to get a prospect to come to your place of business, to think of your firm when he is in the market for your product, or to get him to place an order by return mail. In any event, the effective sales letter requires careful planning. This planning involves the following steps:

1. Determine the aim of your letter. What do you want the reader to do?
2. Determine your market—the kind of individual or individuals to whom you are writing. Are all your readers businessmen, or do they represent all types of professions and occupations?
3. Select the appeals that are adaptable to your market. Why would people want to buy your product? What will it do for them?
4. Organize the facts according to a logical, effective, and easy-to-follow plan.

Determine Your Letter Aim Why are sales letters written? A sales letter may be written to accomplish any one of five purposes: to get the customer to buy your product now, to develop an interest in your product that will induce him to buy later, to keep the name of your organization in the customer's mind, to get the customer to visit your place of business, or to get the customer to try your product or ask questions about it. You must determine which of these purposes you would like your sales letter to accomplish—and build your letter around this one purpose.

If your aim is to get the customer to buy now, you will build your letter around the idea of getting the customer to take immediate action. If the aim of your letter is to get the customer to visit your place of business, then you will make it to his advantage to do so. For example, the Hick's Clothing Centre, to get new customers to visit the store, offered a free gift (most of the gifts were small items like a handkerchief, socks, or neckties) to everyone who would enter the store. Here is the letter that Hick's sent:

> We have a gift for you! At the bottom of this letter is a number—your gift number. Everybody with a numbered letter receives a gift from us—without obligation. Nothing to write and no purchase required. How do you get this gift?
>
> In our store window we have posted a list of numbers, and each number is followed by a handsome gift—a man's suit, a raincoat, a complete lady's ensemble, to mention but a few. Just compare your letter number with those posted in our store window. Then present your letter to me, and I will give you your gift. Come in any time between now and Friday, April 14.
>
> While you are at our store, you will want to get acquainted with the "wonderful difference" in buying clothing in our big, beautiful, exciting house of values. You have never seen such a large selection of men's, women's, and children's clothing! Everything from the tip of your toes (shoes) to the top of your head (hats).

Specializing in Educational Booklets & Training Programs   Tel. 201-736-2255

THE ECONOMICS PRESS, INC. · 270 PLEASANT VALLEY WAY, WEST ORANGE, NEW JERSEY 07052

My Blessing, Not My Doom

The enclosed booklet, we suspect, will still be around long after the writer is dead and buried.

It's an amazing message. It tells people to work better and harder--yet they still like it. We've never published a booklet which brought so many letters of praise from plain, ordinary people--or from company presidents either.

You can read "My Blessing, Not My Doom" today, then read it again six months from now with equal pleasure. More than 4 000 companies have distributed copies to their employees. One actually distributed it twice--30 000 copies each time.

You've never read it? Just open the booklet and try the first two pages.

If you want copies of this message for your employees, they are always available. We reprint periodically to keep it in stock. Just send us your order on the enclosed card--your copies will be shipped immediately.

Sincerely,

John L. Beckley

John L. Beckley
Publisher

This sales letter leaves no doubt as to what the reader is supposed to do.

Come in for your free gift on or before April 14. It will be a pleasure to meet you personally and to present your free gift to you.

Cordially yours,

HICK'S CLOTHING CENTRE

Your gift number is:
14896

Bill Rogers, Manager

In the following letter, the aim is to get the reader to make further inquiry about the service offered.

Dear Mr. Thompson:

Congratulations on your appointment to the position of Office Manager for the Rego Oil Company in Edmonton, announced in last night's Evening Bulletin.

Like most people, you probably dread the chore that accompanies moving from one locality to another. First, the hours of wrapping and packing; and then, additional hours of unpacking and unwrapping. Well, put your mind at ease—Wide World Moving Company is at your service to help make moving painless and pleasant.

Just tell us your moving date. And 24 hours before that date, our corps of courteous, efficient packers will come to your home with all the necessary equipment and supplies. They will carefully wrap and pack every item—from your most delicate china to your grand piano. And everything will be properly packed to avoid any damage. Though we are insured for any loss or damage, our packers and movers do their jobs so well that our claims are phenomenally small.

On moving day, our movers arrive promptly at the designated hour and carefully and quickly load all your belongings into our moving vans. You don't have a care or a worry. And when the van reaches its destination with your belongings, another crew takes over to help you with your unpacking.

Wide World really makes moving a pleasure. So telephone us at 722-3686 and ask our representative to call on you to discuss our low rates and to determine your packing needs.

Very sincerely yours,

Each of these preceding letters had one specific goal, and the letter was built around that goal. A letter that tries to accomplish too many things at the same time usually winds up accomplishing nothing.

Determine Your Market   To whom is the sales letter being sent? to a mass audience—*all* the people in a particular area, regardless of occupation, income, educational background, or to a selected audience whose tastes and interests might be similar? The kind of reader the sales letter will have should determine, to a large extent, the kind of letter that is written. If you are selling air conditioners, are you writing to consumers who want the comfort and convenience of the air conditioner, to retailers who want to make a profit in reselling the air conditioners, or to industrial users who may be more concerned with the economies to be effected by using your particular brand of air conditioner? The same sales letter could not be used very effectively for all three groups, even though the product is the same.

The following letters were sent from the same furniture store. Letter 1 was sent to all customers who previously had made purchases at the store. Letter 2, however, was sent only to businessmen in the community.

Letter 1

Dear Friend:

Put a red circle around May 2 on your calendar! On May 2 our spectacular May Furniture Sale begins—and you will want to be at our store when the doors open at 9 a.m.

Every piece of furniture—lamps, rugs, and bedding, too—will be reduced in price from 10 to 60 percent. Just to give you two examples of the savings in store for you: A beautiful 4-piece mahogany bedroom suite that originally sold for $1475 is reduced to a low $1295. Mattresses and box springs that sold for $159.95 each will be sold at $125.95 each. Every item you purchase during this week-long sale will represent a substantial saving to you.

You won't want to miss this sensational sale, so be here bright and early on May 2. Remember, our Home-Furnishing Account calls for only 10 percent down with the remainder budgeted over a period up to 36 months.

Cordially yours,

Letter 2

Dear Mr. Finch:

Have you taken a good look around your office lately? Is your furniture drab and shabby looking? Does your office give your firm the appearance of success and prosperity—or does it make your clients think "this man must not be doing very well"?

Now is a very good time for you to visit our Office Furniture Department. Every item is reduced 10 percent during the month of July. Our decorator is a specialist in office layout and furnishings. He can help you select appropriate matching furniture, rugs, and draperies—and his advice is free for the asking. You will be under no obligation to make your purchases from us, but you can't beat our low prices and large selection anywhere else in Redwood City.

Call 848-9371 and ask for Mr. Draper. He will be happy to make an appointment to visit your office and help you with your redecorating problems.

You can't afford to miss this once-a-year sale of office furniture and furnishings. So—to take advantage of expert free advice and substantial savings—call or come in to see us today.

Sincerely yours,

Select Appropriate Appeals   When the writer of sales letters has determined the market he wishes to reach, he must then determine the appeals his product will have for the reader. Although the air conditioner discussed on page 430 will do the same thing for everyone who uses it, different people will be moved to buy it for different reasons. The home consumer probably is primarily concerned with comfort and relaxation; the office or industrial user, with increased efficiency of employees. Some appeals, however, are effective for every kind of audience. Most people like to save money, so the thrift of operation of the air conditioner may appeal to both the home consumer and the office or industrial user.

XEROX

Better service
Extra service
Faster service

Competition in banking has never been more spirited. Today,
Xerox can make it convenient for you to offer new services
that will bring people in. And that's sure to give your
bank an edge on competition.

You need take only 10 seconds from your busy schedule to make
the initial step towards supplying these "extra" services
that will draw the flow of new business in your direction.

Use the enclosed postpaid card to send for your own copy of
IMPROVED BANKING SERVICES. This 16-page brochure is filled
with interesting facts and profitable ideas that Xerox has
gathered from in-depth studies with bankers throughout the
country.

It offers actual examples of how your bank can solidify present accounts and promote additional business.

It details dozens of ways in which your bank can simplify
procedures, speed information, and reduce costs.

We firmly believe this book can be a big dividend to your
bank. Its purpose is to assist you in building better
business.

                              Sincerely,

                              C. J. Clarke
                              National Sales Manager

CJC:jw
Encl.

The appeals of, and market for, this effective sales letter are readily apparent.

A sales letter for air conditioners sent to home consumers might read like this:

Dear Mr. Carmichael:

Do you remember the prolonged heat and humidity of last summer? For five nights in a row the temperature did not go below 30°C!

Another "long, hot summer" is coming, bringing with it many uncomfortable days and nights. But this year, you don't have to let the hot weather get you down. Relax and enjoy life this summer!

The new Icecap Air Conditioner has just arrived at our store. Not only is it beautiful—it is beautifully cool! The Arctic model will comfortably cool the average 5-room home, providing 24 hours of relaxing comfort and permitting restful sleep. In addition, you breathe pure air, free of the dust and pollen to which so many of us are allergic. Its quiet operation and low-voltage consumption make the Icecap a pleasure to own.

Why sacrifice comfort when, for a few cents a day, you can own and operate the Icecap? Come in today. You'll want to see and try Icecap, the ultimate in modern air conditioning.

Cordially yours,

Notice that several appeals are used in this letter—pleasure, comfort, health, and thrift. From these appeals, buying points must be developed. For example:

Appeal	Buying Point Developed
Pleasure	Helps you to relax and enjoy your home
Comfort	Helps you to get a restful night's sleep
Health	Purifies air; helps people with allergies
Thrift	Low initial cost and cost of operation

A letter attempting to sell air conditioners for office use might read this way:

Dear Mr. Buckley:

How would you like to increase the efficiency of your office workers by 10 percent this summer? Tests in over one hundred business offices using the Icecap Air Conditioners have proved that worker efficiency increased 10 percent after the Icecap was installed.

Increased worker efficiency means greater profits for your organization—thus the Icecap pays for itself in just a few short years—and, if you would like to spread this cost, you have 36 months in which to pay. In addition, improvements in the new model make your operating costs low. A Polar unit consumes only 25 cents' worth of electricity each working day. Isn't that a small sum to pay for the comfort and increased working efficiency of your employees?

Won't you call us today and ask us to send our engineer to determine the air-conditioning needs of your office? Each day's delay in installing Icecap costs you money.

Very sincerely yours,

Notice that the emphasis here is upon increased worker efficiency, low initial cost, and low operating cost. Since the primary purpose of a business is to make a profit, increasing worker efficiency and keeping costs low both contribute to this profit motive. The buying points developed from these appeals are three:

Appeal	Buying Point Developed
Thrift	Low initial cost
Thrift	Low operating cost
Profit	Increased worker efficiency

The sales correspondent has a choice of many different appeals. Those he uses depend upon the aim of his letter, the nature of his product, and the kind of market he is trying to reach. People usually spend their money for these reasons:

For comfort (air conditioner)
To make money (stocks)
To save money (storm windows)
To save time (pressure cooker)
To imitate others (buckskin shoes)
To be different (exclusive hat)
For health (toothpaste)
For enjoyment (television set)
For cleanliness (soap)
To avoid effort (power lawn mower)
To enhance personal appeal (perfume)
For convenience (automobile)
To safeguard possessions (fire insurance)

To escape physical pain (corn and callus remedy)
To gratify curiosity (new household gadget)
To protect family (life insurance)
To be in style (new coat)
To avoid trouble (casualty insurance)
To take advantage of opportunities (investment property)
To protect reputation (charitable contribution)
To satisfy appetite (candy)
For beautiful possessions (colored telephone)

Of course, some appeals may be used to satisfy a number of desires. For example, a fur stole has several appeals—to keep warm, to appear attractive, to be in style, to impress others, and to save money (investment).

An Effective Letter Plan

You are now ready to begin composing your sales letter. You must, therefore, gather all the facts about your product and the various appeals that may be used and organize them according to an effective plan. This plan calls for four steps, the ABCD's of sales letters:

1. Attracting attention
2. Building interest and desire
3. Convincing the reader
4. Directing favorable action

Let's take a look at what is involved in each of these steps.

Attracting Attention   A sales letter can attract the reader's attention even before it has been removed from the envelope. The envelope may be a color—instead of the traditional white. It may contain a picture or a phrase, as does the one on page 432.

One company that sells Holland tulip bulbs has its sales letters sent from Holland, using a Dutch postage stamp and postmark.

...as in "accommodation"
"reservation"
"information"
"transportation"

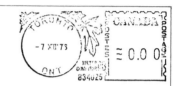

travelation limited

57 mobile drive toronto ontario M4A 1H5 canada

Mr. & Mrs. H. Vanstone
56 Claywood Road
Willowdale, Ontario
M2N 2R2

Courtesy Travelation Limited

This envelope attracts attention through color, design, a picture, and a slogan.

When the letter has been removed from the envelope, it can continue to attract attention through these devices:

1. Tinted stationery
2. An unusual letterhead design
3. A colored typewriter ribbon
4. An unusual letter style, such as the hanging-indented or inverted-paragraph style discussed in Unit 43
5. An unusual style of type, such as a script type
6. Typing the entire letter in capital letters or certain words or sentences all in capitals
7. Underscoring key words or phrases
8. Using italicized words for emphasis
9. Using dashes or exclamation points for emphasis, such as: "Call us today—tomorrow may be too late!"

All these devices are aimed at attracting attention. However, be sure not to "gimmick" the letter to the extent that these eye-catchers get in the way of the message.

The opening paragraph of the letter—in fact, the very first sentence—should excite curiosity or start a train of thought or attract attention in some way that will make the reader continue reading the letter. These opening sentences may be either questions or statements, but they should be original and concise. Questions should not be phrased so that they could be answered by a mere "Yes" or "No." Statements should contain a startling, new, interesting, or different fact. Here are some examples of opening sentences that have proved effective.

Pertinent questions:

"How can you become the best-dressed woman in town?"
"Where can you save 4 cents on each litre of fuel oil you buy for your home?"
"How much is your family worth to you?"
"If you lost your job today, how would you pay your bills?"

Startling or significant statements:

"They said it couldn't be done, but *we* did it!"
"Electric typewriters increase production 10 percent!"
"You can't afford to be without one!"
"Three out of four families use hospital service at least once each year."

The device selected to attract attention should be determined primarily by one or more of these factors:

1. The kind of firm sending the letter (Is it a conservative bank or a store selling gardening supplies?)
2. The nature of the product (Is it a religious book or a book of contemporary fiction?)
3. The kind of audience to receive the letter (Are they doctors or plumbers?)

Building Interest and Desire   When you have succeeded in getting the reader's attention, you must hold that attention. The best way to hold it is to build interest—by vividly describing your product so that the reader can virtually experience it. With colorful, descriptive words and expressions like those listed below, you can make the reader feel, taste, or smell it as well as see it—and you can also cause the reader to "see" himself using your product and getting satisfaction from it. To stimulate the reader to buy your product, you must use appeals that will awaken his emotions.

The Objective	*Suggested Appeal*
To sell floor wax:	"It's a bright shine. A tough shine. An easy-to-wipe-up shine."
To sell canned frozen oyster stew:	"Savory oyster stew with plump, pampered oysters."
To sell laundry soap flakes:	"Softness—you can feel it in the *flakes* . . . feel it in the *clothes!*"
To convince readers to send for a catalogue from a plant nursery:	"Lifelike illustrations you can almost smell and touch!"

The Objective	*Suggested Appeal*
To sell oranges:	"Big, plump wedges . . ."
To sell hardwood paneling:	"The soft beauty and warmth of fine hardwoods."
To sell porcelain bathroom fixtures:	"The porcelain finish is glass-smooth."
To sell small cars:	"The man who is fed up with bigger, thirstier cars switches to _____ ."
To sell air travel:	"For travel elegance, fly with us!"
To sell electric typewriters:	"A pleasure to type; a pleasure to sign; a joy to read."
To sell golf balls:	"The sweet click at the tee is the music of the finest ball in golf."
To sell soft drinks in cans:	"And cans chill so fast, keep the flavor fresh and full of zip."
To sell a station wagon:	"From a frisky, sturdy little work horse to the jauntiest little sedan of them all!"
To sell a soft drink:	"You'll really welcome the cold, crisp taste that so deeply satisfies . . . the cheerful lift that's bright and lively."
To sell a deodorant:	"New roll-on deodorant with staying power."
To sell an air deodorant:	"Makes air smell flower-fresh."
To sell mustard:	"A mustard that is shy, retiring, is no mustard at all; a great mustard should manage to be a delightful contradiction of emphatically hot and delicately mild."
To sell fruit punch:	"The circus-red color, the candy-and-ice-cream taste."
To sell shampoo:	"Hair so satin-bright, satin-smooth, too!"

Suppose you write a letter to sell stereo phonographs. You attract the reader's attention in the first paragraph by asking, "How would you like to bring the concert hall into your living room?" You hope that the reader is interested—or at least curious enough—to find out how this can be done. So you vividly describe your product, appealing to his desire for relaxation. You continue your letter:

You have just come home after a tiring day at work. You relax your body in the comfort of your favorite chair. But you must relax your mind, too, freeing it of the many tensions of the day. You flip the switch on your Magnasound Stereo. Suddenly the room is filled with the soft tones of your favorite music.

You are carried away to the concert hall—every note, every tone is as clear as though the orchestra were performing in your living room. Soon both your mind and your body are completely at ease, and the cares and tensions of the day are forgotten.

Notice how the paragraph builds interest by emphasizing the desire for relaxation.

Convincing the Reader   If you have done your work well to this point, the reader is already partially convinced. At least, you have developed his interest to a strong degree. If he really wants to buy, he can find reasons for doing so. Nevertheless, you must still convince the reader that it will be to his advantage to own the Magnasound Stereo. In fact, you must be able to convince him that he really cannot afford NOT to buy it. Therefore, you are ready now to bring out other features of the product that will convince him. You have attempted to sell the reader on the beautiful performance he can expect from the Magnasound and the effect that performance will have on his pleasure and relaxation. Now, what other features might appeal to him? He certainly would like to have a piece of furniture that will enhance the beauty of his living room and give pleasure to others, so you tell the reader:

Your guests, too, will appreciate the true concert-hall fidelity when you invite them to your home for an evening of listening pleasure. They are sure to comment on the beautiful cabinet—whether you select mahogany, cherry, or walnut. Both inside and out, you will own the finest stereo phonograph anywhere at this low price.

Now the reader may think, "Well, this Magnasound is going to cost more than I can afford." You must convince him that this is not so. Therefore, your letter might continue:

The magnificient Magnasound can be yours for only $50 down and $25 a month for 36 months. Your old phonograph can probably be used as a down payment, and your monthly payments will not begin until August.

Directing Favorable Action   You have now reached the point where, if each of the preceding steps has accomplished its purpose, you must move the reader to act. Some action-getting suggestions that you might use are these:

1. Enclose a return envelope or postal card
2. Suggest that the reader "act now before it is too late"
3. Offer special inducements for prompt action

The letter you write to sell the Magnasound Stereo Phonograph, therefore, might conclude as follows:

If you act before May 15, you may select $25 worth of records from those we have in stock as a FREE addition to your music library. Won't you come in today and listen to the Magnasound?

A Typical Sales Letter   On the following page is an example of an outstanding sales letter, showing each of the steps in the ABCD's of sales letter writing.

Dear Mr. Chapman:

Attracting attention

How would you like to turn your lawn-mowing chores into a pleasant activity? The Madras Riding Mower can do just that —and here's how:

Building interest and desire

The Madras Riding Mower has many features few other reel mowers have:
1. You can sit in a comfortably padded seat while you mow your lawn.
2. The Madras has an automatic starter that requires only a flip of a switch.
3. The Madras has a 9 ℓ capacity fuel tank—no stopping to fill the tank during mowing.
4. It has such an easy steering wheel that anyone can steer the Madras with little effort.
5. The Madras bags leaves and clippings so that no raking is necessary.

Convincing the reader

Nowhere can you get such value as you get with Madras. Take your choice of the 6 horsepower motor at $602.50, an 8 horsepower at $802.50, and the new 10 horsepower at $966.50. Your dealer will give you a generous trade-in on your present mower and can arrange low monthly payments on the balance. So why deny yourself the pleasure of the easy-operating Madras?

Directing favorable action

Visit your dealer today to see the many models he has available. If you will present this letter when you purchase a Madras during the month of May, your dealer will give you without charge a 22 ℓ gasoline can with a handy pouring spout—a $6.95 value.

Yours for a pleasant summer,

Follow-Up Sales Letters

Frequently, more than one sales letter will be sent to a prospective customer to convince him to buy. In selling higher priced items, for instance, more than one letter may be necessary to do the job. If no action results from the first letter sent, one or more additional letters may follow. These follow-up letters often comprise what is called a sales campaign or a "wear-out" series. Sometimes as many as eight letters will be sent, depending upon the product, its cost, and the nature of the market. Each letter in the series is spaced about ten days apart. An attempt is made to vary the appeal in each letter with the hope that one of the appeals will ultimately convince the reader to take action. Preferably, the letters will be short and each will concentrate on one principal sales feature.

If possible, the opening paragraph of each letter should be so constructed that the additional letter seems a natural development. Suppose that, in the first letter attempting to sell the Magnasound Stereo, you enclosed a postal card for the prospective

THE BONACCORD HOTEL

57 BONACCORD ST.

MONCTON, NEW BRUNSWICK E1C 5K8

TEL. 858-2075

November 19, 19--

Dear Customer:

At last we have what you are looking for. At last
we are ready to make you the most contented customer
who ever did business with us. At last our new conference
rooms are open and ready for business.

However, holding a conference is more than just a
suitable room, so may we introduce our

CONFERENCE PLANNING SERVICE

Full details of this service are given in the
enclosed folder. We can now handle small or large groups,
from in town or from out of town, for one day or for as
long as you like. Our business rooms are fully equipped
with screens, chalkboards, electrical outlets, and mikes.

But conferences are not all work. Our banquet
facilities are excellent - as you know from past experience.
Our bedrooms are comfortable, and our swimming pool is an
excellent place to relieve the tensions of the day.

Let's discuss your next conference requirements.
We enjoy your company.

Sincerely,

Lucien Lacosse, Manager
Conference Planning Service

Enc.

This sales letter attracts attention, builds interest, directs action. Obviously, the "enclosed
folder" is aimed to convince the reader to take further action.

customer to let you know that he would like to have a five-day home trial. Since the postal card was not returned, the second letter in the series might begin:

> We note that you have not yet taken advantage of our 5-day no-obligation trial of the wonderful Magnasound. Perhaps you feel that you will be obligated to buy. May we assure you that this will not be the case. At the end of five days, just telephone us to pick up the Magnasound. No questions will be asked; no sales pressure will be exerted. If the trial use of the Magnasound does not convince you, we don't want you to buy it.

Another letter in the series might appeal to the economical side of the reader by stating:

> After March 1, all phonographs will increase 10 percent in price. If you act now, you will save yourself $90, a saving that will enable you to buy several of your favorite record albums.

Communication Problems

Application Exercises

A ■
For each reason for buying given on page 431, name at least one other product or service that might be bought.

B ■
Write an opening sentence that might be used in a sales letter for each of the products or services listed on pages 433 and 434.

C ■
Assume that your class is going to put on a play in the school auditorium to raise money to send the football team to another city for a championship game. Write a letter that could be sent to each member of the PTA, urging him to attend the play.

D ■
Write a sales letter that would be sent to *each* student in the school, urging him to buy a yearbook. Write another sales letter that would be sent only to graduating seniors.

E ■
Choose a product (such as a sports car or a phonograph record album) and write an appropriate sales letter. Define the group to whom you will write, and make your letter appeal to that group.

Word Study

A ■
Words often confused: detract, distract; carton, cartoon.

B ■

Should *a* or *an* precede these words?

1	hour	**3**	umpire	**5**	history
2	woman	**4**	owner	**6**	European

C ■

Which of the following commonly used words are misspelled?

1	receive	**3**	occasion	**5**	untill
2	beleive	**4**	occurence	**6**	seperate

Communication in Action: *Obtaining Information*

As assistant manager of a hotel, you are responsible for authorizing all cheques cashed for guests. The cashier has sent Mr. Pickens to you. He wishes to cash a personal cheque for $50. What questions will you ask Mr. Pickens before you approve his cheque for payment? With another student, enact the scene as you think it might happen. Remember, you must get the information you need, yet retain the good-will of the guest.

UNIT □ 52

Using Writing Skills To Get a Job

Perhaps the most important writing you will ever do is that which pertains to getting a position. Your worth as a prospective employee is often measured largely by the letter you write applying for a job and the supporting employment data you supply in written form. An effective application letter can open doors to a bright future; a poor one could quickly close those doors. While an application letter alone will rarely get you a job, it may lead to a personal interview—its main purpose. Employers often receive hundreds of applications for one job, and they cannot possibly interview each person who applies. Therefore, the personnel recruiter uses the application letter and other written documents as a basis on which to select those who will be called for a personal interview.

Today, many people obtain employment without writing letters of application—and that may be the case with you, too, in your first job. However, as you gain experience, you are likely to become ambitious for better and better jobs. These ''better'' jobs very often call for written applications.

The Qualifications Summary

Before you start your campaign for the job you want, you should decide just what it is that you have to sell to an employer. Employment papers are sales instruments, and they must be prepared just as carefully as a sales letter. They must present you in the best possible light. The first step in the job-getting campaign is to prepare a *qualifications summary*. A qualifications summary—sometimes called a *data sheet*, a personal record, or a *résumé*—is a description of your qualifications. It usually includes a statement of your education, your employment record (experience), a list of references, and other data. A qualifications summary is highly useful. It may accompany a letter of application, be presented to an employer at the interview, or be mailed to a prospective employer without a formal letter of application. The *act of preparing* the qualifications summary is just as valuable as the summary itself, for it forces you to think about yourself—what you have to offer an employer and why he should hire you. Thus, it becomes a self-appraisal. Everyone brings something unique to a position, but usually only after he prepares a qualifications summary does he realize his true worth.

Appearance Counts   Because the qualifications summary is a sales instrument, it should be as attractive as you can make it. Of course, it should be typewritten, perfectly balanced on the page, and free from errors and noticeable erasures. Qualifications summaries vary in length from one page to as many as four pages, depending on how much you have to say about yourself. On your first application, you can probably do the job in one page or at the most, two; but as you gather experience and obtain more education, your summaries will get longer and more detailed.

It Must Be Tailored to Fit   A qualifications summary is tailored carefully to the job for which you are applying. Thus, it is an individual thing. Never try to copy someone else's qualifications summary or to use the same one over and over. You must find out what the job you are seeking demands and tailor the qualifications summary accordingly. For example, if you apply for a job requiring a very fast rate of dictation speed, you will want to emphasize your skill in shorthand. You will make absolutely sure that the employer knows you are a highly skillful shorthand writer and transcriber. On the other hand, if the secretarial job you want requires little in the way of shorthand but a good deal of talent in letter writing, you will mention your shorthand skill only briefly but emphasize your writing ability. And so on.

The Main Categories

The form of the qualifications summary varies according to individual taste and anticipated employer preference. The form illustrated on page 441 is an example of an effective arrangement. Notice that it contains four main headings: "Position Applied For," "Experience," "Education," and "References." The information at the top of the form includes the name, address, and telephone number of the applicant. This is all the personal data needed here; you will supply other personal

```
                                    JOHN J. MEYERS
                                    65 Dunwood Road
                                    Weston, Ontario  M9R 3W7
                                    Telephone (416) 244-5119
```

POSITION APPLIED FOR   General Bookkeeper

EXPERIENCE

July 1975 to   Terhune's Department Store, Weston--Accounts receivable
present   bookkeeper

                        Duties: Posting and balancing customers' accounts,
                        preparing statements, aging accounts receivable

                        Reason for leaving: Seeking more responsibility

                        Starting salary: $85   **Present salary: $140**

January 1973 to   Phil's Army and Navy Store, Weston--Stock clerk
July 1975   (Saturdays and evenings; full time during summer)

                        Duties: Organization of stock, selling during rush
                        periods.

Summers, 1972 and   Self-employed--farm work and lawn tending
1971

September 1968 to   Weston Daily News--newspaper route
January 1970

EDUCATION   **Graduate, 1975, of Weston High School**

                        Major Subjects: Bookkeeping (strong B average with
                                         A's in modern date processing)
                                         Office Machines (calculators, adding
                                         machines)
                                         Business Mathematics (A's and B's)
                                         Business Management

                        Extracurricular: **Treasurer of junior class**
                                         Business manager of yearbook
                                         President 1974-1975, Future Businessmen's Club
                                         Member, Debating Society

                        Honors: **Outstanding Business Student Award,**
                                         1974-1975

REFERENCES (with permission)

Miss Marilyn Hamm, Head Bookkeeper   **Mr. Philip Kaplan, Owner**
Terhune's Department Store   **Phil's Army and Navy Store**
67 Alton Street, Weston, Ontario   **342 Cranton Avenue, Weston, Ontario**
M9P 3B7   **M9P 1V1**
(Telephone 244-3967)   **(Telephone 244-7263)**

                   Mr. Joseph Lennon, Advisor, FBLA Club
                   Weston High School
                   890 Fleming Road, Weston, Ontario
                   M9M 2R2
                   (Telephone 244-8683)

Qualifications summary—also called a data sheet, résumé, or personal record—presents
the writer's job qualifications in an attractive, easy-to-read form.

details, such as height, weight, date of birth, etc., on the application blank that the company will ask you to complete. Some applicants attach a small photo at the top of the qualifications summary, but this is not required.

Job Applied For   The employer wants to know, first of all, the specific job for which you are applying. It is best to find out in advance whether there is a vacancy in the company to which you are applying and to specify that position by its correct title, such as "Secretary to the Assistant Credit Manager." If you don't know the specific job title, it is satisfactory to write "Bookkeeper," "Sales Trainee," "Receptionist," etc.

Education   For most high school students, the Education section of the qualifications summary will be the most important, since work experience will at this point be limited. Therefore, give specific details about your training that qualify you for the position. Study the information presented in the qualifications summary illustrated. Note that the courses emphasized are those that have particular bearing on the position being applied for. Note also that special skills and interests are described. Be sure, on your qualifications summary, to list any honors you have received in school, even though they may not appear to be of great significance to you. Employers *are* interested.

Some people who take part in out-of-school activities mention their hobbies as indications of their broad interests. This is a good idea, especially if these hobbies give the prospective employer a clue to your personality and talents. For example, the hobby of working on cars will impress the manager of an automobile agency or an auto parts store. The hobby of reading will be of interest to a newspaper publisher. If art is your main hobby, this talent will appeal to a large number of employers.

Experience   If you are a recent high school graduate, the employer will not expect you to have had a lot of experience that is related directly to the job for which you are applying. He understands that you have been in school and have used most of your summers for vacation. Nevertheless, any paid work experience, regardless of its nature, will impress an employer, because the mere fact that you have worked reveals that you have some initiative. Therefore, be sure to mention such experience as temporary or part-time after-school, Saturday, or Christmas vacation work. Even volunteer typing or clerical work for a teacher, church, or community agency should be listed.

Include the following facts about your experience:

1. Name and address of your employer (the telephone number is also helpful).

2. Type of work you performed. Give not only the title of the position but also a brief description of the work.

3. Dates of employment. Employers usually prefer that you start your employment listing with your latest employment and work back to the first job. In listing experience by dates, leave no time gaps unaccounted for. For example:

January 1973—September 1973	Did not work during this period; I remained at home.

or

August 1974—July 1975	During this period I was a part-time student at the Franklin Music School. I was not employed.

If you have held one or more full-time positions prior to making the application, state why you left the position and give the starting and ending salaries received. For example: "I left this position because of illness in the family and because I was needed at home. My starting salary was $82.50 a week; when I left, I was receiving $90 a week."

References You will be expected to list the names of people whom the employer can contact for information about you. Common courtesy requires that you obtain permission before using a person's name for reference. The letter requesting such permission is discussed in the next unit. Ordinarily, only three or four names need be listed; but others should be available to attest to your experience, education, and character. If possible, select your references according to the job for which you are applying. And let the reference know what kind of position you are applying for so that he will be guided in his reply. If you are applying for a position as bookkeeper, for example, a reference from someone in that type of work would be more appropriate than one from your family doctor. When you ask someone to write a letter of recommendation, enclose a stamped envelope addressed to the prospective employer.

The following information should be given about each reference:

1. Full name, correctly spelled
2. Title—such as *Mr., Mrs., Dr.*
3. Name of business and address
4. Title of his position
5. Telephone number

Filling Out Employment Applications

Most business firms like to have a standardized record for each employee. You will probably be asked to fill out the company's application form either before or after you have been hired. Frequently, the personnel interviewer uses the application form as he interviews you. Since he is familiar with this form, he can quickly select from it items about which he may question you. Too, the application form provides a great deal of information about the applicant other than the answers to the questions asked—information regarding the legibility of his penmanship, his accuracy and carefulness, his neatness, and his ability to follow written directions.

Here are some suggestions to follow in filling out application forms:

1. Bring with you:
   a. A good quality pen. Most pens provided for public use are not dependable. And a scratchy or an ink-blotched application form will reflect on your neatness.

PERSONNEL DEPARTMENT

McGraw-Hill Ryerson Limited

EMPLOYMENT
APPLICATION

Date _July 10, 19—_

Personal Data

Applying For Position As _Secretary_ ___ Salary desired _$135-$140_ ___ Date available _Immediately_

Name: _Colborne_ _____ _Julia_ _____ _Ellen_ ___ ☐ Male ☒ Female
   (Last)   (First)   (Middle)

Present Address _7 Maple Place Kingston, Ontario K7K 5A8_ _18 years_
   (Street)   (City)   (Province)   (How long at this address)

Permanent Address _same as above_
   (Street)   (City)   (Province)   (How long at this address)

Telephone Number _613_ _555-7040_ ___ Social Insurance No. _706-772-266_
   (Area Code)

Age _18_ ___ Birth Date _June_

Employment Data   Begin with most recent employer

Employed From   Mo-Yr   To   Mo-Yr

Company Name _Fletcher's Department Store_ ___ Salary or Earnings Start _$85_ Finish _$105_

Address _88 Mayflower Street, Kingston, Ont._ ___ Your Title _Clerk-Typist_ _1976_ _File-Clerk_ _1975_

Name and Title of Immediate Supervisor _Mr. Richard Meyer, Office Manager_

Description of Duties
1976 steno pool; typed correspondence, orders, reports, and releases; clerical work included compiling receipt totals. Some telephone work.
1975 Filed correspondence; clerical work as in summer of 1976, some typing.

Reasons For Terminating or considering a change _Return to school._

Employed From   Mo-Yr   To   Mo-Yr
Salary or Earnings Start ___ Finish

Company Name ___ Your Title

Educational Data

SCHOOLS	NAME AND ADDRESS OF INSTITUTION	DATES	GRADUATED?	DEGREE RECEIVED	SUBJECT OF SPECIALIZATION
HIGH SCHOOL	_Kingston Secondary School Kingston, Ontario_	From _Sept 73_ To _June 77_	_Yes_		_Commercial Curriculum_
COLLEGE		From ___ To			
GRADUATE SCHOOL		From ___ To			
TRADE, BUS. NIGHT OR CORRES.		From ___ To			

Parts of an employment application, indicating kinds of information requested.

_b._ Two or more copies of your qualifications summary, one or more for the interviewer and one to use in filling out details on the application blank.

_c._ Your Social Insurance Number, if you have previously worked.

2. Avoid asking unnecessary questions. Become familiar with the type of questions usually asked on an application form.

3. Write legibly. Your handwriting does not need to be fancy, but it must be legible. You should take particular care that any figures you write are clear. If the interviewer has difficulty reading your writing, you will start your interview with one strike against you—if you get as far as an interview!

4. Be accurate and careful. Recheck all the information you have included. Have you given your year of birth where it is asked for, and not this year's date? Is your telephone number correct? Be careful to avoid any readily discernible evidences of carelessness.

5. Don't leave any blanks. If the information asked for does not apply to you, draw a line through that space or mark it, "Does not apply." Otherwise, the interviewer may think you were careless and did not see some of the items.

6. Follow directions exactly. An applicant who cannot follow written directions that he has the opportunity to reread certainly will not be able to follow the many oral instructions given on the job once and not repeated. If the directions say to print, then do so. If the directions call for last name first, don't put your first name first. If you are asked to start your employment record with your last job, then don't list your jobs in chronological order.

Communication Problems

Application Exercises

A ■

Make a list of all the sources of job listings in your community, such as employment agencies (government and commercial), school placement office, etc.

B ■

Prepare a qualifications summary for yourself. Assume that you will graduate from your present course in a few weeks.

C ■

Obtain application forms from two local business concerns. Fill them out just as you would if you were going to apply. Be prepared to discuss these application forms in class.

Word Study

A ■

Words often confused: born, borne; coarse, course.

B ■

What are the adjective forms of these verbs?

1	permit	**3**	benefit	**5**	indulge
2	admire	**4**	extend	**6**	transfer

C ■

Should *ant* or *ent* be added to the following to form the correctly spelled words?

1	defend___	**3**	superintend___	**5**	depend___
2	persist___	**4**	excell___	**6**	descend___

Communication in Action: *Placing a Printing Order*

As chairman of the program committee, you are to have tickets printed for the annual employee dance. Use your own ideas about time, place, and cost. For the ticket, prepare a dummy copy that will give the printer an idea of what you want. Then, make a list of the things you will want to find out before the job is actually assigned to a printer.

UNIT □ 53

Writing Employment Letters

At some time in your career, it is highly likely that you will have occasion to write one or more of the following types of employment letters:

1. A letter of application. This letter may be written in response to a newspaper advertisement; at the suggestion of a relative, friend, teacher, or business acquaintance; or at your own instigation, even though you do not know of a specific job opening in the business to which you write.

2. Letters to various persons asking permission to use their names as reference.

3. A follow-up letter to thank an employment interviewer for the time he gave you and to reemphasize some of your qualifications that particularly fit you for the job.

4. A letter accepting a position.

5. A letter refusing a position.

6. A thank-you letter to each person who helped you in your job-seeking campaign.

7. A letter resigning from a position.

The Letter of Application

A letter of application can get into an executive's office even when it may not be possible for you to do so; thus, it is your personal representative. If the letter is well written, the employer will be interested enough in you to say, "This applicant seems to have promise. I would like to talk with him in person." If the letter is poorly written, the prospective employer will toss it aside without expressing any desire to see the writer in person. Thus, the employer looks upon the application letter as a screening device. Those who write good letters get through the screen; those who don't are left outside. The application letter, then, is important enough to warrant careful thought and planning.

Appearance   The appearance of the application letter gives the employer a clue to the personality and work habits of the writer. A sloppy letter suggests that the writer may not be careful about his own appearance or about his work habits—and this is not the kind of impression you want your letter to make.

The writer of an application letter wants the prospective employer to be favorably impressed and to grant an interview. The physical appearance of the letter can do much to help create this favorable impression. Follow these instructions, therefore, in preparing your letter:

1. Use a good grade of standard bond paper (white). Be certain that it is clean and free from smudges and finger marks both before and after you write your letter.

2. Type your letter of application unless you have been specifically requested to submit an application in your handwriting or unless it is impossible to use a typewriter. If you write your letter by hand, recopy it until you have the best specimen of your handwriting. Here are some suggestions to follow when typing your letter or writing by hand:

When Typing	*When Writing by Hand*
a. Make no strikeovers.	a. Avoid ink smudges.
b. Make very neat erasures. If an erasure can be detected easily, retype the letter.	b. Keep your lines of writing straight. Put a sheet of ruled paper under your stationery sheet.
c. Use a black ribbon that is not so worn that the type is too light or so new that the type is too dark and smudgy.	c. Write slowly and carefully so that each word is readable.
d. Balance your letter neatly on the page, allowing plenty of white space in the margins (at least 3.5 cm all around).	d. See item *d* under *When typing*.

3. Address your letter to a specific person in the organization if it is possible to obtain his or her name.

4. Don't expect to get your letter exactly right the first time. Be willing to rewrite it until it represents you in the best possible light.

5. Never copy an application letter out of a book. Let your letter express your own personality.

Organizing the Letter An application letter is usually accompanied by a qualifications summary such as the one illustrated on page 441. In this case, it is neither necessary nor desirable to describe fully your education and experience; this is the job of the qualifications summary. The letter's main purpose is to transmit the qualifications summary and to supplement it with a personal sales message.

Of course, if you do not send a qualifications summary with your letter of application, then you must include more details about yourself in the letter. (One reason why the qualifications summary is so effective is that no one likes to read a long, rambling letter of application!)

The principal elements of an application letter include:

1. A statement expressing interest in a particular position

2. A statement indicating that a detailed qualifications summary is enclosed and pointing out some of your special qualifications for this particular position. You also may indicate why you wish to be employed by this particular organization.

3. A statement telling where and how you can be reached to make arrangements for a personal interview

These elements need not follow any plan but should be varied to fit the situation.

Beginning the Letter The amount of ''selling'' done in the letter of application depends on how much you want the job and how much competition there is for it. If you know you have a good chance to get the job without special effort, then there is no point in making the letter sound like a sales message. If, however, the job is a once-in-a-lifetime proposition and you know you'll have to compete for it, then you'll probably have to ''pull out the stops.'' In this case, you may want to begin your letter by a challenging question. Following are four beginnings of this type. Caution: Be sure you can meet the challenge!

1. Do you need a salesman who is conscientious, hard-working, and ambitious, who is interested most of all in selling advertising space, who has sold successfully while still in school, who wants to make a career with your organization? If your answer to these questions is ''Yes,'' I believe I can prove to you that I am your man.

2. Can your machine transcribers produce 40 letters a day—letters that any executive would be proud to sign? I can—and I can prove this ability.

3. Is there a place in your organization for a young man who is thoroughly trained in bookkeeping and who is eager to work in data processing?

4. Can you use a secretary in whom you can have complete confidence—in everything from taking your dictation to writing your routine letters?

Another good beginning for an application letter that sells is a summary state-ment of your special qualifications. This type of beginning gives the prospective employer an immediate indication of your ability and training; and, if these qualifi-cations seem to be what he is looking for, he will read further. Here are some examples.

1. My three years of successful employment in the credit department of a large retail store, plus excellent training in writing letters, should qualify me for the position of credit correspondent in your company.

2. A thorough course in secretarial training at the Kingsport High School has provided me with the skills and knowledge probably required in the secretarial position adver-tised in the Evening Register on May 18.

3. My recent experience as a receptionist for the National Carbon Company has given me an excellent background for the receptionist position available in your Stationery Division.

When you have been told about a vacancy by another person—an employee of the organization or a friend of the person to whom you are writing or a teacher or guidance counselor—it is often effective to use that person's name (with his permis-sion) in your opening paragraph. For example:

1. Mr. James Alden, a friend of my father, has told me that you need a secretary. I have had four years of experience as a private secretary and believe I have the qualifica-tions you require.

2. Miss Irene Lawrence, who is employed in your advertising department, indicated that you are looking for an advertising assistant. Would my two years of experience as a copywriter and layout specialist be of interest to you?

3. My business teacher, Mrs. Katherine Lovell, has talked with me about the excellent opportunities in your accounting department. I should like to be considered for the position of junior accountant.

Developing the Body of the Letter   In the body of the letter, you should offer support for the statements made in the opening paragraph. Emphasize the highlights of your educational background and business experience, making reference to the enclosed qualifications summary. You may also indicate why you would like to be employed by the firm to which you are applying. Following this suggested plan, the second paragraph of your application letter might read like one of the following:

1. I can take dictation at 120 words a minute, operate a switchboard, answer routine letters, and type accurately and rapidly. I have also had training in modern filing pro-cedures. For the past two years I have had an opportunity to become familiar with these business activities in the offices of Bryant and Lane, Limited.

2. As you will see from the enclosed qualifications summary, my training and experience have equipped me to fill the position of assistant to the art director in your firm. I have always been interested in advertising, and I am particularly eager to work for an outstanding textile manufacturer.

Concluding the Letter A good conclusion in any letter tells the reader what you wish him to do. In a letter of application, you would like the reader to grant a personal interview. Therefore, ask for an interview and make your request easy to grant. Here are some suggested ways to accomplish this:

1. May I have an appointment for a personal interview? You may telephone me at 825-4878.
2. I need only a few minutes to tell you why I believe I am the man you need to fill your vacancy. May I have an interview? Just jot down a convenient day and hour on the enclosed return postal card.

If the prospective employer is located some distance away, the applicant may write:

I am planning to be in Westerville on June 9 and 10. May I see you on either of those days?

Sample Letters The following letter of application for a position as stenographer was written by a high school student with limited business experience.

Letter 1

3207 Shelley Street
Victoria, B.C. V8P 4A5
May 16, 19—

Mr. George S. Dickerson
Personnel Director
Atlas Manufacturing Company
748 Market Street
Victoria, B.C. V8T 2E4

Dear Mr. Dickerson:

Mr. Lawrence, who is in charge of placement at Larkin High School, has told me that there is an opening in your organization for a competent stenographer. If I may have a few minutes of your time, I should like to tell you why I think I can satisfactorily fill that opening.

You will notice on the enclosed qualifications summary that I have had two years of shorthand dictation and transcription training at Larkin High School and have achieved a high standard of speed in both shorthand and typewriting. While in school, I worked part time in the principal's office, where I took dictation, typed, filed, and performed the duties of a receptionist. Last summer, I worked full time as a vacation replacement stenographer at the Bridgeford Lumber Sales Ltd. I enjoyed my work as a stenographer and am confident that I can adequately fill your vacancy.

I can be ready to start work on June 19.

You may reach me at 742-8906 any day after 3:30 p.m. I hope that I may have the privilege of a personal interview at your convenience.

Sincerely yours,

Letter 2 was written by a young man applying for a bookkeeping position.

Letter 2

21 Shelby Drive
Kentville, Nova Scotia
B4N 3S1

Box 176
The Herald
Kentville, Nova Scotia
B4N 3W4

Gentlemen:

Two years of high school bookkeeping, followed by a year of accounting in the evening school program at Middletown Business School, have given me a thorough preparation in all phases of bookkeeping work.

I am presently employed as an accounts receivable clerk, but I should like to find a position where I can make wider use of my bookkeeping training and where I shall have an opportunity to get into a more advanced phase of accounting. I plan to continue my accounting training through an evening school program.

The enclosed qualifications summary provides the details of my education and experience and suggests a number of people from whom you may obtain information about my character and ability.

May I have a personal interview? I may be reached by telephone at 971-6967, Ext. 413, from 9 a.m. to 5 p.m. or at 262-8734 after 6 p.m.

Sincerely yours,

Requesting References

Almost every prospective employer likes to have information regarding the character, training, experience, and work habits of job applicants. You may need to supply only the name, title, and address of references, leaving to the interested prospective employer the task of obtaining the references he desires. Under some circumstances, you may request that the person speaking on your behalf write a letter of reference directly to the prospective employer. (In most cases, a letter of reference that you carry with you is not too effective.)

Before using a person's name as a reference, you should request his permission to do so. This permission may be obtained in person, by telephone, or by a letter such as the following:

Dear Mrs. Hudson:

I am applying for the position of assistant records supervisor that is now open at the Burndy Corporation in Bridgeton.

Since I was a student in your Office Practice class, where I had excellent filing instruction, I should like permission to use your name as a reference.

I am enclosing a return postal card for your reply.

Sincerely yours,

If you are writing to request that a reference be sent directly to a prospective employer, you may say:

> Dear Mr. Martin:
>
> I am applying for a bookkeeping position with Cooper Wire Ltd.
>
> You will remember that I worked part time for you at the Simcoe Lock Co. Ltd. Would you be willing to send a letter of reference for me to Mr. W. L. Watkins, Personnel Director at the Cooper Wire Ltd? I am enclosing an addressed, stamped envelope for your convenience.
>
> Sincerely yours,

Follow-Up Letters

The Interview Follow-Up   If your application letter has succeeded in obtaining a personal interview for you, the next letter you should write will follow the personal interview. This letter may serve one or more of the following purposes:

1. To thank the interviewer for the time and courtesy extended to you
2. To let the interviewer know you are still interested in the position
3. To remind the interviewer of the special qualifications you have for this position
4. To return the application form that the interviewer may have given you to take home to complete
5. To provide any additional data requested by the interviewer that you may not have had available at the time of the interview

Here is a letter that accomplishes all five purposes:

> Dear Mr. Mason:
>
> Thank you for talking with me yesterday about the vacancy in your credit department. You gave me a very good picture of what would be expected of anyone who fills this position.
>
> I am very much interested in the job you have available and feel that my experience with the Lyons Automobile Company during the past two years would prove a definite asset in fulfilling the duties.
>
> The completed application form you requested is enclosed. A transcript of my school grades is being sent to you by the principal of the high school I attended.
>
> I hope that you will consider my application favorably. Please let me know if I may provide you with any additional information. Thank you again for your courtesy.
>
> Sincerely yours,

The Letter of Acceptance   If you are notified by mail that you are being offered the position for which you applied, you should write a letter of acceptance. This letter does the following:

1. Acknowledges the offer
2. Notifies your employer-to-be of your acceptance
3. Reassures the employer that he has chosen the right person
4. Informs the employer when you can report for work

The letter of acceptance may read:

Dear Mr. Wilton:

Thank you for your letter of June 19 offering me a stenographic position in your bank.

I accept! You can be sure that I will do my best to be an effective worker.

Our graduation activities end on Friday, June 26. Thus, with your permission, I'll report to your office on Monday, June 29, at 8:30 a.m., ready to begin.

Again, thank you, Mr. Wilton, for your confidence in me. I'll do my best to be worthy of it.

Sincerely yours,

The Letter of Refusal   Perhaps you have been offered a position for which you made application, but you have also received another offer that you feel is better. You should return the courtesy extended to you by writing a tactful, friendly letter of refusal. This letter may read:

Dear Mr. Wilton:

Thank you for offering me the position of junior stenographer at Metro Finance. It would have been pleasant working with you and the other fine people there.

Just two days before receiving your offer, though, I accepted another job.

I appreciate the time and effort you and your people spent in considering me.

Sincerely yours,

Thank-You Letters   The persons who have written reference letters for you undoubtedly helped you obtain a position. You should be courteous enough to let them know that you have accepted the position. You might write:

Dear Miss Axelrod:

Thank you for the recommendation you sent to the Mason Building Corporation.

You will be pleased to know that I did get the job as secretary to Mr. George P. Felter, advertising manager.

Until I see you in person to express my gratitude, let me assure you that I do appreciate your help.

Sincerely yours,

The Letter of Resignation

Occasionally, you may need to write a letter resigning from a position. (Of course, you should discuss your resignation with your supervisor before writing a letter.) Regardless of your reason for resigning, your letter should be friendly in tone and tactful. Some day you may want this employer to give you a reference, and you want him to remember you favorably. The following letter is a good example of a letter of resignation.

Dear Mr. Norvell:

In order to accept a position with the Mackin Insurance Company, I wish to resign from my present position, effective June 30.

I have enjoyed my work at the Industrial Life Insurance Company; but in the new position, I shall have more opportunity to use my stenographic training. In addition, there appear to be more opportunities for advancement.

Thank you for the many kindnesses that have made my work here for the past two years such a pleasant and worthwhile experience.

Sincerely yours,

Communication Problems

Application Exercises

A ■

The following advertisements appeared in yesterday's edition of your local newspaper. Write a letter of application answering one of these advertisements.

BOOKKEEPER for Consolidated Printing Ltd. High school graduate, some experience. Apply to Mr. D. C. McComb.	SECRETARY, General Insurance Company. Good dictation and typing skills. Write routine letters. Must be accurate and fast. Apply to Personnel Director.	CLERK for Rockport Manufacturing Ltd. Some typing, filing, and ability to work with numbers. Apply to Supervisor of Personnel, James Davis.

B ■

Write a letter to one of your business teachers requesting permission to use his or her name as a reference.

C ■

You have had a personal interview for one of the jobs in Exercise A. Write a follow-up letter to the person who interviewed you.

D ■

You receive a letter notifying you that you have been selected to fill the vacancy for which you applied. Write a letter accepting the position.

E ■

Suppose you preferred to accept another position; write a letter refusing the position offered to you in Exercise D.

F ■

Write a letter to the business teacher who wrote a letter of reference for you, notifying the teacher that you have accepted a position.

G ■

You have been employed in the office of Redding Supply for the past eighteen months. A friend in the Metropolitan Construction Company Ltd. has told you of a vacancy there, and you have been offered the position. It pays more than you are now receiving; the opportunities for advancement seem better; and the firm is more convenient to your home. You decide to leave your present job. Assume that you have discussed this new job with your present supervisor, and he asks you to put your resignation in writing. Write the letter.

Word Study

A ■

Words often confused: decent, descent, dissent; imitate, intimate.

B ■

In each of these sentences select from the words within parentheses the one that conveys the meaning correctly.

1 Under a city (ordnance, ordinance) Christmas trees in public places may not be lighted.
2 The speaker's veiled (illusion, allusion, delusion) to "the enemies within" was understood by all.
3 The (areas, arrears, arias) of the two plots are nearly the same.
4 I have promised to make a (canvas, canvass) for new members for our Glee Club.
5 Why is Texas called the "(Loan, Lone) Star State"?

C ■

Only one letter is missing from each of the following. Spell the words correctly.

1	acordance	3	recurence	5	promisory
2	anser	4	inteligent	6	conscientous

Communication in Action: Innocent Bystander

You are a salesperson in the floor-covering section of a large store. Your telephone rings, and it is a customer asking about rug-cleaning fluid. This item is not carried in your department but in the housewares section. When you tell the caller that you will transfer his call, he says, "This makes the third time I have been given the run-around—everyone transfers me to someone else. Don't you people know what you're doing down there?" What would you say?

UNIT □ 54

Public Relations Letters

There is no doubt that effectively written sales letters help to stimulate business—if they didn't, they would not be so widely used. However, the letter that tries to convince the reader to buy is not the only kind of letter that helps to make sales. In addition to the kind of sales letter described in Unit 51, the alert businessman uses letters to build public relations—and good public relations ultimately create sales.

The term *public relations* is a difficult one to define. In essence, it means that the customer feels that the firm is more interested in a satisfied customer than it is in just making a sale. A business that has conveyed this feeling to its customers does not have to worry about sales. Public relations letters, then, are letters written to show the firm's concern for the customer.

Characteristics of Public Relations Letters

Although public relations letters have as an underlying motive the increasing of sales, they do not "push" a product or service. Instead, they are a subtle means of building goodwill. The writer hopes to impress the firm name and its product or service on the mind of the reader so that, when the need arises for this product or service in the future, the customer will think of the writer's firm.

Public relations letters (sometimes called business-promotion letters), then, are a special type of sales letter that sells indirectly. In fact, the chief difference between public relations and sales letters is that public relations letters *seem* to be selling nothing at all. Instead, they are written with an eye to the future; that is, with the thought that, if you treat your customer well today, perhaps he will buy from you sometime in the future.

Public relations letters are generally written to accomplish one of the following purposes:

1. To express appreciation to customers for their business ("Thank you for your business during the past year.")

2. To capitalize on some special occasion—a holiday or a birthday, for example ("We should like to wish you and your family a joyous holiday season.")

3. To offer to be of service to the customer ("We have opened a branch bank in your neighborhood, and you will find that doing your banking with us will be even more convenient.")

RIVERSIDE SERVICE CENTER
1180 Riverside Avenue
Williamsport, Pennsylvania

24-Hour Emergency Service
Call 283-2883

4-71-007

This colorful thank-you card, with its service message, cannot fail to build goodwill for the sender.

Courtesy Mobil Oil Corporation

They Express Appreciation   You may not feel that you are accomplishing much when you write to a customer thanking him for his business. However, a courteous "thank you" serves as a gesture of goodwill and paves the way for future business with the customer. Don't you like to feel appreciated? When someone thanks you for something you have done, don't you feel an inner glow of satisfaction? So it is when a firm to whom you have given your business takes the time to thank you for your patronage; you certainly feel more kindly toward that firm. The next time you need their type of product or service, you will be more likely to think of dealing with this firm than with any other.

How do you think the recipient of the following letter might react to it?

Dear Mrs. Briggs:

As another year draws to a close, we feel very grateful for having customers like you.

We want you to know how much we appreciate the business you have given us during the past year. We hope that you have derived much satisfaction from your purchases.

Please remember that we are here to be of service to you. During the coming year we hope to continue serving you.

Cordially yours,

Such a letter as this will not sell a specific item, but it will certainly cement good relations. Notice that the letter is written in a friendly style and does not "push" the reader in any way.

They Capitalize on Special Occasions   A holiday, the beginning of a new season, a birthday or an anniversary, the arrival of new merchandise, a new type of product, a new service, or some other special event—any of these may prompt the writing of a letter to your customers. Of course, in letters of this type, you do not attempt to sell a specific item. However, by making the customer aware of the new service or product—or by calling his attention to some special event—you may be indirectly stimulating his desire to buy. In these letters you are attempting to give the customer the impression of doing him a favor rather than trying to make a sale.

For example, in the following letter you are reminding customers with fur coats that it is time to put their coats in storage to protect them from moth damage.

Dear Mrs. Fitzroy:

Spring is here—so can summer be far behind?

With the approach of warm weather, you should start thinking about the proper care of your furs. You can't afford to forget about them now that the cold weather is over—Mr. Moth would like nothing better, for he is always hungry and furs offer him a delicious meal.

Do you know that we have the largest and most up-to-date fur storage facilities in Saint John? When you store your furs with us, they are certain of receiving deluxe care. Look at what this care includes:

1. Our driver will pick up your furs at your home and bring them to us in our specially treated storage truck. Your furs are protected even while in transit!

2. When the furs arrive at their summer home, the pockets and sleeve cuffs will be carefully brushed to remove any possible source of moth damage.

3. Your furs will then be expertly cleaned and refreshed—made to look like new!

4. Sealed in a plastic jacket, your furs will be placed in our cold—b-r-r—storage vaults to rest until you need them again.

5. Next fall, when the air starts getting nippy again, we'll telephone you—and, the following day, your furs will be brought back home again.

Worry-free protection of your furs is yours when you use Garner's Fur Storage Service. Don't let Mr. Moth dine on your furs.

Very sincerely yours,

Opportunities for building goodwill are numerous for the alert businessman. For example, if a personal or business acquaintance wins an honor or is elected to office in an organization, a note of congratulations such as the one at the top of page 460 might be sent.

travelation limited

February 20, 19-

Mrs. Kay Vanstone
56 Claywood Road
Willowdale, Ontario
M2N 2R2

Dear Mrs. Vanstone:

Welcome back!

We hope you enjoyed your recent holiday, and that the arrangements
we made for you enhanced your vacation.

Your experiences are of great interest to us, and any comments you
wish to express concerning accommodation, meals, transportation
provided, etc., or any other aspect of your holiday will be very
much appreciated. From these comments we are able to provide our
clients with the best possible service.

Thank you for your patronage; we hope you will consult us for any
future travel plans.

Yours very truly,

TRAVELATION LIMITED

Janet Rogers

JANET ROGERS C.T.C.
Executive Vice President

JR:mc

57 mobile drive toronto ontario M4A 1H5 canada (416) 752-6464

Courtesy Travelation Limited

This public relations letter does not attempt to sell a specific item. It is designed
to reestablish goodwill—and to bring the reader back.

Dear Mr. Ashley:

With a great deal of pleasure, I read in last evening's Times-Herald of your election to the office of president of Rotary.

Please accept my sincere congratulations upon your receiving this honor. Best wishes to you for a most successful term of office.

Sincerely,

A very simple note, but don't you think Mr. Ashley would appreciate such thoughtfulness? Similarly, good wishes might be extended to a new business establishment or to a business that has moved into new quarters. Any special events such as these offer an ideal opportunity for building good relations with your customers.

They Offer to Be of Service   Another important function of the public relations letter is that of offering to be of service to the customer. Whereas the sales letter says, "Buy," this letter says, "Let us be of service to you."

The following letter was written by a department store to let customers know about a new type of charge account for home furnishings. Again, no particular item is being sold—instead, the impression is given that here is something new the store is doing for the convenience of its customers—and it is doing them a favor by telling them about it.

Dear Mr. Jay:

Martin and Richards has added a new service to make it more convenient for you to buy home furnishings on a deferred-payment plan. May we tell you about this new plan?

Whenever you buy home furnishings totaling $50 or more, tell the salesman to open a Home-Furnishings account for you. This will automatically spread your payments over a 12-month period, with each month's payment added to your regular monthly charge account. For example, suppose you purchase new living-room furniture totaling $150. You pay nothing down; but, each month, when you receive your regular monthly statement, you will find a charge for $12.95 to apply on your home-furnishings payment, plus a very small carrying charge. Isn't this an easy way to handle your home-furnishings charges? No separate payments or payment books to worry about. All your payments are included on your regular monthly statement.

The next time you need any home furnishings costing $50 or more, remember to say, "Please open a Home-Furnishings account for me."

Sincerely yours,

When a new family moves into the community, some progressive businesses send a welcome to the new residents and offer to be of service. If the service is not a costly one, an invitation to try the service with no charge or at a reduced cost is not an uncommon gesture. For example, here is a letter written by a dry-cleaning establishment to new residents who move into the community it serves:

Welcome to the Rogers family . . . .

We are delighted to have you as residents of Hazelwood and hope that you enjoy living and working here as much as we do.

We hope that you will give us an opportunity to show you the excellent dry-cleaning, pressing, and laundering service we make available to Hazelwood residents—and at low cost, too! Our courteous drivers will pick up and deliver your clothing, or you may prefer to bring it to either our Market Street or our Randolph Avenue store. Both have convenient drive-in windows, so that you don't even need to get out of your car—and you save 10 percent by using our cash-and-carry service.

We are enclosing an introductory card that entitles you to a 50 percent discount on your first order—no matter how large or how small. Won't you come in to see us and let us give you a personal welcome to Hazelwood?

Sincerely yours,

Communication Problems

Application Exercises

A ■

List as many circumstances as you can under which public relations letters might be written.

B ■

Assume that you are employed by the Industrial Life Insurance Company and that you wish to enlarge your field of operations. You therefore plan to write letters to the parents of each new baby whose birth is announced in the local newspaper. Write an appropriate congratulatory letter that will indirectly sell your insurance.

C ■

One of your customers, Mr. William Gaines, has just been elected to serve on the City Council. Write him an appropriate letter that will help develop good public relations.

D ■

You are employed to handle the correspondence for a local dairy. What is your best source of new customers? Write an indirect sales letter that would be appropriate to send to this source of new customers.

E ■

As manager of the Townsend Automobile Service Company, you wish to call attention to your new "Quick-Wash" automobile washing service. Write an appropriate letter to your customers, announcing this service.

Word Study

A ■

Words often confused: annul, annual; emigrant, immigrant.

B ■

Select from the pronouns within the parentheses the one that is correct in each sentence.

1 I will make my explanations to no one but (he, him).
2 Is Jack as tall as (he, him)?
3 If only the winner could have been (we, us)!
4 There is no doubt as to (who, whom) is to blame.
5 (We, Us) boys have signed up for active service.

C ■

Using standard spellings, respell these clever names that manufacturers have devised for their products.

1	Ry-Krisp Crackers	4	My-T-Fine Pudding Mix
2	Spic and Span Cleanser	5	Pepomint Lifesavers
3	Cut-Rite Waxed Paper	6	Sunkist Oranges

Communication in Action: Planned Absence

Today at the office you learn that you cannot come to work tomorrow. You have a very good reason. Which of the following would you use in dealing with your supervisor: (*a*) Telephone him tomorrow? (*b*) Tell him today? (*c*) Just forget it on the theory that he will not find out? (*d*) Ask your co-workers to tell him in the morning? (*e*) Some other way? Discuss.

UNIT □ 55

Social–Business Letters

Many people feel that business is impersonal and that one's business life should be kept separate from one's social life. To do so would be nearly impossible. In fact, success in business depends to a great extent upon the depth of good feeling that exists between a business and its customers, vendors, associates, and even competitors.

Why Social-Business Correspondence?

Some of the people with whom you do business become personal friends; a great many of them become known to you on more than a strictly formal business basis.

Sympathy card for me—from your secretary.

The business executive receives invitations from his business associates outside the company to attend social functions; sometimes he receives favors or gifts from close business friends. From time to time, a business person whom he knows receives a promotion or a special honor. Or a business acquaintance may be struck by a personal tragedy—serious illness, an operation, or a death in the family. These situations call for letters to be written and provide opportunities for building friendly relations.

Social-business letters are just as appropriate as letters to your weekend host or to personal friends who have been especially thoughtful. The businessman who takes the time to write social-business letters will be remembered, and such letters will reflect personal credit on him. They will undoubtedly build goodwill for his company, even though this is not the underlying purpose of social-business letters.

You already know that all special favors should be acknowledged by a personal letter. If a friend invites you to spend a weekend, you will write a thank-you note upon returning home. When someone presents you with a gift for your birthday, Christmas, graduation, or some other special occasion, you always write a letter of appreciation. Likewise, acts of kindness while you are hospitalized or during periods of personal grief should always be acknowledged by letter. If someone helps you obtain a job, secures hard-to-get concert theatre tickets, or goes out of his way to be thoughtful, a letter of appreciation should be written. In business, the same courtesies should be shown.

Kinds of Social-Business Letters

Many executives who every day write effective business letters dealing with business matters find it difficult to compose social-business letters. As a junior correspondent, you may be asked to write some of these social-business letters. Here is an excellent opportunity to reveal your abilities.

Letters Expressing Thanks   A businessman who receives a gift or is granted a special favor should acknowledge the gift or favor and express his appreciation. The following are examples of thank-you letters of a type frequently written by business executives and employees. Note especially in the first example the position of the inside address. Frequently in social-business letters, the inside address is placed at the foot of the letter. Each letter illustrates a different style that may be used in writing social letters for personal or business use.

For a Gift

Dear Ralph:

I was delighted to receive the Old World maps you so thoughtfully sent to me. They are going to be framed for my office, and they will look mighty handsome with our new mahogany paneling.

Thank you very much. Perhaps the next time you visit us, you can see to what good use I am putting your most thoughtful gift.

Sincerely yours,

Mr. Ralph Jensen
Dexter Publishing Company
Don Mills, Ontario
M3B 2T1

For Favors

RONALD ASTOR

1215 Glendale Avenue   Victoria, B.C. V9A 2S3

June 25, 19—

Mr. Charles P. Randolph
32 Lydia Avenue
Winnipeg, Manitoba
R3A 1K6

Dear Mr. Randolph:

I appreciate so very much your thoughtfulness in getting tickets for Mrs. Astor and me to "Lady Beautiful." We enjoyed this musical show enormously—and the seats were just about perfect.

Thank you for helping to make our visit to Winnipeg a memorable one.

Cordially yours,

44 Ronson Boulevard
Duncan, B.C.
December 26, 19 —

Dear Helen:

Mrs. Fitzroy called last week asking me to show her my complete line of cosmetics. She mentioned that you had recommended me to her.

I feel sure that this opportunity to display my wares to Mrs. Fitzroy represents an enormous potential in sales. It is up to me now to come through — you have certainly done your part and more.

Thank you, Helen! I'll telephone you next week to let you know if I succeed. Perhaps we can arrange to have dinner together.

Sincerely,

Letters of Congratulation   The following are examples of letters of congratulation. These letters are usually written by the person who is to sign them, especially when the writer is a personal friend of the individual whom he is congratulating.

To a Business Acquaintance

Dear Tom,

I was pleased to hear that you have been promoted to Assistant Sales Manager of the Chemical Division of Dustrand Company Ltd. This news came as no surprise to me; I had picked you out long ago as a person who was going places! I am very happy to see your abilities recognized—I know you will do an excellent job in your new position.

Please accept my sincere personal congratulations. And tell Bea that Ann and I rejoice in your good fortune. Doesn't this call for some kind of celebration—on us, of course! How about dinner—the four of us—on the 20th? We can make arrangements when I see you next Monday at the Windjammers Club.

Sincerely,

To an Employee   Whenever a businessman takes the time to recognize a milestone in the career of one of his employees, his thoughtfulness is certain to be rewarded in terms of a more productive employee. How do you think Marcia would react to the following letter from her employer?

Dear Marcia,

In the ten years you have been with Drysdale's you have seen our company grow from a small local factory to a nationwide organization. Responsible for this remarkable growth are highly productive and faithful employees like you. It is a pleasure for me to write this letter of congratulation on your tenth anniversary, for it gives me an opportunity to thank you for your contribution to our success.

As head of our filing department, you have set up a highly flexible and effective system for handling the increasing volume of records. I am sure you have heard the often-repeated statement around the office, "If you don't know, ask Marcia." This is indeed a tribute to your efficiency.

I look forward to working with you in the years ahead. When I think of the slogan, "Drysdale's is people," I can't help calling to mind a picture of Marcia Haskins and all those like her who help to make our organization the congenial, effective group it is today.

Sincerely yours,

Letters of Condolence   Letters of condolence are among the most difficult to write. Such letters should be brief and dignified. Obviously, the writer should not be maudlin or recall too vividly the grief recently suffered. Such letters are nearly always written by the person signing them—rarely by a secretary or an assistant. Some businessmen prefer to send a sympathy card rather than a letter, feeling that cards can convey much more effectively the delicate words of consolation. Following is an example of a letter of condolence:

Dear Mark,

I was saddened to learn of the death of your mother last week. Please accept my sincere sympathy.

When my mother passed away two years ago, a friend sent me a copy of the enclosed poem by Thaddeus Milburn. I have received much consolation from the poetic words, and I thought they might help to comfort you as they did me.

My thoughts are with you and your family in your hour of grief.

Sincerely yours,

For a more personal touch, the letter should be written by hand rather than on the typewriter. However, except in the case of a close, personal friend, a typewritten message is acceptable. When the typewriter is used, the inside address is usually placed at the foot of the letter.

Formal Invitations and Replies   Occasionally, business people receive formal invitations—to an open house, to a special party to honor a distinguished person or a special anniversary, or to a formal social gathering. Such invitations are usually engraved or printed and are written in the third person.

Handwritten invitations are written on plain white note paper. In some instances, invitations are typewritten; but this practice is not recommended. Note both the printed and the handwritten invitations on the page opposite.

The Literary Club
requests the pleasure of your company
at a tea
in honor of
John Whitleaf
on Saturday, May the sixth
at four o'clock
Suite 13 of the Howard Building

Please reply

Formal Invitations

Mr. and Mrs. George Randolph
request the pleasure of the company of
Mr. and Mrs. Lawrence Wentlow
at dinner
on Monday, the fourth of April
at eight o'clock
8106 Keats Road

R.S.V.P.

Mr. William Gregory
accepts with pleasure
the kind invitation of
The Literary Club
to attend a tea on
Saturday, May the sixth
at four o'clock
Suite 13 of the Howard Building

Formal Acceptance

Mr. and Mrs. Lawrence Wentlow
regret that a previous engagement
prevents their accepting
the kind invitation to dinner
at the home of
Mr. and Mrs. George Randolph
on Monday, the fourth of April

Formal Refusal

Replies to formal invitations are often requested, as indicated in the illustrations by *Please reply* or *R. S. V. P.* (an abbreviation of the French *Répondez, s'il vous plaît,* which means "Please answer"). If the invitation is written in the third person, the reply is also written in the third person and follows the wording and arrangement of the invitation. On page 467 are also shown a formal acceptance and a formal refusal of invitations.

The Expert Letter Writer

To be classified as an expert business correspondent, you must be able to write letters that do not deal directly with business transactions. There is a social side to business that calls for the writing of social-business letters, letters that would be written by a thoughtful person in a similar situation in private life. Because these letters are admittedly difficult to write, the junior correspondent who can compose them will be a well-rounded, proficient writer of business letters.

Communication Problems

Application Exercises

A ■

Assume that a friend of your employer, whom you have often gone out of your way to help, sends you a gift at Christmas (you may decide what the gift is) in appreciation of your courtesy to him. Write him a thank-you letter.

B ■

A friend of yours recommended to Mr. Henry Lowell that he consider placing all his printing work with your firm. Write an appropriate letter of appreciation to this friend.

C ■

You read in last night's local newspaper that a business acquaintance received a promotion. Write a letter of congratulation.

D ■

One of your employees was named "Junior Executive of the Year" by the local Junior Chamber of Commerce. Write him a letter that shows how proud your firm is to have the type of employee he represents.

E ■

One of your employees receives a 25-year pin for loyalty to the firm. Write him a letter in honor of this event.

F ■

The father of a good business friend of yours died this week. Write your friend a letter of condolence.

G ■

Prepare a formal invitation to attend an open house in honor of the new offices your firm has opened. This invitation is to be printed and sent to all the firm's customers.

H ■

You have received two formal invitations for dinner on the same evening. You must accept one and refuse the other. Write the appropriate acceptance and refusal.

Word Study

A ■

Words often confused: liable, libel; ingenious, ingenuous.

B ■

Which of the three words following each of these phrases is closest in meaning to the italicized word in the phrase?

1 *Visionary* plans. Successful, tried, fanciful.
2 *Perceptible* change. Great, appreciable, invisible.
3 A *pretentious* wardrobe. Showy, unnecessary, well-selected.
4 An *unbiased* opinion. Unfair, impartial, inconsistent.
5 An *inimitable* style of writing. Tiresome, commonplace, matchless.

C ■

Where are apostrophes needed in the following sentences?

1 If youll play the violin, shell sing a solo.
2 Theyre all wearing their galoshes. Where are yours?
3 Its time for the baby to have its nap.
4 We require a two weeks notice on all orders.
5 Whose brief case is this?

Communication in Action: *Listening*

Your instructor will read a short article. Listen carefully, trying to absorb every important detail. Be prepared to give an accurate oral summary of the article.

PART □ 10

Memorandums,
Reports,
and Other Written
Communications □

Letters are not the only means of transmitting written messages in business. In the following three units, you will learn how to prepare a multitude of other types of written communications. As you study the material in this section of your textbook and as you do your writing practice, keep in mind the fact that principles of effective writing apply to *all* writing, regardless of the form of the communication. Be assured that the knowledge and skill you acquire as a result of your work in Part 10 will contribute markedly to your overall writing effectiveness.

Writing
Memorandums

The main difference between a memorandum and a letter is that the memorandum is written to a person in one's own company, while a letter is written to someone outside the company. Memorandums are used to communicate with other employees, regardless of where the employees may be located—whether in the same building or in a branch office hundreds of miles away.

Because the interoffice memorandum form was developed to save time, the formality of an inside address, salutation, and complimentary closing is omitted. In other respects, however, office memorandums and letters have a great deal in common, as you will see from the following discussion.

The Tone of Memorandums

In most companies, memorandums are written in first person, just as business letters are. There is no hard-and-fast rule about tone in memorandums, however. The manner in which they are written will depend upon the preferences of the management in the company by which you are employed. Those who maintain that interoffice correspondence should be formal believe that information will be presented more accurately and read more objectively if "I" and "we" are kept out of the message. They believe that, in a memo written in first person, it is easy to confuse fact with opinion.

In these companies, where business relationships are quite formal and the executives are not on a first-name basis, memorandums are likely to be written in the third person, thus:

"It is believed that . . ." (instead of "I believe")
"It will be seen that . . ." (instead of "You can readily see that")
"It is recommended that . . ." (instead of "I recommend")
"The requested report has been completed . . ." (instead of "I have completed the report you asked for")

However, the trend is decidedly away from the stiff, formal writing style that characterized business letters and memorandums several years ago.

The tone of the memorandum is influenced also by the position held by the writer in relation to that held by the person to whom he is writing. Obviously, a person writing to the company president is less likely to be casual and breezy than if he were writing to an equal in rank. However, the personality of the individual receiving the memorandum is what actually determines its tone. The president may like informality, for example, whereas a minor executive might insist on complete objectivity and an impersonal writing style.

Writing the Memorandum

There are usually three main parts to a memorandum:

1. The heading
2. The subject
3. The message

The Heading   The heading of a memorandum is usually printed. Here is one example.

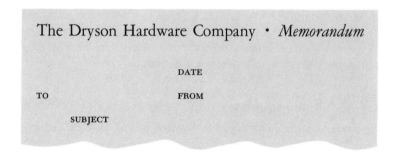

In the TO and FROM sections, the business title of each of the persons is often included, particularly when the memorandum is being sent to a person whose office is in another city. Note that in the FROM section the writer does not use Mr., Dr., or a similar title of respect.

TO: Mr. Gordon Kessler, Office Manager
FROM: Ralph Sisson, Treasurer

The Subject   The subject, a brief statement telling what the memorandum is about, helps the reader to prepare himself for the contents. For example, the subject may read:

SUBJECT: Changes in the Personnel Requisition Form

The Message   The message is usually in three parts. The first part tells the reader why the memorandum is written. This may include telling the reader what you are going to do and how. The second part conveys the information—the details—telling the reader what you said you were going to tell him, in the manner you indicated. Finally, the memorandum gives suggestions for future action or requests guidance on future action. Note how these parts stand out in the memorandum illustrated on the next page.

Note that a title precedes addressee's name, but not writer's

BULMER LTD. *memorandum*

April 27, 19—

TO: Mr. Vernon O. Harris, Advertising Manager

FROM: Milton David

Keep subject brief, specific

SUBJECT: Advertising Space in Office Equipment Magazines in 19—

Why the memorandum is being written

The analysis of advertising space in the four leading trade magazines you asked for in your memorandum of January 16 has now been completed.

Twelve issues (January through December, 19—) of each of the four leading trade magazines in the office equipment field were analyzed. The pages of advertising for each magazine for the entire year were then totaled and averaged.

Information the report is to convey

These averages are as follows:

Office Equipment World	— 32
Today's Office	— 29
Modern Office Equipment	— 26
Office Facts	— 19

Suggested future action

I am attaching the monthly figures from which these averages were obtained. In preparing the report, I also classified the types of advertising—furniture, machines, stationery and forms, and miscellaneous. If these figures would be of interest to you, please let me know. It will take only a short time to put them in tabulated form.

M. D.

When Are Memorandums Written?

Many business firms tell their employees to put in writing all important information that crosses their desks. Written records help to fix responsibility. If you are sending important papers or documents to another person, for example, it is best to transmit them by memorandum so that, if they become lost, there will be no question as to whether or not they were actually sent.

TO: Mr. Leland Warren   DATE: June 4, 19—

FROM: Sarah Freeman

SUBJECT: Safeway Meat Comparison Test

The Safeway Meat Comparison report that you asked to see is enclosed.

Would you please return the report to me when you have finished with it. Incidentally, Mr. Walston has asked that this report not be circulated outside the company.

S. F.

OFFICE MEMORANDUM

ITEM
INCORPORATED

TO   Mr. C. C. Blackwell, Sales Manager   **FROM**   R. J. Keene, Advertising Manager

LOCATION   Room 604, 3d Floor   **LOCATION**   Room 312, 8th Floor

SUBJECT   Monthly Advertising Report   **DATE**   April 3, 19--

Following is the monthly summary of the advertising expenditures for March:

MAGAZINE ADVERTISING

	Space	Cost
Modern Business	$\frac{1}{2}$ page	$375.00
Office Supervision	1 page	200.00
Today's Manager	$\frac{1}{4}$ page	90.00
Equipment Dealer	$\frac{1}{4}$ page	35.00
Total Magazine Advertising		$700.00

CIRCULAR ADVERTISING

	Quantity	Unit	Cost
Circular B (Mfg. List)	3 000	.113	$ 340.00
Circular X (Office Mgr. List)	2 800	.099	278.00
NBI Letter (General List)	6 000	.079	472.00
Total Circular Advertising			$1 090.00

Total Spent During March $1 790.00
(February: $1 782.00)

Of special interest is the new printing rate on the NBI Letter. Although the rates for Circular B and Circular X have increased slightly over last month, we were able to lower the unit rate on the NBI Letter from .098 to .079 because of the new size and format.

Mr. John Kingston of Premier Printing is now getting new cost estimates on Circulars B and X, based on our revised design of these pieces. We are hopeful that we can bring our total costs down to $1 600 and still have more effective circulars.

R. J. Keene

Memorandum displaying statistical matter in easy-to-read tabular form.

The following is an example of a request correctly written in the form of a memorandum.

DATE: May 2, 19—

TO: Mr. Charles L. Coleman, Office Manager

FROM: Patricia Ann Thompson

SUBJECT: Request for Extended Vacation

As you know, I plan to attend my sister's wedding in Halifax in June; and I am taking my two weeks' vacation allowance for the occasion.

After the wedding, I plan to drive my mother to Annapolis Royal, to visit her sister, who is hospitalized. May I extend my vacation two extra days for the purpose of making this trip? My vacation, therefore, would begin on Monday, June 8; and I would return on Wednesday, June 24, instead of Monday, June 22. Naturally, I do not expect salary for these two extra days.

May I have your decision on this request sometime this week so that I may let my family know my plans?

P. A. T.

Displaying Detailed Matter

A memorandum containing a great many details will be easier to read if each point is numbered in 1-2-3 order, each number starting a new paragraph. Enumerations also help the reader to refer by number to specific points when he is replying.

When the memorandum contains statistical matter, the writer should display this material in tabulated form for easier reading. Note the example on the opposite page.

Communication Problems

Application Exercises

A ■
Write a brief memorandum announcing a meeting of one of the clubs to which you belong.

B ■
Write a request to your supervisor asking that your vacation be changed from the two weeks beginning July 5 to the two weeks beginning July 12. Point out that during the week of July 5 you have some personal business that prevents your going away at that time.

C ■
Send a memorandum to your teacher, summarizing a meeting or class discussion in which you recently participated.

D ■
Your office manager would like to set up a standard form for printed memos. Draw up a sample memorandum form and send it to him, together with a memorandum indicating the standards you followed.

E ■
The business teacher asks for a memorandum summarizing the new equipment needed in the business department next fall. Prepare a detailed memorandum.

Word Study

A ■
Words often confused: passed, past; charted, chartered.

B ■

Match each simple definition in column A to the word in column B to which it applies.

A	B
1 To sparkle	a adjacent
2 Quiet	b liberate
3 Situated near	c peculiar
4 To serve as a witness	d glisten
5 To set free	e tranquil
	f deceive
	g polite
	h testify

C ■

What are the superlative forms of the following adjectives and adverbs?

1 early	3 empty	5 many
2 economical	4 good	6 thin

Communication in Action: Formality in the Office

Office custom differs as to the use of first names. Some companies insist that all employees use the title *Miss, Mrs., Ms.,* or *Mr.* when referring or talking to another employee. In other companies, there is no rule. Discuss how a new employee should address his co-workers and his superiors when he starts to work.

UNIT □ 57

Writing Reports

In a small business, the owner or manager can keep in close personal touch with everything that goes on in the firm. When the president or manager of the company wants information, he merely goes to the person who can supply it and asks a question such as: "Jim, how's that new production plan working?"

In most businesses, however, the owner or manager cannot possibly keep in touch personally with all the operations in the firm he heads. Even the various department heads haven't sufficient time to supervise personally all the activities under their direction. Many businesses are so large and complex that a firm may be

scattered throughout a particular section of the country or throughout all of Canada—
in fact, much business activity is now on a worldwide basis. When a businessman
needs information, he must often get it through a written report.

What Is a Business Report?

Essentially, a report is a presentation of facts and/or ideas. The report may
be periodic—that is, submitted at regular intervals—or it may be yearly. A monthly
report from the advertising manager telling the sales manager how much money
was spent on advertising would be a periodic report, as would a weekly report on
absenteeism submitted by each department manager to the general manager. On
the other hand, a report on production in each department as compared with production in the preceding year would have to be made on a yearly basis.

There are many types of reports, serving many purposes. Some reports are
analytical; some are reports of experiments; some give the results of surveys and
investigations; and some tell the owners the progress being made in the business.
Reports may go from employees to management; or they may be made to stockholders, supervisors, employees, or customers.

The memorandum form discussed in Unit 56 may be used for most reports
written in business, even reports as long as five or six pages. Often, however, longer
reports are more formal and a memorandum or *letter of transmittal* may accompany
the report. A letter of transmittal serves several purposes in a formal report:

1. Tells why the report is being made
2. Gives the purpose and scope of the report
3. Acknowledges sources of information and help

Some types of businesses frequently use the longer, more formal report. An
engineering firm, for example, requires greatly detailed reports on huge construction jobs; in fact, several reports may be required on each phase of the job. A company specializing in market analysis (product testing, plant location, advertising
media, and the like) has need for many formal reports—actually, the report is the
end product of its business. Chemical, petroleum, drug, and similar manufacturing
enterprises require formal reports from research and laboratory personnel who are
conducting experiments on new products.

Preparing a Formal Report

The pattern of the formal report varies with the type of business for which it
is prepared. Many companies adopt their own standard pattern for reports. Regardless of form, most longer reports will contain the following basic parts:

1. Introduction
2. Summary
3. Body
4. Conclusions and recommendations

Introduction The introduction includes a background statement as to why the report was written, what its purpose is, how the data were gathered, what the report does *not* include (delimitations), and what materials and equipment were used. Such a background statement is necessary in every report. By knowing the "why" and "how" of a report, the reader is better able to evaluate the findings and the conclusions.

Suppose you have been asked to survey the office equipment in the company by which you are employed. The company management has had numerous complaints from office workers in recent months that the equipment these people must operate is antiquated and inadequate. Management has had conflicting reports from various supervisors and has decided to employ a specialist—that's you—to give them an unbiased report on the true situation. This is how you might introduce your report:

SURVEY OF OFFICE EQUIPMENT AT MELSON'S, LTD.

Purpose

This report has been prepared at the request of J. K. Ronzoni, manager of office services for Melson's, Ltd. The purpose of the report is to determine whether the existing office equipment in the company is adequate to serve growing needs. By "equipment" is meant such office machines as typewriters, adding machines, calculators, duplicating machines, bookkeeping machines, and other data processing equipment. This report does not include a survey of office furniture, such as desks, tables, chairs, and similar items.

How the Report Was Prepared

In gathering data for this report, all department heads were interviewed, as well as every employee who, as his primary responsibility, operates an office machine. These employees include typists, stenographers, bookkeepers, secretaries, duplicating machine operators, computing machine operators, and general office clerks. One full day was spent in each department observing the various operators at work. In each case, the machine was thoroughly examined in terms of the job it is intended to do.

Summary The next part of the formal report is the summary. The summary is a brief presentation of the findings, and it is placed early in the report so that a busy executive will not need to read the entire report to get the gist of it. The summary may be only a paragraph in length or it may be several pages, depending upon the amount of material that has been gathered. Following is a partial summary of the report on the survey of office machines:

Summary

This investigation reveals that a large number of the office machines now used at Melson's, Ltd., are in need of replacement. The following tables summarize the age and condition of the present equipment.

TABLE 1

TYPEWRITERS

Model	Total Machines	Year of Manufacture			Condition		
		Pre-1965	1965-70	1971-74	Good	Fair	Poor
Royal	18	7	7	4	9	3	6
IBM Electric	6	3	3		1	3	2
Olivetti-Underwood	11	7	3	1	4	3	4
Remington	8	6	2		1	4	3
SCM	4		1	3	3	1	

Body   The body of the report is a detailed presentation of the pertinent facts that have been gathered. These facts must be carefully assembled and clearly presented. And the report writer must be sure of the accuracy of the data included. If he needs to check ten times before he is certain that the figures and statements are correct, then he checks ten times. There is no excuse for careless assumptions or errors in a written report; those who read the report depend entirely upon the writer's honesty and accuracy.

Conclusions and Recommendations   Up to this point, a report tells why it was written and what was found. Perhaps this is all that is required, and a statement of the writer's conclusions is not necessary. In some cases, however, if no conclusions are given, the report may have an "up-in-the-air" effect. If the report writer has been asked to include his conclusions and recommendations in the report, this may mean that the executive who asked for the report has faith in the writer's judgment. The writer's conclusions tell the executive what the data gathered mean to the writer and what he thinks should be done about the matter reported on. If conclusions and recommendations are not asked for, the writer must use his best judgment.

The subject matter of the report may not require a conclusion—the report may be a fact-finding one that leaves no room for a personal observation. The nature of the report and the wishes of the person who requested the report will determine whether or not a statement of conclusions is necessary. In any event, conclusions can be drawn only from the data in the report—not from observations that have not been proved by the actual findings included in the body of the report. In the case of the office machines survey, a statement of conclusions and recommendations might begin as follows:

Conclusions and Recommendations

On the basis of this investigation, the facts reveal that our office equipment is generally old and is inadequate for our purposes. If the company is to expand its customer services as planned, more and newer equipment will be needed to do the job. Office personnel are often slowed down by mechanical failures of the equipment they are operating. These operators, for the most part, are skillful, hard-working people; but they cannot produce at their maximum with the present equipment.

The following steps are recommended:

1. That a plan be considered whereby each office machine is replaced on a periodic basis; for example, every five years

2. That the company study the possibility of a service contract with a reputable office machines company to keep all machines in efficient operating condition

3. That a system be installed whereby machine failures are reported more promptly to the supervisor

There might be a dozen or more such recommendations.

Tone of the Formal Report

Most formal reports are written in the third person. The readers of these reports are interested mainly in the data that have been gathered. If personal pronouns, such as *I, you,* and *they* are used, the report may lose some of its objectivity—personalities do sway opinions. As mentioned before, however, there are no basic rules that will apply to all companies.

The good report writer prefers the understatement to the overstatement. For example, in presenting his conclusions and recommendations, he would *not* say:

Obviously, the facts show clearly that we should reorganize the sales promotion department.

Instead, he would say:

On the basis of the findings, consideration of a reorganization of the sales promotion department would seem desirable.

The good report writer would *not* say:

In my opinion, supervisors are not giving adequate time to the training of workers in their departments.

Instead, he would say:

Some of the workers appear to lack adequate training, and the supervisors may find the setting up of special classes for these workers to be a very worthwhile project.

The writer of formal reports must look upon himself as an objective reporter who has no ax to grind. The closer he sticks to the facts and the more objectively he reports them, the more valuable his report will be to those who must make the final decisions.

Mechanics of Report Writing

Expert typing and setting up of a report will increase the forcefulness of the communication by helping the reader to read rapidly and to absorb quickly the main points.

The long, formal report usually consists of the following parts:

1. Cover
2. Title page
3. Letter of transmittal
4. Table of contents
5. Introduction or preface
6. Summary
7. Body of the report
8. Conclusions and recommendations
9. Supplementary material or appendix

Also included may be a bibliography; special supplementary material such as folders, photographs or drawings, charts, maps, and, in rare instances, an index.

Reports should be typed on plain white bond paper, standard size. All reports should be double spaced, and each page after the first should be numbered. A left margin of approximately 15 typewriter spaces should be allowed for binding. Top and bottom margins should be 10 to 12 line-spaces, and the right margin 10 typewriter spaces.

Most long, formal reports require a title page. The following illustrates the title page that might be prepared for the office machines survey report:

SURVEY OF OFFICE EQUIPMENT NEEDS
AT MELSON'S, LTD.

March 12, 19—

Prepared for: J. K. Ronzoni
Manager of Office Services

Prepared by: Wilson Shepherd

Headings The report writer should be generous in the use of headings throughout the report. In typing headings, the following points should be observed:

1. Headings of equal value should be typed alike throughout the report.

2. Headings that indicate principal divisions are usually centred and capitalized. They may also be letterspaced (one blank space between letters within words and three spaces between words) and underscored.

3. Subordinate, or secondary, headings may be written flush with the left margin or indented. They may also be written outside the margin or centred within the body of the report. Whatever style is adopted should be followed consistently throughout the report.

4. Main headings are usually preceded by two line-spaces and followed by one line-space. All other headings are usually preceded and followed by one blank line-space.

5. Unless the heading is in the form of a question, no punctuation should be used after separate-line heads. However, a run-in paragraph heading, i.e., a heading that is not separated from the regular text material, requires a period.

The following headings may be used in a report that contains a number of subdivisions. Headings are listed in order of importance.

<u>TITLE</u>

(Centre on page; type in all capitals; underscore each word.)

MAIN HEADINGS

(Centre on page; type in all capitals.)

<u>Subheadings</u>

(Centre on page; begin each word with a capital letter; underscore entire subheading.)

<u>Marginal Headings</u>

(Type heading on a separate line, beginning at the margin; double space above and below; begin each important word with a capital letter; underscore each word.)

<u>Paragraph Headings</u>. (Start these headings with the usual five-space paragraph indention; begin each important word with a capital letter; underscore each word. A period is placed after the heading and two spaces occur between it and the first word of the paragraph.)

Binding When the report is completed, it may be bound at the side with staples (usually three vertical staples close to the left edge) or fastened at the top with a paper clip. Some reports are placed inside a special folder made for the purpose; others are bound by special backing paper of a heavy stock.

Communication Problems

Application Exercises

A ■

Assume that you have been asked by your office manager to prepare a report on the improvement of the office forms used by your firm. He wants to know what forms are being used, how they are used, who uses them, what forms might be simplified or discontinued, what standard forms are available from firms specializing in the preparation of office forms, what has been the experience of other firms with office forms, and any other information that would be helpful in improving your office forms.

1 Prepare an outline of this proposed report, even though you are not going to gather the information.
2 Describe the procedures you would use in gathering the information and preparing the report.
3 List the sources of information you would use.

B ■

Your supervisor (your instructor) has asked you to investigate the method of handling coffee breaks in five firms in your area. Assume that you have interviewed five employees of different firms. Prepare a report of your findings.

C ■

Type an attractive title page for the report you prepared in Exercise A.

D ■

Your instructor would like a report on the work experience of students in this class. Prepare this report, using a chart to summarize the findings.

Word Study

A ■

Words often confused: suit, suite, sweet; rout, route, root.

B ■

Each of these sentences murders the King's English in some way. Correct the gross errors.

1 Everyone was there except my brother and I.
2 Him and me goes fishing every Sunday.
3 May I have the lend of your fountain pen?
4 I had ought to be going.
5 May I have this here piece of cake?

C ■

In each of these words, the sound of *sh* occurs at the point indicated by the blank spaces. Spell the words.

1	finan___al	3	defi___ent	5	man___on
2	ses___on	4	pa___ence	6	na___on

Communication in Action: *A Delivery Error*

You place an order by telephone to a local stationery store for ten columnar pads of a particular size for use in the accounting department. Two weeks later the delivery-man brings in ten *cartons*, each carton containing a gross of pads. Of course, it is a mistake; but you know the driver is not to blame—his delivery ticket shows ten *cartons*. How would you handle this problem?

UNIT □ 58

Writing Telegrams, Minutes, and News Releases

In addition to letters, memorandums, and reports, there are three other types of written communications that business employees may have occasion to prepare. These are telegrams, minutes of meetings, and news releases. The extent to which each is used often depends upon the type of business and the nature of the business activity.

Communicating by Telegraph

One of the fastest methods of sending a written communication is by telegraphing. When the businessman wishes a message to arrive in the shortest possible time and wishes to have a written record of it, he usually telegraphs. For long distances, a telegram is cheaper than a telephone call. Also, a telegram often can reach a person who cannot be reached by telephone. Perhaps the two most important advantages of telegraph communications are the speed of delivery and the written record they provide.

Another advantage of the telegram is that it attracts attention. People look upon telegrams as urgent and demanding of immediate action. For this reason, telegrams

```
CN                    Telecommunications

send this message subject to the terms on back
dépêche à expédier aux conditions énoncées au verso

                                        St-Hyacinthe, Quebec, June 11, 19--


            Harry Grafton, Jr.
            Grafton Tile Company
            Cheltham Road
            Burlington, Ontario


            20 dozen #85 shipped today.

                                    Ed Willis
                                    Barrett and Company

            hsb
```

check mots		full rate plein tarif X	day letter lettre de jour	night letter lettre de nuit	tolls coût
charge account no. numero du compte 546291		cash number numéro de caisse			
sender's name for reference only nom de l'expéditeur pour référence seulement Barrett and Company					
address and telephone adresse, téléphone 347 South Jackson Street; (302) 555-2200					6102b

Courtesy CNTelecommunications

Full-rate domestic telegram, with message well under the 15-word limit.

are often used in sales promotion even though their speed and "for-the-record" advantages are not important. They are also sometimes used to collect delinquent accounts—telegrams often get action where letters and telephone calls do not.

Two principal companies provide telegraphic services in Canada—Canadian National Telecommunications and Canadian Pacific Telecommunications. Telegraph messages may be filed (placed) at any one of the hundreds of CN and CP offices throughout the country, or they may be filed by telephone. Messages may be sent prepaid or collect. Delivery may be made by telephone, by messenger, or by mail. If you receive a telegraph message by telephone, you may request the telegraph company to mail you a copy of the telegram.

Recent changes in tariff (rates) were approved by the federal government. These changes have an effect, not only upon the basis of word counts for rate purposes, but also upon the classes of service. The classes of service now available are:

Full-Rate Telegram   The full-rate telegram is the fastest telegraphic communication, for it is transmitted immediately after being received in the telegraph office and is usually dispatched to the addressee within a few minutes. The cost of a telegram is based on the distance it is to be sent and on the number of words it contains. The minimum charge for a full-rate telegram is based upon 15 words. Therefore, you can send 15 words as cheaply as you can send five or ten. Additional words beyond 15 are charged for by the word.

Night Letter   The night letter is approximately 20 percent cheaper to send than the full-rate message. It may be filed at any time up to 12 midnight for delivery between 8 a.m. and 12 noon the following morning. Thus, under most circumstances, it is not so fast as the full-rate telegram. The minimum charge is for 35 words; additional words are charged for in groups of 25.

Composing the Message   Because telegraph messages are charged for according to the number of words they contain, they should be kept brief. The able composer of wires, therefore, has the ability to pack into the fewest possible words a clear and complete message. Intent as he is on keeping the number of words to a minimum, however, he knows that sacrificing clearness and completeness to brevity is false economy. If he needs the sixteenth word in a full-rate telegram in order to be sure that the message will be understood, he will use that sixteenth word.

In Canada, word count practices differ from those applicable in the United States. One significant difference is that each numeral in a figure is counted as one word. For example, *17* would be charged as two words, whereas, *seventeen* would be charged as one word.

Suppose you wish to wire for a hotel reservation. You could compose the following message:

Would appreciate your reserving for me a single room with bath, medium priced, for the night of Wednesday, August 17. Will arrive before 9 p.m. Please confirm this reservation.

This full-rate message contains 30 words, a total of 15 words more than the 15 on which the minimum charge is based. The extra words are not needed, and they represent a waste of money. Here is the revised message, containing 15 words:

Reserve single room, bath, medium priced, for August seventeen. Will arrive before 9 p.m. Confirm.

Look at the following rather chatty rush-delivery telegram:

Ship immediately green topper, size 16, on our order No. 48263. Customer leaving for Florida Monday and wants to take topper with her.

Twenty-eight words were used to say what could have been said in thirteen words, like this:

Rush green topper, size 16, on order 48263.

Without adding cost, you could revise the message to emphasize the urgency of the request, "Rush green topper, size sixteen, on order 48263 by the seventeenth."

Telegrams are often of assistance in collecting bad debts. The "Hurry, hurry!" air that surrounds a telegram often gets results that are not achieved by letters. Here is a telegram that is a "last ditch" effort to collect from a customer who has ignored all collection letters:

Unless your account is paid in full by September 15, our attorney will start legal action.

(17 words)

Seventeen words were used in this telegram, but the wording could have been held to 15 by writing "is fully paid" instead of "is paid in full" and expressing the date in words.

Very often only a slight revision is necessary to fit the message into the minimum-rate number of words. In the following message, responding to a telegram, the code word "Retel" could be substituted for "Re your telegram." Also, the word "and" could be omitted.

Re your telegram have shipped order numbers 174296, 164598, and 16776. Check carrier.

(27 words)

Minutes of Meetings

In the typical business, many committees operate within the company. Each department may have several committees that meet periodically—usually once a week, every two weeks, or monthly. If you are working in the sales department, for example, there may be committees on advertising, sales conferences, commissions, forms control, and so on. The purpose of committees is to discuss various problems and to make recommendations to management.

Minutes of Informal Meetings   The written record of the proceedings of a meeting is called the *minutes* of the meeting. Since most meetings in business are informal (that is, do not follow the rules of parliamentary procedure), the minutes are also informal. The minutes usually include the date, time, and place of the meeting; the name of the presiding officer; a list of those present (and, frequently, those absent); and the time of adjournment. Discussions should be summarized.

Usually the minutes are signed by the person who took them and sometimes by the presiding officer as well. Minutes are usually duplicated, and copies are sent to each person present at the meeting and to other designated officials. Following are the minutes of a meeting of a recreation committee.

MINUTES OF THE MEETING

of the

EMPLOYEE RECREATION COMMITTEE

Lovejoy Company Ltd.

2 p.m.

April 14, 19—

Presiding:	Vincent L. Hamm, Chairman	
Present:	Anne David	Lars Lindstrom
	John Eulan	LaSalle Meredith
	Oscar Fields	George Prescott
Absent:	Phil Andrews	
	Mary Hallock	

The primary question discussed was whether or not Lovejoy Company Ltd. should encourage company-sponsored recreational activities for employees during the summer.

Mr. Fields stated that he believes most people are too busy during the summer months to participate in company recreational activities. Many belong to local softball leagues, skin-diving clubs, sailing groups, etc. Others would rather be with their families. He believes we should abandon the recreation program for the summer.

Ms. David said that the Women's Club will probably prefer to remain active through the summer. They have several activities already planned—sight-seeing tours, beach parties, and boat trips.

Mr. Eulan mentioned that the library has received several new films on European travel, and arrangements could be made to show these in the building during the summer months. He recommended that a special bulletin be prepared on these films and suggested a title like "Armchair Travels." Many of the employees are of Italian and Irish descent, and color films about these countries are of special interest.

Mr. Lindstrom recommended that a questionnaire be prepared and issued to each employee to find out whether an organized program of recreation is desirable this summer.

Mr. Hamm endorsed Mr. Lindstrom's idea and appointed Messrs. Andrews, Lindstrom, and Meredith and Ms. Hallock as a committee to draw up the questionnaire. After the questionnaire is approved, it will be turned over to the Personnel Department for duplicating and distribution.

The meeting was adjourned at 3:45 p.m.

(Signed) *Anne David*

Anne David, Secretary

Minutes of Formal Meetings   Minutes of meetings that follow parliamentary procedures more closely are somewhat different in form from the informal minutes illustrated above. Note in the following example the use of topical headings for easy reference. Note, too, how the recorder has briefly summarized the speaker's remarks.

THE SOONER COUNTY CLUB OF TORONTO
MINUTES OF MEETING, JULY 27, 19—

TIME AND PLACE	The regular monthly meeting of the Sooner County Club of Toronto was called to order by the President, Jordan Thomas, on Friday, July 27, 19—, at 14:00, in the Pioneer Room of the Bismarck Hotel.
MINUTES	The minutes of the last meeting were read and approved.
	The following report was given by Clif Downs, the Treasurer.

TREASURER'S REPORT	Balance on hand, July 1, 19—	$1676.40
	Collected during the year	
	(July 1, 19— to June 30, 19—)	3042.12
		Total $4718.52
	Paid out during the year	3004.19
	Balance on hand, July 1, 19—	$1714.33

The Treasurer's report was accepted.

COMMITTEE REPORTS	The report of the Nominating Committee was given by the Chairman, Paul Rykers. A slate of nominees for next year is to be presented at the next meeting.
	The report of the Half-a-Century Celebration was given by the Chairman, Verna Millstone. Two area banquets are being held on August 21—Mississauga and Aurora. Arrangements are being handled by local chairmen.
OLD BUSINESS	The question of whether dues of the organization should be increased was brought up for further discussion. It was moved, seconded, and passed, THAT DUES FOR THE CURRENT YEAR BE INCREASED TO $5 A YEAR AND THAT A SPECIAL ASSESSMENT BE PERMITTED IF ADDITIONAL FUNDS ARE REQUIRED.
NEW BUSINESS	After a discussion about designing a gold "Sooner" pin for the members, a committee consisting of Paula Myers, Chairman, Fred Weir, Ed Maestro, and Clyde Morris was appointed to report at the next meeting.
PROGRAM	Meredith Cave introduced Mr. Alexander Hayhurst, whose topic was "What's New in the Sooner County." Mr. Hayhurst's remarks are summarized briefly here. "The Sooner County is experiencing rapid economic growth. Many new industries have moved there—including chemical, manufacturing, and government enterprises. New sources of water supply—many artificial lakes have been built—make it an attractive place from both a recreational and an industrial standpoint. There is still a large supply of labor, too. Transportation is improving rapidly each year—two new highways are now under construction."
	Mr. Hayhurst urged all members of the club to boost the Sooner

The meeting adjourned at 16:45.

C. A. Miller

C. A. Miller, Secretary

Resolutions   Resolutions to express sympathy, appreciation, congratulations, and the like are often passed at formal meetings. The form of resolutions follows a rather definite pattern, as illustrated here.

Notice that the paragraphs giving the reasons for the resolution are introduced by the word *WHEREAS* (followed by a comma) and that the paragraphs stating the action to be taken are introduced by the word *RESOLVED* (also followed by a comma).

IN MEMORIAM

Resolution Adopted by
The Board of Directors of the Plainfield Sales Company
On the death of Morris Erlich, a member of the Board

WHEREAS, our beloved colleague passed away on March 6, 19—; and

WHEREAS, Mr. Erlich had served the company long and faithfully, being one of its most sympathetic and hardest working members; and

WHEREAS, his wise counsel and unselfish services will be missed not only by the members of the Board and the officials of the organization but also by the community at large: Therefore, be it

RESOLVED, That we, his fellow Board members, take this means of expressing our deep appreciation for his untiring and unselfish service to the Plainfield Sales Company and to the community; and, be it

RESOLVED, further, That we extend our sincerest sympathies to his widow, Mrs. Sara Erlich; to his son, Mr. Steve Erlich, Chicoutimi, Quebec, and to his brother, Mr. L. G. Erlich, Lachine, Quebec; and, be it

RESOLVED, further, That a copy of these resolutions be included in the minutes of the Board of Directors of the Plainfield Sales Company; that a copy be sent to the members of the immediate family; and that a copy be supplied to the press of the city.

Adopted, unanimously, by the Board of Directors of the Plainfield Sales Company, this ninth day of March, 19—.

(Signed) *David Munhall*
Chairman of the Board

(Signed) *P. E. Mayberry*
Secretary

News Releases

All businesses are eager to get as much publicity as possible in newspapers and magazines, on radio or television—wherever there is a reading or listening audience. Larger businesses—even colleges—employ publicity directors whose job is to attract public attention to the organization. The old saying attributed to a movie star, "I don't care what you say about me as long as you spell my name correctly," indicates how valuable publicity is to some people. Most businesses, however, want only stories that show them in a favorable light, for public confidence is at stake.

The physical form in which the planned news or publicity is given to news outlets is called a *news release*. Any subject that the businessman thinks may be of public interest or may bring his name before the public may be the basis for a news release. It may be an announcement of the promotion of a major executive or of a new product or service, a retirement, a death, an honor for an employee, the election of employees to civic posts, company anniversary celebrations, and the like. News releases are usually written, or at least approved, by one executive in an organization. In larger firms, a department of public relations or of publicity handles such releases. In smaller firms, releases may be written by various executives. To prevent inaccurate or conflicting information from leaking out, however, these releases are usually channeled through one executive.

The purpose of the news release is to get into print or on the air. Newspaper, magazine, radio, and television editors receive hundreds of news releases every day from all types of businesses and individuals. The editor appraises these releases by one basic rule: Is this item of current, specific interest to our readers or listeners?

Form of the News Release The style in which releases are written is highly important. Since an editor cannot use them all, everything else being equal, he will usually print those that require the least amount of additional checking and editing. Therefore, a release should give complete information and follow as closely as possible the newspaper style of writing.

News releases should be typed and may be reproduced by stencil or photo-offset. Carbon copies should never be sent to an editor. Releases should be kept as brief as possible—rarely more than a page and a half. The shorter and more interesting the news release, the better its chance of getting into print.

Companies that issue a great many news releases have special forms on which to write them. Reporting a story on a special news release form is much more effective than writing a letter. Editors like to be able to read quickly; they cannot waste time going through the formalities of a letter. Like a letterhead, a news release form usually contains the name, address, and telephone number of the company. This information, however, may be placed at the bottom of the form. In addition, the name of the person who issued the release and who is authorized to give additional information is included.

Note the following about the news release illustrated on page 494:

1. The news release is double spaced. This is a "must" for all news releases so that the editor has room to make changes in the copy.

2. The side margins are generous, and plenty of space is left at both top and bottom. This space permits room for the editor to add typesetting instructions.

3. At the beginning of the story, a brief headline is given so that the editor may learn quickly what the release is about. For example, "New Plastic Skin-Diving Equipment Announced" or "New Vice-President Appointed" or "Printing Press Handles Sheets 275 cm Wide." (The editor will nearly always write his own headline, and the writer of the news release should not be disappointed if his is not used.)

4. Note the term at the top of the form, "For Release upon Receipt." This means that the story may be printed immediately upon receipt. Sometimes the firm likes

NEWS *from* **artco** **FOR RELEASE**

MANUFACTURING COMPANY
135 FRANKLIN AVENUE
VANCOUVER 6. B.C.
LAWRENCE 5-5100

UPON RECEIPT

Gerald F. Fresno

NEW DISPOSABLE ASH TRAY ANNOUNCED

An ash tray that is economical enough to dispose of after use will be on the market by July 1, it was announced by Artco Manufacturing Company, Vancouver, B.C. The product is made of papier-mâche and is especially treated with a thin asbestos coating. Fire from cigarette, cigar, and pipe ashes will not burn it.

Made to sell for under a nickel, this new ash tray is the housewife's answer to the drudgery of cleaning ash trays after each use. This new product--under the brand name of Ashkleen-- is collapsible, permitting the housewife to fold it so that the cigarette butts are "canned"--no mess while disposing. It comes in a variety of designs and colors, to suit any decor.

A special feature of the Ashkleen is that cigarettes do not have to be snubbed out--they may be placed in the bottom of the tray, where they will extinguish themselves. A cleverly con- structed vacuum chamber does the trick.

Ashkleen is packaged in lots of a dozen. They may be bought after July 1 in leading department and variety stores.

-XXX-

News release typed on special letterhead. Main idea is summarized in first paragraph.

to issue a news release several days in advance of the time it is to be used, in which case it will be marked, "To Be Released on July 1" or "Not to be Released Before July 1."

5. At the end of the release, the following symbol appears: —xxx—. The three x's stand for "30," the telegrapher's signal of former days signifying "the end."

If the news release is long, subheads inserted between paragraphs of news text will help break the monotony of type.

If there is more than one page, the word *more* is added in parentheses at the end of each page except the last page.

Writing the News Release　Whether your story heads for the wastebasket or the composing room may depend mostly upon the words you use in your first paragraph. The first paragraph should summarize the basic idea of the story. It should stand by itself if need be, giving the *who, what, why, when,* and *where,* as stories appearing in newspapers generally do. For example:

> Appointment of Gregg W. Kahn as general sales manager of the Verona Plastics Company, Moncton, New Brunswick, has been announced by Gilbert A. Olgar, president.

This release may be revised by the editor of the newspaper or magazine as follows:

> Gregg W. Kahn has been named general sales manager of Verona Plastics Company, Moncton, New Brunswick.

In any case, the news angle to the story is Mr. Kahn's appointment, rather than Mr. Olgar's participation. Put the accent on Kahn, where it belongs, and don't write this:

> Gilbert A. Olgar, president of Verona Plastics Company, Moncton, New Brunswick, has announced the appointment of Gregg W. Kahn as general sales manager.

After the lead paragraph is written, move on to the secondary, or background, facts. For example:

> He succeeds R. Robert Lewis, who retired October 1.

Additional background worth noting may then be given. For instance:

> The new sales manager joined the firm in 1956 as a salesman. In 1965 he was made district manager and in 1970 was appointed assistant sales manager.

If the editor has to "kill," i.e., leave out, part of the release because of space limitations, he will "kill" it from the bottom up. Therefore, the most important information should come first.

On the following page is an example of a well-written news release.

FROM: F. G. Renkin, Jr.
            Fisher Drug Company
            Montreal, Quebec

RELEASE: IMMEDIATE

BLACK NAMED ADVERTISING MANAGER AT FISHER

Appointment of Shelton T. Black as advertising manager of the Fisher Drug Company, Montreal, has been announced by Douglas Sherman, president.

Mr. Black succeeds Donald H. Chevalier, who retired October 1 after thirty years.

The new advertising manager joined the firm in 1956 as a stenographer in the chemical division. In 1960, he was made executive assistant to the sales manager; and in 1970, he was appointed assistant advertising manager.

In commenting on his new post, Mr. Black paid tribute to the fine work done by his predecessor. "Our basic advertising policy remains unchanged," said Mr. Black. "We shall continue to search for new media and new methods, of course; but for the time being we will concentrate our efforts in trade magazines and newspapers."

Mr. Black lives in Mount Royal, a suburb of Montreal. He has three children. Always actively interested in community affairs, Mr. Black is a member of the local committee for the United Appeal, and is presently chairman of the Welfare Council of Mount Royal.

Communication Problems

Application Exercises

A ■

Your employer wishes to send the following message from your office (Windsor, Ontario) to the Kelowna, B.C. branch as quickly as possible. It is 4:30 p.m. when he gives you the message he wishes typed and delivered to the telegraph office. What class of message would you recommend? Why? How many words are in the message? Can you save the firm some money by reducing the number of words? If so, reword the message.

> WE HAVE NOT RECEIVED THE ORDER FOR 50 PAIRS OF LA VOGUE SHOES. WE NEED THEM NOT LATER THAN MARCH 5. PLEASE CHECK INTO THIS AND ANSWER BY TELEGRAM.

B ■

Type the revised telegram from Exercise A on an official form.

C ■

You are asked to reserve a room for your employer, Ralph Dixon, at the Sheraton-Cadillac Hotel in Windsor for April 5 and 6. He does not plan to arrive until late on April 5. Mr. Dixon would like a medium-priced, outside room. He would like a confirmation. Prepare a full-rate telegram, using as few words as possible.

D ■

Write the minutes for a class session or a meeting, using the informal form discussed in this unit.

E ■

Prepare a formal set of minutes for an actual meeting you attended. If you have not attended such a meeting, you may make up the necessary information.

F ■

Prepare a news release for one of your school activities—a sports event or a special meeting of one of the clubs to which you may belong.

G ■

Your employer is being promoted from assistant office manager to office manager. Prepare a news release, supplying the necessary names and background information.

Word Study

A ■

Words often confused: wave, waive; bearing, baring, barring.

B ■

Select a single word that may be substituted for each of the following phrases.

1	during the time that	**4**	in connection with
2	in this day and age	**5**	at the present time
3	reach a decision	**6**	in order that

C ■

What are the present participial (*ing*-ending) forms of the following?

1	vary	**3**	compel	**5**	equal
2	accumulate	**4**	benefit	**6**	delay

Communication in Action: *Clichés*

Clichés are phrases that have been used over and over so many times that they are worn out. Because they are worn out, they make writing and speaking dull and uninteresting. Rewrite the following clichés, using fresh, new words:

1. We traveled *far and wide;* in fact, we *circled the globe* many times.
2. It is a situation that I *view with alarm,* yet I am *helpless to interfere.*
3. The child is *as playful as a kitten* and *sleeps like a log;* when he awakes, he is full of *boundless energy.*
4. She was scared; she was as *white as a sheet* and her *hair stood on end.*

PART □ 11

The Art of Effective Speaking □

Would you like to learn how to be successful in all relationships that involve talking? Would you like to know why some persons are popular and others are not? If so, you will be particularly interested in studying the following seven units, because they teach you how to "put your best foot forward" with everyone you meet. You will learn how to meet the public, in person and by telephone; how to be successful when you are interviewed for employment; how to be a good committee leader or member; how to give a successful talk. And a very important fringe benefit is that all your knowledge can be used to promote your social success!

Setting
the
Stage

How often and for how long do you talk during your waking hours? If you are in school, you recite in class, contribute to discussions, give oral reports. Probably your success in most extracurricular activities depends on the quality of ideas you express through speech. At other times you talk socially with your classmates, if only to ask, "Wodja do lasnight?" If you are in an office, you doubtless spend much time in talking—giving instructions or explanations, asking questions, promoting good business relations, selling goods or services, selling an idea, or selling your qualities as a person.

You talk much more than you write; therefore, you are usually measured more by your speech than by your writing. Your speech is something that is individually and particularly yours; and to many people, your speech is you. The words you use, the way you put them together, plus your tone, pitch, volume, rate, enunciation, and pronunciation all add up to a "you" that can be rated by others. To receive a "high rating," you need special training in oral communication. You need to know how to converse and how to be a good discussion-group member. You need to know what to say and how to say it.

The Setting Is Important

Effective speech, however, depends on factors other than the spoken word. The setting is important, too. For example, the actors in a Broadway play would surely have their lines learned and polished to the highest degree. Now suppose that the plot builds up to a very tender love scene, but the scene is played outdoors on a busy street. With this background, the beauty of the words would be lost on an audience. But, of course, you would never see anything like this. Producers and directors are experts in creating surroundings that heighten the effect of words, so this scene probably would be played in a setting of moonlight and soft music.

The example just given, although somewhat far-fetched, does illustrate that atmosphere can contribute much to successful speaking. Therefore, before learning to speak effectively, you need to study how to create a favorable impression that will set the stage for the best reception of what you say. Setting the stage is the topic of this first unit in oral communication.

An impression is the sum total of many factors. Learning, however, involves studying and mastering the separate elements that make up the total. Among the elements that help a speaker make a favorable first impression are the following:

1. Attractive dress and good grooming
2. Good posture and carriage
3. Pleasant facial expressions
4. Good manners
5. Lack of distracting mannerisms

Appropriate Dress

What is an appropriate wardrobe? Today's fashion magazines display a wide variety of styles, colors, and fabrics at a wide variety of prices. This should make it easier to choose, but somehow it doesn't. Here are a few guidelines to help you decide what clothes to choose.

1. Keep up with fashion trends, but don't blindly follow the extreme fashion fads.
2. Choose simple, clean-cut styles which can be mixed or matched.
3. Have a selection of scarfs, pins, and ties to provide variety in your appearance.
4. Don't be afraid of bright colors, but make sure they suit you and the surroundings where you work.
5. Remembering that your clothing must always be scrupulously clean, choose wash-and-wear, crease-resistant fabrics to make it easier for you to stay neat all day.
6. Beware of bargains that fall apart at the seams! If drycleaning is necessary, a low-priced garment may not be the bargain it seems.

Simply put, an appropriate wardrobe is one in which you feel comfortable and confident, one that will not offend anyone else. Choose clothing that will not wilt as the day goes on. This will create a favorable impression.

Good Grooming

Grooming means taking care of the appearance of something. As mentioned above, clothes must be scrupulously clean with all buttons, etc., intact to give that well-cared-for appearance. By looking after your clothes you make a double investment: (1) You save money by making your clothes last longer, and (2) you help create an attractive appearance that builds self-confidence.

But is that all that is necessary? No. It will not matter how well-dressed you appear if you yourself are not also well groomed. You are an important entity, and as such you are worthy of meticulous attention to personal hygiene. Let's look at three areas where you can really work wonders for yourself.

Diet Be sure always to begin the day with a good breakfast and to continue with nutritious meals throughout the day. Nothing, of course, is gained by skipping meals. What might be

Courtesy Eastman Kodak Company

Good posture gives the impression of an alert mind and an outgoing personality.

saved financially will perhaps be paid out in doctors' bills. You know the basic rules for good eating habits. Follow them for better health and for a feeling of well-being.

Exercise and Sleep   The old adage, "All work and no play makes Jack a dull boy" is as true today as it ever was. Exercise and relaxation are essential to good health; so are rest and sleep. Eyes sparkle and skin glows when you are well-rested and healthy—and both give a more favorable impression.

Personal Hygiene   Never would you offend someone by being rude. However, unless you are very careful about personal hygiene, you may offend someone unwittingly. Remember the day is long, but you must be as smart and as fresh at closing time as you are at starting time. Probably this is the area that contributes most directly to your feeling of confidence and self-respect—so be sure at all times!

Good Posture and Carriage

First impressions are important. The manner in which you sit, stand, or move about can leave one who first meets you with a favorable or a not-so-favorable impression.

Models, who are always in the public eye, spend hours practising the most attractive way in which to move, stand, or sit in order to convey the message they wish to impart. What kind of message do you want to give to those whom you meet? Let's look at some interpretations of the way to stand, sit, or move.

Bad Impressions

If you	then you may
sprawl when you sit,	be lazy.
rest your weight on one leg and hip when you stand,	tire or lose interest quickly and have no drive.
shuffle along with your head down,	not work well with others and have no force of character.

Good Impressions

If you	then you are probably
sit down gracefully, and then sit up straight,	alert and ready to listen attentively.
stand erect with your weight evenly balanced,	an upright, honest person.
walk purposefully with your head up,	ambitious, industrious, and self-directing.

These first impressions may be very inaccurate indeed, but they are hard to erase. So concentrate on making a good first impression!

Pleasant Facial Expressions

The models mentioned above also use facial expressions to keep their audience interested. Do you think you would be as interested in the fashion the model is displaying if that model did not have a vibrant, pleasant expression? If, through practice, a model can "switch on" a pleasant expression, so can you develop a way of showing your interest and enthusiasm that will create a favorable impression.

The first step is to *feel* really, sincerely interested and enthusiastic. Some people feel it is unsophisticated to show emotion, and others are too shy. However, a genuine interest in people and a keen zest for life—perhaps two of the chief ingredients for personal fulfilment and happiness—are the qualities which help one to "look pleasant." A pleasant facial expression—an important "display" for you, another type of model—comes more easily when it reflects a healthy glow from within. It is not even necessary, therefore, to smile or to grin in order to look pleasant, but it is necessary to *feel* pleasant.

No matter how pleasant your expression may be, it is of no value if you hang your head or don't look at the person who is talking to you. If he only sees the top of your head, he has no way of knowing how you really feel; in fact, he may feel you have something to hide! Be sure, therefore, to let people see your alert, interested, enthusiastic expression at all times.

Learning to look pleasant, interested, and alert is purely an individual achievement. We all must consciously work at producing a favorable impression.

Good Manners

Another very important factor in creating a favorable impression is the manifestation of good manners. The atmosphere of polish that surrounds the fortunate people who quite naturally do and say the correct thing at the correct time commands the respect and admiration of all who have an opportunity to observe them. These models of good taste and breeding, however, did not reach the state of being natural without learning and practice and without brushing up at intervals. Your own manners may be excellent, but even you may need to study the following discussion and the suggestions given.

The Basis Is Courtesy   The basis of good manners is courtesy, and the basis of courtesy is consideration for others. Without courtesy, good manners are only a veneer. This is the opinion held by many people whose jobs involve rating and grading others. For example, one interviewer used a special device to rate the manners of male applicants. When an applicant entered his office, he dropped a book, paper, or pen and watched to see whether the applicant would instinctively pick it up. This was his way of rating the good manners based on natural courtesy rather than on the principles contained in a book of etiquette.

Do not, however, minimize the importance of knowing and observing the rules of etiquette. Natural courtesy, while basic, is not enough for correct behavior. You must know such things as how to make and acknowledge introductions properly. You should know when it is appropriate for a man or woman to shake hands, when it is proper for a man or woman to stand. You should, in short, be familiar with all the rules that govern correct social and business relationships. This means that you need to know and to review periodically the contents of an etiquette book. There are some slight differences between social and office etiquette, and these you can learn by studying a book on office etiquette. However, in the absence of any reference book, always be guided by common sense and an awareness of the feelings of those around you.

Introductions   Lack of space here prohibits a full discussion of social correctness, but there are two very practical suggestions that can be given. The first has to do with making introductions. Do not try to learn the various rules—presenting a man to a woman, a younger to an older person, and so on. Just determine quickly which of the two people you wish to honor or which has the more important position. Then say that person's name *first*. By so doing, you will find your introduction procedures automatically correct. For instance, if you were introducing anybody at all to your mother, you would say, "Mother, may I present . . . ," "Mother, I'd like you to know . . . ," or "Mother, this is . . . ." If you wished to introduce your boss, Mr. Martin, and a young man who is with you, you would say, "Mr. Martin, this is . . . ." You might call this a Quick Trick that will prevent those first embarrassing moments of silence that occur while you are trying to remember the various methods of presentation.

The second suggestion is that you learn to shake hands in a manner that will give an impression of decision and determination, of having a mind of your own. You will clasp hands firmly, with no pump-handle arm motion. Now, "firmly" does not mean "bone crushing." You use just enough hand pressure to avoid having your acquaintance think that he got hold of a dead fish by mistake. Your handclasp may be more important to you than you realize. You may be shaking hands with one of those people who staunchly maintain that a handclasp tells all about character and ability. If this act tells a story, let that tale be favorable to you.

Lack of Distracting Mannerisms

The young man who sits at the desk beside yours may be tops in grooming, posture, manners, and facial expressions. But what about his habit of cracking his knuckles? And what about the new girl who, when she comes to tell you something, stands behind you and breathes down your neck or chews gum? And so it goes. A sincere, ambitious person works very hard to improve himself and still is defeated by some defect of which he is not aware.

Logically, then, a finishing touch to your study of the elements of creating a favorable impression is a study of your own mannerisms. In your stage setting there must be nothing to detract from the impression you have worked so hard to produce. You will find that the recommended self-study is quite difficult because you may have distracting, annoying, or tiresome habits and not perceive that you have them. For best results, study first the people around you. Watch to see if they have any behavior quirks. Whenever you observe a mannerism that you think is objectionable, say to yourself, "Do I do that?" After you have had practice in looking for these faults in others, you will be more likely to see your own faults.

Studying your own personal mannerisms and eliminating any that are undesirable are necessary tasks if you wish to protect your investment. There is little profit in presenting a fine appearance and in being polite and well mannered if you consistently do something that rasps the nerves of your colleagues.

Communication Problems

Application Exercises

A ■

Ask yourself the following questions to determine how you set your stage for speaking. Answer each question with "usually," "sometimes," or "rarely." Check your answers with members of the class to see whether they agree with you. Then, from your answers, make a list of the items that you need to practice.

My Personality

1 Am I likable and congenial so that other people want to be around me?
2 Am I optimistic instead of pessimistic or gloomy when presented with a new problem or a new situation?
3 Do I like to be with other people and make the first move to meet new people?
4 Do I look for ways to pay genuine compliments about people to themselves and to others?
5 Am I tolerant of the way other people act or think, avoiding direct criticism or argument?

First Impressions

1 Do I take the initiative to meet, greet, and introduce strangers?
2 Am I consciously thinking about the other person's interests and his comforts (instead of my own) when I talk with him?
3 Do I try to find ways of being helpful to the other person when I talk with him?
4 Do I avoid controversial topics when I enter a conversation with a new friend?
5 Do I avoid talking about personal aches and pains, strong personal likes or dislikes, rumors, and personal prejudices?

My Personal Appearance

1 Do I know what appropriate business dress is?
2 Do I usually feel well dressed?
3 Are my clothes clean, pressed, and in good repair when I wear them?
4 Do I practise strict personal rules of cleanliness and good grooming?
5 Do my personal health habits contribute to my appearance?

My Facial Expressions

1 When I first meet people, does my facial expression indicate genuine interest instead of feigned interest?
2 Am I usually willing to reveal how I feel through my facial expressions instead of covering my feelings with a noncommittal, dead-pan expression?
3 Do my facial expressions reflect the way I want to be understood?
4 Do I avoid showing indifference toward others in my facial expressions?
5 Do I refrain from reflecting my own personal problems or sad feelings in my facial expressions?

My Mannerisms

1 Do I present an attitude of alertness, instead of an "I don't care" attitude, in the way I move about?
2 Do my movements indicate a quiet poise and a purposefulness in living as opposed to an uncertain, frightened, or nervous outlook?
3 Is my posture straight without being stiff?
4 When I walk, is my weight well distributed on both legs?
5 Do I avoid meaningless, jerking movements of the body and hands when I talk?

B ■

Designate a day as "Business Dress and Grooming Day." As a result of a class discussion, make a list of "Tips on Business Dress and Grooming" from the good characteristics of dress and grooming you observe among your classmates.

C ■

In pantomime, try to express before the class some mannerisms of walk, hand movements, or facial expressions that distract and impede communication. Then, express the opposite positive characteristic that would help you set a positive stage for your speech. Was the class able to guess the point you were trying to make?

Word Study

A ■

Words often confused: later, latter; biannual, biennial.

B ■

Which of the following place names are misspelled?

1	St. Catharines, Ont.	3	St. John's, Nfld.	5	Winnipeg, Man.
2	Saanich, B.C.	4	Saint John, N.B.	6	Longueuil, Que.

C ■

Match the definitions in List B with the foreign words and phrases in List A. Then, look up the pronunciations of the foreign words and phrases.

	A		B
1	hoi polloi	a	a social blunder
2	modus operandi	b	boredom
3	nouveau riche	c	the masses
4	coup d'etat	d	the violent overthrow of a government by a small group
5	faux pas		
6	raison d'être	e	a method of procedure
7	ennui	f	a person newly rich
8	esprit de corps	g	the common spirit of enthusiasm within a group
		h	reason for being

Communication in Action: *Handling a Difficult Caller*

A policyholder in the insurance company where you work telephones, asking for your boss, Mr. Halleck. You tell the caller that Mr. Halleck is out of the office for the day. The policyholder insists on telling you his troubles. He is irate because your company purchased three new typewriters from a competing office machines firm. He wonders why, since he is a policyholder in your company, he is not given more consideration; and he threatens to cancel his insurance. Exactly what would you say to the caller? Write a summary of the conversation for your employer.

UNIT □ 60

Developing a Flexible Voice

How you say something can be nearly as important as what you say and how you appear while saying it. Your voice plays a tremendous role in the effect your words have upon your listeners. For example, your voice can soothe a person or make him angry, thus helping or hindering a situation. And the first time a person hears you, he is likely to classify you in his mind as gay or solemn, interesting or dull, lively or lethargic.

Since most persons in business talk more than they write, voice quality can work for or against you and your company. For example, what would be the effect on public relations if a switchboard operator had an irritatingly nasal voice, if a receptionist talked so low that visitors could not hear half of what was said, or if a salesperson spoke so slowly that the listeners became exasperated?

Your Voice Quality

Voice quality is determined by four main factors: *volume, pitch, tone,* and *tempo.* The effectiveness of one's voice depends also on *enunciation* and *pronunciation.* The first four factors will be discussed in this unit; the remainder, in Unit 61.

In order to improve your voice you must be able to control your breathing, for on *breath control* depend the volume, pitch, and tone of your voice and the tempo at which you speak. Breath control depends both on correct posture and on deep breathing. The latter is not possible without the former. Good posture enables a person to breathe into his lungs the maximum amount of air and also to control the amount of air expended.

Deep breathing adds to the resonance of your tones. Deep breathers have more air with which to vibrate the vocal cords, and they can talk without tiring for a greater length of time than can shallow breathers. Be sure to breathe from the *diaphragm,* as singers do. The diaphragm is that muscle partition that separates the chest from the abdominal cavity. If your shoulders move when you breathe, your breathing is too shallow; you are breathing only with the top part of your chest.

Volume   *Intensity, force,* and *volume* are all synonyms for the quality in your voice that enables you to be heard. And a speaker must be heard or he loses his audience. Since good breath control is essential for volume, you should practice correct breathing if you have trouble being heard.

When you speak to your class or school assembly, make sure that you can be heard by the persons in the back row. How much force you use will be determined by such factors as the size of your audience, the size and acoustics of the room, and whether or not you are using a microphone. When talking to a small group in a small room, of course, you should lower your volume so as not to deafen your hearers. Under all circumstances, however, be sure to begin each sentence with enough force to carry you through to the end.

Pitch   *Pitch* refers to whether a sound is high or low and the degree of highness or lowness. A shrill voice is much too high. A moderately low voice is usually the most pleasing. If your voice is unpleasantly high, you can lower it by making a conscious effort to do so over a long period of time.

If possible, record your voice on a tape recorder and listen to it several times. Try to hear your voice as others hear it, and ask your friends or classmates to criticize it. Practice lowering your voice and then record the same material a second time to see if there has been any improvement.

It is evident that no one can speak at the same pitch all the time without becoming monotonous. Therefore, you must vary your pitch according to the meaning of what you are saying. Besides telling your listeners whether a given sentence is a question or a statement, variations in pitch give nuances of meaning to your message and thus add interest.

Notice the different shades of meaning that emerge as you read the following sentences and emphasize the italicized words:

She gave him the books.	(She did, not someone else.)
She *gave* him the books.	(They were a gift.)
She gave *him* the books.	(Only he received the books.)
She gave him *the* books.	(The particular books.)
She gave him the *books.*	(Not something else.)

Tone   It is your *tone* of voice that reveals your attitudes and feelings to your listeners. If you are happy, that fact is instantly obvious; so, too, are anger and sadness revealed unless you are on your guard. Try not to let your tone of voice sound impatient, belligerent, bored, or discontented—unless, of course, you have a good reason for wanting to sound that way. In business relations as well as in social life, try to use a pleasant and cheerful tone whenever possible.

However, variations in tone as well as in volume and pitch will add interest to your speech. This is particularly true when telling a story or when reading something aloud. Think about what you are saying when you are talking or reading orally; then, suiting your tone to your meaning will not be difficult.

Tempo   The rate of speed at which you talk is called *tempo*. Your habitual speaking rate reveals much about the "you" behind your voice. Rate also can determine whether your speech is understandable; therefore, speaking at an appropriate rate is very important. The general tendency among many young speakers—and some older speakers, too—is to try to talk as fast as they think. This is not only impossible, but it is also a major threat to intelligible speech. Prove it to yourself by saying the following three sentences at top speed.

> We do not have three-ply thread in stock.
>
> Mr. Melvin is forever talking about health and wealth.
>
> A postscript is needed for the sixth letter you transcribed.

Supposing that these messages were given at the rate you just used, can you see that a listener would not be able to understand: (1) what is not in stock, (2) what "Mr. Whosit" is talking about, or (3) what has to be added to what? So check your speed. Slow down to a tempo that makes your every word intelligible.

Use pauses to stress major points. By pausing between major points or after important statements, you can add variety to a speech and give emphasis to the points you want the audience to remember.

Changing the tempo contributes to the variety, as well as to the clarity of what you say. Important words may be spoken slowly; unimportant words or phrases, more rapidly.

The Physical Tools of Speech

As was said previously, the volume, pitch, and tone of your voice and the tempo at which you speak depend to a great extent on breath control. But they also depend on how well you use your other physical tools of speech—your jaw, your lips, and your tongue. And the correct use of these physical tools determines how clearly and distinctly you speak.

The Jaw   A rigid jaw is a common fault with those who muffle their speech. You see, most sounds issue through the mouth; and sounds forced through a locked jaw are bound to be muffled and indistinguishable. Try this: lock your jaw tight and pronounce these words—*open, able, ideal, bound.* You probably had difficulty in understanding yourself!

Your jaw should move freely between an open and a closed position as the various vowels are sounded. An effective speaker opens his jaw wide on such diphthong sounds as *ow* but almost shuts the jaw when he sounds the *oo* in *boom*. To get the free-moving feeling of a relaxed jaw, practice is necessary. First, try out individually or in a group the following words to be sure you have unlocked your jaw.

open	mine	able	round
dough	responsible	ideal	brown

You usually talk in complete thoughts, so the best way to learn this free-moving jaw action is to practice phrases and sentences. If these are intelligently and faithfully practiced, your speech will never again suffer from a rigid jaw!

down and out	Name the day to harvest the hay.
high in the sky	The dime is mine to find a blind for his yacht.
out of bounds	The honest Yankee yelled for help.
yelps and yells	The quality of mind determines its power.
around the house	Round and round he goes in honest confusion.
pot of gold	The long shadows fade into darkness.
down the hatch	The cake dough was baked and baked and baked and baked.
going home	Home is where the heart is.

The Lips   Lazy lips are frequently the cause of unintelligible speech. Some nearly inarticulate speakers use only one lip position, but good speakers use a variety of lip positions to pronounce different words. For instance, *who, lose,* and *shoe* should be said with rounded lips. *Key, see,* and *cat* must be said with the lips widely stretched. *Use* and *how* require different lip positions. The lips jut out for *shoe* and *church*.

Practice the following phrases and sentences, using maximum lip movement.

friend in need	Peter Piper picked a peck of pickled peppers.
office merger	She sells seashells by the seashore.
triumphant march	How now, brown cow?
British viewpoint	The bond of friendship was broken.
mimeograph stencil	Which was the witch?
rapidly weighed	For the sake of safety, sound your horn.
passive resistance	"Hippety, hippety, hop," he said, "the mouse ran up the
watered stock	clock."
	The whistling west wind whipped the whispering trees.

The Tongue   Effective use of the tongue depends to a great extent on its placement in regard to the teeth, which act as a backstop or baffle for the tongue. Try this: Keep your tongue away from your teeth and say "this." Now repeat the word, this time touching your tongue to your teeth, and notice the improved clarity. To get the feel of an active tongue, say, "the tip of the tongue, the tip of the tongue, the tip of the tongue." Did you notice how rapidly your tongue moved?

Now practice the following phrases and sentences. Be sure that you activate your tongue.

actually colder	Nothing was lost but a delightful time.
attempted assault and	Needles, pins, spools of thread, and lovely linen laces
battery	were his stock in trade.

automobile battery	Her tale was not strictly factual; yet not fictional either.
loose-fitting clothes	Thirty thousand thermos bottles were auctioned.
zest of children	Linger a little longer, lovely lady.
health, wealth, and	The sixth letter was smoothly dictated.
happiness	The third-rate theatres appealed to the holiday crowd of
through thick and thin	shoppers.
this and that and those	It was a delightful time to be alone at home.
and them	
thirty thick thistles	

Speaking clearly and distinctly is called *articulating* or *enunciating*. The discussion of enunciation will be continued in the next unit.

Communication Problems

Application Exercises

A ■

Your employer telephones long distance for a list of people who have called the office since he left. Give him the following names and telephone numbers for him to call. Remember to make maximum use of your jaw, lips, and tongue. *Note:* You may want to spell difficult names. For example: "Monoghan Dictating Sales (M-o-n-o-g-h-a-n) of Bathurst, New Brunswick. Mr. Raymond Zulauf (Z-u-l-a-u-f), the Personnel Director, would like you to call at (Area Code 506) 291-3434.

Company and City	*Person Calling*	*Telephone Number*
Atomic Office Equipment Sales Leduc, Alberta	Warren Morrissey	(Area Code 403) 243-0331 Ext. 2535
Cahaw Copymaker Pictou, Nova Scotia	Victor Swoverland	(Area Code 902) 682-3200
Ideson and Skinner Enderby, B.C.	Mrs. Marcella Hotchkiss, Secretary to Mr. Ideson	(Area Code 604) 753-0388
Office Electronics Portage, Manitoba	Mr. Merle C. Dowson, Purchasing Agent	(Area Code 204) 562-1763
W-D Office Machines Company Kitchener, Ontario	Mr. J. C. Dulgeroff, Partner	(Area Code 519) 323-2421

B ■

In the shipping department, you are reading the quantities and stock numbers of an order as the shipping clerk checks the merchandise to be trucked to customers.

Pair off, one of you reading from the packing slip and the other checking the merchandise. Be sure you speak distinctly. Be sure, too, that the packing slips agree with the merchandise that is ready to be shipped. Make a note of any errors in numbers or quantities of merchandise.

From the packing slips:		*Merchandise ready to be shipped:*	
QUANTITY	STOCK NUMBER	QUANTITY	STOCK NUMBER
6 boxes	29 x 4028	52 m	66 x 2738
3 dozen	29 x 370	5 m	37 x MT9212
52 m	66 x 2739	5 each	1Y x 1580L
5 m	37 x MT9212	3 dozen	29 x 370
4 each	1Y x 1580L	6 boxes	29 x 4028

C ■

In which of the following words is the *u* pronounced as in *human?*

1	recuperate	4	upheaval	7	Tuesday
2	institute	5	student	8	column
3	utterance	6	illustrate	9	gratitude

Word Study

A ■

Words often confused: lesson, lessen; incite, insight.

B ■

What letter should appear in the blank space in each of these words?

1	perc__late	3	sep__rate	5	p__rsuade
2	attend__nce	4	controver__y	6	vet__ran

C ■

In these sentences, match the italicized word with the best synonym given in parentheses.

1 His musical composition was remarkable for its many *nuances* of tone. (varieties, volumes, shadings)
2 The assignment was not easy, but he needn't have acted so *belligerent* about it. (irritable, combative, petty)
3 The sentence sounded odd because the wording was so *archaic*. (inverted, ambiguous, antiquated)

Communication in Action: *Sharing the Load*

You are one of two stenographers with equal responsibility for operating a lawyer's office. Among other jobs, you have taken the responsibility for the files; your co-worker, for telephone calls. This morning the boss asks for 26 folders to be pulled from the files—and he needs them immediately. Your co-worker is not busy. What would you say to her to sell her on the idea of helping you?

UNIT □ 61

Enunciation and Pronunciation

A person applying for a position may be carefully groomed and may give the outward appearance of being a promising employee. He would not be guilty of chewing gum or cleaning his nails during an interview. But, if he tells the employment manager that he saw the position for which he is applying advertised in a "noospaper," that he can begin working on "Febuary 1," and that he really would like to work for this "kumpni," how long will the illusion of promise last? It has probably already vanished, just because the job applicant gave evidence of faulty *pronunciation* and poor *enunciation.*

    Pronunciation is the sounding of words *correctly. Enunciation,* which was introduced in the preceding unit, is the sounding of words *distinctly.* Both good pronunciation and good enunciation are necessary for the person who wishes not only to be understood, but also to make a good impression on others.

What Causes Poor Enunciation?

Listen to yourself. Do you run words together, leaving out some sounds? Do you say "dijago" for *did you go?* "meetcha" for *meet you?* "gawna" for *going to?* This is the sort of speech that educated persons try to avoid, because it is usually associated with nonstandard English.

    Poor enunciation results from running words together, from leaving out letters or syllables, or from adding unwanted letters or syllables. Let us look first at a group of useful and common words that are sadly mistreated when letters or even whole syllables are dropped.

Lost Consonants   The final consonants most often dropped are *t*, *d*, and *g* when the letters are in combination with some other consonant. Thus, *fact* becomes "fac"; *yield* becomes "yiel"; and *going* becomes "goin." The *wh* sound, too, frequently is carelessly pronounced; for example, "wat" for *what*. Practice saying the following phrases aloud until you are sure you do not slight the sounds of the underlined consonants.

recognized candidate	February second
tourist list	three hundred thirty-three
factual arrangement	through thick and thin
current account	lingering and longing
collect payment	being a linguist
competent party	test of strength
demand payment	assistant management
trust fund	seemingly strict
next payment	bonded debt outstanding
kept a strict accounting	judgment for the tenant
arranging pictures	attempted bankrupt
earned discount	outstanding print
consigning the prints	whistle while thinking
width and length	why white wheels

Lost Vowels   When two vowels occur together in a word, the sound of one often tends to be slighted. Thus, *li-on* becomes an indistinct "line." Too, a single vowel used as a syllable is frequently overlooked and not sounded. A careless person will say "captal," completely ignoring the single-vowel syllable *i*. Pronounce the word correctly—"cap-i-tal." In the following list, be sure you *see* each vowel; and be sure you do not lose any vowel sounds when you practice saying these phrases:

metropolitan area	especially positive
federal cabinet	terrible presentiment
ridiculous accident	indirect but definite
municipal regulation	generally separate
cruel lion	variable regulation
excellent family	family history
accurate and regular	usually interesting
alphabetical list of liabilities	popular battery
eleven manufacturers	separate poem
variable capital	original company
temporarily separated	indirectly responsible
ivory tower	positive verification
veteran general	particularly quiet

Lost Syllables   It is only a step for a person who drops consonant and vowel sounds to drop syllables from words, too. Such a person "c'lects stamps" instead of "col-lects." It is as though he wished to make a contraction (shortened form) out of every word he speaks. Now practice saying the phrases below, being sure to pronounce all the syllables.

accidentally hurt (not *accidently*)	five-year *guarantee* (not *garntee*)
little people (not *lil*)	detailed *itinerary* (not *itinree*)
laboratory technician (not *labatory*)	*generally* acceptable (not *genrally*)
just *obligation* (not *obgation*)	*occasionally* wrong (not *occasionly*)

Addition of Letters or Syllables   Just as serious an enunciation fault as dropping sounds is the frequent mistake of adding extra sounds.

As you say aloud the following italicized words, watch to see if you ordinarily add extra incorrect sounds to them.

a fine *athlete* (not *athalete*)	in *remembrance* (not remember̲ance)
the *height* of fashion (not *heighth*)	*disastrous* results (not *disasterous*)
across the street (not *acrost*)	*entrance* examination (not *enterance*)
broken *umbrella* (not *umberella*)	a *hindrance* to progress (not *hinderance*)
one roll of *film* (not *filum*)	
drowned duck (not *drownded*)	a *mischievous* child (not *mischevious*)
grievous fault (not *grievious*)	a good *preventive* (not *preventative*)
rhythm for dancing (not *rhythum*)	a *burglar* alarm (not *burgular* or *alarum*)
pop *singer* (not *sing-ger*)	

One remedy for these types of enunciation errors is attention to spelling. If you spell these words correctly, you will be more likely to pronounce them correctly and enunciate them distinctly. If you misspell them, you may also mispronounce them.

Some Troublemakers   Some words are more difficult to enunciate than others. They require an even slower rate, to allow maximum use of jaw, lips, and tongue. You will be surprised to know that most of these words are short, three- to five-letter words. They usually include one or more sounds that are difficult to distinguish. Thus, *ache* requires both the long *a* sound and a definite hard *k* sound.

Most of your practice so far has been in phrases and sentences. Yet, if you learn to pronounce the following words out of context so that each one is intelligible, you have arrived!

ache	corn	fife	jig	nap	peat	tang
at	darn	gas	kite	nick	race	tent
balk	earn	grow	lay	oils	rogue	vamp
beau	else	heed	map	our	scab	wag
climb	fill	jam	nab	path	tan	wield

Why We Pronounce as We Do

We all learned to talk by imitating the speech of those around us; first, of members of the family; then, of neighbors and friends; later, of schoolmates, teachers, co-workers, and others with whom we came into contact. Some of the pronunciations we imitated may have been incorrect.

Those who come from homes where most words are correctly sounded do have an advantage over those from homes where mistakes in pronunciation are more common— whether from carelessness or lack of training or because of foreign-language background. Nevertheless, everyone can master habits of good pronunciation if he will but try. The secret is to pattern your pronunciation after the speech of educated persons such as teachers, ministers, and radio and television speakers.

What Makes a Pronunciation Correct?   Who decides whether a certain pronunciation is correct? Doubtless your answer is "the dictionary." This answer is only partially correct.

Even though the dictionary is the book to which we go to determine correct pronunciation, this does not mean that dictionary editors arbitrarily choose certain pronunciations as correct. Instead, they first record the pronunciations that are used by the largest number of the best educated and most cultured speakers in the country. Then, they select the most frequently used of these pronunciations.

Regional Differences   However, the best educated and most cultured people in one part of the country, or throughout the English-speaking world, may pronounce a certain word differently from the way that a cultured American, Englishman, or Canadian would pronounce it. For example, a cultured American Southerner is likely to say "cayn't" for *can't* or "moah" for *more,* while an English-born person might say "pahk" for *park* or "hawf" for *half,* and so on.

So accustomed have residents in various areas become to certain speech patterns that they do not detect any difference between these forms and the forms given in the dictionary. Often, when they do grasp the differences, they are not willing to adopt the standard pronunciation because they do not wish to be "different." The sensible solution seems to be to observe how the best educated persons *in your community* speak and then to adopt their standards.

The Dictionary and Pronunciation   Sometimes two or more pronunciations for a word are given in the dictionary. In such cases, the first pronunciation is usually considered preferable, although the others are acceptable. In this textbook, *Webster's Seventh New Collegiate Dictionary* is the standard for both pronunciation and spelling. Therefore, only the first pronunciation of a word is considered.

As you learned in Unit 2, pronunciations are indicated by a phonetic alphabet and by accent marks. Each dictionary has its own method of indicating the sounds of letters. Refer to the front pages of your dictionary for a key to the markings.

Frequent Mispronunciations

Irrespective of home or regional environment, however, certain types of mispronunciations are prevalent. In order to make it easier for you to overcome tendencies to mispronounce words, these words are grouped for study in the following categories:

Incorrect Vowel Sounds   Many words are mispronounced because certain vowels are incorrectly sounded.

The Sound of Long "u"   You recall the would-be employee mentioned at the start of this unit who referred to a "noospaper." This use of the ōō sound instead of the correct long *u* sound (heard in *human*) is, unfortunately, a common error. It makes a decidedly unpleasant impression on hearers who are speech-conscious.

Read the following words aloud, concentrating on using the long *u* sound.

annuity	neurotic	due
new	revenue	duke
New York	institution	duty
numerous	substitution	municipal
neuritis	latitude	tube
neuralgia	multitude	culinary

Troubles with "a"   In another group of words, the sound of long *a* (the sound in *hate*) is incorrectly replaced by the sound of short *a* (the sound in *hat*).

The following words are typical of this group. Again, read the list aloud.

āviator	gāla	stātus
blātant	ignorāmus	tenācious
dāta	lātent	ultimātum
flāgrant	rādiator	verbātim

In the following words, the short *a* should be used instead of the long *a*.

Ărab	măltreat	păgeant
deprăvity	păgination	Spokăne

Troubles with "i"   In some words, the sound of long *i*, as heard in *wide*, is incorrectly replaced by the short *i* sound heard in *hit*.

alumnī	grīmy	stīpend

On the other hand, in these words, the short *i* should be used rather than the long *i*.

finance	Ĭtalian	respĭte
financial	ĭtalics	

Substituting One Vowel for Another   In another type of mispronunciation, an entirely different vowel is substituted for the correct one. In the following words, the letters that are often thus replaced are underscored. Read the list aloud, clearly enunciating the underlined letters. If in doubt about any pronunciation, consult your dictionary. This type of mispronunciation also is often closely linked with misspelling.

accurate	just	preparation
description	mathematics	privilege
despair	optimistic	restaurant
divide	particular	sacrilegious
escalator	percolator	separate
existence	permanent	

Incorrect Accent Many common errors are caused by placing the stress, or accent, on the wrong syllable of a word.

1. In the following words, the accent should be on the *first* syllable.

'dic-tionary	'ad-mirable	'ap-plicable
'for-midable	'am-icable	'com-parable
'the-atre	'in-teresting	'in-famous
'pref-erable	'kil-ometre	

2. In these words, the accent should be on the *second* syllable.

ac-'cli-mate	om-'nip-otence	con-'do-lence
re-'mon-strate	ir-'rev-ocable	de-'mon-strative
ob-'lig-atory	su-'per-fluous	ex-'traor-dinary

3. In these words, the accent should be on the *final* syllable.

al-'ly	dis-'charge	po-'lice
bou-'quet	fi-'nance	a-'dult
de-'tail	re-'search	rou-'tine
di-'rect		

Silent Letters Among the chief stumbling blocks to correct spelling are silent letters that occur in many of our most frequently used words. Because we do not hear these letters, they do not constitute a serious threat to correct pronunciation except in a few important words in which letters that should be silent are often sounded. As you read aloud the following words, make a special effort *not* to sound the letters that are underscored.

almond	posthumous	salve	vehement
often	salmon	sword	vehicle
indict	mortgage	corps	

Just Plain Tricky Many words often mispronounced cannot be classified under any of the groupings just listed. There is only one way of mastering the correct pronunciations of these offenders. Concentrate on each one, first looking it up in your dictionary and then repeating it many times. Here are representative words of this type.

absorb	deaf	once
absurd	denunciate	partner
apron	err	peremptory
associate	gist	perhaps
association	homogeneous	perspiration
attorney	hundred	possess
bona fide	library	prerogative
clothes	luxurious	quay
censure	luxury	reservoir
codicil	martial	soot
column	medieval	strength
congratulations	mercantile	suppose
coupon	negotiate	tremendous

Some Tips to Help You

These miscellaneous suggestions will help you in your battle against mispronunciation and poor enunciation.

1. Be especially careful in pronouncing personal names. People resent having their names mispronounced just as they resent having them misspelled. If a girl wants to be called "Jo-'an" rather than "Jōn," then follow her preference.

2. Likewise, be careful in pronouncing geographic names. Often, the spelling is no guide to pronunciation. If you are uncertain, check the gazetteer in your dictionary. Following are a few geographic names that bear watching. You may be surprised when you verify their pronunciations.

Abilene	Edinburgh	Norfolk	Nanaimo
Worcester	Haverhill	Southampton	Sault Ste. Marie
Cannes	Illinois	Valparaiso	Longueuil
Cherbourg	Lima, Peru	Versailles	Miramichi

3. Be especially careful with foreign words and phrases. Some very amusing (and embarrassing) mistakes can be made by pronouncing them, especially French words, as they are spelled. The dictionary gives the closest approximation possible to the English sounds.

4. Guard against running words together, making such sounds as "wotcha doon?" (what are you doing?), "shoulda" (should have), "willyuh?" (will you?), or "jeet?" (did you eat?). Nothing more quickly brands a person as illiterate as does slovenly enunciation.

5. When you learn a new word, learn its correct pronunciation at once. In other words, when you look up the spelling and meaning of a word, notice also its pronunciation and practice it.

6. When you speak to a group of people, speak more slowly than you do in ordinary conversation and enunciate carefully.

The person who faithfully carries out the suggestions outlined in this unit will surely acquire an enviable reputation for correct speech.

Communication Problems

Application Exercises

A ■

How many words can you think of that contain the following silent letters?

    1 Words beginning with silent *p*
    2 Words beginning with silent *k*
    3 Words beginning with silent *w*
    4 Words containing a silent *s*
    5 Words containing a silent *l*

B ■

How many syllables has each of these words?

1	accidentally	4	umbrella	7	drowned
2	remembrance	5	elm	8	idea
3	grievous	6	hindrance	9	learned (adj.)

C ■

Make a list of run-together phrases, such as "dijago?" (page 515), that you have heard—phrases or sentences that are unintelligible or difficult for the listener to translate. Be ready to enact a conversation in class in which you use some of these jumbled phrases. Then repeat the conversation, this time using good enunciation. What elements made your speech poor in the first conversation? What elements contributed to your good enunciation in the second conversation? Discuss.

D ■

Each of the following words means one thing when accented on the first syllable and something else when accented on the final syllable. Write definitions for the words in each pair and indicate what part of speech each word is.

1	desert	4	produce	7	contest
2	extract	5	digest	8	object
3	minute	6	absent	9	rebel

E ■

1 In which of the following words should the *i* be sounded as in *ice:* admirable, finance, grimy, reptile?

2 In which of the following words should the *i* not be sounded as in *ice:* alumni, respite, stipend?

3 In which of the following words is the *a* sounded as in *make:* obstacle, tenacious, task, depravity?

4 In which of the following words is the *a* sounded as in *cat:* status, verbatim, fatuous?

F ■

The following words are spelled as they are often incorrectly enunciated. A letter or a syllable has been added or dropped. Respell all words correctly.

1	accelrate	4	labratory	7	probly
2	Febuary	5	strenth	8	sufferage
3	filum	6	sophmore	9	acrosst

G ■

On page 523 is a list of short words that must be enunciated very carefully in order to be understood. Dictate any ten of these (mix them up) for the rest of the class to write as a spelling list. Pronounce each word once only and allow three to four seconds for each to be written. See how many in the class were able to understand all the words dictated.

aid	dab	fifth	job	need	pitch	tap
air	dams	gab	kick	new	pump	tell
awe	deaf	gem	knee	nip	rap	touch
bait	earl	gill	law	oft	rave	tuck
barge	elk	hack	lathe	or	rug	vast
cape	fame	hit	merge	owe	sheik	waif

Communication in Action: *Small-Group Discussion Technique*

The small-group discussion technique is often used to solve problems. It is based on the idea that two heads are better than one. Here is the way it works: Divide your class into small groups of four, five, or six. Then, in each group: (1) Make sure everyone is acquainted. (2) Elect a chairman. (3) Agree quickly on a recorder who will take notes and later report the major points of the discussion to the entire class. (4) Make sure that everyone understands the problem you are to discuss. (5) Be sure that everyone enters into the discussion.

Here is the problem: What are some ways to encourage students to make more effective use of their time in studying?

When you are through, evaluate this discussion process.

UNIT □ 62

Meeting
the
Public

Business People Meet the Public

Hundreds of salespeople and retail, wholesale, and manufacturing agents talk with countless callers daily, both in person and by telephone. By untold thousands, business people in offices also meet and talk with the public—to receive reservations at travel agencies, airlines, railroads, and theatres; to receive or pay money at collection windows in department stores, banks, and utility companies; to receive orders for services or repairs; to receive complaints and make adjustments; to give information at garages, office machines companies, and other service organizations; and to render personal services in medical centres, doctors' offices, and other professional establishments. Millions of people earn their living primarily through meeting the public in person or by telephone.

In a business office, almost everyone meets the public at one time or another. The receptionist or switchboard operator usually makes the initial contact, transferring a call or referring a caller to the appropriate person or office. In smaller offices, a clerk-typist, file clerk, bookkeeper, or stenographer may be asked to help callers, in addition to performing his other duties. And just about everyone in an office has a telephone at his elbow for use in his job. Anyone planning to enter business, therefore, can expect to be responsible for some aspect of meeting the public; and he should be prepared to discharge this responsibility to the best of his ability.

To be a good business host, then, you need to augment the training you already have by giving careful attention to the basic rules for meeting callers. You need to learn, also, how these rules may be applied to meeting a caller in person and to meeting the public by telephone.

Basic Rules for Meeting the Public

The rules for meeting the public—in person or by telephone—have as their foundation courtesy, consideration, and friendly warmth. These are the same qualities that make a visitor in your home feel welcome, comfortable, and at ease. Applied specifically to business callers, the rules are these:

1. Give Prompt Attention to All Callers. Recognize a caller's presence immediately. If he is calling by telephone, answer his call promptly—before the second ring if possible. Have you ever waited and waited for a telephone call to be answered? Have you ever had to stand and wait for someone to attend to you in a store, feeling completely ignored? If so, you know that you became increasingly uncomfortable as you waited, even angry. You hung up the telephone receiver, or you turned on your heel and walked out of the store. In a well-run business, this does not happen. Salespersons, for example, are trained to recognize a caller immediately. If a clerk is busy with one customer, he will glance and nod at a waiting customer or say pleasantly, "I'll be with you in a moment." Then the caller knows that he is not being overlooked. As you meet the public, you must follow the same procedure and give prompt attention to all callers.

2. Greet Callers Pleasantly. The tone of voice you use to greet people should be cheerful and friendly. Even an irate caller will feel better when he hears your pleasant, "Good morning, Mr. Jabson. How nice of you to call." Of course, if you don't mean it, it is best not to say it; your tone of voice and your facial expressions will show your caller that you are not sincere.

Vary your greeting. Treat each visitor as though he were in some way special—he is! And try to make the greeting fit the occasion. For example, an automobile sales-

"Friendly warmth" is essential in an employee who constantly meets the public.

Courtesy American Telephone and Telegraph

man approaching a customer who is behind the wheel of a new demonstrator might say, "It's a comfortable feeling to sit behind the wheel of a new car, isn't it?" One of the following greetings may fit other situations: "Good morning." "What may I show you?" "Whom do you wish to see?" "How may I help you?" "What a pleasant surprise!" "We were expecting you." "How nice of you to call." "How are you today?" Just adding the name of the person, if you know it, will make the greeting special for the caller. Often, too, the same words may be varied by a change in emphasis or in the way they are said.

3. *Treat All Callers as Honored Guests.* Be friendly and courteous to everyone. Never let a caller's voice or appearance influence what you say to him. Some very important people do not dress expensively; and not everyone has had the advantage of voice training. It would be unwise to assume that a modestly attired person or a person with a thick accent is not worthy of your consideration. Every caller deserves the same courteous and considerate treatment.

You must be prepared to have some irritable or even discourteous callers. Treat these people with an understanding smile and gloss over their discourtesies. You represent the firm, and these people are your guests. If you must make some response, express sympathy: "I'm sorry you feel that way." Your own graciousness will often mollify the caller's anger and might even make him friendly again toward you and your company.

4. *Obtain Needed Information.* Before you can refer a caller to someone else, you must find out the caller's name and the reason for his call. You can then relay this information to your boss, who will determine whether he or someone else will handle the call.

Because people sometimes resent being asked about their business, it takes a polished business host to elicit the needed information without endangering pleasant relations. To a telephone caller, you might say, "May I tell Mr. Johnson who is calling, please?" When greeting a caller in person, you might point a pen over a pad and say pleasantly, "Your name is . . . ?" And, as you write the name on the pad, you will probably repeat, "Oh, yes, Mr. Jeffrey L. Adams." Next, you would ask, "And you would like to see Mr. Evans about . . . ?" and also write his answer on your pad. Filling in a leading question is a natural thing to do, so your caller usually will freely and willingly supply the information you need.

5. *Save the Caller's Time.* Let a caller know if he has to wait. On the telephone, if the wait is to be longer than two or three minutes, it is usually better to take the number and call back. You can say, "I'll have to get the information from the files, Mr. Poston. It will take about five minutes to do so. May I have your number and call you back?"

Let a caller know how long he must wait, even if it is a relatively short time. You might say, "I'm sorry, but Mr. Jenson will not be available for at least another hour. Would you like to make an appointment for later?" Or, "Mr. Jenson is in a meeting but should be free in about five minutes." The caller will appreciate your consideration.

6. *Be Discreet.* Protect your employer in what you say—and don't say. If your boss is late in arriving at the office, for example, don't say, "Mr. Duncan has not come in yet this morning." The tactful thing to say is, "Mr. Duncan is not in the office just now. I expect him in a few minutes." Make certain that your remarks reflect favorably on your employer.

Protect your employer's business, also. Certain business information is confidential, and you must keep it so. Imagine what a visitor would think of your company (and you) if you were indiscreet enough to say, "Business is so poor that Mr. Duncan had to let fifty workers go last week." A prospective customer would not be favorably impressed! So be discreet in what you say.

7. *Keep Within Your Authority.* Know the limits of your authority and don't exceed them. If you think your company will replace a defective part, for example—but it is not your responsibility to make adjustments—don't say, "Certainly we'll replace this for you. Just take it to the service department." Both you and your company will be embarrassed if for some reason the service department is unable to make the adjustment. Keep within your authority by saying, "Why don't you talk with Mr. Johnson in the service department?" Be sure you know the names of the people in your company who are authorized to make various kinds of decisions. You can then help callers by referring them to the appropriate person, and you will be keeping within your authority.

8. *Say "No" Gracefully.* Some decisions that you must convey to a caller will be unfavorable to him. Be pleasant but firm. Your knowledge of how to say "No" in a letter will help you. Review Unit 50 so that, when you must refuse a caller, you can do so without losing his goodwill.

9. *Show a Genuine Desire to Serve.* The good host usually extends his guests an extra courtesy or adds a thoughtful touch to make the visit memorable. In business, too, the good host will be on the lookout for the little extra that makes the difference. One business host, for example, helped an out-of-town caller who was concerned about his plane reservation. "While you're talking with Mr. Smith," she said, "I'll call the airline to reconfirm your reservation." As a result, the caller was able to give his full attention to the business at hand; and a new customer was made.

With these basic rules in mind, you are ready to receive the public—in person or by telephone. In greeting telephone callers, however, you need to know certain additional techniques.

Telephone Techniques

Telephone techniques differ somewhat from techniques for greeting callers in person because of the nature of voice-to-voice conversation and the technical equipment used.

Rules for Voice-to-Voice Conversation   A telephone caller is unable to see the other person's facial expressions or surroundings, so he is dependent entirely upon the voice at the other end of the line. In voice-to-voice meetings, therefore, you should do the following:

1. *Identify Yourself Immediately.* The caller cannot see you. He needs to know whether or not he has the right number, company, or person. A switchboard operator usually identifies only the firm's name: "Joplin and Lewis"; "Bannister's Wholesale"; or "This is Abigail and Blakeman Furniture Company." In answering an office or departmental telephone, identify both the office and yourself. You might say: "Dr. Ritter's office, Miss Gallagher speaking"; "Personnel, Mrs. Jamieson"; or "Good morning. This is the sales department, George Nance speaking." "Accounting, Leavitt" is technically correct, but the abruptness of the identification might confuse some people; and the purpose of this identification is to indicate who you are. Whatever greeting you use, remember that on the telephone you must identify yourself at once.

Courtesy Bell Telephone Magazine

Keeping pencil, paper, and message forms near the telephone will make it easy to take down information.

2. Keep the Caller Informed. The telephone caller can't see what is happening, so you must tell him. If you must leave the line to get some information, excuse yourself, saying, "I can find that information in just a few moments, if you wish to hold the line." Of course, all delays must be explained; and best business practice requires that you report to the caller every minute. You can make an appropriate remark like, "We're still trying to locate Mr. Poston," or "I'm sorry, Mr. Poston is still talking on the other line. Do you wish to wait, or shall I have him call you?"

You must also let your caller know verbally that you are following what he says. He can't see the nod of your head or your facial expression to know that you are still with him. You can show that you are listening attentively by a simple verbal response such as "Yes," "I see," etc.

3. *Be Ready to Take Down Information.* Have pencil, paper, and message forms ready for use near the telephone. Then you won't delay the caller with, "Will you wait while I get a pencil?" Be sure, too, to verify the message. After taking the message illustrated on page 529, you would verify the information by saying: "You would like Mr. Firman to call you regarding free servicing of your refrigerator under our Company Service contract, Mrs. Kislak—and you want service today. Let's see, you spell your name K-I-S-L-A-K? And your number is 555-1372? Thank you. Good-bye."

How to Use the Telephone   The telephone is a sensitive instrument. Knowing how to use it correctly will enable you to greet telephone callers courteously and efficiently. Follow these suggestions:

1. Hold your lips from a half to one inch from the mouthpiece. Don't let the mouthpiece slip down under your chin, and don't cut off your voice by holding your hand over the mouthpiece.

2. Adjust your voice to the equipment. Remember, you don't have to shout over the telephone. Use your natural voice. But enunciate clearly so that you will be understood.

3. Transfer calls efficiently and expeditiously. To transfer a call from the outside to another extension within the company, say to the caller, "If you will hold on for just a moment, I'll have your call transferred." How you get the attention of the operator depends on the phone system in your company. You may need to depress the cradle button several times, or just once—firmly. When the operator answers, say, "Will you please transfer this call to Mr. Alison on extension 2317."

4. Avoid irritating mechanical noises. If you must leave the line, place the receiver on a book or magazine. The noise made when the receiver is bumped

TO: *Mr. Firman*

HERE'S A MESSAGE FOR YOU

Mrs. Jerome Kislak

OF

PHONE NO. *555-1372*   EXT.

☒ TELEPHONED   ☐ WILL CALL AGAIN

☐ RETURNED YOUR CALL ☐ CAME TO SEE YOU

☒ PLEASE PHONE   ☐ WANTS TO SEE YOU

Wants refrigerator serviced free under our CS contract— wants service today

TAKEN BY   DATE *8/12*   TIME *10:20*

FORM 51-50540

Telephone message form saves time for the person taking down information.

or dropped on a desk is magnified over the wire and will not be appreciated by the caller. At the completion of a call, place the receiver gently in the cradle for the same reason. Of course, the courteous telephone host will allow the caller to replace the receiver before he does.

Communication Problems

Application Exercises

A ■

Your office manager asks you to write an S.O.P. (standard operating procedure) of one page or less for all office workers who receive telephone calls. Write a memorandum covering especially the following points of procedure:

1 Supplies and materials to be available at each telephone
2 Promptness in answering calls
3 Proper identification
4 Practice in handling delays
5 Personal calls during business hours

B ■

Suppose you are a salesperson who calls on customers in person and by telephone. Make a list of the techniques you would use in selling your product by telephone and then in person.

C ■

Mr. Elkton has left word that he is not to be disturbed. Yet a caller insists, "But I must see Mr. Elkton. I'm leaving town and won't be back for six months." What would you say? Select one of the following; then defend your answer in a paragraph. Discuss in class.

1 "I'm sorry, Mr. Elkton isn't seeing anyone today."
2 "Mr. Elkton is going to be in conference all afternoon, but let me talk with his secretary again."
3 "Mr. Elkton can't be disturbed."
4 "Why didn't you say so? I'll see whether he can work you in."

D ■

Select one of the following situations to enact before the class. How would you give the unfavorable decision to the caller?

1 The contract to build an addition on your plant was awarded to a competitor of the caller at a saving of $10 000.
2 A caller wishes to charge some merchandise, but he has exceeded his credit limit and has not paid a recent overdue invoice.

3 Your employer does not wish to see a caller. "He's nothing but a time waster," your employer has said.

Word Study

A ■

Words often confused: cooperation, corporation; eligible, illegible.

B ■

Give the nouns that may be formed from these verbs.

1	clothe	**3**	expend	**5**	annoy
2	devote	**4**	expand	**6**	unite

C ■

Complete the following by adding *ary, ery,* or *ory*—whichever is correct.

1	diction_____	**3**	necess_____	**5**	direct_____
2	embroid_____	**4**	hist_____	**6**	sal_____

Communication in Action: *Ethical Behavior*

Use the small-group technique to discuss the following situation for five minutes. In reporting back to the entire group, formulate a principle of ethics that you believe should govern such behavior.

Situation: Tom "borrowed" $2 from the office petty cash fund. He put it back the same day, so no one knew about it.

UNIT □ 63

The Employment Interview

Of all oral communication, none is more important to the business person than the employment interview; for his career may depend on its success. The employment interview is also one of the best examples of total communication, because it is in the interview that the job applicant is able to show that he possesses the communication skills required in a business job.

Preparing for the Interview

An employment interviewer judges a job applicant on how well he knows his own qualifications, how well he knows the job, and how effectively he is able to relate the two. Careful planning and preparation for the interview are required. Study the following suggestions thoroughly, for the way you apply them will be a big factor in determining your standing among the other applicants.

Know Your Qualifications   Before the interview, be sure you have collected and reviewed the needed information about your personal qualifications. If you wrote a letter of application (as discussed in Unit 53), refresh your memory about what you said. If you prepared a qualifications summary (Unit 52), memorize the facts you included. Have a transcript of school credits at hand and review the subjects you have taken. Have available, too, a list of class activities in which you have participated, clubs and organizations you belong to, honors you have won, and your hobbies and favorite sports. Know your school average and your attendance record. How embarrassing to be asked about your personal qualifications and not be able to remember exactly!

On his desk, the interviewer may have written information such as your application letter or form, your qualifications summary, school records, statements from previous employers, and letters of reference. In all probability, he will ask you about these records in order to expand or clarify them. And the interviewer will note how accurately your knowledge of your qualifications tallies with the written records he has before him. Prepare yourself, therefore, by collecting and reviewing all data on your qualifications. And have the information at the tip of your tongue so that you can answer questions readily and accurately.

Know the Job   Many employers advertise for experienced applicants to fill a position because they believe an experienced person is more likely to know the job —what is expected and how to perform. But the requirement of experience is not the handicap it may at first seem to an inexperienced applicant. The latter may be able to compensate for his lack of experience by learning all he can about the specific job for which he is applying. He is then prepared to show the interviewer that he makes up for lack of experience by a realistic understanding of what the job involves.

To learn about a job, you can talk with employees in that field. Before you leave school, you might invite a recent graduate who is now working in the company of your choice to speak to the class. If you have an opportunity to do so, take a field trip through the offices or plant. Read about the products manufactured or about the services or goods sold. Through friends, you may even be able to learn something about the people who own or operate the company and about the particular person who will interview you. The more you know about the job, the company, and the people you will meet, the better equipped you will be to relate your abilities to the specific job.

In dictation I can take 60 words a minute, with gusts up to 80 words.

Relate Your Qualifications to the Job   Well-intentioned, well-qualified applicants have been known to enter a personnel office with a general statement such as, "I want to apply for a job." This shows a lack of wisdom and an immaturity not wanted in business. The person might as well say that he has not considered what job he wishes to apply for, what qualifications are needed, or how his qualifications are related to the needs of the job. This applicant usually does not get past the receptionist. To avoid such a disappointment, you must prepare for the employment interview by considering how your abilities fit you for the specific job for which you are applying.

Conducting Yourself During the Interview

Having prepared carefully for the interview, try to radiate self-confidence and poise as you enter the employment office. At the interview, however, you will also be judged on decorum; that is, on the propriety of your dress and conduct as well as what you say.

Your Appearance   Meticulous care in grooming and in the selection of clothing, as discussed in Unit 59, is of major importance to you as an applicant. The clothing you wear to the interview should be neat, clean, comfortable, and, of course, appropriate. As the interviewer talks with you, he will notice such details as nails, teeth, make-up, and hair. A full eight hours of sleep the night before will contribute to your fresh, alert appearance. On the other hand, any detail of appearance and dress that attracts unfavorable attention will count against you. The trained interviewer knows that there is a direct relation between personal habits and work habits— slovenly appearance, slovenly work; neat appearance, neat work. Make your appearance speak favorably for you at the interview.

Your Manner and Manners   Good manners are often taken for granted; but any lapse or omission is noticed immediately. Practice the following five tips on common courtesy and etiquette.

1. Be on Time or a Few Minutes Early. Not only is it rude to be tardy for an appointment, but lack of punctuality may make the interviewer wonder whether you as an employee would be late often. The interviewer might also conclude that you do not really want the job since you are late. Rushing to arrive on time will leave you breathless, however; so start early enough to allow for unforeseen delays.

Shaking hands in a firm, friendly way will let the interviewer know you have confidence in yourself.
Courtesy Seneca College

2. Meet the Unexpected with Poise, Tact, and Humor. If the interviewer is not ready to see you, take a seat and occupy yourself while you're waiting. Imagine the childish impression a person makes who says, "But Mr. White told me that he would see me at ten o'clock."

3. Follow the Lead of the Interviewer. Remember, you are his guest. Shake hands if he offers to do so, and grasp his hand firmly. A limp handshake indicates weakness. Wait for an invitation before seating yourself. It is the host's privilege to seat you where and when he wishes. You are being a good guest if you follow the interviewer's lead.

4. Exhibit Tact and Graciousness in Your Conversation. Listen carefully. Don't interrupt, even if the interviewer is long-winded and you think of something you wish to tell him right away. Follow his conversation leads and show him that you understand the implications of what he says. Don't bore him with long, overly detailed answers; but do give him more than a meek "Yes" or "No" in answer to his questions. Of course you would not contradict him or imply that you think he is wrong; this is rude under any circumstances.

5. Show Appreciation for the Interviewer's Time and Interest. At the close of the interview, remember to thank the interviewer, just as you would thank your host when leaving his home. Don't let the excitement and tension of the interview make you forget this courtesy. Failing to show appreciation spoils an otherwise effective interview.

Your Speech and Conversation   The speech principles you have studied will aid you in demonstrating your oral communication. Have you worked to improve your voice? How is your enunciation, vocabulary, and pronunciation? Do you still say "yeah" when you mean "yes"? If you have worked hard and applied all you have learned, you can forget how your voice and speech sound; they will do you credit. You can concentrate on what you say.

Did you know that what you say reflects your attitudes and tells what kind of person you are? During the interview, for example, if you betray that you are overly interested in salary, your lunch hour, vacation, sick leave, or short working hours, you may reveal that you are more interested in loafing than in working. And interviewers have a responsibility to employ people who want to work!

Typical Interview Questions   Understanding the intent of the interviewer's questions will help you answer more intelligently. Here are some typical interview questions, with the reasons behind them and suggestions as to what you might say in reply.

1. Why Have You Selected This Kind of Work? The interviewer wishes to know how interested you are in the work and what your goals are. An answer like "Oh, I just need a job" shows lack of purpose. Isn't the following a better answer? "I've wanted to be a secretary ever since I started school. That was my reason for studying stenography. I believe I'll like this type of job, too." This person knows what she wants from a job; she has interest; and she has a purpose.

2. If You Had Your Choice of Job and Company, What Would You Most Like to Be Doing and Where? Watch your answer to this question! The interviewer is trying to gauge just how satisfied you will be working in this job and in this company. The best answer, if you can truthfully say so, is: "Mr. Shaw, the job I want is the one for which I am now applying. The company? Yours. Before too long, I hope to have proved myself and to have been promoted to greater responsibility."

3. What Are Your Hobbies? The interviewer is not interested in swapping information about his stamp collection. He wants to find out whether you have broad interests, for a person who has few outside interests is likely to become listless about himself and about his job. Be ready to list briefly your major interests in hobbies and sports.

4. In What Extracurricular Activities Have You Participated? To what clubs do you belong? What offices have you held? What honors have you received? These and similar questions are asked to determine the scope of your interest in people—whether you are able to work with people and whether you have leadership qualities. These are the characteristics of a well-rounded, well-adjusted individual. In preparing for the interview, review your extracurricular activities so that you can give the facts without hesitation.

5. Would You Be Willing to Work Overtime? Employers like to see a willingness, even an eagerness, to perform well in a job. Overtime may be required seldom; but, if it is, employers want to have people who will accept this responsibility. You would be entering a job with the wrong attitude if you were not willing to work overtime when necessary.

Communication Problems

Application Exercises

A ■

Make a list of your personal and educational qualifications to fill one of the following positions: secretary, clerk-typist, bookkeeper, key-punch operator, receptionist, retail salesclerk. From the standpoint of an interviewer, make a similar list of qualifications you now lack for the job.

B ■

Make a list of your leisure-time pursuits. Include all extracurricular activities, clubs, offices held, and honors won that you might mention in the employment interview.

C ■

Make a check list of grooming and dress that you could use as a reminder before going to the employment office for an interview.

D ■

As personnel manager for the largest industry in your community, you have an opening for a general clerical worker. Make a list of questions you might ask an applicant and explain what each answer would tell you about the potential employee. In class, enact the interview, using your questions.

Word Study

A ■

Words often confused: breath, breathe, breadth; indignant, indigent, indigenous.

B ■

1 Does the prefix *re* in *reorganize, reenter, reunion, reestablish* impart to the words the meaning of: beyond, again, under, after?
2 Does the prefix *mis* in *misinformed, misrule, misrepresent, misapply* impart to the word the meaning of: wrongly, throughout, partly, before?
3 Does the suffix *ician* in *electrician, musician, technician* impart to the words the meaning of: a specialist in, service of, the quality of, state of?
4 Does the suffix *ist* in *journalist, organist, humorist, specialist* impart to the words the meaning of: the study of, the act of, the science of, one who?

C ■

Replace the italicized words with correctly formed contractions.

1 We regret that we *cannot* grant this request.
2 *Let us* take a firm stand on this question.
3 *I have* no idea *who is* coming.
4 Miss Wood, you *need not* retype this table.
5 The statement just *does not* make sense.
6 *It is* a long road that has no turning.

Communication in Action: Shake Hands or Not?

Does a man ever shake hands with a woman when they are introduced? When is it appropriate? Does a woman ever rise when being introduced? If so, under what circumstances? When does a man rise upon being introduced? Enact the various situations suggested by these questions.

UNIT □ 64

Participating in Conferences and Meetings

Who isn't at some time called upon to participate in group activities? It may be a small club, a religious group, an extracurricular or special-interest club at school, a civic club or service organization, an adult educational or recreational group, or a political or fraternal group. Most people participate in one or more such organizations.

In business, management increasingly depends upon group thinking to plan and to help make problem-solving decisions. Many business groups and committees are organized to make use of the talents and ideas of employees. Often the work of each person in the group—members as well as the leader or leaders—is assessed by superiors to help determine who should be promoted. Why? Management can observe how well a person works in a group and how effectively he communicates with others—an important basis for advancement. Therefore, it is wise for every person who plans to enter business to know how to participate in group work.

The Group Member

For every leader in a group there are usually many more working members. You, therefore, will probably serve more often as a member than as a leader. Knowing and practicing the following principles will help you to be a valuable group member.

Four Principles to Follow

1. Respect the Opinions of All Other Group Members. It is easy to respect the opinions of people whom you like and whose ideas agree with yours. A good group member, however, respects the opinions of all others. He is courteous to everyone; and, because he is open minded, he is attentive to each member of the group.

You already know the rules of common courtesy and consideration that a group member should practice: Listen with courteous attention and respond with pertinent comments. The test of an effective group member, however, is whether he listens attentively and responds courteously *even to those whom he may dislike or with whom he may disagree.* Discourteous behavior—fidgeting, gazing into space, or trying to strike up an unrelated private conversation—marks the group member as a poor risk for promotion. The courteous person, on the other hand, is considerate of everyone at all times. He may have strong convictions, but he does not close his mind to a different point of view. He knows that, by considering the ideas and beliefs of others, he will grow and learn; he will gain a new respect for the thinking of others; and he will become a more effective person.

2. Use Only Your Share of Talking Time. Every member has a contribution to make to a group. Some people, however, have an exaggerated opinion of the value of their ideas; and they attempt to monopolize a meeting. The good group member knows that everyone has an equal right and responsibility to express himself; and, by limiting his own talking, he makes sure that he does not rob others of their fair share of talking time.

3. Help to Harmonize Differences of Opinion. Because he is able to see the points of value in each opposing view, the good group member often helps to harmonize differences. He not only recognizes merit but also encourages compromise when different factions take conflicting positions. He might say, for example, "There is value in your proposal, and I can see how it would work under certain circumstances. Yet, there is merit in the other plan, too. Shall we take the best from each?" By emphasizing areas of agreement, the good group member is able to harmonize differences of opinion.

4. Help to Keep the Discussion Pertinent. It's easy in a group for some members to let their talking wander from the discussion at hand. The good group member keeps his own remarks pertinent to the subject and also helps channel the ideas of others to the topic at hand. He may do it by identifying the goal or purpose of the group: "As I understand it, our purpose is to . . ." Or, when the discussion begins to wander, he may ask, "Let's see now, what is it we hope to accomplish in this meeting?" He may help to summarize progress made or point out stumbling blocks to achieving the goal. To keep the discussion pertinent, the good member acts as a conscience to let the group know whether or not it is getting the job done.

Attitudes to Avoid   To be sure, you must know the positive principles that constitute good group membership; but just as important as these principles is your understanding of the attitudes and practices that prevent effective group work. An understanding of these attitudes and practices will help you avoid pitfalls, and it will make you better able to harmonize differences of opinion and to keep a discussion on the main track. The attitudes and practices of the following types of people hinder the smooth progress of a group:

Selfish-Interest Pleader   "I don't care what the rest of you think—what I want to see is this . . . ," says the selfish-interest pleader. He has decided what *he* wants. Everything he says and does is intended to help him get his way despite the good ideas of others.

The Blocker   The blocker is opposed to every new idea. "That isn't the way to do it. Here's what we've been doing for years . . . ." or "That's an idiotic idea. It won't work." Whatever the idea is, the blocker is against it. He often displays a negative, stubborn resistance. He opposes in a disagreeable manner and frequently without reason.

The Aggressor   The aggressor is usually unaware of the feelings of others. He may try to build his own importance by deflating the ego of others: "That's a silly thing to do. If I were doing it, here is how I'd go about it." (But, alas, such a person usually avoids doing much!) He may attack the group, its purposes, or the importance of the topic. He usually attempts to assert his superiority by trying to manipulate the group. As the name implies, the aggressor wants to dominate.

The Sympathy Seeker   The sympathy seeker may accept responsibility to do something for the group, but then he doesn't carry it through: "I thought Joe was supposed to do that," or "I was just so busy that I couldn't get that done." Alibis, confessions of shortcomings, and exaggeration of personal problems are all used to gain the sympathy of the group. Such a person would like the group to compliment him for his weaknesses!

The Disinterested Bystander   The disinterested bystander may make a display of his lack of involvement. Through playboy tactics, he may attempt to disrupt. Or he may patronize the group with a frozen smile that permits him to escape mentally from the boring proceedings.

Success as a Group Member   Study your role in a group. Make sure that you practice the principles that contribute to group success. And eliminate all actions that might prevent you from being a good group member. Remember, it is from among the good group members that a leader is usually selected.

The Group Leader

A person who consistently blocks group action will not need to know how to lead a group. He won't be given the opportunity. You, however, who know and practice the positive principles that help a group to function, will soon be selected for a leadership post—an honor, but also a serious obligation. Before you take on the responsibility of chairman for a group, therefore, make sure that you know the duties involved in planning and conducting a meeting.

Planning a Meeting   As chairman of a group, you will usually plan all meetings—whether programs or business meetings. If the group does not have a constitution or bylaws to define your responsibilities, you can usually assume that you are responsible for all aspects of planning—place and time, publicity, pattern of the program, and speakers and other participants.

The Program   The first step is to write a plan for the program. This plan should answer the following questions: (1) What is the purpose of the meeting? (2) What theme or topic is to be considered? (3) Where and when will the meeting be held? Should reservations for a room or hall be made now? (4) Who will attend? (5) How many will attend? (6) What publicity will be needed? (7) How much money is available for speakers, arrangements, decorations, etc.? (8) What persons or committees should be appointed to make arrangements, sell tickets, publicize, act as hosts, etc.? (9) What form or pattern should the program take—speaker or symposium of speakers, demonstration, panel discussion, mock television or radio program, panel, with audience questions and answers, debate, small group discussions— brainstorming, or other?

Delegating Authority   At this point in planning, you may feel overwhelmed by the size of the job ahead of you. Don't be, however; for an important characteristic of the leader is his ability to delegate authority. Specific tasks are assigned to other people, and usually in writing. Delegate as many details as you can, but be sure to follow up on each assignment. Carbons of letters of committee appointments or of letters written to the speakers can be used as a tickler file. To avoid any last minute slip-up, send out reminders to all committees and speakers at least two weeks before the meeting. If you have carefully planned and effectively delegated responsibility, you can go before the group with a feeling of confidence that the meeting you conduct will be a good one.

The Agenda   In an agenda for a business meeting, the discussion items should be listed in the order of expected controversy. For instance, the first item will be the one most likely to meet with almost total agreement. Next will come the item on which the leader expects less agreement, and so on. A sound psychological principle is behind this practice. If a group starts by agreeing, the members will be in a congenial and positive frame of mind that will carry over to succeeding discussion topics. If an untrained leader starts his meeting with the "big question"—the topic likely to provoke the widest difference of opinion—he may wonder why nothing was accomplished at the meeting.

Conducting a Meeting   You, the chairman, set the tone for the meeting as you follow the agenda or program. If you are stiff and formal, the other people on the program are likely to be stiff and formal, too. If you are natural and informal (but in good taste, of course), the others on your program will probably be natural and informal, too. Most audiences today prefer a chairman who conducts an informal kind of meeting, whether or not parliamentary procedure is used.

Parliamentary Procedure   The bylaws of most clubs state that business will be conducted according to Robert's *Rules of Order.* Robert's *Rules* are to parliamentary procedure what Emily Post and Amy Vanderbilt are to etiquette; and, as chairman, you will need to know some of the basic principles of Robert's *Rules* and how to apply them. For example, you should know how to call a meeting to order and how to determine whether or not a quorum is present; how to make and follow an agenda; how to recognize members who wish to make a motion; what an appropriate motion is and how it is seconded, amended, and voted upon; and how to adjourn a meeting. Most organizations will appoint a parliamentarian to help the group leader, but the chairman who possesses a working knowledge of the rules is that much ahead.

Introducing a Speaker   An introduction should be short and simple and should include: (1) some gracious remark that will make the speaker feel warmly welcome; (2) a statement of the speaker's topic; (3) a brief summary of the speaker's background or special interests; and (4) presentation of the speaker by name. The announcement of the name of the speaker is usually made last, so that it serves as a signal for the speaker to leave his chair and begin his talk.

Responding to a Speech   The chairman, of course, wishes the meeting to end on a high note. After an effective talk, he needs to say very little. Even after a poor speech, the chairman shouldn't say too much. One or two comments about the importance of the talk or a short anecdote to leave the audience in good spirits is all that is needed. You should thank the speaker, express appreciation to those who helped plan the meeting, and adjourn.

Communication Problems

Application Exercises

A ■

Which of the following statements were made by people who practice principles of good group membership? Do any of the statements represent an attitude that is likely to hinder group progress?

"What you are saying, then, is that we should hold the meeting in January."
"I don't know about the rest of you, but I'm tired."
"When I was in the Jaycees, we didn't do it like that."
"I wonder, as I listen to your arguments, just how your plan will help us pay our club's debts and keep us from going deeper into the red."

B ■

(*a*) Write a plan of an important program for a group to which you belong. Include a speaker. Use the questions on page 541 as your guide. (*b*) Write the introduction you will use to present the speaker.

C ■

Write a letter to the person you have selected to be the speaker, requesting him to address your group.

D ■

Write a letter appointing a chairman for one of the following committees: (*a*) decorations, (*b*) host, (*c*) arrangements, (*d*) publicity.

Word Study

A ■

Words often confused: censor, censure; read, reed, red.

B ■

From the modifiers enclosed in parentheses, select the correct form for each sentence.

1 Of the two file cabinets, I prefer the (tallest, taller).
2 Our late start has hurt our chances (some, somewhat).
3 I do not like (that, those) kind of play.
4 Tom is (sure, surely) qualified for that job.
5 I am (real, really) pleased to know he passed.

C ■

Choose the item that answers each of the following questions correctly.

1 Which one of the following compound nouns *should* be hyphenated: vice president, real estate, air conditioning?
2 Which one of the following compound nouns should *not* be hyphenated: per-cent, son-in-law, cure-all?
3 Which one of the following expressions should *not* contain hyphens: an up-to-date chart, New-York theatres, large-sized coats, six-year cycle?
4 Which one of these words containing prefixes should *not* be hyphenated: ex-chairman, de-emphasize, re-invest?

Communication in Action: Writing a Telegram

Purchase Order No. 2578-S was mailed by your company to Klaff and Kline on February 5. The order (for office chairs) was marked *Urgent*. Confirmation was received from Klaff and Kline on February 10 and delivery promised by March 1. It is now March 5 and the chairs have not arrived. Compose a telegram to Klaff and Kline to find out "why" and "when."

UNIT □ 65

Giving a Talk

Almost every person must, at some time, talk before an audience. His remarks may be brief, perhaps only long enough to introduce a speaker. Or he may be a member of a panel, talking about one phase of the subject under discussion. He may give a five- or ten-minute talk, or he may be asked to present the main speech at a meeting.

Whatever the length of the talk, everyone who is invited to speak should feel complimented by the invitation. If you are asked to give a talk, someone must believe that you have ideas, suggestions, or experiences that are of value to others. But perhaps you do not feel confident that you will be able to communicate these ideas to others. You realize that a really effective talk is the result of more than just knowing your subject. The good speaker not only knows what he is talking about, but he also knows how to prepare and deliver his speech. He has learned the techniques of preparing and giving a talk, the techniques that you will learn in this unit.

Preparing the Talk

A good talk involves careful preparation. The speaker-to-be must be ready to cover his subject thoroughly and must work hard to organize the talk before giving it. Therefore, when preparing a talk, you must follow these principles:

1. Determine Your Purpose and Topic. First of all, you must know the purpose of your talk. Are you going to inform, explain, convince, entertain, or combine two or several of these purposes? Only when you know *why* you are going to talk will you be able to select the subject of the talk. Ask yourself these questions: Why was I asked to speak to this audience? What is the occasion and reason for this meeting? How long am I expected to talk? What does the group expect to gain from listening to me? What do I hope the audience will find valuable in listening to me? Am I personally in harmony with the interests and background of this group? How can I capture the audience's interest? The answers to these questions will guide you in selecting a topic that will be timely and interesting.

2. Consider Your Audience. Who is your audience? What is their age range, sex, educational and social background, economic status, experience, and interests? A talk presented before one group may have little appeal for another. For example, a discussion of electronic computers that would be exciting to office workers might cause a group of actors or pipe fitters to go to sleep. Failure to know and to consider the audience might seriously impair the effectiveness of the talk.

3. Limit Your Subject. Don't select a four-hour subject for a ten-minute speech! It is better to make two or three specific points in a talk—and do the job well—than to ramble about on too broad a topic. The secretary who talked about "Office Automation" would have presented a more interesting talk had she limited her topic to "How the Electronic Computer Affects My Job." Limit your subject so that you can emphasize two or three specific points in the time allotted to you.

4. Collect and Organize Your Materials. Collect much more information about your subject than you will use. Use small cards to jot down ideas as they occur. Use your own personal experiences; talk with people around you; read newspapers, magazines, books. Take copious notes from as many sources as you can. As you organize the material you have collected, you will be able to select the most important ideas to include in your outline.

5. Prepare Your Outline. A good outline is a "must" in preparing a talk. Refresh your knowledge of outlining by reviewing Unit 23. Your card notes, arranged and rearranged according to major ideas and in order of importance, are the raw materials for organizing the outline. Note, in the following sample, that only important ideas are included.

YOUR JOB OPPORTUNITIES IN BUSINESS

I. Introduction
    A. Response to the chairman and a few remarks and pleasantries about the audience and occasion
    B. Importance of the topic to the audience
    C. Preview of the major points to be discussed
        1. Put your best foot forward to get the job
        2. Learn and advance in the job
        3. Satisfactions I receive from my job
II. Put your best foot forward to get the job
    A. Job seekers who fail
    B. The average job hunter
    C. The superior job hunter who does put his best foot forward
III. Learn and advance in the job
    A. *Etc.*
    B. *Etc.*
IV. Satisfactions I receive from my job
    A. *Etc.*
    B. *Etc.*
  V. Concluding remarks

6. Arouse and Hold Interest. The success of your outline, and later of your talk, will depend on how well you are able to arouse and hold the interest of your audience. Make sure that you have variety and spice in your talk. Insert an amusing

Courtesy Seneca College
Make use of visuals when presenting complicated ideas to a group.

anecdote here and there. Emphasize new ideas. You can hold interest by using personal experiences and examples. Your talk should have a certain element of suspense as the plot unfolds. Complicated ideas, such as figures or statistics, should be omitted, simplified, or supplemented by charts and graphs. As you prepare your talk, consider carefully how you will arouse and hold the interest of the group.

7. **Talk, Don't Read or Recite.** How should you prepare your talk? Should you write your speech word for word, use only your outline, use notes on cards, or plan to talk without notes? These methods are all used by speakers to prepare their talks. Some people prefer not to speak from a written manuscript because they feel that their talk would sound stilted. Whatever method you select, be sure that your talk will sound natural—not like oral reading or a class recitation.

A written talk will be of value as you practise your presentation. It will enable you to fix each idea in your memory and to time your delivery. Having memorized the *what* and *how* of your talk, you can then use brief notes when you deliver it.

8. *Practise, Practise, Practise.* As you practise, try to anticipate the conditions of the actual talk. Imagine your audience in front of you. Stand erect and look at the audience. Talk loud enough for the person in the farthest corner of the auditorium to hear you.

Make slow and deliberate movements. Use hand gestures sparingly, and then only as they seem natural to you. And, if a mirror is available, practise your talk in front of it. The person you see there should be your severest critic, as he tells you about your facial expressions and your platform appearance. Perhaps you can enlist the help of family and friends, too, to listen and offer suggestions. Don't be satisfied with your practice until the talk flows along from idea to idea without the aid of a written text.

Delivering the Talk

Now that your talk is ready, how well are you going to deliver it? The following pointers will help you to present eloquently the thoughts and ideas that you have so carefully prepared.

Platform Manners and Bearing　Face the fact that you will be nervous as you wait for your introduction. The careful preparation of your talk will lessen, but will not overcome entirely, your natural nervousness. If you find yourself afflicted with a case of stage fright, take a good, deep breath before you open your mouth. This will relax your vocal cords. Then console yourself with the thought that you must be a very intelligent person. The speakers who are not at all nervous are either those who give talks very frequently or those who do not know enough to be frightened. A little nervous anticipation is good for you. It will key you up and give your delivery an added sparkle.

Tips to Talkers　Study carefully the following tips. They represent the principles of giving a good talk; and if you know them and use them, your audiences will say, "What a fine speaker!"

　1. Check Your Volume. You know how disgruntled, disinterested, and bored listeners are if they can't hear what a speaker says. Don't let this happen to your audience. If possible, before the meeting check your volume in the hall or room where you are to speak. Have someone stand in the back of the room to tell you when he can hear you perfectly. If you cannot make this test, or if there is any question about being heard, ask at the beginning of your talk whether everyone can hear you; then adjust your volume accordingly.

　2. Keep Your Chin Up. The good speaker holds his head high. Besides looking well, this posture helps him to project his voice out to the audience. You, then, will be careful to keep your chin up so that your words will reach your listeners, instead of dribbling down your shirt front.

　3. Use a Conversational Tone. Remember that you are talking to an audience, not giving an oration. Your voice should reflect the warm, easy, conversational tone that you would use if you were talking to a group of your very good friends. Also remember that you will destroy any warmth created by your tone if you allow a critical, scolding, or sarcastic note to creep in.

4. Look at Your Audience. An audience responds favorably to a speaker who seems to be talking directly to each person in the audience. One way of making your listeners feel that you are talking to each one individually is to look directly at the assembled people. Look at those in the middle section, then at those to the right, and then to the left. As you look, you may see nothing but a blur, a mass of faces. Let your eyes rest on different sections of the blur, and the audience will feel that you are giving a person-to-person talk. And, with experience, you will begin to see the faces and expressions of individual listeners.

5. Conceal Your Nervousness. Do your knees shake when you give a talk? Then arrange to stand behind a lectern. When nervous, do you shift from one hip to the other? Conceal this telltale sign of anxiety by training yourself always to stand with your weight evenly distributed on both feet. Do your hands feel as big as hams and do you twist those hands when you are nervous? If so, you might be wise to keep your hands out of sight, perhaps clasped behind your back. Whenever possible, avoid holding a paper; for nervousness may cause the paper to rattle like a leaf in a hurricane. Your talk, you see, will be easier and more comfortable if the audience thinks that *you* are easy and comfortable.

6. Break Yourself of Objectionable Mannerisms. Do you know whether or not you have objectionable mannerisms? When you talk, do you toy with objects, clear your throat or wet your lips frequently, punctuate everything with "uh" or "anda", or overuse slang expressions? You may not know that you have any such mannerisms, so ask some of your friends to watch and listen and report on any that they may observe. A speaker who has even one annoying habit cannot give a successful talk, for mannerisms distract the audience and obstruct the thoughts you are trying to convey.

7. Use Only the Time Allotted. If your assignment is to talk for five minutes, don't talk for six minutes. A program involving different speakers is usually timed to the last minute; anyone who does not keep to his time limit forces other speakers to shorten their talks. Not only is the long-winded talker thought inconsiderate, but he is also marked as egotistical. He evidently thinks that what he has to say is so important that the other speakers can be disregarded. To avoid going over the time limit, you might ask the chairman of the meeting to give you warning when you have only one minute of your allotment left.

8. Observe How Your Audience Reacts. You can, and should, train yourself to watch the audience and to be sensitive to its changing moods. If, as you talk, you see a blankness on the faces before you, this is the signal that your listeners need perking up. You might then tell one of the amusing stories you keep in reserve. Remember, however, that jokes are like dynamite in that they are effective only if used intelligently.

If your audience seems tired, if the hour is late, or if the previous talks have been overlong, you have two choices open to you: accept the situation as a challenge and give such an interesting and sparkling performance that everyone will be jolted out of his lethargy, or have pity on your audience and cut your talk to the bare essentials. You might decide that it is better to omit most of your speech rather than to give it before a weary audience.

9. Watch Your Last Few Words. A beginning talker frequently betrays his inexperience by lowering his voice as he says the last few words or by dashing off his ending in a hurried rattle. Of course, a beginner is happy to see the end in sight and is eager to get the ordeal over. What a pity, though, to spoil the effect of a fine talk with a poor finish! Remember to keep your pitch up and to observe good timing to the very end.

Communication Problems

Application Exercises

A ■

The following major topics were selected from preliminary notes for a talk on "Your Job as a Secretary." Rearrange them in order of their greatest-to-least importance to an audience of seniors in high school. Be prepared to justify your selection of the three most important and the three least important topics.

> Preparation for a secretarial position; what I failed to learn in school; how I applied for my job; the job interview; my letter of application; employment tests and how I took them; my first day at work; the number of stenographers and secretaries in my company; how I learned my job; my supervisor and co-workers; planning for and obtaining my promotion to secretary; job benefits in salary, vacation, retirement, sick leave, etc.; what I do in my job; the little things that please my boss; my most embarrassing mistake; office customs of behavior and dress; how I prepare an itinerary and make reservations for a trip; handling callers in person and on the telephone; how I handle incoming correspondence; methods I use to take dictation and transcribe; filing; problems that puzzle me about my job.

B ■

List on the left side of your paper the three most important topics you selected in Application Exercise A. On the right, list the sources of information you would use to prepare further for your talk.

C ■

Select one of the following job classifications about which you think your class would like information. Collect and organize your information and make an outline for a five-minute talk. Prepare your talk and give it to the class.

Bookkeeper or accountant
Public accountant and auditor
Administrative assistant to the company president
Secretary or stenographer
Receptionist or messenger

Retail salesclerk
Automobile (or other specialty) salesperson
Key-punch operator
Payroll clerk

Word Study

A ■

Words often confused: overdo, overdue; sole, soul.

B ■

Should *sometime, some time,* or *sometimes* appear in the following blank spaces?

1   I have not been to the movies for _____ .
2   The furniture should be delivered _____ tomorrow.
3   The bus passed the corner _____ ago.
4   _____ the sun shines during a shower.
5   Mr. Dennison will give _____ to the report tomorrow.
6   An inexpensive purchase is _____ false economy.

C ■

Which of the following sentences contain incorrect uses or incorrect forms of abbreviations? Give the correct substitutions.

1   Enclosed is your policy no. 84756, showing change of beneficiary.
2   The Dr. will be here in a half hour.
3   Mr. Jas. Graham, Jr., is in the reception room.
4   Please have some flowers sent to Miss. Young.
5   Our agent sails for S. America on Mon.
6   My aunt has been invited to speak to the C.N.I.B..

Communication in Action: Say It Better

Rewrite the following letter. Simplify the content and keep it friendly.

We were forced to discontinue some time ago Wearwell tires as a stock item in our inventory and are therefore unable to fill your kind order for four of them. In consequence of this, therefore, we regretfully return your cheque made in our favor for $113.35 and request that you write us again.

INDEX

a, repetition of in series, 150
Abbreviations, 252–258
  acceptance of as words, 12, 255
  avoidance of, 256
  dictionary vocabulary of, 21
  firm names, 253
  geographical names, 256
  government agencies, 254
  in historical dates, 255
  organization names, 254
  personal titles, 252–253
  plurals of, 96, 257
  sentences ending with, 185
  shortened forms and, 12, 255
  time, statements of, 255, 266
  words always abbreviated, 255–256
  words never abbreviated, 256
Absolute adjectives, 149–150
Academic degrees, punctuation with, 216
Accent, incorrect, 520
Acceptance
  of formal invitation, *illus.*, 467
  of position, 452–453
Accuracy, importance of, 300, 312, 328, 364
Acknowledgment letters, 369–375
  business papers, 371
  collection, 412
  confirmation, 372, 374
  orders, 371–372; *illus.*, 373
  reasons for writing, 369–370
  receipt of money, 370
  reservations, 371
  secretary's responsibility for, 389
Addressing of envelopes, 348
Adjectives, 147–153
  absolute, 149–150
  or adverbs, choice of, 156–157, 159, 160; *Quick*
    Tricks, **156, 159, 160**
  balancing, 285
  commas with, 220–221; *Quick Trick,* **220**
  comparison of, 147–150
    all in, 149
    double, 148–149
    other in, 149
  compound, 150–151
  defined, 147
  pitfalls in use of, 152
  proper, capitalization of, 246–247
Adjustment letters, 321, 395–402
  exactness in, 396–397
  types of, 398–401
Administrative Management Society, 351
Adverbial connectives, punctuation with, 207
Adverbs, 155–162
  or adjectives, choice of, 156–157, 159–160;
    Quick Tricks, **156, 159, 160**
  conjunctive, 155–156, 213, 281–282
  correct position of, 157–158
  defined, 155
  simple, 155
Afterthoughts, dash with, 198
Agenda, meeting, 541
Ages
  figures for, 265
  spelled out, 265
Aggressive attitude, avoidance of, 540

agree to and *agree with,* 164
Agreement
  of predicate
    with compound subject, 140–146; *Quick*
      Trick, **142**
    with simple subject, 128–140
  of pronoun with antecedent, 129
    relative, 143–144; *Quick Trick,* **144**
Agreements, confirming of, 372, 374
all
  in comparisons, 149
  correct verb with, 131
all (of), 166
almost and *most,* 160
Alphabetical letters
  in parentheses, punctuation of, 184, 234
  plurals of, 96
  silent, 520
  use of instead of names, 254
a.m., 255, 266
American Management Association, 52
among and *between,* 166
Ampersand in firm names, 209
and
  for *but,* 175
  pitfalls in use of, 283–284
  subjects joined by, 141
and which for *which,* 175
and who for *who,* 175
angry with and *angry at,* 164
Antecedents, agreement of, 129 143–144
Antonyms, 291
Apostrophe
  in contractions, 237
  in invented words, 237
  for omitted figures in dates, 237, 262
  in plurals, 96
  in possessives, 103–106, 237
Appeals
  in collection letters, 409, 411
  in sales letters, 428, 430–431, 433–434
Appearance
  of letter of application, 447
  personal, 501–505
    at employment interview, 533–534
  of qualifications summary, 440
Application, letters of, 322, 439, 446–451, 533
Application forms
  credit, *illus.*, 404
  employment, 443, 445; *illus.*, 444
Appointments, 2
  letters confirming, 372
  letters requesting, 364–365
Appositives
  possessive of, 106
  pronouns as, 120–121; *Quick Trick,* **121**
  punctuation of, 121, 215–216
  restrictive, *Quick Trick,* **116**
Appreciation, letters of, 453, 457–458, 464
Archaic words, 13–14
are, our, 108
Art, works of, titles of
  capitalization of, 248
  quotation marks with, 229
Article titles, quotation marks with, 229
Articulation, 513

as
   being that for, 176
   case of pronoun after, 119
   like for, 176
as . . . as and *so . . . as*, 176
as if
   correct verb with, 90
   like for, 176
as regards, 164–165
as though
   correct verb with, 91
   like for, 176
Association names (*see* Organization names)
at and *to*, 166
Attention, attraction of in sales letters, 431–433, 436
Attention line, 341–342
Attitude, importance of
   in business letters, 304, 306
   in group participation, 539–540
Audience
   consideration of, 544–545
   holding interest of, 547–549
Authority
   delegation of, 541
   exceeding of, 526–527
Auxiliary verbs, 80–81, 87–89

Balanced sentence, 284–286
because instead of *that*, 176
behind, 167
being that, 176
"Being" verbs, 87–88
beside and *besides*, 166
between and *among*, 166
Blind carbon copy notation, 345
Blocked letter style, 355; *illus.*, 353
Book titles
   capitalization of, 248
   italics with, 248
both (of), 166
"Bridging" words, 281–282
Buildings, capitalization of names of, 244
Business communication, 1–16
   aim of, 297–298
   completeness in, importance of, 300
   demands in, avoidance of, 303
   effective, hallmarks of, 297–300
   empathy in, 298–299, 303, 396
   goals in, setting of, 4–5
   grammar and, 4, 67–72
   human relations and, 299, 302
   letters (*see* Business letters)
   listening in (*see* Listening)
   oral (*see* Speech; Talks)
   persuasion in, 298
   purpose in, importance of, 297
   skills essential to, 2–5
   standards of, 299–300
Business letters, 2, 4, 310, 319–469 (*see also* Business communication; Business writing)
   acceptance of position, 452–453
   accuracy in, importance of, 300, 312, 328, 364
   accusations in, avoidance of, 303
   acknowledgment (*see* Acknowledgment letters)
   adjustment, 321, 395–402
      exactness in, 396–397
      types of, 398–401

Business letters (*cont.*)
   application, 322, 439, 446–451, 533
   appreciation, 453, 457–458
   attention line in, 341–342
   blocked style, 355; *illus.*, 353
   carbon copies of, 357
      courtesy, 365–366
   claim, 321, 393–395 (*see also* Adjustment letters)
   clarity in, 299–300, 331
   cohesiveness in, 331–332
   collection (*see* Collection letters)
   completeness of, 331, 361–362, 380
   complimentary closings, 250, 342–343
   concise, 331
   cost of writing, 322
   courtesy in, 328–329, 362, 369, 380–381
   credit, 321, 403–406
   effective
      attitude and, 304, 306
      psychology of, 302–307; *illus.*, 305
      qualities of, 326–335
   effectiveness of, measurement of, 322
   empathy in, 396
   erasures in, 357
   everyday, 360
   expressions to avoid in, 332–335
   follow-up
      employment, 452–453
      sales, 436, 438
      secretary's responsibility for, 389–390
   form, 371, 377
   friendliness in, 329, 380–381
   full-blocked style, 351; *illus.*, 352
   goodwill and, 319–320, 330, 458–459, 527
   hanging-indented style, 355; *illus.*, 354
   headings, 338–340
   helpfulness in, 379–380
   incoming, processing of, 385–386
   incomplete inquiries, 416–417
   indented style, 355; *illus.*, 354
   inside address, 341; *illus.*, 355
   negative words in, avoidance of, 306, 397
   notations in, 345, 385; *illus.*, 384
   order, 320, 364 (*see also* Orders)
   paragraphing of, 332
   parts of, 338–347; *illus.*, 343
      placement of, 345–347; *table*, 346
   planning of, 323–324
   postal cards used instead of, 364, 371, 377
   "problem," 303–304, 415–423
   promptness in answering, 378–379, 396
   public relations, 321–322, 456–461; *illus.*, 459
   punctuation styles, 351, 356
   reasons for writing, 319–320
   refusal (*see* Refusal letters)
   request (*see* Request, letters of)
   resignation, 453–454
   response, of, 376–382
   sales (*see* Sales letters)
   salutations in, 250, 341
   second pages of, 347–348
   secretary's responsibility for, 383–392
   semiblocked style, 355; *illus.*, 353
   Simplified, 340, 351; *illus.*, 352
   sincerity in, 329–330
   social- (*see* Social-business letters)
   stationery for, 356–357
   tact in, 303, 362

Business letters (*cont.*)
  thank-you, 457–458
    for employment references, 453
    transmittal, 360, 366, 479; *illus.,* 367
  typewriting quality and, 357
Business papers, acknowledgment of, 371
Business-promotion letters, 321–322, 456–461;
  illus., 459
Business reports (*see* Reports)
Business writing (*see also* Business letters)
  explicitness in, 273–279
  polished, 281–288
  reference sources for, 290–291, 312–313
  skill in, importance of, 2–3, 5, 309
  types of, 309–314
but, 158
  and for, 175
Buying points, development of, 430–431

Cablegrams, 311
Callers, greeting of, 2, 523–531
  basic rules for, 524–527
  telephone techniques, 527–530
Capitalization, 243–251
  after colon, 196
  commercial products, 246
  compass points, 244
  complimentary closings, 250
  days of week, 246
  in dictionary, 19, 21
  family titles, 250
  first words, 243
    of parenthetical elements, 236
  geographical names, 244–245
  governmental bodies, 245
  headings, 248
  historical events and documents, 246
  holidays, 246
  letter parts, 250
  months, 246
  nicknames, 247
  official titles, 249
  organization names, 245
  personal names, 243–244
  personal titles, 248–249
  proper adjectives, 246–247
  publication titles, 248
  religious days, 246
  school subjects, 250
  shortened forms, 247–248
  works-of-art titles, 248
Carbon copies, 357
  courtesy, 365–366
Carbon copy notations, 345
Carriage, importance of, 502–504
Caveat emptor, 45
Centuries, spelled out, 261
certainly, use of, *Quick Trick,* 159
Cities, names of
  abbreviation and, 256
  capitalization of, 244
  punctuation following, 216
Claim letters, 321, 393–395 (*see also* Adjustment
  letters)
Clarity
  in business letters, 299–300, 331
  figures to ensure, 264

Clauses
  compound sentence, punctuation of, 193–195,
    203–204
  incomplete, 286
  independent, 73, 193, 203
  misplaced, 274–275
  nonrestrictive, punctuation of, 212–219
  parenthetical, 125, 213
  relative-pronoun, 143–145; *Quick Trick,* 144
  restrictive, 212
  short, punctuation of, 204
  subordinate, 155
    following main clause, punctuation of, 208–
      209
    introductory, punctuation of, 208
  "that," punctuation of, 215, 275–276
  there at beginning of, 137
  "which," punctuation of, 215, 275–276
  who or *whom* in, 123–125
Collection letters, 321, 407–413
  acknowledging payment, 412
  appeals in, 409, 411
  persuasive, 408–409
  reminders, 407–408; *illus.,* 410
  series of, 411–412; *illus.,* 413
  telegrams as, 488–489
Collective nouns, 130–131
Colon, 195–197
  capitalization after, 196
  or dash, choice between, 197
  before listed items, 195–196
  period instead of, 196
  quotation marks with, 230
Comma, 202–226
  with academic degrees, 216
  with adjectives, 220–221; *Quick Trick,* 220
  with adverbial connectives, 207
  with appositives, 121, 215–216
  in compound sentences, 194, 203–204; *Quick*
    Trick, 203
  in "dashed" material, 199
  in dates, 216
  in direct address, 222
  emphasis indicated by, 223
  interrupting elements set off by, 209, 212–214
  with introductory phrase, 207
  with introductory word, 206–207, 282
  with names in filing order, 223
  with nonrestrictive elements, 212–219
  in numbers, 223
  omission of, rules for, 209, 217, 224
  omissions indicated by, 221
  parenthetical elements set off by, 213
  quotation marks with, 230
  in repeated expressions, 223
  in series, 204–206
  with subordinate clauses, 208–209
  unrelated numbers separated by, 223
  with "which" clauses, 215, 275–276
Comma-for-period fault, 186
Commercial products, capitalization of, 246
Common nouns, 93 (*see also* Nouns)
Communication (*see* Business communication)
Company policy, interpretation of, 307
Comparison of adjectives, 147–150
Comparisons, balancing, 284
Compass points
  abbreviation of, 256
  capitalization of, 244

Complement
 of *to be*, 113, 116
 and verb, punctuation of, 217
Complimentary closings, 250, 342–343
Compound adjectives, 150–151
Compound nouns
 plurals of, 98
 possessive forms, 105
Compound sentence, punctuation of, 193–195,
 203–204; *Quick Trick*, 203
Compound subject, 75–76
 omission of comma in, 209
 personal pronouns in, *Quick Tricks*, 114–115
 predicate agreement with, 140–146; *Quick Trick*,
 142
Conclusions in formal reports, 481–482
Condolence, letters of, 466
Conferences, participation in, 538–543
Confirmation, letters of, 372, 374
Confirmogram, *illus.*, 371
Congratulation, letters of, 465–466
Congressional sessions, numbers in, 260, 261
Conjunctions, 171–178
 coordinate, 171, 173–174, 203
 correlative, 172, 174
 defined, 171
 omission of, 194
 pitfalls in use of, 175–177
 subordinate, 172, 208
Conjunctive adverbs, 155–156, 213, 281–282
Consonants, dropping of, 516
Contractions, 237
Conversation, art of, 36, 535
Coordinate conjunctions, 171, 173–174, 203
Correlative conjunctions, 172, 174
Correspondence (*see* Business letters)
Courtesy
 in business letters, 328–329, 362, 369, 380–
 381
 in greeting callers, 525–526
 in listening, 41, 538–539
 manners and, 505
Courtesy carbons, 365–366
Credit application form, *illus.*, 404
Credit letters, 321, 403–406
Critical listening, 42–45

Dash, 197–200
 or colon, choice between, 197
 emphasis indicated by, 198, 234
Data sheet, 440–443; *illus.*, 441
Date stamp, 385; *illus.*, 384
Dateline, styles of, 340
Dates
 A.D. and B.C. in, 255
 figures for, 264–265
 omission of, apostrophe for, 237, 262
 punctuation of, 216
Day letters, 488
Days of week
 abbreviation of, 256
 capitalization of, 246
Decades, spelled out, 261
Decimals, figures for, 262
Declarative sentence, punctuation of, 183, 190
Definite pronoun reference, 277–278
Degrees, academic, punctuation of, 276
Desire, building of in sales letter, 433–436

Dictionary, 10–12, 17–23, 313
 choice of, 17
 desk, 17; *illus.*, 20
 preview of, 18
 pronunciation guide in, 18, 19, 518
 reference section in, 21
 word references in, 18–19
different from, 165
Digest of mail, 386
Dignity, titles of, 253
Direct address, use of comma in, 222
Direct questions, punctuation of, 189
Direct quotations, 226–227, 243
Discount, terms of, figures for, 262
Discounts, unearned, refusal of, 420, 422
discrepancy in and *between*, 164
Document titles
 historical, capitalization of, 246
 not quoted, 230
Dollars (*see also* Money)
 even amounts of, 185
Double negatives, 158
Doubt, punctuation to express, 234, 235
Dress, business, 502, 533–534

-elect, with titles, 249
Empathy
 in business communication, 298–299, 303, 396
 in listening, 42
Emphasis
 colon for, 196
 comma for, 223
 dash for, 198, 234
Employment data, 439–445 (*see also* Employment
 letters)
 application form, 443, 445; *illus.*, 444
 qualifications summary, 440–443, 532; *illus.*,
 441
Employment interview, 531–537
 applicant's conduct at, 533–536
 preparation for, 532–533
Employment letters, 322
 acceptance, 452–453
 application, 322, 439, 446–451, 533
 follow-up, 452–453
 refusal, 453
 requesting references, 451–452
 resignation, 453–454
 thank-you, 453
Enclosure notations, 345
English, standard, 14, 300, 312
Enumerations (*see* Listed items)
Enunciation, 513, 515–517, 521
Envelopes, 357
 addressing of, 348
 for sales letters, 431; *illus.*, 432
Erasures, 357
Essay titles, quotation marks with, 229
etc., punctuation after, 205–206
Etiquette
 business, 505, 534–535
 social, 505–506
ex-, with titles, 249
except for *unless*, 176
Exclamation point, 190–191
 with dash, 199
 with parentheses, 234–236
 with quotation marks, 230–231

Explanatory elements, punctuation of, 195, 214–217, 228
Explicitness in business writing, 273–279
Eye hygiene, 57

f, fe, nouns ending in, plurals of, 97
Facial expressions, importance of, 504–505
Family titles, capitalization of, 250
Figures (*see also* Numbers)
  for ages, 265
  for dates, 264–265
  for house, street, and ZIP Code numbers, 266–267
  for statements of time, 265–266
  for sums of money, 263–264
  numbers written in, 261–263
  omission of in dates, 237, 262
  plurals of, 96
Firm names
  abbreviation of, 253
  ampersand in, 209
  Inc. after, 216
Flowing sentences, 282
Follow-up letters
  employment, 452–453
  sales, 436, 438
  secretary's responsibility for, 389–390
Foreign words and phrases
  plurals of, 100, 136
  pronunciation of, 521
  translations of, quoted, 229
Form letters, 371, 377
Formal invitations, 466–468; *illus.,* 467
Formal reports (*see* Reports)
former, with titles, 249
Fractions, isolated, 260
Friendliness, importance of, 329, 380–381
from and *off,* 167
Full-blocked letter style, 351; *illus.,* 352
Full-rate telegram, 487

Gender, 129
Geographical names
  abbreviation of, 256
  capitalization of, 244–245
  pronunciation of, 521
Gerund, possessive before, 108
good and *well,* 160
Goodwill, building of, 319–320, 330, 458–459, 527
Government agencies, abbreviation of, 254
Government officials, titles of, capitalization of, 249
Governmental bodies, capitalization of, 245
Graduation years, figures for, 262
Grammar, 4, 67–72
  intentionally poor, quoted, 228
Grooming, importance of, 502, 533–534
Group leadership, 540–542
Group membership, 538–540

half, correct verb with, 131
Handbooks, 312
Handshake, 506
Hanging-indented letter style, 355; *illus.,* 354
hardly, correct use of, 158
have, use of *of* for, 167–168

Headings
  business letter, 338–340
  capitalization of, 248
  formal report, 484
  interoffice memorandum, 474
  punctuation after, 184
help (from), 168
Historical documents, capitalization of, 246
Historical events
  capitalization of, 246
  figures for well-known years, 262
Holidays, capitalization of, 246
Homonyms, 107
Honorable
  abbreviation of, 253
  the with, 253
House numbers, figures for, 266
Human relations in business communication, 299, 302
Humor, quotation marks to indicate, 228
Hyphens, 18
  in compound adjectives, 150–151; *Quick Trick,* **151**
  in compound nouns, 98, 105
  in official titles, 249

identical with, 165
Identification initials, business letter, 344
if, correct verb with, 90–91
Imperative sentence, punctuation of, 183, 190
in and *into,* 166–167
in back of, 167
in regard to, 164
Inc., punctuation with, 216
Incoming mail, processing of, 385–386
Indefinite pronouns, 137–138
Indented letter style, 355; *illus.,* 354
Independent clauses, punctuation with, 203
Indirect question, punctuation of, 183
Infinitive phrase, 207
Infinitives, 84
  complement of *to be,* 113, 116
  split, 84
  subject of, 113, 116
Information
  from callers, obtaining of, 526, 528
  refusals to give, 420
  requests for, 363
Inside address, business letter, 341; *illus.,* 355
inside (of), 166
Interest, building of in sales letters, 433–436
Interest rates, figures for, 262
Interoffice memorandums, 310–311, 473–477
  display of content, 477
  parts of, 474–475
  psychology, use of in, 303
  tone of, 473–474
Interrogative sentence (*see also* Questions)
  who, whom in, 122–123; *Quick Trick,* 122
Interrupted quotations, 227
Interrupting elements, punctuation of, 209, 212–214
Interview, employment (*see* Employment interview)
Intransitive verbs, *Quick Tricks,* **88, 89**
Introduction of formal report, 480
Introductions, making of, 506
  speakers, 541

Introductory clause, punctuation after, 208
Introductory phrase, punctuation after, 207
Introductory words, punctuation with, 194, 206–207, 282
Invented words, apostrophe in, 237
Inverted sentence order, 76–77, 129
Invitations
  formal, 466–468; *illus.,* **467**
  refusal of, 419–420
Irregular verbs, 82–83
Italics, titles set in, 229
  words in, 228

Jargon, 12
Jaw, rigid, effect of on speech, 511–512
Joint ownership, apostrophe to indicate, 105
Jr., punctuation with, 216

kind(s), errors in use of, 152

Language, framework of, 67–72
late, in titles, 249
lay and *lie,* 89–90
Leadership, group, 540–542
Letterheads, 338–339; *illus.,* **339**
Letters
  of alphabet (*see* Alphabetical letters)
  business (*see* Business letters)
lie and *lay,* 89–90
like
  for *as, as if,* or *as though,* 176
  instead of *that,* 176
Linking verbs, 156
Lip movement, effect of on speech, 512
Listed items
  colon preceding, 195–196
  in parentheses, 184, 234
  no punctuation following, 184–185
Listening, 2, 3, 5, 33–46
  basic rules for, 41–42
  in business and industry, 33–36
  conversationalist's role in, 36
  courtesy in, 41, 538–539
  critical, 42–45
  effective, need for, 35–36
  empathic, 42
  hearing and, 36
  and note-taking, 37–38, 45
  purpose of, determination of, 40–41
  readiness for, 41
  and reading, 36–37
  rephrasing speaker's words, *chart,* **44**
  vocabulary improvement by, 11, 14
Literature, sales, letter requesting, 364
Ltd., punctuation with, 216

Magazine titles, italics with, 229
Mail, incoming, processing of, 385–386
Mannerisms, undesirable, 506, 548
Manners, importance of, 505–506
  in delivery of talk, 547
  at employment interview, 534–535
Marginal notations, 385; *illus.,* **384**
Measures
  abbreviation of, 256
  figures for, 262

Meetings
  minutes of, 311, 489–491
  parliamentary procedure in, 541–542
  participation in, 538–543
  planning of, 540–541
  resolutions passed at, 491–492
Membership, group, 538–540
Memorandums, interoffice (*see* Interoffice memorandums)
Metric Measures, 261
Military datelines, 340
Military divisions, numbered, words for, 260, 261
Minutes of meetings, 311, 489–491
  formal, 490–491
  informal, 489–490
Modifiers (*see* Adjectives)
Money
  receipt of, acknowledgment of, 370
  sums of
    figures for, 263–264
    spelled out, 264
Months
  abbreviation of, 256
  capitalization of, 246
most and *almost,* 160

Names
  of cities
    abbreviation and, 256
    capitalization of, 244
    punctuation following, 216
  in direct address, punctuation of, 222
  in filing order, 223
  firm
    abbreviation of, 253
    ampersand in, 209
    Inc. after, 216
  geographical
    abbreviation of, 256
    capitalization of, 244–245
    pronunciation of, 521
  government agencies, abbreviation of, 254
  organization
    abbreviation of, 254
    capitalization of, 245
    possessive forms of, 104
  personal (*see* Personal names)
  of states
    abbreviation of, 256
    capitalization of, 244
    punctuation with, 216
  street
    abbreviation of, 256
    capitalization of, 244
    numbered, spelled out, 266–267
Negative attitude, avoidance of, 304, 306
Negative words, avoidance of, 306, 397
Negatives, double, 158
never, 158
  and *not,* 158
News releases, 311–312, 492–496; *illus.,* **494**
Newspapers, names of, not quoted, 229
Nicknames, capitalization of, 247
Night letters, 488
No., when used, 255
Nominative case of pronouns, 111–114; *Quick Trick,* 113
Nonrestrictive elements, punctuation of, 212–219
nor, subjects joined by, *Quick Trick,* 142
Normal sentence order, 76–77, 129

ot and *never*, 158
ote-taking, listening and, 37–38, 45
*ouns
  collective, 130–131
  common, 93
  compound, 98, 105
  plurals of (*see* Plurals)
  possessive forms of (*see* Possessive case)
  proper, 93
    capitalization of (*see* Capitalization)
  singular, no change in, 99
umber, a or *the,Quick Trick,* 135
umbers (see also Figures)
  approximate, 260
  in Congressional sessions, 260, 261
  consecutive, 263
  even, 260
  large, spaces, 224
  mixed, 260
  in parentheses, punctuation of, 184, 234
  sentences beginning with, 260
  in series, 262
  unrelated, commas between, 223
  written in figures, 261–263
  written as words, 259–261

o, nouns ending in, plurals of, 97
Object and verb, punctuation of, 217
Objective case of pronouns, 111–112, 116
of for *have*, 167–168
off, off of, and *off from,* 168
Official titles, capitalization of, 249
oh, punctuation with, 191
Omissions, comma used to indicate, 221
only, correct use of, 158
opposite (to), 168
or, subjects joined by, *Quick Trick,* 142
Order letters, 320, 364 (*see also* Orders)
Orders
  acknowledgment of, 371–372; *illus.,* 373
  delays in filling, letters on, 418
  refusals of, 418–419
  telephoned, confirmation of, 374
Ordinal endings, 264
Organization names
  abbreviation of, 254
  capitalization of, 245
  possessive form of, 104
other, in comparisons, 149
our, are, 108
Outline
  capitalization of first words of, 243
  punctuation of, 184–185
  of talk, 545
outside (of), 166

Paragraphing of business letters, 332
Paragraphs, transitions between, 282, 331–332
Parallel structure, 173–175
Parentheses, 233–236
  exclamation point with, 234–236
  letters and numbers in, 184, 234
  period with, 236
  question mark with, 234–236
Parenthetical elements (*see also* Parentheses)
  capitalization of first words of, 236
  commas with, 213
  who, whom clause in, 125

Parliamentary procedure, 541–542
part from and *part with,* 164
Participial phrase, 207
Participles, 81–83
Penmanship, 4
Percentages, figures for, 262
Period, 183–188 (*see also* Abbreviations)
  instead of colon, 196
  omission of, rules for, 184–185
  parentheses with, 236
  quotation marks with, 230
Period fault, 185–186
Periodical titles, not quoted, 229
Personal appearance, 501–505
  at employment interview, 533–534
Personal names
  capitalization of, 243–244
  letters used instead of, 254
  plurals of, 94–95
  pronunciation of, care in, 521
  titles with (*see* Personal titles)
Personal pronouns, 103–127
  antecedents of, agreement with, 129
  as appositives, 120–121; *Quick Trick,* 121
  in compounds, *Quick Tricks,* 114–115
  masculine or feminine, choice of, 129
  nominative case of, 111–114; *Quick Trick,* 113
  objective case of, 111-112, 116
  possessive case of, 107–108, 111
  self-ending, 119–120
Personal titles
  abbreviation of, 252–253
  capitalization of, 248–249
  plurals of, 94–95
  punctuation with, 216
Phrases
  hackneyed, 289
  infinitive, 207
  introductory, punctuation after, 207
  misplaced, 274
  nonrestrictive, punctuation of, 212–219
  prepositional, 163, 207
    interrupting, 209
  restrictive, 212
  short, exclamation point after, 190–191
  transitional, 281–282
  verb, 80–81
Place names (*see* Geographical names)
plan to, 165
Plurals, 19, 93–102
  abbreviations, 96, 257
  alphabetical letters, 96
  apostrophe in, 96
  common, 94
  compound nouns, 98
  dictionary information on, 19
  figures, 96
  foreign nouns, 100, 136
  nouns always plural, 100
  nouns ending in *f, fe,* 97
  nouns ending in *o,* 97
  nouns ending in *y,* 95
  personal names, 94–95
  personal titles, 94–95
  two, nouns with, 98
  vowel changes to form, 95–96
p.m., 255, 266
Poems, titles quoted, 229

Policy, company, interpretation of, 307
Possessive case, 103-110
  apostrophe in formation of, 103-106, 237
  before gerund, 108
  joint ownership, 105
  of nouns, 103-106
    compound, 105
  of organization names, 104
  ownership word, *Quick Trick*, 104
  of personal pronouns, 107-108, 111
  separate ownership, 106
Postal cards, use of, 364, 371, 377
Postal Code, 348
Predicate, 74 (*see* also Subject; Verbs)
  agreement of
    with compound subject, 140-146; *Quick Trick*, 142
    with simple subject, 128-140
  and subject, omission of comma between, 209
Predicate nominative, 113
Prepositional phrase, 163, 207
  interrupting, 209
Prepositions, 163-170
  balancing, 285-286
  defined, 163
  illiterate use of, 167-168
  specific, words requiring, 164-165
  troublesome, 166-167
Professional life, reading in, 52-53
Promptness
  in answering letters, 378-379, 396
  at employment interview, 534
  in greeting callers, 524
Pronoun reference, definite, 277-278
Pronouns
  antecedents of, 129, 143-144
  indefinite, 137-138
  personal (*see* Personal pronouns)
  relative, 143-145; *Quick Trick*, 144
Pronunciation, 515, 517-521
  correct
    determinants of, 518
    importance of, 10, 521
  dictionary guide to, 18, 19, 518
  regional differences and, 518
  tips on, 521
Proper nouns, 93 (*see* also Nouns)
Public, meeting of (*see* Callers, greeting of)
Public relations letters, 321-322, 456-461; *illus.*, 459
Publication titles
  capitalization of, 248
  quoted, 229
Punctuation (*see* also individual marks of punctuation)
  of business letters, 351, 356

Qualifications summary, 440-443, 532; *illus.*, 441
Question mark, 189-190 (*see* also Questions)
  dash and, 199
  quotation marks with, 230-231
  parentheses with, 234-236
Questions
  direct, punctuation of, 189
  indirect, punctuation of, 183
  requests phrased as, 183-184
  series of, 189-190

Quotation marks, 226-233 (*see* also Quotations)
  with colon, 230
  comma with, 230
  with direct quotations, 226-227
  exclamation point with, 230-231
  with explained or defined words, 228
  humor indicated by, 228
  overuse of, avoidance of, 228
  period with, 230
  poor grammar indicated by, 228
  with question mark, 230-231
  with semicolon, 230
  single, 227
  with slang, 228
  titles enclosed in, 229-230
  with translations, 229
  with unfamiliar terms, 228
Quotations
  changes in, avoidance of, 227
  direct, 226-227, 243
  interrupted, 227
  within quotations, 227

raise and *rise*, 89, 90
Reading, 2, 3, 5, 51-63
  comprehension in, increasing of, 59-60
  environment and, 58
  eye hygiene and, 57
  lighting conditions for, 58
  listening and, 36-37
  personal, 52
  in professional life, 52-53
  purposeful, 53-55
  in school life, 51-52
  speed in, increasing of, 58-59
real and *really*, 159
Receptionist duties (*see* Callers, greeting of)
Recommendations in formal report, 481-482
Reference books, 290-291, 312-313
References, employment, 443
  letters requesting, 451-452
  thank-you letters for, 453
Refusal letters
  credit, 405-406
  employment, 453
  information, 420
  invitations, 419-420
  manuscript, *illus.*, 421
  orders, 418-419
  unearned discounts, 420, 422
Regional differences, pronunciation and, 518
Regular verbs, 82
Relative-pronoun clause, 143-145; *Quick Trick*, 144
Religious days, capitalization of, 246
Reminder card, *illus.*, 407
Reminder letters, 407-408; *illus.*, 410
Repetitions
  commas with, 223
  dash with, 198
Reports, 311, 478-485
  binding of, 484
  headings in, 484
  parts of, 483
  preparation of, 479-482
  title page, *illus.*, 483
  titles of, 230
  tone of, 482

Request, letters of, 320, 359-366
  characteristics of, 360-363
  employment references, 451-452
  order, 320, 364
  postal cards used instead of, 364
  reasons for writing, statement of, 362
  secretary's responsibility for, 388-389
  types of, 363-365
  unreasonable, 417-418
Requests in form of questions, 183-184
Reservations
  acknowledgment of, 371
  for employer, making of, 388
Resignation, letter of, 453-454
Resolutions, meeting, 491-492
Respect, titles of, 253
Response, letters of, 376-382
Restrictive appositives, Quick Trick, 116
Restrictive clauses and phrases, 212
Résumé, employment, 440-443; illus., 441
retroactive to, 165
Reverend
  abbreviation of, 253
  the with, 253
rise and raise, 89, 90
Roget's Thesaurus, 290-291
Roman numerals, punctuation after, 184

Sales letters, 321-322, 424-438; illus., 426, 429,
  437
  aim of, determination of, 425, 427
  appeals in, 428, 430-431, 433-434
  buying points in, development of, 430-431
  follow-up, 436, 438
  market determination and, 427-428
  plan for, steps in, 431-436
    attention, attracting of, 431-433, 436
    favorable action, direction of, 435, 436
    interest and desire, building of, 433-436
    reader, convincing of, 435, 436
Sales literature, letter requesting, 364
Salutations, 250, 341
scarcely, correct use of, 158
School life, reading in, 51-52
School subjects, capitalization of, 250
Secretary
  letters written by, 386-391
  in employer's absence, 390-391
  responsibility of for correspondence, 383-392
self-ending pronouns, 119-120
Semiblocked letter style, 355; illus., 353
Semicolon, 193-195, 204
  quotation marks with, 230
  in series, 206
Sentence, 73-78
  abbreviation at end of, 185
  balanced, 284-286
  colon introducing, 196
  complete and incomplete, Quick Trick, 73
  compound, punctuation of, 193-195, 203-204;
    Quick Trick, 203
  declarative, punctuation of, 183, 190
  definition of, 73
  flowing, 282
  imperative, punctuation of, 183, 190
  interrogative (see also Questions)
    who, whom in, 122-123; Quick Trick, 122
  numbers at beginning of, 260

Sentence (cont.)
  predicate of (see Predicate)
  run-on, 186
  subject of (see Subject)
  there at beginning of, 137
Sentence order, normal and inverted, 76-77, 129
Separate ownership, apostrophe used to indicate,
  106
Series
  a and the in, repetition of, 150
  comma in, 204-206
  numbers in, 262
  of questions, punctuation of, 189-190
  semicolon in, 206
Sermon titles, quoted, 229
set and sit, 89, 90
Ship names, quoted, 229
Shortened forms
  abbreviations and, 12, 255
  capitalization of, 247-248
Simple adverbs, 155
Simple subject, 75-76
  predicate agreement with, 128-140
Simplified Letter style, 340, 351; illus., 352
since, correct use of, 176
Sincerity, importance of, 329-330
Single quotation marks, 227
Singular nouns, no change in, 99
Singular verbs, plurals of, 128-147
sit and set, 89, 90
Slang, 13-15
  quotation marks with, 228
so . . . as and as . . . as, 176
Social-business letters, 322, 462-469
  condolence, 466
  congratulations, 465-466
  formal invitations and replies, 466-468; illus.,
    467
  thank-you, 464
Social life
  importance of listening in, 36
  vocabulary and, 10
some and somewhat, Quick Trick, 160
sort(s), errors in use of, 152
Speaker, introduction of, 541
Speaking, 2, 3, 5 (see also Speech; Talks)
  listening and, 37
Special occasions, letters on, 458, 460
Speech
  effective, 501
  in employment interview, 535
  enunciation and, 513, 515-517, 521
  pronunciation and, 515, 517-521
  voice quality and, 509-511
  physical tools of, 511-513
Spelling, 4, 10
Split infinitive, 84
Standard English, 14, 300, 312
State names
  abbreviation of, 256
  capitalization of, 244
  punctuation with, 216
Stationery, 356-357
Street names
  abbreviation of, 256
  capitalization of, 244
  numbered, spelled out, 266-267

Subject, 74
  collective-noun, 130–131
  complete, 74
  compound, (see Compound subject)
  indefinite-pronoun, 137–138
  of infinitive, 113, 116
  nominative-case, 112
  and predicate, omission of comma between, 209
  simple, 75–76
  agreement with predicate, 128–140
Subject line
  in business letter, 342
  in interoffice memorandum, 474
Subordinate clauses, 123, 155, 172, 208-209
Subordinate conjunctions, 172, 208
Summarizing word, dash with, 198
Summary of formal report, 480
sure and surely, 159
Surprise, punctuation to express, 234, 235
Syllables
  addition of in enunciation, 517
  dropping of, 516–517
Symbols
  chemical, 254
  plurals of, 96
Synonyms, 10, 19, 290–291

Tabulated items (see Listed items)
Tact, importance of, 303, 362, 526, 535
Talks, 544–550
  delivery of, 547–549
  preparation of, 544–547
  suggested outline for, 545
Telegrams, 300, 311, 486–489; illus., 487
  classes of, 487–488
  as collection letters, 488–489
  confirmation of, 374
  word count for, 488–489
Telephone, 2
  handling callers by, 527–530
  message sheet, illus., 529
  orders received over, confirmation of, 374
Tense, 81–83
than, case of pronoun after, 119
thank-you letters
  business, 453, 457–458
  social-business, 464
that
  clauses introduced by, punctuation after, 215,
    275–276
  instead of because, like, where, 176
the
  in geographical names, 244
  with Honorable or Reverend, 253
  repetition of in series, 150
their, they're, there, 107
them and those, correct use of, 152
there, sentence or clause beginning with, 137
Thesaurus, use of, 290–291
those and them, correct use of, 152
Time, statements of
  abbreviations in, 255, 266
  figures for, 265
  spelled out, 265
24-hour clock, 266
Title page, report, illus., 483

Titles
  of dignity, 253
  document, 230, 246
  family, capitalization of, 250
  hyphenated, 249
  official, capitalization of, 249
  personal (see Personal titles)
  publication
    capitalization of, 248
    quoted, 229
  report, 230
  of respect, 253
to and at, 166
to be
  complement of, 113, 116
  forms of, 87–88
Tongue, correct use of, 512–513
Transitional phrases, 281–282
Transitional words, 155–156, 281–282, 331–332
Transitive verbs, Quick Trick, 88
Translations, quotation marks with, 229
Transmittal letters, 360, 366, 479; illus., 367
Typewriting quality in business letters, 357

Unearned discounts, refusal of, 420, 422
unless, except, or without for, 176
Unreasonable requests, 417–418

Variety in use of words, 288–293
Verb phrases, 80–81
Verbs, 79–92 (see also Predicate)
  with as if, 90
  with as though, 91
  auxiliary, 80–81, 87–89
  balancing, 285
  "being," 87–88
  and complement, punctuation of, 217
  defined, 79
  with half, 131
  with if, 90–91
  infinitives (see Infinitives)
  intransitive, Quick Tricks, 88, 89
  irregular, 82–83
  linking, 156
  main, 80–81, 87
  and objects, punctuation of, 217
  principal parts of, 81–82; table, 83
  regular, 82
  singular or plural, choice of, 128–147
  transitive, Quick Trick, 88
  troublesome, 89–90
  with wish, 91
very, use of, Quick Trick, 159
Visitors, (see Callers, greeting of)
Vocabulary, 9–16 (see also Words)
  changing, 12–14
  good, characteristics of, 9–10
  improvement of, plan for, 10–12
  in social life, 10
  up-to-date, maintenance of, 14–15
Voice, flexible, development of, 509–513
Vowels
  incorrectly sounded, 518–519
  omitted in enunciation, 516
  plurals formed by changes in, 95–96

Weights, figures for, 262
well and good, 160
where instead of that, 176
where at, 169
where to, 169
which
    instead of and which, 175
    punctuation after, 215, 275–276
who instead of and who, 175
who, whom, 116
    in clauses, 123–125
    in interrogative sentences, 122–123; Quick Trick,
    122
whose and who's, 108
wish, correct verb with, 91
with regard to, 164
without for unless, 176
Words (see also Vocabulary)
    abbreviations of (see Abbreviations)
    antonyms, 291
    archaic, 13–14
    "bridging," 281–282
    confusion in use of, 23–27
    defined or explained, quotation marks with, 228
    division of, 17–19
    first, capitalization of, 236, 243
    foreign (see Foreign words and phrases)
    hyphenated, 18, 98, 105, 150–151; Quick Trick,
    151

Words (cont.)
    introductory, punctuation with, 194, 206–207,
    282
    invented, apostrophe in, 237
    meanings of
        changes in, 13
        context and, 13, 24
    misplaced, 273–274
    negative, avoidance of, 306, 397
    new, 12
    nonrestrictive, punctuation of, 212–219
    numbers written as, 259–261
    overused, list of, 289
    restrictive, 212
    shortened forms of, 12, 247–248, 255
    slang, 13–15
        quotation marks with, 228
    synonyms, 10, 19, 290–291
    transitional, 155–156, 281–282, 331–332
    unfamiliar, quotation marks with, 228
    variety in use of, 288–293
Works-of-art titles, capitalization of, 248
Writing (see Business writing)

y, nouns ending in, plurals of, 95
your and you're, 107–108

ZIP Code numbers, 266, 267, 348